# *Rick Steves'*
# ITALY
# 2003

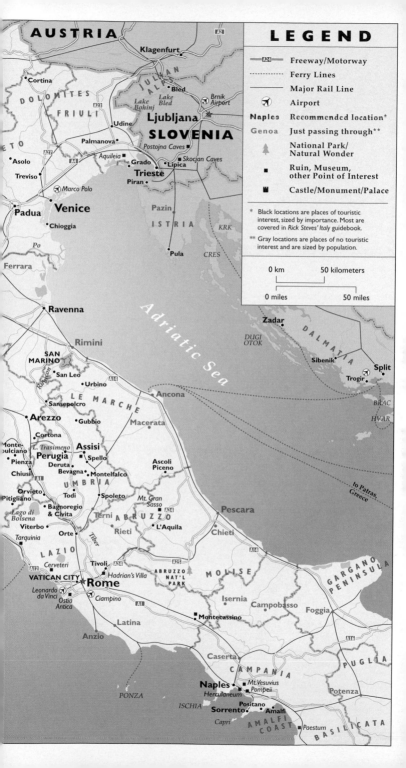

# LEGEND

| | |
|---|---|
| ▬A24▬ | Freeway/Motorway |
| ---- | Ferry Lines |
| ⎯⎯ | Major Rail Line |
| ✈ | Airport |
| **Naples** | Recommended location* |
| Genoa | Just passing through** |
| ♠ | National Park/ Natural Wonder |
| ■ | Ruin, Museum, other Point of Interest |
| ♜ | Castle/Monument/Palace |

\* Black locations are places of touristic interest, sized by importance. Most are covered in *Rick Steves' Italy* guidebook.

\*\* Gray locations are places of no touristic interest and are sized by population.

0 km        50 kilometers

0 miles        50 miles

**AUSTRIA**

Cortina

DOLOMITES

FRIULI

Klagenfurt

JULIAN ALPS

Lake Bohinj

Lake Bled

Bled

Brnik Airport ✈

Udine

Palmanova

**Ljubljana**

**SLOVENIA**

Asolo

Aquileia

Postojna Caves

Treviso

Grado

Lipica

**Trieste**

Marco Polo ✈

Piran

Skocjan Caves

**Venice**

Padua

Chioggia

PAZIN

ISTRIA

KRK

Po

Ferrara

Pula

CRES

**Ravenna**

*Adriatic Sea*

**Zadar**

DUGI OTOK

DALMATIA

Rimini

**SAN MARINO**

San Leo

Sibenik

Urbino

Trogir ✈

**Split**

LE MARCHE

Ancona

BRAC

Sansepolcro

HVAR

**Arezzo**

Gubbio

Macerata

Cortona

Monte-pulciano

L. Trasimeno

**Assisi**

Pienza

**Perugia**

Spello

Chiusi

Deruta

Bevagna

Montefalco

Ascoli Piceno

to Patras, Greece

UMBRIA

Todi

Orvieto

Pitigliano

Spoleto

Mt. Gran Sasso

Pescara

Lago di Bolsena

Bagnoregio & Civita

ABRUZZO

Terni

Viterbo

Orte

Tiber

Rieti

**L'Aquila**

Chieti

Tarquinia

LAZIO

Cerveteri

Tivoli

Hadrian's Villa

ABRUZZO NAT'L PARK

MOLISE

GARGANO PENINSULA

**VATICAN CITY**

Leonardo da Vinci ✈

**Rome**

Ostia Antica

Ciampino ✈

Isernia

Campobasso

Foggia

Latina

Montecassino

Caserta

PUGLIA

Anzio

CAMPANIA

PONZA

**Naples**

Mt. Vesuvius

Herculaneum

Pompeii

Potenza

ISCHIA

**Sorrento**

Positano

Amalfi

Capri

AMALFI COAST

Paestum

BASILICATA

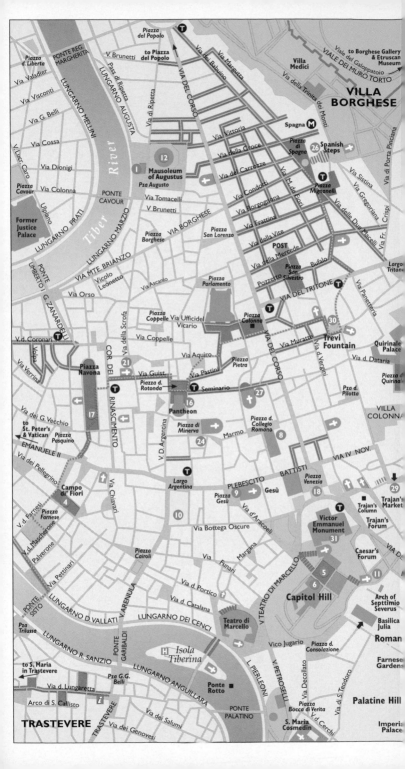

# CENTRAL ROME SIGHTS

1. Altar of Peace
2. Arch of Constantine
3. Baths of Diocletian
4. Campo de' Fiori
5. Capitol Hill
6. Capitol Hill Museum
7. Colosseum
8. Galleria Doria Pamphilj
9. Gesu Church
10. Largo Argentina
11. Mammertine Prison
12. Mausoleum of Augustus
13. National Museum
14. Nero's Golden House
15. Palatine Hill
16. Pantheon
17. Piazza Navona
18. Piazza Venezia
19. Roman Forum
20. San Clemente Church
21. San Luigi dei Francesi Church
22. Santa Maria della Vittoria Church
23. Santa Maria Maggiore
24. Santa Maria Sopra Minerva Church
25. Santa Susanna Church
26. Spanish Steps (Piazza di Spagna)
27. St. Ignazio Church
28. St. Peter-in-Chains Church
29. Trajan's Column, Forum, and Market
30. Trevi Fountain
31. Victor Emmanuel Monument
32. Termini Train Station
33. Main Tourist Info

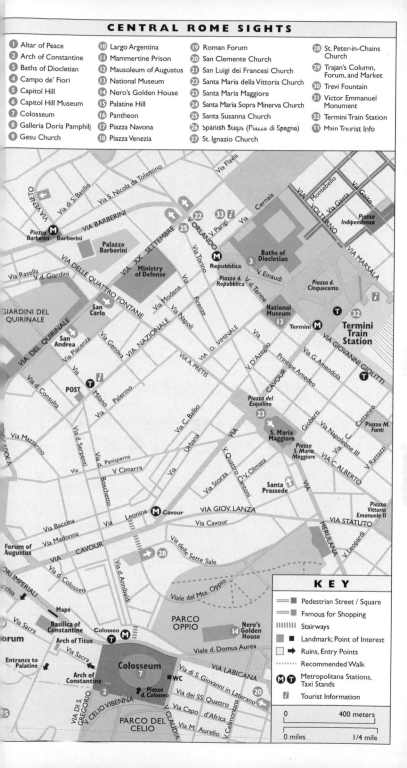

## KEY

- ▬▬ Pedestrian Street / Square
- ═══ Famous for Shopping
- ||||||| Stairways
- ■ Landmark; Point of Interest
- □ ➡ Ruins, Entry Points
- ········ Recommended Walk
- Ⓜ Ⓣ Metropolitana Stations, Taxi Stands
- 🄸 Tourist Information

```
0                    400 meters

0 miles              1/4 mile
```

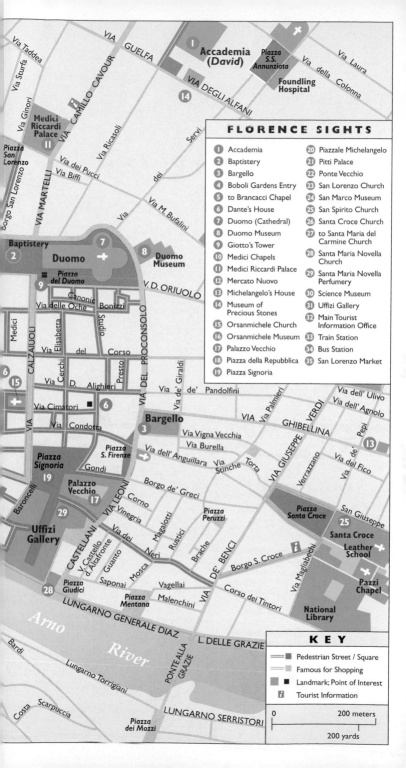

## FLORENCE SIGHTS

1. Accademia
2. Baptistery
3. Bargello
4. Boboli Gardens Entry
5. to Brancacci Chapel
6. Dante's House
7. Duomo (Cathedral)
8. Duomo Museum
9. Giotto's Tower
10. Medici Chapels
11. Medici Riccardi Palace
12. Mercato Nuovo
13. Michelangelo's House
14. Museum of Precious Stones
15. Orsanmichele Church
16. Orsanmichele Museum
17. Palazzo Vecchio
18. Piazza della Repubblica
19. Piazza Signoria

20. Piazzale Michelangelo
21. Pitti Palace
22. Ponte Vecchio
23. San Lorenzo Church
24. San Marco Museum
25. San Spirito Church
26. Santa Croce Church
27. to Santa Maria del Carmine Church
28. Santa Maria Novella Church
29. Santa Maria Novella Perfumery
30. Science Museum
31. Uffizi Gallery
32. Main Tourist Information Office
33. Train Station
34. Bus Station
35. San Lorenzo Market

### KEY

- Pedestrian Street / Square
- Famous for Shopping
- Landmark; Point of Interest
- *i* Tourist Information

0 — 200 meters
200 yards

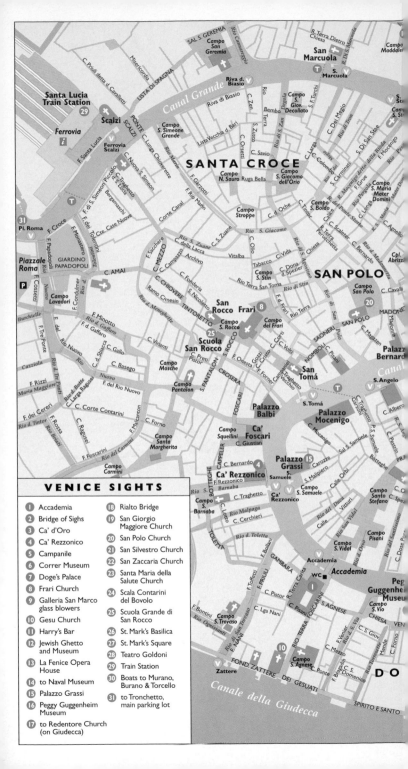

This map shows the sights of Venice. Labeled locations include:

Santa Lucia Train Station, Ferrovia, Scalzi, Ponte Scalzi, Piazzale Roma, Pi. Roma, Giardino Papadopoli, Canal Grande, Riva d. Biasio, Riva di Biasio, San Marcuola, S. Marcuola, Campo San Geremia, Campo S. Simeone Grande, Ferrovia Scalzi, SANTA CROCE, Campo N. Sauro, Ruga Bella, Campo S. Giacomo dell'Orio, Campo Stroppe, Campo S. Maria Mater Domini, SAN POLO, Campo San Polo, Campo S. Stin, Campo S. Boldo, San Rocco, Frari, Scuola San Rocco, Campo S. Rocco, Campo del Frari, San Tomá, S. Tomá, Palazzo Balbi, Palazzo Mocenigo, Palazzo Bernardo, Palazzo Grassi, Ca' Foscari, Campo S. Margherita, Campo Santa Margherita, Ca' Rezzonico, Campo S. Samuele, Campo S. Stefano, Campo S. Vidal, Accademia, Peggy Guggenheim Museum, Campo S. Vio, Zattere, FONDAMENTA ZATTERE DEI GESUATI, Canale della Giudecca, SPIRITO E SANTO, Campo Carmini, Campo Pantaion, Campo Mosche, Campo Squellini, Campo Lavadori, Campo Pisani, Campo S. Trovaso, Campo S. Agnese.

## VENICE SIGHTS

1. Accademia
2. Bridge of Sighs
3. Ca' d'Oro
4. Ca' Rezzonico
5. Campanile
6. Correr Museum
7. Doge's Palace
8. Frari Church
9. Galleria San Marco glass blowers
10. Gesu Church
11. Harry's Bar
12. Jewish Ghetto and Museum
13. La Fenice Opera House
14. to Naval Museum
15. Palazzo Grassi
16. Peggy Guggenheim Museum
17. to Redentore Church (on Giudecca)
18. Rialto Bridge
19. San Giorgio Maggiore Church
20. San Polo Church
21. San Silvestro Church
22. San Zaccaria Church
23. Santa Maria della Salute Church
24. Scala Contarini del Bovolo
25. Scuola Grande di San Rocco
26. St. Mark's Basilica
27. St. Mark's Square
28. Teatro Goldoni
29. Train Station
30. Boats to Murano, Burano & Torcello
31. to Tronchetto, main parking lot

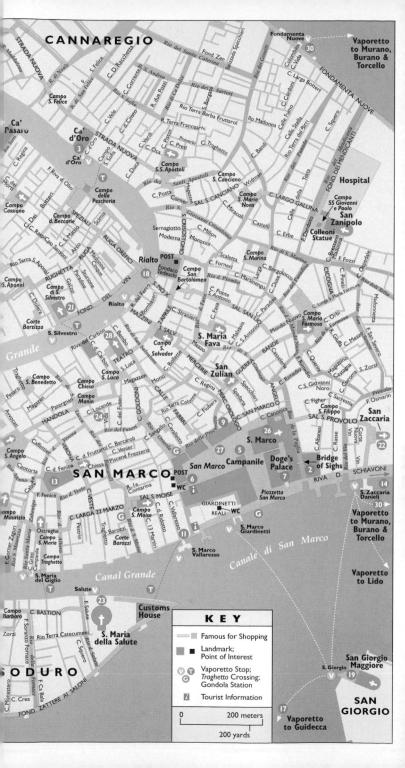

# Rick Steves'
# ITALY
# 2003

AVALON
TRAVEL

**Other ATP travel guidebooks by Rick Steves**
*Rick Steves' Best of Europe*
*Rick Steves' Europe 101: History and Art for the Traveler* (with Gene Openshaw)
*Rick Steves' Europe Through the Back Door*
*Rick Steves' Mona Winks: Self-Guided Tours of Europe's Top Museums*
    (with Gene Openshaw)
*Rick Steves' Postcards from Europe*
*Rick Steves' France* (with Steve Smith)
*Rick Steves' Germany, Austria & Switzerland*
*Rick Steves' Great Britain*
*Rick Steves' Ireland* (with Pat O'Connor)
*Rick Steves' Scandinavia*
*Rick Steves' Spain & Portugal*
*Rick Steves' Amsterdam, Bruges & Brussels* (with Gene Openshaw)
*Rick Steves' Florence* (with Gene Openshaw)
*Rick Steves' London* (with Gene Openshaw)
*Rick Steves' Paris* (with Steve Smith and Gene Openshaw)
*Rick Steves' Rome* (with Gene Openshaw)
*Rick Steves' Venice* (with Gene Openshaw)
Rick Steves' Phrase Books: French, German, Italian, Portuguese,
    Spanish, and French/Italian/German

Avalon Travel Publishing, 1400 65th Street, Suite 250, Emeryville, CA 94608

Printed in the USA by R.R. Donnelley. First printing January 2003.
Distributed by Publishers Group West.

ISBN 1-56691-464-7    •    ISSN 1084-4422

For the latest on Rick's lectures, guidebooks, tours, and public television
series, contact Europe Through the Back Door, Box 2009, Edmonds, WA
98020, 425/771-8303, fax 425/771-0833, www.ricksteves.com, or e-mail:
rick@ricksteves.com.

**Europe Through the Back Door Managing Editor:** Risa Laib
**Europe Through the Back Door Editor:** Jill Hodges
**Avalon Travel Publishing Editor:** Mia Lipman
**Avalon Travel Publishing Series Manager:** Laura Mazer
**Copy Editor:** Leslie Miller
**Research Assistance:** Sarah Murdoch, Heidi Sewell
**Production & Typesetting:** Kathleen Sparkes, White Hart Design
**Cover Design:** Janine Lehmann
**Interior Design:** Linda Braun
**Maps & Graphics:** David C. Hoerlein, Rhonda Pelikan, Zoey Platt
**Cover photo:** Santa Croce, Florence © John Elk III
**Front matter color photos:** p. i, Tuscan vineyards © Mary Liz Austin; p. iv,
    Trevi Fountain, Rome © Richard T. Nowitz; p. v, Rialto Bridge, Venice ©
    John Elk III; p. xii, Val d'Orcia hills © Terry Donnelly

# CONTENTS

# Top Destinations in Italy

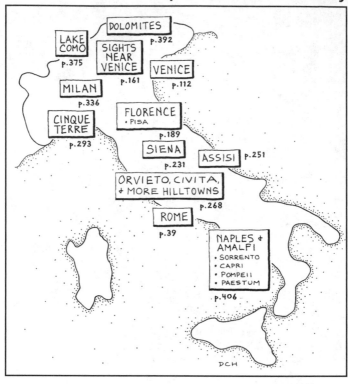

DOLOMITES p.392

LAKE COMO p.375

SIGHTS NEAR VENICE p.161

VENICE p.112

MILAN p.336

FLORENCE • PISA p.189

CINQUE TERRE p.293

SIENA p.231

ASSISI p.251

ORVIETO, CIVITA, & MORE HILLTOWNS p.268

ROME p.39

NAPLES & AMALFI
• SORRENTO
• CAPRI
• POMPEII
• PAESTUM
p.406

DCH

# INTRODUCTION

This book breaks Italy into its top big-city, small-town, and rural destinations. It then gives you all the information and opinions necessary to wring the maximum value out of your limited time and money in each of these destinations.

If you plan a month or less in Italy and have a normal appetite for information, this lean and mean little book is all you need. If you're a travel info fiend (like me), you'll find this book sorts through all the superlatives and provides a handy rack upon which to hang your supplemental information.

Italy is my favorite country. Experiencing its culture, people, and natural wonders economically and hassle-free has been my goal for over 25 years of traveling, researching, and tour guiding. With this book, I pass on to you the lessons I've learned, updated (in mid-2002) for 2003.

*Rick Steves' Italy* is a tour guide in your pocket, offering a comfortable mix of big cities and cozy towns, from brutal but *bello* Rome to *tranquillo*, traffic-free Riviera villages. It covers the predictable biggies and adds a healthy dose of "Back Door" intimacy. Along with marveling at Michelangelo's masterpieces, you'll enjoy a *bruschetta* snack as a village boy rubs fresh garlic on your toast. I've been selective, including only the top sights. For example, after visiting dozens of hill towns, I recommend just the best four (Siena, Assisi, Orvieto, and Civita).

The best is, of course, only my opinion. But after more than two busy decades of travel writing, lecturing, and tour guiding, I've developed a sixth sense for what tickles the traveler's fancy.

## This Information Is Accurate and Up-to-Date

This book is updated every year. Most publishers of guidebooks that cover a country from top to bottom can afford an update only every two or three years. Since this book is selective, I'm able to personally update it each summer. Even with an annual update, things change. But if you're traveling with the current edition of this book, I guarantee you're using the most up-to-date information available (for the latest, check www.ricksteves.com/update). This book will help you have a smooth, inexpensive trip. Use this year's edition. People who try to save a few bucks by traveling with an old book are not smart. They learn the seriousness of their mistake ... in Italy. Your trip costs about $10 per waking hour. Your time is valuable. This guidebook saves lots of time.

## Planning Your Trip

This book is organized by destinations. Each destination is a mini-vacation on its own, filled with exciting sights and comfortable, good-value places to stay. In the following chapters, you'll find:

**Planning Your Time,** a suggested schedule with thoughts on how best to use your limited time.

**Orientation,** including tourist information, city transportation, and an easy-to-read map designed to make the text clear and your arrival smooth.

**Sights with ratings:** ▲▲▲—Don't miss; ▲▲—Try hard to see; ▲—Worthwhile if you can make it; no rating—Worth knowing about.

**Sleeping** and **Eating,** with addresses and phone numbers of my favorite hotels and restaurants.

**Transportation Connections** to nearby destinations by train, and route tips for drivers.

The **appendix** is a traveler's tool kit, with telephone tips, a climate chart, events calendar, and survival phrases.

Browse through this book, choose your favorite destinations, and link them up. Then have a great trip! You'll travel like a temporary local, getting the absolute most out of every mile, minute, and dollar. You won't waste time on mediocre sights because, unlike other guidebook authors, I cover only the best. Since your major financial pitfalls are lousy, expensive hotels, I've worked hard to assemble the best accommodations values for each stop. And as you travel the route I know and love, I'm happy you'll be meeting some of my favorite Italian people.

## Trip Costs

Six components make up your trip cost: airfare, surface transportation, room and board, sightseeing/entertainment, shopping/miscellany, and gelato.

**Airfare:** Don't try to sort through the mess. Find and use a good travel agent. A basic round-trip USA-to-Milan (or Rome) flight should cost $700 to $1,000, depending on where you fly from and when (cheapest in winter). Always consider saving time and money in Europe by flying "open jaw" (into one city and out of another).

**Surface Transportation:** For a three-week whirlwind trip to all my recommended destinations, allow $300 per person for public transportation (train and buses) or $500 per person (based on 2 people sharing a car) for a three-week car rental, tolls, gas, and insurance. Car rental is cheapest if arranged from the United States. Some train passes are available only outside of Europe. You might save money by getting an Italian railpass or buying tickets as you go (see "Transportation," page 13).

**Room and Board:** You can thrive in Italy on $70 a day for room and board (allow $80/day for Rome). This $70/day budget allows $10 for lunch, $20 for dinner, and $40 for lodging (based on 2 people splitting the cost of an $80 double room that includes breakfast). If you've got more money, I've listed great ways to spend it. And students and tightwads can enjoy Italy for as little as $40 a day ($20 for a bed, $20 for meals and snacks). But budget sleeping and eating require the skills covered later in this chapter (and in more depth in my book *Rick Steves' Europe Through the Back Door*).

**Sightseeing and Entertainment:** In big cities, figure about $5 to $7 per major sight (museums, Colosseum), $2 for minor ones (climbing church towers), and $25 to $30 per person for splurge experiences (such as tours and gondola rides). An overall average of $15 a day works for most. Don't skimp here. After all, this category directly powers most of the experiences all the other expenses are designed to make possible.

**Shopping and Miscellany:** Figure $1 per postcard, coffee, and soft drink and $2 per gelato. Shopping can vary in cost from nearly nothing to a small fortune. Good budget travelers find that this category has little to do with assembling a trip full of lifelong and wonderful memories.

## Exchange Rate

I've priced things throughout this book in euros.

---

1 euro (€) = about $1.

---

Just like the dollar, the euro is broken down into 100 cents. You'll find coins ranging from 1 cent to 2 euros, and bills from 5 euros to 500 euros.

## Prices, Times, and Discounts

The opening hours and telephone numbers listed in this book are accurate as of mid-2002—but once you pin Italy down, it wiggles. At each major destination, ask the local tourist information office for a current list of the city's sights, hours, and prices. Any guidebook on Italy starts to yellow even before it's printed.

In Italy—and in this book—you'll use the 24-hour clock. It's the same through 12:00 noon, then keep going—13:00, 14:00 . . . . For anything over 12, subtract 12 and add p.m. (14:00 is 2:00 p.m.).

Don't expect discounts on sights in Italy if you're a youth or senior. Discounts are generally available only to people that are members of the European Union and "reciprocating countries," meaning countries that offer discounts to European youth and seniors—which America doesn't.

## When to Go

Italy's best travel months are May, June, September, and October. November through April usually has pleasant weather, with generally none of the sweat and stress of the tourist season (but expect shorter hours, more lunchtime breaks, and fewer activities).

Peak season offers the longest hours and the most exciting slate of activities—but terrible crowds and, at times, suffocating heat. During peak times, many resort-area hotels maximize business by requiring that guests buy dinner in their restaurants. August, the local holiday month, isn't as bad as many make it out to be, but big cities tend to be quiet (with discounted hotel prices), and beach and mountain resorts are jammed (with higher hotel prices). If you anticipate crowds, arrive early in the day or call hotels in advance (call from one hotel to the next; your fluent-in-Italian receptionist can help you).

Summer temperatures range from the 70s in Milan to the high 80s and 90s in Rome. Air-conditioning, when available, usually doesn't kick in until June 1 and shuts off September 30. Most midrange hotels come with air-conditioning—a worthwhile splurge in the summer. Spring and fall can be cold, and many hotels do not turn on their heat. In the winter, it often drops to the 40s in Milan and the 50s in Rome. (See climate chart in the appendix.)

## Sightseeing Priorities

Depending on the length of your trip, here are my recommended priorities:

| | |
|---|---|
| 3 days: | Florence, Venice |
| 5 days, add: | Rome |
| 7 days, add: | Cinque Terre |
| 10 days, add: | Civita and Siena |
| 14 days, add: | Sorrento, Naples, Pompeii, Amalfi, Paestum |
| 18 days, add: | Milan, Lake Como, Varenna, Assisi |
| 21 days, add: | Dolomites, Verona, Ravenna |

(This includes everything on the "Whirlwind Three-Week Tour" map on page 9.)

Considering that you're likely to go both broke and crazy driving in Italian cities, and how handy and affordable Italy's trains and buses are, I'd do most of Italy by public transportation. If you want to drive, consider doing the big, intense stuff (Rome, Naples area, Milan, Florence, and Venice) by train or bus and renting a car for the hill towns of Tuscany and Umbria and for the Dolomites. A car is a worthless headache on the Riviera and in the Lake Como area.

## Red Tape, Business Hours, and VAT Refunds

You need a passport but no visa or shots to travel in Italy.

**Business Hours:** Traditionally, Italy uses the siesta plan. People work from about 8:00 to 13:00 and from 15:30 to 19:00, Monday through Saturday. Many businesses have adopted the government's new recommended 8:00 to 14:00 workday. In tourist areas, shops are open longer.

**VAT Refunds for Shoppers:** Wrapped into the purchase price of your Italian souvenirs is a Value Added Tax (VAT) that's generally about 17 percent. If you purchase more than €155 worth of goods at a store that participates in the VAT refund scheme, you're entitled to get most of that tax back. Personally, I've never felt that VAT refunds are worth the hassle, but if you do, here's the scoop.

If you're lucky, the merchant will subtract the tax when you make your purchase (this is more likely to occur if the store ships the goods to your home). Otherwise, you'll need to:

Get the paperwork. Have the merchant completely fill out the necessary refund document, called a "cheque." You'll have to present your passport at the store.

Have your cheque(s) stamped at the border at your last stop in the European Union by the customs agent who deals with VAT refunds. It's best to keep your purchases in your carry-on for viewing, but if they're too large or dangerous (such as knives) to carry on, then track down the proper customs agent to inspect them before you check your bag. You're not supposed to use your purchased goods before you leave. If you show up at customs wearing your new shoes, officials might look the other way—or deny you a refund.

To collect your refund, you'll need to return your stamped documents to the retailer or its representative. Many merchants work with a service, such as Global Refund or Cashback, which have offices at major airports, ports, or border crossings. These services, which extract a 4 percent fee, can refund your money immediately in your currency of choice or credit your card (within two billing cycles). If you have to deal directly with the retailer, mail the store your stamped documents and then wait. It could take months.

## Banking

You'll want to spend local hard cash. The fastest way to get it is by using plastic: your ATM, credit, or debit card at a cash machine (Bancomat). To withdraw cash, you'll need to use your four-digit PIN (numbers only, no letters, seven-digit PIN won't work) with your bank card. Before you go, verify with your bank that your card will work.

Visa and MasterCard are more commonly accepted than American Express. Bring two cards in case one is demagnetized, eaten by a machine, or rejected by a temperamental ATM. (If your card is rejected, try again, and request a smaller amount; some cash machines won't let you take out more than about €150—don't take it personally). Just like at home, credit or debit cards work easily at larger hotels, restaurants, and shops, but smaller businesses prefer payment in hard cash.

If you bring traveler's checks, use them only as a backup. Regular banks have the best rates for cashing traveler's checks. For a large exchange, it pays to compare rates and fees (Bank of Sicily consistently has good rates). Banking hours are generally 8:30–13:30 & 15:30–16:30 Monday through Friday, but can vary wildly. Banks are slow; simple transactions can take 15 to 30 minutes. Post offices and train stations usually change money if you can't get to a bank.

Use a money belt. Thieves target tourists. A money belt (order online at www.ricksteves.com or call 425/771-8303 for our free newsletter/catalog) provides peace of mind and allows you to carry lots of cash safely.

Don't be petty about changing money. The greatest avoidable money-changing expense is wasting time every few days to return to a bank. Change a week's worth of money, get big bills, stuff them in your money belt, and travel!

## Language Barrier

Many Italians in larger towns and the tourist trade speak at least some English. Still, you'll get more smiles and results by using at least the Italian pleasantries. In smaller, nontouristy towns, Italian is the norm. See the "Survival Phrases" near the end of this book (excerpted from *Rick Steves' Italian Phrase Book*).

Note that Italian is pronounced much like English, with a few exceptions, such as: *c* followed by *e* or *i* is pronounced *ch* (to ask, *"Per centro?"*—"To the center?"—you say, pehr CHEN-troh). In Italian, *ch* is pronounced like the hard *c* in Pinocchio (*chiesa*—church—is pronounced kee-AY-zah). Give it your best shot. Italians appreciate your efforts.

## Travel Smart

Many people travel through Italy thinking it's a chaotic mess. They feel any attempt at efficient travel is futile. This is dead wrong—and expensive. Italy, which seems as orderly as spilled spaghetti, actually functions quite well. Only those who under-stand this and travel smart can enjoy Italy on a budget.

Your trip to Italy is like a complex play—easier to follow and really appreciate on a second viewing. While no one does the same trip twice to gain that advantage, reading this book in its entirety before your trip accomplishes much the same thing.

Reread entire chapters as you travel, and visit local tourist information offices. Upon arrival in a new town, lay the ground-work for a smooth departure; write down the schedule for the train or bus you'll take when you depart. Buy a phone card (or cell phone) and use it for reservations, reconfirmations, and double-checking hours. Use taxis in the big cities, bring along a water bottle, and linger in the shade. Connect with the cultures. Set up your own quest for the best gelato, sculpture, cheesy souvenir, or whatever. Enjoy the friendliness of the local people. Ask questions. Most locals are eager to point you in their idea of the right direc-tion. Keep a notepad in your pocket for organizing your thoughts. Those who expect to travel smart, do.

Sundays have the same pros and cons as they do for travelers in the United States. Sightseeing attractions are generally open but have shorter hours, shops and banks are closed, and minor transportation connections are more frustrating (e.g., no bus service to or from Civita). City traffic is light. Rowdy evenings are rare on Sundays. Saturdays are virtually weekdays with earlier closing hours. Hotels in tourist areas are often booked up on Easter week-end, in August, and on Fridays and Saturdays. Religious holidays and train strikes can catch you by surprise anywhere in Italy.

Plan ahead for banking, laundry, post-office chores, and picnics. Mix intense and relaxed periods. Every trip (and every traveler) needs at least a few slack days. Pace yourself. Assume you will return. Drink your water *con gas*.

## Tourist Information

During your trip, your first stop in each town should be the tourist office (abbreviated "TI" in this book, and "i," "*turismo*," and "APT" in Italy). While Italian TIs are about half as helpful as those in other countries, their information is twice as important. Prepare. Have a list of questions and a proposed plan to double-check. If you're arriving late, telephone ahead (and try to get a map for your next destination from a TI in the town you're departing from).

Be wary of the travel agencies or special information services that masquerade as TIs but serve fancy hotels and tour companies. They are crooks and liars selling things you don't need.

While the TI is eager to book you a room, use its room-finding service only as a last resort. Across Europe, room-finding services are charging commissions from hotels, taking fees from travelers, and blacklisting establishments that buck their material-istic rules. They are unable to give hard opinions on the relative value of one place over another. The accommodations stakes are too high to go potluck through the TI. You'll do better going direct with the listings in this book.

## Italy's Best Three-Week Trip

| Day | Plan | Sleep in |
|-----|------|----------|
| 1 | Arrive in Milan | Milan |
| 2 | Milan to Lake Como | Varenna |
| 3 | Lake Como | Varenna |
| 4 | To Dolomites via Verona (pick up car at Lake Como) | Castelrotto |
| 5 | Dolomites | Castelrotto |
| 6 | To Venice | Venice |
| 7 | Venice | Venice |
| 8 | To Florence | Florence |
| 9 | Florence | Florence |
| 10 | To Cinque Terre | Vernazza |
| 11 | Cinque Terre | Vernazza |
| 12 | To Siena | Siena |
| 13 | Siena | Siena |
| 14 | To Orvieto | Orvieto |
| 15 | Orvieto | Orvieto |
| 16 | To Sorrento via Pompeii | Sorrento |
| 17 | Sorrento | Sorrento |
| 18 | To Paestum | Sorrento |
| 19 | To Rome, drop car | Rome |
| 20 | Rome | Rome |
| 21 | Rome | Rome |
| 22 | Rome, fly home | |

This trip is designed to be done by car, but works fine by rail with a few modifications. An Italy Rail Card (8 days in 1 month) works well—pay out of pocket for short runs, such as Milan to Varenna, or the hops between villages in the Cinque Terre. While you can fly into Milan or Rome, I'd choose Milan and work my way south, flying out of Rome. Upon landing in Milan, go directly to Lake Como to relax and get over jet lag. Then see Milan for a half day, but sleep in cozier Verona. Consider basing in Bolzano in the Dolomites. From Venice, go straight to the Cinque Terre (2 direct trains/day), then do Florence and Siena. A car is efficient in the hill towns of Tuscany and Umbria, but a headache elsewhere. Sorrento is a good home base for Naples and the Amalfi Coast. Skip Paestum unless you love Greek ruins. To save Venice for last, start in Milan, seeing everything but Venice on the way south, then sleeping through everything you've already seen by catching the night train from Naples to Venice. This saves you a day and gives you an early arrival in Venice.

## Whirlwind Three-Week Tour of Italy

## Italian Tourist Offices in the United States

Before your trip, contact the nearest Italian TI, briefly describe your trip, and request information. You'll get the general packet and, if you ask for specifics (individual city maps, a calendar of festivals, good hikes around Lake Como, info on wine-tasting in Umbria, and so on), an impressive amount of help. If you have a specific problem, they're a good source of sympathy.

Contact the office nearest you...

In **New York:** 630 5th Ave. #1565, New York, NY 10111, brochure hotline 212/245-4822, 212/245-5618, fax 212/586-9249, e-mail: enitny@italiantourism.com.

In **Illinois:** 500 N. Michigan Ave. #2240, Chicago, IL 60611, brochure hotline 312/644-0990, 312/644-0996, fax 312/644-3019, e-mail: enitch@italiantourism.com.

In **California:** 12400 Wilshire Blvd. #550, Los Angeles, CA 90025, brochure hotline 310/820-0098, 310/820-1898, fax 310/820-6357, e-mail: enitla@earthlink.net.

**Web sites:** www.italiantourism.com (Italian Tourist Board in the United States), www.museionline.it (museums in Italy, in English), and www.fs-on-line.com (Italian rail schedules).

## Tips on Sightseeing in Italy

• Churches offer some amazing art (usually free), a cool respite from heat, and a welcome seat. A modest dress code (no bare shoulders or shorts for anyone) is enforced at larger churches, such as Venice's St. Mark's and the Vatican's St. Peter's. Some churches have coin-operated audioboxes that describe the art and history. A deposit in the coin box near a piece of art often illuminates the art (and presents a better photo opportunity). Whenever possible, let there be light.

• Reservations are advisable for some of the more famous museums (Florence: Uffizi and Accademia) and mandatory at others (Milan: Da Vinci's *Last Supper*, Padua: Scrovegni Chapel, Rome: Borghese Gallery and Nero's Golden House).

• Hours listed anywhere can vary. On holidays, expect shorter hours or closures. In summer, some sights are open late, allowing easy viewing without crowds. Ask the local TI for a current listing of museum hours. You can confirm sightseeing plans each morning with a quick 10-cent telephone call asking, "Are you open today?" (*"Aperto oggi?"*; ah-PER-toh OH-jee) and "What time do you close?" (*"A che ora chiuso?"*; ah kay OH-rah kee-OO-zoh). I've included telephone numbers for this purpose.

• Art historians and Italians refer to the great Florentine centuries by dropping a thousand years. The *Trecento* (300s), *Quattrocento* (400s), and *Cinquecento* (500s) were the 1300s, 1400s, and 1500s.

• In Italian museums, art is dated with A.C. (for Avanti Cristo, or B.C.) and D.C. (for Dopo Cristo, or A.D.). O.K.?

• Audioguides are becoming increasingly common at museums. These small portable devices give you information in English on what you're seeing. After you dial a number that appears next to a particular work of art, you listen to the spiel (cutting it short if you want). Though the information can be dry, it's usually worthwhile (about €4; extra for 2 earphones).

• About half the visitors at Italian museums are English (not Italian) speakers. If a museum lacks audioguides and the only English you encounter explains how to pay, politely ask if there are plans to include English descriptions of the art. Think of it as a service to those who follow.

• In museums, rooms can begin closing about 30 to 60 minutes before actual closing time. Don't save the best for last.

• WCs at museums are usually free and clean.

## Recommended Guidebooks

Especially if you'll be traveling beyond my recommended destinations, you may want some supplemental information. When you consider the improvements they'll make in your $3,000 vacation, $30 for extra maps and books is money well spent. Especially for several people traveling by car, the weight and expense are negligible. One budget tip can save the price of an extra guidebook.

Lonely Planet's *Italy* is thorough, well-researched, and packed with good maps and hotel recommendations for low- to moderate-budget travelers, but it's not updated annually. Use it only with a one- or two-year-old copyright. The hip *Rough Guide to Italy* (British researchers, more insightful) and the highly opinionated *Let's Go: Italy* (by Harvard students, better hotel listings) are great for students and vagabonds. If you're a low-budget train traveler interested in the youth and night scene (which I have basically ignored), get *Let's Go: Italy*. The Italy section in the bigger *Let's Go: Europe* is sparse.

**Cultural and Sightseeing Guides:** The colorful Eyewitness series is popular with travelers (editions include Italy, Florence/Tuscany, Venice, Rome, and Sicily). They are fun for their great, easy-to-grasp graphics and photos, and just right for people who want only factoids. But the Eyewitness written content is relatively skimpy, and the books weigh a ton. I buy them in Italy (no more expensive than in the United States) or simply borrow them for a minute from other travelers at certain sights to make sure I'm aware of that place's highlights. The tall, green Michelin guides to Italy and Rome have minimal information on room and board, but include great maps for drivers and lots of solid encyclopedic coverage of sights, customs, and the culture (sold in English in Italy). The Cadogan guides to various parts of Italy offer an insightful look at the rich and confusing local culture. Those heading for Florence or Rome should read Irving Stone's *The Agony and the Ecstasy* for a great—if romanticized—rundown on Michelangelo, the Medici family, and the turbulent times of the Renaissance.

## Rick Steves' Books and Videos

*Rick Steves' Europe Through the Back Door 2003* gives you budget travel skills for minimizing jet lag, packing light, planning your itinerary, traveling by car or train, finding budget beds without reservations, changing money, avoiding rip-offs, outsmarting thieves, hurdling the language barrier, staying healthy, taking great photographs, using your bidet, and much more. The book also includes chapters on 35 of my favorite "Back Doors," six of which are in Italy.

**Rick Steves' Country Guides** are a series of eight guidebooks—including this book—covering Great Britain, Ireland,

France, Spain/Portugal, Germany/Austria/Switzerland,
Scandinavia, and the Best of Europe. These are updated annually;
most are available in bookstores in December, the rest in January.

My **City Guides** cover Rome, Venice, Florence, Paris,
London, and—new for 2003—*Rick Steves' Amsterdam, Bruges &
Brussels*. These practical guides offer in-depth coverage of the
sights, hotels, restaurants, and nightlife in these grand cities, along
with illustrated tours of their great museums. To make your visit
to Italy's super cities more meaningful, consider getting the Rome,
Venice, or Florence city guides. They're updated annually and
come out in December and January.

*Rick Steves' Europe 101: History and Art for the Traveler* (with
Gene Openshaw, 2000) gives you the story of Europe's people,
history, and art. Written for smart people who were sleeping in
their history and art classes before they knew they were going to
Europe, *101* really helps resurrect the rubble.

*Rick Steves' Mona Winks: Self-Guided Tours of Europe's Top
Museums* (with Gene Openshaw, 2001) gives you easy-to-follow,
self-guided tours of Europe's top 25 museums and cultural sites.
Nearly half of the book is devoted to Italy, with tours of Rome
(Colosseum, Forum, Pantheon, National Museum of Rome,
Borghese Gallery, Vatican Museum, and St. Peter's Basilica),
Venice (St. Mark's, Doge's Palace, and Accademia Gallery), and
Florence (Uffizi Gallery, Bargello, Michelangelo's *David*, and a
Renaissance walk through the town center). If you want to enjoy
the great sights and museums of Italy, *Mona* will be a valued friend.

In Italy, a phrase book is as fun as it is necessary. My *Rick
Steves' Italian Phrase Book* will help you meet the people and
stretch your budget. It's written by a monoglot who, for more
than 25 years, has fumbled through Italy struggling with all the
other phrase books. Use this fun and practical communication aid
to make accurate hotel reservations over the telephone, ask for a
free taste of cantaloupe-flavored gelato at the *gelatería*, have the
man in the deli make you a sandwich, and tell your cabbie that
if he doesn't slow down, you'll throw up.

My latest television series, *Rick Steves' Europe*, features five new
shows on Italy: Venice, Veneto (sights near Venice), Florence, Siena/
Assisi, and the Cinque Terre. Between the new series and the earlier
*Travels in Europe* series (more than 80 shows total), I've hosted
and written 15 half-hour shows on Italy. These air throughout the
United States on public television stations. Each episode is also available on an information-packed home video (order online at www
.ricksteves.com or call 425/771-8303 for our free newsletter/catalog).

*Rick Steves' Postcards from Europe*, my autobiographical book,
packs more than 25 years of travel anecdotes and insights into the

ultimate 3,000-mile European adventure. Through my guidebooks, I share my favorite European discoveries with you. *Postcards* introduces you to my favorite European friends. Half of *Postcards* is set in Italy: Venice, Florence, Rome, and the Cinque Terre.

All of my books are published by Avalon Travel Publishing (www.travelmatters.com).

## Maps

The maps in this book, drawn by Dave Hoerlein, are concise and simple. Dave, who is well-traveled in Italy, designed the maps to help you locate recommended places and the tourist offices, where you can pick up more in-depth maps of the city or region (cheap or free).

For a map of Italy, consider my Rick Steves' Italy Planning Map—geared to travelers' needs—with sightseeing destinations listed prominently. On the back of the Italy map, you'll find city maps of Rome, Venice, and Florence (order online at www.rick-steves.com, or call 425/771-8303; other maps in the series are Europe, France, and Britain/Ireland).

Train travelers can do fine with a simple rail map (such as the one that comes with your railpass) and city maps from the TI as they travel. But drivers shouldn't skimp on maps. Excellent maps are available throughout Italy at bookstores, newsstands, and gas stations. Get a good 1:200,000 map to get the most out of your miles; study the key to get the most sightseeing value out of your map.

## Tours of Italy

Travel agents will tell you about normal tours of Italy, but they won't tell you about ours. At Europe Through the Back Door, we offer one-week getaways to **Rome**, to **Venice**, and to **Florence** (departures March–Dec, 20 people max).

Our longer Italy tours come with two great guides and a big, roomy bus. The 20-day **Best of Italy** tour features all of the biggies and our favorite "back doors" (April–Oct, 24–26 people). The 15-day **Village Italy** adventure laces together intimate towns (April–Oct, 20–22 people). For more information, call 425/771-8303 or visit www.ricksteves.com.

## Transportation

### By Car or Train?

Each mode of transportation has pros and cons. Public transportation is one of the few bargains in Italy. Trains and buses are inexpensive and good. City-to-city travel is faster, easier, and cheaper by train than by car. Trains give you the convenience and economy of doing long stretches overnight. By train, I arrive relaxed and well-rested—not so by car.

Parking, gas (about $4 per gallon), and tolls are expensive in Italy. But drivers enjoy more control, especially in the countryside. Cars carry your luggage for you, generally from door to door— especially important for heavy packers (such as chronic shoppers and families traveling with children). And groups know that the more people you pack into a car or minibus, the cheaper it gets per person.

## Trains

To travel by train cheaply in Italy, you can simply buy tickets as you go. But Italy's train ticket system and its fast-train supplements confound even the locals, so I'd pay more and go with the Italian State Railway's Italy Rail Card (see chart on page 17). Although the Rail Card covers most supplements, it doesn't cover reservations (purchased separately for around €4).

Avoid big-city train station ticket lines whenever you can. At travel agencies, such as CIT or American Express, you can make reservations, buy tickets (including Kilometric Tickets— see below), pay for supplements, and reserve a *cuccetta* (overnight berth). The cost is the same or minimally higher (about €2), the lines and language barrier are smaller, and you'll save time.

Whether you're traveling alone or with others, consider Italy's **Kilometric Ticket**. Unlike the Rail Card, the Kilometric Ticket doesn't cover fast-train supplements, but it's especially economical for groups. One to five people can split 3,000 kilometers (1,900 miles) of travel on it for around $105 second class, $160 first class (buy it in Italy at CIT travel agencies or major train stations; valid 2 months). The Kilometric Ticket is a little booklet with 20 coupons, each good for a one-way journey for any or all of the listed travelers. Before you board the train, go to a railway clerk at the ticket window (or a CIT travel agent), and state where you're going, and the clerk will subtract from your total the number of kilometers your journey takes (kids 4–11 "cost" only half as many kilometers as an adult). If any segment of your journey requires a supplement (usually just a few dollars, up to $15 for the fastest trains), pay it at this time, when your ticket is being filled out by the clerk. (If your ticket is first class, get a first-class supplement.) You can stop en route; you're allowed an additional six hours to complete trips less than 200 kilometers (or 24–48 hours with unlimited stops for trips longer than 200 kilometers). Don't tear out any of the pages of your Kilometric Ticket. Note that you need to validate your ticket before boarding (see below).

The **Tariffa Famiglia** discount is available for two or more adults traveling with one or more children (ages 4–11) when they

## Deciphering Italian Train Schedules

At the station, look for the big yellow posters labeled *Partenze*—Departures (ignore the white posters, which show arrivals).

Schedules are listed chronologically, hour by hour, showing the trains leaving the station throughout the day. The first column *(Ora)* lists the time of departure. The next column *(Treno)* shows the type of train. The third column *(Classi Servizi)* lists the services available (first- and second-class cars, dining car, couchettes, etc.) and, more important, whether you need reservations (usually denoted by an *R* in a box). The next column lists the destination of the train *(Principali Fermate Destinazioni)*, often showing intermediate stops, followed by the final destination, with arrival times listed throughout in parentheses. Note that *your* final destination may be listed in fine print as an intermediate destination. If you're going from Milan to Florence, scan the schedule and you'll notice that virtually all trains that terminate in Rome stop in Florence en route. Travelers who read the fine print end up with a greater choice of trains. The next column *(Servizi Diretti e Annotazioni)* has pertinent notes about the train, such as "also stops in . . ." *(ferma anche a . . .)*, "doesn't stop in . . ." *(non ferma a . . .)*, "stops in every station" *(ferma in tutte le stazioni)*, and so on. The last column lists the track *(Binario)* the train departs from. Confirm the *binario* with an additional source: a ticket seller, the electronic board listing immediate departures, TV monitors on the platform, or the railway officials who are usually standing by the train unless you really need them.

For any odd symbols on the poster, look at the key at the end. Some of the phrasing can be deciphered easily, such as *servizio periodico* (periodical service—doesn't always run). For the trickier ones, ask a local or railway official or simply take a different train.

buy first- or second-class point-to-point tickets in Italy. One child travels free, and any additional children travel for half price. All members of the group must travel together.

Before boarding the train, you must **validate** (stamp) your train documents in the machine near the platform. This includes whatever you need to take a particular trip, which can be as simple as a single ticket, or can involve a combination of the pertinent

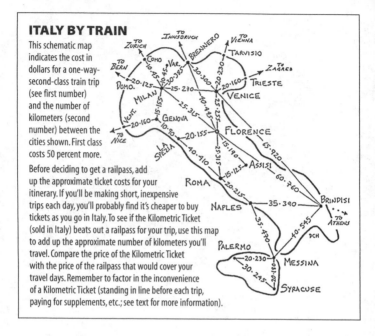

## ITALY BY TRAIN

This schematic map indicates the cost in dollars for a one-way-second-class train trip (see first number) and the number of kilometers (second number) between the cities shown. First class costs 50 percent more.

Before deciding to get a railpass, add up the approximate ticket costs for your itinerary. If you'll be making short, inexpensive trips each day, you'll probably find it's cheaper to buy tickets as you go in Italy. To see if the Kilometric Ticket (sold in Italy) beats out a railpass for your trip, use this map to add up the approximate number of kilometers you'll travel. Compare the price of the Kilometric Ticket with the price of the railpass that would cover your travel days. Remember to factor in the inconvenience of a Kilometric Ticket (standing in line before each trip, paying for supplements, etc.; see text for more information).

page of a Kilometric Ticket, a supplement, seat reservation, or a *cuccetta* (overnight berth) reservation. You don't need to stamp Eurailpasses or Italy Rail Cards.

For travel exclusively in Italy, a 17-country **Eurailpass** is a bad value. If you're branching out beyond Italy, the Eurail Select-pass ($502 for 10 days in 2 months—2002 price) allows you to tailor a pass to your trip, provided you're traveling in three adjacent countries directly connected by rail or ferry. For instance, you could choose France–Italy–Greece or Germany–Austria–Italy. New in 2002, the France and Italy pass combines just those countries (but if your route crosses Switzerland, the Selectpass is a better choice).

**Youth** and **seniors** can buy €25 cards at any train station to get discounts on their train travel in Italy (20 percent discount on second-class or first-class tickets, valid for 6 months). If you're under 26, ask for a Carta Verde. If you're 60 or over, request a Carta d'Argento.

You'll encounter several **types of trains** in Italy. Along with the various milk-run trains, there are the slow IR (Interregional) and *directo* trains, the medium *expresso*, the fast IC (Intercity), and the bullet-train Eurostar Italia (a.k.a. the T.A.V., which stands for *Treno Alta Velocita*). The Eurostar Italia, which requires about a

Prices listed are for 2002. My free *Rick Steves' Guide to European Railpasses* has the latest on 2003 prices. To get the railpass guide or an order form, call us at 425/771-8303 or visit www.ricksteves.com/rail. Italy passes are also sold in Italy at travel agencies and major train stations.

See the text in this section for money-saving local options in Italy.

## ITALY FLEXI RAIL CARD

|  | 1st Class Individual | 1st Class Saver | 2nd Class Individual | 2nd Class Saver | 2nd Class Youth |
|---|---|---|---|---|---|
| Any 4 days in 1 month | $239 | $203 | $191 | $162 | $159 |
| Any 8 days in 1 month | 334 | 284 | 268 | 227 | 223 |
| Any 12 days in 1 month | 429 | 365 | 343 | 292 | 286 |

Kids 4-11: half adult or saver price, under 4: free. Saver price per person for two or more.

## ITALY RAIL & DRIVE PASS

Any 3 days of rail travel + 2 days of Hertz car rental in 1 month.

| Car Category | 1st Class | 2nd Class | Extra car day |
|---|---|---|---|
| Economy | $251 | $195 | $41 |
| Compact | 265 | 215 | 61 |
| Intermediate | 273 | 222 | 67 |
| Small Automatic | 289 | 222 | 67 |

Rail & Drive prices are approximate per person, two traveling together. Solo travelers pay about 20% more. For more info, call your travel agent or Rail Europe at 800/438-7245.

## FRANCE 'N ITALY PASS

|  | 1st Class Individual | 1st Class Saver | 2nd Class Individual | 2nd Class Saver | 2nd Class Youth |
|---|---|---|---|---|---|
| Any 4 days in 2 months | $279 | $239 | $239 | $209 | $199 |
| Extra rail days (max 6) | 28 | 25 | 25 | 22 | 21 |

Kids 4-11: half adult or saver price, under 4: free. Youthpasses are for travelers under age 26 only. Saver prices are per person for two or more.

Be aware of your route. Many daytime connections from Paris to Italy pass through Switzerland (an add'l $40 2nd class or $60 1st class if not covered by your pass). Most night trains, and routes via Nice, Torino, or Modane, will bypass Switzerland (consult a good timetable for details). On a Paris-Venice night route, a morning change in Milan avoids Switzerland.

## EURAIL SELECTPASSES

This pass covers travel in three adjacent countries. For details, visit www.ricksteves.com/rail or see *Rick Steves' Guide to European Railpasses.*

|  | 1st Class Selectpass | 1st Class Saverpass | 2nd Class Youthpass |
|---|---|---|---|
| 5 days in 2 months | $346 | $294 | $243 |
| 6 days in 2 months | 380 | 322 | 266 |
| 8 days in 2 months | 444 | 378 | 310 |
| 10 days in 2 months | 502 | 428 | 352 |

Saverpass: price is per person for two or more traveling together at all times.
Youthpasses: Under age 26 only. Kids 4-11 pay half adult fare; under 4: free.

## Italy's Public Transportation

KEY:  — RAIL   --- BUS   ···· SHIP

*NOT TO SCALE*   ⊙ GOOD OVERNIGHT STOPS

€16 supplement even if you have a railpass, provides two-thirds of the train service from Rome to Milan, Florence, Venice, or Naples. Even with supplements, fast trains are affordable (e.g., a second-class Rome-to-Venice ticket costs about $50 with express supplement). Buying supplements on the train comes with a nasty penalty.

**First-class** tickets cost 50 percent more than **second-class**.

While second-class cars go as fast as their first-class neighbors, Italy is one country where I would consider the splurge of first class. The easiest way to upgrade a second-class ticket once on-board a crowded train is to nurse a drink in the snack car.

Trains can fill up, even in first class; if a popular train route originates at your departure point (e.g., you're catching the Milan-to-Venice train in Milan), arrive a minimum of 15 minutes before the departure time to snare a seat. If you anticipate a crowd, you can get a firm seat reservation in advance for about €4.

Newsstands sell up-to-date regional and all-Italy **timetables** (€4, ask for the *orario ferroviaro*). There is an all-Italy telephone number for train information: tel. 848-888-088 (daily 7:00–21:00, automated, in Italian, get an Italian speaker to listen for you). On the Web, check http://bahn.hafas.de/bin/query.exe/en or www.fs-on-line.com.

Italian trains are famous for their thieves. Never leave a bag unattended. There have been cases of bandits gassing an entire car before looting the snoozing gang. I've noticed that police now ride the trains, and things seem more controlled. Still, for an **overnight** trip, I'd feel safe only in a *cuccetta* (a berth in a special sleeping car with an attendant who keeps track of who comes and goes while you sleep—approximately €13 in a 6-bed compartment, €18 in a less cramped 4-bed compartment).

Many stations have **baggage storage** (*deposito* or *bagagli*) where you can safely leave your bag for €3 per 12-hour period (payable when you pick up the bag). Some larger stations also have lockers, but they are a bit complicated to figure out (the smiley slot takes bills).

**Strikes** are common. Strikes generally last a day, and train employees will simply say, "*Sciopero*" (strike). But in actuality, sporadic trains, following no particular schedule, lumber down the tracks during most strikes.

## Car Rental

Research car rental before you go. It's cheaper to arrange for car rentals through your travel agent while still in the United States. Rent by the week with unlimited mileage. If you need a car for three or more weeks, it's cheaper to lease; you'll save money on insurance and taxes. Explore your drop-off options (south of Rome can be a problem).

For peace of mind, I purchase collision damage waiver (CDW) insurance, which covers the value of the car (sometimes entirely, but more often with a small deductible) in case of an accident. CDW costs from $10 to $25 a day, depending on the car and the company. Figure roughly $150 per week. A few "gold" credit cards

## Standard European Road Signs

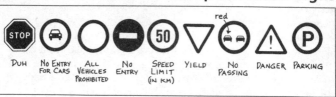

DUH   NO ENTRY FOR CARS   ALL VEHICLES PROHIBITED   NO ENTRY   SPEED LIMIT (IN KM)   YIELD   NO PASSING   DANGER   PARKING

include CDW coverage if you pay for the rental with the card; quiz your credit-card company on the worst-case scenario.

Theft insurance (different from CDW insurance) is mandatory when you're renting a car for use in Italy. The insurance usually costs about $10 to $15 a day, payable when you pick up the car.

A rail-and-drive pass (such as a EurailDrive, Europass Drive, Selectpass Drive, or Italy Rail and Drive) can be put to thoughtful use. Certain areas are great by car, such as the Dolomites and the hill towns of Tuscany and Umbria, while most of Italy is best by train.

### Driving

Driving in Italy is frightening—a video game for keeps, and you only get one quarter. All you need is a U.S. driver's license and a car. According to everybody but the Italian police, international driver's permits are not necessary. The police fine you if they can't read your license.

**Autostradas:** Italy's freeway system is as good as our interstate system, but you'll pay about a dollar for every 10 minutes of use. (I paid €20 for the four-hour drive from Bolzano to Pisa.) While I favor the autostradas because I feel they're safer, cheaper (saving time and gas), and less nerve-racking than smaller roads, savvy local drivers know which toll-free "superstradas" are actually faster and more direct than the autostrada (e.g., Florence to Pisa). For more information, visit www.autostrade.it.

**Gas:** Most cars take unleaded gas (from green pumps, available everywhere). Autostrada rest stops are self-service stations open daily without a siesta break. Small-town stations are usually cheaper and offer full service but shorter hours. Many 24-hour-a-day stations are entirely automated, with machines that trade gas for paper money.

**Metric:** A liter is about a quart, four to a gallon; a kilometer is about six-tenths of a mile. Figure kilometers to miles by cutting them in half and adding back 10 percent of the original (120 km: 60 + 12 = 72 miles, 300 km: 150 + 30 = 180 miles).

**Parking:** White lines generally mean parking is free. Blue

## Driving in Italy

lines mean you'll have to pay—usually €0.75 to €1 per hour. If there's no meter, there is probably a roving attendant who will take your money. Study the signs. Many free zones are cleared out (by car owners or tow trucks) one day a week for street cleaning. Often the free zones have a 30- or 60-minute time limit. *Zona disco* has nothing to do with dancing. Italian cars have a time disk (a cardboard clock), which you set at your arrival time and lay on the dashboard so the attendant knows how long you've been parked. This is a fine system that all drivers should take advantage of. (If your rental car doesn't come with a *zona disco*, pick one up at a tobacco shop or just write your arrival time on a piece of paper and place it on the dashboard.) Garages are safe, save time, and help you avoid the stress of parking tickets. Take the parking voucher with you to pay the cashier before you leave.

**Theft:** Cars are routinely vandalized and stolen. Try to make your car look locally owned by hiding the "tourist-owned" rental company decals and putting a local newspaper in your back window.

# Telephones, Mail, and E-mail

Smart travelers use the telephone every day, especially in Italy, to check opening hours, confirm hotel reservations, and phone home.

**Phone Cards:** There are two kinds of phone cards—those that you insert into the phone instead of coins, and long-distance scratch-off PIN cards that can be used from virtually any phone (you dial a toll-free number and enter your PIN code). The Italian Telecom phone system sells both kinds.

Insertable phone cards are sold in varying denominations at tobacco shops, post offices, and machines near phone booths (many phone booths indicate where the nearest phone card sales outlet is located). Rip off the perforated corner to "activate" the card before you insert it into the phone.

PIN cards are usually the least expensive way to call back to the United States (about 10 min/$1). They're sold at small news-stands and hole-in-the-wall long-distance phone shops (Telecom brand also sold at tobacco shops and post offices). Since you don't insert these cards into a phone, you can use them from most phones, including the one in your hotel room (if it's set on pulse, switch it to tone). Because there are so many brand names, ask for an inter-national telephone card (*carta telefonica prepagate internazionali*, pron. KAR-tah teh-leh-FOHN-ee-kah pray-pah-GAH-tay in-ter-naht-zee-oh-NAH-lee); specify that you want a card for making calls to America or Canada to avoid getting the PIN cards that are only good within particular regions in Italy. After you buy a card, scratch off and reveal your Personal Identification Number, dial the toll-free access number, punch in your PIN, and talk. If the PIN doesn't work on one phone, try another phone. Get a low denomination in case the card is a dud.

The orange SIP public telephones are everywhere and take cards or coins. About a quarter of the phones are broken (which could explain why so many Italians carry cell phones). The rest of the phones work reluctantly. Dial slowly and deliberately, as if the phone doesn't understand numbers very well. Often a recorded message in Italian will break in, brusquely informing you that the phone number does not exist (*non-esistente*), even if you're dialing your own home phone number. Dial again with an increasing show of confidence, in an attempt to convince the phone of your num-ber's existence. If you fail, try a different phone. Repeat as needed.

When spelling out your name on the phone, you'll find *a* (pronounced "ah" in Italian), *i* (pronounced "ee"), and *e* (pronounced "ay") are confusing to Americans. Say "*a*, Aosta," "*e*, Empoli," and "*i*, Italia" to clear up that problem. If you plan to access your voice mail from Italy, be advised that you can't always dial extensions or secret codes once you connect (you're on vacation—relax).

**Dialing within Italy:** Italy has a direct-dial phone system (no area codes). To call anywhere within Italy, just dial the number. For example, the number of one of my recommended Florence hotels is 055-293-451. To call it from the Florence train station, dial 055-293-451. If you call it from Venice, it's the same: 055-293-451.

Italian phone numbers vary in length; a hotel can have, say, a 10-digit phone number and an 11-digit fax number.

Italy's toll-free numbers start with 800 (like U.S. 800 numbers, though in Italy you don't dial a "1" first). In Italy, you can dial these 800 numbers—called *freephone* or *numero verde* (green number)—free from any phone without using a phone card or coins.

**Dialing International Calls:** When calling internationally, dial the international access code (00 if you're calling from Europe, 011 from the U.S. or Canada), the country code of the country you're calling (39 for Italy; see appendix for list of other countries), and the local number. To call the Florence hotel (mentioned above) from the United States, dial 011 (the U.S. international access code), 39 (Italy's country code), then 055-293-451. To call my office from Italy, I dial 00 (Europe's international access code), 1 (the U.S. country code), 425 (Edmonds' area code), and 771-8303. European time is six/nine hours ahead of the East/West Coasts of the United States.

Hotel-room phones are reasonable for calls within Italy (the faint beeps stand for €0.10 phone units) but a terrible rip-off for calls to the United States (unless you use a PIN card or your hotel allows toll-free access to your calling card service—see below).

**Calling Card Services:** Since direct-dialing rates have dropped, calling cards (offered by AT&T, MCI, and Sprint) are no longer the good value they used to be. In fact, they are a rip-off. You'll likely pay $3 for the first minute with a $4 connection fee; if you get an answering machine, it'll cost you $7 to say "Sorry I missed you." Simply dialing direct (even from your hotel room) is generally a much better deal.

**Cell Phones:** Many travelers in Italy buy cheapie cell phones—about $70 on up—to make local and international calls. The cheapest phones work only in Italy; the pricier phones work throughout Europe (but it'll cost you about $40 per country to outfit the phone with the necessary chip and prepaid phone time). Because of their expense, cell phones are most economical for travelers staying in one country for two weeks or more. If you're interested, stop by one of Italy's ubiquitous phone shops or at a cell-phone counter at a department store. Find an English-speaking clerk to help you. To understand all the extras, get a brand that has instructions in English. Confirm with the clerk whether the phone works only in Italy or elsewhere in Europe

Learn how to use the phone while in the store—make a call to the store or, for fun, to the clerk's personal cell phone. You'll need to pick out a policy; different policies offer, say, better rates for making calls at night or for calling cell phones rather than fixed phones, etc. I get the basic fixed rate: a straight 30 cents per minute to the U.S.A. and 15 cents per minute to any fixed or cell phone in the home country at any hour. Receiving calls is generally free. When you run out of calling time, buy more time at a newsstand. Upon arrival in a different country, purchase a new chip (which comes with a new phone number). But if you're on a budget, skip cell phones and buy PIN phone cards instead.

**Mail:** Mail service is miserable throughout Italy. Postcards get last priority. If you must have mail stops, consider a few pre-reserved hotels along your route or use American Express offices. Most American Express offices in Italy will hold mail for one month. This service is free to AmEx cardholders (and available for a small fee to others). Allow 14 days for U.S.-to-Italy mail delivery, but don't count on it. Federal Express makes pricey two-day deliveries. Phoning is so easy that I've completely dispensed with mail stops. If possible, mail nothing precious from Italy.

**E-mail:** E-mail use among Italian hoteliers is increasing. I've listed e-mail addresses when possible. Some family-run pensions can become overwhelmed by the volume of e-mail they receive, so be patient if you don't get an immediate response. Internet Service Providers (ISPs) can change with alarming frequency, so if your e-mail message to a hotel bounces back, use a search engine (such as www.google.com) to find the hotel name and see if it has a new Web site; if that doesn't work, fax or call the hotel.

Cybercafés and little hole-in-the-wall Internet access shops (offering a few computers, no food, and cheap prices) are popular in most cities. If the extension dot-com (.com) doesn't work, try .it for Italy.

In cities, when you see a cluster of orange public phones in a room off a busy street, you might see several computers in the batch. With these, you can use your phone card to access the Internet. You won't be comfortable (no seat), you'll get cut off if your phone card runs out of time, but this can be a handy, quick way to check your e-mail.

If you're planning to log on from your laptop in your hotel room, you'll need an ISP that has local phone numbers for each country you'll visit. While an American modem cable plugs into European phone jacks, you may have to tweak your settings to have your computer recognize a pulse instead of the U.S. dial Bring a phone jack tester that reverses line polarity as needed.

# Sleeping

For hassle-free efficiency, I favor hotels and restaurants handy to sightseeing activities. Rather than list hotels scattered throughout a city, I describe two or three favorite neighborhoods and recommend the best accommodations values in each, from $20 bunks to plush $200 doubles with all the comforts.

Sleeping in Italy is expensive. Cheap big-city hotels can be depressing. Tourist information services cannot give opinions on quality. A major feature of this book is its extensive listing of good-value rooms. I like places that are clean, small, central, quiet at night, traditional, inexpensive, and friendly, with firm beds—and those not listed in other guidebooks. (In Italy, for me, 6 out of 9 attributes means a keeper.)

## Hotels

Double rooms listed in this book will range from about $50 (very simple, toilet and shower down the hall) to $200 (maximum plumbing and more), with most clustering around $80 (with private bathrooms). Prices are higher in big cities and heavily touristed cities, and lower off the beaten path. Three or four people can economize by requesting larger rooms. Solo travelers find that the cost of a *camera singola* is often only 25 percent less than a *camera doppia*. Most listed hotels have rooms for anywhere from one to five people. If there's room for an extra cot, they'll cram it in for you.

The Italian word for "hotel" is *hotel*, and in smaller, non-touristy towns, *albergo*. A few places have kept the old titles, *locanda* or *pensione*, indicating that they offer budget beds.

You normally get close to what you pay for. Prices are fairly standard. Shopping around earns you a better location and more character, but rarely a cheaper price.

However, prices at nearly any hotel can get soft if you do any of the following: arrive direct (without using a pricey middleman like the TI), offer to pay cash, stay at least three nights, or visit off-season. Breakfasts are legally optional (though some hotels insist they're not). Initial prices quoted often include breakfast and a private bathroom. Offer to skip breakfast for a better price.

You'll save $10 to $20 if you ask for a room without a shower and just use the shower down the hall. Generally, rooms with a bath or shower also have a toilet and a bidet (which Italians use for quick sponge baths). Tubs usually come with a frustrating "telephone shower" (handheld nozzle). If a shower has no curtain, the entire bathroom showers with you. The cord that dangles over the tub or shower is not a clothesline. You pull it when you've fallen and can't get up.

## Sleep Code

To help you sort easily through these listings, I've divided the rooms into three categories based on the price for a standard double room with bath:

**Higher Priced**—Most rooms more than €180.
**Moderately Priced**—Most rooms less than €180.
**Lower Priced**—Most rooms less than €130.

To pack maximum information into minimum space, I use this code to describe accommodations in this book. When there is a range of prices in one category, that means the price fluctuates with the season, size of room, or length of stay. Prices listed are per room, not per person.

**S** = Single room or price for one person using a double.

**D** = Double or twin room. "Double beds" are often two twins sheeted together and are usually big enough for non-romantic couples.

**T** = Three-person room (often a double with a single bed moved in).

**Q** = Four-adult room (an extra child's bed is usually cheaper).

**b** = Private bathroom with a toilet and shower or tub.

**s** = Private shower or tub only. (The toilet is down the hall.)

**CC** = Accepts credit cards (Visa and MasterCard, rarely American Express).

**no CC** = Does not accept credit cards; pay in local cash.

**SE** = Speaks English. This code is used only when it seems predictable that you'll encounter English-speaking staff.

**NSE** = Does not speak English. Used only when it's unlikely you'll encounter English-speaking staff.

According to this code, a couple staying at a "Db-€85, CC, SE" hotel would pay a total of 85 euros (about $85) for a double room with a private bathroom. The hotel accepts Visa or Italian cash. The staff speaks English.

Double beds are called *matrimoniale*, even though hotels aren't interested in your marital status. Twins are *due letti singoli*.

When you check in, the receptionist will ask for your passport and keep it for a couple of hours. Hotels are required to register each guest with the police. Relax. Americans are notorious for making this chore more difficult than it needs to be.

Rooms are safe. Still, zip cameras and keep money out of sight. More pillows and blankets are usually in the closet or available on request. In Italy, towels and linen aren't always replaced every day. Hang your towel up to dry.

Many hotel rooms have a TV and phone. Rooms in fancier hotels usually come with a tiny safe, a small stocked fridge (called a *frigo* bar, pron. FREE-goh bar; if it's noisy at night, unplug it), and air-conditioning (sometimes you pay an extra per-day charge for this). Conveniently, many business-class hotels drop their prices in July and August, just when the air-conditioned comfort they offer is most important.

Most hotel rooms with air conditioners come with a control stick (like a TV remote) that generally has the same symbols and features: fan icon (click to toggle through wind power, from light to gale); louver icon (choose steady airflow or waves); snowflake and sunshine icons (cold air or heat, depending on season); clock ("O" setting: run x hours before turning off; "I" setting: wait x hours to start); and the temperature control (20° or 21° Celsius is the normal sleeping temperature).

The hotel breakfast, while convenient, is often a bad value— €8 for a roll, jelly, and usually unlimited *caffè latte*. You can sometimes request cheese or salami (about €2.50 extra). I enjoy taking breakfast at the corner café. It's OK to supplement what you order with a few picnic goodies.

You can usually save time by paying your bill the evening before you leave instead of paying in the busy morning, when the reception desk is crowded with tourists wanting to pay up, ask questions, or check in.

**Hotels near Airports:** If you have an early-morning flight, I'd suggest staying in the center of town and getting to the airport via bus, train, or taxi. But if you really want a hotel near an airport for the first or last night of your trip, try www.worldairportguide.com.

## Other Accommodations

**Hostels:** While bed-and-breakfasts (*affitta camere*) and youth hostels (*ostello della gioventù*) are not as common in Italy as elsewhere in Europe, I've listed many in this book. Big-city hostels normally overrun with the *Let's Go* crowd, but small-town hos can be an enjoyable way to save money and make friends.

*Agriturismo:* Drivers who want to explore rural Italy will probably enjoy staying at an *agriturismo*—a B&B on a working farm. There are up to 2,000 of these rural B&Bs in Italy. The Orvieto chapter of this book contains more information, several *agriturismo* listings, and helpful resources.

## Making Reservations

It's possible to travel at any time of year without reservations, but, given the high stakes and the quality of the gems I've found for this book, I'd recommend making reservations. You can call long in advance from home or grab rooms a few days to a week in advance as you travel. (If you have difficulty, ask the fluent receptionist at your current hotel to call for you.) If you like more spontaneity (or if you're traveling off-season), you might make a habit of calling between 9:00 and 10:00 on the day you plan to arrive, when the hotel clerk knows who'll be checking out and just which rooms will be available. I've taken great pains to list telephone numbers with long distance instructions (see "Telephones," page 22; also see the appendix). Use the telephone, the convenient telephone cards, or your cell phone. Most hotels listed are accustomed to English-only speakers. A hotel receptionist will trust you and hold a room until 16:00 without a deposit, though some will ask for a credit-card number.

If you know where you want to stay each day (and you don't need or want flexibility), reserve your rooms a month or two in advance. To reserve from home, telephone first to confirm availability, then fax or e-mail your formal request. Phone and fax costs are reasonable, e-mail is a steal, and simple English is usually fine. To fax, use the handy form in the appendix (or online at www .ricksteves.com/reservation). If you don't get an answer to your fax request, consider that a "no." (Many little places get 20 faxes a day after they're full, and they can't afford to respond.)

A two-night stay in August would be "2 nights, 16/8/03 to 18/8/03" (Europeans write the date in this order—day/month/year—and hotel jargon uses your day of departure).

If you receive a response from the hotel stating its rates and room availability, it's not a confirmation. You must confirm that you indeed want a room at the given rate. One night's deposit is generally required. A credit card is often accepted as a deposit (though you may need to send a signed traveler's check or, rarely, a bank draft in the local currency). To make things easier on your-self and the hotel, be sure you really intend to stay at the hotel on dates you requested. These family-run businesses lose money when they turn away customers while holding a room for someone who doesn't show up. Understandably, some hotels bill no-shows

# Tips on Tipping

Tipping in Italy isn't as automatic and generous as it is in the United States, but for special service, tips are appreciated, if not expected. As in the United States, the proper amount depends on your resources, tipping philosophy, and the circumstance, but some general guidelines apply.

**Restaurants:** Tipping is an issue only at restaurants that have waiters and waitresses. If you order your food at a counter, don't tip.

At restaurants with table service, menus list if there is a *pane e coperto* charge (bread and cover charge, usually €1–2 per person) and if service is included (*servizio incluso*, generally 15 percent). If the service is included, there's no need to tip beyond that, but if you like to tip and you're pleased with the service, throw in €1 to €2 euros per person.

If service is not included (*servizio non incluso*), tip about 10 percent by rounding up or leaving the change from your bill. Leave the tip on the table or hand it to your server. It's best to tip in cash even if you pay with your credit card. Otherwise the tip may never reach your waitress.

**Taxis:** To tip the cabbie, round up. For a typical ride, round up to the next euro on the fare (to pay a €13 fare, give €14); for a long ride, to the nearest 10 (for a €75 fare, give €80). If the cabbie hauls your bags and zips you to the airport to help you catch your flight, you might want to toss in a little more. But if you feel like you're being driven in circles or otherwise ripped off, skip the tip.

**Special services:** It's thoughtful to tip a couple of euros to someone who shows you a special sight and who is paid in no other way (such as the man who shows you an Etruscan tomb in his backyard). Tour guides at public sites sometimes hold out their hands for tips after they give their spiel; if I've already paid for the tour, I don't tip extra, though some tourists do give a euro or two, particularly for a job well done. I don't tip at hotels, but if you do, give the porter a euro for carrying bags and leave a couple of euros in your room at the end of your stay for the maid if the room was kept clean. In general, if someone in the service industry does a super job for you, a tip of a couple of euros is appropriate . . . but not required.

**When in doubt, ask.** If you're not sure whether (or how much) to tip for a service, ask your hotelier or the TI; they'll fill you in on how it's done on their turf.

for one night. *If you must cancel, give at least two days' notice.* Long distance is cheap and easy from public phone booths. Don't let these people down—I promised you'd call and cancel if for some reason you won't show up.

Reconfirm your reservations a few days in advance for safety. Don't needlessly confirm rooms through the tourist office; they'll take a commission.

# Eating Italian

The Italians are masters of the art of fine living. That means eating...long and well. Lengthy, multicourse lunches and dinners and endless hours sitting in outdoor cafés are the norm. Americans eat on their way to an evening event and complain if the check is slow in coming. For Italians, the meal is an end in itself, and only rude waiters rush you. When you want the bill, mime-scribble on your raised palm or ask for it: "*Il conto?*"

Even those of us who liked dorm food will find that the local cafés, cuisine, and wines become a highlight of our Italian adventure. Trust me, this is sightseeing for your palate, and even if the rest of you is sleeping in cheap hotels, your taste buds will relish an occasional first-class splurge. You can eat well without going broke. But be careful; you're just as likely to blow a small fortune on a disappointing meal as you are to dine wonderfully for €20.

## *Restaurants*

When restaurant-hunting, choose places filled with locals, not the place with the big neon signs boasting, "We speak English and accept credit cards." Restaurants parked on famous squares generally serve bad food at high prices to tourists. Locals eat better in lower-rent locales. Family-run places operate without hired help and can offer cheaper meals. The word *osteria* (normally a simple, local-style restaurant) makes me salivate.

For unexciting but basic values, look for a *menu turistico* (also called *menu del giorno*—menu of the day), a three- or four-course, set-price meal (price includes service charge, no need to tip). Galloping gourmets order à la carte with the help of a menu translator. (The *Marling Italian Menu Master* is excellent. *Rick Steves' Italian Phrase Book* has enough phrases for intermediate eaters.) Some restaurants have self-serve antipasti buffets, offering a variety of cooked appetizers spread out like a salad bar (pay per plate, not weight; usually costs around €6–8); a plate of antipasti combined with a pasta dish makes a healthy, affordable, interesting meal.

A full meal consists of an appetizer (antipasto, €2.50–5), a course (*primo piatto*, pasta or soup, €4–7), and a second course *piatto*, expensive meat and fish dishes, €5–10). Vegetables

## Eating with the Seasons

Italian cooks love to serve you fresh produce and seafood at its tastiest. If you must have porcini mushrooms outside of October and November, they'll be frozen. To get the freshest veggies at a fine restaurant, request *"Un piatto di verdure della stagione, per favore."* (A plate of seasonal vegetables, please.) Here are some examples of what's fresh when:

| | |
|---|---|
| **April–May:** | Calamari, squid, green beans, and zucchini flowers |
| **April, May, Sept, Oct:** | Black truffles |
| **May–June:** | Mussels, asparagus, zucchini, cantaloupe, and strawberries |
| **May–Aug:** | Eggplant |
| **Oct–Nov:** | Mushrooms and white truffles |
| **Fresh year-round:** | Clams, meats, and cheese |

*(contorni, verdure)* may come with the *secondo* course or cost extra (€3) as a side dish.

Seafood and steak is sometimes sold by weight (if you see "100 g" or *"l'etto"* by the price on the menu, you'll pay that price *per* 100 grams—about a quarter pound). Some special dishes come in large quantities meant for two people; the shorthand way of showing this on a menu is "X2" (meaning "times two").

Restaurants normally pad the bill with a cover charge (*pane e coperto*, around €1) and a service charge (*servizio*, 15 percent); see Tips on Tipping, page 29.

As you will see, the euros add up in a hurry. Light and budget eaters get by with a *primo piatto* each and a shared antipasto. Italians admit that *secondi* are the least interesting aspect of the local cuisine.

### Delis, Cafeterias, Pizza Shops, and Tavola Calda (Hot Table) Bars

Italy offers many cheap alternatives to restaurants. Stop by a *rosticceria* for great cooked deli food; a self-service cafeteria (called "free flow" in Italian) that feeds you without the add-ons; a *tavola calda* bar for an assortment of veggies; or a Pizza Rustica shop for stand-up or take-out pizza.

Pizza is cheap and everywhere. Key pizza vocabulary: *capricciosa* (generally ham, mushrooms, and artichokes), *funghi* (mushrooms), *margherita* (tomato sauce and mozzarella), *ma* (tomato sauce, oregano, garlic, no cheese), *quattro formagg*

## Ordering Food at *Tavola Caldas*

| | | |
|---|---|---|
| "Heated, please." | "*Scaldare, per favore.*" | skahl-DAH-ray, pehr fah-VOH-ray |
| "A taste, please." | "*Un assaggio, per favore.*" | oon ah-SAH-joh, pehr fah-VOH-ray |
| plate of mixed veggies | *piatto misto di verdure* | pee-AH-toh MEES-toh dee vehr-DOO-ray |
| artichoke | *carciofo* | kar-CHOH-foh |
| asparagus | *asparagi* | ah-spah-RAH-jee |
| beans | *fagioli* | fah-JOH-lee |
| green beans | *fagiolini* | fah-joh-LEE-nee |
| broccoli | *broccoli* | BROK-oh-lee |
| canteloupe | *melone* | may-LOH-nay |
| carrots | *carote* | kah-ROT-ay |
| ham | *prosciutto* | proh-SHOO-toh |
| mushrooms | *funghi* | FOONG-ghee |
| potatoes | *patate* | pah-TAH-tay |
| rice | *riso* | REE-zoh |
| spinach | *spinaci* | speen-AH-chee |
| tomatoes | *pomodori* | poh-moh-DOH-ree |
| zucchini | *zucchine* | zoo-KEE-nay |
| breadsticks | *grissini* | gree-SEE-nee |

*Excerpted from *Rick Steves' Italian Phrase Book*

(4 different cheeses), and *quattro stagioni* (different toppings on each of the 4 quarters for those who can't choose just 1 menu item). If you ask for *peperoni* on your pizza, you'll get green or red peppers, not sausage. Kids like *diavola* (closest thing in Italy to American "pepperoni") and *margherita* (tomato and cheese). At Pizza Rustica take-out shops, slices are sold by weight (100 grams, or *un etto*, is a hot, cheap snack; 200 grams, or *due etti*, makes a light meal).

For a fast, cheap, and healthy lunch, find a *tavola calda* bar ith a buffet spread of meat and vegetables and ask for a mixed e of vegetables with a hunk of mozzarella *(piatto misto di re con mozzarella)*. Don't be limited by what you can see. like a salad with a slice of cantaloupe and a hunk of cheese, hip that up for you in a snap. Roll up to the bar and, ted finger and key words in the chart in this chapter, you can get a fine mixed plate of vegetables. If something's a mystery, ask for *un assaggio* (a little taste).

## Italian Bars/Cafés

Italian "bars" are not taverns, but cafés. These local hangouts serve coffee, mini-pizzas, sandwiches, and cartons of milk from the cooler. Many dish up plates of fried cheese and vegetables from under the glass counter, ready to reheat. This is my budget choice, the Italian equivalent of English pub grub.

For quick meals, bars usually have trays of cheap, ready-made sandwiches (*panini* or *tramezzini*)—some kinds are delightful grilled. To save time for sightseeing and room for dinner, my favorite lunch is a ham and cheese *panini* at a bar (called *tost*, grilled twice to get really hot). To get food "to go," say, "*Da portar via*" (for the road). All bars have a WC *(toilette, bagno)* in the back, and the public is entitled to use it.

Bars serve great drinks—hot, cold, sweet, or alcoholic. Chilled bottled water *(natural* or *frizzante)* is sold cheap to go.

**Coffee:** If you ask for "*un caffè*," you'll get espresso. Cappuccino is served to locals before noon and tourists any time of day. (To an Italian, cappuccino is a breakfast drink and a travesty after anything with tomatoes.) Italians like it only warm. To get it hot, request "*Molto caldo*" (very hot) or "*Più caldo, per favore*" (hotter, please; pron. pew KAHL-doh, pehr fah-VOH-ray).

Experiment with a few of the options...

- *caffè macchiato* (pron. mah-kee-AH-toh*)*: coffee with only a little milk
- *caffè latte*: coffee with lots of hot milk, no foam
- *caffè Americano*: espresso diluted with water
- *caffè corretto*: espresso with a shot of liqueur
- *caffè freddo*: sweet and iced espresso
- *cappuccino freddo*: iced cappuccino
- *caffè hag*: espresso decaf (decaf is easily available for any coffee drink)

**Beer:** Beer on tap is "*alla spina.*" Get it *piccola* (33 cl/11 oz), *media* (50 cl/17 oz), or *grande* (a liter/34 oz).

**Wine:** To order a glass (*bicchiere*; pron. bee-kee-AY-ree) of red *(rosso)* or white *(bianco)* wine, say, "*Un bicchiere di vino rosso/ bianco.*" *Corposo* means full-bodied. House wine often comes in a quarter-liter carafe *(un quarto)*. Trendy wines with small production (such as Brunello di Montalcino) are good but overpriced. There are better values on wines with greater production and les demand (such as Frescobaldi Montisodi).

**Prices:** You'll notice a two-tiered price system. Drinkin cup of coffee while standing at the bar is cheaper than drin¹ it at a table. If you're on a budget, don't sit without first checking out the financial consequences.

If the bar isn't busy, you'll often just order and pay when you leave. Otherwise: 1) decide what you want; 2) find out the price by checking the price list on the wall or the prices posted near the food, or by asking the barman; 3) pay the cashier; and 4) give the receipt to the barman (whose clean fingers handle no dirty euros) and tell him what you want.

### Picnics

In Italy, picnicking saves lots of euros and is a great way to sample local specialties. In the process of assembling your meal, you get to deal with the Italians in the market scene. On days you choose to picnic, gather supplies early. You'll probably visit several small stores or market stalls to put together a complete meal, and many close around noon. While it's fun to visit the small specialty shops, a local *alimentari* is your one-stop corner grocery store (most will slice and stuff your sandwich for you if you buy the ingredients there). A *supermercato* gives you more efficiency with less color for less cost.

Juice-lovers can get a liter of O.J. for the price of a Coke or coffee. Look for "100% *succo*" (juice) on the label. Hang onto the half-liter mineral-water bottles (sold everywhere for about €0.50). Buy juice in cheap liter boxes, drink some and store the extra in your water bottle. (I drink tap water—*acqua del rubinetto*.)

Picnics can be an adventure in high cuisine. Be daring. Try the fresh mozzarella, *presto* pesto, shriveled olives, and any UFOs the locals are excited about. Shopkeepers are happy to sell small quantities of produce. But in a busy market, a merchant may not want to weigh and sell small, three-carrot-type quantities. In this case, estimate generously what you think it should cost, and hold out euros in one hand and the produce in the other. Wear a smile that says, "If you take the money, I'll go." He'll grab the money. A typical picnic for two might be fresh rolls, 100 grams of cheese, 100 grams of meat (100 grams = about a quarter pound, called *un etto* in Italy), two tomatoes, three carrots, two apples, yogurt, and a liter box of juice. Total cost—about €10.

## Culture Shock—Accepting Italy as a Package Deal

We travel all the way to Italy to enjoy differences—to become ~mporary locals. You'll experience frustrations. Certain truths ~ we find "God-given" or "self-evident," like cold beer, ice in ~s, bottomless cups of coffee, hot showers, and bigger being ~are suddenly not so true. One of the benefits of travel is ~pening realization that there are logical, civil, and even better alternatives. A willingness to go local ensures that you'll enjoy a full dose of Italian hospitality.

If there is a negative aspect to the image Italians have of Americans, it is that we are big, loud, aggressive, impolite, rich, and a bit naive. While Italians, flabbergasted by our Yankee excesses, say in disbelief, "*Mi sono cadute le braccia!*" ("I throw my arms down!"), they nearly always afford us individual travelers all the warmth we deserve.

## Send Me a Postcard, Drop Me a Line

If you enjoy a successful trip with the help of this book and would like to share your discoveries, please fill out and send the survey at the end of this book to me at Europe Through the Back Door, Box 2009, Edmonds, WA 98020. I personally read and value all feedback. Thanks in advance—it helps a lot.

For our latest travel information on Italy, tap into our Web site at www.ricksteves.com. To check on any updates for this book, visit www.ricksteves.com/update. My e-mail address is rick@ricksteves.com. Anyone is welcome to a free issue of our *Back Door* quarterly newsletter.

Judging from all the positive feedback and happy postcards I receive from travelers who have used this book, it's safe to assume you'll enjoy a great, affordable vacation—with the finesse of an independent, experienced traveler. Thanks, and *buon viaggio!*

# BACK DOOR TRAVEL PHILOSOPHY
From *Rick Steves' Europe Through the Back Door*

*Travel is intensified living—maximum thrills per minute and one of the last great sources of legal adventure. Travel is freedom. It's recess, and we need it.*

*Experiencing the real Europe requires catching it by surprise, going casual ... "through the Back Door."*

*Affording travel is a matter of priorities. (Make do with the old car.) You can travel—simply, safely, and comfortably—anywhere in Europe for $80 a day plus transportation costs. In many ways, spending more money only builds a thicker wall between you and what you came to see. Europe is a cultural carnival, and, time after time, you'll find that its best acts are free and the best seats are the cheap ones.*

*A tight budget forces you to travel close to the ground, meeting and communicating with the people, not relying on service with a purchased smile. Never sacrifice sleep, nutrition, safety, or cleanliness in the name of budget. Simply enjoy the local-style alternatives to expensive hotels and restaurants.*

*Extroverts have more fun. If your trip is low on magic moments, kick yourself and make things happen. If you don't enjoy a place, maybe you don't know enough about it. Seek the truth. Recognize tourist traps. Give a culture the benefit of your open mind. See things as different but not better or worse. Any culture has much to share.*

*Of course, travel, like the world, is a series of hills and valleys. Be fanatically positive and militantly optimistic. If something's not to your liking, change your liking. Travel is addictive. It can make you a happier American, as well as a citizen of the world. Our Earth is home to six billion equally important people. It's humbling to travel and find that people don't envy Americans. They like us, but, with all due respect, they wouldn't trade passports.*

*Globe-trotting destroys ethnocentricity. It helps you understand and appreciate different cultures. Travel changes people. It broadens perspectives and teaches new ways to measure quality of life. Many travelers toss aside their hometown blinders. Their prized souvenirs are the strands of different cultures they decide to knit into their own character. The world is a cultural yarn shop. And Back Door Travelers are weaving the ultimate tapestry. Come on, join in!*

# ITALY

- 310,000 square kilometers, or 120,000 square miles (a little larger than Arizona)
- 60 million people (195 people per square kilometer, 500 people per square mile)
- 1,300 kilometers (800 miles) long, 160 kilometers (100 miles) wide

*Bella Italia!* It has Europe's richest, craziest culture. If you take it on its own terms, Italy is a cultural keelhauling that actually feels good.

Some people, often with considerable effort, manage to hate it. Italy bubbles with emotion, corruption, stray hairs, inflation, traffic jams, body odor, strikes, rallies, holidays, crowded squalor, and irate ranters shaking their fists at each other one minute and walking arm in arm the next. Have a talk with yourself before you cross the border. Promise yourself to relax and soak in it; it's a glorious mud puddle.

There are two Italys: The north is industrial, aggressive, and "time is money" in its outlook. The south is crowded, poor, relaxed, farm-oriented, and traditional. Families here are very strong and usually live in the same house for many generations. Loyalties are to family, city, region, soccer team, and country—in that order.

Economically, Italy has had its problems, but somehow things have always worked out. Today, Italy is the Western world's seventh-largest industrial power. Its people earn more per capita than the British. Italy is the world's leading wine producer. It is sixth in cheese and wool output. Tourism is big business. Cronyism, which complicates my work, is an integral part of the economy.

Italy, home of the Vatican, is Catholic, but the dominant religion is life—motor scooters, soccer, fashion, girl-watching, boy-watching, good coffee, good wine, and *la dolce far niente* ("the sweetness of doing nothing"). The Italian character shows itself on the streets in the skilled maniac drivers and the classy dressers who star in the ritual evening stroll, or *passeggiata*.

The language is fun. Be melodramatic and talk with your hands. Hear the melody; get into the flow. Italians are outgoing. They want to communicate, and they try harder than any other Europeans. Play with them.

Italy, a land of extremes, is also the most thief-ridden country you'll visit. Tourists suffer virtually no violent crin but there are plenty of petty purse-snatchings, pickpocketings, and shortchangings. Wear your money belt! The scruffy-looking women and children loitering around the major museums aren't there for the art.

Take advantage of the cheap, colorful, and dry-but-informative city guidebooks sold on the streets. Use the information telephones you'll find in most historic buildings. Just set the dial on English, pop in your coins, and listen. The narration is often accompanied by a brief slide show.

Some important Italian churches require modest dress: No shorts or bare shoulders on men, women, and sometimes even children. With a little imagination (except at the ultrastrict Vatican's St. Peter's), those caught by surprise can improvise something—a jacket for your knees and maps for your shoulders. I wear a super-lightweight pair of long pants for my hot and muggy big-city Italian sightseeing.

While no longer a cheap country, Italy is still a hit with shoppers. Glassware (Venice), gold, silver, leather, prints (Florence), and high fashion (Rome and Milan) are good souvenirs, but do some price research at home so you'll recognize the good values.

*La dolce far niente* is a big part of Italy. Zero in on the fine points. Don't dwell on the problems. Accept Italy as Italy. Savor your cappuccino, dangle your feet over a canal (if it smells, breathe through your mouth), and imagine what it was like centuries ago. Ramble through the rabble and rubble of Rome and mentally resurrect those ancient stones. Look into the famous sculpted eyes of Michelangelo's *David* and understand Renaissance man's assertion of himself. Sit silently on a hilltop rooftop. Get chummy with the winds of the past. Write a poem over a glass of local wine in a sun-splashed, wave-dashed Riviera village. If you fall off your moral horse, call it a cultural experience. Italy is for romantics.

# ROME
## (ROMA)

Rome is magnificent and brutal at the same time. Your ears will ring, if you're careless you'll be run down or pickpocketed, and you'll be frustrated by the kind of chaos that only an Italian can understand. You may even come to believe Mussolini was a necessary evil.

But Rome is required, and if your hotel provides a comfortable refuge, if you pace yourself and accept (and even partake in) the siesta plan, if you're well-organized for sightseeing, and if you protect yourself and your valuables with extra caution and discretion, you'll do fine. You'll see the sights and leave satisfied.

Rome at its peak meant civilization itself. Everything was either civilized (part of the Roman Empire, Latin- or Greek-speaking) or barbarian. Today, Rome is Italy's political capital, the capital of Catholicism, and a splendid . . . "junk pile" is not quite the right term . . . of Western civilization. As you peel through its fascinating and jumbled layers, you'll find its buildings, cats, laundry, traffic, and 2.6 million people endlessly entertaining. And then, of course, there are the magnificent sights.

Tour St. Peter's, the greatest church on earth, and scale Michelangelo's 100-meter-tall (330-foot) dome, the world's largest. Learn something about eternity by touring the huge Vatican Museum. You'll find the story of Creation, bright as the day it was painted, in the recently restored Sistine Chapel. Do the "Caesar Shuffle" through ancient Rome's Forum and Colosseum. Savor Europe's most sumptuous building—the Borghese Gallery—and take an early evening "Dolce Vita Stroll" down the Via del Corso with Rome's beautiful people. Enjoy an after-dark walk from Trastevere to the Spanish Steps, lacing together Rome's Baroque and bubbly nightspots.

## Rome Area

TO PISA
TARQUINIA
TO VITERBO & CIVITA DI BAG.
TO ORVIETO & FLORENCE
RIVER TIBER
A-1
S-22
REST STOP
VIA SALARIA
S-4
LAGO BRACCIANO
CERVETERI
VIA CASSIA
GRANDE RACCORDO ANULARE
-RING FREEWAY-
A-12
ROMA
CIVITA-VECCHIA
S-1
VIA AURELIA
VAT. CITY
VIA TIBURTINA
SS-5
TIVOLI
HADRIAN'S VILLA
TERMINI STATION
EUR
FRASCATI
DA VINCI **AIRPORT** FIUMICINO
OSTIA ANTICA
S-148
VIA APPIA
CIAMPINO AIRPORT
A-2
CASTEL-GANDOLFO
MEDITERRANEAN SEA
S-7
**NOTE:** NOT TO SCALE    DCH
TO NAPOLI

## Planning Your Time

For most travelers, Rome is best done quickly. It's a great city, but it's exhausting. Time is normally short, and Italy is more charming elsewhere. To "do" Rome in a day, consider it as a side trip from Orvieto or Florence, and maybe before the night train to Venice. Crazy as that sounds, if all you have is a day, it's a great one.

**Rome in a day:** Vatican (2 hours in the museum and Sistine Chapel and 1 hour in St. Peter's), taxi over the river to the Pantheon (picnic on its steps), then hike over Capitol Hill, through the Forum, and to the Colosseum. Have dinner on Campo de' Fiori and dessert on Piazza Navona.

**Rome in two to three days:** Day one, do the "Caesar Shuffle" from the Colosseum and Forum over Capitol Hill to the Pantheon. After a siesta, join the locals strolling from Piazza del Popolo to the Spanish Steps (see my recommended "Dolce Vita Stroll," page 87). Have dinner near your hotel.

On the second day, see the Vatican City (St. Peter's, climb dome, tour the Vatican Museum). Spend the evening walking Trastevere to Campo de' Fiori—an atmospheric place for —to the Trevi Fountain (see "Night Walk Across Rome," page 82). With a third day, add the Borghese Gallery (reservations required) and the National Museum of Rome.

## Orientation

Sprawling Rome actually feels manageable once you get to know it. The old core, with most of the tourist sights, sits in a diamond formed by the train station (in the east), Vatican (west), the Borghese Gardens (north) and the Colosseum (south). The Tiber River runs through the diamond from north to south. To give an idea of scale, it takes about an hour-plus to walk from the train station to the Vatican.

Consider Rome in these layers:

**The ancient city** had a million people. The best of the classical sights stand in a line from the Colosseum to the Pantheon.

**Medieval Rome** was little more than a hobo camp of 50,000—thieves, mean dogs, and the pope, whose legitimacy required a Roman address. The medieval city, a colorful tangle of lanes, lies between the Pantheon and the river.

**Window-shoppers' Rome** twinkles with nightlife and ritzy shopping near Rome's main drag, Via del Corso—in the triangle formed by Piazza del Popolo, Piazza Venezia, and the Spanish Steps. (See Dolce Vita Stroll, page 87.)

**Vatican City** is a compact world of its own with two great, huge sights: St. Peter's Basilica and the Vatican Museum.

**Trastevere**, the seedy, colorful, wrong-side-of-the-river neighborhood/village, is Rome at its crustiest—and perhaps most "Roman."

**Baroque Rome** is an overleaf that embellishes great squares throughout the town with fountains and church facades.

Since no one is allowed to build taller than St. Peter's dome, the city has no modern skyline. And the Tiber River is ignored. After the last floods (1870), the banks were built up very high and Rome turned its back on its naughty, unnavigable r:

## Tourist Information

While Rome has three main tourist information offices or so TI kiosks scattered around the town at major tou are handy and just as helpful. If all you need is a map, f TI and get one at your hotel.

The main TI, near Piazza della Repubblica's huge covers the city and the region. It's a five-minute walk o of the train station (Mon–Sat 9:00–19:00, next to car de Via Parigi 5, free Internet access to Rome tourism sites .romaturismo.com, tel. 06-3606-4399). It's air-conditio crowded, and more helpful than the station TI (see be it has seats and a study table.

# Downtown Rome

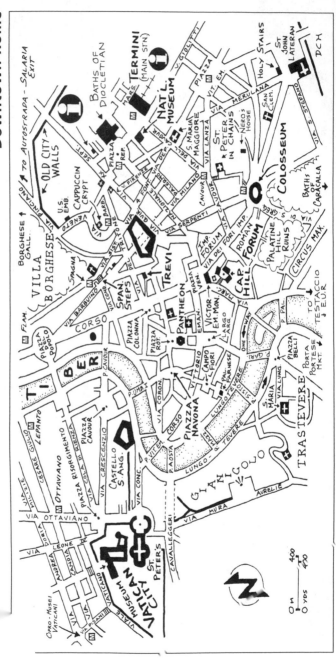

You'll also find TIs at the airport (daily 9:00–19:00, tel. 06-6595-6074) and the train station (daily 8:00–21:00, near track 3, accessible from platforms or lobby, marked "Informazioni Turistiche/Tourist Info," crowded, combined with travel agency, tel. 06-4890-6300).

At any TI, ask for a city map, a listing of sights and hours (in the free *Tesori di Roma* booklet), and *L'Evento*, the free bimonthly entertainment guide for evening events and fun. All hotels list an inflated rate to cover the hefty commission any TI room-finding service charges. Save money by booking direct.

Smaller TIs (daily 9:00–18:00) include kiosks near the Forum (on Piazza del Tempio della Pace), at Via del Corso (on Largo Goldoni), in Trastevere (on Piazza Sonnino), on Via Nazionale (at Palazzo delle Esposizioni), at Castel Sant' Angelo, Santa Maria Maggiore, and at San Giovanni in Laterano. For more information, call 06-3600-4399 (daily 9:00–19:00).

*Roma c'è* is a cheap little weekly entertainment guide with a helpful English section (at the back) on musical events and the pope's schedule for the week (new edition every Thu, sold at newsstands for €1, www.romace.it, Web site in Italian).

## Arrival in Rome

Rome's main train station, **Termini**, is a minefield of tourist services: a TI (daily 8:00–21:00, off-season 9:00–20:00), train info office (daily 7:00–21:45), ATMs, 24-hour thievery, luggage lockers (near track 24), the main city-bus hub (in front of train station), a subway stop, and the handy, cheery Ciao Self-Service Ristorante (daily 11:00–22:30, WC at entrance, near east end of station; although there are several Ciao bars scattered throughout the station, the most comfortable is this sit-down Ristorante). In the modern mall downstairs, under the station, you'll find a grocery (oddly named "Drug Store," daily 7:00–24:00), late-hours banks, a pharmacy (daily 7:30–22:00), public showers, and Internet access at Thenetgate (daily 6:00–23:30, near Dunkin' Donuts, cheapest to buy a €4 60-minute card). The station has some sleazy sharks with official-looking cards. In general, avoid anybody selling anything at the station if you can.

**By Bus:** Long-distance buses (e.g., from Siena and Assisi) arrive at Rome's small **Tiburtina** station, which is on Metro line B, with easy connections to the main train station (a straight shot 4 stops away) and the entire Metro system.

Most of my hotel listings are easily accessible by foot (those near the Termini train station) or by Metro (those in the Colosseum and Vatican neighborhoods). The train station has its own Metro stop (Termini).

**By Plane:** If you arrive at the airport, catch a train (hrly, 30 min, €9) to Rome's train station or take (or share) a taxi to your hotel. For details, see "Transportation Connections," below.

# Dealing with (and Avoiding) Problems

**Theft Alert:** With sweet-talking con artists meeting you at the station, well-dressed pickpockets on buses, and thieving gangs of children at the ancient sites, Rome is a gauntlet of rip-offs. There's no great physical risk, but green tourists will be scammed. Thieves strike when you're distracted. Don't trust kind strangers. Keep nothing important in your pockets. Assume you're being stalked. (Then relax and have fun.) Be most on guard while boarding and leaving buses and subways. Thieves crowd the door, then stop and turn while others crowd and push from behind. The sneakiest thieves are well-dressed businessmen (generally with something in their hands); lately many are posing as tourists with Tevas, fanny packs, and cameras. Scams abound: Don't give your wallet to self-proclaimed "police" who stop you on the street, warn you about counterfeit (or drug) money, and ask to see your wallet.

If you know what to look out for, the gangs of children picking the pockets and handbags of naive tourists are not a threat but an interesting, albeit sad, spectacle. Gangs of city-stained children (sometimes as young as 8–10 years old), too young to be prosecuted but old enough to rip you off, troll through the tourist crowds around the Colosseum, Forum, Piazza Repubblica, and train and Metro stations. Watch them target tourists who are overloaded with bags or distracted with a video camera. The kids look like beggars and hold up newspapers or cardboard signs to confuse their victims. They scram like stray cats if you're onto them. A fast-fingered mother with a baby is often nearby. The terrace above the bus stop near the Colosseum Metro stop is a fine place to watch the action and maybe even pick up a few moves of your own.

**Reporting Losses:** To report lost or stolen passports and documents or to file an insurance claim, you must file a police report (at the train station with Polizia at track 1 or with Carabinieri at track 20, also at Piazza Venezia). To replace a passport, file the police report, then go to your embassy (see below). To report lost traveler's checks, call your bank (Visa—tel. 800-874-155, Thomas Cook/MasterCard—tel. 800-872-050, American Express—tel. 800-872-000), then file a police report. To report stolen or lost credit cards, call the company (Visa—tel. 800-877-232 or 800-819-014, MasterCard—tel. 800-870-866, American Express—tel. 800-874-333), then file a police report. All of these toll-free 800 numbers are Italian (dialed free in Italy), American.

**Embassies:** United States (Mon–Fri 8:30–13:00 & 14:00–17:30, Via Vittorio Veneto 119/A, tel. 06-46741, www.usembassy .it) and Canada (Via Zara 30, tel. 06-445-981, www.canada.it).

**Emergency Numbers:** Police—tel. 113. Ambulance—tel. 118.

**Hit and Run:** Walk with extreme caution. Scooters don't need to stop at red lights, and even cars exercise what drivers call the "logical option" of not stopping if they see no oncoming traffic. As Vespa scooters become electric, they'll get quieter (hooray) but more dangerous for pedestrians. Follow locals like a shadow when you cross a street (or spend a good part of your visit stranded on curbs).

**Staying/Getting Healthy:** The siesta is a key to survival in summertime Rome. Lie down and contemplate the extraordinary power of gravity in the eternal city. I drink lots of cold, refreshing water from Rome's many drinking fountains (the Forum has 3). There's a pharmacy (marked by a green cross) in every neighborhood, including a handy one in the train station (daily 7:30–22:00, located downstairs, at west end), and a 24-hour pharmacy on Piazza dei Cinquecento 51 (next to train station on Via Cavour, tel. 06-488-0019). Embassies can recommend English-speaking doctors (see "Embassies," above). Consider MEDline, a 24-hour home medical service (tel. 06-808-0995, doctors speak English). Anyone is entitled to free emergency treatment at public hospitals. The hospital closest to the train station is Policlinico Umberto 1 (entrance for emergency treatment on Via Lancisi, translators available, Metro: Policlinico). The American Hospital, a private hospital on the outskirts, is used to helping Yankees (tel. 06-225-571).

## Helpful Hints

**Train Tickets and Reservations:** Get train tickets and railpass-related reservations and supplements at travel agencies, rather than deal with the congested train station. The cost is either the same or there's a minimal charge. Your hotel can direct you to the nearest travel agency. Quo Vadis, near the Vatican, is helpful (Via della Conciliazione, 22-24, tel. 06-6880-4941, fax 06-6880-3191, e-mail: qv.viaggi@tiscalinet.it). American Express is near the Spanish Steps (Mon–Fri 9:00–17:30, Sat 9:00–12:30, no train tickets sold on Sat, closed Sun, Piazza di Spagna, 00187 Roma, tel. 06-67641).

**Bookstore:** Try American Bookstore (Via Torino 136, Metro: Repubblica, tel. 06-474-6877).

**Internet Access:** EasyEverything on Piazza Barberini (access from €0.50, open 24/7, 350 terminals, www.easyeverything.com).

**Laundry:** Your hotel can point you to the nearest launderette (usually open daily 8:00–22:00, about €6 to wash and dry a 15-pound load). The Bolle Blu chain comes with Internet access

(€4.25/hr, near train station at Via Milazzo 20, Via Palestro 59, and Via Principe Amedeo 116, tel. 06-446-5804).

**Web Sites on Rome:** www.romaturismo.com (music, exhibitions, events, in English), www.wantedinrome.com (job openings and real estate, but also festivals and exhibitions, in English), and www.vatican.va (the pope's Web site, in English).

## Getting around Rome

Sightsee on foot, by city bus, or by taxi. I've grouped your sightseeing into walkable neighborhoods.

Public transportation is efficient, cheap, and part of your Roman experience. It starts running around 5:30 and stops around 23:30, sometimes earlier. After midnight, there are a few very crowded night buses, and taxis become more expensive and hard to get. Don't try to hail one—go to a taxi stand.

Buses and subways use the same ticket. You can buy tickets at newsstands, tobacco shops (*tabacchi*, marked by a black-and-white T sign), or at major Metro stations or bus stops, but not on board. Since many Metro stations have no human ticket-sellers and the machines are either broken or require exact change (helps to put in smallest-value coins first), it's easier to buy a few tickets above ground at newsstands or *tabacchi* (€0.80, good for 75 min—Metro ride and unlimited buses); all-day bus/Metro passes cost €3.25 (for more info, visit www.atac.roma.it). Fancy new tickets with bar codes eventually will replace the plain paper tickets. Until then, buses and the Metro have two different validation machines; if you've got a new ticket, use the one with the slot on top.

Buses (especially the touristic #64) and the subway are havens for thieves and pickpockets. Assume any commotion is a thief-created distraction.

**By Metro:** The Roman subway system (Metropolitana) is simple, with two clean, cheap, fast lines that intersect at Termini train station. While much of Rome is not served by its skimpy subway, these stops are helpful: Termini (train station, National Museum of Rome at Palazzo Massimo, recommended hotels), Repubblica (Baths of Diocletian/Octagonal Hall, main TI, recommended hotels), Barberini (Cappuccin Crypt, Trevi Fountain), Spagna (Spanish Steps, Villa Borghese, classy shopping area), Flaminio (Piazza del Popolo, start of recommended Dolce Vita Stroll down Via del Corso), Ottaviano (St. Peter's and Vatican City), Cipro-Musei Vaticani (Vatican Museum, recommended hotels), Colosseo (Colosseum, Roman Forum, recommended hotels), and E.U.R. (Mussolini's futuristic suburb).

**By Bus:** Bus routes are clearly listed at the stops. Ask the for a bus map. Punch your ticket in the orange stamping

## Metropolitana: Rome's Subway

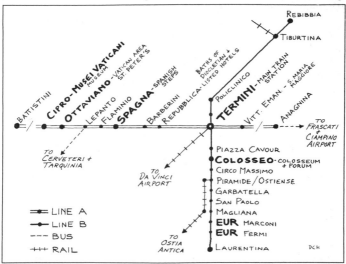

machine as you board (even if you've already stamped it for the
Metro)—or you are cheating. Riding without a stamped ticket
on the bus, while relatively safe, is stressful. Inspectors fine even
innocent-looking tourists €52. If the validation machine won't
work, you can write the date, time, and bus number on the ticket.
Ideally, buy a bunch of tickets from a tobacco shop or newsstand
first thing, so you can hop a bus without first having to search for
a tobacco shop that's open.

Here are a few buses worth knowing about:

**#64:** Termini (train station), Piazza della Repubblica (sights),
Via Nazionale (recommended hotels), Piazza Venezia (near
Forum), Largo Argentina (near Pantheon), St. Peter's Basilica.
Ride it for a city overview and to watch pickpockets in action
(can get horribly crowded).

**#40:** This express route is especially helpful—it's the same
route as #64, but with fewer stops, crowds, and pickpockets.

**#8:** This tram connects Largo Argentina with Trastevere
(get off at Piazza Mastai).

**#H:** Express connecting Termini train station and Trastevere,
with a few stops on Via Nazionale (for Trastevere, get off at Piazza
Belli, just over bridge).

**#492:** Stazione Tiburtina, Piazza Barberini, Piazza Venezia,
Piazza Cavour (Castel Sant' Angelo), Piazza Risorgimento (near
Vatican Museum).

#714: Termini, Santa Maria Maggiore, San Giovanni in Laterano, Terme di Caracalla (Baths of Caracalla).

Rome has cute *electtrico* minibuses that wind through the narrow streets of old and interesting neighborhoods (daily except Sun). These are handy for sightseeing and fun for simply joyriding:

*Electtrico* #116: Through the medieval core of Rome from Campo de' Fiori to Piazza Barberini via the Pantheon.

*Electtrico* #117: San Giovanni in Laterano, Colosseo, Via dei Serpenti, Trevi Fountain, Piazza di Spagna, Piazza del Popolo.

"J" (for Jubilee) buses are bigger, come with a hostess, and provide more convenient access to some places farther out, such as St. Peter's (Cavalleggeri stop) and the Catacombs. Purchase tickets (€1) on the bus (info: tel. 800-076-287).

**By Taxi:** I use taxis in Rome more often than in other cities. They're relatively cheap and useful for efficient sightseeing in a big, hot city. Taxis start at about €2.75 (surcharges of €1 on Sun, €2.75 for night hours of 22:00–7:00, €1 surcharge for luggage, €7.25 extra for airport, tip about 10 percent by rounding up to the nearest euro). Sample fares: Train station to Vatican-€9; train station to Colosseum-€6; Colosseum to Trastevere-€7. Three or four companions with more money than time should taxi almost everywhere. It's tough to wave down a taxi in Rome. Find the nearest taxi stand. (Ask a local or in a shop, "*Dov'è una fermata dei tassi?*" Some are listed on my maps.) Unmarked, unmetered taxis at train stations and the airport are usually a rip-off. Taxis listing their telephone number on the door have fair meters—use them. To save time and energy, have your hotel call a taxi; the meter starts when the call is received. (To call a cab on your own, dial 06-3570, 06-4994, or 06-88177.)

## Tours of Rome

**Scala Reale**—Tom Rankin (an American architect in love with Rome and his Roman wife) runs Scala Reale, a company committed to sorting out the rich layers of Rome for small groups with a longer-than-average attention span. Their excellent walking tours vary in length from two to four hours and start at €16 per person. Try to book in advance, since their groups are limited to six and fill up fast. Their fascinating "Rome Orientation" walks lace together lesser-known sights from antiquity to the present (tel. 06-474-5673, 888/467-1986 in the U.S., www.scalareale.org, e-mail: info@scalareale.org).

If you're interested in week-long classes on Rome, look into the Institute for Roman Culture, an innovative, educational organization run by Tom Rankin and his colleague, archaeologist Darius (see www.romanculture.org for prices, details, and booking).

## Daily Reminder

**Sunday:** These sights are closed: Vatican Museum (except for the last Sunday of the month, when it's free) and the Catacombs of San Sebastian. The Pantheon and E.U.R.'s Museum of Roman Civilization close early in the afternoon.

**Monday:** Many sights are closed: National Museum of Rome, Borghese Gallery, Capitol Hill Museum, Octagonal Hall and Museum of the Bath (both at Baths of Diocletian), Etruscan Museum, Castel Sant' Angelo, Trajan's Market, Protestant Cemetery, E.U.R.'s Museum of Roman Civilization, and Ostia Antica. All of the ancient sites and the Vatican Museum, among others, *are* open. The Baths of Caracalla close early in the afternoon.

**Tuesday:** All sights are open except for Nero's Golden House.

**Wednesday:** All sights are open except for the Catacombs of San Callisto.

**Thursday:** All sights are open except for the Cappuccin Crypt.

**Friday/Saturday:** All sights are open.

**Through Eternity**—This company, which offers four walking tours led by native English speakers, gets mixed reviews from readers who like it or dislike it depending on the quality of their particular guide. The tours include St. Peter's and the Vatican Museum (€35, museum entry not included, 5.5 hrs, daily except Sun); the Colosseum and Roman Forum (€20, 2.5 hrs, daily); Rome at Twilight (€20, nightly); and a Wine Sampling Tour (€35, nightly, includes a glass at 4 or 5 wine bars and dinner). Call to get the schedule and to book in advance (max of 25 people, tel. 06-700-9336, cellular 347-336-5298, private tours possible, www.througheternity.com, e-mail: info@througheternity.com).

**Rome Walks**—Students working for this company give tours in fluent English. Sample tours include the Colosseum/Forum Walk (€33, includes Colosseum admission, 2.5 hrs); the Palatine Hill/Mouth of Truth Walk (€33, includes Palatine admission, 2 hrs); a Scandal Tour (€25, 2 hrs to dig up the dirt on Roman emperors, royalty, and popes); a Vatican City Walk (€45, includes admission to Vatican Museum, 4.5 hrs); and a Twilight Rome Evening Walk (€25, 2 hrs). Look online for the latest (www.romewalks.com) and book in advance by e-mail (info@romewalks.com) or phone (cellular 347-795-5175, private tours also available). You'll need to give your hotel name and phone number. Your guide will call or e-mail you to let you know the meeting place.

# Tips on Sightseeing in Rome

**Museums:** Plan ahead. The marvelous Borghese Gallery and Nero's Golden House both require reservations. For the Borghese Gallery, it's safest to make reservations well in advance of your trip (for specifics, see page 65). You can wait until you're in Rome to call for a reservation time at Nero's Golden House, but it's wise to book ahead (see page 52).

A special **combo-ticket,** which costs €20, covers the National Museum of Rome, Colosseum, Palatine Hill, Baths of Caracalla, Crypt Balbi (medieval art), Museum of the Bath (Roman inscriptions), and Palazzo Altemps (so-so sculpture collection). The combo-ticket allows you to see seven sights for the price of three (purchase at participating sites, valid for 5 days). When you buy this, you can upgrade to a "Coupon Servizi" pass for an extra €5, giving you tours or audioguides at each site (normally €4 each, see page 10 for description). The big plus of this ticket is that you avoid the long lines at the Colosseum (if you purchase it at a participating site other than the Colosseum).

Get a current listing of **museum hours** from one of Rome's TIs: ask for the booklet *Tesori di Roma* (Treasures of Rome). Some museums may stay open later in summer (usually on Sat).

**Churches:** Churches open early (around 7:00), close for lunch (roughly 12:00–15:00), and close late (around 19:00). Kamikaze tourists maximize their sightseeing hours by visiting churches before 9:00 and seeing the major sights that stay open during the siesta (St. Peter's, Colosseum, Forum, Capitol Hill Museum, National Museum of Rome) while Romans are taking it cool and easy.

Many churches have "modest dress" requirements, which means no bare shoulders, miniskirts, or shorts—for men, women, or children. This dress code is only strictly enforced at St. Peter's. Elsewhere, you'll see many tourists in shorts touring many churches.

**Miscellaneous tips:** Carry a plastic water bottle that can be refilled at Rome's many public drinking spouts. Use museum and restaurant toilets when you can, because public restrooms are scarce.

**Hop-on, Hop-off Bus Tour**—The ATAC city bus tour offers your best budget orientation tour of Rome. In under two hours, you'll have 80 sights pointed out to you (by a live guide in English and maybe one other language). If you've got a little more time and money, you can get out at any of the nine stops and catch a later bus (though stops are poorly marked and the included map is useless). While the guide's spiel is limited to simple identification of the sights, this tour provides an efficient and economical orientation to Rome. The stops are: Piazza Barberini, Via Veneto, Villa Borghese, Piazza Cavour, St. Peter's Square, Corso Vittorio Emanuele (for Piazza Navona), Piazza Venezia, Colosseum, and Via Nazionale. I'd take the nonstop tour for €7.75; the hop-on-and-off tour is €13. Bus #110 departs every 30 minutes, at the top and bottom of the hour, from in front of the Termini train station (near platform C, buy tickets at info kiosk there—marked "i bus"—or buy on the bus and pay about 10 percent more, runs March–Sept 9:00–20:00, Oct–Feb 10:00–18:00, tel. 06-4695-2252).

**Archeobus**—This handy hop-on, hop-off bus runs hourly from the west side of Piazza Venezia way out the Appian Way. By far the easiest way to see the sights down this ancient Roman road, it includes a basic, uninspired two-hour (longer if there's traffic) tour in Italian and English in an air-conditioned minibus (buy €7.75 tickets at green kiosk on Piazza Venezia, valid 9:00–17:00, tel. 06-4695-4695).

## Sights—From the Colosseum Area to Capitol Hill

Beware of gangs of young thieves, particularly between the Colosseum and the Forum; they're harmless if you know their tricks (see Theft Alert in "Helpful Hints," above).

▲**St. Peter-in-Chains Church (San Pietro in Vincoli)**—Built in the fifth century to house the chains that held St. Peter, this church is most famous for its Michelangelo statue. Check out the much-venerated chains under the high altar, then focus on Moses (free, Mon–Sat 7:00–12:30 & 15:30–19:00, Sun 7:30–12:30, a short walk uphill from the Colosseum, modest dress required).

Pope Julius II commissioned Michelangelo to build a massive tomb, with 48 huge statues, crowned by a grand statue of this egomaniacal pope. The pope had planned to have his tomb placed in the center of St. Peter's Basilica. When Julius died, the work had barely been started, and no one had the money or necessary commitment to Julius to finish the project. Michelangelo finished one statue—Moses—and left a few unfinished statues: Leah and Rachel flanking Moses in this church, the "prisoners" now in Florence's Accademia, and the "slaves" now in Paris' Louvre.

This powerful statue of Moses—mature Michelangelo—is worth studying. The artist worked on it in fits and starts for 30 years. Moses has received the Ten Commandments. As he holds the stone tablets, his eyes show a man determined to stop his tribe from worshiping the golden calf and idols...a man determined to win salvation for the people of Israel. Why the horns? Centuries ago, the Hebrew word for "rays" was mistranslated as "horns."

▲**Nero's Golden House (Domus Aurea)**—The barren remains of Emperor Nero's "Golden House" were reopened to the public in 1999. The original entrance to the house was all the way over at the Arch of Titus in the Forum. This massive house once sprawled across the valley (where the Colosseum now stands) and up the hill—the part you tour today. Larger even than Bill Gates' place, it was a pain to vacuum. A colossal, 33-meter-tall (100-foot) bronze statue of Nero towered over everything. The house incorporated an artificial lake (where the Colosseum was later built) and a forest stocked with game. It was decorated with the best multicolored marble and the finest frescoes. No expense was too great for Nero—his mistress soaked daily in the milk of 500 wild asses kept for her bathing pleasure.

Nero (ruled A.D. 54–68) was Rome's most notorious emperor. He killed his own mother, kicked his pregnant wife to death, crucified St. Peter, and—most galling to his subjects—was a bad actor. When Rome burned in A.D. 64, Nero was accused of torching it to clear land for an even bigger house. The Romans rebelled and Nero stabbed himself in the neck, crying, "What an artist dies in me!"

While only hints of the splendid, colorful frescoes survive, the towering vaults and the basic immensity of the place are impressive. As you wander through rooms that are now underground, look up at the holes in the ceiling. Imagine how much of old Rome still hides underground...and why the subway is limited to two lines.

Visits are allowed only with an escort (30 people, about every 30 min) and a reservation (€6.20, Wed–Mon 9:00–19:45, last entry at 18:40, closed Tue, tour lasts 50 min, audioguides-€2, but listen to the intro before entering or you'll be forever behind, 200 meters northeast of Colosseum, through a park gate, up a hill, and on the left). Guided tours in English are offered twice daily (€8.50); to reserve a place, call 06-3996-7700. If you just show up (particularly on a late afternoon on a weekday), you could luck out and get on a tour; if tours aren't booked up, the remaining seats are sold to drop-ins.

▲▲▲**Colosseum**—This 2,000-year-old building is *the* great example of Roman engineering. Using concrete, brick, and their trademark round arches, Romans constructed much larger buildings than the Greeks. But in deference to the higher Greek culture, they finished their no-nonsense megastructure by pasting all three orders of Greek columns (Doric, Ionic, and Corinthian) as exterior decorations. The Flavian Amphitheater's popular name, "Colosseum," comes from the colossal statue of Nero that once stood in front of it.

Romans were into "big." By putting two theaters together, they created a circular amphitheater. They could fill and empty its 50,000 numbered seats as quickly and efficiently as we do our superstadiums. Teams of sailors hoisted canvas awnings over the stadium to give fans shade. This was where ancient Romans, whose taste for violence was the equal of modern America's, enjoyed their Dirty Harry and *Terminator*. Gladiators, criminals, and wild animals fought to the death in every conceivable scenario. The floor of the Colosseum is missing, exposing underground passages. Animals were kept in cages here and then lifted up in elevators; they'd pop out from behind blinds into the arena. The gladiator didn't know where, when, or by what he'd be attacked.

**Cost and Hours:** €8 (exact change preferred, includes Palatine Hill visit within 24 hours, also covered by €20 combo-ticket, valid 7 days, daily 9:00–19:00, or one hour before sunset, Metro: Colosseo, tel. 06-3974-9907). Instead of waiting in line (sometimes an hour long) at the Colosseum to purchase a ticket, buy your Colosseum ticket at the Palatine Hill entrances nearby—inside the Forum entry (near Arch of Titus) and on Via di San Gregorio (facing Forum entry, with Colosseum at your back, go left on street). The €20 combo-ticket—covering the Colosseum, Palatine Hill, Baths of Caracalla, National Museum of Rome, Museum of the Bath, and more—also allows you to walk right into the Colosseum (if you've purchased it in advance at the Palatine Hill entrances or other participating sites; valid for 5 days; for details, see "Tips on Sightseeing in Rome," page 50). Or you can reserve a ticket in advance for an additional €1.50 fee (pick up at side window of Colosseum ticket office, call 06-3996-7700 to book, automated info in English).

**Tours:** You can rent an audioguide tour at the ticket office (€4 for 2 hours of use) or take a guided tour in English (€3.50, 60 min, offered several times daily, check at ticket office for schedule).

**Nearby:** Outside the entrance of the Colosseum, vendors sell handy little *Rome, Past and Present* books with plastic overlays to un-ruin the ruins (marked €11, offer €8). A WC is behind the Colosseum (facing ticket entrance, go right; WC is under stairway). The modern-day gladiators outside the Colosseum expect a fee if you snap a photo of them. A couple of fine eateries are close by; see page 106.

▲**Arch of Constantine**—The well-preserved arch, which stands between the Colosseum and the Forum, commemorates a military coup and, more importantly, the acceptance of Christianity in

## The Forum Area

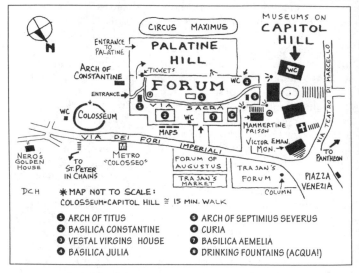

CIRCUS   MAXIMUS

MUSEUMS ON
CAPITOL
HILL

PALATINE
HILL

FORUM

ENTRANCE
TO
PALATINE

ARCH OF
CONSTANTINE

TICKETS

ENTRANCE

WC

COLOSSEUM

VIA   SACRA

WC

MAPS

MAMMERTINE
PRISON

VICTOR EMAN.
MON.

VIA   DEI   FORI

IMPERIALI

NERO'S
GOLDEN
HOUSE

TO
ST. PETER
IN CHAINS

METRO
"COLOSSEO"

FORUM OF
AUGUSTUS

TRAJAN'S
MARKET

TRAJAN'S
FORUM

COLUMN

TO
PANTHEON

PIAZZA
VENEZIA

DCH   *MAP NOT TO SCALE:
COLOSSEUM≅CAPITOL HILL ≅ 15 MIN. WALK

❶ ARCH OF TITUS
❷ BASILICA CONSTANTINE
❸ VESTAL VIRGINS HOUSE
❹ BASILICA JULIA

❺ ARCH OF SEPTIMIUS SEVERUS
❻ CURIA
❼ BASILICA AEMELIA
❽ DRINKING FOUNTAINS (ACQUA!)

the Roman Empire. In A.D. 312, the ambitious Emperor Constantine (who had a vision he could win under the sign of the cross) defeated his rival, Maxentius. Constantine, who became sole emperor, legalized Christianity.

▲▲▲**Roman Forum (Foro Romano)**—This is ancient Rome's birthplace and civic center, and the common ground between Rome's famous seven hills (free admission to Forum, €8 for Palatine Hill, both keep the same hours: daily 9:00–19:00 or an hour before dark, Metro: Colosseo, tel. 06-3974-9907).

A €4 audioguide helps decipher the rubble (rent at gift shop at entrance on Via dei Fori Imperiali). Guided tours in English are offered once daily (€3.50); ask for information at the ticket booth at the Palatine Hill (near Arch of Titus). Sidewalk vendors sell cheap city guidebooks, such as the small red *Rome, Past and Present*, showing helpful before-and-after pictures (marked €11— offer €8).

With the help of the map in this section, follow this basic walk. Enter the Forum near the Arch of Constantine:

**1.** Start by the small **Arch of Titus** (drinking fountain opposite) overlooking the remains of what was the political, social, and commercial center of the Roman Empire. The Via Sacra— the main street of ancient Rome—cuts through the Forum from here to Capitol Hill and the Arch of Septimius Severus on the opposite side. On the left, a ticket booth welcomes you to the

Palatine Hill (described below)—once filled with the palaces of Roman emperors. Study the Arch of Titus—carved with propaganda celebrating the A.D. 70 defeat of the Jews, which began the Diaspora that ended with the creation of Israel in 1947. Notice the gaggle of soldiers carrying the menorah.

**2.** Ahead of you on the right are the massive ruins of the **Basilica of Constantine.** Follow the path leading there from the Via Sacra. Only the giant barrel vaults remain, looming crumbly and weed-eaten. As you stand in the shadow of the Basilica of Constantine, reconstruct it in your mind. The huge barrel vaults were just side niches. Extend the broken nub of an arch out over the vacant lot and finish your imaginary Roman basilica with rich marble and fountains. People it with plenty of toga-clad Romans. Yeow.

**3.** Next, hike past the semicircular Temple of Vesta to the **House of the Vestal Virgins.** Here, the VVs kept the eternal flame lit. A set of ponds and a marble chorus line of Vestal Virgins mark the courtyard of the house.

**4.** The grand **Basilica Julia,** a first-century law court, fills the corner opposite the Curia. Notice how the Romans passed their time; ancient backgammon-type game boards are cut into the pavement.

**5.** The **Arch of Septimius Severus,** from about A.D. 200, celebrates that emperor's military victories. In front of it, a stone called Lapis Niger covers the legendary tomb of Romulus. To the left of the arch, the stone bulkhead is the Rostra, or speaker's platform. It's named for the ship's prows that used to decorate it as big shots hollered, "Friends, Romans, countrymen...."

**6.** The plain, intact brick building near the Arch of Septimius Severus was the **Curia,** where the Roman senate sat. (Peek inside.) Roman buildings were basically brick and concrete, usually with a marble veneer, which in this case is long lost.

**7.** The **Basilica Aemilia** (second century B.C.) shows the floor plan of an ancient palace. This pre-Christian "basilica" design was later adopted by medieval churches. From here, a ramp leads up and out (past a WC and a fun headless statue to pose with).

▲**Palatine Hill**—The hill above the Forum contains scanty remains of the imperial palaces and the foundations of Rome, from Iron Age huts to the legendary house of Romulus (under corrugated tin roof in far corner). We get our word *palace* from this hill, where the emperors chose to live. The Palatine was once so filled with palaces that later emperors had to build out. (Looking up at it from the Forum, you see the substructure that supported these long-gone palaces.) The Palatine museum has sculptures and fresco fragments but is nothing special. From the pleasant garden, you'll get an overview of the Forum. On the far side, look down into an emperor's private stadium and then beyond at the dusty Circus Maximus, once a chariot course. Imagine the cheers, jeers, and furious betting. But considering how ruined the ruins are, the heat, the hill to climb, the €8 entry fee, and the relative difficulty in understanding what you're looking at, the Palatine Hill is a disappointment.

**Cost and Hours:** €8, includes Colosseum visit within 24 hours, also covered by €20 combo-ticket, daily 9:00–19:00, or one hour before sunset, Metro: Colosseo. The main entrance and ticket office—which also sells Colosseum tickets, enabling smart sightseers to avoid that long line—is near the Arch of Titus and the Colosseum. Another Palatine entrance is on Via di San Gregorio.

**Tours:** Audioguides cost €4. Guided tours in English are offered once daily (€3.50); ask for information at the ticket booth.

▲**Mammertine Prison**—The 2,500-year-old, cistern-like prison, which once held Saints Peter and Paul, is worth a look (donation requested, daily 9:00–12:30 & 14:30–18:30, at the foot of Capitol Hill, near Forum's Arch of Septimius Severus). When you step into the room, you'll hit a modern floor. Ignore that and look up at the hole in the ceiling, from which prisoners were lowered. Then take the stairs down to the level of the actual prison floor. As you descend, you'll walk past a supposedly miraculous image of Peter's face, created when a guard pushed him into the wall. Downstairs, you'll see the column to which Peter was chained. It's said that a miraculous fountain sprang up in this room so Peter could baptize other prisoners. The upside-down cross commemorates Peter's upside-down crucifixion.

Imagine humans, amid fat rats and rotting corpses, awaiting slow deaths. On the walls near the entry are lists of notable prisoners (Christian and non-Christian) and the ways they were executed: *strangolati*, *decapitato*, *morto di fame* (died of hunger)....

## Sights—Capitol Hill Area

There are several ways to get to the top of Capitol Hill. If you're coming from the north (Piazza Venezia), take the grand stairs located to the right of the big, white Victor Emmanuel Monument (described below). Coming from the Forum, take either the steep staircase or the winding road, which converge at a great Forum overlook and a refreshing water fountain. Block the spout with your fingers; water spurts up for drinking. Romans, who call this *il nasone* (the nose), joke that a cheap Roman boy takes his date out for a drink at *il nasone*.

▲▲**Capitol Hill (Campidoglio)**—This hill was the religious and political center of ancient Rome. It's still the home of the city's government. Michelangelo's Renaissance square is bounded by two fine museums and the mayoral palace. Its centerpiece is a copy of the famous equestrian statue of Marcus Aurelius (the original is behind glass in the museum, a few steps away).

Michelangelo intended that people approach the square from the grand stairway off Piazza Venezia. From the top of the stairway, you see the new Renaissance face of Rome with its back to the Forum, facing the new city. Notice how Michelangelo gave the buildings the "giant order"—huge pilasters make the existing two-story buildings feel one-storied and more harmonious with the new square. Notice also how the statues atop these buildings welcome you, then draw you in. The terraces just downhill (past either side of the mayor's palace) offer fine views of the Forum.

▲▲**Capitol Hill Museum**—This museum encompasses two buildings (Palazzo dei Conservatori and Palazzo Nuovo), connected by an underground passage that leads to the vacant Tabularium and a panoramic overlook of the Forum (€8, Tue–Sun 9:00–20:00, last entry 19:00, closed Mon, Jan 1, May 1, and Dec 25, tel. 06-3996-7800).

For an orientation to the museum's two buildings, face the equestrian statue on Capitol Hill Square (with your back to the grand stairway). The Palazzo Nuovo is on your left and the Palazzo dei Conservatori is on your right (closer to the river). Ahead is the mayor's palace (Palazzo Senatorio); below it and out of sight are the Tabularium and underground passage.

You can buy your ticket at either building (but if you want to rent a €3.60 audioguide, go to Palazzo dei Conservatori).

The **Palazzo dei Conservatori** is one of the world's oldest museums, at 500 years old. Outside the entrance, notice the marriage announcements and, possibly, wedding-party photo ops. Inside the courtyard, have a look at giant chunks of a statue of Emperor Constantine; when intact, this imposing statue held court in the Basilica of Constantine in the Forum. The museum is worthwhile, with lavish rooms and several great statues. Tops is the original (500 B.C.) Etruscan *Capitoline Wolf* (the little statues of Romulus and Remus were added in the Renaissance). Don't miss the *Boy Extracting a Thorn* or the enchanting *Commodus as Hercules*. The second-floor painting gallery—except for two Caravaggios—is forgettable. The café upstairs, with a splendid patio with city views, is lovely at sunset.

Connect the two museums with the underground passage that leads to the **Tabularium**. Built in the first century A.D., this once held the archives of ancient Rome. The word *Tabularium* comes from tablet, on which the Romans wrote their laws. You won't see any tablets, but you will see a superb head-on view of the Forum from the windows.

The **Palazzo Nuovo** houses mostly portrait busts of forgotten emperors. But it has three must-see statues: the *Dying Gaul*, the *Capitoline Venus* (both on the first floor up), and the original gilded bronze equestrian statue of Marcus Aurelius (behind glass in museum courtyard). This greatest surviving equestrian statue of antiquity was the original centerpiece of the square. While most such pagan statues were destroyed by Dark Age Christians, Marcus was mistaken for Constantine (the first Christian emperor) and therefore spared.

**From Capitol Hill to Piazza Venezia**—Leaving Capitol Hill, descend the stairs leading to Piazza Venezia. At the bottom of the stairs, look left several blocks down the street to see a condominium actually built around surviving ancient pillars and arches of Teatro Marcello—perhaps the oldest inhabited building in Europe.

Still at the bottom of the stairs, look up the long stairway to your right (which pilgrims climb on their knees) for a good example of the earliest style of Christian church. While pilgrims find it worth the climb, sightseers can skip it. As you walk toward Piazza Venezia, look down into the ditch on your right and see how modern Rome is built on the forgotten frescoes and mangled mosaics of ancient Rome.

**Piazza Venezia**—This vast square is the focal point of modern Rome. The Via del Corso, which starts here, is the city's axis, surrounded by Rome's classiest shopping district. In the 1930s, Mussolini whipped up Italy's nationalistic fervor here from a balcony above the square (to your left with back to Victor Emmanuel Monument). Fascist masses filled the square screaming, "Four more years!" or something like that. Fifteen years later, they hung Mussolini from a meat hook in Milan.

**Victor Emmanuel Monument**—This oversized monument to an Italian king was part of Italy's rush to overcome the new country's strong regionalism and create a national identity after unification in 1870. It's now open to the public, offering a new view of the Eternal City (free, 242 steps to the top, long hours).

Romans think of the monument not as an altar of the fatherland but as "the wedding cake," "the typewriter," or "the dentures." It wouldn't be so bad if it weren't sitting on a priceless acre of ancient Rome and if they had chosen better marble (this is too in-your-face white and picks up the pollution horribly). Soldiers guard Italy's *Tomb of the Unknown Soldier* as the eternal flame flickers. At this level, stand with your back to the flame and see how Via del Corso bisects Rome.

**▲Trajan's Column, Market, and Forum**—This offers the grandest column and best example of "continuous narration" from antiquity. Over 2,500 figures scroll around the 40-meter-high (130-foot)

column, telling of Trajan's victorious Dacian campaign (circa
A.D. 103, in present-day Romania), from the assembling of the
army at the bottom to the victory sacrifice at the top. The ashes
of Trajan and his wife were held in the mausoleum at the base
while the sun once glinted off a polished bronze statue of Trajan
at the top. Today, St. Peter is on top. Study the propaganda that
winds up the column like a scroll, trumpeting Trajan's wonderful
military exploits. You can see this close up for free (always open
and viewable, just off Piazza Venezia, across the street from the
Victor Emmanuel Monument). Viewing balconies once stood on
either side, but it seems likely Trajan fans came away only with a
feeling that the greatness of their emperor and empire was beyond
comprehension (for a rolled-out version of the column's story, visit
the Museum of Roman Civilization at E.U.R., below). This column
marked **Trajan's Forum**, which was built to handle the shopping
needs of a wealthy city of over a million. Commercial, political, religious, and social activities all mixed in the forum.

For a fee, you can go inside **Trajan's Market** (boring) and
part of Trajan's Forum; the entrance is uphill from the column
on Via IV Novembre. The market was once filled with shops
selling goods from all over the Roman Empire (€6.20, summer
Tue–Sun 9:00–18:30, winter Tue–Sun 9:00–16:30, closed Mon,
tel. 06-679-0048).

## Sights—Pantheon Area
▲▲▲**Pantheon**—For the greatest look at the splendor of Rome,
antiquity's best-preserved interior is a must (free, Mon–Sat 8:30–
19:30, Sun and holidays 9:00–18:00, tel. 06-6830-0230). Because
it became a church dedicated to the martyrs just after the fall of
Rome, the barbarians left it alone, and the locals didn't use it as
a quarry. The portico is called Rome's umbrella—a fun local
gathering in a rainstorm. Walk past its one-piece granite columns
(biggest in Italy, shipped from Egypt) and through the original
bronze doors. Sit inside under the glorious skylight and enjoy
classical architecture at its best.

The dome, 47 meters/142 feet high and wide, was Europe's
biggest until the Renaissance. Michelangelo's dome at St. Peter's,
while much higher, is one meter (about 3 feet) smaller. The bril-
liance of this dome's construction astounded architects through
the ages. During the Renaissance, Brunelleschi was given permis-
sion to cut into the dome (see the little square hole above and to
the right of the entrance) to analyze the material. The concrete
dome gets thinner and lighter with height—the highest part is
volcanic pumice.

This wonderfully harmonious architecture greatly inspired

Raphael and other artists of the Renaissance. Raphael, along with Italy's first two kings, chose to be buried here.

As you walk around the outside of the Pantheon, notice the "rise of Rome"—about five meters (15 feet) since it was built. Nearest WCs are at McDonald's and bars on the square. Great gelato is nearby (see page 105).

▲▲Churches near the Pantheon—The Church of San Luigi dei Francesi has a magnificent chapel painted by Caravaggio (free, Fri–Wed 7:30–12:30 & 15:30–19:00, Thu 7:30–12:30, sightseers should avoid Mass at 7:30 and 19:00, modest dress recommended).

The only Gothic church you'll see in Rome is Santa Maria sopra Minerva. On a little square behind the Pantheon to the east, past the Bernini statue of an elephant carrying an Egyptian obelisk, this Dominican church was built *sopra* (over) a pre-Christian temple of Minerva. Before stepping in, notice the high-water marks on the wall (right of door). Inside, you'll see that the lower parts of the frescoes were lost to floods. (After the last great flood, in 1870, Rome built the present embankments, finally breaking the spirit of the Tiber River.)

Rome was at its low ebb, almost a ghost town, through much of the Gothic period. Little was built during this time (and much of what was built was redone Baroque). This church is a refreshing exception.

St. Catherine's body lies under the altar (her head is in Siena). In the 1300s, she convinced the pope to return from France to Rome, thus saving Italy from untold chaos.

Left of the altar stands a little-known Michelangelo statue, *Christ Bearing the Cross*. Michelangelo gave Jesus an athlete's or warrior's body (a striking contrast to the more docile Christ of medieval art), but left the face to one of his pupils. Fra Angelico's simple tomb is farther to the left, on the way to the back door. Before leaving, head over to the right (south transept), pop in a coin for light, and enjoy a fine Filippo Lippi fresco showing scenes from the life of St. Thomas Aquinas.

Exit the church via its rear door (behind the Michelangelo statue), walk down Fra Angelico lane (spy any artisans at work), turn left, and walk to the next square. On your right, you'll find the Chiesa di St. Ignazio church, a riot of Baroque illusions. Study the fresco over the door and the ceiling in the back of the nave. Then stand on the yellow disk on the floor between the two stars. Look at the central (black) dome. Keeping your eyes on the dome, walk under and past it. Church building project runs out of money? Hire a painter to paint a fake, flat dome. (Both churches open early, take a siesta—Santa Maria

## Pantheon Area

TO SPANISH STEPS

PONTE UMBERTO

TIBER

LUNGOTEVERE MARZIO

ANCIENT STADIUM ENTRANCE

CORONARI

TRE SCALINI

PIAZZA NAVONA

MUSEUM OF ROME

CAMPO DE' FIORI

LARGO ARGENTINA (CAT HOSPICE)

PALAZZO FARNESE

LUNGOTEVERE SISTO

PONTE SISTO

TO TRASTEVERE

S. LUIGI (CARAVAGGIO)

PIAZZA COLONNA

PARL.

UFF. VIC.

GIO.

PALMA AQUIRO

SALV.

SEMINARIO

PANTHEON

VITTORIO

ARG.

CESTARI

S. MARIA SOPRA MINERVA

E M A N U E L E

GESÙ

ARACOELI

CAMPODOGLIO

VIA DEL TRITONE

VIA

SABINA

MURATTE

TREVI

DATA

SAN IGNAZIO

PIAZZA VENEZIA

V.E.

FORI IMP

TO COLO.

F O R U M

200 YARDS

200 METERS

N

Ⓣ -TAXI STAND

DCH

sopra Minerva closes at 12:00, St. Ignazio at 12:30—reopen around 15:30, and close at 19:00. Modest dress is recommended.)

A few blocks away, back across Corso Vittorio Emmanuele, is the rich and Baroque **Gesu Church** (daily 7:00–12:00 & 15:00–20:00), headquarters of the Jesuits in Rome. The Jesuits powered the Church's Counter-Reformation. With Protestants teaching that all roads to heaven did not pass through Rome, the Baroque churches of the late 1500s were painted with spiritual road maps that said they did.

Walk out the Gesu Church and two blocks down Corso V. Emmanuele to the **Sacred Area** (Largo Argentina), an excavated square facing the boulevard, about four blocks south of the Pantheon. Stroll around this square and look into the excavated pit at some of the oldest ruins in Rome. Julius Caesar was assassinated near here. Today, it's a refuge for cats—some 250 of them are cared for by volunteers. You'll see them (and their refuge) at the far (west) side of the square.

▲**Galleria Doria Pamphilj**—This gallery, filling a palace on Piazza del Collegio Romano, offers a rare chance to wander through a noble family's lavish rooms with the prince who calls this downtown mansion home. Well, almost. Through an audio-guide, the prince lovingly narrates his family's story, including how the Doria Pamphilj (pron. pahm-FEEL-yee) family's cozy relationship with the pope inspired the word nepotism. High-lights include paintings by Caravaggio, Titian, and Raphael, and portraits of Pope Innocent X by Velázquez (on canvas) and Bernini (in marble). The fancy rooms of the palace are interest-ing, with a mini-Versailles–like hall of mirrors and paintings stacked to the ceiling in the style typical of 18th-century galleries (€8, includes fine audioguide, Fri–Wed 10:00–17:00, closed Thu, from Piazza Venezia walk 2 blocks up Via del Corso and take a left, tel. 06-679-7323, www.doriapamphilj.it).

▲**Trevi Fountain**—This bubbly Baroque fountain of Neptune with his entourage, worth ▲ by day and ▲▲ by night, is a minor sight to art scholars but a major nighttime gathering spot for teens on the make and tourists tossing coins. (For more information, see "Self-Guided Walks in Rome," page 82.)

## Sights—East Rome, near the Train Station

These sights are within a 10-minute walk of the train station. By Metro, use the Termini stop for the National Museum and the Piazza Repubblica stop for the rest.

▲▲▲**National Museum of Rome in Palazzo Massimo**— This museum houses the greatest collection of ancient Roman art anywhere, and includes busts of emperors and a Roman copy of the *Greek Discus Thrower*. The ground floor is a historic yearbook of marble statues from the second century B.C. to the second century A.D., with rare Greek originals.

The first floor is peopled by statues from the first through fourth centuries A.D. To see the second-floor collection of frescoes and mosaics that once decorated Roman villas, you must reserve an entry time for a free, 45-minute tour led by an Italian- (and sometimes English-) speaking guide; if interested, book the next available tour when you buy your ticket. Finally, descend into the basement to see fine gold jewelry, dice, an abacus, and vault doors leading into the best coin collection in Europe, with fancy magni-fying glasses maneuvering you through cases of coins from ancient Rome to modern times.

**Cost and Hours:** €6, covered by €20 combo-ticket, Tue–Sun 9:00–19:45, closed Mon, open some summer Saturdays until

## East Rome

23:00, last entry 45 min before closing. An audioguide costs €4
(buy ticket first, then get audioguide at bookshop). The museum
is about 100 meters (330 feet) from the Termini train station.
As you leave the station, it's the sandstone-brick building on
your left. Enter at the far end, at Largo di Villa Peretti (Metro:
Termini, tel. 06-481-4144).

**Baths of Diocletian**—Around A.D. 300, Emperor Diocletian
built the largest baths in Rome. This sprawling meeting place,
with baths and schmoozing spaces to accommodate 3,000 bathers
at a time, was a big deal in ancient Rome. While much of it is

still closed, three sections are open: the Octagonal Hall, the Church of St. Mary of the Angels and Martyrs (both face Piazza della Repubblica), and the Museum of the Bath (across from the train station); see descriptions below.

▲▲Octagonal Hall—The Aula Ottagona, or Rotunda of Diocletian, was a private gymnasium in the Baths of Diocletian. Built around A.D. 300, these functioned until 537, when the barbarians cut Rome's aqueducts. The floor would have been seven meters (23 feet) lower (look down the window in the center of the room). The graceful iron grid supported the canopy of a 1928 planetarium. Today, the hall's a gallery, showing off fine bronze and marble statues—the kind that would have decorated the baths of imperial Rome. Most are Roman copies of Greek originals... gods, athletes, portrait busts. Two merit a close look: the *Defeated Boxer* (first century B.C., Greek and textbook Hellenistic) and the *Roman Aristocrat*. The aristocrat's face is older than the body. This bronze statue is typical of the day: Take a body modeled on Alexander the Great and pop on a portrait bust (free, Tue–Sat 9:00–14:00, Sun 9:00–13:00, closed Mon, borrow the English-description booklet, handy WC hidden in the back corner through an unmarked door).

▲Church of St. Mary of the Angels and Martyrs (Santa Maria degli Angeli e dei Martiri)—From Piazza della Repubblica, step through the Roman wall into what was the great central hall of the baths and is now a church (since the 16th century) designed by Michelangelo. When the church entrance was moved to Piazza Repubblica, the church was reoriented 90 degrees, turning the nave into long transepts and the transepts into a short nave. The 12 red granite columns still stand in their ancient positions. The classical floor was five meters (15 feet) lower. Project the walls down and imagine the soaring shape of the Roman vaults (free, Mon–Sat 7:00–18:30, Sun 8:00–19:30, closed to sightseers during Mass).

Museum of the Bath (Museo Nazionale Romano Terme di Diocleziano)—This museum, located on the grounds of the ancient Baths of Diocletian, has a misleading name. Rather than featuring the baths, it displays ancient Roman inscriptions on tons of tombs, steles, and tablets. Although well-displayed and described in English, the museum is difficult to appreciate quickly, and most travelers will find more history presented on a grander scale in the National Museum of Rome a block away (€5, covered by €20 combo-ticket, Tue–Sun 9:00–19:45, last entry 45 min before closing, closed Mon, Viale E. De Nicola 79, entrance faces Termini station, tel. 06-4782-6152).

▲Santa Maria della Vittoria—This church houses Bernini's statue of a swooning *St. Teresa in Ecstasy* (free, daily 7:00–13:00 &

15:00–19:00, on Largo Susanna, about 5 blocks northwest of train station, Metro: Repubblica). Once inside the church, you'll find St. Teresa to the left of the altar.

Teresa has just been stabbed with God's arrow of fire. Now the angel pulls it out and watches her reaction. Teresa swoons, her eyes roll up, her hand goes limp, she parts her lips...and moans. The smiling, Cupid-like angel understands just how she feels. Teresa, a 16th-century Spanish nun, later talked of the "sweetness" of "this intense pain," describing her oneness with God in ecstatic, even erotic, terms.

Bernini, the master of multimedia, pulls out all the stops to make this mystical vision real. Actual sunlight pours through the alabaster windows; bronze sunbeams shine on a marble angel holding a golden arrow. Teresa leans back on a cloud and her robe ripples from within, charged with her spiritual arousal. Bernini has created a little stage setting of heaven. And watching from the "theater boxes" on either side are members of the family that commissioned the work.

**Santa Susanna**—The home of the American Catholic Church in Rome, Santa Susanna holds Mass in English daily at 18:00 and Sunday at 9:00 and 10:30. Their excellent Web site in English, www.santasusanna.org, contains tips for travelers (Via XX Settembre 15, near recommended Via Firenze hotels, Metro: Repubblica, tel. 06-4201-4554).

## Sights—North Rome:
## Villa Borghese and nearby Via Veneto

▲**Villa Borghese**—Rome's scruffy "Central Park" is great for people-watching (plenty of modern-day Romeos and Juliets). Take a row on the lake or visit the park's fine museums.

▲▲▲**Borghese Gallery**—This private museum, filling a cardinal's mansion in the park, offers one of Europe's most sumptuous art experiences. Because of the gallery's slick mandatory reservation system, you'll enjoy its collection of world-class Baroque sculpture—including Bernini's *David* and his excited statue of Apollo chasing Daphne, as well as paintings by Caravaggio, Raphael, Titian, and Rubens—with manageable crowds.

The essence of the collection is the connection of the Renaissance with the classical world. Notice the second-century Roman reliefs with Michelangelo-designed panels above either end of the portico as you enter. The villa was built in the early 17th century by the great art collector Cardinal Borghese, who wanted to prove that the glories of ancient Rome were matched by the Renaissance.

In the main entry hall, opposite the door, notice the thrilling relief of the horse falling (first century A.D., Greek). Pietro

Bernini, father of the famous Bernini, completed the scene by adding the rider.

Each room seems to feature a Baroque masterpiece. The best of all is in Room 3: Bernini's *Apollo Chasing Daphne*. It's the perfect Baroque subject—capturing a thrilling, action-filled moment. In the mythological story, Apollo races after Daphne. Just as he's about to reach her, she turns into a tree. As her toes turn to roots and branches spring from her fingers, Apollo is in for one rude surprise. Walk slowly around. It's more air than stone.

**Cost and Hours:** €8, Tue–Sun 9:00–19:30, sometimes on Sat. until 23:00 June–Sept, closed Mon. No photos are allowed.

**Reservations:** Reservations are mandatory and easy to get in English over the Internet (www.ticketeria.it) or by phone (tel. 06-32810; if you get an Italian recording, press 2 for English; office hours: Mon–Fri 9:00–19:00, Sat 9:00–13:00, office closed Sat in Aug). Every two hours, 360 people are allowed to enter the museum. Entry times are 9:00, 11:00, 13:00, 15:00, and 17:00 (plus 19:00 and 21:00 if open late on Sat, June–Sept). Reserve a *minimum* of several days in advance for a weekday visit, at least a week ahead for weekends. When you reserve, request a day and time (which you'll be given if available), and you'll get a claim number. While you'll be advised to come 30 minutes before your appointed time, you can arrive a few minutes beforehand. But don't be late, as no-show tickets are sold to standbys.

Visits are strictly limited to two hours. Concentrate on the first floor, but leave yourself 30 minutes for the paintings of the Pinacoteca upstairs; highlights are marked by the audioguide icons. The fine bookshop and cafeteria are best visited outside your two-hour entry window.

If you don't have a reservation, just show up (or call first and ask if there are openings; a late afternoon on a weekday is usually your best bet). Reservations are tightest at 11:00 and on weekends. No-shows are released a few minutes after the top of the hour. Generally, out of 360 reservations, a few will fail to show (but more than a few may be waiting to grab them).

**Tours:** Guided English tours are offered at 9:10 and 11:10 for €5; reserve with entry reservation (or consider the excellent audioguide tour for €4).

**Location:** The museum is in the Villa Borghese park. A taxi (tell the cabbie your destination: gah-leh-REE-ah bor-GAY-zay) can get you within 100 meters (330 feet) of the museum. Otherwise, Metro to Spagna and take a 15-minute walk through the park.

**Etruscan Museum (Villa Giulia Museo Nazionale Etrusco)—**
The Etruscan civilization thrived in this part of Italy around 600

B.C., when Rome was an Etruscan town. The Etruscan civilization is fascinating, but the Villa Giulia Museum is extremely low-tech and in a state of disarray. I don't like it, and Etruscan fans will prefer the Vatican Museum's Etruscan section. Still, the Villa Giulia does have the famous "husband and wife sarcophagus" (a dead couple seeming to enjoy an everlasting banquet from atop their tomb; sixth century B.C. from Cerveteri), the *Apollo from Veio* statue (of textbook fame), and an impressive room filled with gold sheets of Etruscan printing and temple statuary from the Sanctuary of Pyrgi (€4.20, Tue–Sun 9:00–19:00, plus June–Sept Sat 21:00–23:45, closed Mon, closes earlier off-season, Piazzale di Villa Giulia 9, tel. 06-320-1951).

▲**Cappuccin Crypt**—If you want bones, this is the place. The crypt is below the church of Santa Maria della Immaculata Concezione on Via Veneto, just up from Piazza Barberini. The bones of more than 4,000 monks who died between 1528 and 1870 are in the basement, all artistically arranged for the delight—or disgust—of the always wide-eyed visitor. The soil in the crypt was brought from Jerusalem 400 years ago, and the monastic message on the wall explains that this is more than just a macabre exercise. Pick up a few of Rome's most interesting postcards (donation, Fri–Wed 9:00–12:00 & 15:00–18:00, closed Thu, Metro: Barberini, tel. 06-487-1185). A painting of St. Francis by Caravaggio is upstairs. Just up the street, you'll find the American Embassy, Federal Express, and fancy Via Veneto cafés filled with the poor and envious looking for the rich and famous.

**Ara Pacis (Altar of Peace)**—This will reopen in 2005, once restoration is complete. In 9 B.C., after victories in Gaul and Spain, Emperor Augustus celebrated the beginning of the Pax Romana by building this altar of peace. Peace is almost worshiped here. The north and south walls show a procession with realistic portraits of the imperial family in Greek Hellenistic style. It's a fine combination of Roman grandeur and Greek elegance. Even when the altar is not open, it can sometimes be seen through the windows (a long block west of Via del Corso on Via di Ara Pacis, on east bank of river near Ponte Cavour, nearest Metro: Spagna).

## Sights—West Rome: Vatican City Area

▲▲▲**St. Peter's Basilica**—There is no doubt: This is the richest and most impressive church on earth. To call it vast is like calling God smart. Marks on the floor show where the next-largest churches would fit if they were put inside. The ornamental cherubs would dwarf a large man. Birds roost inside, and thousands of people wander about, heads craned heavenward, hardly noticing each other. Don't miss Michelangelo's *Pietà* (behind bulletproof

## Vatican City Overview

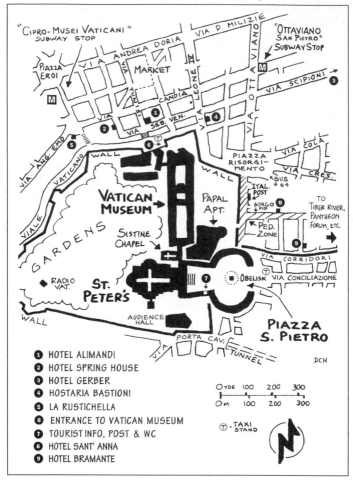

"CIPRO - MUSEI VATICANI" SUBWAY STOP

VIA D. MILIZIE

"OTTAVIANO SAN PIETRO" SUBWAY STOP

VIA ANDREA DORIA

PIAZZA EROI

MARKET

VIA SCIPIONI

CANDIA

VIA SEB. VEN.

VIA OTTAVIANO

VIA LEONE

VIA COLA

PIAZZA RISORGI-MENTO

VIA CRES.

VIA VATICANO

WALL

WALL

BUS # 64

ITAL. POST

VATICAN MUSEUM

PAPAL APT.

BORGO PIO

GARDENS

SISTINE CHAPEL

PED. ZONE

TO TIBER RIVER, PANTHEON FORUM, ETC.

VIA CORRIDORI

RADIO VAT.

ST. PETER'S

OBELISK

VIA CONCILIAZIONE

WALL

AUDIENCE HALL

PIAZZA S. PIETRO

PORTA CAV.

TUNNEL

DCH

- ❶ HOTEL ALIMANDI
- ❷ HOTEL SPRING HOUSE
- ❸ HOTEL GERBER
- ❹ HOSTARIA BASTIONI
- ❺ LA RUSTICHELLA
- ❻ ENTRANCE TO VATICAN MUSEUM
- ❼ TOURIST INFO, POST & WC
- ❽ HOTEL SANT' ANNA
- ❾ HOTEL BRAMANTE

0 YDS 100 200 300
0 M 100 200 300

Ⓣ - TAXI STAND

N

glass) to the right of the entrance. Bernini's altar work and seven-story-tall bronze canopy *(baldacchino)* are brilliant.

For a quick self-guided walk through the basilica, follow these points (see map on page 70):

**1.** The atrium is larger than most churches. Notice the historic doors (the Holy Door, on the right, won't be opened until the next Jubilee Year, in 2025—see point 13 below).

**2.** The purple, circular porphyry stone marks the site of Charlemagne's coronation in A.D. 800 (in the first St. Peter's church that stood on this site). From here, get a sense of the immensity of the church, which can accommodate 95,000 worshipers standing on its six acres.

**3.** Michelangelo planned a Greek-cross floor plan rather than the Latin-cross standard in medieval churches. A Greek cross, symbolizing the perfection of God, and by association the goodness of man, was important to the humanist Michelangelo. But accommodating large crowds was important to the Church in the fancy Baroque age, which followed Michelangelo, so the original nave length was doubled. Stand halfway up the nave and imagine the stubbier design Michelangelo had in mind.

**4.** View the magnificent dome from the statue of St. Andrew. See the vision of heaven above the windows: Jesus, Mary, a ring of saints, rings of angels, and, on the very top, God the Father.

**5.** The main altar sits directly over St. Peter's tomb and under Bernini's 21-meter-tall (70-foot) bronze canopy.

**6.** The stairs lead down to the crypt to the foundation, chapels, and tombs of popes. (Do this last, since it leads you out of the church.)

**7.** The statue of St. Peter, with an irresistibly kissable toe, is one of the few pieces of art that predate this church. It adorned the first St. Peter's church.

**8.** St. Peter's throne and Bernini's starburst dove window is the site of a daily mass (Mon–Sat at 17:00, Sun at 17:45).

**9.** St. Peter was crucified here when this location was simply "the Vatican Hill." The obelisk now standing in the center of St. Peter's square marked the center of a Roman racecourse long before a church stood here.

**10.** For most, the treasury (in the sacristy) is not worth the admission.

**11.** The church is filled with mosaics, not paintings. Notice the mosaic version of Raphael's *Transfiguration*.

**12.** Blessed Sacrament Chapel.

**13.** Michelangelo sculpted his *Pietà* when he was 24 years old. A *pietà* is a work showing Mary with the dead body of Christ taken down from the cross. Michelangelo's mastery of the body is obvious in this powerfully beautiful masterpiece. Jesus is believably dead, and Mary, the eternally youthful "handmaiden" of the Lord, still accepts God's will... even if it means giving up her son.

The Holy Door (just to the right of the *Pietà*) was bricked shut at the end of the Jubilee Year 2000 and won't be opened until 2025. Every 25 years, the Church celebrates an especially festive year derived from the Old Testament idea of the Jubilee Year (originally every 50 years), which encourages new beginnings and the forgiveness of sins and debts. In the Jubilee Year 2000,

## St. Peter's Basilica

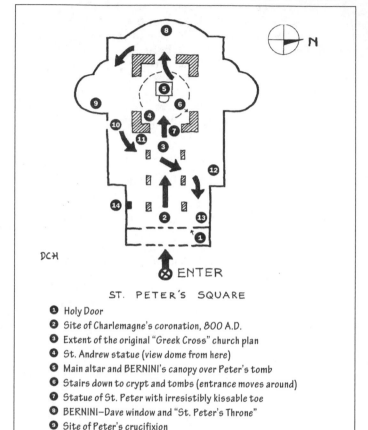

N

DCH

⊗ ENTER

ST. PETER'S SQUARE

❶ Holy Door
❷ Site of Charlemagne's coronation, 800 A.D.
❸ Extent of the original "Greek Cross" church plan
❹ St. Andrew statue (view dome from here)
❺ Main altar and BERNINI's canopy over Peter's tomb
❻ Stairs down to crypt and tombs (entrance moves around)
❼ Statue of St. Peter with irresistibly kissable toe
❽ BERNINI—Dave window and "St. Peter's Throne"
❾ Site of Peter's crucifixion
❿ Museum entrance
⓫ RAPHAEL—"Transfiguration" mosaic
⓬ Blessed Sacrament Chapel
⓭ MICHELANGELO—Pieta
⓮ Elevator to roof and dome-climb (entrance moves around)

the pope tirelessly—and with significant success—promoted debt relief for the world's poorest countries.

   **14.** An elevator leads to the roof and the stairway up the dome (€5, allow an hour to go up and down). The dome, Michelangelo's last work, is (you guessed it) the biggest anywhere. Taller than a football field is long, it's well worth the sweaty climb for a great view of Rome, the Vatican grounds, and the inside of the basilica—particularly heavenly while there is singing. Look around—Rome has no modern skyline. No building is allowed to exceed the height of St. Peter's. The elevator takes you to the rooftop of the nave. From there, a few steps take you to a balcony at the base of the dome looking down into the church interior. After that, the one-way, 300-step climb (for some people claustrophobic) to the cupola begins. The rooftop level (below the dome) has a gift shop, WC, drinking fountain, and a commanding view.

**Dress Code:** The church strictly enforces its dress code: no shorts or bare shoulders (men and women); no miniskirts. You might be required to check any bags at a free cloakroom near the entry.

**Hours of Church:** Daily May–Sept 7:00–19:00, Oct–April 7:00–18:00. All are welcome to join in the hour-long Mass at the front altar (Mon–Sat at 8:30, 10:00, 11:00, 12:00, & 17:00; Sun and holidays 9:00, 10:30, 12:10, 13:00, 16:00, & 17:30). The church is particularly moving at 7:00, while tourism is still sleeping. Volunteers who want you to understand and appreciate St. Peter's give free 90-minute tours (depart from TI daily at 14:15; also Mon, Wed, and Fri at 15:00; confirm schedule at TI, tel. 06-6988-1662); the tours are generally excellent but non-Christians can find them preachy. Seeing the *Pietà* is neat; understanding it is divine.

**Cost and Hours of Dome:** The view from the dome is worth the climb (€5 elevator plus 300-step climb, May–Sept daily 8:00–18:00, Oct–April daily 8:30–17:00).

▲▲▲**Vatican Museum**—The six kilometers (3.75 miles) of displays in this immense museum—from ancient statues to Christian frescoes to modern paintings—are topped by the Raphael Rooms and Michelangelo's glorious Sistine Chapel. (If you have binoculars, bring them.)

Even without the Sistine, this is one of Europe's top three or four houses of art. It can be exhausting, so plan your visit carefully, focusing on a few themes. Allow two hours for a quick visit, three or four for time to enjoy it. The museum has a nearly impossible-not-to-follow, one-way system (although, for the rushed visitor, the museum does clearly mark out four color-coded visits of different lengths—A is shortest, D longest). Tip: The Sistine Chapel has an exit (optional) that leads directly to St. Peter's Basilica, saving you the 10-minute walk back to the Vatican Museum exit; if you want to squirt out at the Sistine, see the Pinacoteca painting gallery first (described below) and don't get an audioguide (which needs to be returned at the entry/exit).

Start, as civilization did, in Egypt and Mesopotamia. Next, the Pio Clementino collection features **Greek and Roman**

## Vatican City

This tiny independent country of just over 100 acres, contained entirely within Rome, has its own postal system, armed guards, helipad, mini–train station, and radio station (KPOP). Politically powerful, the Vatican is the religious capital of 800 million Roman Catholics. If you're not a Catholic, become one for your visit.

Small as it is, Vatican City has two huge sights: St. Peter's Basilica (with Michelangelo's *Pietà*) and the Vatican Museum (with the Sistine Chapel). A helpful TI is just to the left of St. Peter's Basilica (Mon–Sat 8:30–19:00, closed Sun, tel. 06-6988-1662; Vatican switchboard tel. 06-6982, www.vatican.va). The thief-infested bus #64 stops right at the basilica. The nearest Metro stops are a 10-minute walk away from either sight: For St. Peter's, the closest stop is Ottaviano; for the Vatican Museum, it's Cipro-Musei Vaticani.

**Post Office:** The Vatican post, with offices on St. Peter's Square (next to TI) and in the Vatican Museum, is more reliable than Italy's mail service (Mon–Sat 8:30–19:00). The stamps are a collectible bonus. Vatican stamps are good throughout Rome, but to use the Vatican's mail service (rather than Italy's), you need to mail your cards from the Vatican; write your postcards ahead of time. (Note that the Vatican won't mail cards with Italian stamps.)

**Tours:** The Vatican TI conducts free 90-minute tours of St.

statues. Decorating its courtyard are some of the best Greek and Roman statues in captivity, including the *Laocoön* group (first century B.C., Hellenistic) and the *Apollo Belvedere* (a second-century Roman copy of a Greek original). The centerpiece of the next hall is the *Belvedere Torso* (just a 2,000-year-old torso, but one that had a great impact on the art of Michelangelo). Finishing off the classical statuary are two fine fourth-century porphyry sarcophagi; these royal purple tombs were made (though not used) for the Roman emperor Constantine's mother and daughter. They were Christians—and therefore outlaws—until Constantine made Christianity legal (A.D. 312). The tombs, crafted in Egypt at a time when a declining Rome was unable to do such fine work, have details that are fun to study.

After long halls of tapestries, old maps, broken penises, and fig leaves, you'll come to what most people are looking for: The Raphael Rooms (or *stanza*) and Michelangelo's Sistine Chapel.

These outstanding works are frescoes. A fresco (meaning

Peter's (depart daily from TI at 14:15 also; Mon, Wed, and Fri at 15:00; confirm schedule at TI, tel. 06-6988-1662). Tours are the only way to see the Vatican Gardens; book at least a day in advance by calling 06-6988-4466 (€9, Mon–Sat 10:00–12:00, tours start at Vatican Museum tour desk and finish on St. Peter's Square). To tour the necropolis of St. Peter's and the saint's tomb, call the Excavations Office at 06-6988-5318 (€8, 2 hrs, office open Mon–Fri 9:00–17:00).

**Seeing the Pope:** Your best chances for a sighting are on Sunday and Wednesday. The pope usually gives a blessing at noon on Sunday from his apartment on St. Peter's Square (except Aug–Sept, when he speaks at his summer residence at Castel Gandolfo, 40 km, or 25 miles, from Rome; train leaves Rome's Termini station at 8:35, returns after his talk). On Wednesday at 10:30, the pope blesses the crowds at St. Peter's from a balcony or canopied platform on the square (except in winter, when he speaks at 11:00 in the 7,000-seat Aula Paola VI Auditorium, next to St. Peter's Basilica). To find out the pope's schedule or to book a free spot for the Wednesday blessing (either for a seat on the square or in the auditorium), call 06-6988-4631. The weekly entertainment guide *Roma c'è* always has a "Seeing the Pope" section. If you don't want to see the pope, minimize crowd problems by avoiding these times.

"fresh" in Italian) is technically not a painting. The color is mixed into wet plaster, and, when the plaster dries, the painting is actually part of the wall. This is a durable but difficult medium, requiring speed and accuracy, as the work is built slowly, one patch at a time.

After fancy rooms illustrating the "Immaculate Conception of Mary" (a hard-to-sell, 19th-century Vatican doctrine) and the triumph of Constantine (with divine guidance, which led to his conversion to Christianity), you enter the first room completely done by **Raphael** and find the newly restored *School of Athens*. This is remarkable for its blatant pre-Christian classical orientation, especially since it originally wallpapered the apartments of Pope Julius II. Raphael honors the great pre-Christian thinkers— Aristotle, Plato, and company—who are portrayed as the leading artists of Raphael's day. The bearded figure of Plato is Leonardo da Vinci. Diogenes, history's first hippie, sprawls alone in bright blue on the stairs, while Michelangelo broods in the foreground— supposedly added late. Apparently, Raphael snuck a peek at the

Sistine Chapel and decided that his arch-competitor was so good he had to put their personal differences aside and include him in this tribute to the artists of his generation. Today's St. Peter's was under construction as Raphael was working. In the *School of Athens*, he gives us a sneak preview of the unfinished church.

Next (unless you detour through the refreshingly modern Catholic art section) is the brilliantly restored **Sistine Chapel**. The Sistine Chapel, the pope's personal chapel, is where, upon the death of the ruling pope, a new pope is elected. The College of Cardinals meets here and votes four times a day until a two-thirds-plus-one majority is reached and a new pope is elected.

The Sistine is famous for Michelangelo's pictorial culmination of the Renaissance, showing the story of Creation, with a powerful God weaving in and out of each scene through that busy first week. This is an optimistic and positive expression of the High Renaissance and a stirring example of the artistic and theological maturity of the 33-year-old Michelangelo, who spent four years on this work.

Later, after the Reformation wars had begun and after the Catholic army of Spain had sacked the Vatican, the reeling Church began to fight back. As part of its Counter-Reformation, a much older Michelangelo was commissioned to paint the *Last Judgment* (behind the altar). Brilliantly restored, the message is as clear as the day Michelangelo finished it: Christ is returning, some will go to hell and some to heaven, and some will be saved by the power of the rosary.

In the recent and controversial restoration project, no paint was added. Centuries of dust, soot (from candles used for lighting and Mass), and glue (added to make the art shine) were removed, revealing the bright original colors of Michelangelo. Photos are allowed (without a flash) elsewhere in the museum, but as part of the deal with the company who did the restoration, no photos are allowed in the Sistine Chapel.

For a shortcut, a small door at the rear of the Sistine Chapel allows groups and individuals (without an audioguide) to escape directly to St. Peter's Basilica. If you exit here, you're done with the museum. The Pinacoteca is the only important part left. Consider doing it at the start. Otherwise it's a 10-minute, heel-to-toe slalom through tourists from the Sistine Chapel to the entry/exit.

After this long march, you'll find the **Pinacoteca** (the Vatican's small but fine collection of paintings, with Raphael's *Transfiguration*, Leonardo's unfinished *St. Jerome*, and Caravaggio's *Deposition*), a cafeteria (long lines, mediocre food), and the underrated early-Christian art section, before you exit via the souvenir shop.

**Cost and Hours:** €10, March–Oct Mon–Fri 8:45–15:45; Sat 8:45–13:45; Nov–Feb Mon–Sat 8:45–13:45, closed Sun except last Sun of the month (when it's free, crowded, and open 8:45–13:45). Last entry is about 90 minutes before the closing time (12:20 when museum closes at 13:45, 14:20 when museum closes at 15:45). The Sistine Chapel sometimes shuts down 30 minutes early.

The museum is generally hot and crowded. Saturday, the last Sunday of the month, and Monday are the worst; afternoons are best.

The museum is closed on many holidays (mainly religious ones) including—for 2003: Jan 1 and 6, Feb 11, March 19, Easter and Easter Monday (April 20 and 21), May 1 and 29, June 19, Aug 14 and 15, Nov 1, and Dec 8 and 25.

Modest dress (no short shorts or bare shoulders for men or women) is appropriate and often required. Museum tel. 06-6988-4947.

**Tours:** A tour in English is offered once daily at 11:00 (€16.50, 2 hrs, call 06-6988-4466 to reserve). You can rent a €5 audioguide (but if you do, you lose the option of taking the shortcut from the Sistine Chapel to St. Peter's, because the audioguide must be returned at the Vatican Museum entrance).

▲**Castel Sant' Angelo**—Built as a tomb for the emperor; used through the Middle Ages as a castle, prison, and place of last refuge for popes under attack; and today, a museum, this giant pile of ancient bricks is packed with history.

Ancient Rome allowed no tombs—not even the emperor's—within its walls. So Hadrian grabbed the most commanding position just outside the walls and across the river and built a towering tomb (circa A.D. 139) well within view of the city. His mausoleum was a huge cylinder (64 meters wide, 21 meters high; or 210 feet wide, 70 feet high) topped by a cypress grove and crowned by a huge statue of Hadrian himself riding a chariot. For nearly a hundred years, Roman emperors (from Hadrian to Caracalla in A.D. 217) were buried here.

In the year 590, the Archangel Michael appeared above the mausoleum to Pope Gregory the Great. Sheathing his sword, the angel signaled the end of a plague. The fortress that was Hadrian's mausoleum eventually became a fortified palace, renamed for the "holy angel."

Since Rome was repeatedly plundered by invaders, Castel Sant' Angelo was a handy place of last refuge for threatened popes. The elevated corridor connecting Castel Sant' Angelo with the Vatican was built in 1277. In anticipation of long sieges, rooms were decorated with papal splendor (you'll see paintings by Crivelli, Signorelli, and Mantegna). In the 16th century, during a sack of

Rome by troops of Charles V of Spain, the pope lived inside the castle for months with his entourage of hundreds (an unimaginable ordeal, considering the food service at the top-floor bar).

After you walk around the entire base of the castle, take the small staircase down to the original Roman floor. In the atrium, study the model of the castle in Roman times and imagine the niche in the wall filled with a towering "welcome to my tomb" statue of Hadrian. From here, a ramp leads to the right, spiraling 125 meters (410 feet). While some of the fine brickwork and bits of mosaic survive, the marble veneer is long gone (notice the holes in the wall which held it in place). At the end of the ramp, stairs climb to the room where the ashes of the emperors were kept. These stairs continue to the top, where you'll find the papal apartments. Don't miss the Sala del Tesoro (treasury), where the wealth of the Vatican was locked up in a huge chest. Do miss the 58 rooms of the military museum. The views from the top are great—pick out landmarks as you stroll around—and a restful coffee with a view of St. Peter's is worth the price.

**Cost, Hours, Tours:** €5, Tue–Sun 9:00–19:00, plus June–Sept Sat 21:00–23:45, closed Mon. You can take an English-language tour with an audioguide (€3.60) or live guide (€4.20, Tue–Fri at 15:00, Sat at 12:15 and 16:30, confirm times, tel. 06-3996-7600, Metro: Lepanto or bus #64, near Vatican City).

**Ponte Sant' Angelo**—The bridge leading to Castel Sant' Angelo was built by Hadrian for quick and regal access from downtown to his tomb. The three middle arches are actually Roman originals and a fine example of the empire's engineering expertise. The angels were designed by Bernini and finished by his students.

## Sights—South Rome

If you visit Ostia Antica (see page 82), you can maximize sight-seeing efficiency by visiting any of the sights in south Rome on your return.

▲**St. Paul's Outside the Walls (Basilica San Paolo Fuori le Mura)**—One of the greatest churches in Christendom, St. Paul's was originally built in 324, then destroyed by fire in the 1820s. Today, it's mammoth and pristine, rebuilt true to the ancient basilica plan. It feels sterile, but in a good way—like you're already in heaven. Along with St. Peter's Basilica, San Giovanni in Laterano, and Santa Maria Maggiore, this church is part of the Vatican rather than Italy. St. Paul is supposed to be buried under the altar (without his head, which San Giovanni in Laterano got). Alabaster windows light the vast interior, fifth-century mosaics decorate the triumphal arch leading to the altar, and mosaic portraits of all 264 popes, from St. Peter to John Paul II, ring the place—with blank spots ready for future popes. Find John Paul II (to right of the high altar: Jo Paulus II, no date) and John Paul I (to his right, with a reign of one month and three days). Wander the ornate yet peaceful cloister (closed 13:00–15:00). The courtyard leading up to the church is typical of early Christian churches; even the first St. Peter's had this kind of welcoming zone (free, daily 7:00–18:00, modest dress code enforced, Via Ostiense 186, Metro: San Paolo).

▲**Montemartini Museum (Musei Capitolini Centrale Montemartini)**—This museum houses a dreamy collection of 400 ancient statues, set evocatively in a classic 1932 electric power plant among generators and Metropolis–type cast-iron machinery. While the art is not as famous as the collections you'll see downtown, the effect is fun and memorable—and you'll encounter absolutely no tourists (€4.20, Tue–Sun 9:30–19:00, closed Mon, Via Ostiense 106, a short walk from Metro: Garbatella, tel. 06-574-8042).

**Baths of Caracalla (Terme di Caracalla)**—Today, it's just a shell—a huge shell—with all of its sculptures and most of its mosaics moved to museums. Inaugurated by Emperor Caracalla in A.D. 216, this massive complex could accommodate 1,600 visitors at a time. Today, you'll see a two-story, roofless brick building surrounded by a garden, bordered by ruined walls. The two large rooms at either end of the building were used for exercise. In between the exercise rooms was a pool flanked by two small, mosaic-floored dressing rooms. Niches in the walls once held statues. In its day, this was a remarkable place to hang out. For ancient Romans, the baths were a social experience.

The Baths of Caracalla functioned until Goths severed the aqueducts in the sixth century. In modern times, operas were performed here from 1938 to 1993. For the same reason concerts no longer take place in the Forum—to keep the ruins from becoming more ruined—the performances were discontinued (€5, covered by €20 combo-ticket, Mon 9:00–17:30, Tue–Sun 9:00–19:30, last entry 1 hour before closing, audioguide-€4, fine €8 guidebook—can read in shaded garden while sitting on a chunk of column, Metro: Circus Maximus, and a 5-min walk south along Via delle Terme di Caracalla, tel. 06-575-8628). Several of the baths' statues are now in Rome's Octagonal Hall; the immense *Toro Farnese* (a marble sculpture of a bull surrounded by people) snorts in Naples' Archaeological Museum.

**Testaccio**—Four fascinating but lesser sights cluster at the Piramide Metro stop between the Colosseum and E.U.R., in the gritty Testaccio neighborhood. (This is a quick and easy stop as you return from E.U.R., or when changing trains en route to Ostia Antica.)

Working-class since ancient times, Testaccio has recently gone trendy-bohemian, and visitors will wander through an awkward mix of yuppie and proletarian worlds, not noticing—but perhaps feeling—the "keep Testaccio for the Testaccians" graffiti.

**Pyramid of Gaius Cestius:** The Mark Antony/Cleopatra scandal (around the time of Christ) brought exotic Egyptian styles into vogue. A rich Roman magistrate, Gaius Cestius, had a pyramid built as his tomb. Made of brick covered in marble, it was completed in just 330 days (as stated in its Latin inscription) and fell far short of Egyptian pyramid standards. Later incorporated into the Aurelian Wall, it's now next to the Piramide Metro stop.

**Porta Ostiense:** This formidable gate (also next to Piramide Metro stop) is from the Aurelian Wall, begun in the third century under Emperor Aurelius. The wall, which encircled the city, was 20 kilometers (12 miles) long and eight meters (26 feet) high, with 14 main gates and 380 22-meter-tall (72-foot) towers. Most of what you'll see today is circa A.D. 400. The barbarians reconstructed this gate in the sixth century. (For more on the wall, visit the Museum of the Walls at Porta San Sebastian; see "Ancient Appian Way," below.)

**Protestant Cemetery:** The *Cimitero Acattolico per gli Stranieri al Testaccio* (cemetery for the burial of non-Catholic foreigners) is a Romantic tomb-filled park, running along the wall just beyond the pyramid. From the Piramide Metro stop, walk between the pyramid and the Roman gate on Via Persichetti, then go left on Caio Cestio to the gate of the cemetery. Ring the bell (donation box, April–Sept Tue–Sun 9:00–18:00, Oct–March 9:00–17:00, closed Mon).

Originally, none of the Protestant epitaphs were allowed to make any mention of heaven. Signs direct visitors to the graves of notable non-Catholics who have died in Rome since 1738. Many of the buried were diplomats. And many, such as poets Shelley and Keats, were from the Romantic Age; they came on the Grand Tour and—"captivated by the fatal charms of Rome," as Shelley wrote— never left. Head left toward the pyramid to find Keats' tomb, in the far corner. At the pyramid, look down on Matilde Talli's cat hospice (flier at the gate). Volunteers use donations to care for these "Guardians of the Departed" who "provide loyal companionship to these dead."

**Monte Testaccio:** Just behind the Protestant Cemetery (as you leave, turn left and continue 2 blocks down Caio Cestio) is a 35-meter-tall (115-foot) ancient trash mountain. It's made of broken *testae*—broken earthenware jars used to haul mostly wine 2,000 years ago, when this was a gritty port warehouse district. After 500 years of sloppy dock work, Rome's lowly eighth hill was built. Because the caves dug into the hill stay cool, trendy bars, clubs, and restaurants compete with gritty car-repair places for a spot. The neighborhood was once known for a huge slaughterhouse and a Gypsy camp that squatted inside an old military base.

Now it's home to the Villagio Globale, a site for concerts and techno-raves. For a youthful and lively night scene, adventurers might consider a trip out to Monte Testaccio (Metro: Piramide).

# Ancient Appian Way (*Via Appia Antica*)

Since the fourth century B.C., this has been Rome's gateway to the East. The first section was perfectly straight. It was the largest, widest, fastest road ever, the wonder of its day, called the "Queen of Roads." Eventually, this most important of Roman roads stretched 700 kilometers (430 miles) to the port of Brindisi—where boats sailed for Greece and Egypt. Twenty-nine such roads fanned out from Rome. Just as Hitler built the autobahn system in anticipation of empire maintenance, the emperors realized the military and political value of a good road system. A central strip accommodated animal-powered vehicles, and elevated sidewalks served pedestrians. As it left Rome, the road was lined with tombs and funerary monuments. Imagine a funeral procession passing under the pines and cypress and past a long line of pyramids, private mini-temples, altars, and tombs.

Hollywood created the famous image of the Appian Way lined with Spartacus and his gang of defeated and crucified slave rebels. This image is only partially accurate. Spartacus was killed in battle.

**Tourist's Appian Way:** The road starts about three kilometers (less than 2 miles) south of the Colosseum at the massive San Sebastian Gate. The Museum of the Walls, located at the gate, offers an interesting look at Roman defense and a chance to scramble along a stretch of the ramparts (€2.60, Tue–Sun 9:00–19:00, closed Mon, tel. 06-7047-5284). A kilometer (0.6 mile) down the road are the two most historic and popular catacombs, those of San Callisto and San Sebastian (described below). Beyond that, the road becomes pristine and traffic-free, popular for biking and hiking.

To reach the Appian Way, take the Archeobus from Piazza Venezia (see "Tours of Rome," page 48) or take the Metro to the Colli Albani stop, then catch bus #660 to Via Appia Antica—its last stop and the start of an interesting stretch of the ancient road. The segment between the third and 11th milestones is most interesting.

You can rent bikes at the Appian park office on weekends and holidays. To reach the office by bus (either Archeobus or city bus), get off at the park entrance—the Sede Parco Appia Antica stop (€2.50/hr, Via Appia Antica 42, tel. 06-512-6314, www.parcoappiaantica.org).

▲▲**Catacombs**—The catacombs are burial places for (mostly) Christians who died in ancient Roman times. By law, no one was allowed to be buried within the walls of Rome. While pagan Romans were into cremation, Christians preferred to be buried. But land was expensive and most Christians were poor. A few wealthy, landowning Christians allowed their land to be used as burial places.

The 40 or so known catacombs circle Rome about five kilometers (3 miles) from its center. From the first through the fifth centuries, Christians dug an estimated 600 kilometers (375 miles) of tomb-lined tunnels, with networks of galleries as many as five layers deep. The tufa—soft and easy to cut, though it becomes very hard when exposed to air—was perfect for the job. The Christians burrowed many layers deep for two reasons: to get more mileage out of the donated land, and to be near martyrs and saints already buried there. Bodies were wrapped in linen (like Christ's). Since they figured the Second Coming was imminent, there was no interest in embalming the body.

When Emperor Constantine legalized Christianity in 313, Christians had a new, interesting problem. There would be no more persecuted martyrs to bind them and inspire them. Thus the early martyrs and popes assumed more importance, and Christians began making pilgrimages to their burial places in the catacombs.

In the 800s, when barbarian invaders started ransacking the tombs, Christians moved the relics of saints and martyrs to the safety of churches in the city center. For a thousand years, the catacombs were forgotten. Around 1850, they were excavated and became part of the romantic Grand Tour of Europe.

Finding abandoned plates and utensils from ritual meals in the candlelit galleries led 18th- and 19th-century Romantics to guess that persecuted Christians hid out and lived in these catacombs. This Romantic legend grew. But catacombs were not used for hiding out. They are simply early Christian burial grounds. With a million people in Rome, the easiest way for the 10,000 or so early Christians to hide out was not to camp in the catacombs (which everyone, including the government, knew about), but to melt into the city.

The underground tunnels, while empty of bones, are rich in early Christian symbolism, which functioned as a secret language. The dove symbolized the soul. You'll see it quenching its thirst (worshiping), with an olive branch (at rest), or happily perched (in paradise). Peacocks, known for their "incorruptible flesh," symbolized immortality. The shepherd with a lamb on his shoulders was the "good shepherd," the first portrayal of Christ as a kindly leader of his flock. The fish was used because the first letters of these words—"Jesus Christ, Son of God, Savior"— spelled "fish" in Greek. And the anchor is a cross in disguise. A second-century bishop had written on his tomb: "All who understand these things, pray for me." You'll see pictures of people praying with their hands raised up—the custom at the time.

All catacomb tours are essentially the same. The **Catacombs of San Callisto** (a.k.a. Callixtus), the official cemetery for the Christians of Rome and burial place of third-century popes, is the most historic. Sixteen bishops (early popes) were buried here. Buy your €5 ticket and wait for your language to be called. They move lots of people quickly. If one group seems ridiculously large (over 50 people), wait for the next tour in English (Thu–Tue 8:30–12:00 & 14:30–17:30, closed Wed and Feb, closes at 17:00 in winter, Via Appia Antica 110, tel. 06-5130-1580). Dig this: The catacombs have a Web site (www.catacombe.roma.it) focusing mainly on San Callisto, featuring photos, site info, and a history.

The **Catacombs of San Sebastian** (Sebastiano) are 300 meters (985 feet) farther down the road (€5, Mon–Sat 8:30–12:00 & 14:30–17:30, closed Sun and Nov, closes at 17:00 in winter, Via Appia Antica 136, tel. 06-5130-1580).

## E.U.R.

In the late 1930s, Italy's dictator, Benito Mussolini, planned an international exhibition to show off the wonders of his fascist society. But these wonders brought us World War II, and Il Duce's celebration never happened. The unfinished mega-project was completed in the 1950s and now houses government offices and big, obscure museums.

If Hitler and Mussolini won the war, our world might look like E.U.R. (pronounced "ay-oor"). Hike down E.U.R.'s wide, pedestrian-mean boulevards. Patriotic murals, aren't-you-proud-to-be-an-extreme-right-winger pillars, and stern squares decorate the soulless, planned grid and stark office blocks. Boulevards named for Astronomy, Electronics, Social Security, and Beethoven are more exhausting than inspirational. Today, E.U.R. is worth a trip for its Museum of Roman Civilization (described below).

The Metro skirts E.U.R. with three stops (10 min from the Colosseum). Use E.U.R. Magliana for the "Square Colosseum" and E.U.R. Fermi for the Museum of Roman Civilization (both described below). Consider walking 30 minutes from the palace to the museum through the center of E.U.R.

From the Magliana Metro stop, stairs lead uphill to the **Palace of the Civilization of Labor (Palazzo del Civilta del Lavoro)**, the essence of fascist architecture. With its giant, no-questions-asked, patriotic statues and its black-and-white simplicity, this is E.U.R.'s tallest building and landmark. It's understandably nicknamed the "Square Colosseum." Around the corner, Café Palombini is still decorated in a 1930s style and is now quite trendy with young Romans (daily 7:00–24:00, good gelato, pastries, and snacks, Piazzale Adenauer 12, tel. 06-591-1700).

▲**Museum of Roman Civilization (Museo della Civilta Romana)**—With 59 rooms filled with plaster casts and models illustrating the greatness of classical Rome, this vast and heavy museum gives a strangely lifeless, close-up look at Rome. Each room has a theme, from military tricks to musical instruments. One long hall is filled with casts of the reliefs of Trajan's Column. The highlight is the 1:250-scale model of Constantine's Rome— circa A.D. 300 (€4.20, Tue–Sat 9:00–18:45, Sun 9:00–13:30, closed Mon, Piazza G. Agnelli, from Metro: E.U.R. Fermi, walk 10 min up Via dell' Arte, you'll see its colonnade on the right, tel. 06-592-6041).

## Sights—Near Rome

▲▲**Ostia Antica**—For an exciting day trip less than an hour from downtown Rome, pop down to the ancient Roman port of Ostia Antica. It's similar to Pompeii, but a lot closer and, in some ways, more interesting. Because Ostia was a working port town, it shows a more complete and gritty look at Roman life than does wealthy Pompeii. Wandering around today, you'll see the remains of the docks, warehouses, apartment flats, mansions, shopping arcades, and baths that served a once thriving port of 60,000 people. Later, Ostia became a ghost town, and is now excavated. Start at the 2,000-year-old theater, buy a map, explore the town, and finish with its fine little museum (note that museum closes at 13:30).

**Getting There:** To get there, take the Metro's B Line to the Piramide stop (consider popping out to see the ancient Roman pyramid tomb, listed above in South Rome sights). From the Piramide stop, catch the Lido train to Ostia Antica (2/hr, use a Metro ticket). From the train station, cross the road via the blue sky bridge and walk straight down Via della Stazione di Ostia Antica, following signs to *Scavi di Ostia Antica*, about 400 meters (1,300 feet) to the gate.

**Cost and Hours:** €5, Tue–Sun 8:30–18:00 in summer, 9:00–16:00 in winter, closed Mon. Visit the museum in the morning before it closes (Tue–Sun 9:00–13:30, closed Mon, cafeteria in museum, tel. 06-5635-8099).

**Tour:** The well-done audioguide costs €5.

## Self-Guided Walks in Rome

### Night Walk Across Rome: Trastevere to the Spanish Steps

Rome can be grueling. But a fine way to enjoy this historian's rite of passage is an evening walk lacing together Rome's floodlit nightspots. Enjoying fine urban spaces, observing real-life theater vignettes, sitting so close to a Bernini fountain that traffic noises evaporate, watching water flicker its mirror on the marble, jostling with local teenagers to see all the gelato flavors, enjoying lovers straddling more than the bench, jaywalking past flak-proof vested *polizia*, marveling at the ramshackle elegance that softens this brutal city for those who were born here and can imagine living nowhere else—these are the flavors of Rome best tasted after dark. This walk is about three kilometers, or two miles, long (for a short-cut, skip Trastevere and start at Campo de' Fiori instead).

To get to Trastevere, the colorful neighborhood across *(tras)* the Tiber *(tevere)* River, you can take a taxi or ride the bus (from Vatican area—#23; or from Via Nazionale hotels—take the #40 express to Piazza Belli just over bridge, or catch #64, #70, #115, or #640 to Largo Argentina, then transfer to tram #8 and get off at Piazza Mastai). Consider dinner in Trastevere (see "Eating," below).

**Trastevere** offers the best look at medieval-village Rome. The action all marches to the chime of the church bells. Go to Trastevere and wander. Wonder. Be a poet on Rome's Left Bank. This proud neighborhood was long an independent working-class area. It's now becoming trendy, and high rents are driving out the source of so much color. Still, it's a great people scene, especially at night. Start your exploratory stroll at Piazza di Santa Maria in Trastevere. While today's fountain is 17th-century, there has been a fountain here since Roman times.

**Santa Maria in Trastevere**, one of Rome's oldest churches, was made a basilica in the fourth century, when Christianity was legalized (free, daily 7:30–13:00 & 15:00–19:00). It was the first church dedicated to the Virgin Mary. The portico (covered area just outside the door) is decorated with fascinating ancient fragments filled with early Christian symbolism. Most of what you see today dates from around the 12th century, but the granite columns come from an ancient Roman temple, and the ancient basilica floor plan (and ambience) survives. The 12th-century mosaics behind the altar are striking, and notable for their portrayal of Mary—the first showing her at the throne with Jesus in heaven. Look below the scenes from the life of Mary to see ahead-of-their-time paintings (by Cavallini, from 1300) that predate the Renaissance by 100 years.

Before leaving Trastevere, wander the backstreets. Then, from the church square (Piazza di Santa Maria), take Via del Moro to the river and cross on Ponte Sisto, a pedestrian bridge with a good view of St. Peter's dome. Continue straight ahead for one block. Take the first left, which leads down Via di Capo di Ferro through the scary and narrow darkness to Piazza Farnese, with its

## Trastevere

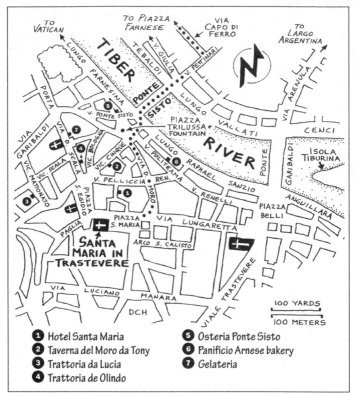

1 Hotel Santa Maria
2 Taverna del Moro da Tony
3 Trattoria da Lucia
4 Trattoria de Olindo

5 Osteria Ponte Sisto
6 Panificio Arnese bakery
7 Gelateria

imposing Palazzo Farnese. Michelangelo contributed to the facade of this palace, now the French Embassy. The fountains on the square feature huge, one-piece granite hot tubs from the ancient Roman Baths of Caracalla.

One block from there (opposite the palace) is **Campo de' Fiori** (Field of Flowers), which is my favorite outdoor dining room after dark (see "Eating in Rome," page 100). The statue of Giordano Bruno, a heretic burned in 1600 for believing the world was round and not the center of the universe, marks the center of this great and colorful square. Bruno overlooks a busy produce market in the morning and strollers after dark. This neighborhood is still known for its free spirit. When the statue of Bruno was erected in 1889, local riots overcame Vatican protests against honoring a heretic. Bruno faces his executioner, the Vatican Chancellory (the big white building in the corner a bit to

# From Campo de' Fiori to the Spanish Steps

his right), while his pedestal reads: "And the flames rose up." The square is lined with, and surrounded by, fun eateries. Bruno also faces La Carbonara restaurant, the only real restaurant on the square. The Forno, next door, is a popular place for hot and tasty take-out *pizza bianco* (plain but spicy pizza bread).

If Bruno did a hop, step, and jump forward, turned right, and marched 200 meters (650 feet), he'd cross the busy Corso Vittorio Emanuele and find **Piazza Navona**. Rome's most interesting night scene features street music, artists, fire-eaters, local Casanovas, ice cream, outdoor cafés (splurge-worthy if you've got time to sit and enjoy the human river of Italy), and fountains by Bernini, the father of Baroque art. The Tartufo "death by chocolate" ice cream (€3.50 to go, €7 at a table) made the Tre Scalini café
(left of obelisk) world-famous among connoisseurs of ice cream and chocolate alike. This oblong piazza is molded around the long-gone Stadium of Domitian, an ancient chariot racetrack.

Leave Piazza Navona directly across from Tre Scalini café,

go (east) past rose peddlers and palm readers, jog left around the guarded building, and follow the brown sign to the **Pantheon** straight down Via del Salvatore (cheap pizza place on left just before the Pantheon, easy WC at McDonald's). Sit for a while and ponder under the Pantheon's floodlit, moonlit portico.

With your back to the Pantheon, head right, passing Bar Pantheon on your right. The Tazza d'Oro Casa del Caffè, one of Rome's top coffee shops, dates back to the days when this area was licensed to roast coffee beans. Look back at the fine view of the Pantheon from here.

With the coffee shop on your right, walk down Via degli Orfani to Piazza Capranica, with the big, plain, Florentine Renaissance-style Palazzo Capranica. Big shots, like the Capranica family, built stubby towers on their palaces—not for any military use . . . just to show off. Leave the piazza to the right of the palace, between the palace and the church. Via in Aquiro leads to a sixth-century B.C. Egyptian **obelisk** (taken as a trophy by Augustus after his victory in Egypt over Mark Antony and Cleopatra). Walk into the guarded square past the obelisk and face the huge parliament building. A short detour to the left (past Albergo National) brings you to some of Rome's most famous gelato. **Gelateria Caffè Pasticceria Giolitti** is cheap to go or elegant, pricey, and worthwhile for a sit among classy locals (open daily until very late, your choice: cone or *bicchierini*—cup, Via Uffici del Vicario 40). Gelato fans will want to visit the nearby **Gelateria della Palma**, also two blocks away, with better gelato (Via della Maddalena 20). Or head directly from the parliament into the next, even grander, square.

**Piazza Colonna** features a huge second-century column honoring Marcus Aurelius, the philosopher-emperor. The big, important-looking palace is the prime minister's residence. Cross Via del Corso, Rome's noisy main drag, and jog right (around the Y-shaped shopping gallery from 1928), heading down Via dei Sabini to the roar of the water, light, and people of the Trevi Fountain.

The **Trevi Fountain** is an example of how Rome took full advantage of water brought into the city by its great aqueducts. This watery Baroque avalanche was built in 1762 by Nicola Salvi, hired by a pope celebrating his reopening of the ancient aqueduct that powers it. Salvi used the palace behind the fountain as a backdrop for Neptune's "entrance" into the square. Neptune surfs through his watery kingdom while Triton blows his conch shell.

Romantics toss two coins over their shoulders, thinking it will give them a wish and assure their return to Rome. That may sound silly, but every year I go through this touristic ritual . . . and it actually seems to work.

Take some time to people-watch (whisper a few breathy *bello*s or *bella*s) before leaving. Facing the fountain, go past it on the right down Via delle Stamperia to Via del Triton. Cross the busy street and continue to the Spanish Steps (ask, *"Dov'è Piazza di Spagna?"*; pron. DOH-veh pee-AHT-zah dee SPAHN-yah), a few blocks and thousands of dollars of shopping opportunities away.

The **Piazza di Spagna** (rhymes with "lasagna"), with the very popular Spanish Steps, got its name 300 years ago, when this was the site of the Spanish Embassy. It's been the hangout of many Romantics over the years (Keats, Wagner, Openshaw, Goethe, and others). The Boat Fountain at the foot of the steps, which was done by Bernini's father, Pietro Bernini, is powered by an aqueduct. The piazza is a thriving night scene. Facing the steps, walk to your right about a block to tour one of the world's biggest and most lavish McDonald's. About a block on the other side of the steps is the Spagna Metro stop, which (usually until 23:30) will zip you home.

### The Dolce Vita Stroll down Via del Corso

This is the city's chic and hip "cruise," from Piazza del Popolo (Metro: Flaminio) down a wonderfully traffic-free section of Via del Corso, and up Via Condotti to the Spanish Steps each evening around 18:00 (Sat and Sun are best). Strollers, shoppers, and flirts on the prowl fill this neighborhood of Rome's most fashionable stores (open after siesta 16:30–19:30). Throughout Italy, early evening is the time to stroll.

Start on **Piazza Popolo**. Historians: This area was once just inside medieval Rome's main entry. The delightfully car-free square is marked by an obelisk that was brought to Rome by Augustus after he conquered Egypt. (It once stood in the Circus Maximus.) The Baroque church of **Santa Maria del Popolo**— with Raphael's Chigi Chapel (pron. kee-gee, third chapel on left) and two Caravaggio paintings (side paintings in chapel left of altar)—is next to the gate in the old wall, on the far side of Piazza del Popolo, to the right as you face the gate (church open Mon–Sat 7:00–12:00 & 16:00–19:00, Sun 8:00–13:30 & 16:30–19:30).

From Piazza del Popolo, shop your way down **Via del Corso**. To rest your feet, join the locals sitting on the steps of various churches along the street.

At Via Pontefici, historians turn right and walk a block to see the massive, rotting, round brick **Mausoleum of Augustus**, topped with overgrown cypress trees. Beyond it, next to the river, is Augustus' Ara Pacis, or Altar of Peace (which should reopen in 2005).

From the mausoleum, return to Via del Corso and the 21st century, continuing straight until **Via Condotti**. Shoppers, take a left on Via Condotti to join the parade to the **Spanish Steps**.

The streets that parallel Via Condotti to the south (Borgogno and Frattini) are just as popular. You can catch a taxi home at the taxi stand a block south of the Spanish Steps (at Piazza Mignonelli, near American Express and McDonald's).

Historians: Ignore Via Condotti. Continue a kilometer (0.6 mile) down Via del Corso—straight since Roman times— to the Victor Emmanuel Monument. Climb Michelangelo's stairway to his glorious (especially when floodlit) square atop Capitol Hill. From the balconies at either side of the mayor's palace, catch the lovely views of the Forum as the horizon reddens and cats prowl the unclaimed rubble of ancient Rome.

## Sleeping in Rome
### (€1 = about $1, country code: 39)

Sleep Code: **S** = Single, **D** = Double/Twin, **T** = Triple, **Q** = Quad, **b** = bathroom, **s** = shower only, **CC** = Credit Cards accepted, **no CC** = Credit Cards not accepted, **SE** = Speaks English, **NSE** = No English. Breakfast is included in all but the cheapest places.

To help you sort easily through these listings, I've divided the rooms into three categories based on the price for a standard double room with bath:

**Higher Priced**—Most rooms more than €180.

**Moderately Priced**—Most rooms €180 or less.

**Lower Priced**—Most rooms €115 or less.

The absolute cheapest beds (dorms or some cramped doubles) in Rome are €18 in small, backpacker-filled hostels. A nicer hotel (around €130 with a bathroom and air-con) provides an oasis and refuge, making it easier to enjoy this intense and grinding city. If you're going door to door, prices are soft—so bargain. Built into a hotel's official price list is a kickback for a room-finding service or agency; if you're coming direct, they pay no kickback and may lower the price for you. Many hotels have high-season (mid-March– June, Sept–Oct) and low-season prices. If traveling outside of peak times, ask about a discount. Room rates are lowest in sweltering August. Easter, September, and Christmas are most crowded and expensive. On Easter weekend (April 18–20 in 2003), April 25, and May 1, the entire city gets booked up.

English works in all but the cheapest places. Traffic in Rome roars. My challenge: To find friendly places on quiet streets. With the recent arrival of double-paned windows and air-conditioning, night noise is not the problem it was. Even so, light sleepers should always ask for a *tranquillo* room. Many prices here are promised only to people who show this book and reserve directly, without using a room-finding service. And many places prefer hard cash.

Bed-and-breakfasts are booming in Rome, offering comfy

doubles in the old center for around €80. The Beehive hostel is
a good contact for booking B&Bs in Rome (www.cross-pollinate
.com, see "Sleeping in Hostels and Dorms," below).

Most hotels are eager to connect you with a shuttle service
to the airport. It's reasonable and easy for leaving, but upon
arrival I think it's easiest to simply catch a cab or the shuttle train.

Almost no hotels have parking, but nearly all have a line on
spots in a nearby garage (about €21/day).

## Sleeping on Via Firenze (zip code: 00184)

I generally stay on Via Firenze because it's safe, handy, central,
and relatively quiet. It's a 10-minute walk from the central train
station and airport shuttle, and two blocks beyond Piazza della
Repubblica and the TI. The Defense Ministry is nearby, so
you've got heavily armed guards watching over you all night.
Virtually all the city buses that rumble down Via Nazionale
(#64, #70, #115, #640, and the #40 express) take you to Piazza
Venezia (Forum) and Largo Argentina (Pantheon). From Largo
Argentina, electric trolley #8 goes to Trastevere (first stop after
crossing the river) and #64 (jammed with people and thieves)
and the #40 express continue to St. Peter's. Farmacia Piram
is the neighborhood 24-hour pharmacy (Via Nazionale 228,
tel. 06-488-4437).

**HIGHER PRICED**
**Residenza Cellini** is a gorgeous new place with six rooms. It
offers "ortho/anti-allergy beds" and four-star comforts and service
(Db-€165, larger Db-€185, €30 discount in off-season—Aug
plus mid-Nov–mid-March, these prices with this book and payment in cash through 2003, elevator, air-con, Via Modena 5,
tel. 06-4782-5204, fax 06-4788-1806, www.residenzacellini.it,
e-mail: residenzacellini@tin.it, SE).

**MODERATELY PRICED**
**Hotel Oceania** is a peaceful slice of air-conditioned heaven.
This 16-room, manor house–type hotel is spacious and quiet,
with spotless rooms, run by a pleasant father-and-son team (Sb-
€105, Db-€135, Tb-€165, Qb-€192, these prices through 2003
with this book only, additional 25 percent off in Aug and winter,
large roof terrace, TV room, CC, Via Firenze 38, 3rd floor,
tel. 06-482-4696, fax 06-488-5586, www.hoteloceania.it, e-mail:
hoceania@tin.it, son Stefano SE, dad Armando serves world-
famous coffee).

**Hotel Aberdeen**, while a more formal place, offers the same
great value, with minibars, phones, and showers in its 36 modern,

# Hotels in East Rome

1. Hotel Oceania & Nardizzi
2. Hotel Aberdeen
3. Residence Adler & Residenza Cellini
4. Hotel Rex
5. Hotel Britannia
6. Hotel Sonya
7. Hotel Pensione Italia
8. Hotel Cortina
9. YWCA Casa per Studentesse
10. Suore di Santa Elisabetta
11. Hotel Montreal
12. Hotel Fenicia & Magic
13. Albergo Sileo
14. Hotel Duca d'Alba
15. Hotel Grifo
16. Pensione per Pellegrini
17. Hotel Paba
18. Hotel Lancelot
19. Casa Olmata Hostel
20. The Beehive Hostel
21. Gulliver's House Rome
22. Hotel Le Petit
23. Pharmacy

air-conditioned, and smoke-free rooms. It's warmly run by Annamaria, with support from her cousins Sabrina, Laura, and Cinzia (Sb-€102, Db-€139, Tb-€164, Qb-€190, prices through 2003 with this book only, €30 less per room in Aug and winter, CC, free Internet access, nearby parking-€21/day, Via Firenze 48, tel. 06-482-3920, fax 06-482-1092, check for deals online at www .travel.it/roma/aberdeen, e-mail: hotel.aberdeen@travel.it, SE).

**Hotel Seiler** is a last resort, with 33 sleepable rooms and too much chipped plaster (Sb-€83, Db-€119, Tb-€145, Qb-€165, these discounted prices good only with this book, CC, fans, elevator, Via Firenze 48, tel. 06-485-550, fax 06-488-0204, e-mail: acropoli@rdn.it, Silvio and Alessia SE).

**LOWER PRICED**
**Residence Adler** offers breakfast on a garden patio, wide halls, and eight quiet, elegant, and air-conditioned rooms in a great location. A good deal, it's run the old-fashioned way by a charming family (Db-€115, Tb-€150, Qb-€180, Quint/b-€195, prices through 2003 with this book only, CC, additional 5 percent off with cash, 15 percent off in Aug, Jan, and Feb; elevator, Via Modena 5, 2nd floor, tel. 06-484-466, fax 06-488-0940, www .hoteladler-roma.com, e-mail: info@hoteladler-roma.com, gracious Sr. Brando Massini NSE but tries).

**Hotel Nardizzi Americana**, with 18 simple, pleasant, air-conditioned rooms and a delightful rooftop terrace, is loosely run (Sb-€90, Db-€110, Tb-€135, Qb-€150, prices through 2003 with this book only, discounts for off-season and long stays, air-con, CC, additional 10 percent off with cash, elevator, Via Firenze 38, 4th floor, tel. 06-488-0368, fax 06-488-0035, SE).

**Hotel Texas Seven Hills**, a stark, institutional throwback to the 1960s, rents 18 dreary rooms (D-€83, Db-€93, often soft prices, CC, single-paned windows, Via Firenze 47, 1st elevator on the right to 3rd floor, tel. 06-481-4082, fax 06-481-4079, www .yellowpage.it/hoteltexas, e-mail: reserva@texas7hills.com, SE).

## Sleeping between Via Nazionale and Basilica Santa Maria Maggiore
### (zip code: 00184 unless otherwise noted)

**HIGHER PRICED**
**Hotel Britannia** stands like a marble fruitcake, offering all the comforts in tight quarters. Lushly renovated with over-the-top classical motifs, its 33 air-conditioned rooms are small but comfortable with bright, modern bathrooms (Sb-€210, Db-€245, cheaper in Aug and off-season, CC, free parking, Via Napoli 64,

tel. 06-488-3153, fax 06-488-2343, www.hotelbritannia.it, e-mail: info@hotelbritannia.it).

**Hotel Rex** is a business-class, modern fortress—a quiet, plain, and stately four-star place with 50 rooms and all the comforts (Sb-€206, Db-€258, Tb-€299, 25 percent less Aug and winter, CC, elevator, air-con, Via Torino 149, tel. 06-482-4828, fax 06-488-2743, e-mail: rex@hotelrex.net, SE).

## MODERATELY PRICED

**Hotel Le Petit** has 11 colorful, cozy rooms with a modern flair (Sb-€80, Db-€135, Tb-€155, 20 percent off in low season, CC, air-con, Via Torino 122, tel. 06-4890-7085, fax 06-474-4645, www.hotel-le-petit.com, e-mail: lepetit@venere.it, SE).

**Hotel Sonya** is a small, family-run, but impersonal place with 23 comfortable, well-equipped rooms, a great location, and decent prices (Db-€119, Tb-€134, Qb-€155, Quint/b-€170, CC, air-con, elevator, facing the Opera at Via Viminale 58, tel. 06-481-9911, fax 06-488-5678, e-mail: hotelsonyaroma@katamail .com, Francesca SE).

**Hotel Cortina** rents 14 modern, air-conditioned rooms on a busy street. Ask for a quieter room on the courtyard or side street (Db-€140 in 2003 with this book, CC, Via Nazionale 18, tel. 06-481-9794, fax 06-481-9220, www.travel.it/roma/hotelcortina, e-mail: hotelcortina@pronet.it, John Carlo and Angelo SE).

## LOWER PRICED

**Hotel Pensione Italia**, in a busy, interesting, and handy locale, is placed safely on a quiet street next to the Ministry of the Interior. Thoughtfully run by Andrea, Isabelle, and Alberico, it has 31 comfortable, airy, clean, and bright rooms (Sb-€75, Db-€100, Tb-€145, Qb-€165, air-con for €8 extra, prices through 2003 with this book and cash only, all rooms 20 percent off mid-July–Aug and winter, elevator, Via Venezia 18, just off Via Nazionale, tel. 06-482-8355, fax 06-474-5550, www.hotelitaliaroma.com, e-mail: hitalia@nettuno.it, SE). Most rooms have a fan. Their fine singles are all on the quiet courtyard and they have eight decent annex rooms across the street.

**Hotel Montreal**, run with care, is a bright, solid, business-class place on a big street a block southeast of Santa Maria Maggiore (Db-€115 but €90 in July–Aug, Tb-€140 but €120 in July–Aug, mention this book, CC, air-con, elevator, good security, 1 block from Metro: Vittorio, 3 blocks west of train station, Via Carlo Alberto 4, 00185 Roma, tel. 06-445-7797, fax 06-446-5522, www.hotelmontrealroma.com, e-mail: info @hotelmontrealroma.com, SE).

**Clarin Hotel**, a plain slumbermill with 21 rooms, is quiet, safe, and run-down (Db-€88, Tb-€109, Qb-€129, prices good with this book and cash, 3 percent extra with CC, Via Palermo 36, tel. 06-4782-5170, fax 06-4788-1393, e-mail: clarinhotel @hotmail.com, Renaldo, Franco, and Marco SE).

## YWCA and Convents

**YWCA Casa Per Studentesse** accepts men and women. It's an institutional place, filled with white-uniformed maids, colorful Third-World travelers, and 75 single beds (€26 per person in 3- and 4-bed rooms, S-€31, Sb-€37, D-€62, Db-€74, includes breakfast except on Sun, elevator, Via C. Albo 4, tel. 06-488-0460, fax 06-487-1028). The YWCA faces a great little street market.

**Suore di Santa Elisabetta** is a heavenly Polish-run convent. While often booked long in advance and a challenge in communication, it's an incredible value (S-€31, Sb-€38, D-€51, Db-€66, Tb-€85, Qb-€103, CC, 23:00 curfew, elevator, fine view roof terrace, a block southwest of Basilica Santa Maria Maggiore at Via dell' Omata 9, tel. 06-488-8271, fax 06-488-4066, a little English spoken).

**Pensione Per Pelligrini** is another nun-run place with 39 big, simple rooms and lots of twin beds. There's a language barrier, but the price is right (S-€34, Sb-€41, D-€67, Db-€82, Tb-€93, breakfast-€4.25, closed Aug, peaceful garden, elevator, just off Piazza Vittorio Emmanuel II, Istituto Buon Salvatore, Via Leopardi 17, no sign, from station take bus #714, #649, or #360 or Metro: Vittorio, tel. 06-446-7147 or 06-446-7225, fax 06-446-1382, Sister Anna Maria SE).

## Sleeping Cheap, Northeast of the Train Station
### (zip code: 00185)

The cheapest hotels in town are northeast of the station. Some travelers feel this area is weird and spooky after dark, but these hotels feel plenty safe. With your back to the train tracks, turn right and walk two blocks out of the station. The first two hotels are located in the same building.

**LOWER PRICED**

**Hotel Fenicia** rents 13 comfortable, well-equipped rooms at a fine price. The bigger rooms upstairs are quieter, but there's no elevator (Sb-€53, Db-€80, Tb-€103, bigger and fancier Db-€93, prices through 2003 with this book only, air-con-€10.50/day, breakfast-€5.25; they say they take CC but, according to readers, sometimes they don't; Via Milazzo 20, tel. & fax 06-490-342, www.hotelfenicia .it, e-mail: info@hotelfenicia.it, Georgio and Anna SE).

**Hotel Magic** has 10 clean, marbled rooms, high enough off the road to escape the traffic noise. It's family-run, though not with much warmth (Sb-€52, Db-€77, Tb-€103, Qb-€114, air-con-€10.50/day, breakfast-€3.75, prices through 2003 with this book only, confirm rates, cheaper in Aug and winter, CC, thin walls, midnight curfew, Via Milazzo 20, 3rd floor, tel. & fax 06-495-9880, www.hotelmagicaroma.com, Carmela, Rosanna, and Caesarina NSE).

**Albergo Sileo** is a shiny-chandeliered, 10-room place. It has a contract to house train conductors who work the night shift, so most of the simple, pleasant rooms are rented from 19:00 to 9:00 only. If you can handle this, it's a great value. During the day, they store your luggage, and though you won't have access to a room, you're welcome to hang out in their lobby or bar (D-€39, Db-€47, Tb-€62, Db for 24 hours-€62—a steal, CC, elevator, Via Magenta 39, tel. & fax 06-445-0246, www.hotelsileo.com, friendly Alessandro and Maria Savioli NSE, daughter Anna SE).

## Sleeping near the Colosseum *(zip code: 00184)*

These places are buried in a Roman world of exhaust-stained, medieval ambience. Take the subway one stop from the train station to the Cavour Metro stop. The *electrico* bus line #117 (San Giovanni in Laterano, Colosseo, Trevi Fountain, Piazza di Spagna, and Piazza del Popolo) connects you with the sights.

**HIGHER PRICED**

**Hotel Duca d'Alba**, a tight and modern pastel/marble/hardwood place, is more professional than homey (Sb-€134, Db-€201, much cheaper July–Aug and winter, extra bed-€21, CC, air-con, safes, phones, TV, elevator, Via Leonina 14, tel. 06-484-471, fax 06-488-4840, check Web site for deals, www.hotelducadalba.com, Angelo SE).

**MODERATELY PRICED**

**Hotel Paba** is a little six-room place, chocolate box–tidy and lovingly cared for by Alberta and Pasquale Castelli. While overlooking busy Via Cavour just two blocks from the Colosseum, it's quiet enough (Db-€124, extra bed-€21, show this book for 5 percent discount, CC, breakfast served in room, air-con, elevator, Via Cavour 266, tel. 06-4782-4902, fax 06-4788-1225, www.hotelpaba.com, e-mail: info@hotelpaba.com, SE).

**Hotel Grifo** has a homey, tangled floor plan with 20 dimly lit, modern rooms and a roof terrace. The double-paned windows almost keep out the Vespa noise (Db-€119, €109 July–Aug, CC, elevator, air-con, some rooms have terraces, 2 blocks off Via Cavour at Via del Boschetto 144, tel. 06-487-1395, fax 06-474-2323, e-mail: hotelgrifo@hotmail.com, Alessandro SE).

**Hotel Lancelot**, a favorite among United Nations workers, is big, with 60 rooms, a shady courtyard, rooftop terrace, bar, and restaurant. It's quiet, safe, well-run by Faris and Lubna Khan, and popular with returning guests (Sb-€93–108, Db-€144, Tb-€168, Qb-€183, add €10 for balcony, CC, air-con, elevator, parking-€11/day, behind Colosseum near San Clemente Church at Via Capo D'Africa 47, tel. 06-7045-0615, fax 06-7045-0640, www.lancelothotel.com, e-mail: info@lancelothotel.com, SE).

## Sleeping near the Palatine (zip code: 00186)

**LOWER PRICED**

**Hotel Casa Kolbe**, located in a former monastery, rents out 63 monkish, spartan rooms with no fans or air-conditioning. With vast public spaces and a peaceful garden, it's popular with groups. But the location is great: it's on the river side of the Palatine ruins, on a quiet side street about a block from a little-used entrance to the Forum (Sb-€62, Db-€78, Tb-€98, Qb-€109, breakfast-€5.25, CC, elevator, garden, courtyard, not handy to public transit so taxi from the station, Via S. Teodoro 44, tel. 06-679-4974 or 06-679-8866, fax 06-6994-1550, Maurizio and Antonio SE).

## Sleeping near Campo de' Fiori (zip code: 00186)

You pay a premium to stay in the old center, but each of these places is romantically set deep in the tangled backstreets near the idyllic Campo de' Fiori and, for many, that's worth the extra money.

**MODERATELY PRICED**

**Casa di Santa Brigida** overlooks the elegant Piazza Farnese. With soft-spoken sisters gliding down polished hallways, and pearly gates instead of doors, this lavish 23-room convent makes exhaust-stained Roman tourists feel like they've died and gone to heaven. If you're unsure of your destiny (and don't need a double bed), this is worth the splurge (Sb-€85, Db-€150, 3 percent extra with CC, great €16 dinners, roof garden, plush library, air-con, physical address: Monserrato 54, mailing address: Piazza Farnese 96, 00186 Roma, tel. 06-6889-2596, fax 06-6889-1573, www.brigidine.org/italia_roma, e-mail: hesselblad@tiscalinet.it, many of the sisters are from India and speak English). If you get no response to your fax or e-mail within three days, consider that a "no." Groups are very welcome here.

**LOWER PRICED**

**Hotel Smeraldo**, with 50 rooms, is well-run, clean, air-conditioned, and a great deal (Sb-€73, D-€73, Db-€114, Tb-€130, roof terrace, CC, Civolo dei Chiodaroli 9, midway between Campo de' Fiori and Largo Argentina, tel. 06-687-5929, fax 06-6880-5495, www.hotelsmeraldoroma.com, e-mail: albergosmeraldoroma@tin.it, SE).

**Hotel Arenula**, the only hotel in Rome's old Jewish quarter (or ghetto), is a fine place in the thick of old Rome, with 50 comfy rooms (Sb-€88, Db-€114, Tb-€134; €26 less in July, Aug, and winter; air-con-€10.50/day, no elevator, CC, just off Via Arenula at Via Santa Maria de' Calderari 47, tel. 06-687-9454, fax 06-689-6188, www.hotelarenula.com, e-mail: hotel.arenula@flashnet.it, SE).

## Sleeping near the Pantheon (zip code: 00186)
These four places are buried in the pedestrian-friendly heart of ancient Rome, each within a four-minute walk of the Pantheon. You'll pay more here—but you'll save time and money by being exactly where you want to be for your early and late wandering.

### HIGHER PRICED
**Hotel Nazionale**, a four-star landmark, is a 16th-century palace sharing a well-policed square with the national parliament. Its 90 rooms are served by lush public spaces, fancy bars, and a uniformed staff. It's a big hotel with a revolving front door, but it's a worthy splurge if you want security, comfort, and the heart of old Rome at your doorstep (Sb-€186, Db-€289, extra person-€62, suite-€439, less in Aug and winter, CC, air-con, elevator, Piazza Montecitorio 131, tel. 06-695-001, fax 06-678-6677, look online for discounts in summer and weekends, www.nazionaleroma.it, e-mail: hotel@nazionaleroma.it, SE).

### MODERATELY PRICED
**Hotel Due Torri** hides out on a tiny, quiet street. It feels professional yet homey, with an accommodating staff, generous public spaces, and 26 comfortable-if-small rooms—four with balconies (Sb-€108, Db-€176, family apartment-€232 for 3 and €258 for 4, CC, air-con, Vicolo del Leonetto 23, a block off Via della Scrofa, tel. 06-6880-6956, fax 06-686-5442, www.hotelduetorriroma.com, e-mail: hotelduetorri@interfree.it, SE).

**Residenza Zanardelli**, a sumptuous little place with six classy and quiet rooms, is two blocks north of Piazza Navona (Db-€135, air-con-€10.50/day, no CC; on busy street but double-paned windows minimize noise; Via G. Zanardelli 7, tiny name next to doorbell, tel. 06-6821-1392 or 06-6880-9760, fax 06-6880-3802).

### LOWER PRICED
**Hotel Navona** is a fine value, offering 41 basic rooms in an ancient building (with a perfect locale) a block off Piazza Navona. Top-floor

## Hotels in the Heart of Rome

TO SPANISH
STEPS & ⑧

TO
TRASTEVERE

| 200 YARDS |
| 200 METERS |

Ⓣ -TAXI
STAND

- ① Casa di Santa Brigida
- ② Hotel Smeraldo
- ③ To Hotel Arenula
- ④ Hotel Due Torri
- ⑤ Hotel Navona
- ⑥ Residenza Zanardelli
- ⑦ Hotel Nazionale
- ⑧ To Residenza Frattina
- ⑨ Hotel Giardino

rooms come with wood-beamed character and more stairs (D-€100, Db-€110, air-con-€16/day, family rooms, no CC, Via dei Sediari 8, tel. 06-686-4203, fax 06-6880-3802, www.hotelnavona.com, e-mail: info@hotelnavona.com; run by a friendly Australian named Corry, his Italian wife Patricia, and her dad Pino, SE).

### Sleeping near the Spanish Steps *(zip code: 00187)*

#### MODERATELY PRICED

**Residenza Frattina** is a pink palace in a posh locale. It has an old-fashioned feel and an unbeatable location on a main pedestrian shopping drag near Piazza di Spagna (Db-€180, Tb-€200, prices are soft, CC, air-con, Via Frattina 23, tel. & fax 06-679-5509, www.residenzafrattinacorso.com, e-mail: residenza.fratina@flashnet.it, SE).

## Sleeping near Piazza Venezia (zip code: 00187)

**MODERATELY PRICED**
**Hotel Giardino**, run by Englishwoman Kate, offers pleasant rooms in a central location three blocks northeast of Piazza Venezia (Sb-€80, Db-€120, these discounted prices good with this book, CC but cash appreciated, double-paned windows, air-con-€7/night, Via XXIV Maggio 51, busy street off Piazza di Quirinale, tel. 06-679-4584, fax 06-679-5155, www.hotel-giardino-roma.com, e-mail: hotel_giardino@libero.it).

## Sleeping in Trastevere (zip code: 00153)
To locate hotels, see the map on page 84.

**MODERATELY PRICED**
**Hotel Santa Maria** sits like a lazy hacienda in the midst of Trastevere. Surrounded by a medieval skyline, you'll feel as if you're on some romantic stage set. Its 18 small but well-equipped, air-conditioned rooms—former cells in a cloister—are all ground floor, circling a gravelly courtyard of orange trees and stay-awhile patio furniture. Because this is the only hotel in Trastevere, you'll pay about 25 percent more—but for poets, it's a deal (Db-€155, Tb-€191, Qb-€217, for this 20–25 percent discount it's cash only and a 3-night minimum, good with this book through 2003, smaller discounts also available with this book for shorter stays and credit cards and during off-season, a block north of Piazza Maria Trastevere at Vicolo del Piede 2, tel. 06-589-4626, fax 06-589-4815, www.htlsanta-maria.com, e-mail: hotelsantamaria@libero.it, Stefano SE).

## Sleeping "Three Stars" near the Vatican Museum (zip code: 00192)
To locate hotels, see the map on page 68.

**HIGHER PRICED**
**Hotel Sant' Anna** is pricey, but located on a charming-for-Rome pedestrian street that fills up with restaurant tables at dinnertime. Its 20 rooms are overly decorated with classical themes, though the furnishings are comfy (Sb-€145, Db-€190, Db-€145 July–Aug and winter, CC, air-con, elevator, courtyard, Borgo Pio 133, near intersection with Mascherino, a

couple of blocks from entrance to St. Peter's, tel. 06-6880-1602, fax 06-6830-8717, www.travel.it/roma/santanna, Viscardo SE).

**Hotel Bramante** sits like a grand medieval lodge in the shadow of the fortified escape wall that runs from the Vatican to Castel San Angelo. The public spaces and the 16 rooms are generously sized, with rough wood beams and high ceilings (Sb-€142, Db-€210, Tb-€239, Qb-€250, 8 percent discount with this book, CC, air-con, no elevator, Vicolo delle Palline 24, tel. 06-6880-6426, fax 06-687-9881, www.hotelbramante.com, e-mail: bramante@excalhq.it, Maurizio and Loredana SE).

## MODERATELY PRICED

**Hotel Alimandi** is a good value, run by the friendly and entrepreneurial Alimandi brothers—Paolo, Enrico, and Luigi—and the next generation, Marta and Germano. Their 35 rooms are air-conditioned, modern, and marbled in white (Sb-€90, Db-€150, Tb-€175, 5 percent discount with this book and cash, CC, closed Jan–mid Feb, elevator, grand buffet breakfast served in great roof garden, small gym, Internet access, pool table, piano lounge, free parking, down stairs directly in front of Vatican Museum, Via Tunisi 8, near Metro: Cipro-Musei Vaticani, reserve by phone, no reply to fax means they are full, tel. 06-3972-6300, toll-free in Italy tel. 800-122-121, fax 06-3972-3943, www.alimandi.org, e-mail: alimandi@tin.it, SE). They offer free airport pickup and drop-off, though you must reserve when you book your room and wait for a scheduled shuttle (every 2 hrs, see their Web site). Maria Alimandi rents out three rooms in her apartment, a 20-minute bus ride from the Vatican (Db-€83, see www.alimandi.org).

**Hotel Spring House** offers 51 attractive rooms—some with balconies or terraces (Db-€135, Tb-€155, Qb-€175, mention this book to get a 15 percent discount July–Aug and Jan–Feb, CC, Internet access, air-con, elevator, free loaner bikes, Metro: Cipro-Musei Vaticani, Via Mocenigo 7, 2 blocks from Vatican Museum, tel. 06-3972-0948, fax 06-3972-1047, www.hotelspringhouse.com, Stefano Gabbani SE).

**Hotel Gerber** is modern and air-conditioned, with 27 businesslike rooms, set in a quiet residential area (Sb-€100, Db-€130, Tb-€150, Qb-€170, 10 percent discount with this book in high season, 15 percent discount in low season, CC, Via degli Scipioni 241, a block from Metro: Lepanto, at intersection with Ezio, tel. 06-321-6485, fax 06-321-7048, www.hotelgerber.it, e-mail: info@hotelgerber.it, friendly pup Kira, Peter and Simonetta SE).

**Hotel Emmaus** offers 30 basic rooms on the south side of St. Peter's, just a communion-wafer's toss from the square (Sb-€105, Db-€150, Tb-€160, Qb-€180, CC, air-con, elevator,

Via delle Fornaci 23, tel. & fax 06-635-658, www.emmaushotel.it, e-mail: emmaus@flashnet.it, SE).

### Sleeping in Hostels and Dorms (zip code: 00184)

For easy communication with young, friendly entrepreneurs, cheap dorm beds, and the very cheapest doubles in town—within a 10-minute hike of the train station—consider the following places:

**Casa Olmata** is a laid-back backpackers' place midway between the Termini train station and Colosseum (dorm beds €17–18, S-€35, bunk bed D-€44, one queen-size D-€55, lots of stairs, laundry service, free Internet access, video rentals, games, rooftop terrace with views, communal kitchen, dinners twice weekly, a block southwest of Basilica Santa Maria Maggiore, Via dell' Omata 36, 3rd floor, tel. 06-483-019, fax 06-474-2854, www.casaolmata.com, e-mail: casaolmata30@hotmail.com, Mirella and Marco).

**The Beehive** is especially good for older vagabonds. This tidy little place has dorms (€18 beds) and double rooms that are a great value (D-€60, Db-€80, T-€90, Tb-€120, Q-€120, Qb-€160, no CC). It's thoughtfully run by a friendly young American couple, Steve and Linda (no curfew or lock-out, 2 blocks south of Basilica Santa Maria Maggiore at Via Giovanni Lanza 99, tel. 06-474-0719, www.the-beehive.com). They hope to move by 2003 to a new location; check their Web site to find their new address.

They also run a B&B booking service (fine private rooms in the old center, offering comparable quality for €65–95—about half the cost of a hotel, www.cross-pollinate.com).

**Gulliver's House Rome** is a fun little hostel in a safe and handy locale, run by helpful Simon and Sara. Its 24 beds in cramped quarters work fine for backpackers (€18 per bunk bed in 8-bed dorm, one D-€57, no CC, closed 12:00–16:00, 1:00 curfew, small kitchen, Via Palermo 36, tel. 06-481-7680, www.gullivershouse.com, e-mail: info@gullivershouse.com).

## Eating in Rome

Romans spend their evenings eating rather than drinking, and the preferred activity is simply to enjoy a fine, slow meal, buried deep in the old city. Rome's a fun and cheap place to eat, with countless little eateries serving memorable €20 meals.

Although I've listed a number of restaurants, I recommend that you just head for a scenic area and explore. Piazza Navona, the Pantheon area, Campo de' Fiori, and Trastevere are neighborhoods packed with characteristic eateries. Sitting with tourists on a famous square enjoying the scene works fine. But for places more out of the way, consider my recommendations.

For Rome's best gelato, see "Eating near the Pantheon," below.

## Eating in Trastevere

Colorful Trastevere is also now pretty touristy. Still, Romans join the tourists to eat on the rustic side of the Tiber River. Start at the central square (Piazza Santa Maria in Trastevere). Then choose: Eat with tourists enjoying the ambience of the famous square, or wander the backstreets in search of a mom-and-pop place with barely a menu. Consider the following places before making a choice (all are in the tangle of lanes between Ponte Sisto and the Piazza Santa Maria in Trastevere—see map on page 84):

At **Taverna del Moro da Tony**, Tony scrambles—with a great antipasti table—to keep his happy eaters (mostly tourists) well-fed and returning. Until we start telling him to "hold the mayo," his bruschetta will come buried in it (Tue–Sun 12:00–24:00, closed Mon, CC, off Via del Moro at Vicolo del Cinque 36, tel. 06-580-9165, SE).

For good home-cooking Roman-style, consider these two fun little places (within a block of each other): **Trattoria da Lucia** (closed Mon, indoor or outdoor seating, Vicolo del Mattonato 2, tel. 06-580-3601, NSE) and the homey **Trattoria de Olindo** (closed Sun, Vicolo della Scala 8, tel. 06-581-8835, NSE).

**Osteria Ponte Sisto**, a rough-and-tumble little place, specializes in traditional Roman cuisine with a menu that changes often. Since it's just outside of the tourist zone, it offers the best value and caters mostly to Romans. It's also easiest to find: As you approach Trastevere, crossing Ponte Sisto (pedestrian bridge), continue across the little square (Piazza Trilussa) and you'll find it on the right (daily 12:30–15:30 & 19:30–24:00, CC, Via Ponte Sisto 80, tel. 06-588-3411, SE).

The fine little **Gelateria alla Scala** (across from the church on Piazza della Scala) dishes up oh-wow pistachio (daily 12:30–24:00).

## Eating on and near Campo de' Fiori

While it is touristy, Campo de' Fiori offers a classic and romantic square setting. And, since it is so close to the collective heart of Rome, it remains popular with locals. For greater atmosphere than food value, circle the square, considering each place. Bars and pizzerias seem to overwhelm the square. The **Taverna** and **Vineria** at numbers 16 and 15 offer good perches from which to people-watch and nurse a glass of wine. The only real restaurant is **La Carbonara**. While famous and atmospheric, it gets mixed reviews (closed Tue, Campo de' Fiori 23, CC, tel. 06-686-4783). Meals on small nearby streets are a better value, but lack that Campo de' Fiori magic.

Nearby, on the more elegant and peaceful Piazza Farnese, **Ostaria da Giovanni ar Galletto** has a dressier local crowd, great outdoor seating, and moderate prices. Giovanni and his son Angelo serve fine food, but sometimes they turn single diners away (closed

Sun, tucked in corner of Piazza Farnese at #102, CC, tel. 06-686-
1714). Of all my listings, Giovanni offers perhaps the best al fresco
dining experience.

**Osteria Enoteca al Bric** is a mod Italian/French bistro–
type place run by a man who loves to cook and serves good wine.
Wine-case lids decorate the wall like happy memories. With
candlelit elegance and no tourists, it's perfect for the wine snob
in the mood for pasta and fine cheese. Choose your bottle (or half
bottle) from the huge selection lining the walls as you enter (open
from 19:30, closed Mon, CC, 100 meters, or 330 feet, off Campo
de' Fiori at Via del Pellegrino 51, tel. 06-687-9533).

**Filetti de Baccala** is a tradition for many Romans. Basically
a fish bar with paper tablecloths and cheap prices, it has grease-
stained, hurried waiters who serve old-time favorites—fried cod
fillets, a strange bitter *puntarelle* salad, and delightful anchovies
with butter—to nostalgic locals (Mon–Sat 17:30–23:00, closed Sun,
a block east of Campo de' Fiori tumbling onto a tiny and atmospheric square, Largo dei Librari 88, no CC, tel. 06-686-4018).

**Trattoria der Pallaro** has no menu but plenty of return
eaters. Paola Fazi—with a towel wrapped around her head, turban-
style—and her family serve up a five-course festival of typically
Roman food for €18, including wine, coffee, and a wonderful
mandarin liqueur. Their slogan: "Here, you'll eat what we want
to feed you." Make like Oliver Twist asking for more soup and
get seconds on the mandarin liqueur (Tue–Sun 12:00–15:00 &
19:00–24:00, closed Mon, indoor/outdoor seating on quiet square,
a block south of Corso Vittorio Emmanuele, down Largo del
Chiavari to Largo del Pallaro 15, tel. 06-6880-1488).

**Ristorante Grotte del Teatro di Pompeo**, sitting atop an
ancient theater, serves good food at fair prices (closed Mon, Via
del Biscione 73, tel. 06-6880-3686). This is great if you want to
dine on a characteristic street busy with strolling people.

*Between Campo de' Fiori and Piazza Navona:* For interesting bar munchies, try **Cul de Sac** on Piazza Pasquino (often
crowded, daily 12:00–18:00 & 19:00–24:00, a block southwest of
Piazza Navona). **L'Insalata Ricca**, next door, is a popular chain
that specializes in hearty and healthy salads (daily 12:00–15:45 &
18:45–22:00, Piazza Pasquino 72, tel. 06-6830-7881). Another
branch is nearby with more spacious outdoor seating (just off
Corso Vittorio Emmanuele on Largo del Chiavari).

### Eating near the Pantheon
You'll find a mix of cafeterias, groceries, restaurants, wine bars,
and gelato shops.

*Cafeterias:* **Brek**, on Largo Argentina just south of the

Pantheon, is an appealing, self-service restaurant with a modern, efficient atmosphere and really cheap prices (daily 12:00–15:30 & 18:30–23:00, skip the sandwiches and pizza slices downstairs and go to the "free flow" cafeteria upstairs, northwest corner of square, Largo Argentina 1, tel. 06-6821-0353).

**Il Delfino**, also on Largo Argentina, is a tired but handy self-service cafeteria that serves throughout the day (daily 7:00–21:00, not cheap but fast). Across the side street, **Frullati di Frutta** sells refreshing fruity frappés.

*Grocery:* The *alimentari* on the Pantheon square will make you a sandwich for a temple-porch picnic. Sit at the base of a column in the shade and munch lunch.

*Restaurants:* **Osteria da Mario**, a great little mom-and-pop joint with a no-stress menu, serves delicious traditional favorites. You'll feel right at home with locals who know a good value. The pop (Mario), who passed away—you'll see his photo on the wall—would be happy with the way his wife and kids are carrying on (Mon–Sat 13:00–15:00 & 19:30–23:00, closed Sun, 2 blocks in front of Pantheon and to the left at Piazza delle Coppelle 51, tel. 06-6880-6349).

**Ristorante Myosotis di Marsili**, a dressy place with black-tie waiters and a coat check, is popular with local politicians and diners classy enough to look into the fish locker and make a knowledgeable choice. It has a traditional yet imaginative menu with a good wine list. Everything here is homemade (Mon–Sat 12:30–15:30 & 19:30–23:30, closed Sun, reservations smart, near Osteria da Mario, 2 blocks in front of Pantheon at Vicolo Della Vaccarella 3, tel. 06-686-5554).

*Wine Bars:* **Enoteca Spiriti**, a wine bar two blocks from the Pantheon, is run by Raffaele, son Matteo, and daughter Daria. They serve great wine ("*corposo*" means full-bodied) by the glass and light meals with integrity. Raffaele and I have designed a treat for travelers with this book: "A Taste of Italy for Two" includes two glasses of fine Amarone wine (or the equivalent in value), fresh bread, and a plate decorated with a tasty variety of Italian cheeses and meats for a total of €20. Choose: cool jazz interior or classic Roman sidewalk exterior (open at 12:30, very busy with local office workers at 13:30, dinner from 19:30, facing Pantheon walk around to the right and take 2 rights to Via S. Eustachio 5, no CC, no phone).

On Piazza de Pietra between the Pantheon and Via del Corso, classy **Osteria dell' Ingegno** (tel. 06-678-0662) and the simpler **Non Solo Bevi** offer hearty salads and good indoor/outdoor seating (daily 12:00–15:00, tel. 06-679-4519). Another Non Solo Bevi *enoteca* is several blocks north, tucked into a distant corner of the pedestrian square Piazza San Lorenzo. At this uncharacteristically

# Restaurants in the Heart of Rome

1. Taverna, Vineria, & La Carbonara Rist.
2. Ostaria da Giovanni ar Galletto
3. Osteria Enoteca al Bric
4. Filetti de Baccala & Trattoria der Pallaro
5. Rist. Grotte del Teatro di Pompeo
6. Cul de Sac bar & L'Insalata Ricca Rist.
7. Brek Rist.
8. Il Delfino Rist. & Frullati di Frutta
9. Osteria da Mario Rist.
10. Rist. Myosotis di Marsili
11. Enoteca Spiriti
12. To Rist. alla Rampa, & Rist. Il Gabriello, Gusto
13. Rist. La Taverna degli Amici
14. Rist. Pizzeria Sacro e Profano
15. Trinity College
16. Giolitti Gelateria
17. Gelateria della Palma
18. Gelateria San Crispino
19. Non Solo Bevi (2 locations)

friendly place, Francesco and Lamberto (Beppo) serve fine wine and delightful toothpick munchies free with a glass. Their coffee *bomba* is memorable (Lucina 15, tel. 06-687-1683).

**Gelato:** Two of Rome's top ice-cream joints are a minute's walk in front of the Pantheon. The venerable **Giolitti's** is good, with cheap take-away prices and elegant Old World seating (just off Piazza Colonna and Piazza Monte Citorio at Via Uffici del Vicario 40, tel. 06-699-1243). But **Gelateria della Palma** is the new king of gelato—fresher, tastier, and with more options, including sugar-free and frozen-yogurt varieties (100 flavors, 2 blocks in front of Pantheon at Via della Maddalena 20, tel. 06-6880-6752).

### Eating near the Spanish Steps

**Ristorante alla Rampa** is a classic old restaurant tucked away just around the corner from the touristy crush of the Spanish Steps. You'll get quality Roman cooking here, with great indoor/outdoor ambience, for a moderate price. They take no reservations, so arrive by 19:30 or be prepared to wait (closed Sun, 100 meters, or 330 feet, east of Spanish Steps at Piazza Mignanelli 18, tel. 06-678-2621).

**Ristorante Il Gabriello** is inviting and small, offering a peaceful and local-feeling respite from all the top-end fashion shops in the area. Claudio serves while his brother cooks traditional Roman cuisine using fresh, organic products from their sister's farm (reasonable prices, dinner only, Mon–Sat 19:00–24:00, closed Sun, air-con, reservations smart, CC, Via Vittoria 51, 3 blocks from Spanish Steps, tel. 06-6994-0810).

**Gusto** is *the* trendy place in Rome today, with a restaurant, pizzeria, and wine bar. The only reason to eat here is to be surrounded by Rome's young and hip—which is not a bad thing (dinner from 19:45, reservations recommended, Piazza Augusto Imperatore 9, tel. 06-322-6273).

### Eating near Piazza Venezia

**Ristorante La Taverna degli Amici** is a dressy yet friendly, candlelit place draped in ivy and tucked away on a sleepy square two blocks toward the Pantheon from the Victor Emmanuel Monument. This is a great and peaceful spot for a break before or after your Capitol Hill sightseeing. The waiters are friendly and the clientele is local and upscale (reserve for dinner to avoid the basement, Tue–Sun 12:30–15:00 & 19:30–24:00, closed Mon, CC, Piazza Margana 36, tel. 06-6920-0493).

For a woody English pub lunch break, **Trinity College** is a fine if smoky place serving creative salads and thriving with locals (just off Via del Corso, 3 blocks from Piazza Venezia at Via del Collegio Romano 6, tel. 06-678-6472).

## Eating near the Trevi Fountain

**Ristorante Pizzeria Sacro e Profano** fills an old church with spicy south Italian (Calabrian) cuisine and some pricey exotic dishes. Run by friendly and helpful Pasquale and friends, this is just far enough away from the Trevi mobs. To avoid a shock when the bill comes, note that seafood is sold here by the *etto* (100-gram unit), not the portion, allow €25–45 per person depending on wine (a block off Via del Tritone at Via dei Maroniti 29, tel. 06-6791-836).

Romans in the know flock to **Gelateria San Crispino** for gelato made from ingredients such as basalmic vinegar, pear, and cinnamon. They only serve in cups because cones degrade the taste (Via della Panetteria 42, tel. 06-679-3924).

## Eating between the Colosseum and St. Peter-in-Chains Church

You'll find good views but poor value in the restaurants directly behind the Colosseum. To get your money's worth, eat a block away from the Colosseum. There are two handy eateries at the top of Terme Di Tito, a block uphill from the Colosseum, near St. Peter-in-Chains church (of Michelangelo's Moses fame).

For a real restaurant meal, try **Ostaria da Nerone**. The Santis family serves traditional Roman cuisine in a homey indoor or outdoor setting (Mon–Sat 12:00–15:00 & 19:00–23:00, closed Sun, Via delle Terme di Tito 96, tel. 06-481-7952). Next door at **Caffè dello Studente**, Pina and Mauro serve typical "bar gastronomia" fare (pizza, toasted sandwiches, various drinks). Stand up at the crowded bar, take away, or enjoy the outdoor tables (Mon–Sat 7:30–21:30, closed Sun, tel. 06-488-3240).

## Eating near Via Firenze and Via Nazionale Hotels

**Snack Bar Gastronomia** is a great local hole-in-the-wall for lunch or dinner (daily 7:00–24:00; fresh meat or veggie sandwiches, fresh squeezed juices, and Greek-style yogurt—yummy with fruit; ask the price first; Via Firenze 34). There's a classic, old-fashioned *alimentari* (grocery) across the street (7:00–19:30).

Popular for its top-quality Sicilian specialties, especially pastries and ice cream, **Pasticceria Dagnino** is frequented by people who work at my recommended hotels (daily 7:00–22:00, in Galleria Esedra off Via Torino, tel. 06-481-8660). Their *arancino*—a rice, cheese, and ham ball—is a greasy Sicilian favorite, and their cannoli is sweet. Direct the construction of your meal at the bar, pay for your trayful at the cashier, and climb upstairs, where you'll find the dancing Sicilian girls (free).

**Hostaria Romana** is a great place for traditional Roman cuisine. For an air-conditioned, classy local favorite, eat here

# Restaurants in East Rome

1. Snack Bar Gastronomia
2. Pasticceria Dagnino
3. Hostaria Romana
4. Ristorante Giovanni
5. Restaurant Target
6. Rist. Cinese Int'l.
7. Monte D.O.C. Vineria
8. Nerone & Caffe dello Studente
9. Cafeteria Nazionale
10. Flann O'Brien

(closed Sun, midway between Trevi Fountain and Piazza Barberini, Via del Boccaccio 1, at intersection with Via Rasella, no reservations needed before 20:00, tel. 06-474-5284). Go ahead and visit the antipasto bar in person to assemble your plate. They're happy to serve an *antipasti misto della casa* and pasta dinner. Take a hard look at their *Specialita Romane* list.

**Ristorante da Giovanni** is a serviceable, hardworking place that's been feeding locals and tired travelers for 50 years (tired €12 *menu*, Mon–Sat 12:00–15:00 & 19:00–22:30, closed Sun and in Aug, CC, just off Via XX Settembre at Via Antonio Salandra 1, tel. 06-485-950).

**Cafeteria Nazionale**, with woody elegance, offers light lunches—including salads—at reasonable prices (Mon–Sat 7:00–20:00, closed Sun, CC, Via Nazionale 26-27, at intersection with Via Agostino de Pretis, tel. 06-4899-1716). The lunch buffet is a delight (€7.50, 12:30–15:00).

**Ristorante Cinese Internazionale** is your best neighborhood bet for Chinese (daily 12:00–15:00 & 18:00–23:00, inexpensive, no pasta, just off Via Nazionale behind Hotel Luxor at Via Agostino de Pretis 98, tel. 06-474-4064).

**Restaurant Target** is a soulless, modern, but handy place serving decent pizza and pasta near recommended hotels (open daily, indoor and outdoor seating, don't expect great service, Via Torino 33, tel. 06-474-0066).

The **McDonald's** restaurants on Piazza della Repubblica (free piazza seating outside), Piazza Barberini, and Via Firenze offer air-conditioned interiors and salad bars.

**Flann O'Brien Irish Pub** is an entertaining place for a light meal (of pasta or something *other* than pasta, served early or late when other places are closed), fine Irish beer, live sporting events on TV, and perhaps the most Italian crowd of all (daily 7:30–23:00, Via Nazionale 17, at intersection with Via Napoli, tel. 06-488-0418).

### Eating near Santa Maria Maggiore
For a classy taste of Tuscany in a woody wine bar filled with local office workers, drop by **Monti D.O.C. Vineria Wine Bar** for lunch (chalkboard shows daily specials, daily 10:00–24:00, 2 blocks from basilica next to recommended Beehive hostel at Via Giovanni Lanza 93, tel. 06-487-2696).

### Eating near the Vatican Museum and St. Peter's
Avoid the restaurant pushers handing out fliers near the Vatican: bad food, expensive menu tricks. Try any of these instead (see map on page 68).

**Antonio's Hostaria dei Bastioni** is tasty and friendly.
It's conveniently located midway on your hike from St. Peter's
to the Vatican Museum, with noisy streetside seating and a
quiet interior (Mon–Sat 12:00–15:00 & 19:00–23:30, closed Sun,
€5.25–6.25 pastas, €7.75 *secondi*, no cover charge, at corner of
Vatican wall, Via Leone IV 29, CC, tel. 06-3972-3034). Antonio
is your gracious host.

**La Rustichella** serves a sprawling antipasti buffet (€7.75
for a meal-sized plate). Arrive when they open at 19:30 to avoid
a line and have the pristine buffet to yourself (Tue–Sun 12:30–
15:00 & 19:30–23:00, closed Mon, near Metro: Cipro-Musei
Vaticani, opposite church at end of Via Candia, Via Angelo
Emo 1, CC, tel. 06-3972-0649). Consider the fun and fruity
**Gelateria Millennium** next door.

Viale Giulio Cesare is lined with cheap **Pizza Rustica**
shops and fun eateries, such as **Cipriani Self-Service Rostic-
cería** (Tue–Sun 10:00–22:00, closed Mon, pleasant outdoor
seating, near Ottaviano subway stop, Viale Guilio Cesare 195).
Restaurants such as **Tre Pupazzi**, which line the pedestrian-only
Borgo Pio—a block from Piazza San Pietro—are worth a look.

Turn your nose loose in the wonderful **Via Andrea Doria**
open-air market, three blocks north of the Vatican Museum
(Mon–Sat roughly 7:00–13:30, until 16:30 Tue and Fri except
summer, corner of Via Tunisi and Via Andrea Doria), or try the
nearby **IN's supermarket** (Mon–Sat 8:30–13:30 & 16:00–20:00,
closed Thu eve, a half block straight out from Via Tunisi entrance
of open-air market, Via Francesco 18).

# Transportation Connections—Rome

Termini is the central station (see "Arrival in Rome," on page 43;
Metro: Termini). Tiburtina is the bus station (4 Metro stops away
from train station; Metro: Tiburtina).

**By train from Rome to: Venice** (6/day, 5–8 hrs), **Florence**
(12/day, 2 hrs, most stop at Orvieto en route), **Pisa** (8/day, 3–4
hrs), **Genova** (7/day, 6 hrs, overnight possible), **Milan** (12/day,
5 hrs, overnight possible), **Naples** (6/day, 2 hrs), **Brindisi** (2/day,
9 hrs), **Amsterdam** (2/day, 20 hrs), **Bern** (5/day, 10 hrs), **Frankfurt** (4/day, 14 hrs), **Munich** (5/day, 12 hrs), **Nice** (2/day, 10 hrs),
**Paris** (5/day, 16 hrs), **Vienna** (3/day, 13–15 hrs). All-Italy train
info: tel. 848-888-088 (automated, in Italian).

**By bus to: Assisi** (3/day, 3 hrs), **Siena** (7/day, 3 hrs).

## Rome's Airports

Rome's two airports—Fiumicino (a.k.a. Leonardo da Vinci) and
the small Ciampino—share the same Web site (www.adr.it).

**Fiumicino Airport:** Rome's major airport has a TI (Mon–Sat 8:00–19:00, closed Sun, tel. 06-6595-4471), ATMs, banks, luggage storage, shops, and bars.

A slick, direct **train** connects the airport and Rome's central Termini train station in 30 minutes. Trains run twice hourly in both directions from roughly 7:30 to 22:00. From the airport, trains depart at :07 and :37 past the hour. From the airport's arrival gate, follow signs to "Stazione/Railway Station." Buy your ticket from a machine or the Biglietteria office (€9, CC). Make sure the train you board is going to "Roma Termini," not "Roma Orte" or others.

Going from the Termini train station to the airport, trains depart at :21 and :51 past the hour, usually from tracks 25 or 26; to reach these tracks, take a 10-minute walk along track 24 to the end of the station (moving walkways are inside the building to the right on the lower level). Check the departure boards for "Fiumicino Aeroporto"—the local name for the airport—and confirm with an official or a local on the platform that the train is indeed going to the airport (€10.30, buy ticket from computerized yellow ticket machines, any *tabacchi* shop in station, or at the desk near entrance to track 26). Read your ticket: If it requires validation, stamp it in a yellow machine near the platform before boarding.

Your hotel can arrange a **taxi** to the airport at any hour for about €40. To get from the airport into town cheaply by taxi, try teaming up with any tourist also just arriving (most are heading for hotels near yours in the center). Splitting a taxi and hopping out once downtown at a taxi stand to take another to your hotel will save you about €15. Avoid unmarked, unmetered taxis.

For **airport information**, call 06-65951. To inquire about flights, call 06-6595-3640 (Alitalia: tel. 06-65643, British Air: toll-free tel. 848-812-266, Delta: toll-free tel. 800-864-114, KLM/Northwest: tel. 06-6501-1441, Lufthansa: tel. 06-6568-4004, SAS: tel. 06-6501-0771, United: tel. 0266-7481).

**Ciampino Airport:** Rome's smaller airport (tel. 06-794-941) handles budget and charter flights. To get to downtown Rome from the airport, take the LILA/Cotral bus (2/hr) to the Anagnina Metro stop, where you can connect by Metro to the stop nearest your hotel.

## Driving in Rome

Greater Rome is circled by the Grande Raccordo Anulare. This ring road has spokes that lead you into the center. Entering from the north, leave the autostrada at the Settebagni exit. Following the ancient Via Salaria (and the black-and-white *Centro* signs), work your way doggedly into the Roman thick of things. This will take you along the Villa Borghese park and dump you right on Via Veneto (where there's an Avis office). Avoid rush hour and drive defensively: Roman cars stay in their lanes like rocks in an avalanche. Parking in Rome is dangerous. Park near a police station or get advice at your hotel. The Villa Borghese underground garage is handy (€18/day, Metro: Spagna).

Consider this: Your car is a worthless headache in Rome. Avoid a pile of stress and save money by parking at the huge, easy, and relatively safe lot behind the Orvieto station (follow P signs from autostrada) and catching the train to Rome (every 2 hrs, 75 min).

# VENICE
## (VENEZIA)

Soak all day in this puddle of elegant decay. Venice is Europe's best-preserved big city. This car-free urban wonderland of a hundred islands—laced together by 400 bridges and 2,000 alleys—survives on the artificial respirator of tourism.

Born in a lagoon 1,500 years ago as a refuge from barbarians, Venice is overloaded with tourists and is slowly sinking (unrelated facts). In the Middle Ages, the Venetians, becoming Europe's clever middlemen for East-West trade, created a great trading empire. By smuggling in the bones of St. Mark (San Marco, A.D. 828), Venice gained religious importance as well. With the discovery of America and new trading routes to the Orient, Venetian power ebbed. But as Venice fell, her appetite for decadence grew. Through the 17th and 18th centuries, Venice partied on the wealth accumulated through earlier centuries as a trading power.

Today, Venice is home to about 65,000 people in its old city, down from a peak population of nearly 200,000. While there are about 500,000 in greater Venice (counting the mainland, not counting tourists), the old town has a small-town feel. Locals seem to know everyone. To see small-town Venice away from the touristic flak, escape the Rialto–San Marco tourist zone and savor the town early and late without the hordes of vacationers day-tripping in from cruise ships and nearby beach resorts. A 10-minute walk from the madness puts you in an idyllic Venice few tourists see.

## Planning Your Time

Venice is worth at least a day on even the speediest tour. Hyper-efficient train travelers take the night train in and/or out. Sleep in the old center to experience Venice at its best: early and late. For a one-day visit, cruise the Grand Canal, do the major sights

# Venice Overview

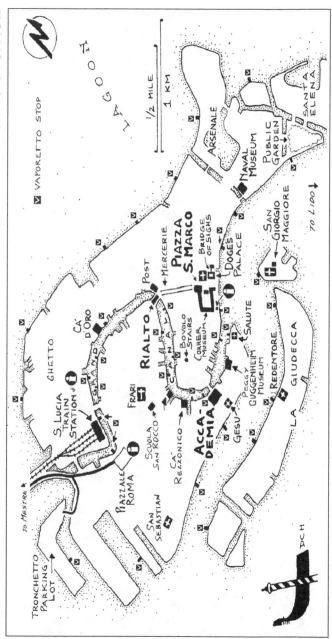

on St. Mark's Square (the square itself, Doge's Palace, and St. Mark's Basilica), see the Church of the Frari (Chiesa dei Frari) for art, and wander the backstreets on a pub crawl (see "Eating in Venice," page 152). Venice's greatest sight is the city itself. Make time to simply wander. While doable in a day, Venice is worth two. It's a medieval cookie jar, and nobody's looking.

## Orientation

The island city of Venice is shaped like a fish. Its major thorough-fares are canals. The Grand Canal winds through the middle of the fish, starting at the mouth where all the people and food enter, passing under the Rialto Bridge, and ending at St. Mark's Square (San Marco). Park your 21st-century perspective at the mouth and let Venice swallow you whole.

Venice is a car-free kaleidoscope of people, bridges, and odor-less canals. The city has no real streets, and addresses are hope-lessly confusing. Each district has about 6,000 address numbers. Luckily, it's easy to find your way, since many street corners have a sign pointing you to the nearest major landmark, such as San Marco, Accademia, Rialto, and Ferrovia (the train station). To find your way, navigate by landmarks, not streets. Obedient visitors stick to the main thoroughfares as directed by these signs and miss the charm of backstreet Venice.

## Tourist Information

There are TIs at the train station (daily 8:00–20:00, crowded and surly); at St. Mark's Square (Mon–Sat 9:45–15:15; with your back to St. Mark's, it's in far left corner of square); and near St. Mark's Square vaporetto boat stop on the lagoon (daily 9:00–18:00, sells vaporetto tickets, rents audioguides at €3.65/hr for self-guided walking tours). Smaller offices are at Tronchetto, Piazzale Roma, and the airport. For a quick question, save time by phoning 041-529-8711. Web sites on Venice: www.govenice.org (official TI site), www.veniceforvisitors.com, and www.meetingvenice.it.

At any TI, pick up a free city map and the free *Leo* bimonthly magazine, which comes with an insert, *Leo Bussola*, listing museum hours, exhibitions, and musical events (in Italian and English). Confirm your sightseeing plans. Ask for the fine brochures out-lining three offbeat Venice walks. The free periodical entertain-ment guide *Un Ospite di Venezia* (a monthly listing of events, nightlife, museum hours, train and vaporetto schedules, emer-gency telephone numbers, and so on) is available at the TI or fancy hotel reception desks (www.aguestinvenice.com).

**Maps:** The €3.10 Venice map on sale at postcard racks has much more detail than the TI's free map, but the "Illustrated

Venice Map" by Magnetic North is by far the best (€6.20, listing nearly every shop, hotel, and restaurant). Also consider the little guidebook (sold alongside the postcards), which comes with a city map and explanations of the major sights.

## Arrival in Venice

A three-kilometer-long (2-mile) causeway (with highway and train lines) connects Venice to the mainland. Mestre, Venice's sprawling mainland industrial base, has fewer crowds, cheaper hotels, and plenty of parking lots, but no charm. Don't stop here, unless you're parking your car in a lot. Trains regularly connect Mestre with Venice's Santa Lucia station (6/hr, 5 min). Don't leave your train at Venezia-Mestre—the next stop is Venezia Santa Lucia (end of the line for Venice).

**By Train:** Venice's **Santa Lucia train station** plops you right into the old town on the Grand Canal, an easy vaporetto ride or fascinating 40-minute walk to St. Mark's Square. Upon arrival, skip the station's crowded TI because the two TIs at St. Mark's Square are better, and it's not worth a long wait for a minimal map (buy a good one, such as Magnetic North's "Illustrated Venice Map" for €6.20, from a newsstand and skip the wait). Confirm your departure plan (stop by train info desk or just study the *partenze*—departure—posters on walls).

Consider storing unnecessary heavy bags, although lines for **baggage check** might be very long (platform 14, €2.60/12 hrs, €5.20/24 hrs, daily 5:00–24:00; there are no lockers).

Then walk straight out of the station to the canal. The dock for **vaporetto** #82 is on your left (for downtown Venice; most recommended hotels; and Grand Canal Cruise—see page 123); the dock for #1, #51 and #52 is on your right (for some recommended hotels). Buy a €3.10 ticket (or €9.30 all-day pass) at the ticket window and hop on a boat for downtown (direction: Rialto or San Marco). Some boats only go as far as Rialto *(solo Rialto)*, so confirm with the conductor.

**By Car:** The freeway ends at Venice in a parking lot on the edge of the island. Follow the green lights directing you to a parking lot with space, probably Tronchetto (across the causeway and on the right), which has a huge, multistoried garage (€15.50/day, half price with discount coupon from your hotel, tel. 041-520-7555). From there, you'll find travel agencies masquerading as TIs and vaporetto docks for the boat connection (#82) to the town center. Don't let taxi boatmen con you out of the cheap €3.10 vaporetto ride. Parking in Mestre is easy and cheap (open-air lots €4.10/day, €5.20/day garage across from Mestre train station, easy shuttle-train connections to Venice's Santa Lucia Station—6/hr, 5 min).

· **By Plane:** Venice's airport on the mainland, 10 kilometers (6 miles) north of the city, has a TI, cash machines, car-rental agencies, a few shops and eateries, and good connections by bus and speedboat to the city center. Airport info: tel. 041-260-611, flight info: tel. 041-260-9260.

Romantics can jet to St. Mark's Square by Alilaguna **speedboat** (easiest transportation to historical center, €9.80, 1/hr, 70 min, runs 6:15–24:00 from airport; 4:50–22:50 from St. Mark's Square, generally departing airport 10 min after the hour, www.alilaguna.com). A **water taxi** zips you directly to your hotel in 30 minutes for €80. **Buses** connect the airport and the Piazzale Roma vaporetto stop: Catch either the blue ATVO shuttle bus (€2.60, 2/hr, 20 min, 5:30–20:40 to airport, 8:30–24:00 from airport, www.atvo.it) or the cheaper orange ACTV bus #5 (€0.75, 1–3/hr, 20–40 min, 4:40–1:00).

## Passes for Venice

To help control (and confuse?) its flood of visitors, Venice now offers cards and passes that cover some museums and/or transportation. For most visitors, the simple Museum Card (for the Doge's Palace and Correr Museum) or Museum Pass will do.

Note that none of these cards or passes cover some of Venice's important attractions—the sights within St. Mark's Basilica, the Campanile, Accademia, Peggy Guggenheim Museum, Scuola Grande di San Rocco, and the Frari Church.

**Museum Card and Museum Pass:** The main **Museum Card** covers the museums of St. Mark's Square: Doge's Palace, Correr Museum, and two museums accessed from within the Correr—the National Archaeological Museum and the Monumental Rooms of Marciana National Library (€9.50, called *"Museum Card per i Musei di Piazza San Marco,"* valid for 3 months; purchase it at the Correr Museum—then use your card at the Doge's Palace to bypass the long line).

The pricier **Museum Pass** includes the St. Mark's Square museums listed above, plus Ca' Rezzonico (Museum of 18th-Century Venice), Mocenigo Palace museum (textiles and costumes), Casa Goldoni (home of the Italian playwright), and museums on the islands—Murano's Glass Museum and Burano's Lace Museum (€15.50, valid for 3 months).

Venice also (pointlessly) offers a couple of other Museum Cards: €8 for the museums of the 18th-century (called *"Museum Card per area del Settecento"*; the museums are Ca' Rezzonico, Casa Goldoni, and Palazzo Mocenigo) and €6 for the island museums (called *"Museum Card per i musei delle isole,"* covering Murano's Glass Museum and Burano's Lace Museum).

## Daily Reminder

**Sunday:** The Church of San Giorgio Maggiore (on island near St. Mark's Square) hosts a Gregorian Mass at 11:00. The Rialto market consists mainly of souvenir stalls today (fish and produce sections closed). These sights are open only in the afternoon: Frari Church (13:00–18:00, closed Sun in Aug) and St. Mark's Basilica (14:00–17:00). The Dalmatian School is closed in the afternoon. It's a bad day for a pub crawl, as most pubs are closed.

**Monday:** All sights are open except for the Rialto fish market, Dalmatian School, and Torcello Museum (on Torcello island). The Accademia and Ca' d'Oro (House of Gold) close early in the afternoon (14:00).

**Tuesday:** All sights are open except the Peggy Guggenheim Museum, Ca' Rezzonico (Museum of 18th-Century Venice), and the Lace Museum (on Burano island).

**Wednesday:** All sights are open except the Glass Museum (on Murano island).

**Thursday/Friday:** All sights are open.

**Saturday:** All sights are open (Peggy Guggenheim Museum until 22:00 April–Oct) except the Jewish Museum.

Are the Museum Cards and Passes worth it? If you want to see just the Doge's Palace, get the Museum Card (€9.50, includes Correr Museum). If you want to add Ca' Rezzonico (€6.70 entry), you'll save money by getting the Museum Pass. With a Museum Card or Pass (sold at participating museums), you'll breeze past any lines.

**Venice Cards:** Personally, I'd skip these, but here's the information. These cards cover Venice's public transportation, the few public toilets, and if you get the "orange" version, some sights.

The **Blue Venice Card** covers all your vaporetto and *traghetto* (gondola crossing of Grand Canal, normally €0.40) rides—plus entry to public toilets: 1 day-€11, 3 days-€23, 7 days-€41; cheaper for "Juniors" under 30. (If all you want is a vaporetto pass, you can get a 24-hour pass for €9.30 at any vaporetto dock; described under "Getting around Venice," page 120.)

The **Orange Venice Card**, which also includes transportation and toilets, gets you into the museums covered by the Museum Pass. It's like getting a Blue Venice Card and a Museum Pass for: 1 day-€26, 3 days-€43, and 7 days-€58; cheaper for "Juniors" under 30.

Hefty supplements—which vary depending on which Venice Card and how many days you get—cover transportation to and from Marco Polo Airport and parking at San Giuliano car park with transportation to the city center.

Venice only issues 30,000 cards a day. You must reserve your card at least 48 hours in advance by going online (www.venicecard.it) or calling 011-30-041-271-4747 from the United States or 899-909-090 within Italy. Pay for the card when you pick it up at one of many offices around Venice (see www.venicecard.it for details).

Note that you don't need a Venice Card of any color to enter the city. A Museum Card or Museum Pass makes the most sense for most travelers.

## Helpful Hints

Venice is expensive for locals as well as tourists. The demand is huge, supply is limited, and running a business is costly. Things just cost more here; everything must be shipped in and hand-trucked to its destination. Perhaps the best way to enjoy Venice is to just succumb to its charms and blow a lot of money.

**Get Lost:** Accept the fact that Venice was a tourist town 400 years ago. It was, is, and always will be crowded. While 80 percent of Venice is, in fact, not touristy, 80 percent of the tourists never notice. Hit the backstreets.

Venice is the ideal town to explore on foot. Walk and walk to the far reaches of the town. Don't worry about getting lost. Get as lost as possible. Keep reminding yourself, "I'm on an island, and I can't get off." When it comes time to find your way, just follow the directional arrows on building corners or simply ask a local, "*Dov'è San Marco?*" ("Where is St. Mark's?") People in the tourist business (that's most Venetians) speak some English. If they don't, listen politely, watching where their hands point, say "*Grazie,*" and head off in that direction. If you're lost, pop into a hotel and ask for their business card—it comes with a map and a prominent "you are here."

**Take Breaks:** Grab a cool place to sit down, relax, and recoup from sightseeing—meditate in a pew in an uncrowded church or buy a cappuccino and a fruit cup in a café.

**Etiquette:** Walk on the right and don't loiter on bridges. Picnicking is technically forbidden (keep a low profile). Dress modestly. Men should keep their shirts on.

**Water:** Venetians pride themselves on having pure, safe, and tasty tap water piped in from the foothills of the Alps; you can actually see the mountains from Venice bell towers on crisp, clear winter days.

**Pigeon Poop:** If bombed by a pigeon, resist the initial response to wipe it off immediately—it'll just smear into your hair. Wait until it dries and flake it off cleanly.

## Services

**Money:** ATMs are plentiful and the easiest way to go. Bank rates vary. I like the Banca di Sicilia, a block toward St. Mark's Square from Campo San Bartolomeo. The American Express change desk is just off St. Mark's Square (see "Travel Agencies," below). Non-bank exchange bureaus, such as Exacto, will cost you $10 more than a bank for a $200 exchange. A 24-hour cash machine near the Rialto vaporetto stop exchanges U.S. dollars and other currencies at fair rates (when it's not out of order).

**Travel Agencies:** If you need to get train tickets, pay supplements, or make reservations, avoid the time-consuming trip to the crowded station by using a downtown travel agency.

Kele & Teo Viaggi e Turismo is good and handy (CC for train tickets only, Mon–Fri 8:30–19:00, Sat 9:00–19:00, Sat afternoon and Sun no train tickets available, at Ponte dei Bareteri on the Mercerie midway between Rialto and St. Mark's Square, tel. 041-520-8722, e-mail: incoming@keleteo.com).

American Express books flights, sells train tickets, and makes train reservations (travel agency: Mon–Fri 9:00–17:30, closed Sat–Sun; change desk: Mon–Sat 7:00–19:30, closed Sun; about 2 blocks off St. Mark's Square at 1471, en route to Accademia, tel. 041-520-0844).

**Rip-offs, Theft, and Help:** While pickpockets work the crowded main streets, docks, and vaporetti (wear your money belt and carry your day bag in front), the dark, late-night streets of Venice are safe. A service called Venezia No Problem tries to help tourists who've been mistreated by any Venetian business (toll-free tel. 800-355-920, for complaints only, not for information).

**"Rolling Venice" Youth Discount Pass:** This worthwhile €2.60 pass gives those under 30 discounts on sights and transportation, plus information on cheap eating and sleeping. In summer, they may have a kiosk in front of the train station (July–Sept daily 8:00–20:00). Their main office, near St. Mark's Square, is open year-round (Mon–Fri 9:00–14:00, closed Sat–Sun, from American Express head toward St. Mark's Square, first left, first left again through "Contarina" tunnel, follow white sign to Commune di Venezia and see the sign, Corte Contarina 1529, 3rd floor, tel. 041-274-7651).

**Church Services:** The **San Zulian Church** (the only church in Venice that you can actually walk around) offers a Mass in English at 9:30 on Sunday (May–Sept, 2 blocks toward Rialto off St. Mark's Square). Gregorians would enjoy the sung Gregorian Mass on Sunday at 11:00 and the rest of the week at 8:00 at **San Giorgio Maggiore Church** (on island of San Giorgio Maggiore, visible from Doge's Palace, catch vaporetto #82 from "San Marco

M.V.E." stop, located 200 meters/650 feet east of St. Mark's Square, at third bridge along waterfront). Call 041-522-7827 to confirm times.

**Laundry:** There is a self-service launderette (open daily) and two full-service laundries (both closed Sat–Sun).

The modern, cheap **Bea Vita** self-serve *lavanderia* is across the canal from the train station (daily 8:00–22:00, from station go over bridge, take first right, first left, first right).

At either of the following full-service laundries, you can get a nine-pound load washed and dried for €16—confirm price carefully. Drop it off in the morning and pick it up that afternoon. (Call to be sure they're open.) Don't expect to get your clothes back ironed, folded, or even entirely dry. **Lavanderia Gabriella** is near St. Mark's Square (Mon–Fri 8:00–19:00, closed Sat–Sun, 985 Rio Terra Colonne, from San Zulian Church go over Ponte dei Ferali, then take first right down Calle dei Armeni, tel. 041-522-1758). **Lavanderia S.S. Apostoli** is near the Rialto Bridge on the St. Mark's side (Mon–Fri 8:30–12:00 & 15:30–19:00, closed Sat–Sun, just off Campo S.S. Apostoli on Salizada del Pistor, tel. 041-522-6650).

**Post Office:** A large post office is off the far end of St. Mark's Square (on the side of square opposite St. Mark's Basilica, Mon–Sat 8:10–18:00, closed Sun, shorter hours off-season), and a branch is near the Rialto Bridge (on St. Mark's side, Mon–Fri 8:10–13:30, Sat 8:10–12:30, closed Sun).

**Haircuts:** I've been getting my hair cut at Coiffeur Benito for 15 years. Benito has been keeping local men and women trim for 25 years. He's an artist—actually a "hair sculptor"—and a cut here is a fun diversion from the tourist grind (€19.50 for women, €16.50 for men, Tue–Sat 8:30–13:30 & 15:30–19:30, closed Sun–Mon, behind San Zulian Church near St. Mark's Square, Calle S. Zulian Gia del Strazzanol 592A, tel. 041-528-6221).

## Getting around Venice

**By Vaporetto:** The public transit system is a fleet of motorized bus-boats called vaporetti. They work like city buses except that they never get a flat, the stops are docks, and if you get off between stops, you may drown. For most, only two lines matter: #1 is the slow boat, taking 45 minutes to make every stop along the entire length of the Grand Canal; #82 is the fast boat that zips down the Grand Canal in 25 minutes, stopping mainly at Tronchetto (car park), Piazzale Roma (bus station), Ferrovia (train station), Rialto Bridge, San Tomá (Frari Church), the Accademia Bridge, and St. Mark's Square. Some #82 boats go only as far as Rialto—confirm with the conductor before boarding. Buy a €3.10 ticket, ideally before boarding (at the booth at the dock) or from a conductor on board (before you sit down or you risk being fined). Families of three or more pay €2.60 per person. A round-trip *(andata e ritorno)* costs €5.20 (good for 2 trips within a day on any line).

A 24-hour pass (€9.30, cheaper for families) pays for itself in three trips. The cheaper "Itinerary Ticket" covers only stops on the Grand Canal and Murano, Burano, and Torcello (€7.75, valid for 12 hours). Also consider the 72-hour (€18.10) and one-week (€31) passes. It's fun to be able to hop on and off spontaneously. Technically, luggage costs the same as dogs—€3.10— but I've never been charged. Riding free? There's a 1-in-10 chance a conductor will fine you €20.

For vaporetto fun, take the Grand Canal Cruise (see page 123); avoid rush hour, when boats are packed heading to St. Mark's Square early in the day and packed heading to the train station late in the day. If you like joyriding on vaporetti, ride a boat around the city and out into the lagoon and back. Ask for the circular route— *circulare*, pronounced "cheer-koo-LAH-ray." It's usually the #51 or #52, leaving from the San Zaccaria vaporetto stop (near the Doge's Palace) and from all the stops along the perimeter of Venice.

**By *Traghetto*:** Only three bridges cross the Grand Canal, but *traghetti* (gondolas) shuttle locals and in-the-know tourists across the Grand Canal at several handy locations (see Downtown Venice map on page 122; routes also marked on pricier maps sold in Venice). Take advantage of these time-savers. They can also save money. For instance, while most tourists take the €3.10 vaporetto to connect St. Mark's with La Salute Church, a €0.40 *traghetto* does the job (free with Venice Blue or Orange Card). Most people stand while riding. *Traghetti* generally run from 6:00 until 20:00, sometimes until 23:00.

**By Water Taxi:** Venetian taxis, like speedboat limos, hang out at most busy points along the Grand Canal. Prices, which average €30 to €40 (about €75 to the airport), are a bit soft. Negotiate and settle before stepping in. For travelers with lots of luggage or small groups, taxi rides can be a worthwhile and time-saving convenience—and extremely scenic to boot.

## Walking Tours of Venice
**Audioguide Tours**—The TI at the lagoon (near St. Mark's Square) rents audioguides for self-guided walking tours of Venice (2 hrs-€5, 24 hrs-€10, just punch the number of what you'd like described—exteriors only).
**Classic Venice Bars Tour**—Debonair local guide Alessandro Schezzini is a connoisseur of Venetian *bacaros*—classic old bars serving traditional *cicchetti* (local munchies). He offers evening

## Downtown Venice

- Vaporetti Stops
- Traghetto Routes

200 YARDS
200 METERS

TO GHETTO, TRAIN STN, ⑲
& TRONCHETTO

TO FONDAMENTA
NUOVE &
BOATS TO
MURANO &
BURANO

CA D'ORO

FISH MKT.

HOSP.

CAMPO S.
GIOVANNI
& PAOLO

RIALTO

POST

CAMPO
S.M.
FORMOSA

CANAL

CAMPO
S.LUCA

CAMPO
MANIN

S. ZAC.

LA FENICE

POST

WC

CAMP.

DOGE'S
PAL.

AMEX

LARGA XXII

S. MOISÈ

CAMPO
S.MARIA
ZOBENIGO

SAN
MARCO

- ❶ HOTEL RIVA
- ❷ LOCANDA PIAVE
- ❸ LOCANDA CASA QUERINI
- ❹ HOTEL CAMPIELLO
- ❺ ALBERGO PAGANELLI
- ❻ ALBERGO DONI
- ❼ HOTEL FONTANA
- ❽ ALBERGO CORONA
- ❾ HOTEL ASTORIA
- ❿ LOCANDA GAMBERO
- ⑪ HOTEL BEL SITO
- ⑫ ALLOGGI ALLA SCALA
- ⑬ LOCANDA STURION &
  HOTEL LOCANDA OVIDIUS
- ⑭ ALBERGO GUERRATO
- ⑮ HOTEL CANADA
- ⑯ HOTEL GIORGIONE
- ⑰ LOCANDA LA CORTE
- ⑱ FORESTERIA DELLA
  CHIESA VALDESE
- ⑲ TO HOTEL GEREMIA

tours that involve stopping and sampling a snack and a glass of wine at three of these. The fee (about €30 per person) includes wine, *cicchetti*, and a great insight into this local tradition (6–8 per group, tours don't depart without a minimum of 6 people, so call a couple of days ahead to arrange and he'll match up smaller parties to form a group, tel. & fax 041-534-5367, cellular 33-5530-9024, e-mail: venische@tiscalinet.it).

**Venicescapes**—Michael Broderick's private theme tours of Venice are intellectually demanding and beyond the attention span of most mortal tourists, but for the curious with stamina, he's enthralling. Michael's challenge: to help visitors gain a more solid understanding of Venice. For a description of all six of his itineraries, see www.venicescapes.org (book well in advance, 4–6-hr tour: €275 for 2, €50 per person after that, plus admissions and transportation, tel. 041-520-6361, e-mail: info@venicescapes.org).

**American Express Tours**—AmEx runs a couple of basic bilingual tours daily (€24, 2 hrs, depart from AmEx office, about 2 blocks off St. Mark's Square in direction of Accademia, 9:00 tour visits St. Mark's Square and the Doge's Palace, 15:00 tour goes to the Frari Church and includes a gondola ride, tel. 041-520-0844).

**Local Guides**—Alessandro Schezzini gets beyond the clichés and into offbeat Venice (€90, 2.5 hrs, listed above under "Classic Venice Bars Tour"). Elisabetta Morelli is a good, licensed guide who can also provide tours in museums (€130, 2 hrs, tel. 041-526-7816, cellular 328-753-5220, e-mail: bettamorelli@inwind.it).

## Grand Canal Tour of Venice

For a ▲▲▲ joyride, introduce yourself to Venice by boat. Cruise the entire Canal Grande from Tronchetto (car park) or Ferrovia (train station) all the way to San Marco. You can ride boat #1 (slow and ideal, 45 min) or #82 (too fast, 25 min, be certain you're on a "San Marco via Rialto" boat because some boats don't go farther than Rialto). The cruise is interesting any time of day, but the least crowded at night, when vaporettos are nearly empty.

If you can't snag a front seat, lurk nearby and take one when it becomes available or find an outside seat in the stern. This ride has the best light and fewest crowds early or late. Twilight is magic. After dark, chandeliers light up the building interiors. While Venice is a barrage on the senses that hardly needs a narration, these notes give the cruise a little meaning and help orient you to this great city. Some city maps (on sale at postcard racks) have a handy Grand Canal map on the back.

**Overview:** Venice, built in a lagoon, sits on pilings driven nearly five meters (15 feet) into the clay (alder wood worked best). About 40 kilometers (25 miles) of **canals** drain the city, dumping like streams into the Grand Canal. Technically, there are three canals: Grand, Giudecca, and Cannaregio. The other 45 "canals" are referred to as *rio* (rivers), but the only natural river is this main street of Venice, about five meters (15 feet) deep. Because of the river's faster current, sediment never settled here.

Venice is a city of **palaces**. The most lavish were built fronting the Grand Canal. This cruise is the only way to really appreciate the front doors of this unique and historic chorus line of mansions dating from the days when Venice was the world's richest city. Strict laws prohibit any changes in these buildings, so while landowners gnash their teeth, we can enjoy Europe's best-preserved medieval city—slowly rotting. Many of the grand buildings are now vacant. Others harbor chandeliered elegance above mossy, empty ground floors. Ages ago, the city was nicknamed "Venice the Red" for the uniform, red brick, dust-colored stucco of its buildings. Today you'll see a bit of the original red along with the modern colors.

Start at **Tronchetto** (the bus and parking lot) or the **train station**. I'll orient by the vaporetto stops.

Venice's main thoroughfare is busy with traffic. You'll see all kinds of **boats**: taxis, police boats, garbage boats, ambulances, and even brown-and-white UPS boats. Venice's sleek, black, graceful **gondolas** are a symbol of the city. While used gondolas cost around €10,000, new ones run up to €30,000 apiece. Today, with over 400 gondoliers joyriding around the churning vaporetti, there's a lot of congestion on the Grand Canal. Watch your vaporetto driver curse the (better-paid) gondoliers.

**Ferrovia vaporetto stop:** The Santa Lucia **train station**, one of the few modern buildings in town, was built in 1954. It's been the gateway into Venice since 1860, when the first station was built. "F.S." stands for "Ferrovie dello Stato," the Italian state railway system. The bridge at the station is the first of only three that cross the Canal Grande.

**Riva di Biasio:** Just past this vaporetto stop, look left down the broad Cannaregio Canal. The twin pink six-story buildings, known as the "skyscrapers," are a reminder of how densely populated the world's original **ghetto** was. Set aside as the local Jewish quarter in 1516, the area became extremely crowded. This urban island (behind the San Marcuola stop) developed into one of the most closely knit business and cultural quarters of all the Jewish communities in Italy. For more information, visit the Jewish Museum in this neighborhood (see "Sights," below).

**San Stae:** Opposite the San Stae stop, look for the faded frescoes (left bank, on lower story). Imagine the grand facades of the Grand Canal at its grandest.

**Ca' d'Oro:** The lacy Ca' d'Oro, or "House of Gold" (left bank, next to vaporetto stop) is considered the most elegant Venetian Gothic palace on the canal. Unfortunately, there's little to see inside (€3, Mon 8:15–14:00, Tue–Sun 8:15–19:15, free peek through hole in door of courtyard). "Ca" refers to "house." Because only the house of the doge (Venetian ruler) could be called a palace, all other palaces are technically "Ca."

Farther along, on the right, the outdoor **fish and produce market** bustles with people in the morning, but is quiet the rest of the day. Find the *traghetto* gondola ferrying shoppers—standing like Washington crossing the Delaware—back and forth.

The huge **post office**, with *servizio postale* boats moored at its blue posts, is on the left just before the Rialto Bridge. Above the post office, the golden angel of the Campanile (bell tower) faces the wind and marks St. Mark's Square, where this tour will end.

**Rialto:** A major landmark of Venice, the **Rialto Bridge** is lined with shops and tourists. The third bridge on this spot, it was built in 1592. Earlier Rialto Bridges could open to let in big ships. After 1592, much of the Grand Canal was closed to shipping and became a canal of palaces. With a span of 42 meters (140 feet) and foundations stretching 200 meters (660 feet) on either side, the Rialto was an impressive engineering feat in its day. Locals call the summit of this bridge the "icebox of Venice" for its cool breeze. Tourists call it a great place to kiss. *Rialto* means "high river bank." The restaurants with views of the bridge feature high prices and low quality.

**Rialto**, a separate town in the early days of Venice, has always been the commercial district, while San Marco was the religious and governmental center. Today, a street called the Mercerie connects the two, providing travelers with human traffic jams and a mesmerizing gauntlet of shopping temptations. The restaurants that line the canal feature great views, midrange prices, and low quality.

**San Silvestro:** We now enter a long stretch of important **merchants' palaces**, each with a proud and different facade. Since ships couldn't navigate beyond the Rialto Bridge (to reach the section of the Grand Canal you just came from), the biggest palaces—with the major shipping needs—lie ahead. Many feature the Roman palace design of twin towers flanking a huge set of central windows. These were showrooms designed to let in maximum sunlight.

Just after the San Silvestro stop, you'll see (on the right) the palace of a 15th-century **"captain general of the sea."** The Venetian equivalents of five-star admirals were honored with twin obelisks decorating their palaces. This palace flies three flags: Italy (green-white-orange), the European Union (blue with ring of stars), and Venice (the lion).

**Sant' Angelo:** Notice how many buildings have a foundation of waterproof white stone (*pietra d'Istria*), upon which the bricks sit high and dry. Many canal-level floors are abandoned; the rising water level takes its toll. The posts—historically and gaily painted with the equivalent of family coats of arms—don't rot under water, but the wood at the water line does.

Look at how the rich marble facades are just a veneer covering no-nonsense brick buildings. Look up at the characteristic **funnel-shaped chimneys**. These forced embers through a loop-the-loop channel until they were dead—required in the days when stone palaces were surrounded by humble wooden buildings and a live spark could make a merchant's workforce homeless.

Take a deep whiff of Venice. What's all this nonsense about stinky canals? All I smell is my shirt. By the way, how's your captain? Smooth dockings? To get to know him, stand up in the bow and block his view.

**San Tomá:** After the San Tomá stop, look down the side canal (on the right, before the bridge) to see the traffic light, the fire station, and the fireboats ready to go.

We now prepare to round the hairpin turn and double back toward St. Mark's. The impressive **Ca' Foscari** (right side) dominates the bend in the canal. Its four stories get increasingly ornate as they rise from the water—from simple Gothic arches at water level, to Gothic with a point, to Venetian-Gothic arches topped with four-leaf clovers, to still more medallions and laciness that look almost Moorish. Wow.

**Ca' Rezzonico:** The grand, heavy, white Ca' Rezzonico, directly at the stop of the same name, houses the Museum of 18th-Century Venice. Across the canal is the cleaner and leaner Palazzo Grassi, which often showcases special exhibitions.

These days, when buildings are being renovated, huge murals with images of the building mask the ugly scaffolding. Corporations hide the scaffolding out of goodwill (and to get their name on the mural).

**Accademia:** The wooden Accademia Bridge crosses the Grand Canal and leads to the Accademia Gallery (right side), filled with the best Venetian paintings. The bridge was put up in 1932 as a temporary one. Locals liked it, so it stayed. Cruising under the bridge, you'll get a classic view of the domed La Salute Church ahead.

The low white building among greenery (on the right, between the bridge and the church) is the **Peggy Guggenheim Museum**. The American heiress "retired" here, sprucing up the palace that had been abandoned in mid-construction; the locals call it the *palazzo non finito*. Peggy willed the city her fine collection of modern art.

Just before the Salute stop (on the right), the house with the big windows and the red and wild Andy Warhol painting on the living-room wall (often behind white drapes) was lived in by rock singer Mick Jagger. In the 1970s, this was notorious as Venice's rock-and-roll-star **party house**.

**Salute:** A crown-shaped dome supported by scrolls stands atop **La Salute Church**. This Church of Saint Mary of Good Health was built to coax God into delivering the Venetians from the devastating plague of 1630 (which eventually killed about a third of the city's population). It's claimed that more than a million trees were piled together to build a foundation reaching below the mud to the solid clay.

Much of the surrounding countryside was deforested by Venice. Trees were exported and consumed locally to fuel the furnaces of Venice's booming glass industry, to build Europe's biggest merchant marine, and to prop up this city in the mud.

Across the canal (left side), several **fancy hotels** have painted facades that hint at the canal's former glory.

As the Grand Canal opens up into the lagoon, the last building on the right with the golden ball is the 16th-century **Customs House** (Dogana da Mar, not open to the public). Its two bronze Atlases hold a statue of Fortune riding the ball. Arriving ships stopped here to pay their tolls.

As you prepare to disembark at San Marco/Vallaresso, look from left to right out over the lagoon. On the left, a wide harbor-front walk leads past the town's most elegant hotels to the green area in the distance. This is the public garden, the largest of Venice's few parks, which hosts the Biennale art show (see page 137). Farther in the distance is the **Lido**, the island with Venice's beach. It's tempting, with sand and casinos, but its car traffic breaks into the medieval charm of Venice.

The dreamy white church that seems to float is the architect Palladio's **San Giorgio Maggiore**. It's just a vaporetto ride away (#82 from San Marco M.V.E. dock). Across the lagoon (to your right) is a residential island called **Giudecca**.

**San Marco/Vallaresso:** Get off at the San Marco/Vallaresso stop. Directly ahead is **Harry's Bar**. Hemingway drank here when it was a characteristic no-name *osteria* and the gondoliers' hangout. Today, of course, it's the overpriced hangout of well-dressed Americans who don't mind paying triple for their Bellinis (peach juice with *prosecco* wine) to make the scene. St. Mark's Square is just around the corner.

## Sights—Venice, on St. Mark's Square

For information on Venice's Museum Card and Museum Pass, see page 116.

▲▲▲**St. Mark's Square (Piazza San Marco)**—Surrounded by splashy and historic buildings, Piazza San Marco is filled with music, lovers, pigeons, and tourists by day and is your private rendezvous with the Middle Ages late at night. Europe's greatest dance floor is the romantic place to be. St. Mark's Square is about the first place in Venice to flood (you might see stacked wooden benches; when the square floods, these are put end to end to make elevated sidewalks).

With your back to the church, survey one of Europe's great urban spaces, and the only square in Venice to merit the title "Piazza." Nearly two football fields long, it's surrounded by the offices of the republic. On the right are the "old offices" (16th-century Renaissance). On the left are the "new offices" (17th-century Baroque). Napoleon, after enclosing the square with the more simple and austere neoclassical wing across the far end, called this "the most beautiful drawing room in Europe."

The clock tower, a Renaissance tower built in 1496, marks the entry to the Mercerie, the main shopping drag, which connects St. Mark's Square with the Rialto. From the piazza, you can see the bronze men (Moors) swing their huge clappers at the top of each hour. In the 17th century, one of them knocked an unsuspecting worker off the top and to his death—probably the first-ever killing by a robot. Notice the world's first "digital" clock on the tower facing the square (with dramatic flips every 5 minutes).

For a slow and pricey evening thrill, invest €6.20 (plus €4 if the orchestra plays) in a beer or coffee at one of the elegant cafés with the dueling orchestras (see Caffè Florian, described below in "Nightlife in Venice.") If you're going to sit awhile and savor the scene, it's worth the splurge. If all you have is €1, buy a bag of pigeon seed and become popular in a flurry. To get everything airborne, toss your sweater in the air.

Venice's best TIs (and WCs) are nearby. One TI is on the square, the other on the lagoon. To find the TI on the square, stand with your back to the church and go to the far corner on your left; the office is tucked away in the arcade (daily 9:00–17:00; near this TI is a €0.50 WC open daily 8:00–21:00—it's a few steps beyond St. Mark's Square en route to the AmEx office and the Accademia; see *Albergo Diorno* sign marked on pavement). The other TI is on the lagoon (daily 9:00–18:00, walk toward the water by the Doge's Palace, go right; nearby WCs open daily 9:00–19:00).

▲▲**St. Mark's Basilica**—Since about A.D. 830, this basilica has housed the saint's bones. The mosaic above the door at the far

## Floods and a Dying City

Venice floods about 60 times a year—normally in March and November—when the wind blowing up from Egypt and high barometric pressure on the lower Adriatic Sea are most likely to combine to push water up to this top end of the sea. (There is no real lunar tide in the Mediterranean.)

Floods start in St. Mark's Square. The entry of the church is nearly the lowest spot in town. (You might see stacked wooden benches; when the square floods, these are put end to end to make elevated sidewalks). The measuring devices at the base of the outside of the Campanile bell tower (near the exit, facing St. Mark's Square) show the current sea level *(livello marea)*. When the water level rises one meter (3 feet), a warning siren sounds. It repeats if a serious flood is imminent. Find the mark showing the high-water level from the terrible floods of 1966 (waist-level, on right).

In 1965, Venice's population was over 150,000. Since the flood of 1966, the population has been shrinking. Today the population is about 65,000 . . . and geriatric. Sad, yes, but imagine raising a family here: The fragile nature of the city means piles of regulations (no biking, and so on), and costs are high—even though the government is now subsidizing rents to keep people from moving out. You can easily get glass and tourist trinkets, but it's hard to find groceries. And floods and the humidity make house maintenance an expensive pain.

left of the church shows two guys carrying Mark's coffin into the church. Mark looks pretty grumpy after the long voyage from Egypt.

The church, built in Eastern style to underline Venice's connection with Byzantium (thus protecting it from the ambition of Charlemagne and his Holy Roman Empire), is decorated by booty from returning sea captains—a kind of architectural Venetian trophy chest.

To enter the church, modest dress is required even of kids (no shorts or bare shoulders). In peak season, there can be long lines of people waiting to get into the church. People who ignore the dress code hold up the line while they plead fruitlessly with—or put on extra clothes under the watchful eyes of—the dress code police.

The church has 4,000 square meters (43,000 square feet) of Byzantine mosaics, the best and oldest of which are in the atrium (turn right as you enter and stop under the last dome—this may be roped off, but dome is still visible). Facing the church, gape up (it's OK, no pigeons), and read clockwise the story of Adam and Eve that rings the bottom of the dome. Now, facing the piazza, look domeward for the story of Noah, the ark, and the flood (two by two, the wicked being drowned, Noah sending out the dove, a happy rainbow, and a sacrifice of thanks).

Step inside the church (stairs on right lead to bronze horses) and notice the marble floor richly decorated in mosaics. As in many Venetian buildings, because the best foundation pilings were made around the perimeter, the interior floor rolls. As you shuffle under the central dome, look up for the Ascension (free, Mon–Sat 9:30–17:00, Sun 14:00–17:00, no photos, tel. 041-522-5205). See the schedule board in the atrium, listing free English guided tours (schedules vary but April–Oct there can be up to 4/day). The church is particularly beautiful when lit (unpredictable schedule, maybe middays 11:00–12:00, Sat–Sun 14:00–17:00, plus 18:45 Mass on Sat). During peak times, the line can be very long. Free reservations may be available at www.alata.it—if the Web site is working (print out your time and present it when you enter, to the left of the general entry).

In the **Galleria and Museum** upstairs, you can see an up-close mosaic exhibition, a fine view of the church interior, a view of the square from the balcony with bronze horses, and (inside, in their own room) the newly restored original horses. These well-traveled horses, made during the days of Alexander the Great (4th century B.C.), were taken to Rome by Nero, to Constantinople/Istanbul by Constantine, to Venice by crusaders, to Paris by Napoleon, back "home" to Venice when Napoleon fell, and finally indoors and out of the acidic air (€1.60, daily 9:45–17:00, winter until 16:00, enter from atrium either before or after you tour church).

San Marco's **treasury** (with included and informative audio-guide free for the asking) and **altarpiece** (€2.10 each, daily 9:45–17:10, 16:10 in winter) give you the best chance outside of Istanbul or Ravenna to see the glories of Byzantium. Venetian crusaders looted the Christian city of Constantinople and brought home piles of lavish loot (until the advent of TV evangelism, perhaps the lowest point in Christian history). Much of this plunder is stored in the treasury *(tesoro)* of San Marco. As you view these treasures, remember most were made in A.D. 500, while western Europe was still rutting in the mud. Beneath the high altar lies the body of St. Mark ("Marxus") and the Pala d'Oro, a golden altarpiece made with 80 Byzantine enamels (A.D. 1000–1300). Each shows a religious scene set in gold and precious stones. Both of these sights are interesting and historic, but neither is as much fun as two bags of pigeon seed.

## Tips on Sightseeing in Venice

**Crowd Control:** Crowds can be a serious problem at the Accademia (to minimize crowds, go early or late); St. Mark's Basilica (consider reserving online at www.alata.it); Campanile bell tower (go late—it's open until 21:00 in the summer); and the Doge's Palace. For the Doge's Palace, you have three options for avoiding the ticket-sales line: Buy your Museum Card or Museum Pass at the Correr Museum (then step right up to the Doge's Palace turnstile, skipping the long line); visit the Doge's Palace at 17:00 (if it's April–Oct), when lines disappear; or book a "Secret Itineraries" tour (see page 132).

**Hours:** The Accademia is open earlier (daily at 8:15) and closes later (19:15 Tue–Sun) than most sights in Venice. Some sights close earlier off-season (e.g., Doge's Palace; Correr Museum; the Campanile; and St. Mark's Museum, Treasury, and Golden Altarpiece).

**Churches:** Modest dress is recommended at churches and required at St. Mark's Basilica—no bare shoulders, shorts, or short skirts. Some churches are closed to sightseers on Sunday morning (e.g., St. Mark's Basilica and Frari Church) and many are closed from roughly 12:00 to 15:00 Monday through Saturday (e.g., La Salute and San Giorgio Maggiore).

▲▲▲**Doge's Palace (Palazzo Ducale)**—The seat of the Venetian government and home of its ruling duke, or doge, this was the most powerful half-acre in Europe for 400 years.

The Doge's Palace was built to show off the power and wealth of the republic and remind all visitors that Venice was number one. In typical Venetian Gothic style, the bottom has pointy arches, and the top has an Eastern or Islamic flavor. Its columns sat on pedestals, but in the thousand years since they were erected, the palace has settled into the mud, and the bases have vanished.

Enjoy the newly restored facades from the courtyard. Notice a grand staircase (with nearly naked Moses and Paul Newman at the top). Even the most powerful visitors climbed this to meet the doge. This was the beginning of an architectural power trip. The doge, the elected-for-life duke or leader of this "dictatorship of the aristocracy," lived with his family on the first floor near the halls of power. From his living quarters (once lavish, now sparse), you'll follow the one-way route through the public rooms of the top floor, finishing with the Bridge of Sighs and the prison.

The place is wallpapered with masterpieces by Veronese and Tintoretto. Don't worry much about the great art. Enjoy the building.

In room 12, the Senate Room, the 200 senators met, debated, and passed laws. From the center of the ceiling, Tintoretto's *Triumph of Venice* shows the city in all her glory. Lady Venice, in heaven with the Greek gods, stands high above the lesser nations, who swirl respectfully at her feet with gifts.

The Armory—a dazzling display originally assembled to intimidate potential adversaries—shows remnants of the military might the empire employed to keep the East-West trade lines open (and the local economy booming). Squint out the window at the far end for a fine view of Palladio's San Giorgio Maggiore Church and the *lido* (cars, casinos, crowded beaches) in the distance.

The giant Hall of the Grand Council (55 meters/180 feet long, capacity 2,000) is where the entire nobility met to elect the senate and doge. Ringing the room are portraits of 76 doges (in chronological order). One, a doge who opposed the will of the Grand Council, is blacked out. Behind the doge's throne, you can't miss Tintoretto's monsterpiece, *Paradise*. At 160 square meters (1,700 square feet), this is the world's largest oil painting. Christ and Mary are surrounded by a heavenly host of 500 saints. Its message to electors who met here: Make wise decisions and you'll ultimately join that holy crowd.

Walking over the Bridge of Sighs, you'll enter the prisons. In the privacy of his own home, a doge could sentence, torture, and jail his opponents secretly. As you walk back over the bridge, squeeze your arm through the marble lattice window and wave to the gang of tourists gawking at you.

**Cost:** €9.50 for Museum Card that also covers the Correr Museum, or get a €15.50 Museum Pass covering several more museums; see page 116 for details. If the line is very long at the Doge's Palace, buy your Museum Card or Pass at the Correr Museum across the square. With that, you can go directly through the Doge's turnstile (you might have to push your way through the throngs).

**Hours:** April–Oct daily 9:00–19:00, Nov–March daily 9:00–17:00, last entry 90 min before closing.

**Tours:** Audioguides cost €5.50. For a live tour, consider the "Secret Itineraries Tour," which follows the doge's footsteps through rooms not included in the general admission price. Call 041-522-4951 at least two or three days in advance to confirm times and reserve a spot; they take only 25 people per tour (€12.50, at 10:00 and 11:30 in English, 1.25 hrs). The cost includes admission only to the Doge's Palace (and allows you to bypass the long line).

While the tour skips the main halls inside, it finishes inside the palace and you're welcome to visit the halls on your own.

▲▲**Correr Museum (Museo Civico Correr)**—The city history museum is now included (whether you like it or not) with the admission to the Doge's Palace. In the Napoleon Wing, you'll see fine neoclassical works by Canova. Then peruse armor, banners, and paintings re-creating festive days of the Venetian republic. The top floor lays out a good overview of Venetian art, including several paintings by the Bellini family. And just before the cafeteria is a room filled with traditional games. There are English descriptions and great Piazza San Marco views throughout (€9.50 Museum Card includes Doge's Palace, or €15.50 Museum Card includes more museums, see page 116 for details, April–Oct daily 9:00–19:00, Nov–March 9:00–17:00, last entry 90 min before closing, enter at far end of square directly opposite church, tel. 041-522-5625).

▲**Campanile di San Marco**—The lofty bell tower was once half as tall—a lighthouse marking the entry of the Grand Canal and part of the original fortress/palace which guarded its entry. Ride the elevator 92 meters (300 feet) to the top of the bell tower for the best view in Venice. This tower crumbled into a pile of bricks in 1902, a thousand years after it was built. For an ear-shattering experience, be on top when the bells ring (€6, June–Sept daily 9:00–21:00, Oct–May until 19:00). The golden angel at its top always faces into the wind. Beat the crowds and enjoy crisp air at 9:00.

## More Sights—Venice

▲▲**Accademia (Galleria dell' Accademia)**—Venice's top art museum, packed with highlights of the Venetian Renaissance, features paintings by Bellini, Veronese, Tiepolo, Giorgione, Testosterone, and Canaletto. It's just over the wooden Accademia Bridge. Expect long lines in the late morning because they allow only 300 visitors in at a time; visit early or late to miss crowds (€6.20, Mon 8:15–14:00, Tue–Sun 8:15–19:15, shorter hours off-season, last entry 45 min before closing, no photos allowed, vaporetto stop: Accademia, tel. 041-522-2247). The dull audioguides (€3.60, €5.20 with 2 earphones, or €6 for a palm-pilot) don't let you fast-forward to works you want to hear about; you have to listen to the whole spiel for each room.

There's a decent pizzeria at the bridge (Pizzeria Accademia Foscarini; see "Eating in Venice," page 152), a public WC under it, and usually a classic shell game being played on top of it (study the system as partners in the crowd win big money). Nearby sights include the Peggy Guggenheim Museum and La Salute Church.

▲**Peggy Guggenheim Museum**—This popular collection of

far-out art offers one of Europe's best reviews of the art styles of
the 20th century. Stroll through Cubism (Picasso, Braque), surreal-
ism (Dalí, Ernst), futurism (Boccione, Carra), American abstract
expressionism (Pollock), and a sprinkling of Klee, Calder, and
Chagall (€6.50, April–Oct Wed–Mon 10:00–18:00, Sat until 22:00,
closed Tue, audioguide-€4, guidebook-€18, free 15 minute tours
given daily in English at 12:00 and 16:00, free baggage check,
pricey café, photos allowed only in garden and terrace—a fine
and relaxing perch overlooking Grand Canal, 5-minute walk from
Accademia, tel. 041-240-5411). The place is run (cheaply) by
American interns working on art history degrees.

▲▲**Frari Church (Chiesa dei Frari)**—My favorite art experience in Venice is seeing art *in situ*—the setting for which it was
designed—and my favorite example is the Chiesa dei Frari. The
Franciscan "church of the friars" and the art that decorates it are
warmed by the spirit of St. Francis. It features the work of three
great Renaissance masters: Donatello, Bellini, and Titian, each
showing worshipers the glory of God in human terms.

In Donatello's wood carving of St. John the Baptist (just to
the right of the high altar), the prophet of the desert—dressed
in animal skins and almost anorexic from his diet of bugs 'n'
honey—announces the coming of the Messiah. Donatello was
a Florentine working at the dawn of the Renaissance.

Bellini's *Madonna and the Saints* painting (in the chapel
farther to the right) came later, done by a Venetian in a more
Venetian style—soft focus without Donatello's harsh realism.
While Renaissance humanism demanded Madonnas and saints
that were accessible and human, Bellini places them in a physical
setting so beautiful it creates its own mood of serene holiness.
The genius of Bellini, perhaps the greatest Venetian painter, is
obvious in the pristine clarity, rich colors (notice Mary's clothing),
believable depth, and reassuring calm of this three-paneled altarpiece. It's so good to see a painting in its natural setting.

Finally, glowing red and gold like a stained-glass window
over the high altar, Titian's *Assumption* sets the tone of exuberant
beauty found in the otherwise sparse church. Titian the Venetian—
a student of Bellini—painted steadily for 60 years . . . you'll see a lot
of his art. As stunned apostles look up past the swirl of arms and
legs, the complex composition of this painting draws you right to
the radiant face of the once dying, now triumphant Mary as she
joins God in heaven.

Be comfortable discreetly freeloading off of passing tours.
For many, these three pieces of art make a visit to the Accademia
Gallery unnecessary (or they may whet your appetite for more).
Before leaving, check out the neoclassical, pyramid-shaped tomb of

Canova and (opposite that) the grandiose tomb of Titian. Compare the carved marble Assumption behind Titian's tombstone portrait with the painted original above the high altar (€2.10, Mon–Sat 9:00–18:00, Sun 13:00–18:00, closed Sun in Aug, last entry 15 min before closing, no visits during services, audioguides €1.60/person, €2.60/double set, modest dress recommended, tel. 041-523-4864).

▲**Scuola di San Rocco**—Next to the Frari Church, another lavish building bursts with art, including some 50 Tintorettos. The best paintings are upstairs, especially the *Crucifixion* in the smaller room. View the neck-breaking splendor with one of the mirrors (*specchio*) available at the entrance (€5.20, includes free and informative audioguide, daily 9:00–17:00, or see a concert here and enjoy the art as an evening bonus—see "Nightlife in Venice," below). For *molto* Tiepolo (14 stations of the cross), drop by the nearby Church of San Polo.

▲**Ca' Rezzonico, the Museum of 18th-Century Venice**—This grand Grand Canal palazzo offers the best look in town at the life of Venice's rich and famous in the 1700s. Wandering among furnishings from that most decadent century, you'll see the art of Guardi, Canaletto, Longhi, and Tiepolo (€6.70, April–Oct Wed–Mon 10:00–18:00, Nov–March 10:00–17:00, closed Tue, last entry 60 min before closing, audioguide-€5.50, vaporetto: Ca' Rezzonico, tel. 041-520-4036).

**Dalmatian School (Scuola Dalmata dei San Giorgio)**—This school (which means "meeting place") is a reminder that Venice was Europe's most cosmopolitan place in its heyday. It was here that the Dalmatian community (people from the present-day region of Croatia) worshiped in their own way, held neighborhood meetings, and worked to preserve their culture. The chapel on the ground floor has the most exquisite Renaissance interior in Venice, with a cycle painted by Carpaccio ringing the room (€3, Tue–Sat 9:30–12:30 & 15:30–18:30, Sun 9:30–12:30, closed Mon, between St. Mark's Square and Arsenale, on Calle dei Furlani, 3 blocks southeast of Campo San Lorenzo, tel. 041-522-8828).

**Jewish Ghetto**—The word "ghetto," which comes from *getti* (the jets of the brass foundry once located here), was inherited by Venice's Jewish community when it was confined to the site of Venice's former copper foundries in 1516. Notice how this ghetto island, dominated by the Campo di Ghetto Nuovo square and connected with the rest of Venice by only three bridges, would be easy to isolate. While little survives from that time or the Jewish community, in its day the square was densely populated—lined with proto-skyscrapers seven to nine stories high. This original ghetto becomes most interesting after touring the Jewish Museum (€3, June–Sept Sun–Fri 10:00–19:30, Oct–May Sun–Fri 10:00–17:30,

closed Sat, English guided tours for €8 leave hourly 10:30–16:30, later in summer, Campo di Ghetto Nuovo, tel. 041-715-359).
**Santa Elena**—For a pleasant peek into a completely untouristy, residential side of Venice, catch the boat from St. Mark's Square to the neighborhood of Santa Elena (at the fish's tail). This 100-year-old suburb lives as if there were no tourism. You'll find a kid-friendly park, a few lazy restaurants, and beautiful sunsets over San Marco.

## Gondola Rides

A rip-off for some, this is a traditional must for romantics. Gondo-liers charge about €62 for a 50-minute ride during the day; from 20:00 on, figure on €77 to €105 (for *musica*—singer and accor-dionist, it's an additional €88 during day, €98 after 20:00). You can divide the cost—and the romance—among up to six people. Glide through nighttime Venice with your head on someone else's shoulder. Follow the moon as it sails past otherwise unseen build-ings. Silhouettes gaze down from bridges while window glitter spills onto the black water. You're anonymous in the city of masks as the rhythmic thrust of your striped-shirted gondolier turns old crows into songbirds. This is extremely relaxing (and I think worth the extra cost to experience at night). Since you might get a narra-tion plus conversation with your gondolier, talk with several and choose one you like who speaks English well. Women, beware... while gondoliers can be extremely charming, local women say any-one who falls for one of these guys "has hams over her eyes."

For a glimpse at the most picturesque gondola workshop in Venice, visit the Accademia neighborhood. Walk down the Accademia side of the canal called Rio San Trovaso. As you approach Giudecca Canal, you'll see the beached gondolas on your right across the canal.

For cheap gondola thrills, stick to the €1.60 one-minute ferry ride on a Grand Canal *traghetto* or hang out on a bridge along the gondola route and wave at (or drop leftover pigeon seed on) romantics.

## Festivals

Venice's most famous festival is **Carnevale** (Feb 21–March 4 in 2003). Carnevale, which means "farewell to meat," originated centuries ago as a wild two-month-long party leading up to the austerity of Lent. In Carnevale's heyday—the 1600s and 1700s—you could do pretty much anything with anybody from any social class if you were wearing a mask. These days, it's a tamer 10-day celebration, culminating in a huge dance lit with fireworks on St. Mark's Square. Sporting masks and costumes, Venetians from kids to businessmen join in the fun. Drawing the biggest crowds of the year, Carnevale has nearly been a victim of its success, driving away many locals (who skip out on the craziness to go ski in the Dolomites).

In 2003, the city hosts the **Venice Biennale International Art Exhibition**, a world-class contemporary art exhibition spread over the sprawling Castello Gardens and the Arsenale. Artists representing 65 nations from around the world offer the latest in contemporary art forms: video, computer art, performance art, and digital photography, along with painting and sculpture (€13, open daily generally March–Nov 10:00–18:00, Sat until 22:00; vaporetto stop: Giardini/Biennale; for details, see www .labiennale.org). This festival is held every other year.

Venetian festival days that fill the city's hotels with visitors and its canals with decked-out boats are **Feast of the Ascension Day** (mid-May), **Feast and Regatta of the Redeemer** (parade and fireworks, July 19 and 20, 2003), and the **Historical Regatta** (old-time boats and pageantry, Sept 1–7, 2003). Each November 21 is the **Feast of Our Lady of Good Health.** On this local "Thanksgiving," a bridge is built over the Grand Canal so the city can pile into the Salute Church and remember how it survived the gruesome plague of 1630. On this day, Venetians eat smoked lamb from Dalmatia (which was the cargo of the first ship let in when the plague lifted).

Venice is always busy with special musical and artistic events. The free monthly *Un Ospite di Venezia* lists all the latest in English (free at TI or from fancy hotels).

## Shopping

Shoppers like Carnevale masks, lace (a specialty of Burano, see below, but sold in Venice as well), empty books with handmade covers, and paintings—especially of Venice. If you're buying a substantial amount from nearly any shop, bargain. It's accepted and almost expected. Offer less and offer to pay cash; merchants are very conscious of the bite taken by credit-card companies.

Popular **Venetian glass** is available in many forms: vases, tea sets, decanters, glasses, jewelry, lamps, sculptures (such as solid-glass aquariums), and on and on. Shops will ship it home for you; snap a photo of it before it's packed up. For simple, easily packable souvenirs, consider glass-bead necklaces (sold cheap at vendors' stalls, expensive at shops).

If you're serious about glass, visit the small shops on Murano Island. Murano's glass-blowing demonstrations are fun; you'll usually see a vase and a "leetle 'orse" made from molten glass.

In Venice, glass-blowing demos are given by various companies around St. Mark's Square for tour groups. **Galleria San Marco,** a tour group staple, offers great demos just off Piazza San Marco every few minutes. They have agreed to let individual travelers flashing this book sneak in with tour groups to see the show (and sales pitch). And, if you buy anything, show this book and they'll take 20 percent off the price listed. (The gallery faces the square behind the orchestra nearest the church at #153, go through it, cross the alley, get in good with the guard, and climb the stairs with the next group, daily 9:30–12:00 & 14:00–17:00, manager Adriano Veronese, tel. 041-271-8650.)

Salizada San Samuele is a nontouristy street with several artsy shops. Livio de Marchi's wood sculpture shop is delightful even when it's closed. Check out the window displays for his latest creations: socks, folded shirts, teddy bears, "paper" sacks, all carved from wood (Mon–Fri 9:30–12:30 & 13:30–18:30, nearest major landmark is Accademia Bridge—on St. Mark's side, Salizada San Samuele 3157, vaporetto stop: San Samuele; if approaching by foot, follow signs to Palazzo Grassi, tel. 041-528-5694, www.liviodemarchi.com).

## Venice Lagoon

The island of Venice sits in a lagoon—a calm section of the Adriatic protected from wind and waves by the neutral breakwater of the *lido.* Four interesting islands hide out in the lagoon.

**San Giorgio Maggiore** is the dreamy island you can see from the waterfront by St. Mark's Square. The impressive church, designed by Palladio, features art by Tintoretto and a bell tower with oh-wow views of Venice (free entry to church, daily 9:30–12:30 & 15:30–18:30, closed Sun to sightseers during Mass; Gregorian Mass sung on Sun at 11:00 and Mon–Sat at 8:00; €3 for bell tower lift, closes 30 min before church's closing time). To reach the island from St. Mark's Square, take the five-minute vaporetto ride on #82, departing from the "San Marco (M.V.E.)" stop, 200 meters (650 feet) east of St. Mark's Square, at the third bridge along the waterfront (Note: This is not the same vaporetto stop as "San Marco.")

The islands of **Murano, Burano,** and **Torcello** are reached easily, cheaply, and slowly by vaporetto. Pick up a free map of the islands from any TI. Depart from San Zaccaria dock nearest the Bridge of Sighs/Doge's Palace. Line #12 connects all three islands, or take #41 to Murano (get off at Murano Colonna), then #12 to the other islands. If you plan to visit even two of these islands, get a 24-hour €9.30 vaporetto pass or a 12-hour €7.75 "Itinerary Ticket" for convenience. Four-hour speedboat tours of these three lagoon destinations leave twice a day from the dock near the

## Venice Lagoon

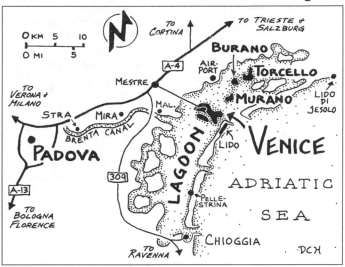

Doge's Palace—look for the signs and booth (€16, usually at 9:30 and 14:30; off-season 1/day at 14:30, tel. 041-523-8835 or 041-522-2159); the tours are speedy indeed, stopping for roughly 35 minutes at each island.

**Murano**, famous for its glass factories, has the Glass Museum, which displays the very best of 700 years of Venetian glassmaking and exhibits of ancient and modern glass art (Museo Vetrario, €4, covered by €15.50 Museum Pass, Thu–Tue 10:00–17:00, last entry 30 min before closing, closed Wed, tel. 041-739-586). You'll be tempted by salesmen offering free speedboat shuttles from Piazza San Marco to Murano. If you're interested in glass, it's handy. You must watch the show, but then you're free to buy or escape and see the rest of the island. Numerous glass factories (*fabbrica* or *fornace*) offer demonstrations all over the island—check one out, and then wander up Via Fondamenta Vetrai toward the Glass Museum. Get off the beaten path by taking the backstreets behind the Duomo on Calle di Conterie for a look at village Venezia. Head to the Faro vaporetto stop and take the #12 to either Burano or Torcello or the #41 back to San Zaccaria.

**Burano**, famous for its lace, is a sleepy island with a sleepy community—village Venice without the glitz. Lace fans enjoy the Lace Museum (Scuola di Merletti, €4.10, covered by €15.50 Museum Pass, Wed–Mon 10:00–17:00, closed Tue, tel. 041-730-034). The park next to Burano's only vaporetto dock is perfect for a waterfront picnic. While the main drag leading from the vaporetto stop into town is lined with shops and packed with tourists, simply wander to the far side of the island and the mood shifts. Explore to the right of the leaning tower for a peaceful yet intensely pastel, small-town lagoon world. Benches lining a little promenade at the water's edge make another tranquil picnic spot. As you head back to the dock, notice the marble tables on Campo Pescaria where the fish market used to be held. Hungry? Try the huge *bruschetta* at Bruschetteria al Vecio Pipa (daily 11:30–16:30, Fondamente San Mauro 397, tel. 041-730-045).

**Torcello** is dead except for its church, which claims to be the oldest in Venice (€5.20 for church, tower, and museum, daily 10:30–17:30 but museum closed Mon, tel. 041-730-761). It's impressive for its mosaics, but not worth a look on a short visit unless you really love mosaics and can't make it to Ravenna.

## Nightlife in Venice

Venice is quiet at night, as tour groups are back in the cheaper hotels of Mestre on the mainland, and the masses of day-trippers return to their beach resorts. **Gondolas** can cost nearly double, but are doubly romantic and relaxing under the moon. Vaporettos are uncrowded, and it's a great time to cruise the Grand Canal on slow boat #1.

Take your pick of traditional Vivaldi **concerts** in churches throughout town. Vivaldi is as trendy here as Strauss in Vienna and Mozart in Salzburg. In fact, you'll find frilly young Vivaldis all over town hawking concert tickets. The TI has a list of this week's Baroque concerts (tickets from €18, shows start at 21:00 and generally last 90 min). If you see a concert at Scuola di San Rocco, you can enjoy the art (which you're likely to pay €5.20 for during the day) for free during the intermission. The general rule of thumb: musicians in wigs and tights offer better spectacle, musicians in black-and-white suits are better performers. Consider the venue carefully.

On St. Mark's Square, the dueling **café orchestras** entertain. Every night, enthusiastic musicians play the same songs, creating the same irresistible magic. Hang out for free behind the tables (which allows you to easily move on to the next orchestra when the musicians take a break) or spring for a seat and enjoy a fun and gorgeously set concert. If you sit awhile, it can be €10 well spent (€6 drink plus a one-time €4 fee for entertainment).

**Caffè Florian,** on St. Mark's Square, is the most famous Venetian café and one of the first places in Europe to serve coffee. It's been the place for a discreet rendezvous in Venice since 1720. Today, it's most famous for its outdoor seating and orchestra, but do walk through its 18th-century, richly decorated rooms, where Casanova, Lord Byron, Charles Dickens, and Woody Allen have all paid too much for a drink (reasonable prices at bar in back, tel. 041-520-5641).

You're not a tourist, you're a living part of a soft Venetian night...an alley cat with money. Streetlamp halos, live music, floodlit history, and a ceiling of stars make St. Mark's magic at midnight. In the misty light, the moon has a golden hue. Shine with the old lanterns on the gondola piers where the sloppy Grand Canal splashes at the Doge's Palace... reminiscing. Comfort the small statues of the four frightened tetrarchs (ancient Byzantine emperors) where the Doge's Palace hits the basilica. Cuddle history.

## Sleeping in Venice
### (€1 = about $1, country code: 39)
Sleep Code: **S** = Single, **D** = Double/Twin, **T** = Triple, **Q** = Quad, **b** = bathroom, **s** = shower only, **CC** = Credit Cards accepted, **no CC** = Credit Cards not accepted, **SE** = Speaks English, **NSE** = No English. Breakfast is included unless otherwise noted. Air-conditioning, when available, is usually only turned on in summer.

To help you sort easily through these listings, I've divided the rooms into three categories based on the price for a standard double room with bath:

**Higher Priced**—Most rooms more than €180.

**Moderately Priced**—Most rooms €180 or less.

**Lower Priced**—Most rooms €130 or less.

Reserve a room as soon as you know when you'll be in town. Book direct—not through any tourist agency. Most places take a credit card number for a deposit. If everything's full, don't despair. Call a day or two in advance and fill in a cancellation. If you arrive on an overnight train, your room may not be ready. Drop your bag at the hotel and dive right into Venice.

I've listed prices for peak season: April, May, June, September, and October. Prices can get soft in July, August, and winter. Hotels sometimes give discounts if you stay at least three nights and/or pay cash. If on a budget, ask for a cheaper room or a discount. Always ask.

Virtually all of these hotels are central. See the map on page 122 for hotel locations. I've listed rooms mainly in two neighborhoods: in the Rialto–San Marco action and in a quiet Dorsoduro area behind the Accademia Gallery. If a hotel has a Web site, check it. Hotel Web sites are particularly valuable for Venice, because they often come with a map that at least gives you the illusion you can easily find the place.

## Sleeping between St. Mark's Square and Campo Santa Maria di Formosa
*(zip code: 30122 unless otherwise noted)*

**MODERATELY PRICED**

**Locanda Piave**, with 27 fine rooms above a bright and classy lobby, is fresh, modern, and comfortable (Db-€139–155, Tb-€190, Qb-€210, family suites-€250 for 4, €280 for 5–6, prices good through 2003 with this book, CC but discount with cash, air-con; vaporetto #51 or #1 to San Zaccaria, to the left of Hotel Danieli is Calle de le Rasse—take it, turn left at end, turn right nearly immediately at square—S.S. Filippo e Giacomo—on Calle Rimpeto La Sacrestie, go over bridge, take second left, hotel is 2 short blocks ahead on Ruga Giuffa 4838/40, Castello, tel. 041-528-5174, fax 041-523-8512, www.elmoro.com/alpiave, e-mail: hotel.alpiave @iol.it, Mirella, Paolo, and Ilaria SE, faithful Molly NSE). They have a couple of apartments for €200 to €232 (for 3–4 people, includes breakfast and kitchenette, cheaper in Aug).

**Locanda Casa Querini,** run by Patty, is an air-conditioned, plush, 11-room place on a quiet square tucked away behind St. Mark's (Db-€130, this special price good only with this book and payment in cash; CC, 3-min walk from St. Mark's Square, exactly halfway between San Zaccaria vaporetto stop and Campo Santa Maria Formosa at Campo San Giovanni Novo 4388, Castello, 30100 Venezia, tel. 041-241-1294, fax 041-241-4231, e-mail: casaquerini@hotmail.com, Silvia SE).

**LOWER PRICED**

**Hotel Riva**, with gleaming marble hallways and bright modern rooms, is romantically situated on a canal along the gondola serenade route. You could actually dunk your breakfast rolls in the canal (but don't). Sandro may hold a corner *(angolo)* room if you ask, and there are also a few rooms overlooking the canal. Confirm prices and reconfirm reservations, as readers have had trouble with both (Sb-€78, 2 D with adjacent showers-€95, Db-€110, Tb-€157, Qb-€190, Ponte dell' Angelo, also spelled Anzolo, Castello 5310, 30122 Venezia, tel. 041-522-7034, fax 041-528-5551). To reach the hotel from St. Mark's Square, face St. Mark's Basilica, walk behind it on the left along Calle de la Canonica, take the first left (at blue "Pauly & C" mosaic in street), continue straight, go over the bridge, and angle right to the hotel.

**Corte Campana** has three comfy, quiet rooms just behind St. Mark's Square (Db-€70–130, Tb-€105–150, Qb-€140–200, buffet breakfast-€11; facing St. Mark's Basilica, take Calle Canonica—to the far left of the church—turn left on Calle dell'

Anzolo and another right on Calle del Remedio, follow signs to Hotel Remedio and enter little courtyard to your right, go up three flights of steps and ring bell at Calle del Remedio 4410, Castello, tel. 041-523-3603, cellular 389-272-6500, e-mail: cortecampana70@hotmail.com, enthusiastic Riccardo SE).

## Sleeping on or near the Waterfront, East of St. Mark's Square
### (zip code: 30122)

These places, about one canal down from the Bridge of Sighs, on or just off the Riva degli Schiavoni waterfront promenade, rub drainpipes with Venice's most palatial five-star hotels. The first two, while a bit pricey because of their location, are professional and comfortable. Ride the vaporetto to San Zaccaria (#51 from train station, #82 from Tronchetto car park).

**MODERATELY PRICED**

**Hotel Campiello,** a lacy and bright little 16-room, air-conditioned place, was once part of a 19th-century convent. It's ideally located 50 meters (165 feet) off the waterfront (Sb-€119, Db-€119–180, CC, 8 percent discount with cash, 30 percent discount mid-Nov–Feb excluding Christmas and Carnevale; behind Hotel Savoia, up Calle del Vin off the waterfront street—Riva degli Schiavoni 4647, San Zaccaria, tel. 041-520-5764, fax 041-520-5798, www.hcampiello.it, e-mail: campiello@hcampiello.it, family-run for 4 generations, sisters Monica and Nicoletta).

**Albergo Paganelli** is right on the waterfront—on Riva degli Schiavoni—and has a few incredible view rooms (S-€90, Sb-€125, Db-€150–181, Db with view-€200, request *con vista* for view, CC, air-con, prices often soft, at San Zaccaria vaporetto stop, Riva degli Schiavoni 4182, Castello, tel. 041-522-4324, fax 041-523-9267, www.hotelpaganelli.com, e-mail: hotelpag@tin.it). With spacious rooms, carved and gilded headboards, chandeliers, and hair dryers, this elegant place is a good value. Seven of their 22 rooms are in a less interesting but equally comfortable *dipendenza* (annex), a block off the canal.

**Hotel Fontana** is a cozy, two-star, family-run place with 14 rooms and lots of stairs on a touristy square two bridges behind St. Mark's Square (Sb-€55–110, Db-€85–170, family rooms, fans, 10 percent discount with cash, quieter rooms on canal side, piazza views can be noisier, 2 rooms have terraces, see Web site for off-season deals, CC; vaporetto #51 to San Zaccaria, find Calle de le Rasse—to left of Hotel Danieli—take it, turn right at end, continue to first square, Campo San Provolo 4701, Castello, tel. 041-522-0579, fax 041-523-1040, www.hotelfontana.it, e-mail: htlcasa@gpnet.it).

**LOWER PRICED**
**Albergo Doni** is a dark, hardwood, clean, and quiet place with 12 dim-but-classy rooms run by a likable smart aleck named Gina (D-€80, Db-€107, T-€108, Tb-€142, ceiling fans, secure telephone reservations with CC but must pay in cash, Riva degli Schiavoni, Calle del Vin 4656, San Zaccaria N., tel. & fax 041-522-4267, e-mail: albergodoni@libero.it, Nicolo and Gina SE). Leave Riva degli Schiavoni on Calle del Vin and go 100 meters (330 feet) with a left jog.

**Albergo Corona** is a homey, confusing, Old World place with eight basic rooms, lots of stairs, and no breakfast (D-€63, vaporetto #1 to San Zaccaria dock, take Calle de le Rasse—to left of Hotel Danieli, turn left at end, take right at square—Campo S.S. Filippo e Giacomo—on Calle Rimpeto La Sacrestie, take first right, then next left on Calle Corona to #4464, tel. 041-522-9174).

## Sleeping North of St. Mark's Square
### (zip code: 30124)

**MODERATELY PRICED**
**Locanda Gambero**, with 32 rooms, is a comfortable and very central three-star hotel run by Sandro (Sb-€77–140, Db-€115–180, Tb-€155–249, Internet in lobby, air-con, CC, 5 percent discount for payment in cash; from Rialto vaporetto #1 dock, go straight inland on Calle le Bembo, which becomes Calle dei Fabbri; or from St. Mark's Square go through Sotoportego dei Dai then down Calle dei Fabbri to #4687, at intersection with Calle del Gambero, tel. 041-522-4384, fax 041-520-0431, e-mail: hotelgambero @tin.it, Christian and Luciana run the day shift, cheery Giorgio the night shift, all SE). Gambero runs the pleasant, Art Deco–style La Bistrot on the corner, which serves old-time Venetian cuisine.

**LOWER PRICED**
**Hotel Astoria** has 24 simple rooms tucked away a few blocks off St. Mark's Square (D-€103, Db-€124, some suites available, €10 discount July–Aug if you pay cash, closed mid-Nov–mid-March, CC, 2 blocks from San Zulian Church at Calle Fiubera #951; from Rialto vaporetto #1 dock, go straight inland on Calle le Bembo, which becomes Calle dei Fabbri, turn left on Calle Fiubera, tel. 041-522-5381, fax 041-528-8981, www.hotelastoriavenezia.it, e-mail: info@hotelastoriavenezia.it, Alberto and Enrico SE).

## Sleeping West of St. Mark's Square
*(zip code: 30124)*

**HIGHER PRICED**
**Hotel Bel Sito**, friendly for a three-star hotel, has Old World character and a picturesque location—facing a church on a small square between St. Mark's Square and the Accademia. With solid wood furniture, its rooms feel elegant (Sb-€130, Db-€195, CC, air-con, elevator, some rooms with views; vaporetto #1 to Santa Maria del Giglio stop, take narrow alley to square, hotel at far end to your right, Santa Maria del Giglio 2517, San Marco, tel. 041-522-3365, fax 041-520-4083, e-mail: belsito@iol.it).

## Sleeping Northwest of St. Mark's Square
*(zip code: 30124)*

**LOWER PRICED**
**Alloggi alla Scala**, a seven-room place run by Signora Andreina della Fiorentina, is homey, central, and tucked away on a quiet square that features a famous spiral stairway called Scala Contarini del Bovolo (small Db-€77, big Db-€87, extra bed-€26, breakfast-€7.75, CC, 5 percent discount for payment in cash, tell her when you reserve if you'll be paying by credit card, sometimes overbooks and sends overflow to her sister's lesser accommodations, Campo Manin 4306, San Marco, tel. 041-521-0629, fax 041-522-6451, daughter Emma SE). To find the hotel from Campo Manin, follow signs to (on statue's left) "Scala Contarini del Bovolo" (€2.10, daily 10:00–17:30, views from top).

## Sleeping near the Rialto Bridge
*(zip code: 30125 unless otherwise noted)*
The first three hotels are on the west side of the Rialto Bridge (away from St. Mark's Square) and the last three are on the east side of the bridge (on St. Mark's side). Vaporetto #82 quickly connects the Rialto with both the train station and the Tronchetto car park.

### On West Side of Rialto Bridge

**HIGHER PRICED**
**Hotel Locanda Ovidius**, with an elegant Grand Canal view terrace, a breakfast room with a wood-beam ceiling, and nine bright, comfortable rooms, is on the Grand Canal (Sb-€77–155, Db-€130–210, Db with view-€185–260, check Web site for special offers, CC, air-con, Calle del Sturion 677a, tel. 041-523-7970, fax 041-520-4101, www.hotelovidius.com, e-mail: info@hotelovidius.com).

**Locanda Sturion**, with air-conditioning and all the modern comforts, is pricey because it overlooks the Grand Canal (Db-€132–202, Tb-€195–265, family deals, canal-view rooms cost about €16 extra, CC, 69 steps to lobby, 100 meters, 330 feet, from Rialto Bridge, opposite vaporetto dock, Calle Sturion 679, San Polo, Rialto, tel. 041-523-6243, fax 041-522-8378, www .locandasturion.com, e-mail: info@locandasturion.com, SE). They require a personal check or traveler's check for a deposit.

**LOWER PRICED**
**Albergo Guerrato**, overlooking a handy and colorful produce market one minute from the Rialto action, is run by friendly, creative, and hardworking Roberto and Piero. Giorgio takes the night shift. Their 800-year-old building is Old World simple, airy, and wonderfully characteristic (D-€82, Db-€106, big top floor Db-€127, T-€103, Tb-€133, Qb-€153, prices promised through 2003 with this book in hand, cash only; €2 maps sold in their lobby; walk over the Rialto away from St. Mark's Square, go straight about 3 blocks, turn right on Calle drio la Scimia—not Scimia, the block before—and you'll see the hotel sign, Calle drio la Scimia 240a, 30125 San Polo, tel. 041-522-7131 or 041-528-5927, fax 041-241-1408, e-mail: hguerrat@tin.it, SE). My tour groups book this place for 50 nights each year. Sorry. If you fax without calling first, no reply within three days means they are booked up. (It's best to call first.) They rent family apartments in the old center (great for groups of 4–8) for around €55 per person.

## On East Side of Rialto Bridge

**HIGHER PRICED**
**Hotel Giorgione**, a professional, four-star hotel in a 15th-century palace, has plush public spaces, pool tables, Internet access, a garden terrace, and 72 spacious rooms with all the comforts (Sb-€90–150, Db-€130–255, pricier superior rooms and suites available, extra bed-€60, 10 percent discount with Web reservations, CC, elevator, air-con, Campo S.S. Apostoli 4587, 30131 Venezia, tel. 041-522-5810, fax 041-523-9092, www.hotelgiorgione.com).

**MODERATELY PRICED**
**Hotel Canada** has 25 small, sleepable rooms (S-€87, Sb-€119, D-€129, Db-€153, Tb-€189, Qb-€236, CC, air-con-€7.75 extra per night; rooms on canal come with view and aroma; rooms facing church are noisier but fresh; Castello San Lio 5659, 30122 Venezia, tel. 041-522-9912, fax 041-523-5852, SE). This hotel is ideally located on a

small, lively square, just off Campo San Lio between the Rialto and St. Mark's Square.

**LOWER PRICED**
**Locanda Novo Venezia**, a charming eight-room place in a 15th-century palazzo, run by industrious Claudio and Ivan, is just off a super square—Campo dei S.S. Apostoli, just north of the Rialto Bridge (Db-€130 with this book, family deals for up to 6 in a room, CC, air-con, Calle dei Preti 4529, Cannaregio, 30121 Venezia, tel. 041-241-1496, fax 041-241-5989, www.locandanovo.com, e-mail: info@locandanovo.com).

## Sleeping near S.S. Giovanni e Paoli
### (zip code: 30122)

**MODERATELY PRICED**
**Locanda la Corte**, a three-star hotel, has 18 attractive, high-ceilinged, wood-beamed rooms—done in pastels—bordering a small, quiet courtyard (Sb-€104, standard Db-€175, superior Db-€185, suites available, CC, air-con; vaporetto #52 from train station to Fondamente Nove, exit boat to your left, follow waterfront, turn right after second bridge to get to S.S. Giovanni e Paolo square; facing Rosa Salva bar, take street to left—Calle Bressana, hotel is a short block away at bridge; Castello 6317, tel. 041-241-1300, fax 041-241-5982, www.locandalacorte.it).

## Sleeping near the Accademia Bridge
### (zip code: 30123 unless otherwise noted)

When you step over the Accademia Bridge, the commotion of touristy Venice is replaced by a sleepy village. This quiet area, next to the best painting gallery in town, is a 10-minute walk from St. Mark's Square and a 15-minute walk from the Rialto. The fast vaporetto #82 connects Accademia Bridge with the train station (in about 15 min) and St. Mark's Square (5 min). The hotels are located near the south end of the Accademia Bridge (see map on page 149), except for the last listing (Fondazione Levi), at the north end of the bridge (St. Mark's side).

## On South Side of Accademia Bridge

**HIGHER PRICED**
**Hotel American** is a small, cushy, three-star hotel on a lazy canal next to the delightful Campo San Vio (a tiny overlooked square facing the Grand Canal). At this Old World hotel with 30 rooms, you'll get better rates Sunday through Thursday (Sb-€105–171, Db-€155–

233, Db with view-€155–269, extra bed-€26–52, CC, air-con, free Internet access in lobby, 30 meters/100 feet off Campo San Vio and 200 meters/650 feet from Accademia Gallery; facing Accademia, go left, forced right, take 2nd left—following yellow sign to Guggenheim Museum, cross bridge, take immediate right to #628 Accademia, tel. 041-520-4733, fax 041-520-4048, check www.hotelamerican .com for deals, e-mail: reception@hotelamerican.com, Marco SE).

**Hotel Belle Arti** is a good bet if you want to be in the old center without the tourist hordes. With a grand entry and all the American hotel comforts, it's a big, 67-room, modern, three-star place sitting on a former schoolyard (Sb-€114–150, Db-€145–210, Tb-€186–255, the cheaper rates apply to July–Aug and winter, CC, plush public areas, air-con, elevator, 100 meters/330 feet behind Accademia Gallery; facing gallery, take left, then forced right, Via Dorsoduro 912, tel. 041-522-6230, fax 041-528-0043, www.hotelbellearti.com, e-mail: info@hotelbellearti.com, SE).

## MODERATELY PRICED
**Pensione Accademia** fills the 17th-century Villa Maravege. While its 27 comfortable and air-conditioned rooms are nothing extraordinary, you'll feel aristocratic gliding through its grand public spaces and lounging in its breezy garden (Sb-€83–123, standard Db-€129–181, superior Db-€155–227, one big family-of-5 room with grand canal view, family deals, CC; facing Accademia Gallery, take first right, cross first bridge, go right, Dorsoduro 1058, tel. 041-523-7846, fax 041-523-9152, www .pensioneaccademia.it, e-mail: info@pensioneaccademia.it).

**Hotel Galleria** has 10 compact and velvety rooms, most with views of the Grand Canal. Some rooms are quite narrow; ask for a larger room (S-€66–90, D-€90–97, Db-€110–140, 2 big canal-view Db-€135, includes breakfast in room, CC, fans, near Accademia Gallery, and next to recommended Foscarini restaurant, 4 extra rooms available near Peggy Guggenheim Museum with varying prices—ask, Dorsoduro 878a, tel. 041-523-2489, tel. & fax 041-520-4172, www.hotelgalleria.it, e-mail: galleria@tin.it, SE).

**Hotel Agli Alboretti** is a cozy, family-run, 24-room place in a quiet neighborhood a block behind the Accademia Gallery. With red carpeting and wood-beamed ceilings, it feels elegant (Sb-€96, 2 small Db-€123, Db-€150, Tb-€180, Qb-€210, CC, air-con; 100 meters, or 330 feet, from the Accademia vaporetto stop on Rio Terra a Foscarini at Accademia 884; facing Accademia Gallery, go left, then forced right, tel. 041-523-0058, fax 041-521-0158, www.aglialboretti.com, e-mail: alborett@gpnet.it, SE).

**Pensione La Calcina**, the home of English writer John Ruskin in 1876, comes with all the three-star comforts in a

# Accademia Area Hotels and Restaurants

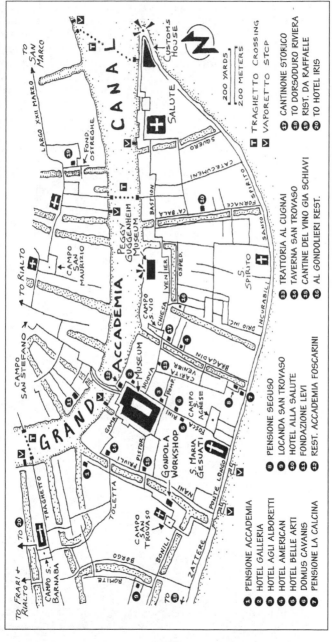

- 1  PENSIONE ACCADEMIA
- 2  HOTEL GALLERIA
- 3  HOTEL AGLI ALBORETTI
- 4  HOTEL AMERICAN
- 5  HOTEL BELLE ARTI
- 6  DOMUS CAVANIS
- 7  PENSIONE LA CALCINA

- 8  PENSIONE SEGUSO
- 9  LOCANDA SAN TROVASO
- 10 HOTEL ALLA SALUTE
- 11 FONDAZIONE LEVI
- 12 REST. ACCADEMIA FOSCARINI

- 13 TRATTORIA AL CUGNAI
- 14 TAVERNA SAN TROVASO
- 15 CANTINE DEL VINO GIA SCHIAVI
- 16 AL GONDOLIERI REST.

- 17 CANTINONE STORICO
- 18 TO DORSODURO RIVIERA
- 19 RIST. DA RAFFAELE
- 20 TO HOTEL IRIS

- ▣  TRAGHETTO CROSSING
- ▼  VAPORETTO STOP

professional yet intimate package. Its 29 rooms are squeaky clean, with good wood furniture, hardwood floors, and a peaceful canal-side setting facing Giudecca (S-€65–77, Sb-€97, Sb with view-€110, Db-€130–145, Db with view-€160–185, prices vary with room size and season, CC, air-con, rooftop terrace, killer sundeck on canal and canalside buffet-breakfast terrace, Dorsoduro 780, at south end of Rio di San Vio, tel. 041-520-6466, fax 041-522-7045, e-mail: la.calcina@libero.it). They also rent apartments nearby (max 2 people, €140–250, air-con and amenities). From the Tronchetto car park or station, catch vaporetto #51 or #82 to Zattere (at vaporetto stop, exit right and walk along canal to hotel).

**Pensione Seguso**, next door to Pensione La Calcina, is almost an Addams-Family-on-vacation time warp. Signora Seguso runs her place as her parents did, with the beds, freestanding closets, lamps, and drapes all feeling like your great-grand-mother's. The upside is the commanding canalside setting. The downside is that dinner is required during high season (Db with dinner-€210 maximum price for 2 people, slow season Db-€140 without dinner, CC, elevator, Zattere 779, tel. 041-522-2340, fax 041-528-6096, e-mail: what's that?).

**Hotel Alla Salute**, a basic retreat buried deep in Dorso-duro, is ideal for those wanting a quiet Venice with three-star comforts (Db-€135, facing the canal Rio delle Fornace near La Salute church, tel. 041-523-5404, fax 041-522-2271, e-mail: hotel.salute.dacici@iol.it).

**Locanda San Barnaba** rents 13 pleasant rooms about 50 meters (165 feet) from the Ca' Rezzonico vaporetto stop (Sb-€70–110, Db-€120–160, superior Db-€130–170, junior suite-€160–210, includes breakfast, CC, air-con, private garden, Calle del Traghetto 2785-2786, tel. 041-241-1233, fax 041-241-3812, www.locanda-sanbarnaba.com, e-mail: info@locanda-sanbarnaba.com).

**LOWER PRICED**
**Domus Cavanis**, across the street from—and owned by—Hotel Belle Arti, is a big, practical, plain place with a garden, renting 30 quiet and simple rooms (Db-€103, extra bed-€50, includes breakfast at Hotel Belle Arti, elevator, TV, phones, reception closes at 23:00, Dorsoduro 895, tel. 041-522-7374, fax 041-522-8505, e-mail: info@hotelbellearti.com).

**Locanda San Trovaso** is sparkling new, with seven classy, spacious rooms—three with canal views—and a peaceful location on a small canal (Sb-€77–95, Db-€115–130, CC, small roof terrace, Dorsoduro 1351; take vaporetto #82 from Tronchetto or #51 from Piazzale Roma or train station, get off at Zattere, exit left, cross bridge, turn right at tiny Calle Trevisan, cross bridge, cross adjacent bridge, take immediate right, then first left, tel. 041-277-1146, fax 041-277-7190, www.locandasantrovaso.com, e-mail: s.trovaso@tin.it, Mark and his son Alessandro SE).

## On North Side of Accademia Bridge

**MODERATELY PRICED**
Recently opened **Locanda Art Déco**, on a street filled with antique and art shops near St. Mark's Square and the Accademia, rents lovingly furnished rooms (Db-€67–165, Tb-€103–215 depending on room and season, CC, air-con, Calle delle Botteghe 2966, near Campo San Stefano, 30124 Venezia, tel. 041-277-0558, fax 041-270-2891, www.locandaartdeco.com, e-mail: info @locandaartdeco.com).

**LOWER PRICED**
**Fondazione Levi**, a guest house run by a foundation that promotes research on Venetian music, offers 21 quiet, institutional yet comfortable rooms (Sb-€57, Db-€93, Tb-€108, Qb-€127, twin beds only, elevator; 80 meters/260 feet from base of Accademia Bridge on St. Mark's side; from Accademia vaporetto stop, cross Accademia Bridge, take immediate left—cross bridge Ponte Giustinian and then go down Calle Giustinian directly to the Fondazione, buzz the "Foresteria" door to the right, San Vidal 2893, 30124 Venezia, tel. 041-786-711, fax 041-786-766, e-mail: foresterialevi@libero.it, SE).

## Sleeping between Frari Church and the Grand Canal
*(zip code: 30125)*

**MODERATELY PRICED**
**Hotel Iris** is a cozy respite, with 19 rooms off the beaten path (S-€70, Sb-€93, D-€99, Db-€135, includes breakfast, air-con, CC; from Campo dei Frari, head south to Campo San Tomá, then take right on Calle del Campanile to Rio della Frescada, hotel is on other side of Ristorante Giardinetto before first bridge to the right, San Polo 2910/A, tel. & fax 041-522-2882, www.irishotel.com).

## Sleeping near the Train Station
*(zip code: 30121)*

**MODERATELY PRICED**
**Hotel San Geremia**, a three-minute walk from the station, offers 20 rooms at decent prices near the Ferrovia vaporetto stop. Head

left outside the station and follow Lista di Spagna to Campo San Geremia. With the bridge in front of you, the hotel is to your left at Campo San Geremia 290/A (Db-€110–145, the higher price is for weekends, CC, self-service laundry and Internet café nearby, tel. 041-716-245, fax 041-524-2342, e-mail: sangeremia@yahoo.it).

## Cheap Dormitory Accommodations

**Foresteria della Chiesa Valdese**, warmly run by the Methodist church, offers dorms and doubles, halfway between St. Mark's Square and the Rialto Bridge. This run-down but charming old place has elegant ceiling paintings (dorm bed-€18, D-€52, Db-€67, family apartment-€103 for 5, must check in and out when office is open: 9:00–13:00 & 18:00–20:00, from Campo Santa Maria di Formosa, walk past Bar all' Orologio to end of Calle Lunga and cross bridge, Castello 5170, 30122 Venezia, tel. & fax 041-528-6797, fax 041-241-6328, e-mail: veneziaforesteria@chiesavaldese.org).

Venice's **youth hostel** on Giudecca Island is crowded and inexpensive (€16 beds with sheets and breakfast in 10- to 16-bed rooms, membership required, office open daily 7:00–9:30 & 13:30–23:00, catch vaporetto #82 from station to Zittele, tel. 041-523-8211). The budget cafeteria welcomes non-hostelers (nightly 17:00–23:30).

# Eating in Venice

While touristy restaurants are the scourge of Venice, and most restaurateurs believe you can't survive in Venice without catering to tourists, there are plenty of places that are still popular with locals and respect the tourists who happen in. First trick: Walk away from triple-language menus. Second trick: Order the daily special. Third trick: Most seafood dishes are the local catch-of-the-day.

For romantic—and usually pricey—meals along the water, see "Eating with a Romantic Canalside Setting," below. For dessert, it's gelato (see end of this chapter).

## Eating between Campo Santi Apostoli and Campo S.S. Giovanni e Paolo

For locations, see map on page 155.

**Antiche Cantine Ardenghi de Lucia e Michael** is a leap of local faith and an excellent splurge. Effervescent Michael and his wife, Lucia, proudly cook Venetian for a handful of people each night by reservation only. You must call first. You pay €50 per person and trust them to wine, dine, and serenade you with Venetian class. The evening can be quiet or raucous depending on who and how many are eating. While the menu is heavy on crustaceans, Michael promises to serve plenty of veggies and fruit as well. Find #6369. There's no sign, the door's locked, and the place looks closed. But knock, say the password (*La Repubblica Serenissima*), and you'll be admitted. From Campo S.S. Giovanni e Paolo, pass the church-like hospital (notice the illusions painted on its facade), go over the bridge to the left, and take the first right on Calle della Testa to #6369 (you must reserve the day before, Tue–Sat 20:00–24:00, closed Sun–Mon, tel. 041-523-7691, cellular 389-523-7691).

The following two colorful *osterias* are good for *cicchetti* (munchies), wine-tasting, or a simple, rustic, sit-down meal surrounded by boisterous local ambience:

**Osteria da Alberto** has the best variety of *cicchetti* (18:15–19:30) and great sit-down meals from 19:30 to 23:00 (CC, closed Sun, midway between Campo Santi Apostoli and Campo S.S. Giovanni e Paolo, next to Ponte de la Panada on Calle Larga Giacinto Gallina, tel. 041-523-8153).

**Osteria al Promessi Sposi** does *cicchetti* with gusto and offers a little garden for sit-down meals (great cod and polenta). This fun place is proud to be Venetian (Thu–Tue 9:00–23:00, closed Wed, a block off Campo S.S. Apostoli and a block inland from Strada Nova at Calle dell' Oca, tel. 041-522-8609).

You'll find pubs opposite Campo St. Sofia across Strada Nova.

### Eating in Dorsoduro, near the Accademia

For restaurant locations, see map on page 149.

**Restaurant/Pizzeria Accademia Foscarini**, next to the Accademia Bridge and Galleria, offers decent €5–7 pizzas in a great canalside setting (Wed–Mon 7:00–23:00 in summer, until 21:00 in winter, closed Tue, Dorsoduro 878C, tel. 041-522-7281).

**Trattoria al Cugnai** is an unpretentious place run by three gruff sisters serving decent food (Tue–Sun 12:00–15:00 & 19:00–21:30, closed Mon, midway between Accademia Gallery and Campo San Vio, tel. 041-528-9238). Enjoy a quiet sit on Campo San Vio (benches with Grand Canal view) for dessert.

**Taverna San Trovaso** is an understandably popular restaurant/pizzeria. Arrive early or wait (CC, Tue–Sun 12:00–14:50 & 19:00–21:50, closed Mon, air-con, 100 meters/330 feet from Accademia Gallery on San Trovaso canal; facing Accademia, take a right and then a forced left at canal). On the same canal, **Enoteca Cantine del Vino Gia Schiavi**—much-loved for its *cicchetti*—is a good place for a glass of wine and appetizers (Mon–Sat 8:00–14:30 & 15:30–20:00, closed Sun, S. Trovaso 992, tel. 041-523-0034). You're welcome to enjoy your wine and finger-food while sitting on the bridge.

**Al Gondolieri** is considered one of the best restaurants for meat—not fish—in Venice. Its sauces are heavy and prices are high, but carnivores love it (Wed–Mon 12:00–13:00 & 19:00–22:00, closed Tue and for lunch Jul–Aug, reservations smart, Dorsoduro 366 San Vio, behind Guggenheim Museum on west end of Rio delle Torreselle, tel. 041-528-6396).

**Cantinone Storico**, also in this neighborhood, is described below under "Eating with a Romantic Canalside Setting."

## Eating near St. Mark's Square
**Osteria da Carla**, two blocks west of St. Mark's Square, is a fun and very local hole-in-the-wall where the food is good and the price is right. They have hearty tuna salads and a daily pasta special along with traditional antipasti, polenta, and decent wine by the glass. While you can eat outside, you don't want table #3 (Mon–Sat 8:00–22:00, closed Sun; from American Express head toward St. Mark's Square, first left down Frezzeria, first left again through "Contarina" tunnel, at Sotoportego e Corte Contarina, sign over door says "Pietro Panizzolo"—it's historic and can't be removed, tel. 041-523-7855, Carlo SE).

## Eating on Campo S. Angelo
**Ristorante Aqua Pazza** (literally, "crazy water") provides good pizza in a wonderful setting on a square (check out the leaning tower over your shoulder) midway between the Rialto, Accademia, and St. Mark's. The owner is from Naples and he delights locals with Amalfi/Naples cuisine. That means perhaps the best—and most expensive—pizza in Venice (Tue–Sun 12:00–15:00 & 19:00–23:00, closed Mon, Campo S. Angelo 3809, tel. 041-277-0688).

## Eating in Cannaregio
For great local cuisine, far beyond the crowds in a rustic Venetian setting, hike to **Osteria Al Bacco** (closed Mon, reservations recommended, Fondamenta Cappuccine, Cannaregio 3054, halfway between train station and northernmost tip of Venice, tel. 041-717-493).

Near the train station, consider **Brek**, a popular self-service cafeteria (at Lista di Spagna 124; with back to station, facing canal, go left on Rio Terra—it becomes Lista di Spagna in 2 short blocks, tel. 041-244-0158).

## Eating with a Romantic Canalside Setting
Of course, if you want a canal view, it comes with lower quality or a higher price. But the memory is sometimes most important.

**Restaurant al Vagon** is popular with tourists because nearly everyone gets a seat right on the canal. The food and prices are

## Venice Restaurants

❶ CANTINA DO MORI
❷ OSTERIA SORA AL PONTE
❸ CANTINA DO SPADE
❹ OSTARIA ALLA BOTTE
❺ ROSTICCERIA SAN BARTOLOMEO
❻ PASTICCERIA PONTE DELLE PASTE
❼ OSTERIA AL PORTEGO
❽ DEVIL'S FOREST PUB & BORA BORA PIZZERIA
❾ OSTERIA AL DIAVOLO E L'AQUASANTA
❿ BAR ALL'OROLOGIO
⓫ CIP CIAP PIZZA
⓬ OSTERIA AL MASCARON
⓭ ENOTECA MASCARETA
⓮ GELATERIA
⓯ LA BOUTIQUE GELATERIA
⓰ ANTICHE CANTINE ARDENGHI
⓱ OSTERIA DA ALBERTO
⓲ OSTERIA AL PROMESSI SPOSI
⓳ REST. AL VAGON
⓴ BENITO'S HAIR SALON
㉑ MICHIELANGELO GELATERIA

acceptable and the ambience glows (moderate prices, Wed–Mon 19:00–22:00, closed Tue, 3-min walk north of Rialto just before Campo S.S. Apostoli, overlooking canal called Rio dei Santi Apostoli, tel. 041-523-7558).

**Ristorante da Raffaele** is *the* place for classy food on a quiet canal. It's filled with top-end tourists and locals who want to pay well for the best seafood. The place was a haunt of the avant-garde a few generations ago. Today, it's on a main gondolier thorough-fare—in fact, many guests arrive or depart by gondola. Make a reservation if you want a canalside table (you do). While the multi-lingual menu is designed for the tourists, locals stick with the daily specials (expensive, CC, Fri–Wed 18:30–22:30, closed Thu, exactly halfway between Piazza San Marco and the Accademia Bridge at Ponte delle Ostreghe, tel. 041-523-2317). Before leaving, wander around inside to see the owner's fabulous old weapons collection.

**Ristorante Cantinone Storico** sits on a peaceful canal in Dorsoduro between the Accademia Bridge and the Peggy Guggenheim Museum. It's dressy, specializes in fish, has six or eight tables on the canal, and is worth the splurge (daily 12:30–14:30 & 19:30–21:30, reservations wise, on the canal Rio de S. Vio, tel. 041-523-9577).

The "Dorsoduro Riviera," the long promenade along the south side of the Dorsoduro (a 5-min walk south of Accademia Bridge), is lined with canalside restaurants away from the crush of touristic Venice. Places immediately south of the Accademia Bridge (near the Zattere vaporetto stop) are decent but more touristic. At the west end (near the S. Basilio vaporetto stop), try **Trattoria B. Basilio** and **Pizzeria Riviera** (a local fave for pizza); both come with local crowds and wet views.

For a Grand Canal view from the Rialto Bridge, consider **Al Buso**, at the northeast end of the Rialto Bridge. Of the several touristy restaurants that hug the canal near the Rialto, this is recommended by locals as offering the best value (daily 9:00–24:00, dine from 11:00–23:00, Ponte di Rialto 5338, tel. 041-528-9078).

## The Stand-Up Progressive Venetian Pub-Crawl Dinner

My favorite Venetian dinner is a pub crawl. A *giro di ombra* (pub crawl) is a tradition unique to Venice—ideal in a city with no cars. (*Ombra* means shade, from the old days when a portable wine bar scooted with the shadow of the Campanile across St. Mark's Square.)

Venice's residential backstreets hide plenty of characteristic bars with countless trays of interesting toothpick munchies *(cicchetti)*. This is a great way to mingle and have fun with the Venetians. Real *cicchetti* (chi-KET-tee) pubs are getting rare in these fast-food days, but locals appreciate the ones that survive.

I've listed plenty of pubs in walking order for a quick or extended crawl below. If you've crawled enough, most of these bars make a fine one-stop, sit-down dinner.

Try fried mozzarella cheese, gorgonzola, calamari, artichoke hearts, and anything ugly on a toothpick. Meat and fish *(pesce;* PESH-shay) munchies can be expensive; veggies *(verdure)* are cheap, around €3 for a meal-sized plate. In many places, there's a set price per food item (e.g., €1). To get a plate of assorted appetizers for €5 (or more, depending on how hungry you are), ask for: *"Un piatto classico di cicchetti misti da €5."*(Pron. oon pee-AH-toh KLAH-see-koh dee cheh-KET-tee MEE-stee da CHING-kway ay-OO-roh.) Bread sticks *(grissini)* are free for the asking.

Drink the house wines. A small glass of house red or white wine *(ombra rosso* or *ombra bianco)* or a small beer *(birrino)* costs about €1. A liter of house wine costs around €3.60. *Vin bon*, Venetian for fine wine, may run you from €1.60 to €2.60 per little glass. *Corposo* means full-bodied. A good last drink is *fragolino*, the local sweet wine—*bianco* or *rosso*. It often comes with a little cookie *(biscotti)* for dipping.

Bars don't stay open very late, and the *cicchetti* selection is best early, so start your evening by 18:00. Most bars are closed on Sunday. When just munching appetizers, you can stand around the bar or grab a table in the back—usually for the same price.

## Cicchetteria *West of the Rialto Bridge*
**Cantina do Mori**, famous with locals (since 1462) and savvy travelers (since 1982), is a classy place for fine wine and *francobollo* (a spicy selection of 20 tiny sandwiches called "stamps"). Choose from the featured wines in the barrel on the bar. Order carefully or they'll rip you off. From Rialto Bridge, walk 200 meters (650 feet) down Ruga degli Orefici away from St. Mark's Square—then ask (Mon–Sat 17:00–20:30, closed Sun, stand-up only, arrive early before the *cicchetti* are gone, San Polo 429, tel. 041-522-5401).

A few steps from the Rialto fish market, you'll find Campo delle Beccarie and two little places serving traditional munchies. On this square, as you face the restaurant Vini da Pinto, **Ostaria Sora al Ponte** is to your right, just over the bridge (each item €0.75, assemble by pointing, Tue–Sun until 22:00, closed Mon, July and Aug closed Sun), and **Cantina do Spade** is in the alley directly behind Vini da Pinto (head around building to your left, take a right through archway; closed Sun).

## *Eating near the Rialto Bridge*
### Eating East of the Rialto Bridge, near Campo San Bartolomeo
**Osteria "Alla Botte" Cicchetteria** is an atmospheric place packed with a young, local, bohemian-jazz clientele. It's good for a *cicchetti* snack with wine at the bar (see the posted, enticing selection of wines by the glass) or for a light meal in the small, smoke-free room in the back (Fri–Tue 10:00–15:00 & 18:00–23:00, closed Wed–Thu and Sun afternoons, 2 short blocks off Campo San Bartolomeo in the corner behind the statue—down Calle de la Bissa, notice the "day after" photo showing a

debris-covered Venice after the notorious 1989 Pink Floyd open-air concert, tel. 041-520-9775).

If the statue on the Campo San Bartolomeo walked backward 20 meters (60 feet), turned left, and went under a passageway, he'd hit **Rosticceria San Bartolomeo**. This cheap—if confusing—self-service restaurant has a likeably surly staff (good €5–6 pasta, great fried *mozzarella al prosciutto* for €1.40, delightful fruit salad, and €1 glasses of wine, prices listed on wall behind counter, no cover or service charge, daily 9:30–21:30, tel. 041-522-3569). Take out or grab a table.

From Rosticceria San Bartolomeo, continue over a bridge to Campo San Lio (a good landmark). Here, turn left, passing Hotel Canada and following Calle Carminati straight about 50 meters (165 feet) over another bridge. On the right is the pastry shop (*pasticceria*) and straight ahead is Osteria Al Portego (at #6015). Both are listed below:

**Pasticceria Ponte delle Paste** is a feminine and pastel *salon de tè*, popular for its pastries and aperitifs. Italians love taking 15-minute breaks to sip a *spritz* aperitif with friends after a long day's work, before heading home. Ask sprightly Monica for a *spritz al bitter* (white wine, *amaro*, and soda water, €1.30; or choose from the menu on the wall) and munch some of the free goodies on the bar around 18:00 (daily 7:00–20:30, Ponte delle Paste).

**Osteria al Portego** is a friendly, local-style bar serving great *cicchetti* and good meals (Mon–Fri 9:00–22:00, closed Sat–Sun, tel. 041-522-9038). The *cicchetti* here can make a great meal, but you should also consider sitting down for an actual dinner. They have a fine little menu.

The **Devil's Forest Pub**, an air-conditioned bit of England tucked away a block from the crowds, is—strangely—more Venetian these days than the *tipico* places. Locals come here for good English and Irish beer on tap, big salads (€6.70, lunch only), hot bar snacks, and an easygoing ambience (daily 8:00–24:00, meals 12:00–15:30, bar snacks all the time, closed Sun in Aug, no cover or service charge, fine prices, backgammon and chess boards available-€2.10, a block off Campo San Bartolomeo on Calle dei Stagneri, tel. 041-520-0623). Across the street, **Bora Bora Pizzeria** serves pizza and salads from an entertaining menu (Thu–Tue 12:00–15:00 & 19:15–22:30, closed Wed, CC, tel. 041-523-6583).

## Eating West of the Rialto Bridge

**Osteria al Diavolo e l'Aquasanta**, three blocks west of the Rialto, serves good pasta and makes a handy lunch stop for sightseers (Wed–Mon 12:00–15:00 & 18:00–24:00, closed

Mon eve and all day Tue, hiding on a quiet street just off Rua
Vecchia S. Giovanni, on Calle della Madonna, tel. 041-277-0307).

**La Rivetta Ristorante** offers several Venetian specialties
under €10 apiece. Scenically located on a canal, it's on the main
drag between the Rialto Bridge and Campo San Polo (open daily,
San Polo 1479, tel. 041-523-1481).

## Eating on or near Campo Santa Maria di Formosa

Campo Santa Maria di Formosa is just plain atmospheric (as most
squares with a Socialist Party office seem to be). For a balmy outdoor meal, you could split a pizza with wine on the square. **Bar all'
Orologio** has a good setting and friendly service but mediocre
"freezer" pizza (happy to split a pizza for pub-crawlers, Mon–Sat
6:00–23:00, closed Sun and in winter at 18:00). For a picnic pizza
snack on the square, cross the bridge behind the canalside *gelateria*
and grab a slice to go from **Cip Ciap Pizza** (Wed–Mon 9:00–
21:00, closed Tue; facing *gelateria*, take bridge to the right; Calle
del Mondo Novo). Pub-crawlers get a salad course at the fruit-
and-vegetable stand next to the water fountain (Mon–Sat, closes
about 19:30 and on Sun).

From Campo Santa Maria di Formosa, follow the yellow sign
to "S.S. Giov e Paolo" down Calle Longa Santa Maria di Formosa,
and head down the street to **Osteria al Mascaron**, a delightful
little restaurant seemingly made to order for pirates gone good
(#5225, Mon–Sat 11:30–15:00 & 19:00–23:30, closed Sun, reservations smart, tel. 041-522-5995). Their *antipasto della casa* (a €13
plate of mixed appetizers) is fun, and the *Pasta Scogliera* (€26,
rockfish spaghetti for 2) makes a grand meal.

**Enoteca Mascareta**, a wine bar with much less focus on
food, is 30 meters (100 feet) farther down the same street (#5183,
Mon–Sat 18:00–24:00, closed Sun, tel. 041-523-0744).

The *gelateria* Zanzibar on the canal at Campo Santa Maria
di Formosa is handy (open 7:00–24:00 in summer, 8:00–21:00
winter; for more, see "Gelato," below).

## Cheap Meals

A key to cheap eating in Venice is **bar snacks,** especially stand-
up mini-meals in out-of-the-way bars. Order by pointing. *Panini*
(sandwiches) are sold fast and cheap at bars everywhere. Basic,
reliable ham-and-cheese sandwiches (white bread, crusts trimmed)
come toasted—simply ask for "toast"; these make a great supplement to Venice's skimpy hotel breakfasts.

For budget eating, I like small *cicchetti* bars (see "Pub-Crawl
Dinner," above); for speed, value, and ambience, you can get a
filling plate of local appetizers at nearly any of the bars.

**Pizzerias** are cheap and easy—try for a sidewalk table at a scenic location. If you want a fast-food pizza place, try **Spizzico** on Campo San Luca.

The **produce market** that sprawls for a few blocks just past the Rialto Bridge (best 8:00–13:00, closed Sun) is a great place to assemble a picnic. The adjacent fish market is wonderfully slimy. Side lanes in this area are speckled with fine little hole-in-the-wall munchie bars, bakeries, and cheese shops.

The **Mensa DLF**, the public transportation workers' cafeteria, is cheap and open to the public (daily 11:00–14:30 & 18:00–22:00). Leaving the train station, turn right on the Grand Canal, walk about 150 meters (500 feet) along the canal, up eight steps, and through the unmarked door.

### Gelato

**La Boutique del Gelato** is one of the best *gelaterias* in Venice (daily 10:00–21:30, closed Dec–Jan, 2 blocks off Campo Santa Maria di Formosa on corner of Salizada San Lio and Calle Paradiso, next to Hotel Bruno, #5727—just look for the crowd).

For late-night gelato at Rialto, try **Michielangelo**, just off Campo San Bartolomeo, on the St. Mark's side of the Rialto Bridge on Salizada Pio X (daily 10:00–22:00). At St. Mark's Square, the **Al Todaro** *gelateria* opposite the Doge's Palace is open late (daily 8:00–24:00, 8:00–20:00 in winter, closed Mon in winter).

## Transportation Connections—Venice

**By train to: Padua** (1/hr, 30 min), **Vicenza** (1/hr, 1 hr), **Verona** (1/hr, 90 min), **Ravenna** (1/hr, 3–4 hrs, transfer in Ferrara or Bologna), **Florence** (7/day, 3 hrs), **Dolomites** (8/day to Bolzano, about hourly, 4 hrs with 1 transfer; catch bus from Bolzano into mountains), **Milan** (1/hr, 3–4 hrs), **Monterosso/Cinque Terre** (2/day, 6 hrs, departs Venice at 10:00 and 15:00), **Rome** (7/day, 5 hrs, slower overnight), **Naples** (change in Rome, plus 2–3 hrs), **Brindisi** (3/day, 11 hrs, change in Bologna), **Bern** (3/day, change in Milan, 8 hrs), **Munich** (2/day, 8 hrs), **Paris** (4/day, 11 hrs), and **Vienna** (4/day, 9 hrs). Train and *couchette* reservations (about €18) are easily made at a downtown travel agency. Italy train info: 848-888-088 (automated, in Italian).

# SIGHTS NEAR VENICE:
## PADUA, VICENZA, VERONA, AND RAVENNA

While Venice is just one of many towns in the Italian region of Veneto (pron. VEN-eh-toh), few venture off the lagoon. Four important towns and possible side trips, in addition to the lakes and the Dolomites, make zipping directly from Venice to Milan or Florence a route strewn with temptation.

## Planning Your Time

The towns of Padua, Vicenza, Verona, and Ravenna are all, for various reasons, good stops. Each town gives the visitor a low-key slice of Italy that complements the high-powered urbanity of Venice, Florence, and Rome. But none is an essential part of the best three weeks Italy has to offer.

Visiting Verona, Padua, and Vicenza couldn't be easier: All are 30 minutes apart on the Venice–Milan line (hrly, 3 hrs). Spending a day town-hopping between Venice and Bolzano or Milan—with 3-hour stops at Padua, Vicenza, and Verona—is exciting and efficient. Trains run frequently enough to allow flexibility and little wasted time. Of the towns discussed below, only Ravenna (2.5 hours from Padua or Florence) is not on the main Venice–Milan train line.

If you're Padua-bound, note that you need to reserve ahead to see the Scrovegni Chapel (see below). Most sights in Verona and Vicenza are closed on Monday.

## PADUA (Padova)

Living under Venetian rule for four centuries seemed only to sharpen Padua's independent spirit. Nicknamed "the brain of Veneto," Padua has a prestigious university (founded 1222) that was home to Galileo, Copernicus, Dante, and Petrarch. The old

## Temptations between Venice and Milan

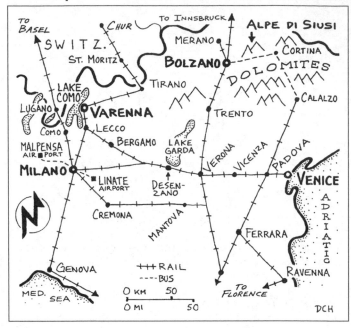

town, even when packed with modern-day students, is a colonnaded time-tunnel experience. And Padua's museums and churches
hold their own in Italy's artistic big league. Note that you need
to book ahead to visit the Scrovegni Chapel, with its great Giotto
paintings (see page 166).

**Arrival in Padua:** Enter the station lobby. To get oriented,
turn around and face the tracks. Look for the two small offices
next to each other, marked *Biglietti e Prenotazioni Internazionali*
(Tickets and International Reservations) and Tourist Information.
To the left of these is an even smaller office, marked Bus Tickets,
which sells city bus tickets (€0.85). At the **TI**, pick up a city map
and list of sights (April–Sept Mon–Sat 8:30–19:00, Sun 8:30–
12:30, Oct–March Mon–Sat 10:00–13:00 & 13:30–16:30, Sun
8:30–12:30, tel. 049-876-7927).

**Day-trippers:** The station has a baggage check office (€3.90,
daily 6:00–24:00). If you have reservations for the Scrovegni Chapel,
that will dictate the order of your sightseeing. But if you don't plan
on seeing the chapel, here's an efficient plan: Take the bus from
the station to the Basilica of St. Anthony, then walk through the
old town, sightseeing your way back to the station (buy your

€0.85 bus ticket at the Bus Ticket office in the station lobby or at a
*tabacchi* stop; catch bus #8, #12, or #18 to Via Luca Belludi, next to
Piazza del Santo and the Basilica of St. Anthony). A taxi into town
costs about €5. (If you have any train business, such as reservations,
note that a CIT travel agency is on the square in front of the station.)

## Sights—Padua

▲▲**Basilica of St. Anthony**—Friar Anthony of Padua, "Christ's
perfect follower and a tireless preacher of the Gospel," is buried
here. For nearly 800 years, his remains and this impressive church
(building started immediately after the death of the saint in 1231)
have attracted pilgrims to Padua (daily in summer 6:30–19:45,
winter 6:30–19:00, modest dress code enforced).

Nod to St. Anthony looking down from the facade, then
start your visit at the information desk just inside the cloisters
(daily 9:00–12:00 & 15:00–18:00, very helpful with an abundance
of St. Anthony–related handouts). Wander around the various
cloisters. In the far end, a fascinating little museum is filled with
votives and folk art recounting miracles attributed to Anthony.

Entering the basilica, you gaze past the crowds and through
the incense haze at Donatello's glorious crucifix hanging over
the altar, and realize this is one of the most important pilgrimage
sites in Christendom.

Along with the crucifix, Donatello's bronze statues—Mary
with Padua's six favorite saints—grace the high altar.

On the left, pilgrims file slowly by the chapel containing
St. Anthony's tomb. This Renaissance masterpiece from 1500
is circled by nine marble reliefs showing scenes and miracles
from the life of the saint. The pilgrims believe Anthony is their
protector—a confidant and intercessor of the poor. And they
believe he works miracles. Votives placed here by the faithful ask
for help or give thanks for miracles they believe he's performed.
By putting their hand on his tomb while saying a silent prayer,
pilgrims show devotion to Anthony and feel the saint's presence.

Next on the pilgrim route is the Chapel of the Reliquaries
(behind the altar), where you can see St. Anthony's robe, vocal
cords (discovered intact when his remains were examined in 1981),
jaw . . . and "uncorrupted tongue" (discovered when the remains
were examined in 1263). These relics—considered miraculously
preserved—befit the saint who couldn't stop teaching, preaching,
and praying.

Outside, on Piazza del Santo, stands Donatello's much-
admired equestrian statue of the Venetian mercenary General
Gattamelata. Even military commanders—such as this powerful
Venetian—wanted to be close to St. Anthony. This statue is

famous as the first statue of this size cast out of bronze since ancient Roman times. On the square, you'll find a handy **TI** and a couple of friendly cafés. A 10-minute stroll up Via del anto takes you back into the center.

**Palazzo della Ragione**—This grand 13th-century palazzo once held the medieval law courts. The first floor consists of a huge hall— 81 meters by 27 meters (265 feet by 90 feet)—that was once adorned with frescoes by Giotto. A fire in 1312 destroyed those paintings, and the palazzo was then decorated with the 15th-century art you see today: a series of 123 frescoes depicting the signs of the zodiac, labors of the month, symbols representing characteristics of people born under each sign, and finally, figures of saints to legitimize the power of the courts in the eyes of the Church. The hall is topped with a keel-shaped roof, which helps to support the structure without the use of columns—quite an architectural feat in its time, considering the building's dimensions. The curious stone in the right-hand corner near the entry is the "Stone of Shame," which was the seat of debtors being punished during the Middle Ages. Instead of being sentenced to death or prison (same thing back then), debtors sat upon this stone, renounced their possessions, and denounced themselves publicly before being exiled from the city. Exhibitions are often held in the palace (€3.60, Feb–Oct Tue–Sun 9:00–19:00, Nov–Jan closes at 18:00, closed Mon).

**▲▲Market Squares: Piazza Erbe and Piazza Frutta**—The stately Palazzo della Ragione (described above) provides a quintessentially Italian backdrop for Padua's almost exotic-feeling market, filling the surrounding squares—Piazza delle Erbe and Piazza della Frutta—each morning. Second only to the produce market in Italy's gastronomic capital of Bologna, this market has been renowned for centuries for having the freshest and greatest selection of herbs, fruits, and vegetables. Beneath the Palazzo della Ragione are various butchers, *salumerie* (delicatessens), cheese shops, bakeries, and fishmongers.

Make a point to explore this scene. Students gather here each evening, spilling out of colorful bars and cafés—drinks in hand— into the square. Their drink of choice is a *spritz*, an aperitif with Campari, Cynar (two bitter, alcoholic liqueurs), white wine, and sparkling water, garnished with an olive and a blood-orange wedge. **Bar Nazionale**, at #41 under the staircase of Palazzo della Ragione, offers outdoor seating for a ringside view of the action. **Bar degli Spritz**, at #36 near the middle of the palazzo at the passageway, is the students' hangout. Get your *spritz* to take away *(da portar via)* and join the young people out on the piazza. This is a classic opportunity to enjoy a real discussion with smart, English-speaking students who see tourists not as pests but as

## Padua

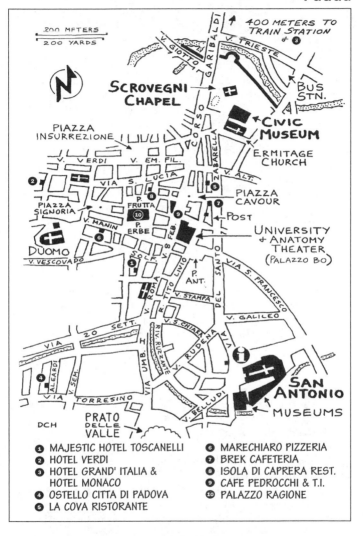

200 METERS
200 YARDS

400 METERS TO TRAIN STATION & ③

SCROVEGNI CHAPEL

BUS STN.

CIVIC MUSEUM

PIAZZA INSURREZIONE

V. VERDI
V. EM. FIL.
VIA S. LUCIA

ERMITAGE CHURCH

PIAZZA CAVOUR

P. FRUTTA
PIAZZA SIGNORIA

POST

DUOMO
V. VESCOVADO
V. MANIN
P. ERBE

UNIVERSITY & ANATOMY THEATER (PALAZZO BO)

VIA S. FRANCESCO

V. ROMA
V. 8 FEB.
SOC F.
TITO LIVIO
DEL SANTO
P. ANT.
V. STAMPA
V. GALILEO

20 SETT.
VIA
V. S. CHIARA
RIV. RIZZANTE
VIA UMB.
RUDENA
ALEARDI
V. SEM.
VIA TORRESINO
BELLUDI

SAN ANTONIO

MUSEUMS

DCH
PRATO DELLE VALLE

❶ MAJESTIC HOTEL TOSCANELLI
❷ HOTEL VERDI
❸ HOTEL GRAND' ITALIA & HOTEL MONACO
❹ OSTELLO CITTA DI PADOVA
❺ LA COVA RISTORANTE
❻ MARECHIARO PIZZERIA
❼ BREK CAFETERIA
❽ ISOLA DI CAPRERA REST.
❾ CAFE PEDROCCHI & T.I.
❿ PALAZZO RAGIONE

interesting people from far away. For an instant conversation starter, ask about the current political situation in Italy or the cultural differences between the north and the south.

Consider dropping by **Café Pedrocchi**, a sumptuously neoclassical café famous as the place where students plotted an uprising in 1848. You can still see a bullet hole in the wall of the Sala

Bianca, where one of the insurgents was killed. Nowadays you get more foam than fervor, but the café is still a marvel of interior design. Each room is decorated in a different style, from simple color schemes (the red, white, and green rooms on the ground floor represent the colors of the Italian flag) to more elaborate Egyptian or Etruscan design. The Sala Verde (green room) is the only room where people can sit and enjoy the beautiful interior without ordering anything or having to pay (at intersection of Oberdan and Febbraio 8, between Piazza delle Erbe and Piazza Cavour, tel. 049-820-5007).

**University of Padua**—This prestigious university, which requires a reservation to tour, is just across the street from Café Pedrocchi. Founded in 1222, it's one of the first, greatest, and most progressive in Europe. Back when the Church controlled university curricula, a group of professors broke free and created this liberal school, independent of Catholic constraints and accessible to people of alternative faiths. A haven for free thinking, it attracted intellectuals from all over Europe. The great astronomer Copernicus made some of his most important discoveries here. And Galileo—notorious for disagreeing with the Church's views on science—called his 18 years on the faculty here the best of his life. Students gather in ancient courtyards, surrounded by memories of illustrious alumni—including the first woman ever to receive a university degree (in 1678).

And just upstairs, Europe's first great **anatomy theater,** from the 1500s, is worth a look. While strictly forbidden by the Church, students would pack this theater to watch professors dissect human cadavers. If the Church came a-knockin', the table could be flipped, allowing the corpse to fall into a river below and be replaced with an animal instead (€2.60, 1 tour daily except Sun, 45 min, request English, book ahead by calling 049-876-7927, university tel. 049-827-3047).

From Piazza Cavour, it's about a 10-minute walk to the station; en route you'll find the town's artistic wonder, the...

▲▲**Scrovegni Chapel (Cappella degli Scrovegni)**—Reserve in advance to see this glorious, recently renovated chapel. It's surrounded by the ruins of a Roman amphitheater, a reminder that Padua was an important Roman town. But the sightseeing thrill here is the chapel, wallpapered by Giotto's beautifully preserved cycle of nearly 40 frescoes, depicting scenes from the lives of Jesus and Mary. Painted by Giotto and his assistants from 1303 to 1305, and considered by many to be the first piece of modern art, this work makes it clear: Europe was breaking out of the Middle Ages. A sign of the Renaissance to come, Giotto placed real people in real scenes. These frescoes were radical for their 3-D nature, lively colors, light sources, emotion, and humanism.

To protect the paintings from excess humidity, only 25 people are allowed in the chapel at a time for a 15-minute visit. To reserve, call 049-201-0020 (Mon–Fri 9:00–19:00, Sat 9:00–13:00) or book online at www.cappelladegliscrovegni.it. Reserve at least four days in advance; earlier is better to guarantee a visit (€11, credit card only).

Arrive one hour before your appointed time to exchange your booking receipt for a ticket. Then consider visiting the neighboring Civic Museum (included with ticket; see below). Be at the chapel 15 minutes before your time slot; it's 100 meters from the ticket desk, outside, and well-signed (daily 9:00–19:00, maybe as late as 22:00, people allowed in every 15 min at :00, :15, :30, and :45 past the hr, last entry 15 min before closing, no photos allowed in chapel). Once you're admitted, you'll have to wait in the anteroom for 15 minutes to establish humidity levels before continuing into the chapel. During your enforced wait, you can watch a multimedia presentation (with English subtitles) on the frescoes, or study a guidebook that you purchased beforehand in the gift shop. Although you have only 15 minutes inside the chapel, it's divine. You're essentially inside a Giotto time capsule, looking back at an artist ahead of his time.

**Civic Museum (Musei Civici Eremitani)**—This museum, next to the Scrovegni Chapel, displays Roman and Etruscan archaeological finds, buckets of rare coins, and 15th- to 18th-century paintings. The highlight is a Giotto crucifix (€4.10, covered by €11 Scrovegni ticket, Tue–Sun 9:00–18:00, until 19:00 in summer, closed Mon, Piazza Eremitani, tel. 049-820-4500).

## Sleeping in Padua
### (€1 = about $1, country code: 39)

Many travelers make Padua a low-stress, low-price home base from which to tour Venice. I'd rather flip-flop it—sleeping in Venice and side-tripping to Padua, 30 minutes away by train.

*In the Center:* **Majestic Hotel Toscanelli** is a big, fancy hotel with 32 pleasant rooms, a touch of charm, and a relatively quiet location on a side street (Sb-€96–116, Db-€140–165, superior rooms and suites available at extra cost, CC, includes a wonderful breakfast, Via dell' Arco 2, several blocks south of Piazza delle Erbe, tel. 049-663-244, fax 049-876-0025, e-mail: majestic@toscanelli.com).

**Hotel Verdi**, much cheaper, has 18 basic rooms and a good attitude (S-€23, D-€36, Via Dondi dell' Orologio 7, bus #10 from station to Teatro Verdi, about four zigzag blocks northwest of Piazza Signori, tel. 049-875-5744).

*Down by the Station:* For elegant four-star comfort, convenience, and prices, it's **Hotel Grand' Italia**. Housed in a palace, its 57 rooms are comfortable, and the breakfast room is bright and inviting (Db-€124–186 depending on season and size, includes breakfast, CC, elevator, air-con, Corso del Popolo 81, right outside train station, tel. 049-876-1111, fax 049-875-0850, www .hotelgranditalia.it, e-mail: info@hotelgranditalia.it).

**Hotel Monaco**, a three-star hotel a few doors away, is plain in comparison, with darkly decorated rooms, but it's a heck of lot cheaper (Db-€108, includes breakfast, CC, elevator, air-con, traffic noise, Piazzale Stazione 3, to the right as you leave the station, tel. 049-664-344, fax 049-664-669, www.monacohotel.it, e-mail: info@monacohotel.it).

*Hostel:* The well-run **Ostello Città di Padova** has four-, six-, and 16-bed rooms (€14 beds with sheets and breakfast, €14.50 in family rooms, bus #3, #8, #12, or #18 from station, Via Aleardi 30, tel. 049-875-2219).

## Eating in Padua

These are all centrally located in the historic core. **La Cova Ristorante/Pizzeria**, at Piazza Cavour, offers a pleasing range of pizza and pasta (Wed–Mon 12:00–15:30 & 18:00–2:00, closed Tue, Piazza Cavour 20, Via P.F. Calvi, tel. 049-654-312). **Marechiaro Pizzeria/Trattoria** is another good bet, just off Piazza delle Erbe (Tue–Sun 12:00–15:00 & 18:00–24:00, closed Mon, Via D. Manin 37, tel. 049-875-8489). **Brek**, tucked into a corner of Piazza Cavour #20, is an easy self-service *ristorante* (daily 11:30–15:00 & 19:30–22:00, tel. 049-875-8489).

For more of a dining experience, consider **Isola di Caprera** for traditional Veneto cuisine (€21 *menu*, cheaper à la carte options, Mon–Sat 12:00–15:00 & 19:30–23:00, closed Sun, CC, air-con, Via Marsilio da Padova 11-15, a half block north of the eastern edge of Piazza della Frutta, tel. 049-876-0244; to reserve, call 664-282-876-0244).

## VICENZA

For many architects, Vicenza is a pilgrimage site. Entire streets look like the back of a nickel. This is the city of Palladio, the 16th-century Renaissance architect who gave us the Palladian style that is so influential in countless British country homes. For the casual visitor, a quick stop offers plenty of Palladio (1508–1580)—the last great artist of the Renaissance. Note that Vicenza's major sights are closed on Monday.

**Tourist Information:** The main TI is at Piazza Matteotti 12 (Mon–Sat 9:00–13:00 & 14:30–18:00, Sun 9:00–13:00, tel. 0444-320-854, www.ascom.vi.it/aptvicenza—site has English translations). The train station sometimes has a bleak TI (Aug–Oct only, if at all). Pick up a map and, if staying the night, an entertainment guide. Architect fans will appreciate the free *Vicenza Città del Palladio* brochure in English. Guided **tours** are offered Saturday at 10:00 (€13, includes admissions to Olympic Theater and other sights—a super deal, April–Oct, 2 hrs, depart from TI on Piazza Matteotti, booking is required, call 0444-320-854 to reserve and confirm time).

**Arrival in Vicenza:** From the train station, it's a 5-minute **walk** up wide Viale Roma to the bottom of Corso Palladio. Or it's a short **bus** ride to Piazza Matteotti and the top of Corso Palladio. For a day trip, consider catching the bus to Piazza Matteotti and doing your sightseeing on the way back to the station. From the station, catch bus #1, #2, or #5 (€0.90, tickets sold at *tabacchi* shop in station and at small white kiosk—marked Vendita Biglietti—across street in the bushes). Validate your ticket in the machine near the back of the bus. Get off at Piazza Matteotti, a skinny, parklike square in front of a white neoclassical building. A **taxi** to Piazza Matteotti costs about €5.50.

At the station, you can store luggage (baggage check-€3.90, daily 6:00–22:00 to the far right as you face the ticket booths) and rent bicycles (€1/hr, €8/day, daily 8:00–20:00).

**Launderette:** The self-service **Lava & Asciuga** is a 10- to 15-minute walk from either the station or central Piazza dei Signori (daily 7:30–22:30, Contra S. Tommaso 46).

**Market Days:** Vicenza hosts a Tuesday market on Piazza dei Signori and a larger Thursday market that also spills into Piazza Duomo, Piazza del Castello, and Viale Roma (8:00–13:00).

## Sights—Vicenza

Most of Vicenza's sights are covered by a Biglietto Unico ticket for €7, sold only at the Olympic Theater. In addition to the theater, this combo-ticket includes the Pinacoteca (paintings, in Palazzo Chiericati on Piazza Matteotti), the Santa Corona Archaeological and Natural History Museum (next to the Church of Santa Corona), and the Basilica Palladiana (in Piazza dei Signori, ticket does not include exhibits held in the basilica).

▲▲**Olympic Theater (Teatro Olimpico)**—Palladio's last work is one of his greatest. Begun in 1580, shortly before Palladio died, the theater was actually completed by his pupil Scamozzi. Modeled after the theaters of antiquity, this is a wood-and-stucco festival of classical columns, statues, and an oh-wow stage bursting with perspective tricks. Behind the stage, framed by a triumphal arch, five streets recede at different angles. Many of the statues in niches are modeled after the people who funded the work. In contrast to the stunning stage, the audience's wooden benches are simple and crude. One of the oldest indoor theaters in Europe and considered one of the world's best, it's still used for performances (€7 Biglietto Unico ticket, Tue–Sun 9:00–17:00, July–Aug until 19:00, last entry 15 min before closing, closed Mon, hours can vary, tel. 0444-222-800, www.olimpico.vicenza.it, WC through entrance to the right).

▲**Church of Santa Corona (Church of the Holy Crown)**— A block away from the Olympic Theater, this church was built in the 13th century to house a thorn from the crown of thorns given to the Bishop of Vicenza by the French king Louis IX (free, Mon 15:00–18:00, Tue–Sun 8:30–12:00 & 15:00–18:00). It has Giovanni Bellini's fine *Baptism of Christ* (c. 1500, put in a coin for light, to the left of the altar). Study the incredible inlaid marble and mother-of-pearl work on the high altar (1670) and the inlaid wood complementing that in the stalls of the choir (1485).

**Archaeological and Natural History Museum**—Next door to the Church of Santa Corona, this humble museum features Roman antiquities (mosaics, statues, and swords) on its ground floor; prehistoric scraps upstairs; and precious little English information throughout (€7 Biglietto Unico, Tue–Sun 9:00–17:00, closed Mon).

**Strolling Corso Palladio**—From the Olympic Theater or Church of Santa Corona, stroll down Vicenza's main drag, Corso Andrea Palladio, and see why they call Vicenza "Venezia on terra firma." A steady string of Renaissance palaces and Palladian architecture is peopled by Vicenzans (considered by their neighbors to be as uppity as most of their colonnades) and punctuated by upper-class *gelaterias*.

After a few blocks, you'll see the commanding **Basilica Palladiana,** under restoration in 2003. (This was not a church, but a meeting place for local big shots.) With its 82-meter-tall (270-foot), 13th-century tower, the basilica dominates the Piazza dei Signori, the town center since Roman times. It was young Palladio's proposal to redo Vicenza's dilapidated Gothic palace of justice in the neo-Greek style that established him as Vicenza's favorite architect. The rest of Palladio's career was a one-man construction boom. Opposite the basilica, the brick-columned **Loggia del Capitaniato**—home of the Venetian governor and one of Palladio's last works—gives you an easy chance to compare early Palladio (the basilica) with late Palladio (the loggia). The ground floor of the basilica is filled with shops. Climb up the 15th-century stairs. You'll see the lion's mouth after a few steps; centuries ago, people used to sneak notes into the mouth,

# Vicenza

- **1** HOTEL CAMPO MARZIO
- **2** HOTEL GIARDINI
- **3** HOTEL PALLADIO
- **4** HOTEL CASTELLO
- **5** L'OSTELLO RIMANE
- **6** AL PESTELLO REST.
- **7** ZI TERESA REST.
- **8** LA MENEGHINA REST.
- **9** SORARU PASTRY SHOP
- **10** BREK RISTORANTE
- **11** PAM SUPERMARKET

anonymously reporting neighbors suspected of carrying communicable diseases, such as the plague. The arcaded upper floor (with a WC in back) contains the entrance to the huge basilica (€7 Biglietto Unico, Tue–Sun 9:00–17:00, closed Mon, frequent exhibitions, Piazza dei Signori). The basilica's ceiling, shaped like an upside-keel, has a nautical feel, augmented by the porthole windows. Set in the wall in front, the winged lion (symbol of St. Mark and Venice) set the course for this little town in the 15th century.

Also in the Piazza dei Signori stand two tall 15th-century columns topped by Jesus and the winged lion. When Venice took over Vicenza in the early 1400s, these columns were added—à la St. Mark's Square—to give the city a Venetian feel. (A rare public WC is behind the basilica; face the belfry and go left through the arch and down the stairs.)

Finish your Corso Palladio stroll at Piazzale Gasperi (where the Pam supermarket is a handy place to grab a picnic for the train ride), dip into the park called Giardino Salvi (for one last Palladio loggia), and then walk five minutes down Viale Roma back to the station. Trains leave about every hour for Milan/Verona and Venice (less than an hour away).

**Villa la Rotonda**—Thomas Jefferson's Monticello was inspired by Palladio's Rotonda (a.k.a. Villa Almerico Capra). Started by Palladio in 1566, it was finished by his pupil Scamozzi. The white, gently domed building, with grand colonnaded entries, seems to have popped out of the grassy slope. Palladio, who designed a number of country villas, had a knack for using the setting for dramatic effect. This private—but sometimes tourable—residence is on the edge of Vicenza (€3 for grounds, mid-March–Oct Tue–Sun 10:00–12:00 & 15:00–18:00, closed Mon; €6 for interior—open only Wed 10:00–12:00 & 15:00–18:00; everything closed Nov–mid-March, Via Rotunda 29, tel. 0444-321-793). To get to the villa from Vicenza's train station, hop a bus (#8, hrly) or take a taxi (about €5.50). For a quick round-trip any time of day, you can zip out by cab (5 min from train station) to see the building sitting regally atop its hill, and then ride the same cab back.

## Sleeping in Vicenza
**(€1 = about $1, country code: 39)**
**Hotel Campo Marzio**, a four-star, American-style, modern place, faces a park on the main drag a few minutes' walk in front of the station (Db-€155–207 depending on season and size of room—"superior" means bigger, includes breakfast, CC, easy parking, air-con, elevator, Viale Roma 21, 36100 Vicenza, tel. 0444-545-700, fax 0444-320-495, www.hotelcampomarzio.com, e-mail: info@hotelcampomarzio.com).

**Hotel Giardini,** with three stars and 17 sleek rooms, has splashy pastel colors and a refreshing feel (Sb-€88, Db-€119, includes breakfast, CC, elevator, air-con, on busy street but has double-paned windows, within a block of Piazza Matteotti/Olympic Theater on Via Giuriolo 10, tel. & fax 0444-326-458, www.hotelgiardini.com, e-mail: hgiardini.vi@iol.it).

**Hotel Palladio** has a shortage of matching bedspreads, but it's decent for a two-star hotel in the city center (25 rooms, S-€36, Sb-€65, D-€62, Db-€72, Tb-€103, includes breakfast, CC, ask for quieter room, a block off Piazza dei Signori, Via Oratoria dei Servi 25, tel. 0444-321-072, fax 0444-547-328, e-mail: hotelpalladio@libero.it).

**Hotel Castello**, on Piazza Castello, has 18 dim, quiet rooms (Sb-€78–98, Db-€98–129, includes breakfast, CC, air-con, Contra Piazza del Castello 24, down alley to the right of Ristorante agli Schioppi, 5-min walk from station, tel. 0444-323-585, fax 0444-323-583, www.hotelcastello.net, e-mail: mail@hotelcastello.net).

*Hostel:* **L'Ostello Rimane,** just a few years old, has a great location on Piazza Matteotti (84 beds, €14 beds in 4- to 6-bed rooms, €15 beds in family room, €16.50 beds in doubles, closes from 9:30–15:30 and at 23:00, no breakfast, Internet access, best to reserve several weeks in advance by fax, tel. 0444-540-???, fax 0444-547-762).

## Eating in Vicenza

The local specialty is marinated cod, called *baccala alla Vicentina*. **Al Pestello** serves typical *cucina Vicentina* a block from the Church of Santa Corona (Santo Stefano 3, Mon–Sat 12:30–14:30 & 19:30–22:30, closed Sun, tel. 0444-323-721). Locals like the romantic **Zi Teresa** for its moderately priced traditional cuisine and pizzas (Thu–Tue 11:30–15:30 & 18:30–24:00, closed Wed, a couple blocks southwest of Piazza dei Signori, Contra S. Antonio 1, at intersection with Contra Proti, tel. 0444-321-411).

**La Meneghina** is an atmospheric pastry shop (on Contra Cavour, a short street between Piazza dei Signori and Corso Palladio, daily 8:00–1:00, closed Mon off-season, tel. 0444-323-305). Nearby, on Piazza dei Signori, the tiny **Soraru** pastry shop has lots of sidewalk tables within tickling distance of the Palladio statue (Thu–Tue 8:30–13:00 & 15:30–20:00, closed Wed, next to basilica, at far end of square from the two tall columns).

A cheap self-service **Brek Ristorante** is just off Piazza del Castello, in the shadow of the arch where Corso Palladio meets Viale Roma (Tue–Sun 11:30–15:00 & 18:30–22:00, closed Mon, Corso Palladio 12, tel. 0444-327-829). A few steps from that same arch is the **Pam supermarket**, perfect for picnics (daily 8:30–20:00, Wed only until 19:30, follow the curve of the road just outside the city wall).

## VERONA

Romeo and Juliet made Verona a household word. But, alas, a visit here has nothing to do with those two star-crossed lovers. You can pay to visit the house falsely claiming to be Juliet's, with an almost believable balcony (and a courtyard slathered with tour groups), take part in the tradition of rubbing the breast of Juliet's statue to ensure finding a lover (or picking up the sweat of someone who can't), and even make a pilgrimage to what isn't "La Tomba di Giulietta." Despite the fiction, the town has been an important crossroads for 2,000 years, and is therefore packed with genuine history. R and J fans will take some solace in the fact that two real feuding families, the Montecchi and the Capellis, were the models for Shakespeare's Montagues and Capulets. And, if R and J had existed and were alive today, they would recognize much of their "hometown."

Verona's main attractions are its wealth of Roman ruins; the remnants of its 13th- and 14th-century political and cultural boom; its 21st-century, quiet, pedestrian-only ambience; and a world-class opera festival each July and August (schedule at www.arena.it). After Venice's festival of tourism, Veneto's second city (in population and in artistic importance) is a cool and welcome sip of pure Italy, where dumpsters are painted by schoolchildren as class projects. If you like Italy but don't need great sights, this town is a joy.

Ask a Veronese to tell you about Papa del Gnoccho (NYO-ko). Every year someone from the San Zeno neighborhood is elected Papa del Gnoccho. On the Friday before Mardi Gras, he's dressed like a king. But instead of a scepter, he holds a huge fork piercing a *gnoccho* (potato dumpling). Lots of people wear costumes, including little kids, who dress as gnocchi. The focal point is the Church of San Zeno; the origin is in medieval times. About 500 years ago, at a time when the Veronese were nearly starving, the prince handed out gnocchi to everyone. Even now, it's customary for the Veronese to eat gnocchi on Friday during Lent.

## Orientation

The most enjoyable core of Verona is along Via Mazzini between Piazza Bra and Piazza Erbe, Verona's market square since Roman times. Head straight for Piazza Bra—and stroll. All sights of importance are located within an easy walk through the old town, which is defined by a bend in the river. For a good day trip, see the Arena and take the self-guided "Introductory Old Town Walk," outlined below.

**Tourist Information:** Verona's TI offices are at the station (Mon–Sat 9:00–18:00, closed Sun, shorter hours off-season, tel. 045-800-0861, www.tourism.verona.it) and at Piazza Bra (July–Aug daily 9:00–19:00, shorter hours off-season; facing the large yellow-white building, TI is across street to your right, tel. 045-806-8680, public WC on Piazza Bra). Pick up the free city map that includes a list of sights, opening hours, and walking tours. Many sights are closed on Monday and are free on the first Sunday of every month. If you're staying the night, ask for the free *Agenda di Verona*, the monthly entertainment guide (it's in Italian, but *concerto di musica classica* is darn close to English).

The **Verona Card** covers bus transportation and most of Verona's sights (€8/day or €12/3 days, sold at museums). A pricier version of the Verona Card (€19.50) includes Gardaland, an Italian Disneyland that's best reached by car.

Verona's historic **churches**—San Zeno, San Lorenzo, Sant' Anastasia, San Fermo, and the Duomo—charge admission (covered by Verona Card or €2 apiece, €5 for a combo-ticket sold at the churches, hours roughly Mon–Sat 9:00–18:00, Sun 13:00–18:00, no photos allowed, no touring during Mass, modest dress expected).

**Opera:** In July and August, Verona's opera festival brings crowds and higher hotel prices (tickets €19.50 154, available through box office tel. 045-800-5151, or online at www.arena.it).

**Internet Access:** Try Internet Train on Via Roma 17a, a couple of blocks off Piazza Bra toward Castelvecchio (Mon–Fri 11:00–22:00, Sat 11:00–20:00, Sun 14:00–20:00, tel. 045-801-3394), Internetfast.it (Mon–Fri 10:00–22:00, Sat 10:00–20:00, Sun 14:00–20:00, Via Oberdan 16/b, just off Porta Borsari toward Piazza Bra, tel. 045-803-3212), or the tiny Realta Virtuale at platform 1 at the train station (Mon–Sat 7:30–19:00, closed Sun).

**Private Guides:** For private guides, consider Marina Menegoi (€95/hour, tel. 045-801-2174, e-mail: milanit@libero.it) or the Verona guide association (tel. 045-810-1322, e-mail: veronaguide@katamail.com).

## Arrival in Verona

Arriving by train, get off at Verona's Porta Nuova station. The train station is modern, but so cluttered with shops it can be hard to get oriented. As you come out of the underground passage from the tracks, an ATM machine is to your right, pay toilets and phones to your left. In the lobby, with your back to the tracks, you'll find the baggage check to your far right (€2.60/12 hrs), and, if you search hard, you'll see the TI (tel. 045-800-861, hours vary), tucked inside an office labeled "Centro Accoglienza e Informazioni." Buses to Verona's airport shuttle you from the train station from 6:00–23:00, departing every 20 minutes.

The 15-minute walk from the station (on busy streets) to Piazza Bra is boring; take the **bus.** Buses leave from directly in front of the station. You need to buy a ticket before boarding (€0.95, from *tabacchi* shop inside station or at white bus kiosk outside at Platform A). Bus information will likely be posted in English on the window of the bus kiosk (or ask, *Che numero per centro?*, pron. kay NOO-may-roh pehr CHEN-troh). You'll probably have a choice of orange bus #11, #12, or #13, leaving from Platform A. Validate your ticket on the bus by stamping it in the machine in the middle of the bus (good for 60 min). Buses stop on Piazza Bra, the square with the can't-miss-it Roman Arena. The TI is just a few steps beyond the bus stop. Buses return to the station from the bus stop just outside the city wall (on the right), where Corso Porta Nuova hits Piazza Bra.

**Taxis** pick up only at taxi stands (at train station and Piazza Bra) and cost about €5.50 for a ride between the train station and Piazza Bra.

## Sights—Verona

**Arena**—This elliptical 140-by-120-meter (160-by-394-foot) amphitheater is the third-largest in the Roman world. Dating from the first century A.D., it looks great in its pink marble. Over the centuries, crowds of up to 25,000 spectators have cheered Roman gladiator battles, medieval executions, and modern plays (including the popular opera festival that takes advantage of the famous acoustics every July and August). Climb to the top for a fine city view (€3.10, Tue–Sun 9:00–18:30, closed Mon and at 15:00 during opera season, info boxes near entry, located on Piazza Bra).

**House of Juliet**—This bogus house is a block off Piazza Erbe (detour right to Via Cappello 23). The tiny, admittedly romantic courtyard is a spectacle in itself, with Japanese posing from the balcony, Nebraskans polishing Juliet's bronze breast, and amorous graffiti everywhere. The info boxes (€0.50 for 2) offer a good history. ("While no documentation has been discovered to prove the truth of the legend, no documentation has disproved it either.") The "museum" is only empty rooms and certainly not worth the €3.10 entry fee (Tue–Sun 9:00–19:00, closed Mon, tel. 045-803-4303).

▲**Piazza Erbe**—Verona's market square is a photographer's delight, with pastel buildings corralling the stalls, fountains, pigeons, and people that have come together here since Roman times, when this was a forum. Notice the Venetian lion hovering above the square, reminding locals since 1405 of their conquerors. During medieval times, the stone canopy in the center held the scales where merchants measured the weight of things they bought and sold, such as silk, wool, even wood. The fountain has bubbled here for 2,000 years. Its statue, originally Roman, had lost its head and arms. After a sculptor added a new head and arms—voilà!—the statue became Verona's Madonna. She holds a small banner that reads: "I want justice and I bring peace."

▲▲**Evening** *Passeggiata*—For me, the highlight of Verona is the *passeggiata* (stroll)—especially in the evening—from the elegant cafés of Piazza Bra through the old town on Via Mazzini (one of Europe's many "first pedestrian-only streets") to the bustling and colorful market square, Piazza Erbe.

**Roman Theater (Teatro Romano)**—Dating from the first century A.D., this ancient theater was discovered in the 19th century and restored. To reach the worthwhile museum, high up in the building above the theater, you can take the stairs or the elevator (to find the elevator, start at the stage and walk up the middle set of stairs, then continue straight on the path through the bushes). The museum displays Roman artifacts (mosaic floors, busts, and clay and bronze votive figures) and a model of the theater; helpful English info sheets are in virtually every room (€2.60, free first

## Verona

- ❶ BUS TO STATION
- ❷ BUS FROM STATION
- ❸ HOTEL TORCOLO
- ❹ HOTEL EUROPA
- ❺ LOCANDA CATULLO
- ❻ HOTEL AURORA
- ❼ HOTEL BOLOGNA
- ❽ HOTEL GIULIETTA E ROMEO
- ❾ TO YOUTH HOSTEL
- ❿ OSTERIA AL DUCA
- ⓫ RISTORANTE GREPPIA & BOTTEGA DEL VINO
- ⓬ ORESTE DAL ZOVO CANTINA
- ⓭ PIZZERIA SALVATORE

Sun of month, Tue–Sun 8:30–19:30, Mon 13:30–19:30, across the river near Ponte Pietra, tel. 045-800-0360). Every summer, the theater stages Shakespeare plays—only a little more difficult to understand in Italian than in Old English.

**Giardini Giusti**—If you'd enjoy a Renaissance garden with mani-cured box hedges and towering cypress trees, you could find this worth the walk and fee (€4.10, daily 9:00–sunset, cross river at Ponte Nuovo, continue 8 blocks up Via Carducci).

## Introductory Old Town Walk

This walk will take you from Piazza Erbe to the major sights and end at Piazza Bra. Allow an hour (including tower climb and dawdling but not detours).

From the center of Piazza Erbe, head toward the river on Via della Costa. The street is marked by an arch with a whale's rib suspended from it. When you pass through the arch, don't worry. The whale's rib has hung there a thousand years. According to legend, it will fall when someone who's never lied walks under it.

The street soon opens up to a square, **Piazza dei Signori**, which has a white statue of Dante center-stage. The pensive Dante seems to wonder why the tourists choose Juliet over him. Dante—expelled from Florence for political reasons—was granted exile in Verona by the Scaligeri family. With the whale's rib behind you, you're facing the brick, crenellated, 13th-century Scaligeri residence. Behind Dante is the yellowish, 15th-century Venetian Renaissance–style Portico of the Counsel. In front of Dante and to his right (follow the white "WC" signs) is the 12th-century, Romanesque **Palazzo della Ragione**.

Enter the courtyard. The impressive staircase—which goes nowhere—is the only surviving Renaissance staircase in Verona. For a grand city view, you can climb to the top of the 13th-century **Torre dei Lamberti** (€1.50 for stairs, €2.10 elevator, Tue–Sun 9:30–21:00, closed Mon). The elevator saves you 245 steps—but you'll need to climb about 45 more to get to the first view platform. It's not worth continuing up the endless spiral stairs to the second view platform.

Exit the courtyard the way you entered and turn right, continuing down the whale-rib street. Within a block, you'll find the strange and very Gothic tombs of the Scaligeri family, who were to Verona what the Medici family were to Florence. Notice the dogs' heads near the top of the tombs. On the first tomb, the dogs peer over a shield displaying a ladder. The story goes that the Scaligeri family got rich making ladders, but money can't buy culture. When Marco Polo returned from Asia boasting of the wealthy Kublai Khan, the Scaligeris wanted to be associated with this powerful Khan by name. But misunderstanding "Khan" as "Cane" (dog), one Scaligeri changed his name to Can Grande (big dog) and another to Can Signori (lead dog).

Continue straight for one long block and turn left on San Pietro Martire (you'll need to step into the street to check the road sign). After one block, you'll reach Verona's largest church, the brick **Church of Sant' Anastasia**. It was built from the late 13th century through the 15th century, but the builders ran out of steam, for the facade was never finished. You can enter the church for €2 (or pay €5 for a combo-ticket that includes other churches, including the Duomo, which we'll stop at later; ask for English brochure), or just peek in over the screen to get a sense of its size. The highlights of the interior are the grimacing hunchbacks holding basins of holy water on their backs (near entrance at base of columns) and Pisanello's fragmented fresco of *St. George and the Princess* (above chapel to right of altar). The story of the church is available in English from the screen at the entry/exit.

Back to the walking tour. Face the church, then go right and walk along the length of it. Take a left on Via Sottoriva. In a block, you'll reach a small riverfront park that usually has a few modern-day Romeos and Juliets gazing at each other rather than the view. Get up on the sidewalk right next to the river. You'll see the red-and-white bridge, **Ponte Pietra**. The white stones are from the original Roman bridge that stood here. After the bridge was bombed in World War II, the Veronese fished the marble chunks out of the river to rebuild it.

You'll also see, across the river and built into the hillside, the **Roman Theater** (description in "Sights," above). Way above the theater is the fortress, Castello San Pietro. We'll be heading toward the Roman bridge. This is your chance to break away, cross the bridge, and visit the Roman Theater; or climb the stairs to the left of the theater for a city view; or take the little road Scalone Castello S. Pietro and climb to the top of the hill to the Castello for an expansive view.

Me? I'm simply passing the bridge on the way to the next church. Leave the riverfront park and take the street to the right, toward the bridge. One block before you reach the bridge (bridge entry clearly marked by an arch in a tower), turn left on Via Cappelletta. After two long blocks, turn right on Via Duomo (the corner is marked by a little church). Straight ahead, you'll see the striped **Duomo**. One of Verona's historic churches, it costs €2 to enter (€5 combo-ticket; English descriptions given at the entrance). Started in the 12th century, it was built over a period of centuries, showing with its bright interior the tremendous leaps made in architecture. (Okay, so the white paint helps.)

The highlights are Titian's *Assumption* and the ruins of an older church. To find the Titian, stand at the very back of the church, facing the altar; the painting is to your left. Mary calmly rides a cloud—direction up—to the shock and bewilderment of the crowd below.

To find the ruins of the older church, walk up toward the altar to the last wooden door on the left. If the door's not open, ask someone for help. Inside are the 10th-century foundations of the Church of St. Elena, turned intriguingly into a modern-day chapel.

Leave the church, returning down Via Duomo. Continue straight ahead on Via Duomo until you reach the Church of Sant' Anastasia. With your back to this church, walk down Corso S. Anastasia.

In five minutes (at a brisk pace), you'll reach the ghostly white **Porta Borsari**, stretching across the road. This sturdy first-century Roman gate was one of the original entrances to this ancient town.

Continue straight (the name of the street changes to Corso Cavour). In a little park next to the castle is a first-century Roman triumphal arch, **Arco dei Gavi.** After being destroyed by French revolutionary troops in 1796, it was rebuilt at this location in the 1900s.

**Castelvecchio,** the medieval castle next to the arch, is now a sprawling art museum displaying Christian statuary, some weaponry, and fine 15th- to 17th-century paintings (€4.20 unless there are special exhibits, free first Sun of month, Tue–Sun 8:30–19:30, last entrance 45 min before closing, closed Mon, audioguide-€3.65 or €5.20 for 2). If you visit the castle, you'll pass outdoors between the museum's buildings; look for the skinny stairway leading up to the ancient wall overlooking the river. Climb up. It's a dead end but offers a great opportunity to shoot arrows at medieval invaders.

From the castle, you have three options. For a view, you can walk out upon the grand bridge that leads from the castle over the river. To get back to Piazza Bra, take the castle's drawbridge; it points the way to Via Roma, taking you to Piazza Bra and a well-deserved rest at a sidewalk café (Brek is good).

Or: A few blocks from the castle is the 12th-century **Basilica of San Zeno Maggiore.** This offers not only a great example of Italian Romanesque but also Mantegna's *San Zeno Triptych* and a set of 48 paneled 11th-century bronze doors that are nicknamed "the poor man's Bible." Pretend you're an illiterate medieval peasant and do some reading. Facing the altar on the far right, you can see frescoes painted on top of other frescoes and graffiti from the 1300s (€2, €5 combo-ticket, March–Oct 8:30–16:00, Nov–Feb until 13:00).

## Sleeping in Verona
**(€1 = about $1, country code: 39, zip code: 37100)**
Prices soar in July and August (during opera season) and any time of year for a trade fair or holiday. The first two are my favorites for their family-run feeling.

*Near Piazza Erbe:* **Hotel Aurora,** just off Piazza Erbe, has friendly family management, a terrace overlooking the piazza, and 19 fresh and newly renovated, air-conditioned rooms (S-€62, Sb-€104, Db-€117, Tb-€145, includes good buffet breakfast, lower prices off-season, reserve with traveler's check or personal check for deposit, CC, elevator, church bells ring the hour early, Piazza Erbe, 37121 Verona, tel. 045-594-717, fax 045-801-0860, www.hotelaurora.biz, SE). Their two quads (each with 2 rooms, a double bed, 2 twins, and bathroom; €191/night) are best for families because the bedrooms aren't private.

*Near Piazza Bra:* Several fine places are in the quiet streets just off Piazza Bra, within 200 meters (650 feet) of the bus stop and well-marked with yellow signs.

**Hotel Torcolo** provides 19 comfortable, lovingly maintained rooms in a good location near Piazza Bra (Sb-€48–73, Db-€82–104, breakfast-€6.20–10.30, prices vary with season, CC, air-con, fridge in room, elevator, garage-€8–10.25/day, Vicolo Listone 3, with your back to the gardens and the Arena over your right shoulder, head down the alley to the right of #16 on Piazza Bra, tel. 045-800-7512, fax 045-800-4058, www.hoteltorcolo.it, well-run by Silvia Pomari, SE).

**Hotel Europa** offers sleek, modern comfort in the same great neighborhood. Nearly half of its 46 rooms are smoke-free, a rarity in Italy (Db-€132 but €160 July–Aug, includes breakfast, call to check for discounts, CC, air-con, elevator, Via Roma 8, 37121 Verona, tel. 045-594-744, fax 045-800-1852, e-mail: hoteleuropavr@tiscalinet.it, SE).

**Hotel Bologna,** within a half block of the Arena, has 30 bright, classy, and well-maintained rooms; attractive public areas; and an attached restaurant (Sb-€96–122, Db-€117–172, Tb-€148–218, includes breakfast, CC, air-con, Piazzetta Scalette Rubiani 3, tel. 045-800-6830, fax 045-801-0602, e-mail: hotelbologna@tin.it).

**Hotel Giulietta e Romeo**, just behind the Arena, is on a quiet side street. Its 30 decent rooms are decorated in dark colors, but on the plus side, they have non-smoking rooms (on first floor) and don't take tour groups (Sb-€62–103, Db-€77–160, includes breakfast, CC, free Internet access in lobby, bike rentals €5/half day, €10/day, air-con, elevator, laundry service, garage-€17/day, Vicolo Tre Marchetti 3, tel. 045-800-3554, fax 045-801-0862, www.giuliettaeromeo.com).

*Between Piazza Bra and Piazza Erbe:* **Locanda Catullo** is a cheaper, quiet, and quirky place deeper in the old town, with 21 good basic rooms up three flights of stairs (S-€39, D-€54, Db-€65, Qb-€124, no CC, no breakfast, left off Via Mazzini onto Via Catullo, down an alley between 1D and 3A at Via Valerio Catullo 1, tel. 045-800-2786, fax 045-596-987, e-mail: locandacatullo@tiscalinet.it, SE a little).

*Hostel:* **Villa Francescatti** is a good hostel (8- to 10-bed

rooms, some family rooms, €12 beds with breakfast, €7.25
dinners, launderette, bus #73 from station during the day or
#90 at night and Sun, over the river beyond Ponte Nuovo at Salita
Fontana del Ferro 15, tel. 045-590-360, fax 045-800-9127). During
busy times, hostel members get priority over nonmembers.

## Eating in Verona

*Near Piazza Erbe:* **Osteria al Duca** has an affordable two-course
*menu* (€13) and lots more options. For dessert, try the chocolate
salami. Family-run with a lively atmosphere, it's popular—go early
(Mon–Sat 12:00–14:15 & 18:45–22:00, closed Sun, Via Arche
Scaligere 2, half block from Scaligeri Tombs, tel. 045-594-474).
Their sister restaurant, **Osteria Giulietta e Romeo**, serves up
the same menu a block away with fewer crowds (Corso Sant'
Anastasia 27, tel. 045-800-9177).

More good choices include **Ristorante Greppia** (Vicolo
Samaritana 3, tel. 045-800-4577) and the pricier **Bottega del
Vino** (closed Tue, Via Scudo di Francia 3, tel. 045-800-4535);
to find these, head from Piazza Erbe up Via Mazzini—they're
within a couple of blocks.

For a fun, local wine/grappa bar (no formal food but an
abundance of fun and hearty bar snacks), try **Oreste Dal Zovo**,
run by Oreste and his wife Beverly from Chicago (March–Dec
8:00–20:00, no chairs, just a couple of benches; it's on the alley—
San Marco in Foro #7—off Porta Borsari, just a block from
Piazza Erbe, tel. 045-803-4369).

*On Piazza Bra:* For fast food with a great view of Verona's
main square, consider the self-service **Brek** (daily 11:30–15:00 &
18:30–22:00, indoor/outdoor seating, cheap salad plates, Piazza
Bra 20, tel. 045-800-4561). **Enoteca Cangrande** serves great
wine (such as the local *pasito bianco)* and delicious food (Tue–Sun
10:00–14:00 & 17:00–2:00, closed Mon, CC, Via Dietro Liston
19/D, one block off Piazza Bra and Via Roma, tel. 045-595-022).

*Near Ponte Nuovo:* **Pizzeria Salvatore**, just across the Ponte
Nuovo bridge (and to the left), serves great pizza on funky, modern
art tables (Tue–Sat 12:00–14:30 & 19:00–23:00, Sun 19:00–23:00,
closed Mon, Piazza San Tomasso 6, tel. 045-803-0366).

## Transportation Connections—Verona

**By train to: Florence** (5/day, 3 hrs, more with transfer in
Bologna; note that all Rome-bound trains stop in Firenze),
**Bologna** (nearly hrly, 2 hrs), **Milan** (hrly, 2 hrs), **Rome** (4/day,
4–6 hrs, more with transfer in Bologna), **Bolzano** (hrly, 90 min,
note that Brennero-bound trains stop in Bolzano).

**Parking in Verona:** Drivers will find lots of free parking at

the stadium or cheap long-term parking near the train station
and city walls. The most central lot is behind the Arena on Piazza
Cittadella (guarded, €1/hr). Street parking costs €0.80 for two
hours (buy ticket at *tabacchi* shop to put on dashboard). The town
center is closed to regular traffic.

# RAVENNA

Ravenna is on the tourist map for one reason: Its 1,500-year-old
churches, decorated with best-in-the-West Byzantine mosaics.
Known in Roman times as Classe, the city was an imperial port
for the large naval fleet. Briefly a capital of eastern Rome during
its fall, Ravenna was taken by the barbarians. Then, in A.D. 540,
the Byzantine emperor Justinian turned Ravenna into the western-
most pillar of the Byzantine Empire. A pinnacle of civilization in
that age, Ravenna was a light in Europe's Dark Ages. Two hundred
years later, the Lombards booted out the Byzantines, and Ravenna
melted into the backwaters of medieval Italy, staying out of historical sight for a thousand years.

Today, the local economy booms with a big chemical industry, the discovery of offshore gas deposits, and the construction of a
new ship canal. The bustling town center is Italy's most bicycle-
friendly (bike paths are in the middle of pedestrian streets, subtly
indicated by white brick paving). Locals go about their business,
while busloads of tourists slip quietly in and out of town for the
best look at the glories of Byzantium this side of Istanbul.

Ravenna's only a 90-minute detour from the main
Venice–Florence train line and worth the effort for those interested in old mosaics. While its sights don't merit an overnight
stop, many find that the peaceful charm of this untouristy and
classy town makes it a pleasant surprise in their Italian wandering.

## Orientation

Central Ravenna is quiet, with a pedestrian-friendly core and
more bikes than cars. On a quick visit to Ravenna, I'd see the
Basilica di San Vitale and its adjacent Mausoleum of Galla
Placidia; the Basilica of St. Apollinare Nuovo; the covered market;
and Piazza del Popolo.

**Tourist Information:** The TI is a 20-minute walk (or a
5-minute pedal) from the train station (Mon–Sat 8:30–19:00,
Sun 10:00–16:00, Via Salara 8, tel. 0544-35404, www.turismo
.ravenna.it). For directions to the TI, see the "Orientation Walk,"
below.

For a private guide, consider Claudia Frassineti (tel. 335-
613-2996, www.abacoguide.it).

**Combo-Tickets:** Many top sights can only be seen by

purchasing a combo-ticket (called *biglietto cumulativo* or Visit Card, €6, sold at participating sights). It includes admission to the Basilica of San Vitale, Mausoleum of Galla Placidia, St. Apollinare Nuovo, Spirito Santo, Battistero Neoniano, and Cappella Arcivescoville. There are no individual admissions to these.

A different combo-ticket (€5) covers admissions to the National Museum and Mausoleum of Teodorico. Pay an extra €1.50 to include the Sant' Apollinare in Classe. Unlike with the other combo-ticket mentioned above, you can buy individual admissions to the sights (National Museum-€4, Tue–Sun 8:30–19:30, off-season until 18:00, closed Mon; Mausoleum of Teodorico-€2.10, daily 8:30–18:00, off-season until 17:30, last entry 30 min before closing; and Sant' Apollinare in Classe-€2.10, Mon–Sat 8:30–19:30; Sun 13:00–19:00).

**Bike Rental:** Bikes are available free from the TI (passport required) or for rent from Coop San Vitale on Piazza Farini (on the left just as you exit train station, tel. 0544-37031).

## Sights—Ravenna

**Orientation Walk**—A visit to Ravenna can be as short as a three-hour loop from the train station. From the station, walk straight down Viale Farini to Piazza del Popolo. This square was built around 1500, during a 60-year period when the city was ruled by Venice. Under the Venetian architecture, the people of Ravenna gather here as they have for centuries. A right on Via IV Novembre takes you a block to the colorful covered market (Mercato Coperto, Mon–Sat 7:00–14:00, closed Sun, good for picnic fixings). The TI is a block away (on Via Salara 8). Ravenna's two most important sights, Basilica di San Vitale and the Mausoleum of Galla Placidia, are two blocks away down Via San Vitale. On the other side of Piazza del Popolo is the Basilica of St. Apollinare Nuovo, also worth a look. From there, you're about a 15-minute walk back to the station.

▲▲**Basilica di San Vitale**—Imagine . . . it's A.D. 540. The city of Rome had been looted, the land was crawling with barbarians, and the infrastructure of Rome's thousand-year empire was crumbling fast. Into this chaotic world came the emperor of the East, Justinian, bringing order and stability, briefly reassembling the empire, and making Ravenna a beacon of civilization. His church of San Vitale—standing as a sanctuary of order in the midst of that chaos—is covered with lavish mosaics: gold and glass chips the size of your fingernail. It's impressive enough to see a 1,400-year-old church. But to see one decorated in brilliant mosaics, still managing to convey the intended feeling that "this peace and stability was brought to you by your emperor and God," is rare indeed.

# Ravenna

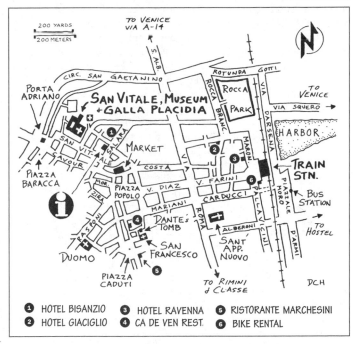

TO VENICE
VIA A-14

200 YARDS
200 METERS

N

CIRC. SAN GAETANINO

S. ALB.

ROTUNDA    GOTTI

PORTA
ADRIANO

ROCCA BRANC.

ROCCA
PARK

VIA DARSENA

TO
VENICE

VIA SQUERO →

**SAN VITALE, MUSEUM
+ GALLA PLACIDIA**

HARBOR

CAVOUR

SAN VIT-ALE

❶

MARKET

❷

❸

TRAIN
STN.

PIAZZA
BARACCA

COSTA

MOR.

PIAZZA
POPOLO

V. DIAZ

V. FARINI

MARON

PIAZZALE MORO

❻

BUS
STATION

ZIR.

MARIANI

CARDUCCI

RASPONI

❹

DANTE'S
TOMB

ROMA

ALBERONI

D'ARMI

TO
HOSTEL

DUOMO

SAN
FRANCESCO

❺

SANT'
APP.
NUOVO

PIAZZA
CADUTI

TO RIMINI
& CLASSE

DCH

| | | |
|---|---|---|
| ❶ HOTEL BISANZIO | ❸ HOTEL RAVENNA | ❺ RISTORANTE MARCHESINI |
| ❷ HOTEL GIACIGLIO | ❹ CA DE VEN REST. | ❻ BIKE RENTAL |

In a medieval frame of mind, study the scene: High above the altar, God is in heaven, portrayed as Christ sitting on a celestial orb. He oversees his glorious creation, symbolized by the four rivers. And running the show on earth is Justinian (left side), sporting both a halo and a crown to show he's leader of the Church and the state. Here, Justinian brings together the military leaders and the church leaders, all united by the straight line of eyes. The bald bishop of Ravenna—the only person who was actually here—is portrayed most realistically.

Facing the emperor (from the right side) is his wife, Theodora, and her entourage. Decked out in jewels and pearls, the former dancer who became Justinian's mistress and then empress carries a chalice to consecrate the new church.

The walls and ceilings sparkle with colorful Bible scenes told with a sixth-century exuberance. This was a time of transition, and many consider the mosaics of Ravenna both the last ancient Roman and the first medieval European works of art. For instance, you'll see a beardless Christ (as he was depicted by ancient Romans) next to a bearded Christ, his standard medieval portrayal.

The church's octagonal design—clearly Eastern—inspired the construction of the Hagia Sofia, built 10 years later in Constantinople. Charlemagne traveled here in about A.D. 800. He was so impressed that when he returned to his capital, Aix le Chapelle (present-day Aachen in Germany), he built what many consider the first great stone building in north Europe—modeled after this church (€6 for combo-ticket, see above, daily 9:00–19:00, off-season until 16:30, tel. 0544-219-938).

▲▲**Mausoleum of Galla Placidia**—Just across the courtyard (and included in San Vitale admission) is this tiny, humble-looking mausoleum, with the oldest—and to many, the best—mosaics in Ravenna. The Mausoleum of Galla Placidia (plah-CHEE-dee-ah) is reputed to be the burial place of this daughter, sister, and mother of emperors, who died in A.D. 450. The little light that sneaks through the thin alabaster panels brings a glow and a twinkle to the very early Christian symbolism (Jesus the Good Shepherd, Mark's lion, Luke's ox, John's eagle, the golden cross above everything) that fills the little room. Cover the light of the door with your hand to see the standard Roman portrayal of Christ—beardless and as the Good Shepherd. The Eastern influence is apparent in the carpet-like decorative patterns (€6 for combo-ticket, daily 9:00–19:00, off-season until 17:30, reservations necessary, call 0544-219-938 to book ahead).

▲▲**Basilica of St. Apollinare Nuovo**—This austere sixth-century church, with a typical early-Christian basilica floor plan, has two huge and wonderfully preserved side panels. One is a procession of haloed virgins, each bringing gifts to the Madonna and the Christ Child. Opposite, Christ is on his throne with four angels, awaiting a solemn procession of 26 martyrs. Ignoring the Baroque altar from a thousand years later, we can clearly see the rectangular Roman hall of justice, or basilica, plan—which was adopted by churches and used throughout the Middle Ages (€6 for combo-ticket, daily 9:30–19:00, off-season until 17:30, tel. 0544-219-938).

▲**Church of Sant' Apollinare in Classe**—Featuring great Byzantine art, this church is a favorite among mosaic pilgrims (€2.10, or €6.50 combo-ticket with National Museum and Mausoleum of Teodorico, Mon–Sat 8:30–19:30, Sun 13:00–19:00, tel. 0544-473-661). It's five kilometers (3 miles) out of town. Catch bus #4 from the station or #44 from Piazza Caduti (3/hr, 10 min, €0.80, buy bus tickets from a tobacco shop).

**Other Sights**—The **Basilica San Francesco** is worth a look for its simple interior and flooded, mosaic-covered crypt below the main altar (daily 7:30–12:00 & 15:00–19:00). Nearby, the **Tomb of Dante** is the true site of his remains. The Dante memorial—often mistaken for a tomb—in Florence's Santa Croce Church is empty (daily 9:00–19:00, off-season daily 9:00–12:00 & 15:00–17:00).

**Overrated Sight**—The nearby beach town of Rimini is an overcrowded and polluted mess.

## Sleeping in Ravenna
**(€1 = about $1, country code: 39, zip code: 48100)**
**Hotel Bisanzio** is a business-class splurge in the city center (Sb-€98, Db-€124, larger Db-€154, Via Salara 30, tel. 0544-217-111, fax 0544-32539).

**Hotel Diana**, with 33 cozy rooms, is an easy walk from San Vitale (Sb-€57, Db-€83, superior and deluxe rooms available, free parking nearby, Via G. Rossi 47, tel. 0544-39164, fax 0544-30001, www.ravennabedandbreakfast.it).

Two cheap hotels near the station are **Al Giaciglio** (S-€33, D-€42, Db-€51, Via R. Brancaleone 42, tel. & fax 0544-39403, SE, reception closes at 24:00) and **Hotel Ravenna** (S-€40, Sb-€45, D-€50, Db-€62, CC, Via Maroncelli 12, tel. 0544-212-204, fax 0544-212-077, SE).

**A Casa di Pino**, about a kilometer (0.6 mile) from the train station, rents two rooms. Engaging Pino Borghi recently opened this B&B in his hometown after a stint running a pension in Portugal (S-€26–34, D-€35–49, extra bed-€15, includes break-fast, Via Baccarini 37, take most any bus to Piazza Caduti, tel. & fax 0544-38524, www.acasadipino.it, e-mail: pinoborghi_ravenna@virgilio.it, SE).

*Hostel:* **Ostello Dante** is a 20-minute walk from the station (€13 bed in 4–6 bed rooms, family rooms available, follow signs for Ostello Dante or catch bus #1 or #70 from the station, Via Nicolodi 12, tel. & fax 0544-421-164, SE).

## Eating in Ravenna
The atmospheric **Ristorante-Enoteca Cá de Ven**—or House of Wine—fills a 16th-century warehouse with locals enjoying quality wine and traditional cuisine. *Piadina* (pron. peeah-DEE-nah) dominates the menu. An unleavened bread that kids are raised on here, it's served with cheese and prosciutto (Tue–Sun 11:00–14:00 & 17:30–22:15, closed Mon, Via C. Ricca 24, 2-min walk from Piazza del Popolo, tel. 0544-30163).

**Ristorante Marchesini** has a classy, self-serve menu that includes some delicious salads (Mon–Fri 12:00–14:30, Sat 19:30–22:30, closed Sun, Via Mazzini 6, 5-min walk from Piazza del Popolo, near Piazza Caduti, tel. 0544-212-309).

**Free Flow Bizantino**, inside the covered market, is another self-serve (Mon–Fri open for lunch only). Or assemble a picnic at the market and enjoy your feast in the shady gardens of the **Rocca Brancaleone** fortress (5-min walk from the station).

For a cheap and traditional lunch or snack, try a *piadina* or *cresciolo* (vegetarian) sandwich from **Pizzeria Cupido** just up Via Cavour, past the covered market. These tasty sandwiches come stuffed with a variety of meats and cheeses for €2.85–4.15. Try the *squaquarella*, filled with a soft regional cheese (Tue–Sun 8:00–20:00, closed Mon, Via Cavour 43, through the archway, tel. 0544-37529).

## Transportation Connections—Ravenna
**By train to: Venice** (3 hrs with transfer in Ferrara: Ravenna to Ferrara, every 2 hrs, 1 hr; Ferrara to Venice, hrly, 90 min), **Florence** (4 hrs with transfer in Bologna: Ravenna to Bologna, 8/day, 90 min; Bologna to Florence, hrly, 90 min). Train info: tel. 848-888-088 (automated, in Italian).

# FLORENCE
## (FIRENZE)

Florence, the home of the Renaissance and birthplace of our modern world, is a "supermarket sweep," and the groceries are the best Renaissance art in Europe.

Get your bearings with a Renaissance walk. Florentine art goes beyond paintings and statues—there's food, fashion, and handicrafts. You can lick Italy's best gelato while enjoying some of Europe's best people-watching.

## Planning Your Time

If you're in Europe for three weeks, Florence deserves a well-organized day. Make reservations in advance for the Uffizi Gallery (best Italian paintings anywhere) and Accademia (Michelangelo's *David*). For a day in Florence, see the Accademia, tour the Uffizi Gallery, visit the underrated Bargello (best statues), and do the Renaissance ramble (explained below).

Art-lovers will want to chisel out another day of their itinerary for the many other Florentine cultural treasures. Shoppers and ice cream–lovers may need to do the same.

Plan your sightseeing carefully. Some sights close Mondays and afternoons. While many spend several hours a day in lines, thoughtful travelers avoid this by making reservations or going late in the day. Places open at night are virtually empty.

## Orientation

The Florence we're interested in lies mostly on the north bank of the Arno River. Everything is within a 20-minute walk of the train station, cathedral, or Ponte Vecchio (Old Bridge). The less impressive but more characteristic Oltrarno (south bank) area is just over the bridge. The huge, red-tiled dome of the cathedral

## Florence Overview

(the Duomo) and its tall bell tower (Giotto's Tower) mark the center of historic Florence.

## Tourist Information

There are three TIs in Florence: across from the train station, near Santa Croce, and on Via Cavour.

The TI across the square from the train station is most crowded—expect long lines (Mon–Sat 8:30–19:00, Sun 8:30–13:00; off-season Mon–Sat 8:30–17:30, Sun 8:30–13:00; with your back to tracks, exit the station—it's across the square in wall near corner of church, Piazza Stazione, tel. 055-212-245, www.firenze.turismo.toscana.it). Note: In the station, avoid the Hotel Reservations "Tourist Information" window (marked *Informazioni Turistiche Alberghiere*) near the McDonald's; it's not a real TI but a hotel reservation business.

The TI near Santa Croce Church is pleasant, helpful, and uncrowded (Mon–Sat 9:00–19:00, Sun 9:00–14:00, shorter hours off-season, Borgo Santa Croce 29 red, tel. 055-234-0444).

Another winner is the TI three blocks north of the Duomo (Mon–Sat 8:15–19:15, Sun 8:30–13:30, closed winter Sun, Via Cavour 1 red, tel. 055-290-832 or 055-290-833; Feltrinelli's bookstore across street, listed under "Helpful Hints," page 192).

At any TI, pick up a map, a current museum-hours listing (extremely important since no guidebook—including this one—has ever been able to predict the hours of Florence's sights),

# Daily Reminder

**Sunday:** Today the Duomo's dome, Science Museum, and the Museum of Precious Stones are closed. These sights close early: the Duomo Museum (at 13:40), Baptistery's interior (at 14:00), and Dante's House (also at 14:00). A few sights are open only in the afternoon: Santa Croce Church (15:00–17:30) and the Brancacci Chapel and Santa Maria Novella (both 13:00–17:00).

The Museum of San Marco, which is open on the second and fourth Sunday of the month until 19:00, closes entirely—as does the Bargello—on the first, third, and fifth Sunday. The Medici Chapels and Modern Art Gallery (in Pitti Palace) close on the second and fourth Sunday.

**Monday:** The biggies are closed—Accademia (David) and Uffizi Gallery—as well as the Vasari Corridor and the Palatine Gallery/Royal Apartments (in Pitti Palace).

The Medici Chapels and Modern Art Gallery (in Pitti Palace) close on the first, third, and fifth Monday of the month. The Museum of San Marco and Bargello close on the second and fourth Monday. The Orsanmichele Church and Boboli Gardens close on the first and last Monday.

Good bets: Duomo Museum, Giotto's Tower, Brancacci Chapel, Michelangelo's House, Dante's House, Science Museum, Palazzo Vecchio (maybe until 23:00 in summer), and churches.

**Tuesday:** All sights are open except for Dante's House, Michelangelo's House, and the Brancacci Chapel. The Science Museum closes early (13:00).

**Wednesday:** All sights are open except for the Medici Riccardi Palace.

**Thursday:** All sights are open. The Museum of Precious Stones stays open late (19:00) while these sights close early: Duomo (15:30) and Palazzo Vecchio (14:00).

**Friday:** All sights are open. The Church of Santa Maria Novella opens late (13:00–17:00) and Palazzo Vecchio closes late (maybe until 23:00 in summer).

**Saturday:** All sights are open, but the Science Museum closes early (13:00). These sights close early on the first Saturday of the month: Duomo (15:30) and the Duomo's dome (15:20). The Museum of San Marco stays open until 19:00. The Accademia, Uffizi, and Palatine Gallery/Royal Apartments may stay open until 22:00 in summer.

and any information on entertainment. The free, monthly *Florence Concierge Information* magazine lists museums, plus lots of information that I don't: concerts and events, markets, sporting events, church services, shopping ideas, bus and train connections, and an entire similar section on Siena. Get yours at the TI or from any expensive hotel (pick one up as if you're staying there).

## Arrival in Florence

**By Train:** The station soaks up time and generates dazed and sweaty crowds. Try to get your tourist information and train tickets elsewhere. (You can get onward tickets and information at American Express—see "Helpful Hints," below.) With your back to the tracks, to your left are most of my recommended hotels; a 24-hour pharmacy (Farmacia Comunale, near McDonald's); city buses; and the entrance to the underground mall/passage that goes across the square to the church Santa Maria Novella (but because the tunnel, especially the surface point near the church, is frequented by pickpockets, stay above ground). Baggage check is near track 16.

**By Car:** From the autostrada (north or south), take the Certosa exit (follow signs to *Centro;* at Porta Romana, go to the left of the arch and down Via Francesco Petrarca). After driving and trying to park in Florence, you'll understand why Leonardo never invented the car. Cars flatten the charm of Florence. Don't drive in Florence, and don't risk parking illegally (fines up to €150). The city has plenty of lots. For a short stay, park underground at the train station (€2/hr). The Fortezza da Basso is clearly marked in the center (€18.50/24 hrs). The least expensive lots are Parcheggio Parterre (Firenze Parcheggi, €10.50/24 hrs, perhaps cheaper with hotel reservation) and Parcheggio Oltrarno (near Porta Romana—pass through gate and on left, €10.50 per day). For parking information, call 055-500-1994.

**By Plane:** Florence has its own airport and Pisa's is nearby. See "Transportation Connections," page 224, for details.

## Helpful Hints

**Theft Alert:** Florence has particularly hardworking thief gangs. They specialize in tourists and hang out where you do: near the train station, the station's underpass (especially where the tunnel surfaces), and major sights. Also, be on guard at two squares frequented by drug pushers (Santa Maria Novella and Santo Spirito). American tourists—especially older ones—are considered easy targets.

**Medical Help:** For a doctor who speaks English, call 055-475-411 (reasonable hotel calls, cheaper if you go to the

# Tips on Sightseeing in Florence

**Make Reservations to Avoid Lines:** Florence has a great reservation system for its top five sights—Uffizi, Accademia, Bargello, Medici Chapels, and the Pitti Palace. You can show up and wait in line, or make a quick and easy telephone booking.

Two sights come with long lines: the Accademia (*David*) and the Uffizi (two-hour lines on busy days). These lines are easily avoided by making a reservation. Frankly, it's stupid not to.

While you can generally make a reservation a day in advance (upon arrival in Florence), you'll have a wider selection of entry times by calling a few days ahead. You dial 055-294-883 (Mon–Fri 8:30–18:30, Sat 8:30–12:00, closed Sun), an English-speaking operator walks you through the process, and two minutes later, you say *grazie* with appointments (15-minute entry window) and six-digit confirmation numbers for each of the top museums and galleries.

If you haven't called ahead, you can make reservations for the top sights at the minor, less crowded sights (such as the Museum of San Marco or Museum of Precious Stones). Clerks at the ticket booths at these sleepy sights can reserve and sell tickets to the major sights—often for admissions the same day—allowing you to skip right past the dreary mob scene.

**Hours of Sights Can Change Suddenly:** Because of labor demands, hours of sights change without warning. Pick up the latest listing of museum hours at a TI, or you'll miss out on something you came to see. Don't delay; you never know when a place will close for a holiday, strike, or restoration.

**More Tips:** The biggies (Uffizi and Accademia) close on Monday. The *Concierge Information* magazine lists which sights are open afternoons, Sundays, and Mondays (best attractions open Mon: Museo dell' Opera del Duomo, Giotto's Tower, Brancacci Chapel, Michelangelo's Casa Buonarroti, Dante's House, Science Museum, Palazzo Vecchio, and churches).

Several museums are closed alternating Sundays and Mondays (e.g., closed first, third, and fifth Sun and second and fourth Mon of each month); use the calendar in the appendix to figure out which day they're closed during your trip. Churches usually close from 12:30 to 15:00 or 16:00. Some museums close at 14:00 and stop selling tickets 30 minutes before that.

I like the €2.60 "new map" of Florence that lists the sights (sold at newsstands). Local guidebooks are cheap and give you a map and a decent commentary on the sights.

clinic at Via L. Magnifico 59). The TI has a list of English-speaking doctors. A 24-hour pharmacy is at the train station.

**Addresses:** Street addresses list businesses in red and residences in black or blue (color-coded on the actual street number and indicated by a letter following the number in printed addresses: n = black, r = red). *Pensioni* are usually black but can be either. The red and black numbers each appear in roughly consecutive order on streets, but bear no apparent connection with each other. I'm lazy and don't concern myself with the distinction (if one number's wrong, I look for the other) and find my way around fine.

**American Express:** American Express offers all the normal services, but is most helpful as an easy place to get your train tickets, reservations, supplements (all the same price as at the station), or even just information on train schedules (Mon–Fri 9:00–17:30, Sat money exchange only 9:00–12:30, CC, 3 short blocks north of Palazzo Vecchio on Via Dante Alighieri 22 red, tel. 055-50981).

**Long-Distance Telephoning:** Small newsstand kiosks sell PIN phone cards that give you cheap international rates (10 minutes/€1).

**Books:** Feltrinelli International, a fine bookstore that sells fiction and guidebooks in English, is a few blocks north of the Duomo and across the street from the TI on Via Cavour (Mon–Sat 9:00–19:30, closed Sun, Via Cavour 20 red, tel. 055-219-524). Edison Bookstore sells CDs and novels on the Renaissance (daily 9:00–24:00, facing Piazza della Repubblica, tel. 055-213-110). Paperback Exchange also sells fiction and guidebooks (cheaper but smaller selection, Mon–Fri 9:00–19:30, Sat 10:00–13:00 & 15:30–19:30, closed Sun, shorter hours in Aug, at corner of Via Fiesolana and Via dei Pilastri, 6 blocks east of Duomo, tel. 055-247-8154).

**Laundry:** The Wash & Dry Lavarapido chain offers long hours and efficient self-service launderettes at several locations (about €6.20 for wash and dry, daily 8:00–22:00, tel. 055-580-480). Close to recommended hotels: Via dei Servi 105 (and a rival Laundromat at Via Guelfa 22 red, off Via Cavour; both near *David)*; Via del Sole 29 red and Via della Scala 52 red (between train station and river), and Via dei Serragli 87 red (across the river in Oltrarno neighborhood).

## Getting around Florence

I organize my sightseeing geographically and do it all on foot. A €1 ticket gives you one hour on the buses, €1.80 gives you three hours, and €4 gets you 24 hours (tickets not sold on bus—except after 21:00, buy in *tabacchi* shops or newsstands, validate on bus).

The minimum cost for a taxi ride is €4, or, after 22:00, €5 (rides in the center of town should be charged as tariff #1). A taxi ride from the train station to Ponte Vecchio costs about €8. Taxi fares and supplements are clearly explained on signs in each cab.

## Tours of Florence

**Walking Tours of Florence**—This company offers a variety of tours (up to 4/day Mon–Sat) featuring downtown Florence, Uffizi highlights, or the countryside, presented by informative, entertaining, native English-speaking guides. The "Original Florence" walk hits the main sights, but gets offbeat to weave a picture of Florentine life in medieval and Renaissance times. You can expect lots of talking, which is great if you like history. Tours, offered year-round regardless of weather, start at their office and are limited to a maximum of 22; extra guides are available if more people show up (€24 for 3-hr Original Florence walk, office open Mon–Sat 8:30–18:00, closed for lunch off-season, Piazza Santo Stefano 2 black, a short block north of Ponte Vecchio; go east on tiny Vicolo San Stefano, in Piazza Santo Stefano at #2; booking necessary for Uffizi tour, private tours available, tel. 055-264-5033, cellular 0329-613-2730, www.artviva.com). The owner of the company, Rosanne Magers, also offers private tours (tel. 055-264-5033, e-mail: walkingtours @artviva.com).

**Florentia**—These top-notch historical walking tours of Florence and Tuscany are led by local scholars. The tours, ranging from introductory city walks to in-depth visits of museums and lesser-known destinations, are geared for thoughtful and well-heeled travelers (semi-private tours start at €45 per person, max 8 per group; private tours start at€180 for half-day tour, reserve in advance, tel. 055-225-535, U.S. tel. 510/549-1707, www.florentia .org, e-mail: info@florentia.org).

**Florence Art Lectures**—These 90-minute talks on the Florentine Renaissance, designed for English-speaking tourists, are held in a classy 13th-century palazzo near the Santa Croce Church (€20, offered May–Sept only, Mon–Sat at 14:30, includes glass of wine, espresso, or cold drink, Piazza Santa Croce 21, tel. 055-245-354, www.florenceart.org). They also offer art lectures combined with a lunch or dinner, as well as museum tours and city walking tours at sunset.

**Local Guide—Paola Migilorini** offers museum tours, city walking tours, and Tuscan excursions by van (€100 for 2-hr walking tour or Uffizi tour, Via S. Gallo 120, tel. 055-472-448, cellular 347-657-2611, www.florencetour.com, e-mail: info@florencetour.com).

## A Florentine Renaissance Walk

Even during the Dark Ages, people knew they were in a "middle time." It was especially obvious to the people of Italy—sitting on the rubble of Rome—that there was a brighter age before them. The long-awaited rebirth, or Renaissance, began in Florence for good reason. Wealthy because of its cloth industry, trade, and banking; powered by a fierce city-state pride (locals would pee into the Arno with gusto, knowing rival city-state Pisa was downstream); and fertile with more than its share of artistic genius (imagine guys like Michelangelo and Leonardo attending the same high school)—Florence was a natural home for this cultural explosion.

Take a walk through the core of Renaissance Florence by starting at the Accademia (home of Michelangelo's *David*) and cutting through the heart of the city to Ponte Vecchio on the Arno River. (A 13-page, self-guided tour of this walk is outlined in my museum guidebook, *Rick Steves' Mona Winks*, and in *Rick Steves' Florence*; otherwise, you'll find brief descriptions below.)

At the Accademia, you'll look into the eyes of Renaissance man—humanism at its confident peak. Then walk to the cathedral (Duomo) to see the dome that kicked off the architectural Renaissance. Step inside the baptistery to view a ceiling covered with preachy, flat, 2-D, medieval mosaic art. Then, to learn what happened when art met math, check out the realistic 3-D reliefs on the doors. The painter, Giotto, also designed the bell tower—an early example of a Renaissance genius excelling in many areas. Continue toward the river on Florence's great pedestrian mall, Via de' Calzaiuoli (or "Via Calz")—part of the original grid plan given to the city by the ancient Romans. Down a few blocks, compare medieval and Renaissance statues on the exterior of the Orsanmichele Church. Via Calz connects the cathedral with the central square (Piazza della Signoria), the city palace (Palazzo Vecchio), and the Uffizi Gallery, which contains the greatest collection of Italian Renaissance paintings in captivity. Finally, walk through the Uffizi courtyard—a statuary think tank of Renaissance greats—to the Arno River and Ponte Vecchio.

## Sights—On a Renaissance Walk through Florence

▲▲▲Accademia (Galleria dell' Accademia)—This museum houses Michelangelo's *David* and powerful (unfinished) *Prisoners*. Eavesdrop as tour guides explain these masterpieces. More than with any other work of art, when you look into the eyes of *David*, you're looking into the eyes of Renaissance man. This was a radical break with the past. Hello, humanism. Man was now a confident individual, no longer a plaything of the supernatural.

And life was now more than just a preparation for what happened after you died.

The Renaissance was the merging of art, science, and humanism. In a humanist vein, *David* is looking at the crude giant of medieval darkness and thinking, "I can take this guy." (David was an apt mascot for a town surrounded by big bully city-states.) Back on a religious track, notice *David*'s large and overdeveloped right hand. This is symbolic of the hand of God that powered David to slay the giant... and enabled Florence to rise above its crude neighboring city-states.

Beyond the magic marble are two floors of interesting pre-Renaissance and Renaissance paintings, including a couple of lighter-than-air Botticellis.

**Cost, Hours, Location:** €6.50 (plus €1.55 reservation fee). Open Tue–Sun 8:15–18:50, until 22:00 on holidays and maybe on summer Sat, closed Mon (last entry 30 min before closing, Via Ricasoli 60, tel. 055-238-8609). No photos or videos are allowed. The museum is most crowded on Sun, Tue, and the first thing in the morning. It's easy to reserve ahead; see page 193 for details.

**Nearby:** Piazza Santissima Annunziata, behind the Accademia, features lovely Renaissance harmony. Brunelleschi's Hospital of the Innocents (Spedale degli Innocenti, not worth going inside), with terra-cotta medallions by Luca Della Robbia, was built in the 1420s and is considered the first Renaissance building. The 15th-century Santissima Annunziata church facing the same square is worth a peek.

▲▲**Duomo**—Florence's Gothic Santa Maria del Fiori cathedral has the third-longest nave in Christendom (free, Mon–Wed and Fri–Sat 10:00–17:00 except first Sat of month 10:00–15:30, Thu 10:00–15:30, Sun 13:30–16:45, tel. 055-230-2885).

The church's noisy neo-Gothic facade from the 1870s is covered with pink, green, and white Tuscan marble. Since nearly all of its great art is stored in the Museo dell' Opera del Duomo (behind the church), the best thing about the interior is the shade. The inside of the dome is decorated by one of the largest paintings of the Renaissance, a huge (and newly restored) *Last Judgment* by Vasari and Zucarri.

Think of the confidence of the age: The Duomo was built with a hole awaiting a dome in its roof. This was before the technology to span it with a dome was available. No matter. They knew that someone soon could handle the challenge... and the local architect Brunelleschi did. The cathedral's claim to artistic fame is Brunelleschi's magnificent dome—the first Renaissance dome and the model for domes to follow.

## Florence Sights

▲**Climbing the Cathedral's Dome**—For a grand view into the cathedral from the base of the dome, a peek at some of the tools used in the dome's construction, a chance to see Brunelleschi's "dome-within-a-dome" construction, a glorious Florence view from the top, and the equivalent of 463 plunges on a StairMaster, climb the dome (€6, Mon–Sat 8:30–19:00 except first Sat of month 8:30–15:20, closed Sun; enter from outside church on south or river side, arrive by 8:30 to avoid a long wait in line). When planning St. Peter's in Rome, Michelangelo rhymed (not in English), "I can build its sister—bigger, but not more beautiful, than the dome of Florence."

▲**Giotto's Tower (Campanile)**—If you're not interested in experiencing dome-within-a-dome architecture, you'll likely feel that climbing Giotto's 82-meter-tall (270-foot) bell tower beats scaling the neighboring Duomo's dome because it's 50 fewer steps, faster, and offers the same view plus the dome (€6, daily 8:30–19:30, last entry 40 min before closing).

▲▲**Museo dell' Opera del Duomo**—The underrated cathedral museum, behind the church at #9, is great if you like sculpture. It has masterpieces by Donatello (a gruesome wood carving of Mary Magdalene clothed in her matted hair, and the *cantoria*, a delightful choir loft bursting with happy children) and by Luca Della Robbia (another choir loft, lined with the dreamy faces of musicians praising the Lord). Look for a late Michelangelo *pietà* (Nicodemus, on top, is a self-portrait), Brunelleschi's models for his dome, and the original restored panels of Ghiberti's doors to the baptistery. This is one of the few museums in Florence open on Monday (€6, Mon–Sat 9:00–19:30, Sun 9:00–13:40, closed on holidays, tel. 055-230-2885). If you find all this church art intriguing, look through the open doorway of the Duomo art studio, which has been making and restoring church art since the days of Brunelleschi (a block toward the river from the Duomo at 23a Via dello Studio).

▲**Baptistery**—Michelangelo said its bronze doors were fit to be the gates of Paradise. Check out the gleaming copies of Ghiberti's bronze doors facing the Duomo. Making a breakthrough in perspective, Ghiberti used mathematical laws to create the illusion of receding distance on a basically flat surface. The earlier, famous competition doors are around to the right (north); Ghiberti, who beat Brunelleschi, got the job of designing these doors.

A local document from A.D. 860 already refers to Florence's oldest building as "ancient." Inside, sit and savor the medieval mosaic ceiling, where it's Judgment Day and Jesus is giving the ultimate thumbs up and thumbs down. Compare that to the "new, improved" art of the Renaissance (€3, interior open Mon–Sat 12:00–19:00, Sun 8:30–14:00, bronze doors are on the outside so always "open"; original panels are in the Museo dell' Opera del Duomo).

▲**Orsanmichele**—This ninth-century loggia (a covered court-yard) was a market used for selling grain (stored upstairs). Later, it was closed in to make a church. Notice the grain spouts on the pillars inside. The glorious tabernacle by Orcagna (1359) takes you back.

Study the sculpture in the niches outside. You can see man stepping out of the literal and figurative shadow of the Church in the great Renaissance sculptor Donatello's *St. George*. Look into George's face; he's a sensitive new-age guy (SNAG). The predella (platform) at the base of this statue shows St. George slaying the dragon to protect the wispy, melodramatic maiden. This was groundbreaking Renaissance emotion and perspective (free, daily 9:00–12:00 & 16:00–18:00, closed first and last Mon of month, on Via Calzaiuoli, enter through the back door, may be closed due to staffing problems). The iron bars spanning the vaults were the Italian Gothic answer to the French Gothic external buttresses. Across the street is...

▲**Museo Orsanmichele**—For some peaceful time alone with the original statues that filled the niches of Orsanmichele, climb to the top of the church (entry behind church, across street). Be there at 9:00, 10:00, and 11:00 daily, when the door is open and art-lovers in the know climb four flights of stairs to this little-known museum containing statues by Ghiberti, Donatello, and others (info in Italian, but picture guides on wall help you match art with artists). Upstairs is a tower room with city views (free). A block away, you'll find the...

▲**Mercato Nuovo**—This market loggia is how Orsanmichele looked before it became a church. Originally a silk and straw market, Mercato Nuovo still functions as a rustic market today (at intersection of Via Calimala and Via Porta Rossa). Prices are soft.

Notice the circled *X* in the center, marking the spot where people hit after being hoisted up to the top and dropped as punishment for bankruptcy. You'll also find Porcellino (a statue of a wild boar, nicknamed "little pig"), which people rub and give coins to in order to ensure their return to Florence. Nearby is a wagon selling tripe (cow innards) sandwiches.

▲**Palazzo Vecchio**—This fortified palace, once the home of the Medici family, is a Florentine landmark. But if you're visiting only one palace interior in town, the Pitti Palace is better. The Palazzo Vecchio interior is wallpapered with mediocre magnificence, worthwhile only if you're a real Florentine art and history fan. The museum's most famous statues are Michelangelo's *Genius of Victory*, Donatello's static *Judith and Holofernes*, and Verrocchio's *Winged Cherub* (a copy tops the fountain in the free courtyard at entrance, original inside).

Scattered throughout the museum are a dozen computer terminals with information in English on the Medici family, Palazzo Vecchio, and the building's architecture and art, including an animated clip showing how Michelangelo's *David* was moved from the square to the Accademia (€5.70, Fri–Wed 9:00–19:00, Thu 9:00–14:00, in summer maybe open until 23:00 on Mon and Fri, ticket office closes 1 hour earlier, WC in second courtyard can be accessed without paying palace admission, tel. 055-276-8465).

Even if you don't go to the museum, do step into the free

courtyard (behind the fake *David*) just to feel the essence of the Medici. Until 1873, Michelangelo's *David* stood at the entrance, where the copy is today. While the huge statues in the square are important only as the whipping boys of art critics and rest stops for pigeons, the nearby Loggia dei Lanzi has several important statues. Look for Cellini's bronze statue of Perseus (with the head of Medusa). The plaque on the pavement in front of the fountain marks the spot where the monk Savonarola was burned in MCCCCXCVIII (for more on the monk, see "Museum of San Marco" listing, below).

▲▲▲**Uffizi Gallery**—The greatest collection of Italian paintings anywhere is a must, with plenty of works by Giotto, Leonardo, Raphael, Caravaggio, Rubens, Titian, and Michelangelo and a roomful of Botticellis, including his *Birth of Venus*. Make a reservation to avoid the long line (see below). Because only 780 visitors are allowed inside the building at any one time, there's generally a very long wait during the day. The good news: No Louvre-style mob scenes. The museum is nowhere near as big as it is great: Few tourists spend more than two hours inside. The paintings are displayed on one comfortable floor in chronological order, from the 13th through 17th centuries.

Essential stops are (in this order): Gothic altarpieces (narrative, pre-Realism, no real concern for believable depth) including Giotto's altarpiece, which progressed beyond "totem-pole angels"; Uccello's *Battle of San Romano*, an early study in perspective (with a few obvious flubs); Fra Filippo Lippi's cuddly Madonnas; the Botticelli room, filled with masterpieces, including a pantheon of classical fleshiness and the small *La Calumnia*, showing the glasnost of Renaissance free-thinking being clubbed back into the darker age of Savonarola; two minor works by Leonardo; the octagonal classical sculpture room with an early painting of Bob Hope and a copy of Praxiteles' *Venus de Medici*—considered the epitome of beauty in Elizabethan Europe; a view through the window of Ponte Vecchio—dreamy at sunset; Michelangelo's only surviving easel painting, the round *Holy Family*; Raphael's noble *Madonna of the Goldfinch*; Titian's voluptuous *Venus of Urbino*; and Duomo views from the café terrace at the end (WC near café).

**Cost, Hours, Reservations:** €8, plus €1.55 for recommended reservation, Tue–Sun 8:15–18:50, until 22:00 on holidays and maybe on summer Sat, closed Mon (last entry 45 min before closing; after entering take elevator or climb 4 long flights of stairs).

Avoid the two-hour peak season midday wait by making a telephone reservation. It's easy, slick, and costs only €1.55 (tel. 055-294-883, explained on page 193). At the Uffizi, walk briskly past the 200-meter-long (650-foot) line—pondering the IQ of this gang—to the special entrance for those with reservations (labeled in English "Entrance for Reservations Only"), give your number, pay (cash only), and scoot right in.

If you haven't called ahead, you may be able to book a ticket at Florence's lesser sights (such as the Museum of San Marco) or even at the Uffizi itself. At the Uffizi, ask the clerk (who stands at the entrance for people with reservations) if you can make a reservation in person. He may direct you to the ticket office where you can secure a reservation for later in the day or the next day (depends on luck and availability). Also, Walking Tours of Florence does a guided tour of the museum Tuesday through Saturday which gets you inside without a wait (see "Tours of Florence," page 195).

Enjoy the Uffizi square, full of artists and souvenir stalls. The surrounding statues honor the earthshaking: artists, philosophers (Machiavelli), scientists (Galileo), writers (Dante), explorers (Amerigo Vespucci), and the great patron of so much Renaissance thinking, Lorenzo (the Magnificent) de' Medici.

▲**Ponte Vecchio**—Florence's most famous bridge is lined with shops that have traditionally sold gold and silver. A statue of Cellini, the master goldsmith of the Renaissance, stands in the center, ignored by the flood of tacky tourism. Notice the "prince's passageway" above. In less secure times, the city leaders had a fortified passageway connecting the Palace Vecchio and Uffizi with the mighty Pitti Palace, to which they could flee in times of attack. This passageway, called the Vasari Corridor, is open to the persistent by request only (€8, Tue–Sat at 9:30, closed Mon, tel. 055-265-4321).

## Sights—Near the Accademia

▲▲**Museum of San Marco**—One block north of the Accademia on Piazza San Marco, this museum houses the greatest collection anywhere of medieval frescoes and paintings by the early Renaissance master Fra Angelico. You'll see why he thought of painting as a form of prayer, and couldn't paint a crucifix without shedding tears. Each of the monks' cells has a Fra Angelico fresco. Don't miss the cell of Savonarola, the charismatic monk who rode in from the Christian right, threw out the Medici, turned Florence into a theocracy, sponsored "bonfires of the vanities" (burning books, paintings, and so on), and was finally burned himself when Florence decided to change channels (€4, daily 8:15–13:50, Sat–Sun until 19:00, but closed first, third, and fifth Sun and second and fourth Mon of each month, tel. 055-238-8608). They can sell tickets (often with immediate reservation) to Uffizi and Accademia.

**Museum of Precious Stones (Museo dell' Opificio delle Pietre Dure)**—This unusual gem of a museum features mosaics of inlaid marble and semiprecious stones. You'll see remnants of the Medici workshop from 1588, including 500 different semi-precious stones, the tools used to cut and inlay them, and room after room of the sumptuous finished product. The fine loaner booklet describes it all in English (€2, Mon–Sat 8:15–14:00, Thu until 19:00, closed Sun, Via degli Alfani 78, around corner from Accademia). This ticket booth can also sell tickets with reservations (perhaps same-day) to the Uffizi and Accademia.

## Sights—Heart of Florence

▲▲▲**Bargello (Museo Nazionale)**—This underrated sculpture museum is behind Palazzo Vecchio in a former prison that looks like a mini–Palazzo Vecchio. It has Donatello's painfully beautiful *David* (the very influential first male nude to have been sculpted in a thousand years), works by Michelangelo, and rooms of Medici treasures cruelly explained in Italian only—mention that English descriptions would be wonderful (€4, daily 8:15–13:50 but closed first, third, and fifth Sun and second and fourth Mon of each month, last entry 30 min before closing, Via del Proconsolo 4, tel. 055-238-8606).

**Dante's House (Casa di Dante)**—Dante's house consists of five rooms in an old building, with little of substance to show but lots of photos relating to his life and work. Although it's well-described in English, it's mainly of interest to literary buffs (€3, Mon and Wed–Sat 10:00–17:00, Sun 10:00–14:00, closed Tue, across the street and around the corner from Bargello, at Via S. Margherita 1).

▲**Medici Chapels (Cappelli dei Medici)**—This chapel, containing two Medici tombs, is drenched in lavish High Renaissance architecture and sculpture by Michelangelo (€6, daily 8:15–17:00 but closed the second and fourth Sun and the first, third, and fifth Mon of each month, tel. 055-238-8602). Behind San Lorenzo on Piazza Madonna is a lively market scene that I find just as interesting. Take a stroll through the huge, double-decker central market one block north.

▲**Piazza della Repubblica**—This large square, the belly-button of Florence, sits on the site of Florence's original Roman Forum. The lone column is the only remaining bit of Roman Florence except for the grid street plan. Look at the map to see the ghost of Rome: a rectangular fort with this square marking the intersection of the two main roads (Via Corso and Via Roma).

Today's piazza, framed by a triumphal arch, is really a nationalistic statement celebrating the unification of Italy. Florence, the capital of the country (1865–1870) until Rome was liberated, lacked a square worthy of this grand new country. So the neighborhood here was razed to open up a grand modern forum surrounded by grand circa-1890 buildings.

Medieval writers described Florence as so densely built up that when it rained, pedestrians didn't get wet. Torches were used to light the lanes in midday. The city was prickly with noble family towers (like San Gimignano) and had Romeo-and-Juliet-type family feuds. But with the rise of the Medicis (c. 1300), no noble family was allowed to have an architectural ego trip taller then their tower, and nearly all were taken down.

**Science Museum (Museo di Storia della Scienza)**—This is a fascinating collection of Renaissance and later clocks, telescopes, maps, and ingenious gadgets. One of the most talked-about bottles in Florence is the one here containing Galileo's finger. Loaner English guidebooklets are available. It's friendly, comfortably cool, never crowded, and just a block east of the Uffizi (€6.50, Mon and Wed–Fri 9:30–17:00, Tue and Sat 9:30–13:00, closed Sun, Piazza dei Giudici 1, tel. 055-239-8876).

**Church of Santa Maria Novella**—This 13th-century Dominican church, just south of the train station, is rich in art. Along with crucifixes by Giotto and Brunelleschi, there are fine examples of the early Renaissance mastery of perspective. The most famous is the *Holy Trinity* by Masaccio; it's opposite the entrance (€2.60, Mon–Thu and Sat 9:30–17:00, Fri and Sun 13:00–17:00).

A palatial **perfumery** is around the corner 100 meters (330 feet) down Via della Scala at #16 (free but shopping encouraged, Mon–Sat 9:30–19:30, closed Sun). Thick with the lingering aroma of centuries of spritzes, it started as the herb garden of the Santa Maria Novella monks. Well-known even today for its top-quality products, it is extremely Florentine. Pick up the history sheet at the desk and wander deep into the shop. From the back room, you can peek at the S. M. Novella cloister, with its dreamy frescoes, and imagine a time before Vespas and tourists.

## Sights—Santa Croce and Nearby

▲▲**Santa Croce Church**—This 14th-century Franciscan church, decorated by centuries of precious art, holds the tombs of great Florentines (€3, Mon–Sat 9:30–17:30, Sun 15:00–17:30, in winter Mon–Sat 9:30–12:30 & 15:00–17:30, Sun 15:00–17:30, modest dress code enforced, tel. 055-244-619). The loud 19th-century Victorian Gothic facade faces a huge square ringed with tempting touristy shops and littered with tired tourists. Escape into the church.

Working counterclockwise from the entrance, you'll find the tomb of Michelangelo (with the allegorical figures of painting, architecture, and sculpture), a memorial to Dante (no body...

he was banished by his hometown over politics), the tomb of Machiavelli (the originator of hardball politics), a relief by Donatello of the Annunciation, and the tomb of the composer Rossini. To the right of the altar, step into the sacristy, where you'll find a bit of St. Francis' cowl and old sheets of music with the medieval and mobile C clef (two little blocks on either side of the line determined to be middle C). In the bookshop, notice the photos high on the wall of the devastating flood of 1966. Beyond that is a touristy—but mildly interesting—"leather school." The chapels lining the front of the church are richly frescoed. The Bardi Chapel (far left of altar) is a masterpiece by Giotto featuring scenes from the life of St. Francis. On your way out, you'll pass the tomb of Galileo (allowed in by the church long after his death).

The neighboring **Pazzi Chapel** by Brunelleschi is considered one of the finest pieces of Florentine Renaissance architecture (covered by €3 Santa Croce church admission, Thu–Tue 10:00– 18:00, closed Wed, entrance outside church; facing facade it's the door to the right).

▲**Michelangelo's Home (Casa Buonarroti)**—Fans enjoy Michelangelo's house, which has some of his early, much-less-monumental statues and sketches (€6.50, Wed–Mon 9:30– 14:00, closed Tue, English descriptions, Via Ghibellina 70).

## Sights—Florence, South of the Arno River

▲▲**Pitti Palace**—From the Uffizi, follow the elevated passageway (closed to non-Medicis) across the Ponte Vecchio bridge to the gargantuan Pitti Palace, which has five separate museums.

The **Palatine Gallery/Royal Apartments** features palatial room after chandeliered room, their walls sagging with paintings by the great masters. Its Raphael collection is the biggest anywhere (first floor, €6.50, Tue–Sun 8:30–18:50, maybe summer Sat until 22:00, closed Mon, buy tickets on right-hand side of courtyard).

The **Modern Art Gallery** features Romanticism, neoclassicism, and Impressionism by 19th- and 20th-century Tuscan painters (second floor, €5, daily 8:30–13:50 but closed second and fourth Sun and first, third, and fifth Mon).

The **Grand Ducal Treasures**, or Museo degli Argenti, is the Medici treasure chest entertaining fans of applied arts with jeweled crucifixes, exotic porcelain, gilded ostrich eggs, and so on (ground floor, €7.75, nearly the same hours as Modern Art Gallery).

The landscaped **Boboli Gardens** offer a shady refuge from the heat (€2, daily 9:00–18:30, June–Aug until 19:30, winter until 16:30, closed first and last Mon of month, behind palace).

▲**Brancacci Chapel**—For the best look at the early Renaissance master Masaccio, see his restored frescoes here (€3.10, Mon and

Wed–Sat 10:00–17:00, Sun 13:00–17:00, closed Tue, cross Ponte Vecchio and turn right a few blocks to Piazza del Carmine). Since only a few tourists are let in at a time, seeing the chapel often involves a wait. The neighborhoods around here are considered the last surviving bits of old Florence.

▲**Piazzale Michelangelo**—Across the river overlooking the city (look for the huge statue of *David*), this square is worth the 30-minute hike, drive, or bus ride (either #12 or #13 from the train station) for the view of Florence and the stunning dome of the Duomo. After dark, it's packed with local schoolkids, feeding their dates slices of watermelon. Just beyond it is the stark and beautiful, crowd-free Romanesque San Miniato Church.

**Oltrarno Walk**—If you never leave the touristy center, you don't really see Florence. There's more to the city than tourism. Ninety percent of its people live and work—mostly in small shops—where tourists rarely venture. This self-guided tour follows a perfectly straight line (you can't get lost). Cross the Ponte Vecchio and walk west on the road toward Pisa—it changes names, from Borgo San Jacopo and Via di Santo Spirito to Borgo Frediano, until you reach the city wall at Porta San Frediano. Along this route you can check out several of my favorite restaurants (described below). As you walk, consider these points:

After one block, at the fancy **Hotel Lungarno**, belly up to the Arno River viewpoint for a great look at Ponte Vecchio. Recall the story of Kesserling, the Nazi commander-in-chief of Italy who happened to be an art-lover. As the Nazis retreated in 1944, he was commanded to blow up all the bridges. Rather than destroy the venerable Ponte Vecchio, he disabled it by blowing up the surrounding neighborhood. Turn around and cross the street to see the ivy-covered nub of a medieval tower—ruined August 6, 1944.

Along this walk, you'll see plenty of artisans at work and inviting little **shops**. You're welcome to drop in but remember, it's rude not to say "*Buon giorno*" and "*Ciao*." "Can I take a look?" is "*Posso guardare?*" (pron. POH-soh gwahr-DAH-ray).

The streets are busy with *motorini* (Vespas and other motorbikes). While these are allowed in the city, nonresident cars are not (unless they are electric). Notice that parked cars have a *residente* permit on their dash. You'll see a police officer (likely a woman) later on the walk, keeping traffic out.

Look for little architectural details. Tiny shrines protect the corners of many blocks. Once upon a time, the iron spikes on the walls impaled huge candles, which provided a little light. Electricity changed all that, but notice there are no electric wires visible. They're under the streets.

This street is lined with apartment flats punctuated by the

occasional palazzo. The skyline and architecture are typical of the 13th to 16th centuries. Huge **palazzos** (recognized by their immense doors, lush courtyards, and grand stonework) were for big-shot merchants. Many have small wooden doors designed to look like stones (e.g., 3b on Borgo San Frediano). While originally for one family, these buildings are now subdivided, as evidenced by the huge banks of doorbells at the door.

The **Church of Santa Maria del Carmine**, with its famous Brancacci Chapel and Masaccio frescoes, is a short detour off Borgo San Frediano (described above).

A couple of blocks before Porta San Frediano (and its tower), look left up Piazza dei Nerli. The bold yellow schoolhouse was built during Mussolini's rule—grandly proclaiming the resurrection of the Italian empire.

**Porta San Frediano** (c. 1300), is part of Florence's medieval wall, which stretches grandly from here to the river. The tower was originally twice as high, built when gravity ruled warfare. During the Renaissance, when gunpowder dominated warfare, the tower—now just an easy target—was topped. In medieval times, a kilometer-wide strip outside the wall was cleared to deny attackers any cover. Notice the original doors, immense and studded with fat iron nails to withstand battering rams. Got a horse? Lash it to a ring.

Tour over. You passed several fun eateries, and the colorful Trattoria Sabatino is just outside the wall (all described in "Eating in Florence," page 218). *Ciao.*

## Experiences—Florence

▲▲**Gelato**—Gelato is an edible art form. Italy's best ice cream is in Florence—one souvenir that can't break and won't clutter your luggage. But beware of scams at touristy joints on busy streets that turn a simple request of a cone into a €10 "tourist special."

The **Gelateria Carrozze** is very good (daily 11:00–24:00, closes at 21:00 in winter, on riverfront 30 meters, or 100 feet, from Ponte Vecchio toward the Uffizi, Via del Pesce 3). **Gelateria dei Neri** is another local favorite worth finding (2 blocks east of Palazzo Vecchio at Via Dei Neri 20 red, daily in summer 12:00–23:00, closed Wed in winter).

**Vivoli's** is the most famous (Tue–Sun 8:00–24:00, closed Mon, the last 3 weeks in Aug, and winter; opposite the Church of Santa Croce, go down Via Torta a block, turn right on Via Stinche; before ordering, try a free sample of their *riso* flavor—rice).

If you want an excuse to check out the little village-like neighborhood across the river from Santa Croce, enjoy a gelato at the tiny **no-name** *gelateria* at Via San Miniato 5 red (just before Porta San Miniato).

## Shopping

Florence is a great shopping town. Busy street scenes and markets abound, especially near San Lorenzo, near Santa Croce, on Ponte Vecchio, and at Mercato Nuovo (a covered market square 3 blocks north of Ponte Vecchio, listed above in "Sights"). Leather (often better quality for less than the U.S. price), gold, silver, art prints, and tacky plaster mini-*David*s are most popular. Shops usually have promotional stalls in the market squares. Prices are soft in markets. Many visitors spend entire days shopping.

For ritzy Italian fashions, browse along Via de Tornabuoni, Via della Vigna Nuova, and Via Strozzi. Typical chain department stores are Coin (Mon–Sat 9:30–20:00, Sun 11:00–20:00, on Via Calzaiuoli, near Orsanmichele Church); Standa, a discount clothing/grocery chain (Mon–Sat 9:00–19:55, closed Sun, at intersection of Via Panzani and Via del Giglio, near train station) and La Rinascente (Piazza della Repubblica, Mon–Sat 9:00–21:00, Sun 10:30–20:00).

For shopping ideas, ads, and a list of markets, see the *Florence Concierge Information* magazine described under "Tourist Information," above (free from TI and many hotels).

## Side Trips to Fiesole and Siena

For a candid peek at **Fiesole**—a Florentine suburb—ride bus #7 (3/hr, departs from Piazza Adua at the northeast side of the station and also from Piazza San Marco) for about 25 minutes through neighborhood gardens, vineyards, orchards, and large villas to the last stop—Fiesole. This town is a popular excursion from Florence because of its small eateries and its good views of Florence. Catch the sunset from the terrace just below the La Reggia restaurant; from the Fiesole bus stop, face the bell tower and take the very steep Via San Francisco on your left. You'll find the view terrace near the top of the hill.

Connoisseurs of smaller towns (who won't be seeing Siena otherwise) should consider riding the bus to **Siena** (75 min by bus). This can be a day trip or an evening trip. Siena is magic after dark. Confirm when the last bus returns. For more information, see the Siena chapter.

## Sleeping in Florence
**(€1 = about $1, country code: 39)**
Sleep Code: **S** = Single, **D** = Double/Twin, **T** = Triple, **Q** = Quad, **b** = bathroom, **s** = shower only, **CC** = Credit Cards accepted, **no CC** = Credit Cards not accepted, **SE** = Speaks English, **NSE** = No English. Unless otherwise noted, breakfast is included (but usually optional). English is generally spoken.

To help you sort easily through these listings, I've divided the rooms into three categories based on the price for a standard double room with bath:

**Higher Priced**—Most rooms more than €160.
**Moderately Priced**—Most rooms €160 or less.
**Lower Priced**—Most rooms €110 or less.

The accommodations scene varies wildly with the season. Spring and fall are very tight and expensive, while mid-July through August is wide open and discounted. November through February is also generally empty. With good information and a phone call ahead, you can find a stark, clean, and comfortable double with breakfast for about €65, with a private shower for €100 (less at the smaller places, such as the *soggiornos*). You get elegance for €140. Rooms with air-conditioning cost around €100—worth the extra money in the summer. Virtually all of the places are central, within minutes of the great sights. Few hotels escape Vespa noise at night.

Call direct to the hotel. Do not use the TI, which costs your host and jacks up the price. In slow times, budget travelers call around and find soft prices. Ask if you'll get a discount for paying in cash, for staying for three or more nights (or both), or for using this book. And ask if you can skip breakfast (the overpriced breakfasts are legally optional, though some hotels pretend otherwise).

Call ahead. I repeat, call ahead. Places will hold a room until early afternoon. If they say they're full, mention you're using this book.

## Sleeping between the Station and Duomo (zip code: 50123)

### HIGHER PRICED

**Palazzo Castiglioni** offers 16 grand rooms with all the conveniences in a peaceful, 19th-century palazzo package. Most rooms are spacious, several have frescoes, and all make a fine splurge (Db-€165, Db suite-€207, Tb-€207, air-con, elevator, Via del Giglio 8, tel. 055-214-886, fax 055-274-0521, e-mail: pal .cast@flashnet.it, Laura SE).

### MODERATELY PRICED

**Hotel Accademia** is an elegant two-star hotel with marble stairs, parquet floors, attractive public areas, 22 pleasant rooms, and a floor plan that defies logic (Sb-€87, Db-€140, Tb-€170, these discounted prices are promised through 2003 only with this book, CC, air-con, TV, tiny courtyard, Via Faenza 7, tel. 055-293-451, fax 055-219-771, www.accademiahotel.net, e-mail: info@accademiahotel.net, SE).

# Hotels in Florence

- ➊ HOTEL ACCADEMIA
- ➋ HOTEL MORANDI ALLA CROCETTA
- ➌ CASA RABATTI
- ➍ SOGGIORNO PEZZATI
- ➎ HOTEL ENZA
- ➏ SOGGIORNO MAGLIANI
- ➐ HOTEL LOGGIATO DEI SERVITI
- ➑ DUE FONTANE HOTEL
- ➒ OBLATE SISTERS OF THE ASSUMPTION
- ➓ RESIDENZA DEI PUCCI
- ⓫ PALAZZO CASTIGLIONI & HOTEL ALDOBRANDINI
- ⓬ HOTEL BELLETTINI
- ⓭ HOTEL BASILEA
- ⓮ PENSIONE CENTRALE
- ⓯ HOTEL SOLE
- ⓰ SOGGIORNO BATTISTERO
- ⓱ HOTEL PENDINI
- ⓲ PENSIONE MAXIM
- ⓳ ALBERGO FIRENZE
- ⓴ HOTEL ELITE
- ㉑ TORRE GUELFA & ALESSANDRA HOTELS
- ㉒ PENSIONE BRETAGNA
- ㉓ FLORENCE WALKING TOURS

**Residenza dei Pucci**, a block north of the Duomo, has 12 tastefully decorated rooms—in soothing earth tones—with aristocratic furniture and tweed carpeting. It's fresh and bright (Sb-€130, Db-€145, Tb-€165, suite with grand Duomo view-€207 for 2 people, €233 for 4, claim a 10 percent discount through 2003 with this book and payment in cash, breakfast served in room, CC, Via dei Pucci 9, tel. 055-281-886, fax 055-264-314, http://residenzapucci.interfree.it, e-mail: residenzapucci@interfree.it, SE).

**LOWER PRICED**
**Hotel Bellettini** rents 34 bright, cool, well-cared-for rooms with inviting lounges and a touch of class. Its five rooms in an annex two blocks away are higher quality with all the comforts, but you need to come to the main hotel for breakfast (main building: S-€75, Sb-€95, D-€100, Db-€130, Tb-€170, Qb-€210; annex: Sb-€110, Db-€155, Tb-€209, CC, 5 percent discount with this book only if you claim it upon arrival, air-con, free Internet access, Via de' Conti 7, tel. 055-213-561, fax 055-283-551, www.firenze.net /hotelbellettini, e-mail: hotel.bellettini@dada.it, frisky Gina SE).

**Hotel Aldobrandini**, a good budget choice, has 15 decent, clean, affordable rooms, with the San Lorenzo market at its doorstep and the entrance to the Medici Chapel a few steps away (Ss-€42, Sb-€52, D-€67, Db-€83, CC, lots of night noise but has double-paned windows, fans, Piazza Madonna degli Aldobrandini 8, tel. 055-211-866, fax 055-267-6281, Ignazio SE).

**Pensione Centrale**, a traditional-feeling place with 18 spacious rooms, is indeed central, though run without warmth (D-€93, Db-€109, CC, quiet, some air-con rooms, often filled with American students, elevator, Via de' Conti 3, tel. 055-215-761, fax 055-215-216, www.pensionecentrale.it, e-mail: info @pensionecentrale.it). They sometimes send people to a near-by, noisier pension; confirm that your reservation is in fact for this place.

## Sleeping near the Central Market
### (zip code: 50129)

**MODERATELY PRICED**
**Hotel Basilea** offers predictable three-star, air-conditioned comfort in its 38 modern rooms (Db-€110–160 depending on season, CC, elevator, terrace, free e-mail service, Via Guelfa 41, at intersection with Nazionale—a busy street, ask for rooms in the back, tel. 055-214-587, fax 055-268-350, www.florenceitaly .net, e-mail: basilea@dada.it).

**LOWER PRICED**

**Casa Rabatti** is the ultimate if you always wanted to be a part of a Florentine family. Its four simple, clean rooms are run with motherly warmth by Marcella and her husband, Celestino, who speak minimal English (D-€50, Db-€60, €25 per bed in shared quad or quint, prices good with this book, no breakfast, no CC, fans, no sign other than on doorbell, 5 blocks from station, Via San Zanobi 48 black, tel. 055-212-393, e-mail: casarabatti@inwind.it).

**Soggiorno Pezzati Daniela** is another little place with six homey rooms (Sb-€45, Db-€62, Tb-€86, cheaper off-season, no breakfast, no CC, all rooms have a fridge, air-con extra; marked only by small sign near door, Via San Zanobi 22, tel. 055-291-660, fax 055-287-145, www.soggiornopezzati.it, e-mail: 055291660 @iol.it, Daniela SE). If you get an Italian recording when you call, hang on—your call is being transferred to a cell phone.

**Soggiorno Magliani,** central and humble with seven rooms, feels and smells like a great-grandmother's place. It's run with warmth by a friendly family duo, Vincenza and her English-speaking daughter, Cristina (S-€33, D-€43, cash only but secure reservation with CC, no breakfast, double-paned windows, near Via Guelfa at Via Reparata 1, tel. 055-287-378, e-mail: hotel-magliani@libero.it).

## Sleeping East of the Duomo

The first two listings are near the Accademia, on Piazza S.S. Annunziata (zip code: 50122). The third is just off the square.

**HIGHER PRICED**

**Hotel Loggiato dei Serviti**, at the most prestigious address in Florence on the most Renaissance square in town, gives you Renaissance romance with hair dryers. Stone stairways lead you under open-beam ceilings through this 16th-century monastery's elegant public rooms. The 34 cells, with air-conditioning, TVs, minibars, and telephones, wouldn't be recognized by their original inhabitants. The hotel staff is both professional and friendly (Sb-€146, Db-€210, family suites from €263, book a month ahead during peak season, cheaper Aug and winter, CC, elevator, annex Piazza S.S. Annunziata 3, tel. 055-289-592, fax 055-289-595, www.loggiatodeiservitihotel.it, e-mail: info @loggiatodeiservitihotel.it, Simonetta, Francesca, and Andrea SE).

**MODERATELY PRICED**

**Le Due Fontane Hotel** faces the same great square but fills its old building with a smoky, 1970s, business-class ambience. Its 57 air-conditioned rooms are big and comfortable (Sb-€103, Db-€140, Tb-€196, these discounted prices are promised through 2003 but only if you claim them upon reserving, CC, elevator, Piazza S.S. Annunziata 14, tel. 055-210-185, fax 055-294-461, www.leduefontane.it, e-mail: leduefontane@dada.it, SE).

At **Hotel Morandi alla Crocetta**, a former convent, you're enveloped in a 16th-century cocoon. Located on a quiet street, with period furnishings, parquet floors, and wood-beamed ceilings, it draws you in (Sb-€100, Db-€160, breakfast-€11, CC, Via "Laura 50, a block off Piazza S.S. Annunziata, tel. 055-234-4747, fax 055-248-0954, www.hotelmorandi.it, e-mail: welcome @hotelmorandi.it, SE).

**LOWER PRICED**

The **Oblate Sisters of the Assumption** run a 20-room hotel in a Renaissance building with a dreamy garden and a quiet, institutional feel (S-€34, D-€62, Db-€67, elevator, no CC, Borgo Pinti 15, 50121 Firenze, tel. 055-248-0582, fax 055-234-6291, NSE).

## *Sleeping on or near Piazza Repubblica (zip code: 50123)*

These are the most central of my accomodations recommendations, though given Florence's walkable core, nearly every hotel can be considered central.

**MODERATELY PRICED**

**Hotel Pendini**, a well-run three-star hotel with 42 old-time rooms (8 with views of the square), is popular and central, overlooking Piazza Repubblica (Sb-€86–110, Db-€110–150 depending on season, CC, elevator, fine lounge and breakfast room, air-con, Via Strozzi 2, reserve ASAP, tel. 055-211-170, fax 055-281-807, www.florenceitaly.net, e-mail: pendini @dada.it, SE).

**Residenza Giotto** has six bright, modern rooms and a terrace so close to the Duomo you can almost touch it (Sb-€120, Db-€130, Tb-€145, 10 percent discount with this book and payment in cash, breakfast in room, CC, Via Roma 6, 4th floor, tel. 055-214-593, fax 055-264-8568, www.residenzagiotto.it, e-mail: residenzagiotto@tin.it, SE).

**Pensione Maxim**, right on Via Calz, is a big, institutional-feeling place as close to the sights as possible. Its halls are narrow, but the 29 rooms are comfortable and well-maintained (Sb-€83, Db-€113, Tb-€148, Qb-€173, CC but pay first night in cash, Internet access, elevator, Via dei Calzaiuoli 11, tel. 055-217-474, fax 055-283-729, www.hotelmaximfirenze.it, e-mail: hotmaxim @tin.it, Paolo and Nicola Maioli SE).

**LOWER PRICED**

**Soggiorno Battistero**, next door to the baptistery, has seven simple, airy rooms, most with urban noise but also great views, overlooking the baptistery and square. You're in the heart of Florence
(S-€73, Db-€95, Tb-€130, Qb-€140, these prices good with
this book, 5 percent additional discount with cash, breakfast
served in room, Internet access, CC, Piazza San Giovanni 1,
3rd floor, no elevator, tel. 055-295-143, fax 055-268-189, www
.soggiornobattistero.it, e-mail: battistero@dada.it, lovingly run
by Italian Luca and his American wife, Kelly).

**Albergo Firenze**, a big, efficient place, offers good,
basic, and spacious rooms in a wonderfully central, reasonably
quiet locale two blocks behind the Duomo (Sb-€67, Db-€88,
Tb-€126, Qb-€156, cash only, must prepay first night with
a bank draft or traveler's check, elevator, off Via del Corso at
Piazza Donati 4, tel. 055-214-203, fax 055-212-370, SE).

## Sleeping North of the Train Station
### (zip code: 50123)

**MODERATELY PRICED**

**Hotel Beatrice**, a three-star hotel popular with tour groups,
is well-located if you've packed heavy—it's just a block north
of the train and bus stations (Sb-€75–90, Db-€95–142, includes
breakfast, CC, most rooms air-con, elevator, Via Fiume 11, tel.
055-216-790, fax 055-80-711, www.hotelbeatrice.it).

## Sleeping South of the Train Station
## near Piazza Santa Maria Novella
### (zip code: 50123)

From the station (with your back to the tracks), cross the
wide square to reach the Santa Maria Novella church and
continue to the piazza in front of the church (avoid thief-ridden
underground Galleria S. M. Novella tunnel leading from station
under square to church). Piazza Santa Maria Novella, pleasant
by day, gets a little sleazy after dark.

**LOWER PRICED**

**Hotel Pensione Elite**, run warmly by Maurizio and Nadia, is a
fine value, with 10 comfortable rooms and a charm rare in this price
range (Ss-€52, Sb-€72, Ds-€67, Db-€83, breakfast-€6, maybe
CC, fans, at south end of square with back to church, go right to
Via della Scala 12, 2nd floor, tel. & fax 055-215-395, SE).

**Hotel Sole**, a clean, cozy, family-run place with eight
bright, modern rooms, is just off Santa Maria Novella toward

the river (Sb-€47, Db-€78, Tb-€104, no breakfast, no CC, air-con, elevator, curfew at 1:00, Via del Sole 8, 3rd floor, tel. & fax 055-239-6094, friendly Anna NSE, but daughter SE).

## Sleeping near Arno River and Ponte Vecchio
### (zip code: 50123)

**HIGHER PRICED**

**Hotel Torre Guelfa** is topped with a fun medieval tower with a panoramic rooftop terrace. Its 29 rooms vary wildly in size (small Db-from €145, standard Db-€170, Db junior suite-€220, 5 percent discount with cash). Room #15, with a private terrace—€210—is worth reserving several months in advance (CC, huge lobby, elevator, air-con, 2 blocks northwest of Ponte Vecchio, Borgo S.S. Apostoli 8, tel. 055-239-6338, fax 055-239-8577, www.hoteltorreguelfa.com, e-mail: torreguelfa@flashnet.it, Giancarlo, Carlo, and Sandro all SE).

**MODERATELY PRICED**

**Hotel Pensione Alessandra** is a 16th-century, peaceful place with 27 big, modern rooms (S-€82, Sb-€109, D-€119, Db-€150, T-€140, Tb-€181, Q-€155, Qb-€202, CC but 5 percent discount with cash, air-con, Internet access, Borgo S.S. Apostoli 17, tel. 055-283-438, fax 055-210-619, www.hotelalessandra.com, e-mail: info @hotelalessandra.com, SE).

**LOWER PRICED**

**Pensione Bretagna** is an Old World–ramshackle place run by helpful Antonio and Maura. Imagine eating breakfast under a painted, chandeliered ceiling overlooking the Arno River (S-€50, Sb-€59, small Db-€95, Db-€105, Tb-€129, Qb-€150, family deals, prices special with this book in 2003, CC, air-con, Internet access, just past Ponte San Trinita, Lungarno Corsini 6, tel. 055-289-618, fax 055-289-619, www.bretagna.it, e-mail: hotel @bretagna.it). They also run Soggiorno Althea, a cheaper place with nicer rooms, near Piazza San Spirito in the Oltrarno neighborhood (6 rooms, Db-€71, air-con, no breakfast, no reception desk, cellular 388-233-5341, www.florencealthea.it).

## Sleeping in Oltrarno, South of the River
### (zip code: 50125)

Across the river in the Oltrarno area, between the Pitti Palace and Ponte Vecchio, you'll still find small traditional crafts shops, neighborly piazzas, and family eateries. The following places are a few minutes' walk from Ponte Vecchio.

## Florence's Oltrarno Neighborhood

1. HOTEL LA SCALETTA
2. TO HOTEL SILLA
3. PENSIONE SORELLE BANDINI
4. HOTEL LUNGARNO
5. SOGGIORNO PEZZATI ALESSANDRA
6. ISTITUTO GOULD
7. OSTELLO SANTA MONACA
8. TRATTORIA BORDINO
9. RISTORANTE BIBO
10. BORGO ANTICO REST., OSTERIA SANTO SPIRITO, & RICCHI CAFFÈ
11. TRATTORIA CASALINGA
12. CAMMILLO TRATTORIA
13. OSTERIA DEL CINGHIALE BIANCO
14. TRATTORIA ANGIOLINO
15. TO TRATTORIA SABATINO

**HIGHER PRICED**

**Hotel Lungarno** is the place to stay if money is no object. This deluxe, four-star hotel with 70 rooms strains anything stressful or rough out of Italy, and gives you only service with a salute, physical elegance everywhere you look, plus fine views over the Arno and Ponte Vecchio (Sb-€225, Db-€360, Db facing river-€460, fancier suites, great riverside public spaces, CC, 100 meters, or 330 feet, from Ponte Vecchio at Borgo San Jacopo 14, tel. 055-27261, fax 055-268-437, www.lungarnohotels.com, e-mail: bookings@lungarnohotels.com, SE).

**MODERATELY PRICED**

**Hotel La Scaletta,** an elegant, dark, cool place with 13 rooms, a labyrinthine floor plan, lots of Old World lounges, and a romantic and panoramic roof terrace, is run by Barbara, her son Manfredo, and daughters Bianca and Diana (S-€52, Sb-€95, D-€105, Db-€113–130, Tb-€115–150, Qb-€130–170, higher price is for quieter rooms in back, €5–10 discount if you pay cash, CC, air-con in 10 rooms and fans in others, elevator, bar with fine wine at good prices, Via Guicciardini 13 black, 150 meters, or 500 feet, south of Ponte Vecchio, tel. 055-283-028, fax 055-289-562, www.lascaletta.com, e-mail: info@lascaletta.com, SE). Secure your reservation with a personal check or traveler's check. Manfredo loves to cook. If he's cooking dinner, eat here. He serves a €10 "Taste of Tuscany" deal (plate of quality Tuscan meats and cheeses with bread and 2 glasses of robust Chianti)—ideal for a light lunch on the terrace.

   **Hotel Silla,** a classic three-star hotel with 36 cheery, spacious, pastel, and modern rooms, is a fine value. It faces the river and overlooks a park opposite the Santa Croce Church (Sb-€120, Db-€170, Tb-€210, mention this book for a discount, CC, elevator, air-con, Via dei Renai 5, tel. 055-234-2888, fax 055-234-1437, www.hotelsilla.it, e-mail: hotelsilla@tin.it, Laura SE).

   **Pensione Sorelle Bandini** is a ramshackle, 500-year-old palace on a perfectly Florentine square, with cavernous rooms, museum-warehouse interiors, a musty youthfulness, cats, a balcony lounge-loggia with a view, and an ambience that, for romantic bohemians, can be a highlight of Florence. Mimmo or Sr. Romeo will hold a room until 16:00 with a phone call (D-€103, Db-€125, T-€141, Tb-€171, includes breakfast—which during low times is optional, saving €9 per person—no CC, elevator, Piazza Santo Spirito 9, tel. 055-215-308, fax 055-282-761, SE).

**LOWER PRICED**

**Soggiorno Pezzati Alessandra** is a warm and friendly place renting five great rooms in the Oltrarno neighborhood (Sb-€45, Db-€62, Tb-€86, Qb-€108, cheaper off-season, no breakfast, no CC, all rooms have a fridge, air-con extra, Via Borgo San Frediano 6, tel. 055-290-424, fax 055-218-464, e-mail: alex170169 @libero.it, Alessandra). If you get an Italian recording when you call, hang on—your call is being transferred to a cellular phone.

   **Istituto Gould** is a Protestant Church–run place with 33 clean but drab rooms, twin beds, and modern facilities (S-€30, Sb-€35, D-€44, Db-€52, Tb-€63, €20 per person in quads, no breakfast, no CC, quieter rooms in back, Via dei Serragli 49, tel. 055-212-576, fax 055-280-274, e-mail: gould.reception

@dada.it). You must arrive when the office is open (Mon–Fri 9:00–13:00 & 15:00–19:00, Sat 9:00–13:00, no check-in Sun, SE).

**Ostello Santa Monaca**, a cheap hostel, is a few blocks south of Ponte Alla Carraia, one of the bridges over the Arno (€15.50 beds, 4- to 20-bed rooms, breakfast extra, CC, 1:00 curfew, Via Santa Monaca 6, tel. 055-268-338, fax 055-280-185).

## Sleeping Away from the Center

### MODERATELY PRICED
**Hotel Ungherese** is good for drivers. It's northeast of the city center (near Stadio, en route to Fiesole), with easy, free street parking and quick bus access (#11 and #17) into central Florence (Sb-€72, Db-€123, extra bed-€30, these discounted prices available with this book, pay cash to get additional 7 percent discount, rooms are 20 percent less off-season, includes breakfast, CC, air-con, Via G. B. Amici 8, tel. & fax 055-573-474, www.hotelungherese.it, e-mail: hotel.ungherese@dada.it, Giovanni, Francesca SE). It has great singles and a backyard garden terrace (ask for a room on the garden). They can recommend good eateries nearby.

### LOWER PRICED
**Villa Camerata**, classy for an IYHF hostel, is on the outskirts of Florence (€14.50 per bed with breakfast, 4- to 12-bed rooms, must have IYHF card, no CC, ride bus #17 to Salviatino stop, Via Righi 2, tel. 055-601-451).

# Eating in Florence
To save money and time for sights, you can keep lunches fast and simple, eating in one of the countless self-service places and pizzerias or just picnicking (try juice, yogurt, cheese, and a roll for €5). For good sit-down meals, consider the following. Remember, restaurants like to serve what's fresh. If you're into flavor, go for the seasonal best bets—featured in the *Piatti del Giorno* (special of the day) sections of the menus.

## Eating in Oltrarno, South of the River
For a change of scene, eat across the river in Oltrarno (see map on page 216). Here are a few good places just over Ponte Vecchio.

*At Piazza San Felicita:* A block south of Ponte Vecchio is the unpretentious and happy Piazza San Felicita, with two good restaurants. The cozy and candlelit **Trattoria Bordino**, just up the street and actually built into the old town wall (c. 1170), serves tasty and beautifully presented Florentine cuisine "with international influence" (a little pricey, Mon–Sat 12:00–14:30 & 19:30–22:30, closed Sun, Via Stracciatella 9 red, tel. 055-213-048). Right on the square, the more touristy **Ristorante Bibo** serves *"cucina tipica Fiorentina"* with a pink tablecloth-and-black-bowties dressiness and leafy, candlelit outdoor seating (good €15 3-course meal, CC, reserve for outdoor seating, Wed–Mon 12:00–14:30 & 19:00–22:30, closed Tue, Piazza San Felicita 6 red, tel. 055-239-8554).

*On Via di Santo Spirito/Borgo San Jacopo:* Several good and colorful restaurants line this multi-named street a block off the river in Oltrarno. I'd survey the scene (perhaps following the self-guided Oltrarno walk described on page 206) before making a choice.

At **Cammillo Trattoria,** while Cammillo is slurping spaghetti in heaven, his granddaughter Chiara carries on the tradition, mixing traditional Tuscan with "creative" modern cuisine. With a charcoal grill and a team of white-aproned waiters cranking out wonderful food in a fun, dressy-but-down-to-earth ambience, this place is a hit (full dinners about €36 plus wine, Thu–Tue 12:00–14:30 & 19:30–22:30, closed Wed, CC, Borgo San Jacopo 57 red, reservations smart, tel. 055-212-427).

Other inviting places along this street: **Osteria del Cinghiale Bianco** is popular but cramped (around €30 for dinner plus wine, Borgo San Jacopo 43 red, air-con, Thu–Tue 12:00–15:00 & 18:30–23:30, closed Wed, reservations wise, tel. 055-215-706). The more relaxed **Trattoria Angiolino** serves good, old-fashioned local cuisine (about €20 for dinner plus wine, Tue–Sun 12:00–14:30 & 19:30–22:30, closed Mon, Via di Santo Spirito 36 red, tel. 055-239-8976). **Trattoria Sabatino** is spacious and disturbingly cheap, with family character, red-checkered tablecloths, a simple menu, and the fewest tourists of all. A wonderful place to watch locals munch, it's just outside the Porta San Frediano (medieval gate), a 15-minute walk from Ponte Vecchio (Mon–Fri 12:00–14:30 & 19:20–22:00, closed Sat–Sun, Via Pisana 2 red, tel. 055-225-955, NSE). If you eat here, read my self-guided Oltrarno walk (on page tk) before hiking out to the gate.

*At Piazza Santo Spirito:* This classic Florentine square (lately a hangout for drug pushers, therefore a bit seedy-feeling and plagued by Vespa bag-snatchings) has two popular little restaurants offering good local cuisine every night of the week, indoor and on-the-square seating (reserve for on-the-square), moderate prices, and impersonal service: **Borgo Antico** (Piazza Santo Spirito 6 red, tel. 055-210-437) and **Osteria Santo Spirito** (pricier, more peaceful outdoor seating, Piazza Santo Spirito 16 red, tel. 055-238-2383).

**Ricchi Caffè**, next to Borgo Antico, has fine gelato and

# Restaurants in Florence

1 OSTERIA BELLEDONNE
2 RIST. LA SPADA
3 TRATTORIA MARIONE
4 TRATTORIA SOSTANZA-TROIA
5 TRATTORIA IL CONTADINO
6 TRATTORIA DA GIORGIO
7 LA GROTTA DI LEO
8 MERCATO CENTRALE MARKET
9 TRATTORIA LA BURRASCA &
   OSTERIA LA CONGREGA

10 SELF-SERVICE REST. LEONARDO
11 RIST. IL CAVALLINO
12 OSTERIA VINI E VECCHI SAPORI
13 CANTINETTA DEI VERRAZZANO
   & RIST. PAOLI
14 I FRATELLINI WINE
   & SANDWICH SHOP
15 TRATTORIA ICCHE C'E C'E
16 PICNIC SPOT IF
   IT'S NOT TOO HOT

shaded outdoor tables. After noting the plain facade of the Brunel-leschi church facing the square, step inside the café, and pick your favorite of the many ways it might be finished. **Café Cabiria,** next door, is a great local hangout with good light meals and a cozy Florentine funky room in back.

**Trattoria Casalinga** is an inexpensive standby. Famous for its home cooking, it's now filled with tourists rather than locals. But it sends them away full, happy, and with euros left for gelato (Mon–Sat 12:00–14:30 & 19:00–21:45, closed Sun and all of Aug, CC, just off Piazza Santo Spirito, near the church at Via dei Michelozzi 9 red, after 20:00 reserve or wait, tel. 055-218-624).

## Eating North of the River

### Eating near Santa Maria Novella and the Train Station

**Osteria Belledonne** is a crowded and cheery bohemian hole-in-the-wall serving great food at good prices. I loved the meal but had to correct the bill—read it carefully. They take only a few reservations. Arrive early or wait (Mon–Fri 12:00–14:30 & 19:00–22:30, closed Sat–Sun, Via delle Belledonne 16 red, tel. 055-238-2609).

**Ristorante La Spada,** nearby, is another fine local favorite serving typical Tuscan cuisine with less atmosphere and more menu (€11 lunch special, about €20 for dinner plus wine, daily 12:00–15:00 & 19:00–22:30, air-con, near Via della Spada at Via del Moro 66 red, evening reservations smart, tel. 055-218-757).

**Trattoria Marione** serves good home-cooked-style meals to a local crowd in a happy, food-loving ambience (closed Sun, dinners run about €15 plus wine, pretty smoky, Via della Spada 27 red, tel. 055-214-756).

**Trattoria Sostanza-Troia** is a characteristic and well-established place with shared tables and a loyal local following. Whirling ceiling fans and walls strewn with old photos create a time-warp ambience. They offer two seatings, requiring reservations: one at 19:30 and one at 21:00 (dinners for about €15 plus wine, great steaks, lunch 12:00–14:00, closed Sat, Via del Porcellana 25 red, tel. 055-212-691).

Two smoky chow houses for local workers offer a €9, hearty, family-style, fixed-price menu with a bustling working-class/budget-Yankee-traveler atmosphere (Mon–Sat 12:00–14:30 & 18:15–21:30, closed Sun, 2 blocks south of train station): **Trattoria il Contadino** (Via Palazzuolo 69 red, tel. 055-238-2673) and **Trattoria da Giorgio** (across the street at Via Palazzuolo 100 red). Arrive early or wait. The touristy **La Grotta di Leo** (a block away) has a cheap, straightforward menu and edible food and pizza (daily 11:00–1:00, Via della Scala 41 red, tel. 055-219-265). Because these places are a block from the station, they are handy, but the street scene is shabby.

## Eating near the Central and San Lorenzo Markets

For mountains of picnic produce or just a cheap sandwich and piles of people-watching, visit the huge Central Market—**Mercato Centrale** (Mon–Sat 7:00–14:00, closed Sun, a block north of the San Lorenzo street market).

**Trattoria la Burrasca** is a funky, family-run place ideal for Tuscan home cooking. It's small (10 tables) and inexpensive, with pasta for €4. Anna and Antonio Genzano have cooked and served here with passion since 1982. If Andy Capp were Italian, he'd eat here for special nights out. Everything but the desserts is homemade. And, if you want good wine for cheap prices, order it here (Fri–Wed 12:00–15:00 & 19:00–22:00, closed Thu, Via Panicale 6b, at the north corner of Central Market, tel. 055-215-827, NSE).

**Osteria la Congrega** brags that it's a Tuscan wine bar designed to help you lose track of time. In a fresh and romantic two-level setting, creative chef/owner Mahyar has designed a fun, easy menu featuring modern Tuscan cuisine, with top-notch local meat and produce. He offers fine vegetarian dishes. With just 10 uncrowded tables, the restaurant requires reservations for dinner (moderate with €13 dinner plates, CC, daily 12:00–15:00 & 19:00–23:00, Via Panicale 43 red, tel. 055-264-5027).

For a cheap lunch, try **Trattoria San Zanobi's** Pasta Break Lunch (most pastas around €5, Via San Zanobi 33 red, a couple blocks northeast of the Central Market, tel. 055-475-286).

## Eating near the Accademia and Museum of San Marco

**Gran Caffè San Marco**, conveniently located on Piazza San Marco, offers reasonably priced pizzas, sandwiches, and desserts (no cover charge, self-service and restaurant, Piazza San Marco 11 red, across square from Museum of San Marco entrance, tel. 055-215-833).

## Eating near the Cathedral (Duomo)

**Self-Service Restaurant Leonardo** is fast, cheap, air-conditioned, and very handy, just a block from the Duomo, southwest of the baptistery (€3 pastas, €4 main courses, Sun–Fri 11:45–14:45 & 18:45–21:45, closed Sat, upstairs at Via Pecori 5, tel. 055-284-446). Luciano (like Pavarotti) runs the place with enthusiasm.

## Eating near Palazzo Vecchio

Piazza Signoria, the square facing the old city hall, is ringed by beautifully situated yet touristic eateries. Any will do for a reasonably priced pizza. Perhaps the best value is **Ristorante il Cavallino** (€10 fixed-price lunch menu, €16 fixed-price dinner menu, great outdoor seating in shadow of palace, tel. 055-215-818).

**Osteria Vini e Vecchi Sapori** is a colorful hole-in-the-wall serving traditional food, including plates of mixed *crostini* (€0.75 each—you choose), half a block north of Palazzo Vecchio (Tue–Sun 10:00–23:00, closed Mon, Via dei Magazzini 3 red, facing the bronze equestrian statue in Piazza della Signoria, go behind its tail into the corner and to your left, NSE).

**Cantinetta dei Verrazzano** is a long-established bakery/café/wine bar, serving delightful sandwich plates in an elegant old-time setting, and hot focaccia sandwiches to go. The *Specialita Verrazzano* is a fine plate of four little *crostini* (like mini-*bruschetta*) featuring different local breads, cheeses, and meats (€7). The *Tagliere di Focacce*, a sampler plate of mini–focaccia sandwiches, is also fun. Either of these dishes with a glass of Chianti makes a fine, light meal. Paolo describes things to make eating educational. As office workers pop in for a quick bite, it's traditional to share tables at lunchtime (Mon–Sat 12:30–21:00, closed Sun, just off Via Calzaiuoli on a side street across from Orsanmichele Church at Via dei Tavolini 18, tel. 055-268-590).

At **I Fratellini,** a colorful hole-in-the-wall place, the "little brothers" have served peasants rustic sandwiches and cheap glasses of Chianti wine since 1875. Join the local crowd, then sit on a nearby curb or windowsill to munch, placing your glass on the wall rack before you leave (€4 for sandwich and wine, 20 meters, or 65 feet, in front of Orsanmichele Church on Via dei Cimatori).

**Ristorante Paoli** serves great local cuisine to piles of happy eaters under a richly frescoed Gothic vault. Because of its fame and central location, it's filled mostly with tourists, but for a dressy, traditional splurge meal, this is my choice (Wed–Mon 12:00–14:00 & 19:00–22:00, closed Tue, reserve for dinner, €20 tourist menu, à la carte is pricier, CC, midway between old square and cathedral at Via de Tavolini 12 red, tel. 055-216-215). Salads are flamboyantly cut and mixed from a trolley right at your table.

**Trattoria Icche C'è C'è** (dialect for "whatever is, is"; pron. EE-kay CHAY chay) is a small, family-style place where fun-loving Gino serves good traditional meals (moderate, not too touristy, closed Mon, midway between Bargello and river at Via Magalotti 11 red, tel. 055-216-589).

**Osteria del Porcellino**—a rare place that serves late— is delightful and a bit pricey, packed with a mix of locals and in-the-know tourists, and run with style and enthusiasm by friendly chef Enzo (daily 18:00–1:00, summer lunches, indoor/outdoor, CC, Via Val di Lamona 7 red, half a block behind Mercato Nuovo, reserve for dinner, tel. 055-264-148).

**Trattoria Nella** serves good, typical Tuscan cuisine—including the best gnocchi in town—at affordable prices. Arrive early or be disappointed (Mon–Sat 12:00–14:30 & 19:30–22:00, closed Sun, 3 blocks northwest of Ponte Vecchio, Via delle Terme 19 red, tel. 055-218-925).

## Transportation Connections—Florence

**By train to: Assisi** (3/day, 2 hrs, more frequent with transfers, direction: Foligno), **Orvieto** (6/day, 2 hrs), **Pisa** (2/hr, 1 hr), **La Spezia** (for the Cinque Terre, 2/day direct, 2 hrs, or change in Pisa), **Venice** (7/day, 3 hrs), **Milan** (12/day, 3–5 hrs), **Rome** (hrly, 2.5 hrs), **Naples** (10/day, 4 hrs), **Brindisi** (3/day, 11 hrs with change in Bologna), **Frankfurt** (3/day, 12 hrs), **Paris** (1/day, 12 hrs overnight), **Vienna** (4/day, 9–10 hrs). Train info: tel. 848-888-088.

**Buses:** The SITA bus station, a block west of the Florence train station, is user-friendly (but remember, bus service drops dramatically on Sunday). Schedules are posted everywhere, with TV monitors indicating imminent departures. You'll find buses to: **San Gimignano** (hrly, 1.75 hrs), **Siena** (hrly, 75-min *corse rapide* fast buses, faster than the train, avoid the 2-hr *diretta* slow buses), and the **airport** (hrly, 15–30 min). Bus info: tel. 055-214-721 from 9:30 to 12:30; some schedules are in the *Florence Concierge Information* magazine.

**Taxi to Siena:** For around €100, you can arrange a ride directly from your Florence hotel to your Siena hotel. For a small group or for people with more money than time, this can be a good value.

## Airports

The **Amerigo Vespucci Airport** (www.safnet.it), several kilometers northwest of Florence, has a TI, cash machines, car rental agencies, and easy connections by airport shuttle bus with Florence's bus station, a block west of the train station (€4, 2/hr, 15–30 min, from Florence runs 5:30–23:00, from airport 6:00–23:30). Airport info: 055-306-1300, flight info: 055-306-1700 (domestic), 055-306-1702 (international). Allow about €16 to €20 for a taxi.

International flights often land at Pisa's **Galileo Galilei Airport** (also has TI and car rental agencies, www.pisa-airport.com), an hour from Florence by train (runs hrly; if you're leaving Florence for this airport, catch the train at Florence's train station at platform #5). Flight info: 050-500-707.

# PISA

Pisa was a regional superpower in its medieval heyday (11th, 12th, and 13th centuries), rivaling Florence and Genoa. Its Mediterranean empire, which included Corsica and Sardinia, helped make it a wealthy republic. But the Pisa fleet was beaten (in 1284, by Genoa) and its port silted up, leaving the city high and dry, with only its Field of Miracles and its university keeping it on the map.

Pisa's three important sights (the cathedral, the baptistery, and the bell tower) float regally on the best lawn in Italy. Even as the church was being built, the Piazza del Duomo was nicknamed the Campo dei Miracoli, or Field of Miracles, for the grandness of the undertaking. The style throughout is Pisa's very own "Pisan Romanesque," surrounded by Italy's tackiest ring of souvenir stands. This spectacle is tourism at its most crass. Wear gloves.

The Leaning Tower recently reopened after a decade of restoration and topple prevention. To ascend, you'll have to make a reservation when you buy your €15 ticket (for details, see "Sights," below).

## Planning Your Time

Seeing the tower and the square and wandering through the church are 90 percent of the Pisan thrill. Pisa is a touristy quickie. By car, it's a headache. By train, it's a joy. Train travelers may need to change trains in Pisa anyway. Hop on the bus and see the tower. If you want to climb it, go straight to the ticket booth to snare an appointment—usually for a couple of hours later (or check www.duomo.pisa.it before you go to see if you can book online). Sophisticated sightseers stop more for the Pisano carvings in the cathedral and baptistery than for a look at the tipsy tower. There's nothing wrong with Pisa, but I'd stop only to see the Field of Miracles and get out of town. By car, it's a 45-minute detour from the freeway.

## Orientation

**Tourist Information:** One TI is at the train station (summer: Mon–Sat 9:00–19:00, Sun 9:30–15:30; winter: Mon–Sat 9:00–19:00 and possibly closed Sun; to your left as you exit station, tel. 050-42291) and another is near the Leaning Tower (Mon–Fri 9:00–18:00, Sat–Sun 10:30–16:30, outside the medieval wall, hidden behind souvenir stands in a nook of the wall, about 100 meters, or 330 feet, to the left of the gate before you enter the Field of Miracles, tel. 050-560-464). Another TI is at the airport (tel. 050-503-700). Beware of pickpockets in Pisa.

# Pisa

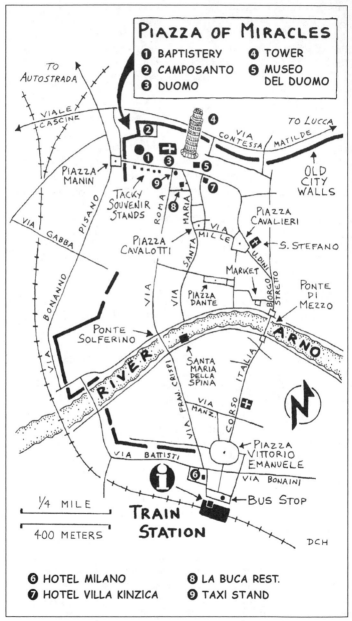

**PIAZZA OF MIRACLES**
1 BAPTISTERY     4 TOWER
2 CAMPOSANTO     5 MUSEO
3 DUOMO            DEL DUOMO

TO AUTOSTRADA
VIALE CASCINE
TO LUCCA
VIA CONTESSA MATILDE
OLD CITY WALLS
PIAZZA MANIN
TACKY SOUVENIR STANDS
VIA GABBA
VIA BONANNO
VIA PISANO
VIA ROMA
VIA SANTA MARIA
PIAZZA CAVALOTTI
PIAZZA CAVALIERI
S. STEFANO
V. DINI
VIA MILLE
MARKET
BORGO STRETTO
PONTE DI MEZZO
PIAZZA DANTE
PONTE SOLFERINO
ARNO RIVER
SANTA MARIA DELLA SPINA
VIA FRAN. CRISPI
VIA MANZ.
CORSO ITALIA
N
VIA BATTISTI
PIAZZA VITTORIO EMANUELE
VIA BONAINI
BUS STOP
¼ MILE
400 METERS
TRAIN STATION
DCH

6 HOTEL MILANO          8 LA BUCA REST.
7 HOTEL VILLA KINZICA   9 TAXI STAND

## Arrival in Pisa

**By Train:** To get to the Field of Miracles from the station, you can **walk** (25–30 min, get free map from TI at station, they'll mark the best route on your map), take a **taxi** (€8, at taxi stand at station or call 050-541-600), or catch a **bus**. The latest information on the bus route to the Field of Miracles is posted in the train information office in Pisa's station lobby (or ask at TI). It's likely bus #3 (3/hr) which leaves from in front of the station, across the street at the big hotel. Buy an €0.80 ticket from the *tabacchi*/magazine kiosk in the station's main hall or at any *tabacchi* shop (good for 1 hr, round-trip OK, 10-minute ride one-way to tower). Confirm the bus route number or risk taking a long tour of Pisa's suburbs. The correct bus will let you off at Piazza Manin, in front of the gate to the Field of Miracles. To return to the station, catch the bus from across the street where you got off (confirm the stop with a local or at the TI).

The train station no longer has a baggage check. If necessary, you could store your bag at the airport (€6/per piece per day); it's only a 5-minute ride on bus #3 (same bus route as to the Field of Miracles but catch bus going in opposite direction) and still make it to the tower on the same bus ticket.

**By Car:** To get to the Leaning Tower, follow signs to the Duomo or Campo dei Miracoli, located on the north edge of town. If you're coming from the Pisa Nord autostrada exit, you won't have to mess with the city center, but you will have to endure some terrible traffic. There's no option better than the €1-per-hour pay lot just outside the town wall a block from the tower.

**By Plane:** From Pisa's airport, take bus #3 into town (€0.80, 3/hr, 5 min) or a taxi (€6). Flight info: 050-500-707 (www.pisa-airport.com).

## Prices

Pisa has a scheme to get you into its neglected secondary sights: the baptistery, cathedral museum (Museo dell' Opera del Duomo), Camposanto cemetery, and fresco museum (Museo delle Sinopie).

For any one monument, you'll pay €5; for two monuments, the cost is €6; for four monuments, it's €8.50; and for the works (including the cathedral), you'll pay €10.50. In comparison, the cathedral alone is a bargain (€2). You can buy any of these tickets at the usually crowded ticket office (behind tower and cathedral entrance), or more easily at the Camposanto cemetery, Museo dell' Opera del Duomo, or Museo delle Sinopie (near baptistery, almost suffocated by souvenir stands); note that you can buy a ticket just for, say, the cathedral at any of these points.

For marathon sightseers, there's a €13 Universalis ticket that covers all of the above sights, the Museo Nazionale di San Matteo, and many others, purchasable only at the Tower of Santa Maria, behind the baptistery.

No matter what ticket you get, you'll have to pay another €15 to climb the Leaning Tower. Tickets for the ascent are sold only at the crowded ticket office behind the tower and duomo.

## Sights—Pisa

▲▲**Leaning Tower**—Started in the 12th century, this most famous example of Pisan Romanesque architecture was leaning even before its completion. Notice how the architect, for lack of a better solution, kinked up the top section. The 294 tilted steps to the top were closed for years, as engineers worked to keep the bell tower from toppling. The formerly clean and tidy area around the tower was turned into a construction zone, as engineers used steam pipes to dry out the subsoil and huge weights to stabilize (but not straighten out) the tower.

Now 30 people an hour can clamber to the top for €15 (Mon–Sat 8:00–17:20, Sun 9:00–17:00). To make the necessary reservation, go straight to the ticket office behind the tower. You choose a time slot (40 minutes) for your visit at the time of purchase; it will likely be a couple of hours before you're able to go up (you could see the rest of the monuments and grab lunch while waiting). There are plans to set up online booking; check www.duomo.pisa.it or call 050-560-547 for the latest.

Note that even though the ticket office sign says the visit is guided, that only means you'll be accompanied by a museum guard to make sure you don't stay up past your scheduled 40-minute appointment time. Not including the climb, you'll have about 25 minutes for vertigo on top.

▲▲**Cathedral**—The huge Pisan Romanesque church (known as the duomo), with its carved pulpit by Giovanni Pisano, is artistically more important than its more famous bell tower (€2, open daily, summer: Mon–Sat 10:00–20:00, Sun 13:00–19:40; spring and fall: Mon–Sat 10:00–17:40, Sun 13:00–17:40; winter: Mon–Sat 10:00–12:45 & 15:00–16:45, Sun 15:00–16:45). Shorts are OK as long as they're not short shorts. Big backpacks are not allowed, nor is storage provided (but ticket-taker might let you leave bag at entrance).

**Baptistery**—The baptistery, the biggest in Italy, is interesting for its great acoustics (open daily, summer: 8:00–19:40; spring and fall: 9:00–17:40; winter: 9:00–16:40; located in front of cathedral). If you ask nicely and leave a tip, the ticket-taker uses the place's echo power to sing haunting harmonies with himself. The pulpit, by Nicola Pisano (1260), inspired Renaissance art to follow, but the same artist's pulpit and carvings in Siena were just as impressive to me—in a more enjoyable atmosphere. Notice that even the baptistery leans nearly two meters (5 feet).

**Other Sights at the Field of Miracles**—For Pisan art, see the **Museo dell' Opera del Duomo**, displaying treasures of the cathedral, including sculptures (12th–14th century), paintings, silverware, and ancient Egyptian, Etruscan, and Roman artifacts (same hours as baptistery; housed behind tower, Piazza Arcivescovado 18).

Skip the **Camposanto** cemetery bordering the cathedral square, even if its "Holy Land dirt" does turn a body into a skeleton in a day (same hours as baptistery).

The **Museo delle Sinopie**, housed in a 13th-century hospital, features the sketchy frescoes that were preparatory work for the frescoes in the cemetery (same hours as baptistery, hidden behind souvenir stands, across street from baptistery entrance).

The much-advertised **Panoramic Walk on the Wall**, which includes just a small section of the medieval wall, isn't worth your time or €2.20 (March–Dec daily 10:00–18:00, entrance near baptistery, at Porta Leone).

**More Sights**—The **Museo Nazionale di San Matteo**, in a former convent, displays 12th- to 15th-century sculptures, illuminated manuscripts, and paintings by Martini, Ghirlandaio, Masaccio, and others (€4.20, Tue–Sat 8:30–19:00, Sun 9:30–13:30, closed Mon, on river near Piazza Mazzini at Lungarno Mediceo, tel. 050-541-865).

Walking between the station and Field of Miracles in the pedestrian zone from Via G. Oberdan to Piazza Vittorio Veneto shows you a student-filled, classy, Old World town with an Arno-scape much like its rival upstream. A little **fruit market** is pinched and squeezed into Piazza Vettovaglie (Mon–Sat 7:00–18:00, near river, between station and tower). A **street market** attracts shoppers Wednesday and Saturday mornings between Via del Brennero and Via Paparrelle (just outside of wall, about 6 blocks east of tower).

## Sleeping and Eating in Pisa
**(€1 = about $1, country code: 39, zip code: 56100)**

Consider **Hotel Milano**, near the station, offering 10 spacious rooms with faded-but-clean bedspreads (D-€47, Db-€65, breakfast extra, CC, air-con, Via Mascagni 14, tel. 050-23162, fax 050-44237, e-mail: hotelmilano@csinfo.it). Or try the pricier **Hotel Villa Kinzica**, with 33 modern rooms within a block of the Field of Miracles—ask for a room with a view of the tower (Db-€104, CC, elevator, most rooms air-con, attached restaurant, Piazza Arcivescovado 2, tel. 050-560-419, fax 050-551-204).

*Eating:* For a quick lunch or dinner, the pizzeria/trattoria **La Buca**—just a block from the tower—has a good reputation among locals (Sat–Thu 12:00–15:30 & 19:00–23:00, closed Fri, CC, at Via Santa Maria and Via G. Tassi, tel. 050-560-660).

**Bar Costa Gelateria** has a good assortment of homemade gelati a block from the Museo dell' Opera del Duomo on Via Santa Maria 100 (daily 8:00–24:00, tel. 050-551-016).

For a cheap, fast, and tasty meal a few steps from the train station, try cheery **La Lupa Ghiotta Tavola Calda.** It's got everything you'd want from a *ristorante* at half the price, with faster service (you can build your own salad—5 ingredients for €4.50, Mon and Wed–Sat 12:00–15:30 & 19:00–24:00, Tue 12:00–15:30, Sun 19:00–24:00, Viale Bonaini 113, tel. 050-21018).

## Transportation Connections—Pisa

**By train to: Florence** (hrly, 1 hr), **La Spezia** (hrly, 1 hr, gateway to Cinque Terre), **Siena** (change at Empoli: Pisa–Empoli, hrly, 30 min; Empoli–Siena, hrly, 1 hr). Even the fastest trains stop in Pisa, and you might be changing trains here whether you plan to stop or not. Train info: tel. 848-888-088.

**By car:** The drive between Pisa and Florence is that rare case where the non-autostrada highway (free, more direct, and at least as fast) is a better deal than the autostrada. When departing for Florence, San Gimignano, or Siena, follow the blue *superstrada* signs (green signs are for the autostrada) for the SS road (along the city wall east from the tower—away from the sea) for Florence (and later Siena). If departing for the Cinque Terre, catch the Genova-bound autostrada. The white stuff you'll see in the mountains as you approach La Spezia isn't snow—it's Carrara marble, Michelangelo's choice for his great art. From Pisa to La Spezia takes about an hour.

# SIENA

Break out of the Venice–Florence–Rome syndrome and savor Italy's hill towns. Experience the texture of Tuscany, the slumber of Umbria, and the lazy towns of Lazio.

For starters, here's one of my favorites. Tuscany's Siena seems to be every Italy connoisseur's pet town. In my office, whenever Siena is mentioned, someone moans, "Siena? I luuuv Siena!" Nearby San Gimignano (see end of chapter) is the quintessential hill town, with Italy's best surviving medieval skyline.

Seven hundred years ago, Siena was a major military power in a class with Florence, Venice, and Genoa. With a population of 60,000, it was even bigger than Paris. In 1348, a disastrous plague weakened Siena. Then, in the 1550s, her bitter rival, Florence, really "salted" her, forever making Siena a nonthreatening backwater. Siena's loss became our sightseeing gain, as its political and economic irrelevance pickled it purely Gothic. Today Siena's population is still 60,000, compared to Florence's 420,000.

Siena's thriving historic center, with red-brick lanes cascading every which way, offers Italy's best Gothic city experience. Most people do Siena, just 50 kilometers (30 miles) south of Florence, as a day trip, but it's best experienced at twilight. While Florence has the blockbuster museums, Siena has an easy-to-enjoy soul: Courtyards sport flower-decked wells, alleys dead-end at rooftop views, and the sky is a rich blue dome. Right off the bat, Siena becomes an old friend.

Pleasing those who dream of a Fiat-free Italy, pedestrians rule in the old center of Siena. Sit at a café on the red-bricked main square. Take time to savor the first European city to eliminate automobile traffic from its main square (1966) and then, just to be silly, wonder what would happen if they did it in your city.

## Planning Your Time

On a quick trip, consider spending three nights in Siena (with a whole-day side trip into Florence and a day to relax and enjoy Siena). Whatever you do, enjoy a sleepy medieval evening in Siena. After an evening in Siena, you can see its major sights in half a day. San Gimignano is an overrun, pint-sized Siena. Don't rush Siena for San Gimignano (with less than 24 hours for Siena, skip San Gimignano). Note that San Gimignano, with good bus connections, also makes an easy day trip from Florence.

## Orientation

Siena lounges atop a hill, stretching its three legs out from Il Campo. This main square, the historic meeting point of Siena's neighborhoods, is for pedestrians only. And most of those pedestrians are students from the local university. Everything I mention is within a 15-minute walk of the square. Navigate by landmarks, following the excellent system of street-corner signs. The typical visitor sticks to the San Domenico–Il Campo axis.

Siena is one big sight. Its essential individual sights come in two little clusters: the square (city hall, museum, tower) and the cathedral (baptistery, cathedral museum with its surprise viewpoint). Check these sights off and you're free to wander.

**Tourist Information:** Pick up a free town map from the main TI at #56 on Il Campo; look for the yellow Change sign—bad rates, good information (Mon–Sat 8:30–19:30, tel. 0577-280-551, www.siena.turismo.toscana.it). The little TI at San Domenico is for hotel promotion only and sells a Siena map for €0.60.

**Museum Passes:** Siena offers a variety of passes. If you're staying for two days or more, consider getting the €16 combo-ticket (called Siena Itinerari d'Arte) that covers eight sights, including Museo Civico, Santa Maria della Scala, Museo dell' Opera, baptistery, Piccolomini Library (in the cathedral), and more (valid for 7 days, sold at participating sites). This pass covers a wider range of sights than the other passes that cost and cover less (e.g., just religious sights or just city museums). In general, if you see two-thirds of the sights covered by a pass, you'll save money.

## Arrival in Siena

**By Train:** The small train station has a bar and bus office. The baggage checkroom and lockers have been closed indefinitely.

The station is located on the outskirts of town. To get to the city center, take a taxi or a city bus. The **taxi stand** is to your far right as you exit the station; allow about €8 to your hotel (for taxis at station, call 0577-44504, for taxis at Piazza Matteotti in the center, call 0577-49222). For the **city bus**, buy a €0.75 ticket from the Bus Ticket Office in the station lobby (daily 6:15–19:30, ask for city map—it's free and just a bus route map, but helps get you started). You can also buy a bus ticket from the blue machine in the lobby (touch screen for English and select "urban" for type of ticket). Then cross the parking lot and the street to reach the sheltered bus stop. Catch any orange city bus to get into town (punch ticket in machine on bus to validate it). You'll end up at one of three stops—Piazza Gramsci/Lizza, Piazza Sale, or Stufa Secca—all within several blocks of each other (buses run about every 7 min, fewer on Sun; if you get off at Stufa Secca's tiny square, you're soon faced with two uphill roads—take the one to the right for one block to reach the main drag, Banchi di Sopra).

To get to Siena's train station from the center of Siena, catch the city bus at Piazza del Sale or Stufa Secca; note that bus stops are rarely marked with a "bus stop" sign, but instead with a posted schedule and sometimes with yellow lines painted on the pavement, showing a bus-sized rectangle and the word "bus." Confirm with the driver that the bus is going to the *stazione* (pron. stat-zee-OH-nay). Purchase your ticket in advance from a *tabacchi* shop.

**By Bus:** Some buses arrive in Siena at the train station (see "Arrival By Train," above), others at Piazza Gramsci (a few blocks from city center), and some stop at both. The main bus companies are Sena and Tran. You can store baggage underneath Piazza Gramsci in Sotopassaggio la Lizza (€2.75, daily 7:00–19:30, no overnight).

**By Car:** Drivers coming from the autostrada take the Porta San Marco exit and follow the *Centro*, then *Stadio*, signs (stadium, soccer ball). The soccer-ball signs take you to the stadium lot (Parcheggio Stadio, €1.50/hr, €12.50/day) at the huge, bare-brick San Domenico Church. The Fortezza lot nearby charges the same. Or park in the lot underneath the railway station. You can drive into the pedestrian zone (a pretty ballsy thing to do) only to drop bags at your hotel. You can park free in the lot below the Albergo Lea, in white-striped spots behind Hotel Villa Liberty, and behind the Fortezza. (The signs showing a street cleaner and a day of the week indicate which day the street is cleaned; that's a €105 tow-fee incentive to learn the days of the week in Italian.)

## Helpful Hints

**Local Guide:** Roberto Bechi, a hardworking Sienese guide, specializes in off-the-beaten-path tours of Siena and the surrounding countryside. Married to an American (Patti) and having run restaurants in Siena and the United States, Roberto communicates well with Americans. His passions are Sienese culture, Tuscan history, and local cuisine. Book well in advance (full-day tours from €65–95 per person, half-day tours from €30–50 per person, tel. & fax 0577-704-789, www.toursbyroberto.com, e-mail: tourrob@tin.it; for U.S. contact, fax Greg Evans at 540/434-4532).

**Internet Access:** In this university town, there are lots of places to get plugged in. **Internet Point** is just off Piazza Matteotti, on Via Paradiso (across street from McDonald's) and **Internet Train** is near Il Campo, at Via di Città 121 (tel. 0577-226-366).

**Markets:** On Wednesday morning, the weekly market—consisting mainly of clothes—sprawls between the Fortress and Piazza Gramsci along Viale Cesare Maccabi and the adjacent Viale XXV Aprile. The produce market is held a block from Il Campo, behind the city hall (Mon–Sat mornings).

**Laundry:** Two modern, self-service places are Lavarapido Wash and Dry (daily 8:00–22:00, Via di Pantaneto 38, near Logge del Papa) and Onda Blu (daily 8:00–21:00, Via del Casato di Sotto 17, 50 meters, or 165 feet, from Il Campo).

## Sights—Siena's Main Square

▲▲▲**Il Campo**—Siena's great central piazza is urban harmony at its best. Like a people-friendly stage set, its gently tilted floor fans out from the tower and city hall backdrop. It's the perfect invitation to loiter. Think of it as a trip to the beach without sand or water.

Il Campo was located at the historic junction of Siena's various competing districts, or *contrada*, on the old marketplace. The brick surface is divided into nine sections, representing the council of nine merchants and city bigwigs who ruled medieval Siena. At the square's high point, look for the *Fountain of Joy*, the two naked guys about to be tossed in, and the pigeons politely waiting their turn to gingerly tightrope down slippery spouts to slurp a drink. (You can see parts of the original fountain, of which this is a copy, in an interesting exhibit at Siena's Santa Maria della Scala museum, listed below.) At the square's low point is the city hall and tower. The chapel located at the base of the tower was built in 1348 as thanks to God for ending the Black Plague (after it killed more than a third of the population).

To say Siena and Florence have always been competitive is an understatement. In medieval times, a statue of Venus stood on Il Campo (where the *Fountain of Joy* is today). After the plague hit Siena, the monks blamed this pagan statue. The people cut it to pieces and buried it along the walls of Florence.

The market area behind the city hall, a wide-open expanse since the Middle Ages, originated as a farming area within the city walls to feed the city in times of siege. Now the morning produce

## Siena Sights

TO HOSTEL
TO TRAIN STATION
FORTEZZA
VIALE FRANCHI
LA LIZZA
VIALE MACCARI
V. GIARI.
STUFASECCA
V. MONT.
PIAZZA SALE
PIAZZA GRAMSCI
BUSES TO FLORENCE
ENOTECA ITALIA
VIALE TOZZI
STADIO
P
25 APR.
PIAZZA MATTEOTTI
100 YDS.
100 m
POST
PIAZZA SALIMBENI
PIAZZA TOLOMEI
V. DEI MILLE
VIA CURTATONE
VIA PARADISIO
McD
VIA DI SAPIENZA
CAMPOREGIO
WC
S. ANT.
PITTORI
S. CAT.
BANCHI DI SOPRA
ROSSI
CECCO
SAN DOMENICO
SANCT. S. CAT.
GALLUZZA
TERME
TERMINI
P. IND.
BANCHI
MUSEO CIVICO
CITY HALL & TOWER
ESTERINA FONT.
COSTONE
V. FONT.
CETO
WC
BANCHI DI SOTTO
BAPT.
FRANC.
VIA PELL.
IL CAMPO
PANT.
DUOMO
VIA DI CITTÀ
SALICOTTO
PORRIONE
PIAZZA DUOMO
CASTORO
WC
CAS. DI SOTTO
SANTA MARIA DELLA SCALA
CAPITANO
MUSIC ACADEMY
PIAZZA MERCATO
CATHEDRAL MUSEUM
STALLOREGGI
S. PIETRO
100 YDS.
100 m
PINACOTECA
-PICTURE GALL.-

① SOTTOPASSAGGIO LA LIZZA ② PALIO MOVIE

market is held here Monday through Saturday. (The public WCs closest to Il Campo are each about a block away: at Via Beccheria—a few steps off Via de Città—and on Casato di Sotto; €0.60.)

▲**Museo Civico**—The Palazzo Publico (city hall), at the base of the tower, has a fine and manageable museum housing a good sample of Sienese art. In the following order, you'll see: the Sala Risorgimento, with dramatic scenes of Victor Emmanuel's unification of Italy (surrounded by statues that don't seem to care); the chapel, with impressive inlaid wood chairs in the choir; and the Sala del Mappamondo, with Simone Martini's *Maesta* (Enthroned Virgin) facing the faded *Guidoriccio da Fogliano* (a mercenary providing a more concrete form of protection). Next is the Sala della Pace—where the city's fat cats met. Looking down on the oligarchy during their meetings were two interesting frescoes showing the effects of good and bad government. Notice the whistle-while-you-work happiness of the utopian community ruled by the utopian government (in the better-preserved fresco) and the fate of a community ruled by politicians with more typical values (in a terrible state of repair). The message: Without justice, there can be no prosperity. The rural view out the window is essentially the view from the top of the big stairs—enjoy it from here (€6.50, combo-ticket with tower-€9.50, daily March–Oct 10:00–19:00, July–Sept until 23:00, Nov–Jan 10:00–16:00, last entry 45 min before closing; audioguide-€3.75 for 1 person, €5.25 for 2; tel. 0577-292-111).

▲**City Tower (Torre del Mangia)**—Siena gathers around its city hall, not its church. It was a proud republic; its "declaration of independence" is the tallest secular medieval tower in Italy. The 100-meter-tall (330-foot) Torre del Mangia was named after a hedonistic watchman who consumed his earnings like a glutton consumes food (his chewed-up statue is in the courtyard, to the left as you enter). Its 300 steps get pretty skinny at the top, but the reward is one of Italy's best views (€5.50, combo-ticket with Museo Civico-€9.50, daily 10:00–19:00, mid-July–mid-Sept until 23:00, Nov–March 10:00–16:00, closed in rain, sometimes long lines, limit of 30 tourists at a time, avoid midday crowd).

▲**Pinacoteca (National Picture Gallery)**—Siena was a power in Gothic art. But the average tourist, wrapped up in a love affair with the Renaissance, hardly notices. This museum takes you on a walk through Siena's art, chronologically from the 12th through the 15th centuries. For the casual sightseer, the Sienese art in the city hall and cathedral museums is adequate. But art fans enjoy this opportunity to trace the evolution of Siena's delicate and elegant art (€4.25, Sun–Mon 8:30–13:15, Tue–Sat 8:15–19:15, plus possibly 20:30–23:30 on Sat in summer, tel. 0577-281-161). From Il Campo, walk out Via di Città to Piazza di Postierla and go left on San Pietro.

## Sights—Siena's Cathedral Area

▲▲▲**Duomo**—Siena's cathedral is as Baroque as Gothic gets. The striped facade is piled with statues and ornamentation, and the interior is decorated from top to bottom. The heads of 172 popes peer down from the ceiling, over the fine inlaid art on the floor. This is one busy interior. (Modest dress is required for entry.)

To orient yourself in this *panforte* of Italian churches, stand under the dome and think of the church floor as a big clock. You're the middle, and the altar is high noon: you'll find the *Slaughter of the Innocents* roped off on the floor at 10:00, Pisano's pulpit between two pillars at 11:00, Bernini's chapel at 3:00, two Michelangelo statues (next to doorway leading to a shop, snacks, and WC) at 7:00, the library at 8:00, and a Donatello statue at 9:00. Take some time with the floor mosaics in the front. Nicola Pisano's wonderful pulpit is crowded with delicate Gothic story-telling from 1268. To understand why Bernini is considered the greatest Baroque sculptor, step into his sumptuous *Cappella della Madonna del Voto*. This last work in the cathedral, from 1659, is enough to make a Lutheran light a candle. Move up to the altar and look back at the two Bernini statues: Mary Magdalene in a state of spiritual ecstasy, and St. Jerome playing the crucifix like a violinist lost in beautiful music.

The Piccolomini altar is most interesting for its two Michel-angelo statues (the lower big ones). Paul, on the left, may be a self-portrait. Peter, on the right, resembles Michelangelo's more famous statue of Moses. Originally contracted to do 15 statues, Michelangelo left the project early (1504) to do his great *David* in Florence.

The Piccolomini Library—worth the €1.50 entry—is brilliantly frescoed with scenes glorifying the works of a pope from 500 years ago. It contains intricately decorated, illuminated music scores and a statue (a Roman copy of a Greek original) of the Three Graces (library open Sun 13:30–19:30, Tue–Sat same as church hours, below). Donatello's bronze statue of St. John the Baptist, in his famous rags, is in a chapel to the right of the library.

**Hours:** The church is open mid-March–Oct daily 7:30–19:30 but Sun 10:15–14:00 is reserved for worship only; Nov–mid-March Mon–Sat 7:30–17:00, Sun 14:30–17:30. In September, when much of the elaborate mosaic floor is uncovered, you'll pay a fee to enter the church (€2.75 for Pavimento Cattedrale).

**Audioguides:** There's a daunting number of audioguides. An audioguide for just the church costs €3.10; to add the library, it's €3.60; and to add the Cathedral Museum (Museo dell' Opera de Panorama), it's €5.25. For the church and museum only, it's €4.25. Two headphones are available at a price break.

▲**Santa Maria della Scala**—This renovated old hospital-turned-museum (opposite the duomo entrance) was used as a hospital as recently as the 1980s. Now it displays a lavishly frescoed hall, a worthwhile exhibit on Quercia's *Fountain of Joy* (downstairs), and a so-so archaeological museum (subterranean, in labyrinthine tunnels). The entire museum is a maze, with various exhibitions and paintings plugged in to fill the gaps.

The frescoes in the **Pellegrinaio Hall** show medieval Siena's innovative health care and social welfare system in action (c. 1442, wonderfully described in English). The hospital was functioning as early as the 11th century, nursing the sick and caring for abandoned children (see frescoes). The good work paid off, as bequests and donations poured in, creating the wealth that's evident in the chapels elsewhere on this floor. The Old Sacristy was built to house precious relics, including a Holy Nail thought to be from Jesus' cross.

Downstairs, the engaging exhibit on Jacopo della Quercia's early-15th-century *Fountain of Joy* doesn't need much English description, fortunately, because there isn't much. In the 19th century, the *Fountain of Joy* in Il Campo was deteriorating. It was dismantled, and plaster casts were made of the originals. Then replicas were made, restoring the pieces as if brand-new. The *Fountain of Joy* that stands in Il Campo today is a replica. In this exhibit, you'll see the plaster casts of the original, eroded panels paired with their restored twins. Statues originally stood on the edges of the fountain (see the statues and drawings). In general, the pieces at the beginning and end of the exhibit are original. If there's a piece in a dim room near the exit of the exhibit, it's likely an original chunk awaiting cleaning.

The **Archaeological Museum**, way downstairs, consists mainly of pottery fragments in cases lining tunnel after tunnel. It's like being lost in a wine cellar without the wine. Unless there's an exhibition, it's not worth the trip.

**Cost and Hours:** €5.25, daily 10:00–18:00, Fri–Sat in summer until 23:00, off-season 11:30–16:30, closed some Sundays. The chapel just inside the museum entrance door is free (as you enter the museum, it's to your left; English description inside chapel entry).

▲**Baptistery**—Siena is so hilly that there wasn't enough flat ground on which to build a big church. What to do? Build a big church and prop up the overhanging edge with the baptistery. This dark and quietly tucked-away cave of art is worth a look (and €2.50) for its cool tranquillity and the bronze panels and angels—by Ghiberti, Donatello, and others—adorning the pedestal of the baptismal font (daily mid-March–Sept 9:00–19:30, Oct 9:00–18:00, Nov–mid-March 10:00–13:00 & 14:30–17:00).

▲▲**Cathedral Museum (Museo dell' Opera e Panorama)**—Siena's most enjoyable museum, on the Campo side of the church (look for the yellow signs), was built to house the cathedral's art. The ground floor is filled with the cathedral's original Gothic sculpture by Giovanni Pisano (who spent 10 years in the late 1200s carving and orchestrating the decoration of the cathedral) and a fine Donatello *Madonna and Child.* Upstairs to the left awaits a private audience with Duccio's *Maesta (Enthroned Virgin)*. Pull up a chair and study one of the great pieces of medieval art. The flip side of the *Maesta* (displayed on the opposite wall), with 26 panels—the medieval equivalent of pages—shows scenes from the Passion of Christ. Climb onto the "Panorama dal Facciatone." From the first landing, take the skinnier second spiral for Siena's surprise view. Look back over the duomo and consider this: When rival republic Florence began its grand cathedral, proud Siena decided to build the biggest church in all Christendom. The existing cathedral would be used as a transept. You're atop what would have been the entry. The wall below you, connecting the duomo with the museum of the cathedral, was as far as Siena got before a plague killed the city's ability to finish the project. Were it completed, you'd be looking straight down the nave—white stones mark where columns would have stood (€5.50, worthwhile €2.60 40-minute audioguide, daily mid-March–Sept 9:00–19:30, Oct 9:00–18:00, Nov–mid-March 9:00–13:30, tel. 0577-283-048).

## Sights—Siena's San Domenico Area

**Church of San Domenico**—This huge brick church is worth a quick look. The bland interior fits the austere philosophy of the Dominicans. Walk up the steps in the rear for a look at various paintings from the life of Saint Catherine, patron saint of Siena. Halfway up the church on the right, you'll see a metal bust of Saint Catherine, a small case containing her finger, and her actual head (free, daily March–Oct 7:00–13:00 & 14:30–18:30, Nov–Feb 9:00–13:00 & 15:00–18:00; WC for €0.60 at far end of parking lot—facing church entrance, it's to your right).

**Sanctuary of Saint Catherine**—Step into Catherine's cool and peaceful home. Siena remembers its favorite hometown girl, a simple, unschooled, but mystically devout girl who, in the mid-1300s, helped convince the pope to return from France to Rome. Pilgrims have come here since 1464. Since then, architects and artists have greatly embellished what was probably a humble home (her family worked as wool-dyers). Enter through the courtyard and walk to the far end. The chapel on your right was built over the spot where Saint Catherine received the stigmata while praying. The chapel on your left used to be the kitchen. Go down the stairs to the left of the chapel/kitchen to reach the saint's room. The saint's bare cell is behind see-through doors. Much of the art throughout the sanctuary depicts scenes from the saint's life (free, daily 9:30–18:00, winter 9:30–13:30 & 15:00–18:30, Via Tiratoio). It's a few downhill blocks toward the center from San Domenico (follow signs to the Santuario di Santa Caterina).

**Nightlife**—Join the evening *passeggiata* (peak strolling time is

19:00) along Via Banchi di Sopra with gelato in hand. **Nannini's** at Piazza Salimbeni has fine gelato (daily 11:00–24:00).

The **Enoteca Italiana** is a good wine bar in a cellar in the Fortezza/Fortress (Mon 12:00–20:00, Tue–Sat 12:00–1:00, closed Sun, sample glasses in 3 different price ranges: €1.55, €2.75, €5.25, bottles and snacks available, CC, cross bridge and enter fortress, go left down ramp, tel. 0577-288-497).

**Shopping**—Shops line Via Banchi di Sopra, the *passeggiata* route. For a department store, try Upim on Piazza Matteotti (Mon–Sat 9:30–19:50, closed Sun). The large, colorful scarves/flags, each depicting the symbol of one of Siena's 17 different neighborhoods (such as the wolf, the turtle, and snail, etc.), are easy-to-pack souvenirs, fun for decorating your home (€7.25 apiece for large size, sold at souvenir stands).

## Siena's Palio

In the Palio, the feisty spirit of Siena's 17 *contrada* (neighborhoods) lives on. These neighborhoods celebrate, worship, and compete together. Each even has its own historical museum. *Contrada* pride is evident any time of year in the colorful neighborhood banners and parades. (If you hear distant drumming, run to it for some medieval action.) But *contrada* pride is most visible twice a year— on July 2 and August 16—when they have their world-famous horse race, the Palio di Siena. Ten of the 17 neighborhoods com- pete (chosen by lot), hurling themselves with medieval abandon into several days of trial races and traditional revelry. On the big day, jockeys and horses go into their *contrada*'s church to be blessed ("Go and win," says the priest). It's considered a sign of luck if a horse leaves droppings in the church.

On the evening of the big day, Il Campo is stuffed to the brim with locals and tourists, as the horses charge wildly around the square in this literally no-holds-barred race. A horse can win even if its rider has fallen off. Of course, the winning neighborhood is the scene of grand celebrations afterward. The grand prize: simply proving your *contrada* is numero uno. All over town, sketches and posters depict the Palio. This is not some folkloristic event. It's a real medieval moment. If you're packed onto the square with 15,000 people who each really want to win, you won't see much, but you'll feel it. While the actual Palio packs the city, you could side-trip in from Florence to see horse-race trials each of the three days before the big day (usually at 9:00 and around 19:30).

▲**Palio al Cinema**—This 20-minute film, *Siena, the Palio, and its History*, helps re-create the craziness of the Palio. See it at the Cinema Moderno in Piazza Tolomei, two blocks from Il Campo (runs May–Sept only, €5.25, with this book pay €4.25, or €7.75

for 2; Mon–Sat 9:30–17:30, English showings generally hourly at
:30 past the hour, schedule posted on door, closed Sun, air-con,
tel. 0577-289-201). Call or drop by to confirm when the next
English showing is scheduled—there are usually seven a day.
At the ticket desk, you can buy the same show on video (discounted from €13 to €10.50 with this book, video must be labeled
"NTSC American System" or it'll be a doorstop at your home).

## Sleeping in Siena
### (€1 = about $1, country code: 39, zip code: 53100)
Sleep Code: **S** = Single, **D** = Double/Twin, **T** = Triple, **Q** = Quad,
**b** = bathroom, **s** = shower only, **CC** = Credit Cards accepted, **no
CC** = Credit Cards not accepted, **SE** = Speaks English, **NSE** =
No English. Breakfast is generally not included. Have breakfast
on Il Campo or in a nearby bar.

To help you sort easily through these listings, I've divided
the rooms into three categories based on the price for a standard
double room with bath:

**Higher Priced**—Most rooms more than €110.
**Moderately Priced**—Most rooms €110 or less.
**Lower Priced**—Most rooms €80 or less.

Finding a room is tough during Easter or the Palio in early July
and mid-August. Call ahead any time of year, as Siena's few budget
places are listed in all the budget guidebooks. While day-tripping
tour groups turn the town into a Gothic amusement park in mid-
summer, Siena is basically yours in the evenings and off-season.

Nearly all hotels listed lie between Il Campo and the Church
of San Domenico (see map on page 243). About a third of the
listings don't take credit cards, no matter how earnestly you ask.
Cash machines are plentiful on the main streets.

### *Sleeping near Il Campo*

#### HIGHER PRICED
These two places are a 10-minute walk from Il Campo.

**Hotel Duomo** is a classy place with 23 spacious rooms
(Sb-€110, Db-€150, Tb-€175, Qb-€200, includes breakfast,
CC, air-con, picnic-friendly roof terrace, free parking, follow
Via di Città, which becomes Via Stalloreggi, to Via Stalloreggi 38,
tel. 0577-289-088, fax 0577-43043, www.hotelduomo.it, e-mail:
booking@hotelduomo.it, Stefania SE). If you arrive by train, take
a taxi (€8); if you drive, go to Porta San Marco and follow the
signs to the hotel, drop off your bags, and then park in nearby
"Il Campo" lot.

**Pensione Palazzo Ravizza**, elegant and friendly, has an

aristocratic feel and a peaceful garden (Db-€148–255, suites available, includes breakfast and dinner, cheaper mid-Nov–Feb, CC, elevator, back rooms face open country, good restaurant, half pension required in summer, free parking, Via Pian dei Mantellini 34, tel. 0577-280-462, fax 0577-221-597, www .palazzoravizza.it, e-mail: bureau@palazzoravizza.it, SE).

**LOWER PRICED**
Each of these listings is forgettable but inexpensive, and just a horse wreck away from one of Italy's most wonderful civic spaces.

**Piccolo Hotel Etruria**, a good bet for a hotel with 19 decent rooms but not much soul, is just off the square (S-€39, Sb-€44, Db-€73, Tb-€91, Qb-€114, breakfast-€4.75, CC, with your back to the tower, leave Il Campo to the right at 2:00, Via Donzelle 1-3, curfew at 0:30, tel. 0577-288-088, fax 0577-288-461, e-mail: hetruria@tin.it, Fattorini family SE).

**Albergo Tre Donzelle,** with its 27 plain, institutional rooms next door to Piccolo Hotel Etruria, makes sense only if you think of Il Campo as your terrace (S-€34, D-€47, Db-€60, CC, Via Donzelle 5, tel. 0577-280-358, fax 0577-223-933, Signora—pron. seen-YOR-ah—Iannini SE).

**Locanda Garibaldi** is a modest, very Sienese restaurant/ *albergo*. Gentle Marcello wears two hats, as he runs a fine, busy restaurant downstairs and seven pleasant rooms up a funky, artsy staircase (Db-€70, Tb-€89, family deals, no CC, takes reservations only a week in advance, half a block downhill off the square at Via Giovanni Dupre 18, tel. 0577-284-204, NSE).

**Hotel Cannon d'Oro,** a few blocks up Via Banchi di Sopra, is spacious and group-friendly (30 rooms, Sb-€66, Db-€82, Tb-€104, Qb-€122, these discounted prices promised through 2003 with this book, family deals, breakfast-€6, CC, Via Montanini 28, tel. 0577-44321, fax 0577-280-868, e-mail: cannondoro @libero.it, Maurizio and Debora SE).

**Albergo La Perla,** a last resort, is a funky, jumbled, 13-room place with a narrow maze of hallways, stark rooms, old bedspreads, miniscule bathrooms, and laissez-faire environment (Sb-€50, Db-€65, Tb-€90, no CC, a block off Piazza Independenza at Via della Terme 25, tel. 0577-47144). Attilio and his American wife, Deborah, take reservations only a day or two ahead. Ideally, call the morning you'll arrive.

## Sleeping near San Domenico Church
These hotels are also within a 10-minute walk of Il Campo. Albergo Bernini and Alma Domus, which enjoy views of the old town and cathedral, are the best values in town.

# Siena Hotels and Restaurants

| | | |
|---|---|---|
| **1** PICCOLO HOTEL ETRURIA | **9** HOTEL CHIUSARELLI | **16** IL VERROCHIO |
| **2** ALBERGO TRE DONZELLE | **10** TO ALBERGO LEA & HOTEL LIBERTY | **17** CIAO CAFETERIA |
| **3** ALBERGO LA PERLA | **11** JOLLY HOTEL SIENA | **18** TO PENSIONE PAL. RAVIZZA |
| **4** TO HOTEL DUOMO | **12** PIZZERIA SPADAFORTE | **19** TO HOTEL SANTA CATARINA & PALAZZO VALLI |
| **5** HOTEL CANNON D'ORO | **13** RISTORANTE GALLO NERO | **20** SOTTOPASSAGGIO LA LIZZA |
| **6** LOCANDA GARIBALDI | **14** OSTERIA IL TAMBURINO | **21** LAUNDROMATS |
| **7** ALBERGO BERNINI | **15** OSTERIA DA DIVO | |
| **8** ALMA DOMUS | | |

**HIGHER PRICED**

**Hotel Villa Liberty** has 18 big, bright, comfortable rooms (S-€75, Db-€130, includes breakfast, CC, only one room with twin beds; elevator, bar, air-con, TVs, courtyard, facing fortress at Viale V. Veneto 11, tel. 0577-44966, fax 0577-44770, www.villaliberty.it, e-mail: info@villaliberty.it, SE).

**Jolly Hotel Siena,** for people who want a four-star hotel, has 126 rooms that are clean but dated. Across the street from Piazza Gramsci, it's convenient if you're arriving by bus and you've got lots of luggage—and money (Sb-€124–160, Db-€170–233, includes breakfast, CC, non-smoking floor, Piazza La Lizza, tel. 0577-288-448, fax 0577-41272, e-mail: siena@jollyhotels.it).

**MODERATELY PRICED**

**Albergo Bernini** makes you part of a Sienese family in a modest, clean home with nine fine rooms. Friendly Nadia and Mauro welcome you to their spectacular view terrace for breakfast and picnic lunches and dinners. Outside of breakfast and checkout time, Mauro, an accomplished accordionist, might play a song for you if you ask (Sb-€77, D-€62, Db-€82, breakfast-€7, less in winter, no CC, midnight curfew, on the main San Domenico–Il Campo drag at Via Sapienza 15, tel. & fax 0577-289-047, www.albergobernini.com, e-mail: hbernin@tin.it, son Alessandro SE).

**Hotel Chiusarelli**, a proper hotel in a beautiful building with a handy location, comes with traffic noise at night—ask for a quieter room in the back (49 rooms, S-€57, Sb-€72, Db-€108, Tb-€146, includes big buffet breakfast, CC, suites available, air-con, pleasant garden terrace, across from San Domenico at Viale Curtatone 15, tel. 0577-280-562, fax 0577-271-177, www.chiusarelli.com, e-mail: info@chiusarelli.com, SE).

**Albergo Lea** is a sleepable place in a residential neighborhood a few blocks away from the center (past San Domenico) with 11 rooms and easy parking (S-€52, Db-€93, Tb-€120, cheaper in winter, includes breakfast, CC, rooftop terrace, Viale XXIV Maggio 10, tel. & fax 0577-283-207, SE).

**LOWER PRICED**

**Alma Domus** is ideal—unless nuns make you nervous, you need a double bed, or you plan on staying out past the 23:30 curfew (no mercy given). This quasi-hotel (not a convent) is run with firm but angelic smiles by sisters who offer clean and quiet rooms for a steal and save the best views for foreigners. Bright lamps, quaint balconies, fine views, grand public rooms, top security, and a friendly atmosphere make this a great value. The checkout time is strictly 10:00, but they will store your luggage in their secure courtyard (Db-€59, Tb-€72, Qb-€90, no CC, ask for view room—*con vista*, elevator, from San Domenico walk downhill with the church on your right toward the view, turn left down Via Camporegio, make a U-turn at the little chapel down the brick steps to Via Camporegio 37, tel. 0577-44177 and 0577-44487, fax 0577-47601, NSE).

## Sleeping Farther from the Center

The first two listings are near Porta Romana.

### HIGHER PRICED

**Hotel Santa Caterina** is a three-star, 18th-century place, best for drivers who need air-conditioning. Professionally run with real attention to quality, it has 22 comfortable rooms with a delightful garden (Sb-€98, small Db-€98, Db-€133, Tb-€179, mention this book to get these prices, includes buffet breakfast, elevator, CC; garden side is quieter but street side—with multipaned windows—isn't bad, fridge in room, parking-€12/day—request when you reserve, 100 meters, or 330 feet, outside Porta Romana at Via E.S. Piccolomini 7, tel. 0577-221-105, fax 0577-271-087, www.hscsiena.it, e-mail: info@hscsiena.it, SE). A city bus runs frequently (Mon–Sat 4/hr, Sun 2/hr) to the town center. A taxi to/from the station runs around €8.

**Palazzo di Valli**, with 11 spacious rooms and a garden, is 800 meters (0.5 mile) beyond Porta Romana (the Roman gate) and feels like it's in the country. Catch the city bus into town (Db-€140, Tb-€170, includes breakfast, CC, parking, Via E.S. Piccolomini, bus to center Mon–Sat 4/hr, Sun 2/hr; tel. 0577-226-102, fax 0577-222-255, Camarda family SE). From the autostrada, exit at Siena Sud in the direction of Porta Romana.

**Frances' Lodge** is a small farmhouse B&B 1.5 kilometers (1 mile) out of Siena. English-speaking Franca and Franco rent four modern rooms in a rustic yet elegant old place with a swimming pool, peaceful garden, eight acres of olive trees and vineyards, and great Siena views (Db-€150–180, Tb-€210, easy parking, near shuttle bus into town, Strada di Valdipugna 2, tel. 0577-281-061, fax 0577-222-224, www.franceslodge.it).

### MODERATELY PRICED

**Casa Laura** has five clean, well-maintained rooms, some with brick-and-beam ceilings (Db-€83 with breakfast, €73 without, cheaper off-season or for 3 nights or more, CC, Via Roma 3, about a 10-min walk from Il Campo toward Porta Romana, closed Nov–March, tel. 0577-226-061, fax 0577-225-240, e-mail: labenci@tin.it, NSE).

**LOWER PRICED**
Siena's **Guidoriccio Youth Hostel** has 120 cheap beds, but, given the hassle of the bus ride and the charm of downtown Siena at night, I'd skip it (office open 15:00–1:00, €13 beds in doubles, triples, and dorms with sheets and breakfast, CC, bus #10 from train station or bus #15 from Piazza Gramsci, Via Fiorentina 89 in Stellino neighborhood, tel. 0577-52212, SE).

# Eating in Siena
Sienese restaurants are reasonable by Florentine and Venetian standards. Even with higher prices, lousy service, and lower-quality food, consider eating on Il Campo—a classic European experience.

**Pizzeria Spadaforte**, at the edge of Il Campo, has a decent setting, mediocre pizza, and tables steeper than its prices (daily 12:00–16:00 & 19:30–22:30, CC, to far right of city tower as you face it, tel. 0577-281-123).

For authentic Sienese dining at a fair price, eat at **Locanda Garibaldi**, down Via Giovanni Dupre at #18, within a block of Il Campo (€15 *menu*, Sun–Fri opens at 12:00–14:00 for lunch and 19:00–21:00 for dinner, arrive early to get a table, closed Sat). Marcello does a nice little *piatto misto dolce* for €2.75, featuring several local desserts with sweet wine.

**Osteria il Tamburino** is friendly, small, and intimate and serves up tasty meals (Mon–Sat 12:00–14:30 & 19:00–20:30, closed Sun, CC, follow Via di Città off Il Campo, becomes Stalloreggi, Via Stalloreggi 11, tel. 0577-280-306).

**Taverna San Giuseppe**, a local favorite, offers traditional food with a creative flair. Reserve or arrive early (Mon–Sat 12:15–14:15 & 17:15–21:45, closed Sun, Via Giovanni Dupre 132, tel. 0577-42286).

**Antica Osteria Da Divo** is the place for a fine €40 meal. The kitchen is creative, the food is fresh and top-notch, and the ambience is candlelit. You'll get a basket of exotic fresh breads. They offer excellent seasonal dishes. The lamb goes baaa in your mouth. And the chef is understandably proud of his desserts (daily 12:00–14:30 & 19:00–22:00, CC, Via Franciosa 29, facing baptistery door, take the far right and walk one long curving block, reserve for summer eves, tel. 0577-286-054).

**Trattoria La Tellina** has patient waiters and great food, including homemade tiramisu. Arrive early to get a seat (Via dell Terme 52, between St. Catherine's House and Piazza Tolomei—where Palio film is shown, tel. 0577-283-133).

**Osteria Nonna Gina** wins praise from locals for its good

quality and prices (Tue–Sun 12:30–14:30 & 19:30–20:30, closed Mon, CC, Piano dei Mantellini 2, 10-min walk from Il Campo, near Hotel Duomo, tel. 0577-287-247).

**Ristorante Gallo Nero** is a friendly "grotto" for Tuscan cuisine. Popular with groups, this "black rooster" serves *ribollita* (hearty Tuscan bean soup) and offers a €23 "medieval *menu*," as well as several Tuscan *menus*, starting at €16 (daily 12:00–15:30 & 19:00–24:00, CC, 3 blocks down Via del Porrione from Il Campo at #65, tel. 0577-284-356).

**Il Verrochio**, a block away—tucked between a church and loggia—serves a decent €13 *menu* in a cozy, wood-beamed setting (daily 12:00–14:30 & 19:00–22:00, closed Wed in winter, CC, Logge del Papa 1, tel. 0577-284-062).

**Le Campane**, two blocks off Il Campo, is classy and a little pricey (daily 12:15–14:30 & 19:15–22:00, closed Mon in winter, CC, indoor/outdoor seating, a few steps off Via di Città at Via delle Campane 6, tel. 0577-284-035).

**Osteria la Chiacchera**, while touristy, is an atmospheric, tasty, and affordable hole-in-the-brick-wall (daily 11:00–24:00, CC, 2 rooms, below Pension Bernini at Costa di San Antonio 4, reservations wise, skip the *trippa*—tripe, tel. 0577-280-631).

### Cheap Meals, Snacks, and Picnics

Snack with a view from a small balcony overlooking Il Campo. Survey these three places from Il Campo to see which has a free table. On Via di Città, you'll find **Gelateria Artigiana,** which has perhaps Siena's best ice cream, and **Barbero d'Oro,** which serves cappuccino and *panforte* (€1.75/100 grams/3.5 oz; balcony with 2 tables, closed Sun). **Bar Paninoteca** is on Vicolo di S. Paolo, on the stairs leading down to Il Campo (sandwiches, has a row of chairs on balcony, closed Mon).

At the bottom of Il Campo, a **Ciao** cafeteria offers easy self-service meals, no ambience, and no views. The crowded **Spizzico**, a pizza counter in the front half of Ciao, serves huge, inexpensive quarter pizzas; on sunny days, people take the pizza, trays and all, out on Il Campo for a picnic (daily 11:00–22:00, non-smoking section—*non fumatori*—in back, CC only in cafeteria, to left of city tower as you face it).

Budget eaters look for *pizza al taglio* shops, scattered through-out Siena, selling pizza by the slice. Picnickers enjoy the market held mornings (except Sun) behind Il Campo, on Piazza del Mercato. Of the grocery shops scattered throughout town, the biggest is called simply **Alimentari;** it's one block off Piazza Matteotti, toward Il Campo. Their pesto is the besto (Mon–Sat 8:00–19:30, Via Pianigiani 5, no sign).

### Sienese Sweets

All over town, **Prodotti Tipici** shops sell Sienese specialties. Siena's claim to caloric fame is its *panforte*, a rich, chewy concoction of nuts, honey, and candied fruits that impresses even fruitcake-haters (although locals prefer a white macaroon-and-almond cookie called *ricciarelli).*

## Transportation Connections—Siena

**By train to: Florence** (9/day, 1.75 hrs, last one at 21:00).

**By bus to: Florence** (2/hr, 1.25–2 hrs, by Tran bus), **San Gimignano** (6/day, 1.25 hrs, by Tran bus, more frequent with transfer in Poggibonsi), **Assisi** (2/day, 2 hrs, by Sena bus; the morning bus goes direct to Assisi, the afternoon bus might terminate at Santa Maria Angeli, from here catch a local bus to Assisi, 2/hr, 20 min), **Rome** (7/day, 3 hrs, by Sena bus, arrives at Rome's Tiburtina station), **Milan** (4/day, 14 hrs). Buses also connect Siena with Montepulciano, Montalcino, Chiusi, Pienza, and the San Galgano Monastery (see More Hill Towns in Orvieto chapter for information on these towns; get schedule in Siena). Schedules get sparse on Sunday.

Buses depart Siena from Piazza Gramsci, the train station, or both; confirm when you purchase your ticket. You can get tickets for Tran buses or Sena buses at the train station (Tran bus office: Mon–Sat 5:50–20:00; for Sena, buy tickets at *tabacchi* shop unless they've opened a separate office in the station), or easier and more central, under Piazza Gramsci at Sottopassaggio La Lizza (Tran bus office: daily 5:50–20:00, tel. 0577-204-225, toll-free tel. 800-373-760; Sena bus office: Mon–Sat 7:45–19:45, Sun 15:30–19:30, tel. 0577-283-203, www.senabus.it).

Sottopassaggio La Lizza, under Piazza Gramsci, has a cash machine (neither bus office accepts credit cards), luggage storage (€2.75/day, €1.50/half day, daily 7:00–19:30, no overnight storage), posted bus schedules, TV monitors (listing imminent departures), an elevator, and expensive WCs (€0.55). If you decide to depart Siena after the bus offices close, you can buy the ticket directly from the driver (and get charged a supplement).

On schedules, the fastest buses are marked *corse rapide*. Note that if a schedule lists your departure point as Via Tozzi or La Lizza, you catch the bus at Piazza Gramsci (Via Tozzi is the street that runs alongside Piazza Gramsci and La Lizza is the name of the bus station).

## SAN GIMIGNANO

The epitome of a Tuscan hill town, with 14 medieval towers still standing (out of an original 72!), San Gimignano is a perfectly preserved tourist trap, so easy to visit and visually pleasing that it's a good stop. In the 13th century, back in the days of Romeo and Juliet, towns were run by feuding noble families. They'd periodically battle things out from the protection of their respective family towers. Pointy skylines were the norm in medieval Tuscany. But in San Gimignano, fabric was big business, and many of its towers were built simply to hang dyed fabric out to dry.

While the basic three-star sight here is the town of San Gimignano itself, there are a few worthwhile stops. From the town gate, shop straight up the traffic-free town's cobbled main drag to Piazza del Cisterna (with its 13th-century well). The town sights cluster around the adjoining Piazza del Duomo. Thursday is market day (8:00–13:00), but for local merchants, every day is a sales frenzy.

**Tourist Information:** The TI is in the old center on Piazza Duomo (daily March–Oct 9:00–13:00 & 15:00–19:00, Nov–Feb 9:00–13:00 & 14:00–18:00, changes money, tel. 0577-940-008, www.sangimignano.com, e-mail: prolocsg@tin.it). To see virtually all of the city's sights, consider a €10.50 combo-ticket (covers Collegiata, Torre Grossa, Museo Civico, archaeological museum, and more).

## Sights—San Gimignano
**Collegiata**—This Romanesque church, with round windows and wide steps, is filled with fine Renaissance frescoes (€3.50, Mon–Fri 9:30–19:30, Sat 9:30–17:00, Sun 13:00–17:00).
**Torre Grossa**—The city's tallest tower can be scaled (€4.25, 60 meters/200 feet tall, March–Oct daily 9:30–19:20, Nov–Feb Sat–Thu 10:30–16:20, closed Fri), but the free *rocca* (castle), a short hike behind the church, offers a better view and a great picnic perch, especially at sunset.
**Museo Civico**—This museum, on Piazza Popolo, has a classy little painting collection with a 1422 altarpiece by Taddeo di Bartolo, honoring Saint Gimignano. You can see the saint with the town in his hands surrounded by events from his life (€3.75, €6.25 combo-ticket with Torre Grossa, same hours as Torre Grossa).

## Sleeping and Eating in San Gimignano
### (€1 = about $1, country code: 39, zip code: 53037)
**Carla Rossi** offers rooms and apartments—most with views—throughout the town (Db-from €60, most around €100, no CC, no breakfast, Via di Cellole 81, tel. & fax 0577-955-041, cellular 36-8352-3206, www.appartamentirossicarla.com, e-mail: cabusini@tin.it, SE). For a listing of private rooms, stop by or call **Associazione Strutture Extralberghiere** (Db-€52, no CC, no breakfast, Piazza della Cisterna, tel. 0577-943-190).

*Eating:* **Osteria del Carcere** has good food and prices (Via del Castello 13, no CC, just off Piazza della Cisterna, tel. 0577-941-905). Shops guarded by wild boar statues sell boar by the gram; carnivores buy some boar (*cinghiale*—cheen-GAH-lay), cheese, bread, and wine and enjoy a picnic in the garden by the castle.

## Transportation Connections— San Gimignano

**To: Florence** (hrly buses, 75 min, change in Poggibonsi; or catch the frequent 20-min shuttle bus to Poggibonsi and train to Florence), **Siena** (5/day, 1.25 hrs, or can change in Poggibonsi to catch train to Siena), **Volterra** (6/day, 2 hrs, change in Poggibonsi and Colle di Val d'Elsa). In San Gimignano, bus tickets are sold at the bar just inside the town gate. The town has no baggage-check service.

**Drivers:** You can't drive within the walled town of San Gimignano, but a car park awaits just a few steps outside.

# ASSISI

Assisi is famous for its hometown boy, St. Francis, who made very good.

Around the year 1200, a simple friar from Assisi challenged the decadence of Church government and society in general with a powerful message of non-materialism, simplicity, and a "slow down and smell God's roses" lifestyle. Like Jesus, Francis taught by example. A huge monastic order grew out of his teachings, which were gradually embraced (some would say co-opted) by the Church. Clare, St. Francis' partner in poverty, founded the Order of the Poor Clares. Catholicism's purest example of simplicity is now glorified in beautiful churches. In 1939, Italy made Francis and Clare its patron saints.

Francis' message of love and sensitivity to the environment has a broad and timeless appeal. But any pilgrimage site will be commercialized, and the legacy of St. Francis is Assisi's basic industry. In summer, this Umbrian town bursts with flash-in-the-pan Francis fans and Franciscan knickknacks. Those able to see past the tacky friar mementos can actually have a "travel on purpose" experience.

## Planning Your Time

Assisi is worth a day and a night. The town has a half day of sightseeing and another half day of wonder. The essential sight is the Basilica of St. Francis. For a good visit, take the Assisi Welcome Walk (below), ending at the basilica. Schedule time to linger on the main square. Hikers enjoy sunset at the castle.

Most visitors are day-trippers. While the town's a zoo by day, it's a delight at night. Assisi after dark is closer to a place Francis could call home.

## Orientation

Crowned by a ruined castle at the top, Assisi spills downhill to its famous Basilica of St. Francis. The town is beautifully preserved and rich in history. The 1997 earthquake did more damage to the tourist industry than to the local buildings. Fortunately tourists are returning—whether art-lovers or pilgrims or both—drawn by Assisi's powerful sights.

**Tourist Information:** The TI is in the center of town on Piazza del Comune (Mon–Sat 9:00–14:00 & 15:30–18:30, Sun 9:00–13:00, tel. 075-812-534; visit www.umbria2000.it for info on Umbria, e-mail: info@iat.assisi.pg.it).

Also on (or just off) Piazza del Comune, you'll find the Roman temple of Minerva, a Romanesque tower, banks, a finely frescoed pharmacy, and an underground Roman Forum.

A combo-ticket *(biglietto cumulativo)* for €5.25 covers three sights—Rocca Maggiore (castle), Pinacoteca (paintings), and the Roman Forum; you'd need to see all three sights to save money (sold at participating sites).

Market day is Saturday on the Piazza Matteotti (which has a good parking garage). Your hotel may give you an Assisi Card, which offers discounts on parking and some restaurants.

## Arrival in Assisi

**By Train and Bus:** City buses connect Assisi's train station with the old town of Assisi on the hilltop (€0.80, 2/hr, about 15–20 min), stopping at Piazza Unita d'Italia (near Basilica of St. Francis), then Largo Properzio (near Basilica of St. Clare), and finally Piazza Matteotti (top of old town). Going to the old town, buses usually leave from the train station at :16 and :46 past the hour. Going to the train station from the old town, buses usually run from Piazza Matteotti at :10 and :40 past the hour, and from Piazza Unita d'Italia at :17 and :47 past the hour. At Piazza Unita d'Italia, there are two bus stops *(fermata bus):* one sign reads *per f.s. S.M. Angeli* (take this bus to get to the train station), and the other reads *per P. Matteotti* (this bus goes to the top of the old town). Note that you can take this bus within Assisi to save a long walk uphill (e.g., visit basilica, walk down to bus stop, then catch bus up to the middle or top of town).

**By Taxi:** Taxis from the station to the old town run about €10. There are legitimate extra charges for luggage and night service, but beware: Many taxis rip off tourists by using tariff #2; the meter should be set on tariff #1 (€2.50 drop). You can check bags at the train station (€2.75, daily 7:00–19:30), but not in the old town. When departing the old town of Assisi, you'll find taxi stands at Piazza Unita d'Italia and the Basilica of St. Clare (or have your hotel call for you, tel. 075-812-600).

**By Car:** Drivers just coming in for the day should follow the signs to Piazza Matteotti's wonderful underground parking garage at the top of the town (which comes with bits of ancient Rome in the walls, €1/hr, or €11/day with Assisi Card—offered by many hotels; open 7:00–21:00, until 23:00 in summer).

## Helpful Hints

**Travel Agency:** You can get train tickets and most bus tickets (but not for Siena) at Agenzia Viaggi Stoppini, between Piazza del Comune and the Basilica of St. Clare (Mon–Fri 9:00–12:30 & 15:30–19:00, Sat 9:00–12:30, closed Sun, Corso Mazzini 31, tel. 075-812-597). For Siena, you buy tickets on the bus (see "Transportation Connections," below).

**Internet Access: Internet World** has several computers and a non-smoking room (Thu–Tue 11:00–13:00 & 14:00–22:00, Wed 16:00–22:00, Via San Gabriele 25, a long block off Piazza del Comune, tel. 075-812-327).

**Guide:** Anne Robichaud, an American who has lived here since 1975, gives pricey though informative tours of the town and the countryside. Make it clear what you want (half day from €66 per person, full day from €99, cooking lessons, tel. 075-802-334, fax 075-813-698, www.annesitaly.com). Thanks to Anne for her help with the following self-guided walk.

## Assisi Welcome Walk

There's much more to Assisi than St. Francis and what all the blitz tour groups see.

This walk, rated ▲▲, covers the town from Piazza Matteotti at the top, down to the Basilica of St. Francis at the bottom. To get to Piazza Matteotti, ride the bus from the train station (or from Piazza Unita d'Italia) to the last stop, or drive there (underground parking with Roman ruins).

**The Roman Arena:** Start 50 meters (165 feet) beyond Piazza Matteotti (at intersection at far end of parking lot, away from the city center—see map). A lane, named Via Anfiteatro Romano, leads to a cozy circular neighborhood built around a Roman arena. Assisi was an important Roman town. Circle the arena counterclockwise (the chain stretched across the road is to keep cars out, not you). Imagine how colorful the town laundry must have been in the last generation, when the women of Assisi gathered here to do their wash. Adjacent to the laundry is a small rectangular pool filled with water; above it are the coats of arms of the town's leading families. A few steps farther, hike up the stairs to the top of the hill for an aerial view of the oval arena. The Roman stones have long been absorbed into the medieval architecture. It was Roman tradition

Assisi

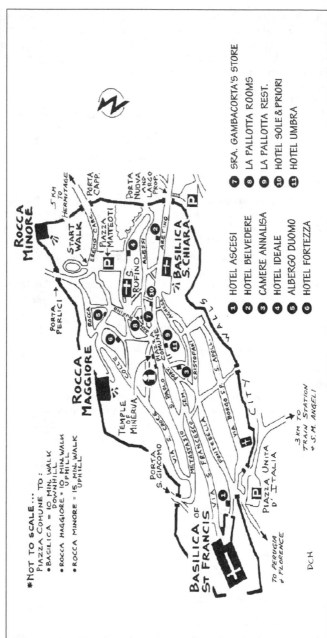

to locate the arena outside of town . . . which this was. Continue on. The lane leads down to a city gate.

**Umbrian view:** Leave Assisi at the Porta Perlici for a commanding view. Umbria, called the "green heart of Italy," is the country's geographical center and only landlocked state. Enjoy the greens: silver green on the valley floor (olives), emerald green 10 meters/33 feet below you (grapevines), and deep green on the hillsides (evergreen oak trees). Also notice Rocca Maggiore (big castle), a fortress providing townsfolk a refuge in times of attack, and, behind you, atop the hill, Rocca Minore (little castle). Now walk back to Piazza Matteotti. Go to the opposite end of this piazza, to the corner with the blobby stone tower. As you walk down the lane next to this tower, you'll see the big dome of the Church of San Rufino. Walk to the courtyard of the church; its big bell tower is on your left.

**Church of San Rufino:** While Francis is Italy's patron saint, Rufino is Assisi's—the town's first bishop (he was martyred and buried here in the third century). The church is 12th-century Romanesque with a neoclassical interior. Enter the church (daily 7:00–13:00 & 14:00–18:00). To your right (in the back corner of the church) is the baptismal font where Francis and Clare were baptized. Traditionally, the children of Assisi are still baptized here.

The striking glass panels in the church floor reveal a recent discovery: ancient foundations dating from Roman times. You're walking on history. After the 1997 earthquake, the church was checked from ceiling to floor by structural inspectors. When they looked under the paving stones, they discovered bodies (it used to be a common practice to bury people in church, until Napoleon decreed otherwise) and underneath the graves, Roman foundations and some animal bones (suggesting the possibility of animal sacrifice). There might have been a Roman temple here. It's plausible, because churches were often built on the sites of ruined Roman temples. Standing at the back of the church (facing the altar), look left at the Roman cistern (enclosed with a black iron fence). This was once the town's water source when under attack.

Underneath the church, alongside the Roman ruins, are the foundations of an earlier Church of San Rufino, now the crypt. When it's open in summer, you can go below to see the saint's sarcophagus (€3, daily 10:00–13:00 & 15:00–18:00). An archaeology museum may open here in 2003.

**Medieval Architecture:** When you leave the church, take a sharp left (on Via Dono Doni—say it fast three times), following the sign to Santa Chiara. Take the first right, down the stairway. At the bottom, notice the pink limestone pavement. The medieval town survives. The arches built over doorways indicate that the buildings date from the 12th through the 14th century. The vaults that turn lanes into tunnels are reminders of medieval urban expansion (mostly 15th century). While the population grew, people wanted to live protected within the walls, so Assisi became more dense. Medieval Assisi had five times the population density of today's Assisi. Notice the floating gardens. Assisi has a flowering balcony competition each June. When you arrive at a street, turn left, going slightly uphill for a block, then jog right, following the "S. Chiara" sign down to the Basilica of St. Clare.

**Basilica of St. Clare (Santa Chiara):** For a description of this stark, impressive church built to honor St. Clare, see "More Sights—Assisi," below.

**Another Umbrian View:** Belly up to the viewpoint in front of the basilica. On the left is the convent of St. Clare; below you, the olive grove of the Poor Clares since the 13th century; and, in the distance, a grand Umbrian view. Assisi overlooks the richest and biggest valley in otherwise hilly and mountainous Umbria. The municipality of Assisi has a population of 29,000, but only 1,000 people live in the old town. The lower town grew up with the coming of the railway in the 19th century. In the haze, the blue-domed church is St. Mary of the Angels (Santa Maria degli Angeli, see description below), the cradle of the Franciscan order, marking the place St. Francis lived and worked. This church, a popular pilgrimage sight today, is the first Los Angeles. Think about California. The Franciscans named L.A. (after this church), San Francisco, and even Santa Clara.

**Arches and Artisans:** From Via Santa Chiara, you can see two arches over the street. The arch at the back of the church dates from 1265. (Beyond it—out of view, the Porta Nuova, from 1316, marks the final expansion of Assisi.) Toward the city center (on Via Santa Chiara, the high road), an arch indicates the site of the Roman wall.

Forty meters (130 feet) before this arch, pop into the souvenir shop at #1b. The plaque over the door explains that the old printing press (a national monument now, just inside the door) was used to make fake documents for Jews escaping the Nazis in 1943 and 1944. The shop is run by a couple of artisans: The man makes frames out of medieval Assisi timbers; the woman makes the traditional Assisi, or Franciscan, cross-stitch.

Just past the gate and on your left is the La Pasteria natural products shop at Corso Mazzini 18b (across from entrance of Hotel Sole). Cooks love to peruse Umbrian wines, herbs, pâtés, and truffles, and sample an aromatic "fruit infusion." Ahead at Corso Mazzini 14d, the small shop (Poiesis) sells olive-wood carvings. Drop in. It's said that St. Francis made the first nativity scene to help teach the Christmas message. That's why you'll see so many of these in Assisi. Even today, nearby villages are enthusiastic about their "living" manger scenes. The Lisa Assisi shop (at Corso Mazzini 25b, across the street and to your right) has a delightful bargain basement with surviving bits of a 2,000-year-old mortarless Roman wall. Ahead of you, the columns of the Temple of Minerva mark the Piazza del Comune (described below). Sit at the fountain on the square for a few minutes of people-watching—don't you love Italy? Within 200 meters (650 feet) of this square, on either side, were the medieval walls. Imagine a commotion of 5,000 people confined within these walls. No wonder St. Francis needed an escape for some peace and quiet. I'll meet you over at the temple on the square.

**Roman Temple/Christian Church:** Assisi has always been a spiritual center. The Romans went to great lengths to make this Temple of Minerva a centerpiece of their city. Notice the columns cutting into the stairway. It was a tight fit here on the hilltop. The stairs probably went down triple the distance you see today. The church of Santa Maria sopra (over) Minerva was added in the ninth century. The bell tower is 13th century. Pop inside the temple/church (Mon–Sat 7:15–19:00, from 8:15 on Sun, closes at 17:00 in winter). Today's interior is 17th-century Baroque. Flanking the altar are the original Roman temple floor stones. You can even see the drains for the bloody sacrifices that took place here. Behind the statues of Peter and Paul, the original Roman embankment peeks through.

A few doors back toward the fountain, step into the 16th-century vaults from the old fish market. Notice the Italian flair for design. Even a smelly fish market was finely decorated. The art style is "grotesque"—literally, a painting in a grotto. This was painted in the early 1500s, a few years after Columbus brought turkeys back from the New World. The turkeys painted here may just be that bird's European debut. (Public WCs are a few steps off Piazza del Comune; near the fountain, go through Via dell' Arco dei Priori, then down the street on the left.)

**Church of San Stefano:** From the main square, hike past the temple up the high road, Via San Paolo. After 200 meters (650 feet), a sign directs you down a lane to San Stefano, which used to be outside the town walls in the days of St. Francis. Legend is that its bells miraculously rang on October 3, 1226, the day St. Francis died. Surrounded by cypress, fig, and walnut trees, it's a delightful bit of offbeat Assisi. Step inside. This is the typical rural Italian Romanesque church—no architect, just built by simple stonemasons who put together the most basic design. The lane zigzags down to Via San Francesco. Turn right and walk under the arch toward the Basilica of St. Francis.

**Via San Francesco:** This was the main drag leading from the town to the basilica holding the body of St. Francis. Francis was a big deal even in his own day. He died in 1226 and was made a saint in 1228—the same year the basilica's foundations were laid—and his body was moved in by 1230. Assisi was a big-time pilgrimage center, and this street was a booming place. Notice the fine medieval balcony just below the arch. A few meters farther down (on the left), cool yourself at the fountain. The hospice next door was built in 1237 to house pilgrims. Notice the three surviving faces of its fresco: Jesus, Francis, and Clare.

## Basilica of St. Francis

A ▲▲▲ sight, the Basilica de San Francesco is one of the artistic and religious highlights of Europe. In 1226, St. Francis was buried (with the outcasts he had stood by) outside of his town on the "Hill of the Damned"—now called the "Hill of Paradise." The basilica is frescoed from top to bottom by the leading artists of the day: Cimabue, Giotto, Simone Martini, and Pietro Lorenzetti. A 13th-century historian wrote, "No more exquisite monument to the Lord has been built."

From a distance, you see the huge arcades "supporting" the basilica. These were 15th-century quarters for the monks. The arcades lining the square leading to the church housed medieval pilgrims.

There are three parts to the church: the upper basilica, the lower basilica, and the saint's tomb (below the lower basilica). Modest dress is required to enter the church—no sleeveless tops or shorts for men, women, or children (free entry, daily 6:30–19:00, relic chapel in lower basilica closes at 18:30, tel. 075-819-0084, www.sanfrancescoassisi.org, e-mail: assisisanfrancesco@krenet.it).

In the 1997 earthquake, the lower basilica—with walls nearly three meters (9 feet) thick—was undamaged. The upper basilica, with bigger windows and walls only one meter (3 feet) thick, was damaged. After restoration was completed, the entire church was reopened to visitors in late 1999.

Start at the lower entrance in the courtyard. Opposite the entry to the lower basilica is the information center Ask about their tours in English—or call or e-mail in advance. (Mon–Sat 9:00–12:00 & 14:00–17:00, Sun 14:00–17:00, tel. 075-819-0084, e-mail: assistours@aol.com; a WC is a half block away—from courtyard, look up the road at the squat brick building; walk alongside the right of it to find the WC). The info center sells an excellent guidebook, *The Basilica of Saint Francis—A Spiritual Pilgrimage* (€2.50, by Goulet, McInally, and Wood) which I used as a source for the following self-guided tour.

The Basilica of St. Francis, a theological work of genius, can be difficult for the 21st-century tourist/pilgrim to appreciate. Since the basilica is the reason most people visit Assisi, and the message of St. Francis has even the least devout blessing the town Vespas, I've designed a *Mona Winks*–type tour with the stress on the place's theology, rather than art history.

At the doorway of the lower basilica, look up and see St. Francis (in a small gold triangle), who greets you with a Latin inscription (arching over the doorway). Sounding a bit like John Wayne, he says the equivalent of "Slow down and be joyful, pilgrim. You've reached the Hill of Paradise, and this church will knock your spiritual socks off." Start with the tomb (turn left into the nave, midway down the nave to your right follow signs and go downstairs to the tomb). Grab a pew (for more light to read by, sit in back).

**The message:** Francis' message caused a stir. He traded a life of power and riches for one of obedience, poverty, and chastity. The Franciscan existence (Brother Sun, Sister Moon, and so on) is a space where God, man, and the natural world frolic harmoniously. Franciscan friars, known as the "Jugglers of God," were a joyful part of the community. In an Italy torn by fighting between towns and families, Francis promoted peace and the restoration of order. (He set an example by reconstructing a crumbled chapel.) While the Church was waging bloody Crusades, Francis pushed ecumenism and understanding. Even today the leaders of the world's great religions meet here for summits.

This rich building seems to contradict the teachings of the poor monk it honors, but it was built as an act of religious and civic pride to remember the hometown saint. It was also designed, and still functions, as a pilgrimage center and a splendid classroom.

**The tomb:** In medieval times, pilgrims came to Assisi because St. Francis was buried here. Holy relics were the "ruby slippers" of medieval Europe. They gave you power—got your prayers answered and helped you win wars—and ultimately helped you get back to your eternal Kansas. Assisi made no bones about promoting the saint's relics, but hid his tomb for obvious reasons of security. Not until 1818 was the tomb opened to the public. The saint's remains are above the altar in the stone box with the iron ties. His four closest friends are buried in the corners of the room. Opposite the altar, up four steps in between the entrance and exit, notice the small gold box behind the metal grill; this contains the remains of Francis' rich Roman patron, Jacopa dei Settesoli. Climb back to the lower nave.

**The lower basilica** is appropriately Franciscan, subdued and Romanesque. The nave was frescoed with parallel scenes from the lives of Christ and Francis—connected by a ceiling of stars.

Unfortunately, after the church was built and decorated, the popularity of the Franciscans meant side chapels needed to be built. Huge arches were cut out of some scenes, but others survive. In the fresco directly above the entry to the tomb, Christ is being taken down from the cross (just the bottom half of his body can be seen, to the left), and it looks like the story is over. Defeat. But in the opposite fresco (above the tomb's exit), we see Francis preaching to the birds, reminding the faithful that the message of the Gospel survives.

These stories directed the attention of the medieval pilgrim to the altar, where, through the sacraments, he met God. The church was thought of as a community of believers sailing toward God. The prayers coming out of the nave (*navis*, or ship) fill the triangular sections of the ceiling—called *vele*, or sails—with spiritual wind. With a priest for a navigator and the altar for a helm, faith propels the ship.

Stand behind the altar (toes to the bottom step) and look up. The three scenes in front of you are, to the right, "Obedience" (Francis wearing a yoke); to the left, "Chastity" (in a tower of purity held up by two angels); and straight ahead, "Poverty." Here Jesus blesses the marriage as Francis slips a ring on Lady Poverty. In the foreground two "self-sufficient" merchants (the new rich of a thriving North Italy) are throwing sticks and stones at the bride. But Poverty, in her patched wedding dress, is fertile and strong, and even those brambles blossom into a rosebush crown.

Putting your heels to the altar and bending back like a drum major, look up at Francis, who traded a life of earthly simplicity for glory in heaven. Now, turn to the right and march . . .

In the corner, steps lead down into the relic chapel. Circle the room clockwise. You'll see the silver chalice and plate Francis used for the bread and wine of the Eucharist (in small, dark, windowed case set into wall, marked *Calice con Patena*). Francis believed that his personal possessions should be simple, but the items used for worship should be made of the finest materials. In the corner display case is a small section of the haircloth worn by Francis as penitence. In the next corner are the tunic and slippers Francis wore during his last days. Next, find a prayer (in a fancy silver stand) that St. Francis wrote for Brother Leo, signed with his tau cross. Next is a papal document (1223) legitimizing the Franciscan order and assuring his followers that they were not risking a (deadly) heresy charge. Finally, see the tunic lovingly patched and stitched by followers of the five-foot, four-inch-tall St. Francis.

Return up the stairs to the lower basilica. You're in the transept. This church brought together the greatest Sienese (Martini and Lorenzetti) and Florentine (Cimabue and Giotto) artists of the day. Look around at the painted scenes. In 1300, this was radical art—believable homespun scenes, landscapes, trees, real people. Study the crucifix (by Giotto) with the eight sparrowlike angels. For the first time, holy people are expressing emotion: One angel turns her head sadly at the sight of Jesus, and another scratches her hands down her cheeks, drawing blood. Mary, previously in control, has fainted in despair. The Franciscans, with their goal of bringing God to the people, found a natural partner in Europe's first modern painter, Giotto.

To see the Renaissance leap, look at the painting to the right. This is by Cimabue—it's Gothic, without the 3-D architecture, natural backdrop, and slice-of-life reality of the Giotto work. Cimabue's St. Francis is considered by some to be the earliest existing portrait of the saint. To the left, at eye level, enjoy the Martini saints and their exquisite halos.

Francis' friend, "Sister Death," was really not all that terrible. In fact, Francis would like to introduce you to her now (above and to the right of the door leading into the relic chapel). Go ahead, block the light and meet her. I'll wait for you upstairs, in the courtyard, next to the fine bookstore. By the way, monks in robes are not my idea of easy-to-approach people, but the Franciscans are still God's jugglers (and most of them speak English).

From the courtyard, climb the stairs to the **upper basilica**. Built later than the lower, the upper basilica is brighter, Gothic (the first Gothic church in Italy, 1228), and nearly wallpapered by Giotto. This gallery of frescoes by Giotto and his assistants shows 28 scenes from the life of St. Francis.

Look for these scenes:

• **A common man spreads his cape before Francis** (immediately to right of altar, as you face altar) out of honor and recognition to a man who will do great things. Symbolized by the rose window, God looks over the 20-year-old Francis, a dandy imprisoned in his selfishness. A medieval pilgrim fluent in symbolism would understand this because the Temple of Minerva (which you saw today on Assisi's Piazza del Comune) was a prison at that time. The rose window, which never existed, is symbolic of God's eye.

• **Francis offers his cape to a needy stranger** (next panel). Prior to this act of kindness, Francis had been captured in battle, held as a prisoner of war, and then released.

• **Francis is visited by the Lord in a dream** (next panel) and told to leave the army and go home.

• **Francis relinquishes his possessions** (two panels down), giving his dad his clothes, his credit cards, and even his time-share condo on Capri. Naked Francis is covered by the bishop, symbolizing his transition from a man of the world to a man of the Church.

• **The pope has a vision** (next panel) of a simple man prop-
ping up his teetering Church. This led to the papal acceptance
of the Franciscan reforms.

• **Christ appears to Francis** being carried by a seraph—
a six-winged angel (other side of church, fourth panel from the
door). For the strength of his faith, Francis is given the marks
of his master, the "battle scars of love"...the stigmata. Throughout his life, Francis was interested in chivalry; now he's joined
the spiritual knighthood.

• **Francis preaches to the birds** (to the right of the exit).
Francis was more than a nature-lover. The birds, of different
species, represent the diverse flock of humanity and nature, all
created and loved by God and worthy of each other's love.

Before you leave, look at the ceiling above the altar and front
entrance to see large tan patches; these careful repairs were made
after the basilica was damaged in the 1997 earthquake. It's a blessing that so many of the frescoes remain.

Near the outside of the upper basilica are the Latin pax
(peace) and the Franciscan tau cross in the grass. Tav ("tau" in
Greek), the last letter in the Hebrew alphabet, is symbolic of
faithfulness to the end. Francis signed his name with this simple
character. Tav and pax. For more pax, take the high lane back to
town, up to the castle, or into the countryside.

## More Sights—Assisi
▲**Basilica of Saint Clare (Basilica di Santa Chiara)**—
Dedicated to the founder of the order of the Poor Clares, this
Umbrian Gothic church is simple, in keeping with the Poor
Clares' dedication to a life of contemplation. The church was
built in 1265, and the huge buttresses were added in the next
century. The interior's fine frescoes were whitewashed in Baroque
times. The Chapel of the Crucifix of San Damiano, on the right
(actually an earlier church incorporated into this one), has the
crucifix that supposedly spoke to St. Francis, leading to his conversion in 1206. Stairs lead from the nave down to the tomb of
Saint Clare. Her tomb is at the far end. The walls depict scenes
from Clare's life and death (1193–1253); the saint's robes are in
a large case between the stairs. The attached cloistered community of the Poor Clares has flourished for 700 years (church open
daily 6:30–12:00 & 14:00–18:00).

**Roman Forum (Foro Romano)**—For a look at Assisi's Roman
roots, tour the Roman Forum, which is actually under Piazza del
Comune. The floor plan is sparse, the odd bits and pieces obscure,
but it's well-explained in English (a 10-page booklet is loaned
to you when you enter) and you can actually walk on an ancient

Roman road. For an orientation, look at the poster for sale at the entry to get an idea of the original setting of forum and temple (€2 entry, or included in €5.25 combo-ticket, daily 10:00–13:00 & 15:00–18:00, closes at 17:00 in winter; from Piazza del Comune, go one-half block down Via San Francesco, it's on your right).

**Pinacoteca**—This small museum attractively displays its 13th- to 17th-century art (mainly frescoes), with general information in English in nearly every room. There's a Giotto Madonna (damaged) and a rare secular fresco (to right of Giotto), but it's mainly a peaceful walk through a pastel world, best for art-lovers (€2.20, included in €5.25 combo-ticket, daily 10:00–13:00 & 14:00–18:00, Via San Francesco 10, on main drag between Piazza del Comune and Basilica of St. Francis, tel. 075-812-033).

▲**Rocca Maggiore**—The "big castle" offers a good look at a 14th-century fortification and a fine view of Assisi and the Umbrian countryside (€2.20, included in €5.25 combo-ticket, daily 10:00–sunset, opens at 9:00 July–Aug). If you're counting euros, the view is just as good from outside the castle, and the interior is pretty bare. For a picnic with the same birdsong and views that inspired St. Francis, leave all the tourists and hike to the Rocca Minore (small castle) above Piazza Matteotti.

## Santa Maria degli Angeli

This flat, modern part of Assisi has one major sight: The basilica that marks the spot where Francis lived, worked, and died.

▲▲**St. Mary of the Angels (Basilica di Santa Maria degli Angeli)**—This huge basilica, towering above the buildings below Assisi, was built around the tiny but historic Porziuncola Chapel (now directly under the dome). When the pope gave Francis his blessing, he was given this *porziuncola*, or "small portion"—a little land with a fixer-upper chapel—on which Francis and his followers established their order. As you enter, notice the sketch on the door showing the original little chapel with the monks' huts around it and Assisi before it had its huge basilica. Francis lived here after he founded the Franciscan Order in 1208, and this was where he consecrated St. Clare as the Bride of Christ. A chapel called Cappella del Transito marks the place where Francis died (behind and to the right of the Porziuncola Chapel). Follow signs to the Roseta (Rose Garden). Francis, fighting off a temptation that he never named, threw himself onto roses. As the story goes, the thorns immediately dropped off the roses. Ever since, thornless roses have grown here. Look through the window at the rose garden (to the right of the statue of Francis petting a sheep). The Rose Chapel (Cappella delle Rose) is built over the place where Francis lived. The bookshop has some books in English and the free *museo* has a few monastic cells

interesting to pilgrims (museum open Mon–Sat 9:00–12:00 &
15:00–18:00, Sun 15:00–18:00).

**Hours:** The basilica is open May–Oct 7:00–18:30, Nov–
April 7:00–12:00 & 14:00 until sunset. There's a little TI to your
right as you face the church (supposedly open daily 9:00–12:00 &
15:00–18:00 but may be closed, tel. 075-80511). A WC is 40
meters (130 feet) to the right of the TI, behind the hedge.

**Transportation Connections:** To get to Basilica di Santa
Maria degli Angeli from Assisi's train station, it's quicker to walk
(exit station left, take first left at McDonald's, 5-minute walk)
than to take the orange city bus' circuitous route (though with
lots of luggage, you might prefer the bus). When you're leaving
the basilica, you can catch the bus directly to the station and on
to the old town of Assisi (as you leave church, stop is to your right,
next to basilica). The orange city buses run twice hourly (buses
to the old town depart the basilica at :10 and :40 after the hour;
tickets cost €0.80 if you buy at *tabacchi* or newsstand, €1.10 if
you buy from driver; 15–20 minute ride up to old town).

It's efficient to visit this basilica either on your way to the old
town of Assisi or when you leave. You can easily walk to the basilica
from the station (baggage check available, €2.75, access through
shop). If you're heading to Siena next, visit the basilica right before
you leave, because that's where you'll catch the bus to Siena (as you
leave basilica, stop is to your right, across the street, buy ticket on
bus); see "Transportation Connections—Assisi," below.

## Sleeping in Assisi
### (€1 = about $1, country code: 39, zip code: 06081)
Sleep Code: **S** = Single, **D** = Double/Twin, **T** = Triple, **Q** = Quad,
**b** = bathroom, **s** = shower only, **CC** = Credit Cards accepted,
**no CC** = Credit Cards not accepted, **SE** = Speaks English,
**NSE** = No English.

To help you sort easily through these listings, I've divided
the rooms into three categories based on the price for a standard
double room with bath:
**Higher Priced**—Most rooms more than €90.
**Moderately Priced**—Most rooms €90 or less.
**Lower Priced**—Most rooms €55 or less.

The town accommodates large numbers of pilgrims on
religious holidays. Finding a room at any other time should be
easy. See the map on page 254 for hotel locations.

### HIGHER PRICED
**Hotel Umbra**, the best splurge in the center, feels like a quiet
villa in the middle of town (25 rooms, Sb-€77, Db-€92, Tb-€120,

includes breakfast, CC, air-con, peaceful garden and view terrace, most rooms have views, good restaurant, dinner only, 100 meters, or 330 feet, below Piazza del Comune at Via degli Archi 6, tel. 075-812-240, fax 075-813-653, www.hotelumbra.it, e-mail: humbra@mail.caribusiness.it, family Laudenzi SE).

**Hotel Dei Priori** is a three-star, palatial place in the old center, with big, quiet, recently renovated rooms that have all the comforts (Db-€100–120, superior Db-€140–160, includes breakfast, CC, elevator, air-con, Corso Mazzini 15, tel. 075-812-237, fax 075-816-804, www.assisihotel.net, e-mail: info @assisihotel.net, SE).

**MODERATELY PRICED**
**Hotel Ideale,** on the top edge of town overlooking the valley, offers 12 bright, modern rooms, view balconies, peaceful garden, free parking, and a warm welcome (Sb-€47, Db-€78, includes big-for-Italy breakfast, CC, most rooms with views, Piazza Matteotti 1, tel. 075-813-570, fax 075-813-020, www .hotelideale.it, e-mail: info@hotelideale.it, sisters Lara and Ilaria SE). This hotel, at the top of the old town, is close to the bus stop (and parking lot) at Piazza Matteotti, easy to reach by public transportation.

**Hotel Sole** is well-located, with 40 spacious, comfortable rooms in a 15th-century building (Sb-€41, Db-€62, Tb-€81, breakfast-€6.25, CC, half its rooms are in a newer annex across the street, some rooms have views and balconies, elevator in annex, Corso Mazzini 35, 100 meters, or 330 feet, before Basilica of St. Clare, tel. 075-812-373, fax 075-813-706, e-mail: soleassisi@hotmail.com, SE).

**Hotel Belvedere**, which offers good views and 16 basic rooms, is run by Enrico and his American wife, Mary (Db-€76, breakfast-€5.25, elevator, 2 blocks past Basilica of St. Clare at Via Borgo Aretino 13, tel. 075-812-460, fax 075-816-812, e-mail: assisihotelbelvedere@hotmail.com, SE). Their attached restaurant is good, by request and reservation only.

**LOWER PRICED**
**Hotel Ascesi** has an inviting little lobby, nine pleasant rooms, and a tiny terrace, located within a block of the Basilica of St. Francis (Sb-€34, Db-€52, breakfast-€3.75, CC, air-con, Via Frate Elia 5, walk up from Piazza Unita d'Italia, take a left at Piazzetta Ruggero Bonghi, see sign on right, tel. & fax 075-812-420, e-mail: hotelascesi@libero.it). This hotel is near the bus stop and parking lot at the bottom of town (Piazza Unita d'Italia), handy if you're packing lots of luggage.

**Hotel La Fortezza** is a simple, modern, and quiet place with seven rooms (Db-€49, Tb-€67, Qb-€78, CC, a short block above Piazza del Comune at Vicolo della Fortezza 19b, tel. 075-812-993, fax 075-819-8035, www.lafortezzahotel.com, e-mail: lafortezza@lafortezzahotel.com, Lorenzo SE).

**Albergo Il Duomo** is tidy and *tranquillo*, with nine rooms on a stair-step lane one block up from San Rufino (S-€29, Sb-€31, D-€35, Db-€42, breakfast-€4.25, CC, Vicolo S. Lorenzo 2; from Church of San Rufino follow sign, then turn left on stair-stepped alley; tel. & fax 075-812-742, www .hotelsanrufino.it, e-mail: info@sanrufino.it, Carlo SE).

**Camere Annalisa Martini** is a cheery home swimming in vines and roses in the town's medieval core. Annalisa speaks English and enthusiastically accommodates her guests with a picnic garden, a washing machine (small load-€3), a refrigerator, and six homey rooms (S-€20, Sb-€23, D-€31, Db-€36, Tb-€47, Qb-€57, 3 rooms share 2 bathrooms, no breakfast, no CC, 1 block from Piazza del Comune, go downhill toward basilica, turn left on Via S. Gregorio to #6, tel. & fax 075-813-536).

**La Pallotta**, a recommended restaurant (see "Eating," below), offers seven clean, bright rooms (note that rooms and restaurant are in different locations). Rooms #12 and #18 have views (Db-€47, CC, view terrace, Via San Rufino 4, go up short flight of stairs outside building to reach entrance, a block off Piazza del Comune, tel. & fax 075-812-307, www.pallottaassisi.it, SE).

**Signora Gambacorta** rents several decent rooms and has a roof terrace on a quiet lane (Via Sermei 9) just above St. Chiara. There is no sign or reception desk, so you'll need to check in at her shop a half block east of Piazza del Comune at San Gabriele 17—look for the sign "Bottega di Gambacorta" (S-€20 Db-€40, Tb-€60, 2-night stays preferred, no breakfast but has kitchen, store open Mon–Wed and Fri–Sat 8:00–13:00 & 16:30–19:30, Thu 8:00–13:00, closed Sun—if you can't arrive when store is open, call when you arrive, tel. 075-812-454, fax 075-813-186, www.ilbongustaio.com/inglese/eerooms.htm, e-mail: geo@umbrars.com, a little English spoken). She also has two apartments for stays of at least four nights (3 rooms-€90/day, 5 rooms-€200/day, kitchen, no breakfast).

*Hostel:* Francis probably would have bunked with the peasants in Assisi's **Ostello della Pace** (€13 beds in 4- to 8-bed rooms, Qb-€15 apiece, includes breakfast, dinner-€8, CC, laundry, lockout 10:00–15:30, get off bus at Piazza Unita d'Italia, then take 10-min walk to Via di Valecchie 177, tel. & fax 075-816-767, Giuseppe SE).

# Eating in Assisi

For a fine Assisian perch and good regional cooking, relax on a terrace overlooking Piazza del Comune at **Taverna dei Consoli** (€13 4-course *menu*, also à la carte, Thu–Tue 12:00–14:30 & 19:00–21:30, closed Wed and Jan, CC, tel. 075-812-516, friendly owner Moreno, who doesn't speak English, recommends the *bruschetta*, *stringozzi*—noodles, *agnello*—lamb, and *cinghiale*—boar). Moreno also runs **Locanda del Podestà** with the same high standards (12:00–15:30 & 19:00–22:00, 5-min walk uphill from basilica, San Giacomo 6C, tel. 075-813-034).

**La Pallotta**, a local favorite run by a friendly, hardworking family, offers regional specialties, such as *piccione* (pigeon), *coniglio* (rabbit), and more typical food (€14.50 *menu*, Wed–Mon 12:00–14:30 & 19:15–21:30, closed Tue, CC, also rents rooms—see listing above, a few steps off Piazza del Comune, through gate across from temple/church, Vicolo della Volta Pinta, tel. 075-812-649).

**Osteria Piazzetta dell Erba** is a fun, little, family-run place a block above Piazza del Comune, serving good, basic Umbrian specialties next to the Gambacorta grocery (Tue–Sun 12:00–14:00 & 19:00–21:45, closed Mon, CC, Via San Gabriele 156, tel. 075-815-352).

**Pizzeria/Tavola Calda dal Carro** is popular, affordable, and friendly (good pizzas and €12 *menu*, closed Wed, Vicolo di Nepis 2, leave Piazza del Comune on Via San Gabriele, then take first right—down a stepped lane, tel. 075-815-249).

**Ristorante San Francesco** is the place to splurge for dinner (Thu–Tue 12:00–14:30 & 19:30–22:00, closed Wed, CC, facing Basilica of St. Francis at Via San Francesco 52, tel. 075-812-329).

For a picnic of Umbrian treats, try **La Bottega dei Sapori** for its good prosciutto sandwiches and speciality items, including truffle paste. Friendly Fabrizio may give you a taste (9:00–20:00, Piazza del Comune 34, tel. 075-812-294).

# Transportation Connections—Assisi

**By train to: Rome** (5/day, 1.75–2.5 hrs), **Florence** (5/day, 2–2.75 hrs, more with transfers at Terontola and Cortona), **Orvieto** (7/day, 2 hrs, transfer in Terontola), **Siena** (6/day, 3.25 hrs, transfers in Chiusi and Terontola; bus is more efficient). Train station: tel. 075-804-0272, train info: tel. 848-888-088.

**By bus to: Rome** (3/day, 3 hrs, departs Assisi's Piazza Unita d'Italia, arrives at Rome's Tiburtina station), **Siena** (1/day, 2 hrs, €8.25, pay driver, departs from Basilica di Santa Maria degli Angeli near Assisi train station; to get from station to basilica, exit station left, take first left at McDonald's; as you face basilica, bus stop is to your left across street). Don't take the bus to Florence (1/day, departs Piazza Unita d'Italia at 6:45 a.m., 2.75 hrs); the train is better.

# ORVIETO, CIVITA, AND MORE HILL TOWNS

Sun-dried tomatoes, homemade pasta, wispy cypress-lined drive-ways following desolate ridges to fortified 16th-century farm-houses, and dusty old-timers warming the same bench day after day while soccer balls buzz around them like innocuous flies... the sun-soaked hill towns of Tuscany and Umbria offer what to many is the quintessential Italian experience.

Tuscany and Umbria have replaced Provence as *the* trendy destination in Europe among Americans. If you really want to do the *Under the Tuscan Sun* thing correctly, you'll need to supplement this book with one specializing in the subtle delights of this area. You'll also need a readiness to encounter plenty of like-minded tourists—especially if you visit any hill town that is a household word among American travelers.

In this chapter, I cover the grand and classic town of Orvieto; my longtime favorite, the tiny, obscure, and (to be honest) dying hilltown of Civita; and a smattering of the most noteworthy towns of Umbria and Tuscany. If you have the time (or a car) and a hankering to see what all the fuss over this region is about, this material will give you the basics.

For a relaxing break from the intensity, traffic, and obligatory museums of big-city Italy, settle down in an *agriturismo*—a farm-house that rents out rooms to travelers (usually for a minimum of a week in high season). These rural B&Bs—almost by defini-tion in the middle of nowhere—provide a good home base from which to find the magic of Tuscany and Umbria. See the end of this chapter for information on *agriturismo* lodgings, some specific listings, and resources for finding out more.

Orvieto and Civita are doable by public transportation. The other hill towns mentioned in the chapter are easier to visit

# Hill Towns

by car. This rugged and hilly region, with its meager public transportation and tortured little roads, seems bigger than it is. With a car and some motion-sickness pills, it's a delight.

## Planning Your Time

Orvieto and Civita are worth a day and an overnight—ideally, an afternoon, night, and morning. Most people start with Orvieto, which is an easy train stop on the Florence–Rome line, then continue to Civita by bus.

Orvieto has a good half day of sightseeing. Spend the night in Orvieto if you want a variety of restaurants, or in Civita if you want peace. Civita is also worth a half day; a chunk of that time is spent hiking to and from the town from Bagnoregio (connected by bus with Orvieto, daily except Sun).

## ORVIETO

Umbria's grand hill town, while no secret, is worth a quick look. The town sits majestically on a big chunk of tufa rock. Streets are lined with exhaust-stained buildings made from the volcanic stuff.

## Hill Towns: Public Transportation

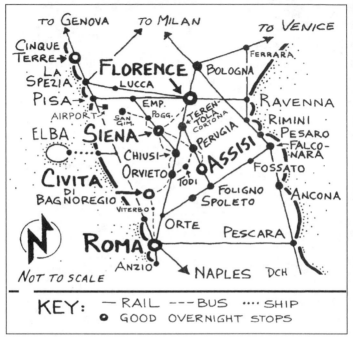

KEY: — RAIL  --- BUS  ···· SHIP
○ GOOD OVERNIGHT STOPS

Orvieto—just off the freeway, with three popular claims to fame (cathedral, Classico wine, and ceramics)—is loaded with tourists by day and quiet by night. Drinking a shot of wine in a ceramic cup as you gaze up at the cathedral lets you experience Orvieto all at once.

Piazza Cahen is a key transportation hub at the entry to the hill-top town. As you exit the funicular, the town center is straight ahead.

**Tourist Information:** The TI is at Piazza Duomo 24 on the cathedral square (Mon–Fri 8:15–14:00 & 16:00–19:00, Sat 10:00–13:00 & 16:00–19:00, Sun 10:00–12:00 & 16:00–18:00, tel. 0763-341-772). Pick up the free city map and ask about train and bus schedules. The TI sells a €1.50 admission ticket for the Chapel of St. Brizio (within the cathedral). For a longer visit, consider buying the €10.50 Carta Unica combo-ticket, which covers entry to the chapel, Archaeological Museum (Museo Claudio Faina e Museo Civico), Underground Orvieto Tours, and Torre del Moro (tower), plus your public transportation (bus and funicular) for one day or five hours of parking (at *parcheggio* Campo della Fiera).

**Market Days:** Drop by Piazza del Popolo with your cloth shopping bag on Tuesday and Saturday mornings.

## Arrival in Orvieto

**By Train:** If you're day-tripping, you can check your bag at the station (€2.75, access from platform; if no one is around, ask at the newsstand in the station).

A handy funicular/bus shuttle will take you quickly from the train station and parking lot to the top of the town. Buy your ticket at the entrance to the *funiculare;* look for the *biglietteria* sign. The €0.85 ticket includes the funicular plus the minibus from Piazza Cahen to Piazza Duomo—where you'll find most everything that matters. Or you can pay €0.65 for the funicular only—the best choice if you're staying at the recommended Hotel Corso. The funicular runs every 10 minutes (Mon–Sat 7:20–20:30, Sun 8:00–20:30).

As you exit the funicular at the top, to your left is a ruined fortress with a garden, WC, and a commanding view, and to your right—St. Patrick's Well (described below), Etruscan ruins, and another sweeping view. Just in front of you is an orange bus waiting to shuttle you to the town center. It'll drop you off at the TI (last stop, in front of cathedral).

If you forgot to check at the station for the train schedule to your next destination (and now the station is far, far below), Orvieto is ready for you. The train schedule is posted at the top of the *funiculare* and also available if you ask at the TI.

**By Car:** Drivers park at the base of the hill at the huge, free lot behind the Orvieto train station (follow the P and *funiculare* signs) or at the pay lot to the right of Orvieto's cathedral (€0.75 for first hour, €0.60/hr thereafter).

## Sights—Orvieto's Piazza Duomo

▲▲**Duomo**—The cathedral has Italy's most striking facade (from 1330), thanks to architect Lorenzo Maitani and many others. Grab a gelato (to the left of the church) and study this fascinating, gleaming mass of mosaics and sculpture.

At the base of the cathedral, the broad marble pillars carved with biblical scenes tell the story of the world from left to right. The pillar on the far left shows the Creation (see the snake and Eve), next is the Tree of Jesse, next the New Testament (look for Mary and a manger, etc.), and on the far right—the Last Judgment (with hell, of course, at the bottom). Each pillar is topped by a bronze symbol of one of the evangelists: angel (Matthew), lion (Mark), eagle (John), and bull (Luke). The bronze doors are modern, by the Sicilian sculptor Emilio Greco. (A museum devoted to Greco's work is to the right of the church; it's labeled simply *Museo.*) In the mosaic below the rose window, Mary is transported to heaven. In the uppermost mosaic, Mary is crowned.

Why such an impressive church in a little tufa town? Because

# Orvieto

**Orvieto**

PORTA MAGGIORE

TO BOLSENA & VITERBO

ETRUSCAN TOMBS

400 METERS
400 YARDS

CAVA MAGALOTTI

PORTO ROMANO

PIAZZA REPUBBLICA

VIALE CARDUCCI

S.T.I

ARCHAEOLOGICAL MUSEUM

POPOLO

VIA DUOMO

PARCO DELLE GROTTE

WC

VIA NEBBIA

PIAZZA XXIX MARZO

DUOMO

VIA POSTIERLA

CAVOUR

VIA ROMA

VIALE CRISPI

ETRUSCAN TEMPLE RUINS

ST. PATRICK'S WELL

PIAZZA CAHEN

FORTRESS RUINS & WC

TO FLOR.

1. Hotel Corso
2. Hotel Duomo
3. Hotel Posta
4. Istituto S.S. Domenicane
5. To Hotel Picchio
6. Hotel Virgilio
7. Buy bus tickets to Civita
8. Museo Emelio Greco
9. Torre del Moro

FUNICULAR

TRAIN STN.

PARKING LOT

TO AUTOSTRADA & CIVITA

TO ROMA

DCH

of a blood-stained cloth. In the 1260s, a Bohemian priest—who doubted that the bread used in Communion was really the body of Christ—came to Rome on a pilgrimage. On his return journey, he worshiped in Bolsena, near Orvieto. During Mass, the bread bled, staining a linen cloth. The cloth was brought to the pope, who was visiting Orvieto at the time. Such a miraculous relic required a magnificent church. You can see the actual cloth from the Miracle of Bolsena displayed in the chapel to the left of the altar.

**Hours of Cathedral:** April–Sept daily 7:30–12:45 & 14:30–19:15; closes at 18:15 March and Oct, and at 17:15 Nov–Feb. Admission is free, but there is a charge for the Chapel of St. Brizio.

**Cost and Hours of Chapel:** The chapel is usually free 7:30–10:00—drop by to check; you'll pay to visit Mon–Sat 10:00–12:45 & 14:30–19:15, Sun 14:30–17:45 (closes an hour earlier in winter). When payment is required, buy the €3 ticket at the TI or the shop across the square; it's included in the €10.50 Carta Unica combo-ticket. Only 25 people are allowed in the chapel at a time.

**Chapel of St. Brizio:** This chapel, to the right of the altar, features Luca Signorelli's brilliantly lit frescoes of the Apocalypse (1449–1451). Step into the chapel and you're surrounded by vivid scenes, including the *Preaching of the Antichrist* (to your left as you enter—the figure standing on far left is a self-portrait of Signorelli, next to Fra Angelico, who worked on the ceiling); the *Calling of the Elect to Heaven* (left of altar—hear that celestial band); the *Damned in Hell* (right of altar—the scariest mosh pit ever); and the *Resurrection of the Bodies* (to your right as you enter; people dreamily climb out of the earth as skeletons chatter in the corner, wondering where to snare some skin). On the same wall is a gripping *pietà*. Fra Angelico started the ceiling and Signorelli finished it, turning the entire room into Orvieto's artistic must-see sight.

After leaving the cathedral, if you want a break at a viewpoint park, exit left and pass the small parking lot. The nearest WCs are in the opposite direction (exit cathedral to the right), down the stairs from the left transept.

**Archaeological Museum (Museo Claudio Faina e Museo Civico)**—Across from the entrance to the cathedral is a fine Etruscan art museum (two upper floors) combined with a miniscule city history museum on the ground floor that features a sarcophagus and temple bits. The Faina art—consisting largely of Etruscan vases, plates, and coins, with some jewelry and bronze dishes—was collected by Mauro Faina and his nephew starting in the late 19th century. They bought some of the art, and dug up the rest in haphazardly conducted excavations. Many of the vases came from the Etruscan necropolis (Crocifisso del Tufo) just outside Orvieto. The English placards in most rooms offer some information, especially on the Faina family (€4.25, included in €10.50 Carta Unica combo-ticket, April–Sept Tue–Sun 9:30–18:00, Oct–March 10:00–17:00, closed Mon, audioguide, WC after ticket desk and on top floor, tel. 0763-341-511). Look out the windows at the duomo's glittering facade.

▲**Museo Emilo Greco**—This museum displays the work of Emilio Greco (1913–1995), the Sicilian artist who designed the doors of Orvieto's cathedral. His sketches and bronze statues show his absorption with gently twisting and turning nudes. In the back left corner of the museum, look for the sketchy outlines of women—simply beautiful. The artful installation of his work in this palazzo, with walkways and even a spiral staircase up to the ceiling, allows you to view his sculptures from different directions (€2.50, €4.50 includes St. Patrick's Well, April–Sept daily 10:30–13:00 & 14:00–18:30, closes 1 hour earlier Oct–March, no English but not essential, next to duomo, marked *Museo*, tel. 0763-344-605).

**Underground Orvieto Tours (Parco delle Grotte)**—Guides weave a good archaeological history into an hour-long look at about 100 meters (330 feet) of caves (€5.50, included in €10.50 Carta Unica combo-ticket, English tours daily at 12:15 and 17:15, confirm times by calling 0763-344-891 or checking with TI). Orvieto is honeycombed with Etruscan and medieval caves. You'll see the remains of an old olive press, two impressive 40-meter-deep (130-foot) Etruscan well shafts, and the remains of a primitive cement quarry; but, if you want underground Orvieto, this is the place to get it.

## More Sights—Orvieto

**Torre del Moro**—For yet another viewpoint, this distinctive square tower comes with 250 steps and an elevator. The elevator goes only partway up, leaving you with a mere 173 steps to scurry up (€2.75, included in €10.50 Carta Unica combo-ticket, April–Oct daily 10:00–19:00, May–Aug until 20:00, Nov–March 10:30–13:00 & 14:30–17:00, terrace on top, at intersection of Corso Cavour and Via Duomo).

**St. Patrick's Well (Posso de S. Patrizio)**—Engineers are impressed by this deep well—53 meters (175 feet) deep and 13 meters (45 feet) wide—designed in the 16th century with a double-helix pattern. The two spiral stairways allow an efficient one-way traffic flow; intriguing now, but critical then. Imagine if donkeys and people, balancing jugs of water, had to go up and down the same stairway. At the bottom is a bridge that people could walk on to scoop up water.

The well was built because a pope got nervous. After Rome was sacked in 1527 by renegade troops of the Holy Roman Empire, the pope fled to Orvieto. He feared that even this little town (with no water source on top) would be besieged. He commissioned a well, which was started in 1527 and finished 10 years later. It was a huge project. Even today, when a local is faced with a difficult task, people say, "It's like digging St. Patrick's Well." The unusual name came from the well's supposed resemblance to the Irish saint's cave. It's not worth climbing up and down a total of 495 steps; a quick look is painless but pricey (€3.50, €4.50

includes Museo Emilio Greco, April–Sept daily 10:00–18:45,
Oct–March closes an hour earlier; the well is to your right as you
exit *funiculare)*. Bring a sweater if you descend to the chilly depths.
**View Walks**—For short, pleasant walks, climb the medieval wall
(access at western end of town, between Piazza S. Gionvenale and
Via Garibaldi) or stroll the promenade park on the northern edge
of town (along Viale Carducci, which becomes Gonfaloniera).

## Sights near Orvieto

**Wine-Tasting**—Orvieto Classico wine is justly famous. For a
short tour of a local winery with Etruscan cellars, visit Tenuta Le
Velette, where English-speaking Corrado and Cecilia Bottai will
welcome you—if you've called ahead to set up an appointment
(€8 for tour and tasting, Mon–Fri 8:30–12:00 & 14:00–17:00, Sat
8:30–12:00, closed Sun, tel. 0763-29144, fax 0763-29114). From
their sign (5 min past Orvieto at top of switchbacks just before
Canale, on Bagnoregio road), cruise down a long, tree-lined drive,
then park at the striped gate (must call ahead; no drop-ins).

## Sleeping in Orvieto
**(€1 = about $1, country code: 39, zip code: 05018)**
Sleep Code: **S** = Single, **D** = Double/Twin, **T** = Triple, **Q** = Quad,
**b** = bathroom, **s** = shower only, **CC** = Credit Cards accepted, **no CC** =
Credit Cards not accepted, **SE** = Speaks English, **NSE** = No English.

To help you sort easily through these listings, I've divided
the rooms into three categories based on the price for a standard
double room with bath:

    **Higher Priced**—Most rooms more than €90.

    **Moderately Priced**—Most rooms €90 or less.

    **Lower Priced**—Most rooms €55 or less.

All of the recommended hotels are in the old town except Hotel
Picchio, which is in a more modern neighborhood near the station.

### HIGHER PRICED

**Hotel Duomo**, centrally located, is super-duper modern, with
splashy art and 17 sleek rooms named after artists who worked on
the duomo (Sb-€63, Db-€93, Db suite-€114, Tb-€114, includes
breakfast, CC, elevator, air-con, double-paned windows keep out
noise, a block from duomo, behind *gelateria* at Via di Maurizio 7,
tel. 0763-341-887, fax 0763-394-973, www.argoweb.it/hotel_duomo,
e-mail: hotelduomo@tiscalinet.it, SE).

### MODERATELY PRICED

**Hotel Corso** is friendly and clean, with 18 comfy, modern rooms,
some with balconies and views (Sb-€59, Db-€81, 10 percent

discount with this book, buffet breakfast-€6.50, CC, air-con, elevator, garage, on main street up from funicular toward duomo at Via Cavour 339, tel. & fax 0763-342-020, www.argoweb.it /hotel_corso, e-mail: hotelcorso@libero.it, SE).

**Hotel Virgilio** has modern but faded and overpriced rooms shoehorned into an old building, ideally located on the main square facing the cathedral (Sb-€62, Db-€85, breakfast-€6, send personal or traveler's check for first night's deposit, CC, elevator, noisy church bells every 15 min, Piazza Duomo 5, tel. 0763-341-882, fax 0763-343-797, www.hotelvirgilio.com, e-mail: info@hotel.virgilio.com, SE). They also have a cheaper *dependencia*—a double and quad in a one-star hotel a few doors away (Db-€57, Qb-€103).

**Hotel Posta** is a five-minute walk from the cathedral into the medieval core. It's a big, old, formerly elegant but well-cared-for-in-its-decline building with a breezy garden, a grand old lobby, and 20 spacious, clean, plain rooms with vintage rickety furniture and good mattresses (S-€31, Sb-€36, D-€43, Db-€56, breakfast-€6, no CC, Via Luca Signorelli 18, tel. & fax 0763-341-909, NSE).

**LOWER PRICED**
The sisters of the **Istituto SS Domenicane** rent 15 spotless twin rooms in their heavenly convent with a peaceful terrace (Sb-€41, Db-€52, 2-night minimum, breakfast-€5.25, no CC, elevator, parking, just off Piazza del Popolo at Via del Popolo 1, tel. & fax 0763-342-910, www.argoweb.it/istituto_sansalvatore /istituto.it.html, NSE).

**Hotel Picchio,** with 19 newly remodeled rooms, is a wood-and-marble place, more comfortable but with less character than others in the area. It's in the lower, plain part of town, 300 meters (985 feet) from the train station (Sb-€36, Db-€48, Tb-€59, ask for the Rick Steves 5 percent discount; some rooms with air-con, fridge, and phone; Via G. Salvatori 17, 05019 Orvieto Scalo, tel. & fax 0763-301-144, e-mail: dan_test @libero.it, family-run by Marco and Picchio, SE). A trail leads from here up to the old town.

Franco Sala, who runs the Antico Forno restaurant and a B&B in Civita, also rents a centrally located **one-bedroom apartment** in Orvieto (€100 up to 4 people, 2-night minimum, kitchen, tel. 0761-760-016).

## Eating in Orvieto
Near the duomo, consider **Pergola**—its affordable menu is popular with locals (Thu–Tue 12:30–14:30 & 19:30–22:00, closed Wed, Via dei Magoni 9, tel. 0763-343-065). **La Palomba** is also a good bet

(Thu–Tue 12:30–14:15 & 19:30–22:00, closed Wed, Via Cipriano Manente, just off Piazza della Repubblica, tel. 0763-343-395).

For a bit of a splurge, try **Antico Bucchero** for its classy candlelit ambience and fine food (Thu–Tue 12:30–15:00 & 19:00–24:00, closed Wed, CC, indoor/outdoor seating, Via de Cartori 4, a half block south of Corso Cavour, between Torre del Moro and Piazza della Repubblica, tel. 0763-341-725).

**Osteria San Patrizio**, near the funicular, is good (12:00–15:00 & 19:00–22:30, closed Sun eve and Mon, Corso Cavour 312, tel. 0763-341-245).

For dessert, try the deservedly popular *gelateria* **Pasqualetti** (daily 12:30–1:00, until 20:30 Nov–March, Piazza Duomo 14, next to left transept of church; another branch is at Corso Cavour 56).

**Enoteca Tozzi**, to the left of the duomo, serves up rustic *panini* sandwiches—try the roast suckling pig (*porchetta*, pron. por-KET-tah) if it's available (9:00–21:00, until 18:00 in winter, Piazza Duomo 13, tel. 0763-344-393).

## Transportation Connections—Orvieto

**By train to: Rome** (19/day, 75 min, consider leaving your car at the large car park behind Orvieto station), **Florence** (14/day, 2.25 hrs), **Siena** (8/day, 2–3 hrs, change in Chiusi; all Florence-bound trains stop in Chiusi). The train station's Buffet della Stazione is surprisingly good if you need a quick focaccia sandwich or pizza picnic for the train ride.

**By bus to Bagnoregio (near Civita):** It's a 70-minute, €1.50 bus ride. Departures in 2002 from Orvieto's Piazza Cahen on the blue Cotral bus, daily except Sunday: 6:20, 9:10, 12:40, 13:55, 15:45, 17:40, and 18:20 (buses stop at Orvieto's train station 5 min later). During the school year (roughly Sept–June), there are additional departures at 7:20 and 7:50. Buy your ticket at the *tabacchi* stop on Corso Cavour (also confirm the schedule) a block up from the *funiculare*. To find the bus stop, face the *funiculare*; the stop is at the far left end of Piazza Cahen where the blue buses are parked (no schedule posted; confirm departure and return times with driver). Once you're in Bagnoregio, you'll find the Bagnoregio–Orvieto bus schedule posted at the bus stop.

## CIVITA DI BAGNOREGIO

Perched on a pinnacle in a grand canyon, the traffic-free village of Civita is Italy's ultimate hill town. Curl your toes around its Etruscan roots.

Civita is terminally ill. Only 15 residents remain as, bit by bit, the town is being purchased by rich big-city Italians who come here to escape. Apart from its permanent (and aging) residents

## Orvieto and Civita Area

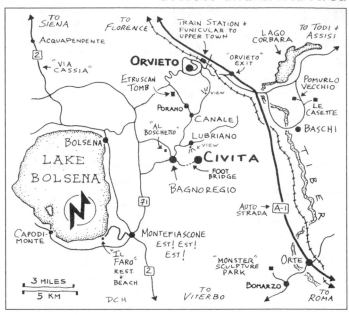

and those who have weekend homes here, there is a group of Americans—introduced to the town through a small University of Washington architecture program—who have bought into the rare magic of Civita. When the program is in session, 15 students live with residents and study Italian culture and architecture.

Civita is connected to the world and the town of Bagno-regio by a long pedestrian bridge—and a Web site (www .civitadibagnoregio.it). While Bagnoregio lacks the pinnacle-town romance of Civita, it's actually a healthy, vibrant community (unlike Civita, the suburb it calls "the dead city"). In Bagnoregio, get a haircut, sip a coffee on the square, and walk down to the old laundry (ask, *"Dov'è la lavanderia vecchia?"*). A Grand Spesa supermarket is 300 meters (985 feet) from the bus stop (Mon–Sat 8:30–13:00 & 17:00–20:00, closed Sun; take main drag from town gate—away from Civita, angle right at pyramid monument). A lively market fills the bus parking lot each Monday.

From Bagnoregio, yellow signs direct you along its long, skinny spine to its older neighbor, Civita. Enjoy the view as you walk up the bridge to Civita. Be prepared for the little old ladies of Civita, who can be aggressive at getting money out of visitors—tourists are their only source of support. Off-season, Civita,

Bagnoregio, and Al Boschetto (see "Sleeping," below) are all deadly quiet—and cold. I'd side-trip in quickly from Orvieto or skip the area altogether.

## Arrival in Bagnoregio, near Civita

If you're arriving by bus from Orvieto, you'll get off at the bus stop in Bagnoregio. Look at the posted bus schedule and write down the return times to Orvieto. (Drivers, see "Transportation Connections," page 283.)

**Baggage Check:** While there's no official baggage-check service in Bagnoregio, I've arranged with Laurenti Mauro, who runs the Bar/Enoteca/Caffè Gianfu, to let you leave your bags there (€1/bag, Fri–Wed 7:00–24:00 with a 13:00–13:30 lunch break, closed Thu; to get to café from Orvieto bus stop where you got off, continue in same direction the Orvieto bus headed and go right around corner).

**From Bagnoregio to Civita:** From Bagnoregio, you can walk or take a little orange shuttle bus to the base of the bridge to Civita. From here, you have to walk the rest of the way. It's a 10-minute hike up a pedestrian bridge that gets steeper near the end. There's no bus—only you and your profound regret that you didn't get in better shape before your trip.

The little shuttle **bus** runs from Bagnoregio (catch bus across from gas station) to the base of the bridge (€1, pay driver, 10-min ride, first bus at 7:39, last at 18:20, 1–2/hr except during 13:00–15:30 siesta). If you'll want to return to Bagnoregio by bus, check the schedule posted near the bridge (at edge of car park, where bus let you off) before you head up to Civita.

To **walk** from Bagnoregio to the base of Civita's bridge (about 20 min, fairly level), take the road going uphill (overlooking the big parking lot), then take the first right and an immediate left onto the main drag, Via Roma. Follow this straight out to the belvedere for a superb viewpoint. From the viewpoint, backtrack a few steps, and take the stairs down to the road leading to the bridge.

## Civita Orientation Walk

Civita was once connected to Bagnoregio. The saddle between the separate towns eroded away. Photographs around town show the old donkey path, the original bridge. It was bombed in World War II and replaced in 1965 with the new **bridge** you're climbing today. The town's hearty old folks hang on the bridge's hand railing when fierce winter weather rolls through.

Entering the town, you'll pass through a cut in the rock (made by Etruscans 2,500 years ago) and under a 12th-century Romanesque **arch**. This was the main Etruscan road leading to the Tiber Valley and Rome.

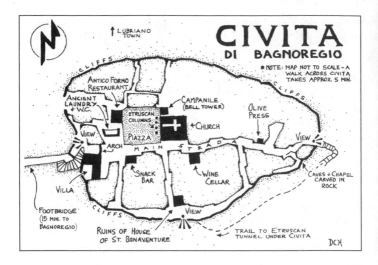

Inside the town gate, on your left is the old **laundry** (in front of the WC). On your right, a fancy wooden door and windows (above the door) lead to thin air. This was the facade of a Renaissance palace—one of five that once graced Civita. It fell into the valley riding a chunk of the ever-eroding rock pinnacle. Today, the door leads to a remaining chunk of the palace—complete with Civita's first hot tub—owned by the "Marchesa," a countess who married into Italy's biggest industrialist family.

Peek into the museum next door if it's open (Wed and Sat–Sun 10:00–13:00, marked *Benvenuti a Civita*) and check out the **viewpoint** a few steps away. Nearby is the site of the long-gone home of Civita's one famous son, Saint Bonaventure, known as the "second founder of the Franciscans."

Now wander to the **town square** in front of the church, where you'll find Civita's only public phone, bar, and restaurant—and a wild donkey race on the first Sunday of June and the second Sunday of September. The church marks the spot where an Etruscan temple, and then a Roman temple, once stood. The pillars that stand like giants' bar stools are ancient—Roman or Etruscan.

Go into the **church**. You'll see frescoes and statues from "the school of Giotto" and "the school of Donatello," a portrait of the patron saint of your teeth (notice the scary-looking pincers), and an altar dedicated to Marlon Brando (or St. Ildebrando).

The basic grid street plan of the ancient town survives. Just around the corner from the church, on the main street, is Rossana and Antonio's cool and friendly **wine cellar** (their sign reads: *bruschette con prodotti locali*). Pull up a stump and let them or their children, Arianna and Antonella, serve you *panini* (sandwiches), *bruschetta* (garlic toast with optional tomato topping), wine, and a local cake called *ciambella*. Climb down into the cellar and note the traditional wine-making gear and the provisions for rolling huge kegs up the stairs. Tap on the kegs in the cool bottom level to see which are full.

The rock below Civita is honeycombed with ancient cellars (for keeping wine at the same temperature all year) and cisterns (for collecting rainwater, since there was no well in town). Many of these date from Etruscan times.

Explore farther down the street but, remember, nothing is abandoned. Everything is still privately owned. After passing an ancient Roman tombstone on your left, you'll come to Vittoria's **Antico Mulino**, an atmospheric collection of old olive presses. The huge press in the entry is about 1,500 years old and was in use as recently as the 1960s (donation requested, give about €1). Vittoria's sons, Sandro and Felice, running the local equivalent of a lemonade stand, toast delicious *bruschetta* on weekends and holidays (roughly 11:00–19:00). Choose your topping (chopped tomato is super) and get a glass of wine for a fun, affordable snack.

Farther down the way and to your left, Maria (for a donation of about €1) will show you through her **garden** with a grand view (Maria's Giardino) and share historical misinformation (she says Civita and Lubriano were once connected). Maria's husband, Peppone, used to carry goods on a donkey back and forth on the path between the old town and Bagnoregio.

At the end of town, the main drag winds downhill past small **Etruscan caves** to your right. The first two were used as stables until last year. The third cave is an unusual chapel, cut deep into the rock, with a barred door—this is the **Chapel of the Incarcerated** (Cappella del Carcere). In Etruscan times, the chapel may have originally been a tomb, and in medieval times, it was used as a jail. When Civita's few residents have a religious procession, they come here, in honor of the Madonna of the Incarcerated.

After the chapel, the paving-stone path peters out into a dirt trail leading down and around to the right to a **tunnel**. Dating from the Etruscan era, the tunnel may have served as a shortcut to the river below. It was widened in the 1930s so farmers could get between their scattered fields more easily, and now the residents use it as a shortcut in fall to collect chestnuts from the trees that cover the hillside. Backtrack to the town square.

Evenings on the town square are a bite of Italy. The same people sit on the same church steps under the same moon, night after night, year after year. I love my cool, late evenings in Civita. If you visit in the morning, have cappuccino and rolls at the small café on the town square.

Whenever you visit, stop halfway up the donkey path and listen to the sounds of rural Italy. Reach out and touch one of the monopoly houses. If you know how to turn the volume up on the crickets, do so.

## Sleeping in Civita and Bagnoregio
**(€1 = about $1, country code: 39, zip code: 01022)**
When you leave the tourist crush, life as a traveler in Italy becomes easy, and prices tumble. Finding a room is easy in small-town Italy. Drivers who would like to experience rural Italy should check the *Agriturismo* section at the end of this chapter for farmhouse B&Bs near Orvieto.

### In Civita
**Civita B&B**, run by Franco Sala, who also owns the Antico Forno restaurant, has three comfortable rooms overlooking Civita's main square. Call a minimum of one day in advance to reserve (D-€57, Db-€67, €13 more for optional half pension, CC, Piazza del Duomo Vecchio, 01022 Civita di Bagnoregio, tel. 0761-760-016, cellular 34-7611-5426, www.civitadibagnoregio.it, e-mail: fsala@pelagus.it). Drivers should request a parking pass when they call.

For information about a fully furnished and equipped two-bedroom **Civita apartment** with a terrace and cliffside garden ($800/week, 1-week minimum Sat to Sat, personal checks OK), call Carol Watts in Kansas (785/539-0815, evenings or weekends, http://homepage.mac.com/cmwatts/civita .html, e-mail: cmwatts@mac.com).

### In Bagnoregio
**Hotel Fidanza**, in Bagnoregio near the bus stop, is tired but decent and the only hotel in town. Of its 25 rooms, #206 and #207 have views of Civita (Sb-€52, Db-€62, breakfast-€5.50, no CC, attached restaurant, Via Fidanza 25, Bagnoregio/Viterbo, tel. & fax 0761-793-444).

Just outside Bagnoregio is **Al Boschetto.** The Catarcia family speaks no English, so have an English-speaking Italian call for you (Sb-€34, D-€44, Db-€49, breakfast-€3, CC, Strada Monterado, Bagnoregio/Viterbo, tel. 0761-792-369). Most of the 25 rooms, while very basic, have private showers. The Catarcia family (Angelino, his wife Perina, sons Gianfranco and Domenico, daughter-in-law Giuseppina, and the grand-children) offers a candid look at rural Italian life. Meals are uneven in quality, and the men are often tipsy (which can pose a problem for women). If the men invite you down deep into the gooey, fragrant bowels of the cantina, be warned: The theme song is *"Trinku Trinka Trinka,"* and there are no rules unless the female participants set them. The Orvieto bus drops you at the town gate (no bus on Sun). The hotel is a 15-minute walk out of town past the old arch (follow *Viterbo* signs); turn left at the pyramid monument and right at the first fork (follow *Montefiascone* sign). Civita is a pleasant 45-minute walk (back through Bagnoregio) from Al Boschetto.

## Eating in and near Civita

In Civita, try **Trattoria Antico Forno**, which serves up pasta at affordable prices (daily for lunch at 12:00 and sporadically for dinner at 19:00, on main square, also rents rooms—see above, tel. 0761-760-016). At **Da Peppone**, the small café/bar on the square, you can get simple treats (daily 9:30–12:30 & 14:00–19:00, closed 17:00 and Mon or Tue in winter).

**Hostaria del Ponte** offers light, creative cuisine at the parking lot at the base of the bridge to Civita (Tue–Sat 12:30–16:00 & 19:30–24:00, Sun 12:30–16:00, closed Mon, great view terrace, tel. 0761-793-565).

In Bagnoregio, check out **Ristorante Nello il Fumatore** (Sat–Thu 12:00–15:00 & 19:00–22:00, closed Fri, on Piazza Fidanza). At **Al Boschetto,** you'll get country cooking, such as bunny (just outside Bagnoregio; see "Sleeping," above).

## Transportation Connections—Bagnoregio

**To Orvieto:** Public buses (7/day, 70 min) connect Bagnoregio to the rest of the world via Orvieto. Departures in 2002 from Bagnoregio, daily except Sunday: 5:30, 6:50, 9:50, 10:10, 13:00, 14:25, and 17:20. During the school year (roughly Sept–June), buses also run at 6:35, 13:35, and 16:40 (for info on Orvieto, see "Connections—Orvieto," above).

**Driving from Orvieto to Bagnoregio:** Orvieto overlooks the autostrada (and has its own exit). The shortest way to Civita from the freeway exit is to turn left (below Orvieto) and follow the signs to Lubriano and Bagnoregio.

The more winding and scenic route takes 20 minutes longer: From the freeway, pass under hill-capping Orvieto (on your right, signs to Lago di Bolsena, on Viale I Maggio), then take the first left (direction: Bagnoregio), winding up past great Orvieto views through Canale, and through farms and fields of giant shredded wheat to Bagnoregio.

Either way, just before Bagnoregio, follow the signs left to Lubriano and pull into the first little square by the church on your right for a breathtaking view of Civita. Then return to the Bagnoregio road. Drive through Bagnoregio (following yellow Civita signs) and park at the base of the steep pedestrian bridge leading up to the traffic-free, 2,500-year-old, canyon-swamped pinnacle town of Civita di Bagnoregio.

## MORE HILL TOWNS

If you haven't gotten your fill of hill towns, here are more to check out. There are three main regions in central Italy, listed here in order of touristic popularity and accessibility: Tuscany, Umbria, and Le Marche.

**Tuscany** is our image of village Italy, with its manicured hills, rustic farms, and towns clinging to nearly every hill. Yet many who visit Tuscany, famous as the cradle of the Renaissance, never get out of the crowds of Florence. You'll find manageable train and bus connections throughout most of the region, but a car is fun.

Landlocked **Umbria**, the "Green Heart of Italy," is known for Assisi, famous worldwide as the hometown of St. Francis. Yet a short distance away from Assisi's touristic bustle, you'll find plenty of pleasant towns with more of the peace that Francis was seeking.

**Le Marche** is much less discovered. Its landscape is more wild and less manicured. The town of Urbino is the region's highlight. To unlock Le Marche's charms, a car is essential.

## TUSCANY

▲▲**Cortona**—Cortona clings by its fingernails to the top of a mountain, dangling above views of the Tuscan and Umbrian landscape below. Frances Mayes' books, such as *Under the Tuscan Sun*, have placed this town in the touristic limelight, just as Peter Mayle's books popularized (and populated) the Luberon region in France. But even before Mayes ever published a book, Cortona was considered one of the classic Tuscan hill towns.

Unlike many hill towns, Cortona is worth visiting for its art alone. The Museo Diocesano has a small but interesting collection, including powerful works by native son Signorelli and two wonderful luminous Fra Angelicos. The Museo dell'Accademia Etrusca, housed in a former palace, has an eclectic collection of paintings, Etruscan artifacts and jewelry, and Egyptian mummies.

Cortona lies above the Terontola station (8 km, or 5 miles, away) on the Florence–Perugia line. Frequent buses connect the station with Piazza Garibaldi and the sights. The **TI** is at Via Nazionale 42 (tel. 0575-630-352). There are lots of cafés for lunch, or assemble a picnic and dine alfresco. Cortona's San

Marco hostel, housed in a remodeled 13th-century palace, is one of Italy's best (Via Maffei 57, tel. 0575-601-392). Drivers will find *agriturismo* listings for farmhouse B&Bs at the end of this chapter.
▲**Chiusi**—This small hill town (rated ▲▲ for Etruscan fans), which was once one of the most important Etruscan cities, is now a key train junction on the Florence–Rome line. The region's trains (to Siena, Orvieto, and Assisi) go through or change at this hub.

Highlights include the Archaeological Museum and the Etruscan tombs located just outside of town near Lago di Chiusi (€4, Mon–Sat 9:00–19:30, Sun 9:00–13:00, Via Porsenna 7, tel. 0578-20177). One of the tombs is multichambered, with several sarcophagi; while another, the Tomba della Scimmia (Tomb of the Monkey) has some well-preserved frescoes. Visiting the tombs requires a guide, arranged through the TI or the Archaeological Museum (5 people allowed to view at a time).

Troglodyte alert! The Cathedral Museum on the main square has an underground labyrinth of Etruscan tunnels (dark, so bring a flashlight). The mandatory guided tour ends in a large Roman cistern from which you can climb the church bell tower for an expansive view of the countryside (museum-€2, labyrinth-€3, combo-ticket-€4, daily 9:30–12:45 & 16:00–19:00, tours 11:00–16:00).

The **TI** is on the main square (daily in summer 9:00–12:30 & 15:30–19:00, otherwise mornings only, tel. 0578-227-667). Trains connect Chiusi with Rome, Florence, Siena, and more. Buses link the station (3 km, or less than 2 miles, away) with the town center.
▲▲**Montepulciano**—Long and skinny, Montepulciano stretches out lazily across a ridge. Due to its time under Medici rule, Montepulciano has an interesting mix of Renaissance buildings. To explore this Tuscan gem on a downhill stroll, take the shuttle bus from Piazza San Agnese up to Piazza Grande (and the TI, tel. 0578-717-484).

At Piazza Grande, the Palazzo Comunale (a mini-version of Florence's Palazzo Vecchio) looms across from Palazzo Contucci. Here you'll find an *enoteca* (wine bar) where you can sample the famous Vino Nobile di Montepulciano. From Piazza Grande, take Viale Sangallo downhill. The road snakes its way past shops, palaces, and *enotecas* through the old Porta al Prato gate back to Piazza San Agnese. Just outside the city walls is the Church of San Biagio, a Renaissance masterpiece by Sangallo.

Buses take you from Montepulciano's train station on the Florence–Rome line to the parking lot below Piazza San Agnese at the bottom of town. From here, it's a 25-minute walk up to Piazza Grande (or a quick bus ride). Buses connect Montepulciano with Siena as well.
▲**Montalcino**—Famous for its Brunello di Montalcino red wines,

this hill town (rated ▲▲▲ for wine-lovers), once part of Siena's empire, is worth a visit for its *enoteca*, housed inside the 14th-century *fortezza* at the edge of town (tel. 0577-849-211, www .enotecalafortezza.it). After sampling a glass of the local *vino*, wander down into the heart of town at Piazza Garibaldi. The TI is on this square (tel. 0577-849-331). Besides the *fortezza* and the Brunello, Montalcino's main sight is the Museo Civico on Via Ricasoli, where you'll find art from the late Gothic/ early Renaissance period. For an atmospheric café, try Antica Fiaschetteria on Piazza del Popolo. Non–wine-lovers may find Montalcino a bit too focused on *vino*, but one sip of Brunello makes even wine skeptics believe that Bacchus was on to something. Note that the Rosso di Montalcino wine is also good at half the price. Those with sweet tooths will enjoy munching Ossi di Morta ("bones of the dead"), a crunchy cookie with almonds.

Buses connect Montalcino with Siena.

▲**Pienza**—In the 1400s, local pope Pius II of the Piccolomini family decided to remodel his hometown in the current Renaissance style. Propelled by papal clout, the town of Corsignano was transformed into a jewel of Renaissance architecture and renamed Pienza. The focal point is the Piazza Pio II, with the Duomo and Palazzo Piccolomini. The TI is in Palazzo Pubblico (tel. 0578-749-071).

Buses connect Pienza with Siena and Montepulciano.

▲▲**Crete Senese Drive**—Sometimes it seems that all of Tuscany is one big scenic route, but my favorite drive is this one between Montepulciano and Montalcino on the S-146 road. This area is known as the Crete Senese ("Crests of Siena"), a series of undulating hills that provides postcard views at every turn. You'll see an endless parade of classic Tuscan scenes, with rolling hills topped with medieval towns, olive groves, rustic stone farmhouses, rows of vineyards, and a skyline punctuated with cypress trees.

**San Galgano Monastery**—Of southern Tuscany's several evocative monasteries, San Galgano is the best. Way off the beaten track, this sight is for drivers only. San Galgano was a 12th-century saint who renounced his past as a knight by miraculously burying his sword up to its hilt into a stone. After his death, a large monastery complex grew up. Today, all you'll see is the roofless, ruined abbey and, on a nearby hill, the Chapel of San Galgano with its fascinating dome and sword in the stone. The adjacent gift shop sells a little bit of everything from wine to postcards to herbs. Other more accessible Tuscan monasteries worth visiting include San Antimo (10 km, or 6 miles, south of Montalcino) and Monte Oliveto Maggiore (25 km, or 15 miles, south of Siena).

One bus a day from Siena stops at San Galgano. Buses

link Montalcino with San Antimo, and Siena with Monte
Oliveto Maggiore.

▲**U.S. Cemetery**—Whatever one's feelings about war, the sight
of endless rows of white marble crosses and Stars of David never
fails to be moving. This particular cemetery is the final resting
place of more than 4,000 Americans who died in the liberation of
Italy during World War II. Their memory lives on in two Italian
cemeteries, one in Nettuno near Rome and this one just south of
Tavernuzze, 12 kilometers (7 miles) south of Florence. Climb the
hill past the perfectly manicured grassy lawn, lined with grave
markers, to the memorial, where maps and history of the Italian
campaign detail the Allied advance (daily mid-April–Sept 8:00–
18:00, Oct–mid-April 8:00–17:00, WC, just off Via Cassia road
that parallels the *superstrada* between Florence and Siena, 3 km,
or 1.9 miles, south of Florence Certosa exit on A-1 autostrada).
Buses from Florence stop just outside the cemetery.

# UMBRIA
▲**Gubbio**—This handsome town climbs Monte Ingino in northeast Umbria. Tuesday is market day, when Piazza 40 Martiri
(named for 40 locals shot by the Nazis) bustles. Nearby, the ruins
of the Roman amphitheater are perfect for a picnic. Head up
Via della Repubblica to reach the main square with the imposing
Palazzo dei Consoli. Farther up, Via San Gerolamo leads to the
funky lift that will carry you up the hill in two-person "baskets"
for a stunning view from the top, where the basilica of St. Ubaldo
is worth a look.

Buses run to Perugia, Rome, and Florence. The TI is at
Piazza Odersi (tel. 075-922-0693).

▲**Deruta**—Pottery-lovers the world over start to salivate when the
name Deruta is mentioned. Colorful Deruta pottery, considered to
be Italy's best, features designs popular since Renaissance times.
The high-quality local clay attracted artisans centuries ago, and
today artists still practice their craft. Deruta is actually two towns:
the upper hill town and the lower strip. The upper town, full of
small shops run by local artisans, warrants a wander; prices and
quality are higher up here. Ceramic fans drop by the Museo
Regionale della Ceramica (closed Tue), in the upper town, next
to the TI on the main square. Below, a commercial strip parallel
to the *superstrada* is lined with larger commercial outlets and factories. Many offer demonstrations of their time-honored craft. Prices
are about one-third cheaper than in the United States, and most
will ship your purchases home with a guarantee of safe delivery.

Buses connect Deruta with Perugia.

▲**Bevagna**—This sleeper of a town south of Assisi has Roman ruins, interesting churches, and more. Locals offer their guiding services for free (usually Italian-speaking only) and are excited to show visitors their town. Get a map at the **TI** on Piazza Silvestri (tel. 0742-361-667) and wander. Highlights are the Roman mosaics, remains of the arena that now houses a paper-making shop, the Romanesque church of San Silvestro, and a gem of a 19th-century theater. Bevagna has all the elements of a hill town except one—a hill. A couple of hours is plenty to see the main sights. For an overnight, consider the fancy Hotel Palazzo Brunamonti (Db-€110, Corso Matteotti 79, tel. 0742-361-932, fax 0742-361-948, www.brunamonti.com, e-mail: hotel@brunamonti.com). Buses connect Bevagna with Foligno.

**Montefalco**—Famous for its Sagrantino wine and its site (Montefalco means Falcon's Mountain), this village is dubbed the "Balcony of Umbria" for its expansive views. Intact medieval walls surround the town. The Museo Civico San Francesco displays frescoes by Gozzoli (Fra Angelico's pupil) of the life of St. Francis. There is no TI, but the people at the museum can answer questions.

A few buses a day run to Bevagna.

▲**Spello**—Umbrian hill town aficionados always include Spello on their list. Just 10 kilometers (6 miles) south of Assisi, this town is much less touristy than its neighbor to the north. Spello will give your legs a workout. Via Consolare goes up, up, up to the top of town. Views from the terrace of the restaurant Il Trombone will have you singing a tune. The **TI** is on Piazza Matteotti 3 (tel. 0742-301-009).

Spello is on the Perugia–Assisi–Foligno train line. Buses run to Assisi.

# LE MARCHE

▲▲**Urbino**—Urbino is famous for being the hometown of the artist Raphael and architect Bramante, yet the town owes much of its fame to the Duke of Montefeltro. This mercenary general turned Urbino into an important Renaissance center, attracting artists such as Piero della Francesca, Uccello, and Raphael's papa, Giovanni Santi.

The Ducal Palace, with more than 300 rooms, is the main course of a visit to Urbino. Highlights include great paintings such as Raphael's *La Muta*, the remarkable *intarsio* (inlaid wood) walls of the duke's study, the vast cellars, and the Renaissance courtyard (€4.20, Sun–Mon 9:00–14:00, Tue–Sat 9:00–19:00). Note that during busy periods, you need to reserve a ticket for the palace in person. For information on how to reserve, call the **TI** (Piazza Duca Federico 35, across from palace, tel. 0722-2613) or the booking office in the palace (tel. 0722-329-057).

Stop by the Oratory of St. John to see its remarkable frescoed interior. Nearby, the Church of San Giuseppe has a dreamy stucco ceiling, with angels peering down through whipped-cream clouds at the huge nativity diorama below. In the adjacent church, a Baroque trompe l'oeil ceiling is worth a look. Fans visit the Casa di Raffaello, but the artist's famous works are in Florence and Rome. For a fabulous view, climb up to the Giardini Pubblici park, where a grassy hillside provides a panorama of Urbino and the hills of Le Marche.

A couple of good restaurants are Taverna degli Artisti (great pizzas, Via Bramante) and Il Coppiere (Via Santa Margherita), where your entire meal, including the post-dinner grappa, can involve truffles, if you like. The *enoteca* on Via Raphael merits a stop, but the action in town is at the bustling Piazza della Repubblica, with an endless parade of students and locals.

Urbino is well off the beaten tourist path. Frequent buses connect Pesaro (on the Ravenna–Pescara train line) with Urbino, terminating at the Borgo Mercatale parking lot below the town, where an elevator lifts you up to the base of the slender towers of the Ducal Palace (or walk 5 min steeply up Via Mazzini to Piazza della Repubblica).

## Agriturismo

*Agriturismo* (or agricultural tourism) began in the 1960s to encourage farmers to remain on their land, produce food, and offer accommodation to tourists. These rural Italian B&Bs are ideal for couples or families traveling by car.

Some properties are simple and rustic, while others are downright luxurious, offering amenities such as swimming pools and stables. The quality of the rooms varies, but they are usually simple, clean, and comfortable. Most serve tasty homegrown food. And most require a minimum-night stay, usually a week. July and August are especially busy. Off-season shorter stays are possible.

Be aware that agricultural tourism is organized "*alla Italiana*," which means, among other things, a lack of a single governing body. You'll find a listing of several *agriturismo* farms below. For more options, go to www.agriturist.it, which lists over 1,700 farms throughout Italy. If you'd prefer to use an agency, consider Farm Holidays in Tuscany. They book rooms and apartments at 300 farms in Tuscany, Umbria, and elsewhere in Italy (Mon–Fri 9:00–13:00 & 15:00–18:00, Via Manin 20, 58100 Grosseto, tel. 0564-417-418, www.it-farmholidays.it, Andrea Mazzanti SE). Book several months in advance for high season (May–Sept). Generally, a 25 percent deposit is required (lost if you cancel), and the balance is due one month before arrival.

For more information on *agriturismo*, visit www.initaly.com, www.italyfarmholidays.com, www.agriturismoitaly.it, www.rent-villas.com, www.italianvillas.com, and www.tuscanyumbria.com.

## *Agriturismo* Listings

### Near Orvieto

**Agriturismo Le Casette,** outside the village of Baschi, is outstanding, with rooms in several restored stone farmhouses clustered around a grassy lawn and a swimming pool with a fabulous view of the green Umbrian landscape (Db-€70, includes breakfast; for a room, breakfast, and a home-cooked dinner, pay €50–60 per person per day; minimum 1-week stays preferred July–Aug, CC, 12 km, or 7 miles, southeast of Orvieto, tel. 0744-957-645, fax 0744-950-500, www.pomurlovecchio -lecasette.it, e-mail: pomurlovecchio@tiscalinet.it, run by charming Minghelli family, Daniela speaks "a leetle" English). The same family also owns **Pomurlo Vecchio**, a 12th-century tower house with three rooms a few kilometers away (same prices, tel. 0744-950-190, fax 0744-950-500).

**Agriturismo Sant' Angelo** rents four apartments in an old stone farmhouse on a hillside near Monte Rufeno Natural Park Reserve, about 20 kilometers (12 miles) northwest of Orvieto. Each apartment has a living room and kitchen and sleeps up to four (2-night stay required). The entire villa also can be rented (apartment for 2 people/2 nights-€310–620 depending on season, weekly-€620–1,033, villa-€2,376–4,132, no CC, pool, horseback riding, mountain bikes, S.S. Cassia Nord Km 136.300, tel. 0763-734-738 or 0763-730-150, cellular 338-366-5475, www.agriturismosantangelo.it, e-mail: info@agriturismosantangelo.it, SE).

**Agriturismo Pomonte Umbria,** a short drive from Civita and Orvieto, offers home-cooked meals, lovely vistas, and seven comfortable rooms in a newly built guest house (€26 per person, includes breakfast, €42-half pension, €52-full pension, CC, Loc. Canino di Orvieto 1, Corbara, 12 km, or 7 miles, east of Orvieto, tel. 076-330-4041, fax 076-330-4080, www.orvienet.it /agriturismo.pomonte, e-mail: info@pomonte.it, SE).

### Near Assisi

**Podere La Fornace** is a renovated farmhouse in the tiny village of Tordibetto, just a few kilometers outside Assisi. The four apartments (with 1–3 bedrooms) have full kitchens and a living room that can sleep an extra person. Local wine, olive oil, and pasta are available on-site; if you stay for a week, they'll include your breakfast ingredients (apartment-€75–240 depending on size and season, 3-night minimum, games for children, swimming pool, bikes, Via Ombrosa 3, tel. 075-801-9537, cellular 338 990 2903, fax 075 801 9630, www.lafornace.com, e-mail: info@lafornace.com, SE).

### In Montalcino
**La Crociona,** a farm and working vineyard in Montalcino (45 min south of Siena), rents seven fully equipped apartments. Fiorella Vannoni and Roberto & Barbara Nannetti offer wine-tasting and cooking classes (Db-€67–105, Qb-€93–155, lower weekly rates, CC, pool, La Croce, Montalcino, tel. 0577-847-133, tel. & fax 0577-848-007, www.lacrociona.com, e-mail: lacrociona@tin.it, SE).

### Near Urbino
At **Locanda della Valle Nuova,** a 185-acre organic farm near Urbino, they raise cattle, pigs, and poultry; grow grapes for their wine; and harvest wheat for their homemade bread and pasta. The six rooms—named by color—are tranquil and cozy (Db-€90 includes buffet breakfast, Db-€125 also includes 5-course evening meal, no CC, 3-night minimum, reserve 1 day in advance, swimming pool, horseback riding, La Cappella 14, Sagrata di Fermingnano, tel. & fax 0722-330-303, www.vallenuova.it, e-mail: gsavini@supereva.it, SE).

### Near Cortona
**Casa San Martino**, in the village of Lisciano Niccone (midway between Cortona and Perugia), is a 250-year-old farmhouse run as a B&B by American Italophile Lois Martin. Using this comfortable hilltop countryside as a home base, those with a car can tour Assisi, Orvieto, and Civita. While Lois reserves the summer (June–Aug) for one-week stays, she'll take guests staying a minimum of three nights for the rest of the year (Db-€160, 10 percent discount for my readers—mention this book when you reserve, includes breakfast, views, pool, washer/dryer, house rental available, Casa San Martino 19, Lisciano Niccone, 20 km, or 12 miles, east of Cortona, tel. 075-844-288, fax 075-844-422). Lois' neighbors, Ernestine and Gisbert Schwanke, run the charming **La Villetta di San Martino B&B** (Db-€110 includes hearty country breakfast, minimum2-night stay, kitchen, sitting room, fireplace, San Martino 36, tel. & fax 075-844-309, e-mail: erni@netemedia.net, SE).

    **Country House Montali** is perched on a hilltop (roughly between Cortona and Chiusi), within an hour's drive of Orvieto and Assisi. The architect owners have restored an old farmhouse and built three single-story houses for guests. Olive trees and trails surround the property, which overlooks nearby Lake Trasimeno. The owners offer vegetarian meals and cooking courses designed to prove that healthy food can be tasty (10 rooms, €67.15–77.50 per person half pension, swimming pool, Via Montali 23, Tavernelle di Panicale, 40 km, or 25 miles, south of Cortona, tel. 075-835-0680, www.montalionline.com, e-mail: montali@montalionline.com, SE).

## Near Siena

**Agriturismo Le Trappoline,** on I Sodi Farm in Chianti about a 20-minute drive east of Siena, is a recently renovated farmhouse with panoramic vistas and ample grounds for country walks. Guests stay in one of four apartments with one or two bedrooms and fully equipped kitchens (€39–80 per bedroom depending on season, must rent entire apartment, 1-week stays usually required, 2-night stays okay off-season, large pool, Località Monti Gaiole, tel. 0577-747-012, www.agrisodi.com, e-mail: info@agrisodi.com, Danilo and Gabriella Casini, some English spoken).

Family-friendly **Agriturismo Il Molinello**, in the clay hills about 30 minutes southeast of Siena, rents four apartments carved out of a medieval mill (€28–60 per bedroom, must rent entire apartment, 1-week stays usually required, off-season discounts, pets and short stays welcome off-season, organic vegetables and fruit, wine tastings, children's toys, large swimming pool, mountain bike rentals, Località Molinello, tel. 0577-704-791, cellular 335-692-5720, fax 0577-705-605, www.molinello.com, e-mail: info@molinello.com, Alessandro and Elisa Draghi SE).

**Parri Nada Farmhouse** is tucked away in the vineyards in the hills of Chianti about a 20-minute drive northeast of Siena. Luca and Elena Masti rent two rooms in their quaint, comfortable farmhouse (D-€70, 1-night rentals okay, pool and private yard, Località Santa Chiara 4, tel. & fax 0577-359-072, cellular 380-321-4681, www.farm-house.it, e-mail: info@farm-house.it).

**Poste Regie**, a B&B in Ancaiano, about 20 minutes west of Siena, rents three double rooms in a restored Tuscan villa on a country road (D-€65, includes breakfast, Via della Montagnola 68, cellular 349-475-4995, fax 0577-45387, www .posteregie.com, e-mail: reservations@posteregie.com, Beatrice Marzolla).

# THE CINQUE TERRE

The Cinque Terre (pron. CHINK-weh TAY-reh), a remote chunk of the Italian Riviera, is the traffic-free, lowbrow, underappreciated alternative to the French Riviera. There's not a museum in sight. Just sun, sea, sand (well, pebbles), wine, and pure unadulterated Italy. Enjoy the villages, swimming, hiking, and evening romance of one of God's great gifts to tourism. For a home base, choose among five villages, each of which fills a ravine with a lazy hive of human activity—calloused locals, sunburned travelers, and no Vespas. Vernazza is my favorite home base. While the Cinque Terre is now well-discovered (www.cinqueterre.it), I've never seen happier, more relaxed tourists.

The chunk of coast was first described in medieval times as "the five lands." Tiny communities grew up in the protective shadows of the castles (in feudal times, the land was the property of the castles), ready to run inside at the first hint of a Turkish "Saracen" pirate raid. Many locals were kidnapped and ransomed or sold into slavery somewhere far to the east. As the threat of pirates faded, the villages grew, with economies based on fish and grapes. Until the advent of tourism in this generation, the towns were remote. Even today, traditions survive, and each of the five villages comes with a distinct dialect and proud heritage. The region has just become a national park, and its natural and cultural wonders will be carefully preserved.

Now that the Cinque Terre is a national park, you need to pay a park entrance fee. You have two options: buying a Hiking Pass or a Cinque Terre Card. The Hiking Pass costs €3 (kids under 4 free; comes with map) and is valid for one day. The pricier Cinque Terre Card covers the park entrance fee and your transportation on the local trains (from Levanto to La Spezia, including all Cinque

Terre towns) plus the shuttle buses that run about twice an hour within each Cinque Terre town (€5.20/1 day, €12.40/3 days, €19.60/week, kids 4–12 half-price, under 4 free; includes map, brochure, and train schedule). A new pass for €13 covers hiking and local trains, shuttle buses, and boats for one day. Passes, valid until midnight of the day they expire, are sold at train stations and some trailheads. Validate your pass (unless it's a Hiking Pass) at a train station by punching it into the yellow machine.

Over the next decade, Italy has quiet plans for the Cinque Terre. For the sake of tranquillity, a new train line will be built inland for the noisy fast trains, leaving the Cinque Terre tracks for just the pokey milk-run trains.

Sadly, a few ugly, noisy Americans are giving tourism a bad name here. Even hip young locals are put off by loud, drunken tourists. They say (and I agree) that the Cinque Terre is a special place.

It deserves a special dignity. Party in Viareggio or Portofino, but be mellow in the Cinque Terre. Talk softly. Help keep it clean. In spite of the tourist crowds, it's still a real community, and we are guests.

## Planning Your Time

The ideal minimum stay is two nights and a completely uninterrupted day. The Cinque Terre is served by the milk-run train from Genoa and La Spezia. Speed demons arrive in the morning, check their bags in La Spezia, take the five-hour hike through all five towns, laze away the afternoon on the beach or rock of their choice, and zoom away on the overnight train to somewhere back in the real world. But be warned: The Cinque Terre has a strange way of messing up your momentum.

The towns are each just a few minutes apart by hourly train or boat. There's no checklist of sights or experiences; just a hike, the towns themselves, and your fondest vacation desires. Study this chapter in advance and piece together your best day, mixing hiking, swimming, trains, and a boat ride. For the best light and coolest temperatures, start your hike early.

Market days perk up the towns from 8:00 to 13:00 on Tuesday in Vernazza, Wednesday in Levanto, Thursday in Monterosso, and Friday in La Spezia.

## Getting around the Cinque Terre

**By Train:** At La Spezia, the gateway to the Cinque Terre, you'll transfer to the milk-run Cinque Terre train. There might be a TI at the station in summer. If not, skip the 20-minute hike to La Spezia's main TI at Via Mazzini near the waterfront (daily in summer 9:00–13:00 & 15:00–18:00; winter Mon–Sat 9:00–13:00 & 14:00–17:00, Sun 9:00–13:00, tel. 0187-718-997).

At the station, buy your €1.20 train ticket or Cinque Terre Card, and take the half-hour train ride into the Cinque Terre town of your choice. Once in the Cinque Terre, you'll get around the villages more cheaply by train but more scenically by boat.

Cinque Terre Train Schedule: Since the train is the Cinque Terre lifeline, many shops and restaurants post the current schedule. Try to get a photocopied schedule—it'll come in handy (comes with Cinque Terre Card).

Trains leave La Spezia for the Cinque Terre villages (last year's schedule, only daily trains listed—there are others that run only weekdays or only Sundays as well) at 7:12, 8:17, 10:08, 11:24, 12:29, 13:20, 14:29, 15:08, 16:18, 18:26, 19:26, 20:26, 21:14, 22:28, and 0:35.

Trains leave Monterosso al Mare for La Spezia (departing

Vernazza about 4 minutes later, last year's schedule) at 6:30, 8:09, 9:08, 10:12, 12:16, 13:14, 14:16, 15:08, 16:16, 17:12, 17:31, 18:22, 18:42, 19:22, 20:12, 22:29, 23:23, and 0:19.

Do not rely on these train times. Check the current posted schedule and then count on half the trains being 15 minutes or so late (unless you're late, in which case they are right on time).

To orient yourself, remember that directions are "*per* (to) Genoa" or "*per* La Spezia." Note that many trains leaving La Spezia skip them all or stop only in Monterosso. The five towns are just minutes apart by train. Know your stop. After leaving the town before your destination, go to the door to slip out before mobs pack in. Since the stations are small and the trains are long, you might get off the train deep in a tunnel, and you might need to flip open the handle of the door yourself.

The train stations should be staffed at all five Cinque Terre towns. Stations sell train tickets; the Cinque Terre Card, which covers the park entrance fee plus train and bus travel on the Cinque Terre (€5.20/1 day, €12.40/3 days, and €19.60/week); and maybe the Hiking Pass (€3 for park entrance fee).

The Cinque Terre Card, which includes the national park entry fee, is convenient, but if you're on a tight budget, you can save a bit of money by buying a one-day Hiking Pass (€3) and paying separately for your train travel.

It's cheap to buy individual train tickets to travel between the towns. Since a one-town hop costs the same as a five-town hop (€1.20) and every ticket is good for six hours with stopovers, save money and explore the region in one direction on one ticket. Stamp the ticket at the station machine before you board.

If you have a Eurailpass, don't spend one of your valuable flexi-days on the cheap Cinque Terre.

**By Boat:** From Easter to late October (through Nov if weather is good), a daily boat service connects Monterosso, Vernazza, Manarola, Riomaggiore, and Portovenere (on Sun, a boat makes an afternoon run to Portofino). Boats provide a scenic way to get from town to town and survey what you just hiked. It's also the only efficient way to visit the nearby resort of Portovenere; the alternative is a tedious train/bus connection via La Spezia. In peaceful weather, the boats are more reliable than the trains. Boats go about hourly, from 10:30 until 18:00 from Monterosso and from 9:00 until 17:10 from Portovenere (about €3 per single hop or €11.50 for an all-day pass to the Cinque Terre towns, buy tickets at little stands at each town's harbor, tel. 0187-777-727). A more frequent boat service connects Monterosso and Vernazza (about hourly to Monterosso, less frequently to Vernazza, tel. 0187-817-452). Schedules are posted at docks, harbor bars, and hotels.

## Events on the Cinque Terre

| | |
|---|---|
| **mid-May** | Monterosso: Lemon Festival |
| **June 22** | Monterosso: Corpus Domini (procession on carpet of flowers) |
| **June 24** | Riomaggiore and Monterosso: Festival in honor of St. John the Baptist |
| **June 29** | Corniglia: Festival of St. Peter and St. Paul |
| **July 20** | Vernazza: Festival for patron saint, St. Margaret |
| **Aug 10** | Manarola: Festival for patron saint, St. Lawrence |
| **Aug 15** | All towns: Ascension of Mary |
| **Sept 8** | Monterosso: Maria Nascente, or "Rising Mary" (fair with handicrafts) |

**By Foot:** A scenic trail runs along the coast, connecting each of the five Cinque Terre towns (see "Hiking," page 302). Sometimes severe rains can wash out trails, especially in winter. Ask around if the trails are open.

# VERNAZZA

With the closest thing to a natural harbor—overseen by a ruined castle and an old church—and only the occasional noisy slurping up of the train by the mountain to remind you of the modern world, Vernazza is my Cinque Terre home.

The action is at the harbor, where you'll find a kids' beach, plenty of sunning rocks, outdoor restaurants, a bar hanging on the edge of the castle (great for evening drinks), and a tailgate-party street market every Tuesday morning. In the summer, the beach becomes a soccer field, where teams fielded by local bars and restaurants provide late-night entertainment. In the dark, locals fish off the promontory, using glowing bobs that shine in the waves.

The town's 500 residents, proud of their Vernazzan heritage, brag that "Vernazza is locally owned. Portofino has sold out." Fearing the change it would bring, keep-Vernazza-small proponents stopped the construction of a major road into the town and region. Families are tight and go back centuries; several generations stay together. Leisure time is devoted to the *passeggiata*—strolling lazily together up and down the main street. Sit on a bench and study the passersby. Then explore the characteristic alleys, called *carugi*. In October, the cantinas are draped with drying grapes. In the winter, the population shrinks as many people move to more comfortable big-city apartments.

A steep five-minute hike in either direction from Vernazza gives you a classic village photo op (for the best light, head toward Corniglia in the morning, toward Monterosso in the evening). Franco's Bar, with a panoramic terrace, is at the tower on the trail toward Corniglia.

Vernazza has ATMs and two banks (in center and top of town). A shuttle bus (free with Cinque Terre Card, otherwise €1.50) runs twice an hour from the top of the main street to the parking lot.

You can buy train tickets, Hiking Passes, and Cinque Terre Cards at the Vernazza train station/TI—staffed by helpful trio Eliano, Diego, and Francesco (daily in summer 8:00–22:00, in winter 8:00–20:00, tel. 0187-812-533, a little English spoken). You can also store luggage here (€0.50/hr). Accommodations are listed near the end of this chapter.

**Internet Access and Laundry:** The slick Internet Point, run by Alberto and Isabella, is in the village center (daily 9:30–20:00, tel. 0187-812-949). The Blue Marlin bar (run by Carmen and Massimo, 6:45–24:00, open daily in Aug, otherwise closed Thu) also offers Internet access plus a self-service laundry (€4.60 wash, €4.60 dry, English instructions, buy tokens at Blue Marlin bar— note hours above, laundry open daily 8:00–22:00, Via Roma 49, tel. 0187-821-149, 30 meters, or 100 feet, below train station).

## Sights—Vernazza

▲▲**Vernazza Top-Down Orientation Walk**—Walk uphill until you hit the parking lot—with a bank, a post office, and a barrier that keeps all but service vehicles out. Vernazza's shuttle buses run locals back and forth up into the hills from this point (€1.50–2.50, free with Cinque Terre Card). The tidy new square is called Fontana Vecchia, after a long-gone fountain. Older locals remember the river filled with townswomen doing their washing. Begin your saunter downhill to the harbor.

Just before the Pension Sorriso sign, you'll see the ambulance barn (big brown wood doors) on your right. A group of volunteers is always on call for a dash to the hospital, 30 minutes away in La Spezia. Opposite that is a big empty lot next to Pension Sorriso. Like many landowners, the owner of the Sorriso had plans to ex- pand, but the government said no. The old character of these towns is carefully protected.

Across from Pension Sorriso is the honorary clubhouse for the ANPI (members of the local WWII resistance). Only five ANPI old-timers survive. Cynics consider them less than heroes. After 1943, Hitler called up Italian boys over 15. Rather than die

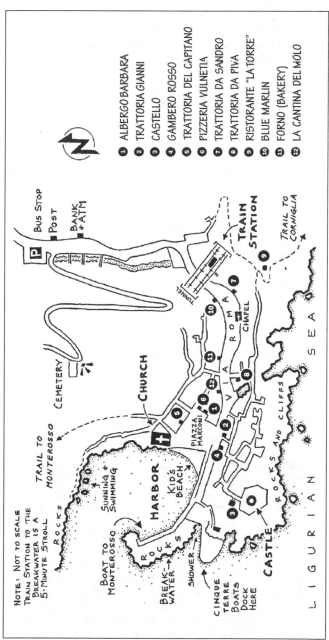

**Vernazza**

1. ALBERGO BARBARA
2. TRATTORIA GIANNI
3. CASTELLO
4. GAMBERO ROSSO
5. TRATTORIA DEL CAPITANO
6. PIZZERIA VULNETIA
7. TRATTORIA DA SANDRO
8. TRATTORIA DA PIVA
9. RISTORANTE "LA TORRE"
10. BLUE MARLIN
11. FORNO (BAKERY)
12. LA CANTINA DEL MOLO

on the front for Hitler, they escaped to the hills. Only to remain free did they become "resistance fighters."

A few steps farther along, you'll see a monument (marble plaque in wall to your left) to those killed in World War II. Not a family was spared. Study this: Soldiers *"morti in combattimento"* fought for Mussolini, some were deported to *Germania*, and "partisans" were killed later fighting against Mussolini.

The tiny monorail *trenino* (as you're facing plaque, look up on the wall on your right) is parked quietly here except in September and October, when it's busy helping locals bring down the grapes. The path to Corniglia leaves from here (it runs above plaque, starting at your left). Behind you is a tiny square playground, decorated with three millstones, which no longer grind local olives into oil. From here, Vernazza's tiny river goes underground.

In the tunnel under the railway tracks, you'll see a door marked "Croce Verde Vernazza" (Green Cross). Posted on the other side of the tunnel is the "P.A. Croce Verde Vernazza" (in a small green display case), the list of volunteers ready for ambulance duty each day of the month.

The train tracks are above you. The second set of tracks (nearer the harbor) was recently renovated to lessen the disruptive noise; locals say it made no difference.

Follow the road downhill. Until the 1950s, Vernazza's river ran open through the center of town from here to the *gelateria*.

Wandering through this main business center, you'll pass many locals doing their *vasca* (laps) past the entrepreneurial Blue Marlin bar (about the only nightspot in town) and the tiny Chapel of Santa Marta (the small stone building with iron grillwork over the window, across from Il Baretto), where Mass is celebrated only on special Sundays. Next you'll see a grocery, *gelateria*, bakery, pharmacy, another grocery, and another *gelateria*.

On the left, in front of the second *gelateria*, an arch leads to what was a beach where the river used to flow out of town. Continue on down to the harbor square and breakwater. Vernazza, with the only natural harbor of the Cinque Terre, was established as the sole place boats could pick up the fine local wine. (The town is named for a kind of wine.) Peek into the tiny street behind the Vulnetia restaurant with the commotion of arches. Vernazza's most characteristic side streets, called *carugi*, lead up from here. The trail (above the church toward Monterosso) leads to the classic view of Vernazza (best photos just before sunset).

▲▲▲**The Burned-Out Sightseer's Visual Tour of Vernazza**— Sit at the end of the harbor breakwater (perhaps with a glass of local white wine or something more interesting from Bar Capitano— borrow the glass, they don't mind), face the town, and see . . .

**The harbor:** In a moderate storm, you'd be soaked, as waves routinely crash over the *molo* (breakwater, built in 1972). The train line (to your left), constructed 130 years ago to tie a newly united Italy together, linked Turin and Genoa with Rome. A second line (hidden in a tunnel at this point) was built in the 1960s. The yellow building alongside the tracks was Vernazza's first train station. You can see the four bricked-up alcoves where people once waited for trains. Vernazza's fishing fleet is down to three small fishing boats (with the net spools); the town's restaurants buy up everything they catch. Vernazzans are more likely to own a boat than a car. In the '70s, tiny Vernazza had one of the top water polo teams in Italy, and the harbor was their "pool." Later, when a real pool was required, Vernazza dropped out of the league.

**The castle:** On the far right, the castle, which is now a grassy park with great views, still guards the town (€1, daily 10:00–18:30, from harbor, take stairs by Trattoria Gianni and follow signs to Castello restaurant, tower is a few steps beyond, see the photo and painting gallery rooms). It's called *Belforte*, or "loud screams," for the warnings it made back in pirating days. The highest umbrellas mark the recommended Castello restaurant (see "Eating," page 310). The squat tower on the water is great for a glass of wine (follow the rope to the Belforte Bar, open Wed–Mon 8:00–24:00, closed Tue, tel. 0187-812-222; inside the submarine-strength door, a photo of a major storm shows the entire tower under a wave).

**The town:** Vernazza has two halves. *Sciuiu*, on the left (literally, "flowery"), is the sunny side, and *luvegu*, on the right (literally, "dank"), is the shady side. The houses below the castle were connected by an interior arcade—ideal for fleeing attacks. The pastel colors are regulated by a commissioner of good taste in the community government. The square before you is locally famous for some of the region's finest restaurants. The big, red, central house, the 12th-century site where Genoan warships were built, used to be a kind of guardhouse.

**Above the town:** The small, round tower above the guardhouse, another part of the city fortifications, reminds us of Vernazza's importance in the Middle Ages, when it was a key ally of Genoa (whose archenemies were the other maritime republics of Pisa, Amalfi, and Venice). Franco's Bar, just behind the tower, welcomes hikers finishing, starting, or simply contemplating the Corniglia–Vernazza hike, with great town views (8:00–22:00). Vineyards fill the mountainside beyond the town. Notice the many terraces. Someone calculated that the vineyard terraces of the Cinque Terre have the same amount of stonework as the Great Wall of China. Wine production is down nowadays, as the younger residents choose less physical work. But locals still work their plots and proudly serve their family wines. A single steel train line winds up the gully behind the tower. This is for the vintner's *trenino*, the tiny service train.

**The church, school, and city hall:** Vernazza's Ligurian Gothic church, built with black stones quarried from Punta Mesco (the distant point behind you), dates from 1318. The gray-and-red house above and to the left of the spire is the local elementary school (which about 25 children attend). High school is in the "big city," La Spezia. The red building to the right of (and below) the schoolhouse is the former monastery and present city hall. Vernazza and Corniglia function as one community. Through most of the 1990s, the local government was communist. In 1999, they elected a coalition of many parties working to rise above ideologies and simply make Vernazza a better place. Finally, on the top of the hill, with the best view of all, is the town cemetery, where most locals plan to end up.

## Cinque Terre Hiking and Swimming

▲▲▲**Hiking**—All five towns are connected by good trails. Experience the area's best by hiking from one end to the other. The entire 11-kilometer (7-mile) hike can be done in about four hours, but allow five for dawdling. While you can detour to dramatic hill-top sanctuaries (one trail leads from Vernazza's cemetery uphill), I'd keep it simple by following the easy red-and-white-marked low trails between the villages. Good hiking maps (about €5, sold everywhere, not necessary for this described walk) cover the expanded version of this hike, from Portovenere through all five Cinque Terre towns to Levanto, and more serious hikes in the high country. Get local advice to make sure trails are open, particularly in spring.

Since I still get the names of the Cinque Terre towns mixed up, I think of the towns by number: Riomaggiore (town #1), Manarola (#2), Corniglia (#3), Vernazza (#4), and resorty Monterosso (#5).

**Riomaggiore–Manarola (20 min):** Facing the front of the train station in Riomaggiore (town #1), go up the stairs to the right, following signs for the Via dell' Amore. The film-gobbling promenade—wide enough for baby strollers—leads down the coast to Manarola. While there's no beach here, stairs lead down to sunbathing rocks.

**Manarola–Corniglia (45 min):** The walk from Manarola (#2) to Corniglia (#3) is a little longer and a little more rugged than that from #1 to #2.

Ask locally about the more difficult nine-kilometer (6-mile) inland hike to Volastra (shuttle buses run hourly to Volastra from Manarola, €2.50). This tiny village, perched between Manarola and Corniglia, hosts the Five-Terre wine co-op; stop by the Cantina Sociale. If you take this high road between Manarola and Corniglia, allow two hours; in return, you'll get sweeping views and a closer look at the vineyards.

**Corniglia–Vernazza (90 min):** The hike from Corniglia (#3) to Vernazza (#4)—the wildest and greenest of the coast—is most rewarding. From the Corniglia station and beach, zigzag up to the town (taking the steeper corkscrew stairs, the longer road, or the shuttle bus). Ten minutes past Corniglia toward Vernazza, you'll see the nude Guvano beach far below (see below). The trail leads past a bar and picnic tables, through lots of fragrant and flowery vegetation, and scenically into Vernazza.

**Vernazza–Monterosso (90 min):** The trail from Vernazza (#4) to Monterosso (#5) is a scenic up-and-down-a-lot trek. Trails are rough (and some readers report "very dangerous") but easy to follow. Camping at the picnic tables midway is frowned upon. The views just out of Vernazza are spectacular.

**Short Hiking Tour**—For a guided tour, consider spending a day with a hardworking and likable American student, Sean Risatti, who liked the Cinque Terre so much he moved in (€40, almost daily April–Oct, departing Monterosso at 10:00 or Vernazza at 10:45, book at cinqueterretrek@hotmail.com or at either Internet point in Monterosso: The Net or Fishnet Internet Lounge). The day—which is a great way to meet other travelers—includes a hike from Vernazza to Manarola, lots of information, special glimpses of the area, and a dinner that evening.

▲**Swimming**—Wear your walking shoes and pack your swim gear. Several of the beaches have showers (no shampoo, please) that may work better than your hotel's. Underwater sightseeing is full of fish—goggles are sold in local shops. Sea urchins can be a problem if you walk on the rocks; consider using Aquasocks or fins.

Here's a beach review:

**Riomaggiore:** The beach is rocky, but clean and peaceful. It's a two-minute walk from the harbor: face the harbor, then take the path to your left. At the La Conchiglia bar, go down the stairs to the right of the bar. Follow the path to the beach.

**Manarola:** Manarola has no sand, but the best deepwater swimming of all. The first "beach," with a shower, ladder, and wonderful rocks (with daredevil high-divers), is my favorite. The second has tougher access and no shower, but feels more remote and pristine (follow paved path around point).

**Corniglia:** This hilltop town has a rocky man-made beach below its station. It's clean and uncrowded, and the beach bar has showers, drinks, and snacks.

The nude Guvano (GOO-vah-noh) beach (between Corniglia

and Vernazza) made headlines in Italy in the 1970s, as clothed locals in a makeshift armada of dinghies and fishing boats retook their town beach. But big-city nudists still work on all-around tans in this remote setting. From the Corniglia train station, follow the road north, go over the tracks, then zigzag below the tracks, following signs to the tunnel in the cliff (walk past the *proprieta privata* sign). When you buzz the intercom, the hydraulic *Get Smart*–type door is opened from the other end. After a 15-minute hike through a cool, moist, and dimly lit unused old train tunnel, you'll emerge at the Guvano beach—and get charged €5 (€4 with this guidebook). The beach has drinking water, but no WC. A steep (free) trail leads from the beach up to the Corniglia–Vernazza trail. The crowd is Italian counterculture: pierced nipples, tattooed punks, hippie drummers in dreads, and nude exhibitionist men. The ratio of men to women is about three to two. About half the people on the pebbly beach keep their swimsuits on.

**Vernazza:** The village has a children's sandy cove, sunning rocks, and showers by the breakwater. There's a ladder on the breakwater for deepwater access. The tiny *acque pendente* (waterfall) cove which locals call their *laguna blu*, between Vernazza and Monterosso, is accessible only by small hired boat.

**Monterosso:** The town's beaches, immediately in front of the train station, are easily the Cinque Terre's best and most crowded. It's a sandy resort with everything rentable...lounge chairs, umbrellas, paddleboats, and usually even beach access. Beaches are free only where you see no umbrellas.

## Cinque Terre Towns

Note: Readers of this book fill Vernazza. For this reason, you might prefer to stay in one of these towns with fewer Americans. See "Sleeping," below, for accommodations for each town.

▲▲**Riomaggiore (town #1)**—The most substantial non-resort town of the group, Riomaggiore is a disappointment from the train station. But walk through the tunnel next to the train tracks (or ride the elevator through the hillside to the top of town), and you land in a fascinating tangle of pastel homes leaning on each other as if someone stole their crutches. There's homemade gelato at the Bar Central on main street, and, if Ivo is there, you'll feel right at home. When Ivo closes, the gang goes down to the harborside with a guitar.

Riomaggiore's **TI** is inside the train station (Mon–Fri 7:00–20:00 in winter, until 22:00 in summer, tel. 0187-920-633). The shuttle bus takes locals and tourists up and down Riomaggiore's steep main street (free with Cinque Terre Card, 2/hr, just flag it down).

**Introductory Walk:** Here's an easy loop trip through Riomaggiore that maximizes views and minimizes walking uphill.

## Riomaggiore

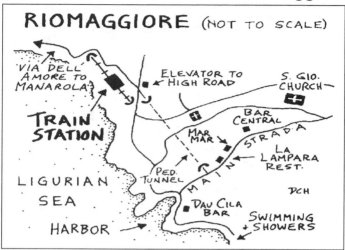

Start at the train station (if you arrive by boat, take the tunnel alongside the tracks to get to the station). From the station, take the elevator up to the top of town (€0.55, free with Cinque Terre Card, entrance at railway tunnel). At the top, go right, following the walkway—with spectacular sea views—around the cliff. Ignore the steps marked *Marina Seacoast* (harbor). Instead, continue along the path; it's a five-minute, fairly level walk to the church. Continue past the church and then take a right down the stairs to Via Columbo, Riomaggiore's main street. Stroll down Via Columbo. Just past the WC, you'll see flower boxes on the street, sometimes blocking it; these slide back electrically to let the shuttle bus get past. On your way down the hill, you'll pass colorful, small shops, including a bakery, a couple of grocery shops, and a self-service laundry (daily 7:30–19:30, next door to Edi Rooms). When Via Columbo dead-ends, on your left you'll find the stairs down to the harbor, boat dock, and a 200-meter (650-foot) trail to the beach (*spiaggia*). To your right is the tunnel, running alongside the tracks, which takes you directly to the station. Either take a train or hop a boat (from the harbor) to your next destination.

For hikes from Riomaggiore, consider the cliff-hanging trail that leads from the beach to a hilltop botanical garden (free with Cinque Terre Card) and old WWII bunkers. Another climbs scenically to the Madonna di Montenero sanctuary high above the town.

Riomaggiore also has a diving center (scuba, snorkeling, boats, Via San Giacomo, tel. 0187-920-014).

## Manarola

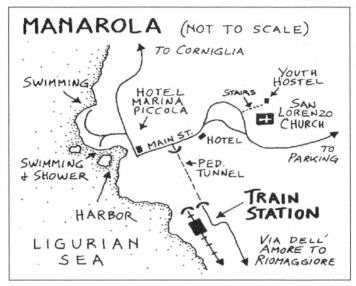

▲**Manarola (town #2)**—Like town #1, #2 is attached to its station by a 200-meter-long (650-foot) tunnel. Manarola is tiny and picturesque, a tumble of buildings bunny-hopping down its ravine to the fun-loving harbor. Notice how the I-beam crane launches the boats. Facing the harbor, look at the hillside to your right, dotted with a bar in the middle. It's Punta Bonfiglio, an entertaining park/game area/bar with the best view playground on the coast. The gate farther up the hillside is the entrance to the cemetery. From here you can get poster-perfect views of Manarola (2-min walk from the harbor on path to Corniglia).

Within Manarola, the shuttle bus takes people between main street and the parking lot (free with Cinque Terre Card, 2/hr, just flag it down). In the middle of town, across from the railway tunnel, you'll see Bar Aristide, which sometimes shows outdoor movies on weekends in August by hanging a screen over part of the tunnel entrance (closed Mon, Via Discovolo 290, tel. 0187-920-000). At the top of the town, you'll find great views, the church, and a cluster of accommodations, including a super hostel (see "Sleeping," page 310).

The simple, wooden, religious scenes that you'll likely see on the hillside are the work of local resident Mario Andreoli. Before his father died, Mario promised him he'd replace the old cross on the family's vineyard. Mario's been adding figures ever

## Corniglia

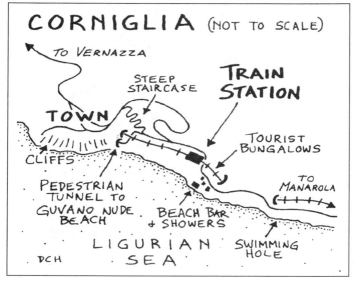

CORNIGLIA (NOT TO SCALE)

TO VERNAZZA

STEEP STAIRCASE

TRAIN STATION

TOWN

CLIFFS

TOURIST BUNGALOWS

PEDESTRIAN TUNNEL TO GUVANO NUDE BEACH

BEACH BAR & SHOWERS

TO MANAROLA

LIGURIAN SEA

SWIMMING HOLE

DCH

since. After recovering from a rare illness, he redoubled his efforts. The scenes, which do change occasionally (a sheep here, an apostle there), are sometimes left up year-round. On religious holidays, everything's lit up: the Nativity, the Last Supper, the Crucifixion, the Resurrection, and more.

▲▲**Corniglia (town #3)**—From the station, a footpath zigzags up nearly 400 stairs to the only town of the five not on water. Take the bus (€1.50, free with Cinque Terre Card, 2/hr). Originally settled by a Roman farmer who named it for his mother, Cornelia (how Corniglia is pronounced), the town and its ancient residents produced a wine so famous that vases found at Pompeii touted its virtues. Today, wine is still its lifeblood. Follow the pungent smell of ripe grapes into an alley cellar and get a local to let you dip a straw into a keg. Remote and less visited, Corniglia has fewer tourists, cooler temperatures, a windy belvedere (on its promontory), a few restaurants, and plenty of private rooms for rent (ask at any bar or shop). Past the train station (toward Manarola) you'll find Corniglia's beach. The well-hung Guvano beach is in the opposite direction (toward Vernazza).

▲▲▲**Vernazza (town #4)**—See beginning of chapter.

▲▲**Monterosso al Mare (town #5)**—This is a resort with cars, hotels, rentable beach umbrellas, crowds, and a thriving nightlife. The town is split into the old and new, connected by a tunnel.

# Monterosso

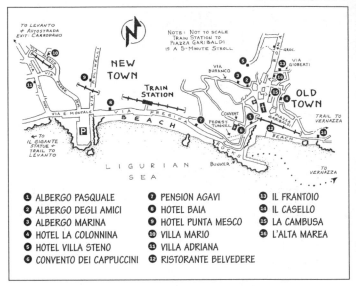

● ALBERGO PASQUALE
● ALBERGO DEGLI AMICI
● ALBERGO MARINA
● HOTEL LA COLONNINA
● HOTEL VILLA STENO
● CONVENTO DEI CAPPUCCINI
● PENSION AGAVI
● HOTEL BAIA
● HOTEL PUNTA MESCO
● VILLA MARIO
● VILLA ADRIANA
● RISTORANTE BELVEDERE
● IL FRANTOIO
● IL CASELLO
● LA CAMBUSA
● L'ALTA MAREA

The train station is in the new town, along with the Cinque Terre park office (*Parco Nazionale delle Cinque Terre*, daily 8:00–22:00, shorter hours in winter, in the station, tel. 0187-817-059, e-mail: parconazionale5terre@libero.it); the **TI** (daily Mon–Sat 10:00–12:45 & 14:15–19:00, Sun 10:00–12:45, closed Nov–Easter, exit station and go left a few doors, tel. 0187-817-506); several recommended accommodations; and a statue—*Il Gigante*. This 14-meter-tall (46-foot) statue, which once held a trident, looks as if it were hewn from the rocky cliff, but it's made of reinforced concrete, and dates from the beginning of the 20th century.

Along the waterfront, in the new part of town or the break-water of the old town, look for all the towns of the Cinque Terre strung out along the coast.

Monterosso's old town contains Old World charm, small crooked streets, and plenty of Internet access.

**Internet Access:** Kate's Fishnet Internet Lounge—a welcoming, well-run center for local information—has several computers and digital camera photo services (daily in summer 10:00–20:00 & 21:30–24:00, in winter Mon 10:00–13:00, Tue–Sun 10:00–13:00 & 16:00–20:00, Via Roma 17, can book accommodations, tel. 0187-817-373, www.fishnet.it). A few steps farther into the alley is The Net, offering 10 high-speed computers, classical music if Renato's on duty, and a free cuppa joe to patrons. Renato and Enzo happily provide information on the Cinque Terre and book accommodations, guides, and scuba diving (Via Vittorio Emanuele 55, tel. 0187-817-288, www.cinqueterrenet.com).

**Boats and Buses:** From the old town harbor, boats run nearly hourly to Vernazza and points beyond.

The shuttle buses that run along the waterfront connect the old and new towns with outlying areas. You can catch the bus at the parking lot (€10.50/day) at the north end of the new town, the train station, or the old town (€1, free with Cinque Terre Card, 1–3/hr, runs 8:00–16:00, 10-min ride between old and new towns).

**Short Hike:** You can easily stroll the short tunnel between the new and old towns, but hikers prefer the trail. It's like a mini–Cinque Terre trail, combining scenery and greenery. Heading from the train station to the old town, take the path to the right of the tunnel entrance. The path leads to views of a German WWII bunker below on the rocks (worth seeing, but not worth climbing down to).

Continuing on the path gets you into the old town. Or, at the point where you see the bunker, take the path up to the top of the hill (where you'll see a statue of St. Francis), and up farther still through the woods to reach a gate (marked *Convento e Chiesa Cappuccini*) leading to a church with a Van Dyck painting of the Crucifixion (accommodations next to church, see "Sleeping," below). You're a world away from the resort town below.

A trail to the right of the church leads up to the cemetery; appreciate its flowers, photos, and your beating heart. Backtrack to the St. Francis statue, and take the trail down into the old town. (Reversing this, if you're going from the old town to the new, take the trail to the right of the tunnel entrance; go right on Zii di Frati to see the church, or continue straight to get to the new town). Allow a total of 30 minutes if you include the church and cemetery.

**Nightlife:** Young travelers and night owls gather at Fast Bar on Via Roma in the old town to mix travel tales and beer (sandwiches and snacks served until midnight, closes 1:30). For nightlife with a sea view, wander up to Il Casello by the *bocce* courts on the road toward Vernazza; its outdoor tables are sandwiched between the old town beaches (Wed–Mon 11:30–2:00, closed Tue, tel. 0187-818-330). Many of the little bars and *enotecas* (wine bars) in the old town stay open late during the summer months—wander the backstreets until you find your favorite.

## Cinque Terre Cuisine 101

A few menu tips: *Accuighe* (pron. ah-CHOO-gay) are anchovies, a local specialty—always served the day they're caught. If you've always hated anchovies (the harsh, cured-in-salt American kind), try them fresh here. *Tegame alla Vernazza* is the most typical main course in Vernazza: anchovies, potatoes, tomatoes, white wine, oil, and herbs. *Pansotti* is ravioli with ricotta and spinach, often served with a hazelnut or walnut sauce … delightful and filling. While antipasto is cheese and salami in Tuscany, here you'll get *antipasti di mare*, a plate of mixed fruits of the sea and a fine way to start a meal. For many, splitting this and a pasta dish is plenty. Try the fun local dessert: *torte della nonna* (grandmother's cake), with a glass of *sciacchetrà* for dunking (see "Wine," below).

▲▲**Pesto**—This is the birthplace of pesto. Basil, which loves the temperate Ligurian climate, is mixed with cheese (half *Parmigiano* cow cheese and half pecorino sheep cheese), garlic, olive oil, and pine nuts, and then poured over pasta. Try it on spaghetti, *trenette*, or *trofie* (made of flour with a bit of potato, designed specifically for pesto). Many also like pesto lasagna. If you become addicted, small jars of pesto are sold in the local grocery stores (you can take it home or spread it on focaccia here).

▲▲**Wine**—The *vino delle Cinque Terre*, respected throughout Italy, flows cheap and easy throughout the region. It is white—great with the local seafood. D.O.C. is the mark of top quality. Red wine is better elsewhere. For a sweet dessert wine, the local *sciacchetrà* wine is worth the splurge (€2.60 per glass, often served with a cookie). While 10 kilos of grapes yield seven liters of local wine, *sciacchetrà* is made from near-raisins, and 10 kilos of grapes make only 1.5 liters of *sciacchetrà*. The word means "push and pull" … push in lots of grapes, pull out the best wine. If your room is up a lot of steps, be warned: *Sciacchetrà* is 18 percent alcohol, while regular wine is only 11 percent. In the cool, calm evening, sit on the Vernazza breakwater with a glass of wine and watch the phosphorescence in the waves.

## Sleeping and Eating on the Cinque Terre
**(€1 = about $1, country code: 39)**

Sleep Code: **S** = Single, **D** = Double/Twin, **T** = Triple, **Q** = Quad, **b** = bathroom, **s** = shower only, **CC** = Credit Cards accepted, **no CC** = Credit Cards not accepted, **SE** = Speaks English, **NSE** = No English. Breakfast is included only in real hotels.

To help you sort easily through these listings, I've divided the rooms into three categories based on the price for a standard double room with bath:

**Higher Priced**—Most rooms more than €100.

**Moderately Priced**—Most rooms €100 or less.

**Lower Priced**—Most rooms €50 or less.

If you're trying to avoid my readers, stay away from Vernazza. Monterosso is a good choice for the younger crowd (more nightlife) and rich, sun-worshiping softies (who prefer firm reservations for hotels with private bathrooms). Wine-lovers and mountain goats like Corniglia. Sophisticated Italians and Germans choose Manarola. Travelers who show up without reservations enjoy Riomaggiore for its easy room-booking services.

While the Cinque Terre is too rugged for the mobs that ravage the Spanish and French coasts, it's popular with Italians, Germans, and Americans in the know. Hotels charge the most and are packed on Easter, in August, and on summer Fridays and Saturdays. August weekends are worst. But €60 doubles abound throughout the year. Outside of August weekends, you can land a comfortable €65 double room in a private home on any day by just arriving in town (ideally by noon) and asking around at bars and restaurants, or simply by approaching locals on the street. This seems scary, but it's true.

For the best value, visit three private rooms and snare the best. Going direct cuts out a middleman and softens prices. Plan on paying cash. Private rooms are generally bigger and more comfortable than those offered by the pensions and they offer the same privacy as a hotel room.

If you want the security of a reservation, make it long in advance for a hotel (small places generally don't take reservations made weeks ahead). If you don't get a reply to your faxed request for a room, assume the place is fully booked.

### Sleeping in Vernazza
### (zip code: 19018)

Vernazza, the essence of the Cinque Terre, is my favorite. There are two recommended pensions and piles of private rooms for rent.

To reserve ahead, call, fax, or e-mail. As a last resort, write: address letters to 19018 Vernazza, Cinque Terre, La Spezia. If you arrive without a reservation, you can call these places from the pay phone at the bottom of the stairs at the train station. Or drop by the nearest shop or bar; most locals know someone who rents rooms.

Anywhere you stay here will require some climbing. Night noises can be a problem if you're near the station.

A new parking lot (€1/hour or €8/day) and a hardworking shuttle service make driving to Vernazza a reasonable option for drivers with nerves of steel. The little shuttle bus runs twice an hour (generally with helpful, English-speaking Beppe behind the wheel).

Usually, when a price range is listed, the lower price is charged during winter (roughly Nov–March) and the higher price the rest of the year. The first two are pensions (see map on page 299 for location), the rest are private rooms.

## MODERATELY PRICED

**Trattoria Gianni** rents 23 small rooms just under the castle. The funky ones are artfully decorated à la shipwreck and are up lots of tight, winding, spiral stairs, and most have tiny balconies and grand views. The new, comfy rooms lack views but have modern bathrooms and a super-scenic, cliff-hanger private garden. Marisa, who rarely smiles at anyone (not just you), requires a two-night minimum and check-in before 16:00 (S-€35, D-€58, sinks and bathrooms down the hall; Db-€70, Tb-€86, CC but 10 percent discount for cash, Piazza Marconi 5, closed Jan–Feb, tel. & fax 0187-812-228, tel. 0187-821-003, e-mail: info@giannifranzi.it, a little English spoken). Pick up your keys at Trattoria Gianni's restaurant/reception on the harbor square and hike up dozens of stairs to #41 (funky, *con vista mare*) or #47 (new, *nuovo*) at the top. (Note: My tour company books this place 50 nights of the season.) Telephone three days in advance and leave your first name and time of arrival.

## LOWER PRICED

**Albergo Barbara**, on the harbor square, is run by kindly Giuseppe and his Swiss wife, Patricia. Their nine clean, modern rooms share three public showers and WCs (S-€36–€47 depending on season, D without view-€43, D with small view-€45, D with big view-€55, bunky family Q-€67, 2-night stay preferred, call before 17:00 on the day of arrival or lose your room, loads of stairs, fans, closed Dec–Jan, Piazza Marconi 30, call to reserve instead of fax, tel. & fax 0187-812-398, cellular 338-793-3261, SE). The two big doubles on the main floor come with grand harbor views and are the best value (top-floor doubles have small windows and small views). The office is on the top floor of the big, red, vacant-looking building facing the harbor.

## *Private Rooms* (Affitta Camere)

These are the best values in Vernazza. The town is honeycombed year-round with pleasant, rentable private rooms and apartments with kitchens (cheap for families). They are usually reluctant to reserve rooms far in advance. It's easiest to call a day or two ahead or simply show up in the morning and look around. The rooms cost about €45–60 for a double, depending on the view, season, and plumbing. Some have killer views, most have lots of stairs and cost the same as a small dark place on a back lane over the train tracks. Little or no English is spoken at these places. Any main-street business has a line on rooms for rent.

## MODERATELY PRICED

**Franca Maria** rents two sharp, comfortable rooms overlooking the harbor square (Db-€42–72, Qb-€83–105 depending on season, the 2 side-by-side doubles can turn into a quad, Piazza Marconi 30, tel. 0187-812-002, fax 0187-812-956, son Giovanni's e-mail: metalgearsolid@inwind.it—he has rooms to rent as well). It's just a few steps up from the harbor—a rarity in vertical Vernazza.

**Martina Callo** rents four fine, lofty rooms overlooking the square, up plenty of steps near the church tower (Db-€50–60, Qb-€93–103; room #1-Qb with harbor view, room #2-Qb huge family room with no view, room #3-Db with grand view terrace, room #4-roomy Db with no view; heating in winter; ring bell at Piazza Marconi 26, tel. & fax 0187-812-365, e-mail: roomartina@supereva.it).

**Affitta Camere da Anna-Maria** offers five pleasant rooms up spiral staircases (Db-€65–67 with view or terrace—the terrace room is best, Via Carattino 64, turn left at pharmacy, climb Via Carattino to #64, tel. 0187-821-082).

**Tonino Basso** rents four super, clean, modern rooms—each with its own computer for free Internet access—near the post office, in the only building in Vernazza that has an elevator. Rooms come with a private bath but no views (Sb-€60, Db-€70, Tb-€100, Qb-€110, CC, tel. 0187-821-264, cellular 335-269-436, fax 0187-821-260, e-mail: toninobasso@libero.it; when you arrive, call cellular number from train station—phones at bottom of stairs—and Tonino will meet you; or the Gambero Rosso restaurant at harbor can find him—but then you'll have to backtrack to get to his rooms).

**Giuseppina's Villa**, a cozy apartment with a low-ceilinged loft, has one window, no view, and a kitchen. The woman at the grocery store nearest the harbor (with *Salumi e Formaggi* on the awning) can check if it's available (€25 per person, Via S. Giovanni Battista 7, only a short climb from harbor, tel. 0187-812-026). Giuseppina also rents a double room up the street (no view, but has a garden, terrace, and kitchen) and her sister owns **Villa Antonia,** two newly remodeled rooms with a shared bath on the main drag (Db-€75, tel. 0187-812-343).

**Nicolina** rents four decent rooms: a large one with a view, two overlooking Vernazza's main drag, and one without any view. Inquire at Pizzeria Vulnetia on the harbor square or reserve in advance by phone (Db-€55-65, Qb with terrace and view-€127, Piazza Marconi 29, tel. & fax 0187-821-193, Frederica).

**Armanda** rents a one-room apartment without a view near the Castello (€62, Piazza Marconi 15, tel. 0187-812-218, cellular 347-306-4760).

**Moggia Manuela** rents rooms at the top of town near the old fountain (Db-€62, Qb-€110, cheaper Nov–mid-April, Via Gavino 22, tel. 0187-812-397, cellular 333-416-374).

**Giuliano Basso** rents three fine rooms that share a view

balcony (Db–€65, CC, open year-round, above train station, direction: Corniglia, take a right before Sorriso's, then take left fork, 5-min walk to harbor, cellular 333-341-4792, www .cdh.it/giuliano, e-mail: giuliano@cdh.it).

**Annamaria Galleno** rents a double room with bath, without a view (€52–60, tel. 0187-821-133).

**Rosa Vitali** rents two apartments, one for three people (has terrace), the other (for 4 people) has windows overlooking the main street (€70–110 a night, tel. 0187-821-181, cellular 340-267-5009).

**LOWER PRICED**
**Egi Rooms,** run by friendly Egidio Verduschi, offers rooms right in the center of the main drag. The common area includes a partial kitchen (no stove but fridge and sink), comfy living room, and shared bath (€25–40 per person depending on season, Via Visconti 9, call a day ahead to reserve, cellular 380-258-1712, e-mail: egidioverduschi@libero.it).

## Eating in Vernazza

If you enjoy Italian cuisine, Vernazza's restaurants are worth the splurge. All take pride in their cooking and have similar prices. Wander around at about 20:00 and compare the ambience.

The **Castello**, run by gracious and English-speaking Monica, her husband Massimo, kind Mario, and the rest of her family, serves great food with great views, just under the castle (Thu–Tue 12:00–15:00 for lunch, 15:00–19:00 for drinks and snacks, 19:00–22:00 for dinner, closed Wed and Nov–April, tel. 0187-812-296).

Four fine places fill the harborfront with happy eaters: **Gambero Rosso**, considered Vernazza's best restaurant, feels classy and costs only a few euros more than the others (Tue–Sun 12:00–15:00 & 19:00–22:00, closed Mon and Nov–March, CC, Piazza Marconi 7, tel. 0187-812-265). **Trattoria del Capitano** might serve the best food for the money (Thu–Tue 12:00–15:00 & 19:00–22:30, closed Wed except in Aug, closed Dec–Jan, CC, tel. 0187-812-201, Paolo SE). **Trattoria Gianni** is also good, especially for seafood (daily 12:30–15:00 & 19:00–22:00 in July–Aug, otherwise closed Wed). **Ristorante Pizzeria Vulnetia** serves regional specialties and the best harborside pizza (Tue–Sun 12:00–16:00 & 18:30–23:00, closed Mon, Piazza Marconi 29, tel. 0187-821-193).

**Trattoria da Sandro**, on the main drag, mixes Genovese and Ligurian cuisine with friendly service, and can be a peaceful alternative to the harborside scene (Wed–Mon 12:00–15:00 & 19:00–22:00, closed Tue, CC, just below train station, Via Roma 60, tel. 0187-812-223, Gabriella SE). The more offbeat and intimate

**Trattoria da Piva** may come with late-night guitar strumming (Tue–Sun 12:00–14:30 & 19:00–22:00, closed Mon, Via Carattino 6, around corner from pharmacy, tel. 0187-812-194).

For basic grub, a grand view, and perfect peace, hike to Franco's **Ristorante "La Torre"** for a dinner at sunset (Wed–Mon 20:00–21:30, sometimes closed Tue, on trail toward Corniglia, tel. 0187-821-082).

The main street is creatively determining tourists' needs and filling them. The **Blue Marlin** bar offers a good selection of sandwiches, salads, and *bruschetta*. Try the **Forno** bakery for good focaccia and veggie tarts, and the several bars for sandwiches and pizza by the slice. Grocery stores make inexpensive sandwiches to order (Mon–Sat 8:00–13:00 & 17:00–19:30, Sun 7:30–13:00). The town's two *gelaterias* are good. **La Cantina del Molo**, the wine shop, will uncork the bottle you buy and supply cups to go (daily 10:30–20:00, until 22:00 in summer, owner makes 5 of the wines, tasting possible). Most harborside bars will let you take your glass on a breakwater stroll.

*Breakfast:* Locals take breakfast about as seriously as flossing. A cappuccino and a pastry or a piece of focaccia does it. The two harborfront bars offer the most ambience (you can walk out with the cup, grab a view picnic bench, and return the cup when you're done). The bakery opens early, offering freshly made focaccia. The Blue Marlin serves a special €6.20 breakfast: ham and cheese focaccia, an assortment of fresh local pastries, juice, and cappuccino (Fri–Wed 6:45–24:00, closed Thu; open daily in Aug; just below station, tel. 0187-821-149).

## Sleeping in Riomaggiore
### (zip code: 19017)

Riomaggiore has organized its private room scene better than its neighbors. Several agencies within a few meters of each other on the main drag (with regular office hours, English-speaking staff, and e-mail addresses) manage a corral of local rooms for rent. Expect lots of stairs. The town's shuttle bus service makes getting in and out of town from the parking lot easier.

### Room-Finding Services
**MODERATELY PRICED**

**Edi's Rooms** rents five fine rooms and 12 apartments—half have views (Db-€52–80, Qb-€104 depending on view, season, and number of people, CC, office open 8:00–20:00 in summer, otherwise 9:00–13:00 & 15:00–19:00, Via Colombo 111, tel. & fax 0187-920-325, tel. 0187-760-842, e-mail: edi-vesigna@iol.it).

**Mar Mar Rooms**, run by Mario Franceschetti, has 12 pleasant rooms, 10 apartments and a mini-hostel (dorm bed-€21, Db apartments-€55–100, seaview rooms maybe €60–80, bunky family deals, can request kitchen and balcony, CC, Internet access and small self-service laundry in office, 30 meters, or 100 feet, above train tracks on main drag next to Lampara restaurant, Via Malborghetto 4, tel. & fax 0187-920-932, e-mail: marmar@5terre.com). The same people run the recommended Albergo Caribana (below) using the same e-mail address; specify what you're interested in when you write. Mar Mar also rents kayaks (double kayaks €8/hr, cheaper by the half day).

**Luciano and Roberto Fazioli** loosely run five apartments, nine rooms, and a basic 11-bed mini-hostel (dorm bed-€15.50–21, D-€50–70, Db-€50–83, apartments-€21–70 per person, open at whim—making it difficult to check in and out, Via Colombo 94, tel. 0187-920-904, e-mail: robertofazioli@libero.it).

## Private Rooms and Hotels
### HIGHER PRICED
For a real hotel, consider **Villa Argentina**. It's on the top ridge of town (15-min walk uphill from "downtown"), with 15 crisply clean, modern rooms, fine balconies (for 9 rooms), and sea views. While this is a good choice for drivers, the little bus that shuttles people (and their luggage) between the top and bottom of town makes this hotel a possibility for train travelers (Db-€120, includes breakfast, no CC, Via de Gasperi 37, go through tunnel from station, wait for bus or walk 15 min uphill, then take a left at parking booth, tel. 0187-920-213, fax 0187-920-213, e-mail: villaargentina@libero.it).

### MODERATELY PRICED
**Michielini Anna** rents four clean, attractive apartments in the center with kitchens and no views (€52/2 people, €93/3 people, €104/4 people mid-April–Sept, less during low season, CC to reserve but please pay cash, cheaper for longer stays, 2 nights preferred June–Sept, across from Bar Central at Colombo 143, ring bell to open door; to call friendly Daniela who speaks good English, call 0187-920-950 or cellular 328-131-1032; for solo-Italiano-speaking mother, try tel. & fax 0187-920-411; e-mail: anna.michielini@tin.it, another e-mail: michielinis@yahoo.it).

**Albergo Caribana** has six modern rooms with views and shared terraces. At the edge of town, it's a five-minute walk to the center. The easy parking makes this especially appealing to drivers (Db-€64–85, depending on season, includes breakfast, Via Sanctuario 114, tel. 0187-920-773, tel. & fax 0187-920-932, e-mail: marmar@5terre.com). The same people run Mar Mar Rooms, a room-finding service (see above), using the same e-mail address; specify what you want when you write.

## Eating in Riomaggiore

**Ristorante La Lampara** serves a *frutti di mare* pizza, *trenete al pesto*, and the aromatic *spaghetti al cartoccio*—spaghetti with mixed seafood cooked in foil (€13 tourist *menu*, Wed–Mon 12:00–15:30 & 18:00–24:00, closed Tue, CC, on Via Colombo just above tracks, tel. 0187-920-120). Groceries and delis (such as Da Simone) on Via Colombo sell food to go, including pizza slices; have your picnic at the harbor.

**Bar Central**, run by friendly Ivo and Alberto, is a good stop for breakfast, cheeseburgers, Internet access, and live music (sometimes in summer). Ivo lived in San Francisco, fills his bar with only the best San Franciscan rock, speaks great English, and can even help you find a room. During the day, Bar Central is a shaded place to relax with other travelers. At night, it offers the only action in town (daily 7:30–1:00, closed Mon in winter only, Via Colombo 144, tel. 0187-920-208, e-mail: barcentr@tin.it). And there's prizewinning gelato next door.

While the late-night fun is at Ivo's Bar Central, take a walk down to the harborside **Dau Cila** bar (10:30–0:30, closed Tue) for jazz, nets, and mellow *limoncino*—a drink of lemon juice, sugar, and pure alcohol (a.k.a. *limoncello* elsewhere in Italy).

## Sleeping In Manarola
### (zip code: 19010)

Manarola has plenty of private rooms. Ask in bars and restaurants. Otherwise, you'll find a modern three-star place halfway up the main drag, a cluster of great values around the church at the peaceful top of town (a 5-min hike above the train tracks), and a salty place on the harbor. The town's handy shuttle bus service makes getting to and from your car easier.

**MODERATELY PRICED**

Up the hill, the utterly normal **Albergo ca' d'Andrean** is quiet, comfortable, modern, and very hotelesque, with 10 big, sunny rooms and a cool garden oasis complete with lemon trees (Sb-€60, Db-€80, breakfast-€6, closed Nov, Via A. Discovolo 101, tel. 0187-920-040, fax 0187-920-452, www.cadandrean.it, e-mail: cadandrean@libero.it, Simone SE).

**Affitta Camere de Baranin** rents eight newly renovated, airy, refreshing rooms (Db-€53–73, Db with view and breakfast-€85, CC to reserve but please pay cash, Internet access; climb stairway against wall beyond church square—with your back to the church, stairway is at 7:00, follow sign to Trattoria dal Billy, Via Rollandi 29, tel. & fax 0187-920-595, www.baranin.com, Sara and Silvia SE).

**La Torretta** has four compact apartments with kitchens, five doubles, and one quad, all attractively designed by the young, English-speaking architect/manager Gabriele Baldini (student Db-€26–36, Db-€52–72, Db apartment-€57–77, Qb-€83–124, prices vary with season, reserve with CC, cancellation fee, views, big garden; with your back to church, it's at 10:00—look left across the square toward the sea, Piazza della Chiesa, Vico Volto 14, tel. & fax 0187-920-327, also rents a Tuscan villa, see www.cinqueterre .net/torretta, e-mail: torretta@cdh.it).

**Marina Piccola** has 10 bright, modern rooms on the water, so they figure a warm welcome is unnecessary (Db-€80 for 1-day stays, otherwise half pension required at €72 per person, CC, Via allo Scalo 16, tel. 0187-920-103, fax 0187-920-966, www .hotelmarinapiccola.com).

**LOWER PRICED**

**Casa Capellini** rents four fine rooms; one has a view balcony, another a 360-degree terrace (D-€42, €36 for 2 or more nights; Db-€47, €42 for 2 or more nights; the *alta camera* on the top, with a kitchen, private terrace, and knockout view-€57, €52 for 2 or more nights; 2 doors down the hill from the church, with your back to the church, it's at 2:00, Via Ettore Cozzani 12, tel. 0187-920-823 or 0187-736-765, e-mail: casa.capellini@tin.it, NSE).

**Ostello 5-Terre,** Manarola's modern and well-run hostel, stands like a Monopoly hotel behind the church square. It's smart to reserve at least two weeks in advance in high season (one week in off-season). You book with your credit card number; if you cancel with less than three days' notice, you'll be charged for one night. This is not a party hostel; quiet is greatly appreciated (May–Sept: beds-€19, Qb-€76, new Db rooms planned for 2003; off-season: beds-€16, Qb-€64, closed early Jan–mid-Feb, CC, 48 beds in 4- to 6-bed rooms, not coed except for couples and families, office closed 13:00–17:00, rooms closed 10:00–17:00, curfew–1:00, off-season: office and rooms closed until 16:00 and curfew at 24:00, open to anyone of any age, laundry, safes, phone cards, Internet access, book exchange, elevator, optional €3.50 breakfast and €4.50–6 dinner, great roof terrace and sunset views, Via B. Riccobaldi 21, tel. 0187-920-215, fax 0187-920-218, www.cinqueterre.net/ostello, e-mail: ostello@cdh.it). They rent bikes, kayaks, and snorkeling gear.

## Sleeping in Corniglia
### (zip code: 19010)

Perched high above the sea on a hilltop, Corniglia has plenty of private rooms (generally Db-€52). To get to the town from the station, catch the shuttle bus or take a 15-minute uphill hike.

If you hike, choose between a long road or lots of stairs. At the top of the stairs, turn left to reach the town (if you've taken the road, just stay on the road). The main drag is Via Fieschi, stretching to the tip of the promontory and its viewpoint park.

## MODERATELY PRICED
For this first listing, take the road (rather than the stairs) up from the station. **Domenico Spora** has eight apartments scattered throughout town, all with views, terraces, and private bath (Db-€65, Qb-€110, Via Villa 19, tel. 0187-812-293, NSE). Her place is about three-fourths of the way up the hill from the station.

For the rest of the listings, if you've taken the stairs up from the station, turn left at the top of the stairs and walk up Via Fieschi.

At the main square, you'll see **La Lanterna** bar, which rents 10 sleepable rooms in town, some with a view (D-€50, Db-€60, also has 6 new rooms in Comeneco a 30-min walk away—better for drivers, tel. 0187-812-291, Via Fieschi 72, www.5terre.com).

**Louisa Cristiana** rents a great apartment with three doubles and a big comfy living room/kitchen with a view terrace on the tiny soccer court near the end of Via Fieschi at the top of the town (Db-€52, grand apartment for 2 people-€103, for 4 people-€114, for 6 people-€130, cheaper in winter, Via Fieschi 215, call English-speaking daughter Cristiana at tel. 0187-812-236—she works at Bar Matteo on Via Fieschi, below main square; also tel. & fax 0187-812-345; daughter rents small apartment for €57).

**Villa Cecio,** more like a hotel, has eight rooms on the outskirts of town (Db-€75, views, on main road 200 meters, or 650 feet, toward Vernazza, tel. 0187-812-038).

## LOWER PRICED
**Pelligrini,** on a quiet side street, offers three comfortable rooms (one with a balcony) that share two baths and a terrace (D-€42; going up Via Fieschi, take a left at Via Solferino, then go right, left, and left to find #34; tel. 0187-812-184 or 0187-821-176).

**Villa Sandra** has five good doubles (D-€47—2 have terraces, Db-€52) and an apartment (Db-€62–68; Via Fieschi 212, tel. & fax 0187-812-384, www.cinqueterre-laposada.com, e-mail: la_posada@libero.it).

## Sleeping in Monterosso
### (zip code: 19016)
Monterosso al Mare, the most beach-resorty of the five Cinque Terre towns, offers maximum comfort and ease. There are plenty of hotels and rentable beach umbrellas, shops, and cars. The TI (Pro Loco) can give you a list of €30-per-person doubles (pricier

for a single) in a private home (Mon–Sat 10:00–12:45 & 14:15–19:00, Sun 10:00–12:45; exiting station, TI is to your left; tel. 0187-817-506) or check with either of the Internet cafés in town.

Monterosso is 30 minutes off the freeway (exit: Carrodano). Parking is easy in the huge, beachfront guarded lot (€10.50/day).

Recommended hotels are listed for the old town and the new town (connected by a tunnel), with a convent-run place in between. To locate hotels, see the map on page 308. My favorite is the Hotel Villa Steno in the old town. To get to the old town from the station, exit left, walk along the waterfront, and go through the tunnel.

## Sleeping in the Old Town

### HIGHER PRICED

The lovingly managed **Hotel Villa Steno** features great view balconies, private gardens off some rooms, air-conditioning, and the friendly help of English-speaking Matteo. Of his 16 rooms, 12 have view balconies (Sb-€85, Db-€130, Tb-€150, Qb-€170, includes hearty buffet breakfast, CC, €10 discount per room per night if you pay cash and show this book, Internet access, self-service laundry—guests only, 10-min hike from train station to the top of old town at Via Roma 109, tel. 0187-817-028 or 0187-818-336, fax 0187-817-354, www.pasini.com, e-mail: steno@pasini.com). Readers get a free Cinque Terre info packet and a glass of the local sweet wine, *sciacchetrà*, when they check in—ask. The Steno has a tiny parking lot (free, but call to reserve a spot).

**Albergo Pasquale** is a modern, comfortable place, run by the same family who owns Hotel Villa Steno (see listing above). It's just a few steps from the beach, boat dock, tunnel entrance (to new town), and train tracks. The air-conditioning minimizes any train noise (Sb-€85, Db-€130, Tb-€150, Qb-€170, includes breakfast, CC, €10 discount per room per night if you pay cash and show this book, readers get a free glass of the local sweet wine—*sciacchetrà*—at check-in, same-day laundry service, Via Fegina 4, tel. 0187-817-550 or 0187-817-477, fax 0187-817-056, e-mail: pasquale@pasini.com, Felicita and Marco SE).

The next two places, next door to each other on a quiet street, both require half pension during peak season: the fancy **Albergo degli Amici** (40 modern rooms, Db-€90–124, breakfast extra, Db with half pension-€150—required July–Aug, CC, no views from rooms, peaceful above-it-all view garden with "sun beds"—lawn chairs with movable sun shades, Via Buranco 36, tel. 0187-817-544, fax 0187-817-424, www.cinqueterre.it/hotel_amici) and the less fancy **Albergo Marina** (23 decent rooms, Db with required half pension-€97–126, CC, elevator, air-con, garden

with lemon trees, next door at Via Buranco 40, tel. & fax 0187-817-242 or 0187-817-613, www.hotelmarinacinqueterre.it).
To get to the Amici and Marina from the old town harbor, go to the left of the arcaded building with the bell tower and turn left after a block; for the next listing go to the right of the arcaded building up Via Roma.

**MODERATELY PRICED**
**Hotel La Colonnina**, a comfy, modern place on a sleepy side street, takes reservations in advance only for three-night stays. For a shorter stay, just call a day or two ahead to see if they have space (Db-€95, no breakfast, elevator, garden, rooftop terrace, Via Zuecca 6, tel. 0187-817-439). In the old town by the train tracks, look for the playground and the square with a statue of Garibaldi; Via Zuecca is directly behind him (the hotel is one block up, to the right).

## Sleeping between the Old and New Towns

**MODERATELY PRICED**
The religious **Convento dei Cappuccini** rents 15 spartan rooms on the hill above the tunnel connecting the old and new parts of town. The terrace, overlooking the garden and a long stretch of coastline, has a tremendous panoramic view. It's a steep hike on foot, or take a taxi (€8) to the cemetery 200 meters/650 feet) away—go around or walk through cemetery to reach the convent. Its door is to the left of the church (S-€34, D-€68, Db-€78, all twins, includes breakfast, dinner extra and optional, reserve ahead, must send a deposit of 30 percent—personal check OK, 19016 Monterosso, tel. 0187-817-531, e-mail: monterosso.convento @libero.it, truly NSE, but e-mail in English is OK). To hike to the convent from the station (15 min), follow the recommended walk listed in Cinque Terre Towns/Monterosso, above.

## Sleeping in the New Town
Turn right leaving the station for the following listings.

**HIGHER PRICED**
The central, waterfront **Hotel Baia** has appealing, high-ceilinged rooms, but the staff is rude (Db-€100–140, includes breakfast, CC, slow elevator, balconies, request view—same price, Via Fegina 88, tel. 0187-817-512, fax 0187-818-322).
   **Hotel Punta Mesco** has 17 new, modern rooms (Db-€104, CC, discount with cash, no views, free parking, exit right from station, take first right, Via Molinelli 35, tel. 0187-817-495, www .hotelpuntamesco.it).

**Villa Adriana**, run by brusque Austrian nuns, has 55 decent, clean rooms divided between a 19th-century villa and an adjacent, modern annex. With a strict 23:00 curfew, a lofty setting (up off the street with a tropical garden as its front yard), and a religious, institutional atmosphere, it's peaceful (Sb-€65, Db-€130, half pension required June–mid-Sept: Sb-€75, Db-€140, CC, double and twins available, some views, attached chapel, elevator, parking, exit right from station, walk along waterfront, turn right at Via IV Novembre, 300 meters, or 985 feet, off beach, Via IV Novembre 23, reception at back of building, tel. 0187-818-109, fax 0187-818-128, SE).

**MODERATELY PRICED**
**Villa Mario**, good for backpackers, has three basic rooms with a view terrace and a squawky bird (Db-€62–72, exit right from station, take second right, walk 5 min uphill, Via Padre Semeria 28, tel. & fax 0187-818-030).

Turn left out of the station for **Pension Agavi,** which has 10 bright, airy rooms (Sb-€47, Db-€85, refrigerators, Fegina 30, tel. 0187-817-171, cellular 336-258-467, fax 0187-818-264, www.paginegialle.it/hotelagavi, e-mail: hotel.agavi@libero.it, spunky Hillary SE).

### Eating in Monterosso's Old Town
**Ristorante Belvedere** is a good bet for good value. Their *Amphora di Pesce*—mixed seafood stew (€42/2 people minimum)—is inspiring (Wed–Mon 12:00–14:30 & 19:00–22:00, closed Tue, CC, right on the harbor, across from Albergo Pasquale, tel. 0187-817-033).

**La Cambusa** serves up traditional Ligurian cuisine to hungry locals and tourists alike (Tue–Sun 12:00–14:30 & 18:45–22:30, closed Mon except July–Aug, Via Garibaldi 10, tel. 0187-817-690).

Lots of shops and bakeries sell pizza and focaccia for an easy picnic at the beach. **L'Alta Marea** offers a specialty fish ravioli, the catch of the day, and huge crocks of fresh, steamed mussels (Thu–Tue 12:00–15:00 & 18:30–22:30, closed Wed, Via Roma 54, tel. 0187-817-170). **Il Frantoio** makes tasty pizza to go (Wed–Fri 9:00–14:00 & 16:00–20:00, closed Thu, Via Gioberti 1, just off Via Roma, tel. 0187-818-333). For a quick salad or sandwich near the beach, try **Il Casello,** next to the *bocce* court on the trail to Vernazza (Wed–Mon 11:30–2:00, closed Tue, tel. 0187-818-330).

## Transportation Connections—Cinque Terre
The five towns of the Cinque Terre are on a milk-run train line described earlier in this chapter. Hourly trains connect each town with the others, La Spezia, and Genoa. While a few

of the milk-run trains go to more distant points (Milan or Pisa), it's faster to change in La Spezia or Monterosso to a bigger train. Train info: Monterosso tel. 0187-817-458 or 848-888-088 (automated in Italian).

**From La Spezia by train to: Rome** (10/day, 4 hrs), **Pisa** (hrly, 1 hr, direction: Livorno, Rome, Salerno, Naples, etc.), **Florence** (hrly, 2.5 hrs, change at Pisa), **Milan** (hrly, 3 hrs direct or 4 hrs with change in Genoa), **Venice** (2 direct 6-hr trains/day).

**From Monterosso by train to: Venice** (2/day, 6 hrs), **Milan** (3/day, 3 hrs), **Genova** (9/day, 1.25 hrs), **Turin** (5/day, 3.25 hrs), **Pisa** (3/day, 1.5 hrs), **Sestri Levante** (hrly, 15 min, most trains to Genova stop here), **La Spezia** (nearly hrly, 20 min), **Levanto** (nearly hrly, 6 min).

## Driving in the Cinque Terre

**Milan to the Cinque Terre (210 km/130 miles):** Drivers speed south by autostrada from Milan, skirt Genoa, and drive along some of Italy's most scenic and impressive freeways toward the port of La Spezia. The road via Parma is faster but less scenic.

All of the Cinque Terre towns except Corniglia have a parking lot and a shuttle bus to get you into town. Monterosso's guarded beachfront lot fills only on August weekends (€10.50/day).

To drive to Monterosso or Vernazza, exit the autostrada at Uscita Carrodano west of La Spezia (note that the drive down to Vernazza is scenic, narrow, and treacherous). To drive to Rio-maggiore, leave the freeway at La Spezia.

You can park your car near the train stations in La Spezia or Levanto (the first town past Monterosso). Confirm that parking is OK and leave nothing inside to steal. In La Spezia, the garage near the station can store your car for about €13 per day.

## NEAR THE CINQUE TERRE

La Spezia, a gateway to the Cinque Terre, is simply a place to stay if you can't find a room in the Cinque Terre (20–30 min away by train). Carrara is a quickie for marble-lovers who are driving between Pisa and La Spezia. The picturesque village of Portovenere, near La Spezia, has scenic boat connections with Cinque Terre towns. Levanto has a long beach and a scenic trail to Monterosso (2.5-hour hike, or easier, 6 min by train). Sestri Levante, on a narrow peninsula flanked by two beaches, is for sunseekers (15 min by train from Cinque Terre). Santa Margherita Ligure (75 min by train from the Cinque Terre) is more of a real town, with actual sights, beaches, and easy connections with Portofino by trail, bus, or boat.

## Cinque Terre Area

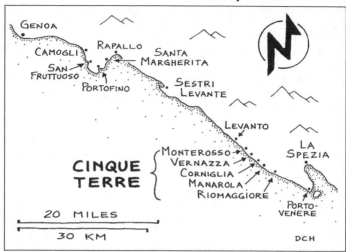

# LA SPEZIA

When all else fails, you can stay in a noisy, bigger town such as La Spezia. While just a quick train ride away from the fanciful Five Terre, La Spezia feels like work-a-day Italy.

The TI is a 20-minute walk from the station, near the waterfront (Mon–Sat 9:00–13:00 & 15:00–18:00, Sun 9:00–13:00, Viale Mazzini 45, tel. 0187-770-900). There's usually a kiosk branch at the station in summer. If not, skip it.

Sights are slim. On Friday mornings, a huge open-air market sprawls along Via Garibaldi (about 6 blocks from station). The pedestrian zone on Via del Prione to the gardens along the harbor makes a pleasant stroll. The **Museo Amedeo Lia** displays Italian paintings from the 13th to 18th centuries (€6.20, Tue–Sun 10:00–18:00, closed Mon, last entry 30 min before closing, no photos allowed, 10-min walk from station at Via Prione 234, tel. 0187-731-100, www.castagna.it/mal).

## Sleeping in La Spezia
### (€1 = about $1, country code: 39)

The first four hotels are within a five-minute walk from the station. The last two are for drivers only. Only the first has air-conditioning.

**HIGHER PRICED**

The grand, old, but newly restored **Hotel Firenze e Continentale** has 68 rooms with all the classy comforts (Sb-€69–80,

Db-€115, maybe €93 in slow time, includes buffet breakfast, CC, air-con, double-paned windows, some non-smoking rooms, elevator, parking-€13/day, Via Paleocapa 7, tel. 0187-713-200, fax 0187 714 930, www.hotelfirenzecontinentale.it, SE).

## MODERATELY PRICED

**Hotel Venezia**, across the street from Hotel Firenze e Continentale, has a plain lobby, but its 19 rooms are modern (Db-€62–87, CC, elevator, Via Paleocapa 10, tel. & fax 0187-733-465, NSE).

**Albergo Parma** is tight, bright, and bleachy clean, with 33 rooms (D-€44, Db-€57, CC, located just below station, down the stairs, Via Fiume 143, tel. 0187-743-010, fax 0187-743-240, some English spoken).

**Hotel Astoria**, with 56 decent rooms, has a combination lobby and breakfast room as large as a school cafeteria. It's a fine backup if the hotels nearer the station are full (Db-€73–103, CC, includes breakfast, elevator, Via Roma 139, take street left of Albergo Parma—Via Milano, go 3 blocks and turn left on Via Roma, tel. 0187-714-655, fax 0187-714-425, e-mail: hotelastoria@tiscali.it).

**Il Gelsomino**, for drivers only, is a small B&B in the hills above La Spezia (3 rooms, D-€62, Db-€75, Tb-€85, views, Via dei Viseggi 9, tel. & fax 0187-704-201, run by Carla Massi).

**Santa Maria del Mare Monastery**, a last resort for drivers, rents 100 comfortable rooms high above La Spezia in a scenic but institutional setting (Db-€78, Castellazzo Stra, tel. 0187-700-365 or 0187-711-332, e-mail: mare@tamnet.it).

# CARRARA

Perhaps the world's most famous marble quarries are just east of La Spezia in Carrara. Michelangelo himself traveled to these valleys to pick out the marble that he would work into his masterpieces. The towns of the region are dominated by marble. The quarries higher up are vast digs that dwarf their hardworking trucks and machinery. The Carrara museum allows visitors to trace the story of marble-cutting here from pre-Roman times until today. For a guided visit, Sara Paolini is excellent (€78/half-day tour, tel. 0585-632-617, cellular 347-888-3833, e-mail: casara00@hotmail.com). She is accustomed to meeting and joining drivers at the Carrara freeway exit.

# PORTOVENERE

While the gritty port of La Spezia offers little in the way of redeeming touristic value, the nearby resort of Portovenere is enchanting. This Cinque Terre–esque village clings to a rocky promontory jutting into the sea, protecting the harbor from the crashing waves. On the harbor, next to colorful bobbing boats, a row of restaurants—perfect for alfresco dining—feature local specialities such as *trenette* pasta with pesto and spaghetti *frutti di mare*.

Local boats take you on excursions to nearby islands or over to Lerici, the town across the bay. Lord Byron swam to Lerici (not recommended). Hardy hikers enjoy the two-hour (or more) hike to Riomaggiore, the nearest Cinque Terre town.

Portovenere is an easy day trip from the Cinque Terre by boat (Easter–late Oct, nearly hrly 10:00–18:00), or take the bus from La Spezia (25 min). In peak season, buses shuttle drivers from the parking lot just outside Portovenere to the harborside square.

**Sleeping:** If you forgot your yacht, try **Albergo Il Genio**, in the building where the main street hits the piazza (Db-€62–83, Piazza Bastreri 8, tel. 0187-790-611). If your *vita* is feeling *dolce*, consider **Grand Hotel Portovenere** (from €108 for viewless double off-season to €375 for view suite in summer with half pension, tel. 0187-792-610, fax 0187-790-661, e-mail: ghp@village.it).

# LEVANTO

Graced with a long, sandy beach, Levanto is packed in summer. The rest of the year, it's just a small, sleepy town, with less colorful charm and fewer tourists than the Cinque Terre towns. Levanto has a new section (gridded-street plan) and a twisty old town (bisected by a modern street), plus a few pedestrian streets, a castle (not open), and a scenic, no-wimps-allowed hike to Monterosso (1.5 hrs).

For an energetic day trip, hike from Monterosso to Levanto, play in the surf (or collapse on the beach), take a look at the town, and catch the boat or the train back home.

From the Levanto train station to the TI, it's a 10-minute walk (head down the stairs in front of the station, cross the bridge, then follow Corso Roma to Piazza Mazzini). Drivers can park free at the train station (there's also a free lot north of TI, but it's near a pay lot—confirm you're in the free one). At the TI, pick up a map (Mon–Sat 9:00–13:00 & 15:00–18:00, Sun 9:00–13:00, longer hours in summer, shorter in winter, tel. 0187-808-125).

The beach is just two blocks away from the TI. During the summer, half the beach is free *(libero)*, the other half is broken up into private sections that require an admission fee. Off-season, roughly October through May, when the sea is free, you can stroll the entire beach. Facing the harbor, the boat dock is to your far left and the diving center is at your far right (you can rent boats in summer at either place).

The old town, several blocks from the TI and beach, clusters around Piazza del Popolo. Until 10 years ago, the town market *(mercato)* was held at the 13th-century loggia in the square. Explore the backstreets. To get to the trailhead to Monterosso:

From Piazza del Popolo, head uphill to the striped church, Chiesa di S. Andrea (with your back to the loggia, go straight ahead—across the square and up Via Don Emanuele Toso to the church). From the church courtyard, follow the sign to the *castello* (castle), go around the castle, and turn left. You'll see the sign for Punta Mesco, the rugged tip of the peninsula. From here you can hike up (1.5 hrs to Monterosso), or—if you have second thoughts—hike down, taking the stairs to the beach. You'll end up near the dock, where you can catch the boat for the Cinque Terre towns.

For picnic supplies, try Levanto's modern, covered *mercato* (Mon–Sat 9:00–13:00, closed Sun, fish and produce market, between train station and TI; the street it's on—only a decade old—hasn't yet been officially named). On Wednesday morning, an open-air market fills the street in front of the *mercato*.

To get to the Cinque Terre, take the train (nearly hrly, 6 min to Monterosso) or the boat (2/day, stops at every Cinque Terre town except Corniglia, Easter–Oct).

# Sleeping in Levanto
## (€1 = about $1, country code: 39, zip code: 19015)
In the popular beach town, a number of hotels require you to take half pension (lunch or dinner) in summer. A self-service **laundry** is at Piazza Staglieno 38 (daily 8:30–23:00).

## MODERATELY PRICED
**Ristorante la Loggia** has eight pleasant rooms perched above the old loggia on Piazza del Popolo (Db-€47–62, includes breakfast, half pension not required, air-con, request balcony, quieter rooms in back, apartment available, attached restaurant, Piazza del Popolo 7, tel. & fax 0187-808-107, www.locandalaloggia.it).

**Albergo Primavera** has 17 comfortable rooms—10 with terraces but no views—just a half block from the beach (Db-€98, Db with half pension required June–Aug-€134, buffet breakfast, closed Nov–Jan, CC, Via Cairoli 5, a block from TI, tel. 0187-808-023, fax 0187-801-588, e-mail: info@primaverahotel .com, friendly staff speaks a little English).

**Hotel Europa**, also a block from the TI, is a good bet, with 22 decent, well-maintained rooms (Db-€88, Db with half pension required April–Aug-€164, CC, roof terrace, elevator, Via Dante Alighieri 41, tel. 0187-808-126, fax 0187-808-594, e-mail: albeurop@tin.it).

## LOWER PRICED
*Hostel:* The **Ostello Ospitalia del Mare** offers 67 beds, bright rooms, Internet access, and a terrace in a well-built building in

the old town (beds-€19–28 in 2-, 4-, 6-, and 8-bed rooms with private bath, includes breakfast and sheets, CC, anyone welcome, not coed except for couples and families, no curfew, office hours daily 8:00–13:00 & 14:30–23:00, Via San Nicolo 1, tel. 0187-802-562, fax 0187-803-696, www.ospitaliadelmare.it, SE).

## Eating in Levanto

**Totano Blu** offers Ligurian specialties and pizzas at reasonable prices in the old town (Fri–Wed 12:00–14:00 & 19:00–22:00, Thu 19:00–22:00, Via Molinelli 10/12, tel. 0187-808-714).
**Osteria Tumelin** is a bit spendier, but has great fresh seafood and ambience (Fri–Wed 12:00–14:30 & 19:00–22:30, closed Thu, Via D. Grillo, across street from loggia, tel. 0187-808-379).

**Antico Caffe' Roma,** a favorite among locals for affordable seafood and pasta, has alfresco dining in the back (Wed–Mon 12:00–15:00 & 19:00–22:00, closed Tue, Piazza Staglieno 10, tel. 0187-808-514).

*Focaccerie, rosticcerie,* and delis with take-out pasta abound on Via D. Alighieri. **Polleria** sells roasted chicken and potatoes to go (Tue–Sun 8:00–12:30 & 16:00–20:00, closed Mon, Via Cairoli 3). **Focacceria il Falcone** has a great selection of focaccia with different toppings (Tue–Sun 9:30–20:00, closed Mon, Via Cairoli 19). Piazza C. Colombo, with its benches and sea view, makes an excellent picnic site. For a shadier setting, lay out your spread on a bench near Piazza Staglieno.

For dessert, sample **Il Penguino Gelateria** on Piazza Staglieno 38 (Thu–Tue 8:00–late, closed Wed) or **Il Porticciolo Gelateria** at the end of Via Cairoli in Piazzeta Marina (closed Mon).

## SESTRI LEVANTE

This peninsular town is squeezed as skinny as a hot dog between its two beaches. The pedestrian-friendly Corso Columbo, which runs down the middle of the peninsula, is lined with shops selling take-away pizza, pastries, and beach paraphernalia. The rocky, forested bluff at the end of the peninsula is inaccessible to the public (it's the huge backyard of the fancy Hotel Castelli). Market day is Saturday at Piazza Aldo Moro (8:00–13:00).

The best, quick visit from the station (luggage storage-€2.60—if the office is closed, ask at the newsstand) starts with a five-minute walk to the TI to get a map (May–Sept Mon–Sat 9:30–12:30 & 15:30–18:30, Sun 9:30–12:30 & 16:30–19:30, Oct–April closes at 17:30 and on Sun; go straight out of station on Via Roma, turn left at fountain in park, TI at next square—Piazza S. Antonio 10, tel. 0185-457-011). Roads fan out from Piazza S. Antonio like spokes. From the TI, you're one "spoke"

away from Corso Columbo (to the left of Bermuda Bar) that runs
up the peninsula. Stroll this street until nearly the end (about
5 min). Just before you get to the large white church at the end,
turn off for either beach (the free public beach, Baia del Silencio,
is on your left). Or head uphill behind the church to the Hotel
Castelli for a drink at their view café (so-so view, reasonably priced
drinks, café is at end of parking lot to your right). On the way up
the hill you'll pass the evocative arches of a ruined chapel, bombed
during World War II, and left as a memorial.

Most people are here for the sun. The beaches are named
after the bays *(baias)* they border. The bigger beach, Baia delle
Favole, is divided up much of the year (May–Sept) into sections
that you pay to enter. The fees, which can soar up to €24 in
August, generally include chairs, umbrellas, and fewer crowds.
There are several small free sections: at the ends and in the middle
(look for *libere* signs). The town's other beach, Baia del Silencio, is
narrow, virtually all free, and packed, providing a good chance to
see Italian families at play. There isn't much more to do than
unroll a beach towel and join in.

You're in good company. Hans Christian Andersen enjoyed
his visit here in the mid-1800s, writing, "What a fabulous evening
I spent in Sestri Levante!" One of the bays—Baia delle Favole—
is named in his honor (*favole* means fairy tale). The last week of
May is a street festival, culminating in a ceremony for locals who
write the best fairy tales (4 prizes for 4 age groups, from pre-
kindergarten to adult). The "Oscar" awards are little mermaids.
The small mermaid curled on the edge of the fountain (behind
the TI) is another nod to the beloved Danish storyteller.

Even Hans found Sestri Levante easy to reach by train, just
15 minutes away from Monterosso (hourly connections with
Monterosso, nearly hourly with other Cinque Terre towns).

## Sleeping and Eating in Sestri Levante
### (€1 = about $1, country code: 39, zip code: 16039)

**HIGHER PRICED**
**Hotel Due Mari** has three stars, 49 fine rooms, and a rooftop
terrace with a super view of both beaches. Ideally, reserve well in
advance (Db-€95–130 depending on view, Db with half pension
required July–Aug-€136–172, CC, some air-con, elevator, garden,
swimming pool with heated seawater, take Corso Columbo to
the end, hotel is behind church, free parking first day—then
€8/day, Vico del Coro 18, tel. 0185-42695, fax 0185-42698,
www.duemarihotel.it, e-mail: hotelduemari@inwind.it, SE).

**Hotel Helvetia**, overlooking Baia del Silencio, is another good three-star bet, with 24 bright rooms, a large view terrace, and a peaceful atmosphere (Db-€114–160 depending on view/balcony, includes breakfast, CC, air-con, elevator, parking-€10/day, from Corso Columbo turn left on Palestro and angle left at square, Via Cappuccini 43, tel. 0185-41175, fax 0185-457-216, www.rainbownet.it/helvetia, SE).

### MODERATELY PRICED

**Hotel Elisabetta**, less central and cheaper, has 38 comfortable rooms on a busy street at the end of Baia delle Favole, a block from the beach (Db-€70–80 depending on season, half pension available but not required, CC, ask for quieter room in back, Via Novara 7, walk straight out of station, then turn right at park, 12-min walk, tel. 0185-41128, fax 0185-487-206, e-mail: albergoelisabetta@libero.it, NSE).

**Hotel dei Fiori** has 15 basic rooms across Piazza S. Antonio from the TI office (Db-€55–68, includes breakfast, CC, double-paned windows, request a *tranquillo* room in back, Via Nazionale 12, tel. & fax 0185-41147, NSE).

## Eating in Sestri Levante

At **L'Osteria Mattana**, where everyone shares long tables, you can mix with locals while enjoying traditional cuisine (Tue–Sun 19:30–22:30, also Fri–Sun 12:30–14:30, closed Mon, Via XXV Aprile 26, take Corso Columbo from TI, turns into XXV Aprile, restaurant on right, tel. 0185-457-633). **Polpo Mario** is classier but affordable, with a good people-watching location on the main drag (Tue–Sun 12:00–14:30 & 19:30–22:30, closed Mon, Via XXV Aprile 163, tel. 0185-480-203). **Ristorante Previna** has good seafood and pizzas at fair prices (closed Wed, Piazza della Repubblica 23, tel. 0185-482-397).

## SANTA MARGHERITA LIGURE

If you need the movie star's Riviera, park your yacht at Portofino. Or you can settle down in the nearby and more personable Santa Margherita Ligure (15 min by bus from Portofino and 75 min by train from the Cinque Terre). While Portofino's velour allure is tarnished by snobby residents and a nonstop traffic jam in peak season, Santa Margherita tumbles easily downhill from its train station. The town has a fun resort character and a breezy promenade.

On a quick day trip, walk the beach promenade, see the small old town, and catch the bus (or boat) to Portofino to see what all the fuss is about. With more time, Santa Margherita makes a fine overnight stop.

**Tourist Information:** Pick up a map at the TI (daily 9:00–

12:30 & 15:00–19:30, in winter Mon–Sat 9:00–12:30 & 14:30–17:30, closed Sun, Via XXV Aprile 2b, tel. 0185-287-485, www.apttigullio.liguria.it).

**Arrival by Train:** To get to the city center from the station, take the stairs marked *Mare* (Sea) down to the harbor. The harbor-front promenade is as wide as the skimpy beach. (The real beaches, which are pebbly, are a 10-min walk farther on, past the port.)

To get to the pedestrian-friendly old town and the TI, take a right at Piazza Veneto (with the roundabout, flags, and park) onto Largo Antonio Giusti. For the TI, angle left on Via XXV Aprile. For the old town (a block off Piazza Veneto), head toward the TI, but turn left on Via Torino, which opens almost immediately onto Piazza Caprera, a square with a church and fruit vendors (Mon–Sat morn) in the midst of pedestrian streets.

Day-trippers: If the train station still doesn't store luggage, you might be able to check it at Hotel Terminus, next to the station (€5/day).

**Internet Access: Internet Point** gives readers with this book a free additional 30 minutes (€5.20/30 min, daily 9:00–21:00, Via Guinchetto 39, off Piazza Mazzini, tel. 0185-293-092, run by owners of recommended Hotel Fasce). **Papiluc's Bar** offers Internet access until 2:00 (see "Eating in Santa Margarita Ligure," page 334).

## Sights—Santa Margherita Ligure

**Villa Durazzo**—If you need a sight more than a beach or hike, wander through this 17th-century villa. It's the distinctive (garish?), green-shuttered, rust-colored building atop the hill, a couple of blocks inland from Piazza Martiri della Libertà. The building has changed aristocratic hands several times, and, in the early 20th century, even served as a grand hotel. It was sold to the city in 1973. The interior has some period furniture, several grand pianos, chandeliers, and paintings strewn with cupids on the walls and ceilings. Even with the furniture, it's a bit stark. You can tour it on your own with an English info sheet, or, if you call ahead—even on the same day—you might snare a tour in English (€5.20, or €6.20 with tour, summer Tue–Sun 9:00–17:00, winter Tue–Sun 9:30–16:00, closed Mon, WC in adjacent building, tel. 0185-205-449).

The **garden** surrounding the villa is laced with dirt trails and stone-mosaic paths. The greenery, unkempt and evocative at the base of the hill, is tamed on top, with manicured hedges, statuary, and a wide mosaic terrace offering a view of the sea and marina. Bring a picnic and find a bench (free, daily 9:00–19:00 in summer, until 17:00 in winter).

**Castle**—The small castle overlooking the harbor, just off Piazza Martiri della Libertà, is open if there's an exhibit; check with the

TI. If the castle is closed, walk uphill just past the castle to the church for the view from its terrace.

**Markets**—Around 16:00 on weekdays, fishing boats dock at the fish market to unload their catch, which is then sold to waiting customers. The market—Mercato del Pesce—is the rust-colored building with arches and columns on Via Marconi, on the harbor, just past the castle. The **open-air market**, a commotion of clothes and produce, is held every Friday morning on Corso Matteotti (between the castle and harbor).

## Side-Trip to Portofino

Santa Margherita Ligure, with its aristocratic architecture, hints of old money, whereas Portofino, with its sleek shops, reeks of the new. Fortunately, a few pizzerias, bars, and grocery shops are mixed in with Portofino's jewelry shops, art galleries, and clothing boutiques, making the town bearable. The *piccolo* harbor, classic Italian architecture, and wooded peninsula can even turn Portofino into an appealing package, if you look past the glitzy wrapping.

Portofino's **TI** is downhill from the bus stop, on your right (daily in summer 10:30–13:30 & 14:00–19:30, in winter Tue–Sun 10:30–13:30 & 14:30–17:30, closed Mon, Via Roma 35, tel. 0185-269-024). Pick up a free town map and a rudimentary hiking map. Trails are signed well enough.

For hikers, the best thing about Portofino is leaving it. Options include the well-trodden path that leads out to the light-house at the point (20 min, nonstop views; the medieval castle en route may still be under restoration in 2003); the pedestrian prom-enade to Paraggi (20 min, parallels main road, ends at ritzy beach where it's easy to catch the bus back to Santa Margherita Ligure); the trail to Santa Margherita Ligure (1 hr); and the trail to San Fruttuoso Abbey (2.5 hrs, steep at beginning and end).

The 11th-century **San Fruttuoso Abbey,** accessible only by foot or boat (from Portofino or Santa Margherita) isn't the main attraction. The intriguing draw is a statue of Christ of the Abyss (Cristo degli Abissi), 18 meters (60 feet) underwater. Boats run from the abbey to the Christ, where you can look down to see him, his arms outstretched, reaching upward.

**Getting to Portofino from Santa Margherita:** Portofino is an easy day trip by bus, boat, or foot.

Catch **bus** #82 from Santa Margherita's train station or at bus stops along the harbor (€1, 2–3/hr, 15 min, buy tickets at bar at station, at bus kiosk at Piazza Veneto—open daily 7:10–19:40, or at any shop that displays a *Biglietti Bus* sign).

The **boat** makes the trip with more class and without the traffic jams (€3.60 one-way, €6 round-trip, hrly in summer,

2/day in spring and fall, 2/day only on Sun in winter, dock is off Piazza Martiri della Libertà, a 2-min walk from Piazza Veneto, call to confirm or pick up schedule from TI, tel. 0185-284-670, www.traghettiportofino.it); the boats run between Rapallo and the San Fruttuoso Abbey, stopping in between at Santa Margherita Ligure and Portofino.

Hikers call the one-hour **Santa Margherita–Portofino hike** one of the best on the Riviera (5 km, or 3 miles, start at Via Maragliano, several blocks past the castle).

## Sleeping in Santa Margherita Ligure
(€1 = about $1, country code: 39, zip code: 16038)

**HIGHER PRICED**

For a room with a view, try **Hotel Laurin.** All of its 43 rooms face the sea, most have terraces, and there's a heated pool and sundeck on the third floor (Sb-€75–105, Db-€119–155 depending on season, air-con, double-paned windows, elevator, Lungomare G. Marconi 3, past the castle, about a 15-min walk from station, CC, tel. 0185-289-971, fax 0185-285-709, www.laurinhotel.it, e-mail: info@laurinhotel.it).

**Hotel Jolanda** is two blocks east of the TI and 100 meters (330 feet) from the sea (Db-€122, superior Db-€130, CC, Via Luisito Costa 6, tel. 0185-287-512 or 0185-287-513, fax 0185-284-763, www.hoteljolanda.it, e-mail: desk@hoteljolanda.it).

**MODERATELY PRICED**

**Hotel Fasce** is a hardworking place with 18 bright rooms and a happy clientele (Sb-€77, Db-€92, Tb-€118, Qb-€138, includes breakfast, happy hour welcome drink, CC, free round-trip train tickets to Cinque Terre for 3-night stays, parking-€16/day, free bikes, English newspapers, roof garden, laundry service-€16, a 10-min walk from the station at Via Bozzo 3, taxi from station costs about €10, tel. 0185-286-435, fax 0185-283-580, www.hotelfasce.it, run enthusiastically by Jane Fasce—an Englishwoman—and her husband, Aristide).

**Hotel Fiorina**, with 55 airy rooms decorated in a light-and-dark color scheme, is on a busy square with quieter rooms in the back. It's family-run with pride and care (Db-€89 with breakfast, Db-€74 without breakfast, half pension possible, CC, fans in every room, sun terrace—no view, Piazza Mazzini 26, 2 blocks inland from pedestrian Piazza Caprera, tel. 0185-287-517, fax 0185-281-855, www.paginegialle.it/hfiorina, e-mail: fiorinasml@libero.it, SE).

At **Hotel Nuova Riviera**, a stately old villa, the Sabini family offers 12 non-smoking rooms (Db-€90, Tb-€116, Qb-€145, discount of €5 per day if you pay cash, includes breakfast, CC, mother Angela cooks dinner—optional, fans in every room, some balconies, Internet access, free parking—first-come, first-served, peaceful garden, 10-min walk from station; walking or driving, follow signs to hospital, on Piazza Mazzini see hotel signs, Via Belvedere 10, tel. & fax 0185-287-403, www.nuovariviera.com, e-mail: info@nuovariviera.com, pleasant daughter Cristina and temperamental son Giancarlo SE). Their annex is cheaper (3 nights preferred, D-€62, T-€88, Q-€104, 4 rooms share 2 bathrooms, includes breakfast, cash only). Note that if you cancel your reservations, you'll be billed for one night. They also rent a nearby apartment by the week (for 2 people-€530, for 4-€830, deposit required, cellular 329-982-2689, e-mail: info@villinomatilde.com).

### By the Train Station
These three hotels, close to the train station, all come with train noise.

**HIGHER PRICED**

**Nuovo Hotel Garden** is tucked away down a side street. From its 31 comfortable rooms to its restaurant, the hotel is high-quality (Db-€58–114 depending on season, CC, terrace, bar, double-paned windows on train side, Via Zara 13, a block from train station—instead of taking the stairs down to harbor, face stairs and go right, tel. 0185-285-398, fax 0185-290-439, www.nuovohotelgarden.com, SE).

**MODERATELY PRICED**

**Hotel Conte Verde,** next door to Nuovo Hotel Garden, rents 33 rooms (some newly remodeled) of varying quality and price. Ask if a room with a big terrace is available (Sb-€50–99, D-€52–78, Db-€70–155, price depends on season and size, includes breakfast, exercise room and hydromassage, CC, garden, 6 free bikes, big public areas, parking-€11/day—call ahead to reserve, Via Zara 1, tel. 0185-287-139, fax 0185-284-211, e-mail: info@hotelconteverde.com, SE).

**Hotel Terminus**, with 24 rooms right at the station, works hard to keep its customers satisfied (Db-€87, includes huge breakfast, CC, terrace, good meals, some view rooms, triple-paned windows, ask for room away from tracks, tel. 0185-286-121, fax 0185-282-546, Angelo SE).

## Eating in Santa Margherita Ligure
**Ristorante il Faro**, which serves good seafood and more, is atmospheric, with rows of wine bottles lining its wainscoted walls (€25 and €30 *menus*, à la carte options, lunch from 12:20, dinner

from 19:20, closed Tue, 2 blocks inland from port, Via Maragliano 24a, tel. 0185-286-867).

**Ristorante "A' Lampara,"** on the same street, is the locals' favorite for affordable Genovese cuisine. Try their specialty fish ravioli—*ravioli di pesce* (Fri–Wed 12:00–14:00 & 19:30–22:00, closed Thu, Via Maragliano 33, tel. 0185-288-926).

**Ristorante il Nostromo,** cheaper and more central, offers a €17 menu plus à la carte options (closed Tue, Via dell' Arco 6, a block off Piazza Veneto, take Via Gramsi and turn inland on Via dell' Arco, tel. 0185-281-390). **Papiluc's Bar,** a rare Internet café that's actually a café, is on the same street, a few doors down (Fri–Wed 6:30–2:00, closed Thu, Via dell' Arco 20, tel. 0185-282-580). **Dal Baffo,** nearby, is a good pizzeria (Wed–Mon 12:00–15:00 & 18:30–1:00, closed Tue, Corso Matteotti 56, tel. 0185-288-987).

**Da Pezzi** is a cheap and cheerful greasy spoon packed with locals munching *farinata* (thin focaccia made from chickpeas) at the bar and enjoying pesto and fresh fish in the dining room (Sun–Fri 11:45–14:00 & 18:00–21:00, closed Sat, on Via Cavour, no reservations accepted).

The Doro Centry **supermarket** is just off Piazza Mazzini (Mon–Sat 8:30–12:30 & 15:30–19:30, Sun 8:30–12:30, Dogali 34, across from Hotel Fiorina).

## Transportation Connections— Santa Margherita Ligure

**By train to: Sestri Levante** (hrly, 30 min), **Monterosso** (hrly, 1 hr), **La Spezia** (hrly, 1.5 hrs), **Pisa** (3/day, 2.25 hrs, more with transfer in La Spezia), **Genoa** (hrly, 45–60 min), **Milan** (4/day, 2 hrs, more with transfer in Genoa), **Ventimiglia** (2/day, 3.5 hrs, to French border, change in Genoa), **Venice** (2/day, 5.25 hrs). For **Florence,** you'll transfer in La Spezia or Pisa or both (allow 3.5–4 hrs).

# MILAN
## (MILANO)

For every church in Rome, there's a bank in Milan. Italy's second city and the capital of Lombardy, Milan is a hardworking, fashion-conscious, time-is-money city of 1.5 million. Milan is a melting pot of people and history. Its industriousness may come from the Teutonic blood of its original inhabitants, the Lombards, or from the region's Austrian heritage. Milan is Italy's industrial, banking, TV, publishing, and convention capital. The economic success of modern Italy can be blamed on this city of publicists and pasta power lunches.

As if to make up for its shaggy parks, blocky fascist architec-ture, and recently bombed-out feeling (World War II), its people are works of art. Milan is an international fashion capital with a refined taste. Window displays are gorgeous, cigarettes are chic, and even the cheese comes gift wrapped.

Three hundred years before Christ, the Romans called this place Mediolanum, or "the central place." By the fourth century A.D., it was the capital of the western half of the Roman Empire. It was from here that Emperor Constantine issued the Edict of Milan, legalizing Christianity. After some barbarian darkness, medieval Milan rose to regional prominence under the Visconti and Sforza families. By the time of the Renaissance, it was called "the New Athens" and was enough of a cultural center for Leonardo to call home. Then came 400 years of foreign dom-ination (Spain, Austria, France, more Austria). Milan was a center of the 1848 revolution against Austria and helped lead Italy to unification in 1870.

Mussolini left a heavy fascist touch on the city's architecture (such as the central train station). His excesses also led to the WWII bombing of Milan. But Milan rose again. The 1959

Pirelli Tower (the skinny skyscraper in front of the station) was a trendsetter in its day. Today, Milan is people-friendly, with a great transit system and inviting pedestrian zones.

Many tourists come to Italy for the past. But Milan is today's Italy, and no Italian trip is complete without visiting it. While it's not big on the tourist circuit, Milan has plenty to see.

And seeing Milan is not difficult. My coverage focuses on the old center. Nearly all the sights and hotels covered are within a 10-minute walk of the cathedral (Duomo), which is one straight eight-minute shot on the Metro from the train station. Milan, no more expensive than other Italian cities, is well-organized and completely manageable.

For a pleasant day trip from Milan, consider Stresa on Lake Maggiore. This resort town has easy boat connections to lovely islands brimming with lush, exuberant gardens. Stresa, about an hour from Milan by train, is covered at the end of this chapter.

## Planning Your Time

OK, it's a big city, so you probably won't linger. Compared to Rome and Florence, Milan's art is mediocre, but the city does have unique and noteworthy sights. To maximize your time, use the Metro and note which places stay open through the siesta.

With two nights and a full day, you can gain an appreciation for the town and see the major sights. (Note that about half of Milan's sights close on Monday.) With 36 hours, I'd sleep in Milan and focus on the center. Tour the Duomo, hit what art you like (Brera Gallery, Michelangelo's last *Pietà*, Leonardo's *Last Supper*— which requires a reservation), browse through the elegant shopping area and the galleria, and try to see an opera. Technology buffs like the Science and Technology Museum, while medieval art buffs dig the city's early Christian churches. People-watchers and pigeon-feeders could spend their entire visit never leaving sight of the Duomo.

Since Milan is a cold Italian plunge, and most flights to the United States leave Milan early in the morning, you may want to start your Italian trip softly by going directly from Milan to Lake Como (1-hour train ride to Varenna), Lake Maggiore (about an hour by train to Stresa—see end of chapter), or the Cinque Terre (4 hours to Vernazza). Then spend a night or two in Milan at the end of your trip before flying home.

**Three-hour tour:** If you're just changing trains in Milan (as sooner or later you will), consider this blitz tour: Check your bag at the station, pick up a city map at the station TI, ride the subway to the Duomo (in front of the train station, follow yellow line 3 direction per San Donato 4 stops to Duomo), peruse the square, explore the cathedral's rooftop and interior, have a scenic coffee in the galleria, spin on the Taurus, see a museum or two (most are within a 10-minute walk of the main square), and return by subway to the station (yellow line 3, direction Zara). Art fans might make time for the Duomo's museum, Leonardo (if you have reservations; Metro: Cadorna or Tram #24 direction Axum), or the Michelangelo (no reservations necessary, Metro: Cairoli).

## Orientation

**Tourist Information:** Milan has two TIs. One is in the central train station (Mon–Sat 9:00–19:00, Sun 9:00–12:30 & 13:30–18:00, tel. 02-7252-4360). At track level (with your back to the tracks), look for the sign "APT Tourist Information" near the blinking orange-and-white T. The TI is tucked away down a corridor next to a Telecom telephone center (Internet access with phone card).

The other TI is on Piazza Duomo (Mon–Fri 8:45–13:00 & 14:00–18:00, Sat–Sun 9:00–13:00 & 14:00–17:00, closes 1 hour earlier Oct–April, tel. 02-7252-4301, www.milanoinfotourist .com). As you face the church, it's to your right in a skinny three-story building.

At either TI, confirm your sightseeing plans and pick up the free map and the classy *Museums in Milan* booklet (with latest museum hours). For events, concerts, films in English, expatriate groups, and cultural insights, ask for the free *Hello Milano* monthly newspaper (www.hellomilano.it) or the less-helpful *Milano Mese* (events are listed in Italian by category rather than date). The 80-page *Where, When, How* booklet—useful, but overkill for most short visits—details several self-guided walking tours and provides a listing of sights, shopping ideas, bookstores, restaurants, nightlife, sports events, and much more (€1.60).

The TI sells a Welcome Card packet for €8, which includes a 24-hour transit pass (value: €3, good on Metro, trams, and buses); a coupon booklet good for discounts on their city bus tour (about €5 off, includes Leonardo's *Last Supper*), Navigli boat cruise, classical music concerts, and several museums; a CD of opera music; and an unnecessary vinyl pouch. This is a decent value if you can manage to fit several of those activities into your day or want the CD.

While I've listed enough sights to keep you hectic for two days, there's much more to see in Milan. Its many thousand-year-old churches make it clear that Milan was an important beacon in the Dark Ages. The TI, the *Where, When, How* booklet, and other local guidebooks can point you in the right direction if you have more time.

# Arrival in Milan

**By Train:** The huge, sternly decorated, fascist-built (in 1931) train station is a city and a sight in itself. You'll get off the train and enter the lobby at track level; another floor is downstairs.

Orient from the track-level lobby with your back to the tracks. On your right: train information (daily 7:00–21:00, validate railpasses here at refund windows #7 or 8, tel. 848-888-088 for automated info in Italian), baggage check (€2.60/12 hrs), and a 24-hour pharmacy (*farmacia*, look for green neon cross). On your left are cash machines (near track 14) and the TI (see above, look for blinking orange T). Out the side exit on the left (down the escalator under the "Gran Bar" sign), you'll find airport shuttle buses (to Malpensa and Linate, run by STAM) lined up. Across the curb from those buses is the handy Passaggi Travel Agency (can help you with your air and rail needs with far fewer lines than inside the station—a real time-saver).

From the track level, go downstairs straight ahead to find train-ticket windows, Hertz/Avis/Europcar offices, and a great and huge supermarket/cafeteria that's hidden away (daily 7:30–24:00, after you descend stairs from track-level lobby, go right to the far end and enter Pellini bar, snake your way through the cafeteria to the SuperCentrale market, also called Supermercato Sigma). Just outside the front of the station is the taxi stand (figure on €8 to Duomo) and escalators, which take you down into the Metro system.

Warning: Locals call the change offices in the train station *ladri auttorizzati* (authorized thieves). Ignore them and their 10 percent commission. Use a cash machine (from track 14, enter the lobby—you'll find a Bancomat cash machine to your left and another across the hall) or exit the station straight ahead and cross the square to Banca Commerciale Italiana (Mon–Fri 8:30–13:30 & 15:00–16:30).

For most quick visits, the giant city is one simple axis from the train station to the Duomo. To get to the Duomo, go straight into the Metro (look for red M) and buy a €1 ticket (from the underground ticket office at the Metro stop—with all prices listed in English over the window, or from a machine—push green button). Follow signs for line 3 (yellow), direction S. Donato, and in eight minutes you'll be facing the cathedral. To return to the station, take the yellow line 3, direction Zara. After one trip on the Metro, you'll dream up other excuses to use it.

**By Car:** Driving is bad enough in Milan to make the €20/day fee for a downtown garage a blessing. If you're driving, do Milan (and Lake Como) before or after you rent. If you have a car, use the well-marked suburban *parcheggi* (parking lots), which offer affordable and safe parking at city-edge subway stations.

**By Plane:** Frequent shuttle trains and buses connect the airports and train station. See "Transportation Connections," page 364.

## Helpful Hints

**Theft Alert:** Be on guard. Milan's thieves target tourists. At the station and around the Duomo, thieves roam dressed as beggars, sometimes in gangs of several too-young-to-arrest children. Watch out for ragged people carrying newspaper and cardboard. If you're ripped off, ask the police to fill out a report; it's necessary if you plan to file a claim with your insurance company (Police Station, *"Questura,"* Via Fatebenefratelli 11, Metro: Turati, tel. 02-62261 or Piazza San Sepolcro 9 behind Pinacoteca Ambrosiana near Duomo, tel. 02-806-051). For lost or stolen credit cards or traveler's checks, contact Visa in Italy at 800-877-232; Master Card at 800-68086; or American Express at 800-864-046 (for credit cards) or 800-72000 (for traveler's checks).

**U.S. Consulate:** Mon–Fri 8:30–17:30, Via Principe Amedeo 2/10, Metro: Turati, tel. 02-290-351.

**Scheduling:** Monday is a terrible sightseeing day, since many museums are closed. August is rudely hot and muggy. Locals who can, vacate, leaving the city pretty quiet. Those visiting in August find the nightlife sleepy; many shops, restaurants, and some hotels closed; and the hotels that are open—empty and discounted. I've indicated which recommended hotels offer air-conditioning, worth the money for a summer visit.

**Travel Agencies Selling Train Tickets:** You can buy train tickets and reserve *couchettes* for the station price without the station lines alongside the station or near the Duomo. At the station, head out the side (under the Gran Bar sign to the airport shuttle buses) and find the Passaggi Travel Agency (Piazza Luigi di Savoia1, tel. 02-669-0531). Near the Duomo, go to CIT, in the center of Galleria Vittorio Emanuele (Mon–Fri 9:00–19:00, Sat 9:00–13:00 & 14:00–18:00, closed Sun, must place order at least 30 min before closing, CC, tel. 02-8637-0228). American Express is also near the Duomo (Mon–Fri 9:00–12:30 & 14:30–17:00, pay cash or use AmEx credit card, up Via Verdi from La Scala, Via Brera 3, tel. 02-7200-3694).

**Bookstores:** The handiest major bookstore is Libreria Feltrinelli, under the Galleria Vittorio Emanuele. The books in English—fiction and guidebooks—are at opposite ends of the store (Mon–Sat 10:00–23:00, Sun 10:00–20:00, shorter hours in Aug, CC, store is huge but entrances are subtle: either enter at Ricordi Mediastore next to McDonald's in center of galleria and go downstairs, or enter through Autogrill restaurant on Piazza Duomo, also sells maps, tel. 02-8699-6903). The American Bookstore is at Via Camperio 16, near the Sforza Castle (Mon 13:00–19:00, Tue–Sat 10:00–19:00, closed Sun, tel. 02-878-920).

**Internet Access:** Major phone offices (e.g., at central train station and in galleria) have phone card–operated computers online which work well. The Leonardo da Vinci Science Museum has a wonderful room filled with computers for free Internet access (see "Sights," below).

**Street Markets:** Milan's most popular flea market is Fiera di Sinigallia, which spills down Viale d'Annunzio every Saturday from 8:30 to 17:00 (Metro: San Agostino, walk down Viale Papiniano—where market starts—to d'Annunzio, where it gets bigger). Small street markets are held every morning except Sunday in various neighborhoods; *Hello Milano* has a complete listing (free at TI). Be wary of pickpockets at any street market.

**Medical Services:** A 24-hour pharmacy is in Central Station; look for the neon green cross. Several international medical clinic/emergency care facilities are in Milan: at Via Cerva 25 (24-hr help, Metro: San Babila, tel. 02-7601-6047); near the center at Via San Paolo 15 (Metro: Duomo, tel. 02-7200-4080), and at Via Mercalli 11 (Metro: Crocetta, call for appointments, tel. 02-5831-9808).

## Getting around Milan

Use Milan's great subway system. The clean, spacious, fast, and easy four-line Metro zips you most anywhere you may want to go and trams and city buses fill in the gaps. A **ticket,** valid for 75 minutes, can be used for one subway, tram, or bus ride, plus a transfer (€1, sold at newsstands, many *tabacchi* shops, and at machines in subway station: push green *rete urbana di Milano* button; note that some machines sell only the €1 ticket—just feed in the money). Other options include: a *carnet* (€9.20 for 10 rides; you get 5 tickets that can be used twice—flip over to use a second time; these can be shared); the **24-hour pass** (€3, worthwhile if you take 4 rides; can usually cover a journey the following morning since it's a 24-hour rather than a 1-day pass); and a **48-hour pass** (€5.50). Transit info: toll-free tel. 800-016-857 (underground ATM Point office at Duomo stop, Mon–Sat 7:45–19:45).

I've keyed sightseeing to the subway system. While most sights are within a few blocks of each other, Milan is an exhausting city for walking. You'll rarely wait more than five minutes for a subway train, and the well-marked trams can be useful (especially to the *Last Supper*, catch #24 near Duomo, see "Sights," below).

## Milan's Metro

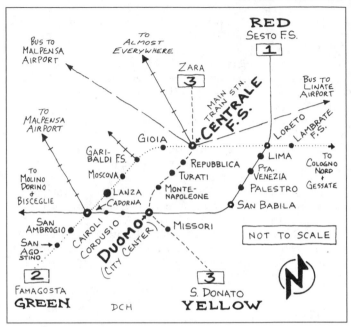

Small groups go cheap and fast by **taxi** (metered, drop charge €3.10 and €0.70 per km, often easier to walk to a taxi stand than to flag down a cab).

## Tours of Milan

**Bus Tours**—The three-hour **Autostradale** city bus tour has a live guide, is a good value, and guarantees you'll see Leonardo's *Last Supper* (useful if you haven't booked ahead for this sight). The two different itineraries also include visits to the Duomo, galleria, and Sforza Castle. Both tours cover entry fees, depart from Piazza Duomo at Via Marconi, and are €5 off with the TI's Welcome Card (€40 for morning tour offered at 9:30 Tue–Sun year-round; €43 for afternoon tour—which includes Brera Art Gallery—offered at 15:00 Tue–Sun April–July and Sept–Oct only, CC, book at TI on Piazza Duomo, tel. 02-3391-0794).

The **Ciao Milano** vintage tram, which does a figure-eight trip around the city with a taped spiel, isn't worth €15.50 for the transportation, because Milan's sights cluster in the center (3/day, multi-lingual tour, you can hop on and off but what's the point, departs Piazza Duomo at roughly 11:00, 13:00, and 15:00, tel. 02-805-5323).

**Walking Tour**—The TI may offer walking tours in 2003 (for information call tel. 02-7252-4301).

**Private Guide**—Lorenza Scorti, a hardworking young woman who speaks good English, knows her local history and how to teach it. She can be booked well in advance (necessary in May and Sept) or with short notice (€100 for 3-hr tour, eves OK, €200/full day, price identical for individuals or groups, tel. 02-4801-7042, e-mail: lorenza.scorti@libero.it).

## Sights—Milan's Cathedral and Museum

▲▲**Duomo (Cathedral)**—The city's centerpiece is the fourth-largest church in Europe—after the Vatican's, London's, and Sevilla's. Get the most out of your visit by starting with the adjacent Duomo Museum, located just outside the church, directly across from the south transept, and described below.

Back when Europe was fragmented into countless tiny kingdoms and dukedoms, the dukes of Milan wanted to impress their counterparts in Germany and France. Their goal was to earn Milan recognition and respect from both the Vatican and the kings and princes of northern Europe by building a massive, richly ornamented cathedral. Even after Renaissance domes were in vogue elsewhere in Italy, Milan's cathedral stayed on Gothic target. The dukes—thinking northerners would relate better to Gothic—loaded it with pointed arches and spires. For good measure, the cathedral was built not of stone but of marble—pink marble of Candoglia, from top to bottom—rafted from a quarry 70 kilometers (43 miles) away to a canal port at the cathedral.

**Interior:** To get inside, dress modestly (no shorts or bare shoulders for anyone of any age).

At 160 meters long and 93 meters wide (525 by 300 feet), with 52 30-meter-tall (100-foot), sequoia-sized pillars inside and more than 2,000 statues, the place seats 12,000 worshipers. If you do two laps, you've done your daily walk.

Built from 1386 to 1810, this construction project originated the Italian phrase meaning "never-ending": "like building a cathedral." It started Gothic (best seen in the apse behind the altar) and was finished in the early 1800s under Napoleon (particularly the noteworthy west façade, which is wonderful late in the day, with the sun low in the sky).

While the church is a good example of the flamboyant, or "flamelike," overripe final stage of Gothic, architectural harmony is not its forte (church free, €3 for 1-hr audioguide, daily 7:00–19:00, Metro: Duomo). For most, the treasury, or *tesoro*, under the altar isn't worth the time or the €1 fee, but if you're going to the Duomo Museum, a combo-ticket purchased here

# Milan

saves you €4 and can't be purchased at the Duomo Museum
(treasury open daily 10:00–12:00 & 14:30–18:00).

Standing inside (at the back rear), notice two tiny lights:
The little red one above the altar marks where a nail from the
cross of Jesus is kept. This relic was brought to Milan by St.
Helen (Emperor Constantine's mother) in the fourth century,
when Milan was the capital of the Western Roman Empire.
It's on display for three days a year (in September). Now look
high to the right and find a tiny pinhole of white light. This
shines a 25-centimeter (10-inch) sunbeam onto the bronze
line running across the floor here at noon (13:00 in summer)
indicating where we are on the zodiac.

Wander deeper into the church up the right aisle. Notice the
windows. Those on the right are 15th century; these mosaics of
colored glass are brilliant and expensive, bought by wealthy families seeking the Church's favor. The windows on the left, dating
from the time of Napoleon, are dimmer, cheaper painted glass.

Belly up to the bar facing the high altar. While the church

is Gothic, the altar was made Baroque—the style of the Vatican in the 1570s (a Roman Catholic statement to counter the Protestant churches of the north that were mostly Gothic). Look up at the arches. Structurally, they are round (providing the necessary strength to hold up the massive roof), but visually, they're Gothic—filled in with decorative fittings to look pointed and fit the general style of the building. Now look to the rear up at the ceiling and see the fancy carving—nope, that's painted. It looks expensive, but, being painted, it was more affordable than carved stone.

**Paleo-Christian Baptistery:** In the rear of the church (buy €1.50 ticket at kiosk, daily 9:30–17:15), climb down into the church that stood here long before the present one. Milan was an important center of the early Christian Church. In Roman times, Mediolanum's street level was three meters (10 feet) below today's level. You'll see the scant remains of an eight-sided baptistery (where Saints Augustine and Ambrogio were baptized) and a little church. Back then, since you couldn't enter the church until you were baptized—which didn't happen until the age of 18—churches had a little "holy zone" just outside for the unbaptized. This included a baptistery.

**Cathedral Rooftop:** This is the most memorable part of a Duomo visit. You'll wander through a fancy forest of spires with great views of the city, the square, and—on clear days—even the Swiss Alps. And, 100 meters (330 feet) above everything, overlooking everything is La Madonnina. This four-meter-tall (13-foot) gilt Virgin Mary is a symbol of the city. In fact, locals refer to their town as "the city of la Madonnina." (Climb stairs for €3; or ride elevator for €5; €7 combo-ticket—sold only at the elevator— includes elevator and Duomo Museum; daily mid-Feb–mid-Nov 9:00–17:30, mid-Nov–mid-Feb 9:00–16:15, enter outside from north transept; clue: in Europe old churches face roughly east.)

▲▲**Duomo Museum (Museo del Duomo)**—To really understand Milan's cathedral, visit the cathedral museum first. While admission is €6, they encourage attendance by selling deeply discounted combo-tickets (€4 includes treasury—purchasable only at treasury; €7 includes elevator to church rooftop—sold only at elevator; €12 covers Pinacoteca Ambrosiana and Museo Diocesano—sold at any participating sight).

The museum is open daily (10:00–13:15 & 15:00–18:00, last entry 30 min before closing, in Ducal Palace next to south side of Duomo, Piazza Duomo 14, Metro: Duomo, tel. 02-860-358).

Here's a tour:

**Room 1:** After you buy your ticket, look up. Greeting you, as he did pilgrims 500 years ago, is God the Father, made of wood, wrapped in copper, and gilded. In 1425, this covered the keystone connecting the tallest arches directly above the high altar of the Duomo.

**Room 2:** Meet St. George. Among the oldest cathedral statues, it once stood on the highest spire and shows nearly 600 years of pollution and aging. Some think this is the face of Duke Visconti—the man who started the cathedral. The museum is filled with originals like this. On the right, finger a raw piece of *marmo di Candoglia*—the material of the church, spires, and statues. The duke's family gave the entire Candoglia quarry to the church for all the marble it would ever need.

**Room 3:** This room (which used to be the stable for the Duke's horses) shows how Gothic was an international style. Gothic craftsmen, engineers, and artists roamed across Europe to work on huge projects such as Milan's cathedral. The statues in this room show the national differences: Peter (near the door, showing off his big keys) is Italian. His expressive face is made even more expressive by his copper-button pupils. The smaller statues (which were models for the big ones) behind glass are German (showing inner strength) and French (most graceful). Pope Martino V, overlooking the room from his perch at the end (to the left as you enter), celebrated the first Mass in the cathedral in 1418 (look at "Papa Martino V" closely—we'll see a 20th-century rendition later in the tour). Study the 15th-century stained-glass windows close up. The grotesque gargoyles (originals), protruding over the door you entered, served two purposes: to scare away evil spirits and to spew rainwater away from the building. Leaving the room, you'll walk under a stylized sun—symbol of both Jesus and the Visconti family.

**Room 5:** A lit panel shows how the church was built in stages from 1386 to 1774. Building resumed whenever the community had the money.

**Room 6:** The brick backdrop reminds us what the church would have looked like if not for the dandy with the rolled-up contract in his hand. That's Galeazzo Sforza, making it official—the church now owns the marble quarry (and it makes money on it to this day). A photo of the contract is opposite.

**Room 7:** The crucifix (again, copper-sheet gilded with real gold nailed onto wood) is 900 years old. It hung in the church that stood here previously, as well as in today's cathedral. The two-sided miniature altar painting has been carried through the city on festival days since the 16th century.

**Room 8:** These statues, from around 1500, are originals. Copies now fill their niches in the church. St. Paul the Hermit (in front of the blue curtain) got close to God by living in the desert. While wearing only a simple robe, he's filled with inner richness.

The intent is for pilgrims to stare into his eyes and feel at peace. (But I couldn't stop thinking of the Cowardly Lion.)

**Room 9** (discreet WC behind wooden door): Five hundred years ago, this sumptuous Flanders-style tapestry hung from the high altar. Note the exquisite detail, down to the tears on Mary's cheeks. In the hall is more fancy fabric—this one has silk, silver, and gold embroidery. The tapestries were gifts from big shots hoping to gain favor with the Church.

**Room 10:** The sketchy red cartoons were designs for huge paintings (see photographs nearly opposite) that still hang between the columns (Oct–Christmas). Notice the inlaid 16th-century marble floor. The black (from Lake Como) and red (from Verona) marble is harder. Go ahead, wear down the white a little more.

**Room 12:** Enter room 12 and turn around to see the artwork lining the wall. The terra-cotta was clay—worked in a creative frenzy and then baked. Study the quick design below the careful marble originals (flanking the doorway you entered). You will notice what 300 years of acidic pigeon droppings do to marble.

The statues all around this room (c. 1600) were sculpted 100 years later than the statues in room 8, and therefore are more expressive.

Find the painting of Saint Carlo Borromeo in the black robe, to your right. The 16th-century saint carries a cross showing the holy nail (the church's top relic) as he leads the plague out of Milan. In the background, see the 13th-century original church's facade with today's church—before spires—behind it.

Start circling the room clockwise. Crespi's monochrome painting of the *Creation of Eve (Creazione di Eva)* came first (1628). From that, the terra-cotta model was made (1629), and this served as the model for the marble statue that still stands above the center door on the church's west portal (1643). Three other sets line the wall.

Opposite *Eve*, see the swirling *Dance of Angels* and its terra-cotta model. This is the original, which decorated the ceiling over the door.

**Room 20:** If the vestments are still on loan from the treasury, you'll find them here, off room 12. Showing off rich red robes with lavish gold brocade, it's like a priestly fashion show from the 16th through 20th centuries.

**Room 13:** Standing like a Picasso is the original (1772) iron frame for the statue of the Virgin Mary that still crowns the cathedral's tallest spire. In 1967, a steel replacement was made for the 33 pieces of gilded copper bolted to the frame. The carved wood face of Mary (in the corner) is the original mold for Mary's cathedral-crowning copper face.

**Room 15:** At the modern doors with the thin orange-white

marble windows, turn right into a tunnel-like hall. Along the left wall, you'll see a painting of the earlier church, competition designs proposing possible facades for the cathedral, and a photo of the actual west portal. Along the right, the evolution of the church and the Ducal Palace (which you're in now).

**Room 16:** This huge wooden model of the cathedral was the actual model—necessary in that pre-computer age—used in the 16th century by the architects and engineers to build the church. The more recent facade wasn't used. Climb around the back to see the spire-filled rooftop, which you'll explore later if you like.

**Room 17:** Look around this room. The art seems a mixture of old and new, but it's all from the 20th century. Notice the vibrant Pope Martin V popping out of the wall (bronze panel to the left as you enter; artist Lucio Fontana). To see the gigantic leap that art has made over the centuries, compare this with the static statue of the same pope in room 3. On the opposite wall, see Fontana's *Ascension of Mary (Mary Assunta)*. She's making a jump shot into heaven. Her veil looks like flowing hair, like the wings of an angel. Without regret, she soars above the grief of the world.

The last rooms are technical, showing the recent restoration work and the stabilization and reinforcement of the main pylons. To exit, retrace your steps.

## More Sights near the Cathedral

▲**Piazza Duomo**—Milan's main square is a classic European scene and a popular local gathering point. Professionals scurry, label-conscious kids loiter, young thieves peruse. For that creepy-crawly, pigeons-all-over-you experience, buy a bag of seed.

Standing in the square, you're surrounded by history. The statue is of Victor Emmanuel II, first king of Italy. He's looking at the grand galleria named for him. Stand midway between the statue and the galleria, which was a gift from the people to their king. The words above the entrance read: To Victor Emmanuel II from the people of Milan.

Behind the statue (opposite the cathedral) is the center of medieval Milan—Piazza Mercanti. The medieval city hall (look for its red brick arches), dating from 1220, marked the center of town back when the entire city stood within its immense fortified walls. The merchant's square is a strangely peaceful place today, with a fine smattering of old-time Milano architecture.

Opposite the galleria are two fascist towers (one houses the TI). Mussolini made grandiose speeches from these balconies. You can still see relief panels illustrating the power of the fascist state. Between these towers and the cathedral (set back a bit) is the palace of Maria Theresa from the late 1700s—when Milan was ruled by the Austrian Hapsburgs.

The Duomo Center (next to TI) is a modern mall with a Virgin Megastore, one-hour photo service, decent Spizzico pizzeria, and handy Ciao cafeteria. For a fine view of the Duomo and the piazza, climb the steps (unless strewn with litter and derelicts) to the balcony above the TI. Behind the Duomo is a vibrant, pedestrian shopping zone along Vittorio Emanuele II.

▲▲Galleria Vittorio Emanuele—Milan is symbolized by its great four-story, glass-domed arcade on the cathedral square. Here you can turn an expensive cup of coffee into a good value by enjoying Europe's best people-watching (or get the same view for peanuts from the strategically placed McDonald's). Bar Zucca (at the entry), with an interior typical of the 1920s, is the birthplace of Campari. (If you try one, you'll pay €3.50 standing or €8 seated.)

Wander around the gallery. Its art is a reminder that the gallery was a gift from the people to the king to celebrate the establishment of Italy as an independent country. Stand under the central dome and enjoy the patriotic mosaics symbolizing the four major continents. The mosaic floor is also patriotic. The white cross in the center is a symbol of the king. The she-wolf with Romulus and Remus (on the south side facing Rome) honors the city, which since 1870 has been the national capital. On the west side (facing Torino, the provisional capital of Italy from 1861–1865), you'll find that city's symbol: a torino (little bull). For good luck, locals step on his irresistible little testicles. Two local girls explained to me that it works better if you spin. Find the poor little bull and just observe for a few minutes . . . it's a cute scene. With so much spinning, the mosaic is replaced every two years.

Also under the galleria dome is the CIT travel agency (sells train tickets and *couchettes*; see "Helpful Hints," above) and a cluster of SIP public phone booths (Internet access with phone card).

Piazza della Scala—This smart, little, traffic-free square, out the back between the galleria and the opera house, is dominated by a statue of Leonardo da Vinci. The statue (from 1870) is a reminder that Leonardo spent many years in Milan working for the Sforza family (Milan's answer to the Medici). Under the great Renaissance genius stand four of his greatest "Leonardeschi." (He apprenticed a sizable group of followers.) The reliefs show his various contributions—painter, architect, and engineer. Leonardo, wearing his hydroengineer hat, designed Milan's canal system complete with locks. (Until the 1920s, Milan was one of Italy's major ports, with canals connecting it to the Po River and Lake Maggiore.)

▲▲La Scala Opera House and Museum—From the galleria, you'll see a statue of Leonardo. He's looking at a plain but famous neoclassical building, possibly the world's most prestigious opera house: Milan's Teatrale alla Scala. La Scala opened in 1778 with an opera by Antonio Salieri (of *Amadeus* fame).

Milan's famous opera house and its adjacent museum are now closed while the venerable hall is renovated, and will reopen in April 2005. Until then, opera buffs can see the museum's extensive collection in the Palazzo Busca at Collegio San Carlo in front of Santa Maria della Grazie, which houses Leonardo's *Last Supper*. The collection features things that mean absolutely nothing to the MTV crowd: Verdi's top hat, Rossini's eyeglasses, Toscanini's baton, Fettuccini's pesto, and original scores, stage sets, costumes, busts, portraits, and death masks of great composers and musicians (€5, Tue–Sun 9:00–18:00, closed Mon, Corso Magenta 71, Metro: Cadorna or Conciliazione, or tram #24 from near Duomo, tel. 02-805-3418).

**Opera:** While La Scala is being renovated, the show will go on at the Theater Arcimboldi (shuttles run theater-goers to and from performances from Piazza Scala starting 18:45–19:00; cost is €1 transit ticket; ask for details when purchasing opera ticket). Schedules vary, but the opera season is nearly year-round (show time 20:00), and ballet and classical concerts are held from October through June. No performances are held in August (for information and booking call Scala Infotel Service, daily 12:00–18:00, CC, tel. 02-7200-3744—live, or tel. 02-860-775—automated booking, or book online at La Scala's fine Web site: www .teatroallascala.org). On the opening night of an opera, a dress code is enforced for men (suit and tie).

Tickets generally go on sale two months before a performance. The expensive seats sell out quickly. At noon on the day of the show, any remaining seats (usually in the affordable, sky-high gallery) are sold at a 50 percent discount at the box office and on the Internet (Web sales cease 1 hour before show time).

▲**Via Speronari**—A block off Piazza Duomo, this is one of Milan's oldest streets and the most charming street in the old center. Via Speronari—named for the spurs once made and sold here—is worth a wander. Streets around here recall their medieval crafts: *speronari*—spurs, *spadari*—swords, *armorari*—armor. The weaponry made on these streets was high fashion among Europe's warrior class . . . like having an Armani dagger. While right in the city center, the neighborhood feels vital. That's because it's also a residential street. Banks of doorbells indicate that families live above the shops. Start at the recommended Hotel Speronari, formerly a dorm for monks from the church across the street. The classy Vino Vino wine shop next door welcomes tasters (€2/glass—daily specials posted at the door, Tue–Sat 9:00–19:30, closed

Sun–Mon). The sign next door—*"L'Ortolan Pusae Vecc de Milan"*—brags in the old Milanese language that this is the oldest fruit and veggie store in the city. The Princip bakery next door is understandably popular. Its brioches are rarely more than a few minutes old. In the back, a busy *tavola calda* serves a quick, fresh, and tasty hot meal (around €4 per plate, 12:00–14:00 only, pay at cashier first).

Where Via Speronari hits Via Torino, go 20 meters (65 feet) to the left to find the **Church of Santa Maria presso San Satiro** hiding behind its Baroque facade (daily 7:30–11:30 & 15:30–18:00). It was the scene of a temper tantrum in 1242, when a losing gambler vented his anger by hitting the baby Jesus in the Madonna-and-Child altarpiece. Blood "miraculously" spurted out, and the beautiful little church has been on the pilgrimage trail ever since. While I've never seen any blood, I'd swear I've seen a 3-D background behind the basically flat altar (a trompe l'oeil illusion by Bramante). This church—squeezed between the earlier church of San Satiro and a street—had no room for a real apse, so, with the help of math, the Renaissance architect Bramante made what looks like an apse. In the north transept, you'll find that original ninth-century church of San Satiro (brother of St. Ambrogio, patron saint of Milan). This tiny church—with surviving bits of Byzantine fresco—predated the rest (note the name means Church of St. Mary at St. Satiro). From this chapel, look back at the main altar to see Bramante's 3-D work collapsed. On the opposite side (near entry)—with dimensions mirroring this old chapel—an eight-sided baptistery by Bramante from the 1480s shows the mathematically based values of the Renaissance. If you have a prayer in need of an extra boost, pop a coin into the box and "light" an electric candle.

**Pinacoteca Ambrosiana**—While a prestigious collection, it contains few recognizable names for most tourists, except for the impressive drawing Raphael used as a design for his *School of Athens* in the Vatican (€7.50, no English descriptions but small English guidebook for €6.20 covers museum's highlights nicely, Tue–Sun 10:00–17:30, last ticket sold at 16:30, closed Mon, a couple of blocks from Piazza Duomo at Piazza Pio XI 2, tel. 02-869-2225).

▲**Brera Art Gallery**—Milan's top collection of Italian paintings (13th–20th centuries) is world class, but it can't top Rome's or Florence's. Established in 1809 to house Napoleon's looted art, it fills the first floor above an art college. On the ground level, wander past the nude *Napoleon* (by Canova) in the courtyard and straight through the art school to a great, cheap cappuccino machine (with all the lingo).

Back in the courtyard, climb the stairway following signs to "Pinacoteca" (€6.20, March–Oct Tue–Sun 8:30–19:15, maybe

June–Sept Sat until 23:00, closed Mon and May 1, last entry 45 min before closing, shorter hours Nov–Feb, Via Brera 28, Metro: Lanza, tel. 02-722-631).

The gallery's highlights include works by Gentile da Fabriano (room IV), the Bellini brothers and Mantegna (his textbook example of feet-first foreshortening, *The Dead Christ*, room VI), Crivelli (for someone new, in room XXI), Raphael *(Wedding of the Madonna*, room XXIV), and Michelangelo Merisi (a.k.a. Caravaggio, *Supper at Emmaus*, room XXIX). Since there are no English descriptions, consider the audioguide (€3.60, or €5.50 for 2 headsets).

▲**Risorgimento Museum**—With a quick 30-minute swing through this quiet, one-floor museum thoughtfully described in English, you'll learn the interesting story of Italy's rocky road to unity: from Napoleon (1796) to the victory in Rome (1870). It's just around the block from the Brera Art Gallery at Via Borgonuovo 23 (free, Tue–Sun 9:00–13:00 & 14:00–17:30, closed Mon, Metro: Montenapoleone).

**Poldi Pezzoli Museum**—This classy house of art features top Italian paintings of the 15th through the 18th centuries, old weaponry, and lots of interesting decorative arts, such as a roomful of old sundials and compasses (€6, Tue–Sun 10:00–18:00, closed Mon, not a word of English, Via Manzoni 12, Metro: Montenapoleone, tel. 02-796-334).

**Bagatti Valsecchi Museum**—This unique 19th-century collection of Italian Renaissance furnishings was assembled by two aristocratic brothers who spent a wad turning their home into a Renaissance mansion. Museum guards pack flashlights for closer examination of fine wood carvings (€6, half price on Wed, Tue–Sun 13:00–17:45, closed Mon, good English descriptions, Via Santo Spirito 10, Metro: Montenapoleone).

▲**Sforza Castle (Castello Sforzesco)**—The castle of Milan tells the story of the city in brick. Built in the late 1300s as a military fortress, it guarded the gate to the city wall (see the diagram on the flip side of the entry sign) and defended the city from enemies "within and without." It was beefed up by the Sforza duke in 1450 in anticipation of a Venetian attack. Later, it was the Renaissance palace of the Sforza family and even housed their in-house genius, Leonardo. During the centuries of foreign rule (16th–19th), it was a barracks for occupying soldiers. Today, it houses several museums.

This immense, much-bombed-and-rebuilt brick fortress—exhausting at first sight—can only be described as heavy. But its courtyard has a great lawn for picnics and siestas, and its free museum is filled with interesting medieval armor, furniture, early Lombard art, an Egyptian collection, and, most important, Michelangelo's unfinished *Rondanini Pietà*. Michelangelo died while still working on this piece, which hints at the elongation of the Mannerist style that would follow. This is a rare opportunity to enjoy a Michelangelo with no crowds (free, Tue–Sun 9:00–17:30, closed Mon; study posted diagram at castle entrance to find museum—marked #12 on diagram, on the right at beginning of second courtyard; between renovation and reorganization the art gets moved around a lot—confirm location of museums at reception or ask museum guards; photos OK without flash, English info fliers throughout, Metro: Cairoli, tel. 02-8846-3701).

A big park, with a couple of cheap eateries, sprawls behind the fortress. At the far end of the park is the monumental Arco della Pace, a triumphal arch commemorating Napoleon's brief rule over "Italy" before Italy was unified.

## Sights—The *Last Supper* and Nearby

Note that the opera museum is located across the street from the *Last Supper* until 2005, when renovation on the opera house is complete (for details, see "La Scala Opera House," above).

▲**Leonardo da Vinci's *Last Supper (Cenacolo)***—You must have a reservation to see this Renaissance masterpiece in the church of Santa Maria delle Grazie. Because of Leonardo's experimental use of oil on chalk rather than the normal fresco technique, deterioration began within six years of its completion. The church was bombed in World War II, but—miraculously, it seems—the wall holding the *Last Supper* remained standing. The 21-year restoration project (completed in 1999) peeled 500 years of touch-ups away, leaving a faint but vibrant scene. In a big, vacant, white-washed room, you'll see faded pastels and not a crisp edge. The feet under the table look like negatives. But the composition is dreamy—Leonardo captures the psychological drama as the Lord says, "One of you will betray me," and the apostles huddle in stressed-out groups of three, wondering, "Lord, is it I?" Some are scandalized. Others want more information. Simon (on the far right) gestures as if to ask a question that has no answer. In this agitated atmosphere, only Judas (fourth from left and the only one with his face in shadow)—clutching his 30 pieces of silver and looking pretty guilty—is not shocked.

The circle meant life and harmony to Leonardo. Deep into a study of how life emanates in circles—like ripples on a pool hit by a pebble—Leonardo positioned the 13 characters in a semicircle. Jesus is in the center, from whence the spiritual force of God emanates.

The room depicted in the painting seems like an architectural extension of the church. The disciples form an apse, with Jesus the altar—in keeping with the Eucharist. Jesus anticipates his sacrifice—his face sad, all-knowing, and accepting. His feet even foreshadowed his crucifixion. Had the door, which was cut out in 1652, not been added, you'd see how Leonardo placed Jesus' feet atop each other, ready for the nail.

The room was a refectory or dining room for the Dominican friars. Traditionally, they'd gather here to eat with a last supper scene on one wall facing a crucifixion scene on the opposite wall.

The perspective is mathematically correct. In fact, restorers found a tiny nail hole in Jesus' right ear, which anchored the strings Leonardo used to establish these lines. The table is cheated out to show the meal. Notice the exquisite lighting. The walls are lined with tapestries (as they would have been) and the one on the right is brighter—to fit the actual lighting in the refectory (with windows on the left). With the extremely natural effect of the light and the drama of the faces, Leonardo created an effective masterpiece.

Reservations are mandatory. To minimize the humidity problem—even though the damage has already been done—25 tourists are allowed in every 15 minutes for just 15 minutes. Prior to your appointment time, you wait in several rooms, while doors close behind you and open up slowly in front of you. The information posted on Leonardo is mainly in Italian. For a reservation, call 028-942-1146 (or from the U.S., call 011-39-028-942-1146) a minimum of three days in advance for a weekday visit, and at least a week ahead for a weekend visit (booking office open Mon–Fri 9:00–18:00, Sat 9:00–14:00, closed Sun). It's a simple two-minute process, and you'll hang up with an appointed entry time and a number (€6.50 entry plus €1 reservation fee, cash only, pay upon arrival). Long-range planners can book up to three or four months in advance.

**Hours of *Last Supper:*** Tue–Sun 8:15–18:45 (last visit), July–Sept also open Sat until 21:45 (last visit), always closed Mon. You'll be asked to show up 15 minutes before your scheduled time (10 minutes should be enough but if you're a minute late, you get no supper). Consider the €2.60 15-minute audioguide (€4.50 with 2 headphones). You might want to listen to it in the waiting room while studying the reproduction of the actual *Last Supper* on that wall until you're let in.

To get to Santa Maria delle Grazie, you can either take the Metro to Cadorna (plus a 5-min walk), or, even better, hop on tram #24 from Via Mazzini (catch it in front of Rolex store at intersection of Via Dogana and Via Mazzini, just off Piazza Duomo), which drops you off in front of the church. The

Science Museum (see below) is two blocks away, and the temporary La Scala Opera House museum is across the street.

People who show up without a reservation can sometimes get in (even if "Sold Out" sign is posted). You'll be told that entry is by reservation only—but if fewer than 25 people show up for a particular time slot, you can get lucky. Still, for guaranteed entry, it's best to call ahead. Note that the city bus tour (see "Tours of Milan," above) includes entry to the *Last Supper*.

▲**National Leonardo da Vinci Science and Technology Museum (Museo Nazionale della Scienza e Tecnica)**—The spirit of Leonardo lives here. Most tourists visit for the hall of Leonardo designs illustrated in wooden models, but Leonardo's mind is just as easy to appreciate by paging through a coffee-table edition of his notebooks in any bookstore. The rest of this immense collection of industrial cleverness is fascinating, with trains, radios, old musical instruments, computers, batteries, telephones, chunks of the first transatlantic cable, and on and on. Some of the best exhibits (such as the Marconi radios) branch off the Leonardo hall (€6.20, Tue–Fri 9:30–16:50, Sat–Sun 9:30–18:30, closed Mon, Via San Vittore 21, bus #50 from Duomo, or Metro: San Ambrogio, tel. 02-485-551). Complain politely about the lack of English descriptions. There's a great Internet access room off the Leonardo hall (free).

## Sights—Away from the Center

**Leonardo's Horse**—This largest equestrian monument in the world is a modern reconstruction of a model created in 1482 by Leonardo da Vinci for the Sforza family. The model was destroyed in 1499 by invading French forces, who used it for target practice. In 1999, American Renaissance art collector Charles Dent decided to build the statue from Leonardo's design. He presented it to the Italians in appreciation for their role in the Renaissance and in homage to Leonardo's genius. The exhibit, described in English, includes statue casts and photos of the construction (free, daily 9:30–18:30, located on outskirts near Meazza soccer stadium and San Siro racetrack; take tram #24 to Stratico Palatino stop—ask conductor when to get off, then head right on Via Palatino, and left on Piazzale dello Sport to #9).

**Soccer**—The Milanese claim that their soccer ( *football* in Italiano) team is the best in Europe. For a dose of Europe's soccer mania (which many believe provides a necessary testosterone vent to keep Europe out of a third big war), catch a match in Milan. Inter and A.C. Milan are the ferociously competitive home teams (tickets-€15–115, A.C. Milan tickets sold at Cariplo banks, Inter tickets at Banca Popolare di Milano, and both at Virgin Megastore in Piazza del Duomo near TI, games held in 85,000-seat Meazza stadium most Sunday afternoons Sept–June, Metro: Lotto—no kidding, or tram #24 from Duomo directly to stadium—last stop, tel. 02-4870-7123).

## World-Class Window-Shopping

The "Quadrilateral," an elegant, high-fashion shopping area around Via Montenapoleone, is fun for shoppers (except in Aug, when most shops close). In this land where fur is still prized, the people-watching is as entertaining as the window-shopping. Notice also the exclusive penthouse apartments with roof gardens high above the scene. Via Montenapoleone and the pedestrianized Via Spiga are the best streets. From La Scala, walk up Via Manzoni to the Metro stop at Montenapoleone, browse down Montenapoleone to Piazza San Babila, then (for less expensive shopping thrills) walk down the pedestrian-only Corso Vittorio Emanuele II to the Duomo. Rinascente is a Nordstrom-type department store with reasonable prices (Mon–Sat 9:00–22:00, Sun 10:00–21:00, good toy selection; faces north side of Duomo on Piazza Duomo) and recommended restaurants (see "Eating," below).

## Nightlife

For evening action, check out the arty, student-oriented Brera area in the old center and Milan's formerly bohemian, now gentrified "Little Venice," the Navigli neighborhood (Metro: Porta Genova). Specifics change quickly so it's best to rely on the entertainment information in periodicals from the TI.

## Sleeping in Milan
**(€1 = about $1, country code: 39)**

Sleep Code: **S** = Single, **D** = Double/Twin, **T** = Triple, **Q** = Quad, **b** = bathroom, **s** = shower only, **CC** = Credit Cards accepted, **no CC** = Credit Cards not accepted, **SE** = Speaks English, **NSE** = No English.

To help you sort easily through these listings, I've divided the rooms into three categories based on the price for a standard double room with bath:

**Higher Priced**—Most rooms more than €150.
**Moderately Priced**—Most rooms €150 or less.
**Lower Priced**—Most rooms €110 or less.

I have tried to minimize traffic noise problems in my listings. All are within a few minutes' walk of Milan's subway system. With Milan's fine Metro, you can get anywhere in town in a flash. Anytime in April, September, October, and November, the city can be completely jammed by conventions, and hotel prices increase by €5 to €60. Summer is usually wide open, though many hotels close in August for vacation. Hotels cater more to business travelers than to tourists. Everyone speaks at least some English.

## Sleeping near the Duomo

The Duomo area is thick with people-watching, reasonable eateries, and the major sightseeing attractions. From the central train station to the Duomo, it's just four stops on a direct Metro line (yellow line 3, direction S. Donato) to Metro: Duomo.

### HIGHER PRICED

**Hotel Grand Duca di York,** with 33 pleasant rooms and lavish public spaces, is oddly stuck in the middle of banks and big-city starkness three blocks southwest of Piazza Duomo (Sb-€102, Db-€156, Tb-€180, includes breakfast, CC, air-con, elevator, closed Aug, near Metro stops: Piazza Cordusio or Duomo, Via Moneta 1/A, 20123 Milano, tel. 02-874-863, fax 02-869-0344, SE).

**Hotel Spadari** is for art-lovers. Designed by the Milanese artist Art Deco, the 40 rooms have billowing drapes, big paintings, and designer doors. It's next door to the recommended Peck deli (see below), two blocks from the Duomo (standard Db-€217–281, no need for pricier suites, includes breakfast, CC, Via Spadari 11, tel. 02-7200-2371, fax 02-861-184, www.spadarihotel.com, e-mail: spadari@tin.it).

### MODERATELY PRICED

**Hotel Gritti**, facing a peaceful square just off Via Torino, is a bright, classy, professionally run three-star hotel that comes with 48 comfortable rooms and a big, sleepy dog, Boris. Run by a jolly trio of English-speaking gentlemen (Mario, Bruno, and Evandro), Hotel Gritti feels like home in a hurry (Sb-€93, Db-€132, Tb-€183, includes big breakfast, same price all seasons, open year-round, family deals, CC but 10 percent off with cash, air-con, some smoky rooms, elevator, 2 blocks southwest of Piazza Duomo, Piazza S. Maria Beltrade 4, 20123 Milano, tel. 02-801-056, fax 02-8901-0999, www.hotelgritti.com, e-mail: info@hotelgritti.com).

**Hotel Santa Marta,** a shiny little hotel on a small street, has 15 fresh, tranquil, and spacious rooms (Db-€129 most of year but €165 during conventions and as low as €98, includes breakfast, CC, air-con, elevator, closed Aug, Via Santa Marta 4, 20123 Milano, tel. 02-804-567, fax 02-8645-2661, e-mail: info@hotel-santamarta.it).

### LOWER PRICED

**Hotel Speronari**, my home in Milan, is perfectly located, safe, and fairly quiet, with 32 bright, clean rooms on a great pedestrian street

# Milan's Center

- **1** Elevator to roof
- **2** Stairs to roof
- **3** CIT Travel Agency, Tel. Center, McD's, & Taurus
- **4** Pinacoteca Ambrosiana
- **5** Hotel Speronari
- **6** London Hotel
- **7** Hotel Giulio Cesare
- **8** Hotel Grand Duca di York
- **9** Hotel Santa Marta
- **10** Hotel Gritti
- **11** Antica Locanda Mercanti
- **12** Hotel Star
- **13** Hotel Nuovo
- **14** La Rinascente Bistrot & Brunch
- **15** Odeon Gelateria
- **16** Peck Grocery & Hotel Spadari
- **17** Trattoria Milanese
- **18** Pizzeria Dollaro
- **19** Ciao Ristorante (2 locations)
- **20** Latteria Rest. & Pizzeria Calafuria Unione
- **21** Rist. Familiare Cimbraccola

full of delis and food shops. Enjoy a free cappuccino upon arrival.
Note that this is a one-star hotel. If you want an elevator, air-
conditioning, and more comfort, please choose any of the pricier
recommended hotels (S-€44, Ss-€52, D-€68, Db-€88, T-€88,
Tb-€119, Qb-€135, these discounted prices promised through
2003 with this book—mention it when you reserve, CC but €3
off per person per night if you pay cash, lots of stairs, no breakfast,
ceiling fans, 200 meters, or 650 feet, off Piazza Duomo, Via Speronari 4, 20123 Milano, tel. 02-8646-1125, fax 02-7200-3178, e-mail:
hotelsperonari@inwind.it, run by the friendly Isoni family: father
Paolo and Gianpaolo, pron. "John Paolo," Maurizio, Carla, and
Fara). For breakfast, I like the Chicco D'Oro Bar across the intersection (from 7:00, closed Sun), or grab a fresh brioche at the
Princip bakery next door to have with your coffee in the Speronari
lobby. If you're flying out of Malpensa Airport, the hotel can get
you there via car much cheaper than a taxi—which charges €80 (2
people-€47, 3 people-€57, 4 people-€68, request 1 day in advance).

**Hotel Nuovo**, with 36 fine, smallish rooms and a lukewarm
reception, is central on a noisy square east of the Duomo near a
pedestrian street (S-€34, D-€52, Db-€83–98, Tb-€108–129,
CC, no breakfast, some air-con, request the third floor for less
noise, no public space, Piazza Beccaria 6, tel. 02-8646-4444, fax
02-7200-1752).

## Sleeping between La Scala and Sforza Castle

### HIGHER PRICED
**Hotel Star** is a comfortable, modern, 30-room place with fancy,
modern plumbing and, more important, a helpful staff (Sb-€108,
Db-€155, includes big breakfast, CC, closed Aug, air-con, fridge,
Via dei Bossi 5, tel. 02-801-501, fax 02-861-787, www.hotelstar.it,
e-mail: reception@hotelstar.it).

### MODERATELY PRICED
**London Hotel**, a 30-room hotel with all the comforts, is warmly
run by the friendly Gambino family (S-€80, Sb-€92, D-€120,
Db-€140, T-€135, Tb-€180, breakfast-€8, cheaper in July and
closed Aug, CC but 10 percent off with cash except during special
events, air-con, elevator, near Metro: Cairoli at Via Rovello 3,
on relatively quiet side street, 20121 Milano, tel. 02-7202-0166,
fax 02-805-7037, www.traveleurope.it/hotellondon.htm, e-mail:
hotel.london@traveleurope.it, Tanya and Licia SE).

**Hotel Giulio Cesare,** across the street from London Hotel,
is bigger, basic, impersonal, and tired but quiet and comfortable
(Sb-€93, Db-€150, 10 percent discount with this book, CC,

air-con, Via Rovello 10, 20121 Milano, tel. 02-7200-3915, fax 02-7200-2179, www.initalia.it/hotel-milano-giuliocesare).

**Antica Locanda dei Mercanti** feels like a library in heaven, well-located and seriously quiet (no TVs, lots of books). It lacks public spaces and a breakfast area but comes with fresh flowers in each of its 14 rooms (standard Db-€133, master Db-€156, Db with air-con and terrace-€215, optional €9 breakfast served in room, no CC except to hold room, fans, elevator, no young children, Via San Tomaso 6, second floor, no sign—only a name on doorbell, Metro: Cordusio, tel. 02-805-4080, fax 02-805-4090, www.locanda.it, e-mail: locanda@locanda.it).

## Sleeping near the Train Station

**LOWER PRICED**
If you like to drop your bag near the station, this is a handy, if dreary, area. The neighborhood between the train station and Corso Buenos Aires, in spite of its shady characters in the park and its 55-year-old prostitutes after dark, is reasonably safe. Many soulless business hotels have desperately discounted prices for those who drop in during slow times. Just walk down Via Scarlatti (leave the station's upper hall—with your back to the tracks—to the left). Decent options include **"The Best" Hotel** (19 rooms, Sb-€75, Db-€110, includes breakfast, CC, Via B. Marcello 83, 5-min walk from station, tel. 02-2940-4757, e-mail: thebesthotel @tiscalinet.it), **Hotel Valley** (small, dark, inexpensive Db-€72–78, Via Soperga 19, tel. 02-669-2777), **Hotel Virgilio** (inexpensive business hotel, S-€36, Sb-€62, D-€65, Db-€83, includes breakfast, Via P.L. da Palestrina 30, tel. 02-669-1337), and **Hotel Andreola Central** (4-star business hotel with occasional door-breaker prices, i.e., Db-€90 on weekends instead of midweek €362 rate, Via Scarlatti 24, tel. 02-670-9141).

# Eating in Milan

This is a fast-food city, but fast food in a fashion capital isn't a burger and fries. The bars, delis, *rosticcerie*, and self-service cafeterias cater to people with plenty of taste and more money than time. You'll find delightful eateries all over town (but many close in Aug for vacation).

I found the price between basic and classy restaurants was negligible (e.g., pastas-€7–10, *secondi*-€8–12, cover-€1–2), so it is worth springing for the places giving the best experience. To eat mediocre food on a famous street with great people-watching, choose an eatery on the pedestrian-only Via Mercanti or Via Dante. To eat with students in trendy little trattorias, explore the Brera neighborhood. To eat well near the Duomo, consider the recommended places below.

Locals like to precede a lunch or dinner with an aperitif (Campari made its debut in Milan). Bars fill their counters with inviting baskets of munchies, which are served free with these drinks. A cheap drink (if you're either likable or discreet) can become a light meal.

Breakfast is a bad value in hotels and fun in bars. It's OK to quasi-picnic. Bring in a banana (or whatever) and order a toasted ham-and-cheese sandwich (called and pronounced *tost*) or croissant with your cappuccino.

## Eating Classy near the Duomo

**Trattoria Milanese**, a classy family-run place, is a splurge (€30 fixed-price *menu* at lunch, à la carte available). It has an enthusiastic and local clientele; the restaurant didn't even bother to get a phone until 1988. Expect a Milanese ambience and quality traditional cuisine (Wed–Mon 12:30–15:00 & 19:30–23:00, closed Tue and mid-July–Aug, CC, air-con, Via Santa Marta 11, 5-min walk from Duomo, near Pinacoteca Ambrosiana, tel. 02-8645-1991).

**Ristorante Bruno** serves Tuscan cuisine with dressy waiters, hearty food, inexpensive desserts, and the best antipasto buffet I've seen (a plate full of Tuscan specialties for €7). You can eat inside or on the sidewalk under fascist columns (Sun–Fri 12:00–15:00 & 19:00–22:45, closed Sat, moderate prices, CC, air-con, Via M. Gonzaga 6, reservations wise, tel. 02-804-364).

**Ristorante al Mercante** is *the* place to dine elegantly inside or outside under historic arches in a peaceful square a block from the cathedral. Follow Via Mercanti away from the Duomo and turn left just after passing the loggia (covered market square); the restaurant is straight ahead on the right. You'll pay extra for the location, but the food is very good (moderately expensive, €16 *secondi*, Mon–Sat 12:00–14:30 & 19:00–22:30, closed Sun, CC, near Piazza Cordusio at Piazza Mercanti 17, tel. 02-805-2198).

**Pizzeria Ristorante al 50 da Geggio** is a bustling little favorite packed with locals eating Tuscan food under fans (Wed–Mon 12:15–13:30 & 19:15–23:30, closed Tue and Aug, moderate prices, good daily specials, Via Torino 50, tel. 02-8645-2244).

The big department store **La Rinascente,** alongside the Duomo, has three rooftop eateries (and a free WC) on the seventh floor, each with a terrace overlooking the ornate top of the cathedral (terrace dining only May–Sept): **Bistrot** is a dressy restaurant serving modern Mediterranean cuisine (5-course Tasting Menu-€62, Mon–Sat 12:00–14:30 & 19:30–22:00, Sun until 20:00, CC, tel. 02-877-120). The **Brunch** is a cafeteria with a much simpler, cheaper menu (Mon–Sat 12:00–15:30 & 18:00–22:00, Sun 12:00–15:30). Anyone can pop up to the **bar** for a look at the cathedral. While you can go through the department store taking escalators, a side entrance (on the Galleria Vittorio Emanuele side) has a direct elevator.

## Eating Simple near the Duomo

Also see **La Rinascente**, above, for its Brunch cafeteria and bar with a view, next to the Duomo.

**Latteria Cucina Vegetariana** serves a good vegetarian Italian lunch. This busy joint is actually a tiny grocery store overrun with dining tables, where local workers enjoy soup, salads, pasta dishes, and affordable prices (€5–8 meals, Mon–Sat 11:30–16:30, closed Sun, just off Via Torino at Via dell' Unione 6, 2 blocks southwest of Duomo, tel. 02-874401, Giorgio Notari).

**Pastarito Pizzarito** is a pasta-and-pizza chain with a wonderful formula. In a bright atmosphere under literal walls of pasta, you can choose from 10 fresh pastas and lots of sauces to create a huge dish (€4.50–9.50); splitting is welcome. Pizzas range from €5 to €8 (daily 12:00–14:30 & 19:30–23:30, CC, air-con, 4 blocks from Duomo, a block behind opera house at Via Verdi 6, tel. 02-862-210).

**Ristorante Pizzeria Calafuria Unione** serves tasty €6 pizzas in a non-smoking room (Mon–Sat 11:00–15:00 & 19:00–1:00, closed Sun and Aug, CC, near where Via Falcone hits Via dell' Unione at Via dell' Unione 8, 2 blocks southwest of Duomo. tel. 02-866-103).

**Ristorante/Pizzeria Al Dollaro** is a mod, happy place with well-fed locals (Mon–Fri 12:00–16:00 & 18:00–24:00, closed Sat at lunch and all day Sun and Aug, air-con, smoke-free section, 4 blocks south of Duomo at Via Paolo da Cannobio 11, tel. 02-869-2432).

**Ciao**, a self-service cafeteria, offers a low-stress, affordable meal on Piazza Duomo (daily 11:30–15:00 & 18:30–23:00, next to TI, on second floor, inexpensive pasta and good salad bar, easy public WC). Bring your tray upstairs to the top terrace floor for views of the Duomo and Square.

Fast-food cheapskates enjoy the best people-watching in Milan inside the galleria at **McDonald's** (salad/pasta plate and tall orange juice for €5).

Floodlit Mary gazes down from the top of the Duomo on the **Odeon Gelateria** for good reason (next to McDonald's on Piazza Duomo, on the far side of square opposite facade of the Duomo, open nightly until 1:00).

## Picnics near the Duomo

For a fun adventure, assemble an elegant dinner **picnic** by hitting the colorful deli, cheese, and produce shops on Via Speronari. The **Princip bakery** is mobbed with locals vying for focaccia, olive breadsticks, and luscious pastries. At the small bar in the back, you get free, fresh munchies with your drink or you can try a cheap meal (about €4 per plate, 12:00–14:00 only, pay cashier first; bakery open Mon–Sat 7:00–20:00, on Via Speronari, off Via Torino, a block southwest of Piazza Duomo).

**Peck** is an aristocratic deli with a fancy coffee/pastry shop upstairs, a gourmet grocery and *rosticceria* on the main level, and an *enoteca* wine cellar in the basement (Mon 15:00–19:30, Tue–Sat 8:45–19:30, closed Sun, Via Spadari 9). The *rosticceria* serves fancy food to go for a superb picnic dinner in your hotel. It's delectable, beautiful, sold by weight (order by the *etto*—100-gram unit—about a quarter pound), and not cheap. Try the risotto.

The **Standa Superfresco supermarket** is within a few blocks of the Duomo (Mon–Sat 8:00–21:00, Sun 9:00–20:00 small deli on ground level, big supermarket in basement, on Via Torino, at intersection with San Maurilio).

## Eating near Sforza Castle

**Le Briciole Pizzeria** draws a local crowd for its good prices, pizza, and varied meat dishes; it's packed by 21:00, go earlier (Tue–Fri and Sun 12:15–14:30 & 19:15–23:30, Sat 19:15–23:30, closed Mon, Via Camperio 17, a block in front of castle, on small street at end of Via Dante, tel. 02-877-185).

**Garbagnati** is a tasty self-service cafeteria on Via Dante 13, a couple of blocks in front of the castle (Mon–Sat 12:00–15:00 only, snacks otherwise, closed Sun; a smaller Garbagnati, with sweets and no seats, is near Peck deli at Via Hugo 3; tel. 02-8646-0672).

Another **Ciao** Autogrill cafeteria is on Via Dante, just off Piazza Cordusio, with outdoor seating on the pedestrian-only street (daily 11:30–22:30).

At **Ristorante Familiare della Cimbraccola,** the atmosphere is more memorable than the food. Stefanini Arnaldo, with his imaginary mother in the kitchen (she's 92 and now retired back in Tuscany) and using the same pots and pans since 1974, throws his entire menu at his guests—a series of uninspired appetizers, pastas, and entrées; endless wine, water, coffee, and *grappa* (firewater); and three desserts—all for €15. The food is Tuscan and plain. After six or eight courses, you'll get a big plate of meats. (This is your cue to say "Oh, my gosh!") The walls are plastered with model ships, pipes, dusty paper money, and pins for each hungry client on a U.S. map (Mon–Sat 19:00–22:30, closed Sun and Aug, an olive toss off Via Dante, midway between Duomo and fortress at Via S. Tomaso 8, tel. 02-869-2250).

### Eating near the Brera Art Gallery

The Brera neighborhood surrounding the Church of St. Carmine is laced with narrow, inviting pedestrian streets. Find your own *ristorante* or consider **Al Pozzo**, which offers Tuscan cuisine (Tue–Fri and Sun 11:00–15:00 & 19:00–24:00, Sat 19:00–24:00, closed Mon, Via S. Carpoforo 7, tel. 02-869-2279). **Caffe Vecchia Brera** serves up tempting sandwiches and savory and sweet crepes from €4 to €7 (Mon–Sat 8:00–14:00, closed Sun, Via dell'Orso 20, tel. 02-8646-1695).

### Eating Cheap near Montenapoleone

For inexpensive, healthy food near the classy shopping street, **Brek** is best. This self-service cafeteria chain is a step above Ciao in quality. One Brek is near one end of Montenapoleone (2 Via dell' Annunciata, 2 blocks from Montenapoleone, tel. 02-653-619), and another is near the other end, a half block off Piazza San Babila (daily 11:30–15:00 & 18:30–22:30, Piazza Giordano 1; on Piazza Babila, with back to "egg monument" and facing fountain, Brek is through arch in building on right, tel. 02-7602-3379). One of the ubiquitous **Ciao** Autogrill cafeterias is also on Piazza San Babila (self-service, at the end of pedestrian zone).

### Eating near the Train Station

Again, it's **Brek**, for better food than you'll find at the station (Mon–Sat 11:30–15:00 & 18:30–22:30, closed Sun; with back to tracks, exit station to left, it's within a block; Via Lepetit 20, tel. 02-670-5149).

## Transportation Connections—Milan

**By train to: Venice** (departures :05 after each hour, 3 hrs), **Florence** (hrly, 3 hrs, also check schedule for trains going to Rome and Naples—these stop in Florence), **Genoa** (hrly, 2 hrs), **Rome** (hrly, 4.5 hrs), **Brindisi** (4/day, 10–12 hrs), **Cinque Terre** (hrly, 3–4 hrs to La Spezia, some direct trains to Monterosso, sometimes changing in Genoa; trains from La Spezia to the villages go nearly hourly), **Varenna** on Lake Como (the small line to Lecco/Sondrio/Tirano leaves every 2 hours for the 1-hour trip to Varenna—maybe 8:15, 9:15, 12:15, 14:16, 16:15, 18:00, 19:10, and 20:15), **Stresa** (hrly, 50–75 min, faster trains require reservations; trains going to Domodossola and some international destinations stop at Stresa), **Como** (around :25 after each hour,

30 min, ferries go from Como to Varenna until 19:00). Train info (automated, in Italian): tel. 848-888-088.

**International destinations: Amsterdam** (4/day, 14 hrs), **Barcelona** (2 changes, 17 hrs—before paying extra for Pablo Casals express, consider flying), **Bern** (7/day, 3 hrs), **Frankfurt** (5/day, 9 hrs), **London** (2/day, 18 hrs), **Munich** (5/day, 8 hrs), **Nice** (5/day, 7–10 hrs), **Paris** (4/day, 7 hrs), **Vienna** (4/day, 14 hrs).

## Milan's Airports

To get flight information for either airport or the current phone number of your airline, call 02-74851 or 02-7485-2200.

**Malpensa:** Most international flights land at the manageable Malpensa Airport, 45 kilometers (28 miles) northwest of Milan. Customs guards fan you through, and even the sniffing dog seems friendly. You'll most likely land at Terminal 1 (international flights) rather than Terminal 2 (charter flights); buses connect the two. Both have cash machines (at Terminal 1, near exit 4 at Banca Nazionale del Lavoro), banks, and change offices. Terminal 1 has a pharmacy, eateries, and a TI (daily 8:00–20:00; when you exit the baggage-carousel area, go right; tel. 02-5858-0080 or 02-5858-0230). At the *tabacchi* shop, buy a phone card and confirm your hotel reservation.

You have three easy ways to get to downtown Milan: by train, shuttle bus, or taxi.

The Malpensa Express **train** zips between Malpensa Airport and Milan's Cadorna station (which is both a Metro stop and a small train station), closer to the Duomo than the central train station (€9.50, sometimes discounted to €6 for Alitalia passengers, 40 min, 2/hr, departing airport at :15 and :45 past the hour, departing Cadorna at :20 and :50 past the hour, runs from 6:00–24:00, no railpasses, tel. 02-27763 or 02-20222, www.ferrovienord.it /webmxp/). At the airport, follow signs (*Treni* and Malpensa Express) down the stairs; you'll go through a glass tunnel to the ticket office. After buying your ticket, take the ramp down to the tracks. If you're leaving Milan to go to the airport, take the Metro to the Cadorna stop, surface, and buy a ticket at the Malpensa Express office in the station. Purchase your ticket before you board, or you'll pay €2.60 extra to buy it on the train.

Two companies run **buses** between Malpensa Airport and Milan's central train station. The buses are virtually identical in everything except price, using the same departure points: in front of the airport and from Piazza Luigi di Savoia at the east side of the train station. Buy your ticket from the driver for the 50-minute trip. Each company's buses depart every 20 to 30 minutes, but because the schedules are generally staggered, you'll find buses running every 10 to 15 minutes. The cheaper Malpensa Shuttle bus costs €4.20 (runs from station 4:30–22:30, from airport 6:40–0:15, at airport buy ticket on bus or at Airport 2000 office between exits 5 and 6, catch bus at exit 5, tel. 02-5858-3185, www.malpensa-shuttle.com). The Malpensa Bus Express costs €5 (from station 5:10–22:30, from airport 6:30–23:50, catch bus at exit 6, pay driver).

**Taxis** into Milan cost up to €80 (insist on meter, avoid hustlers in airport halls).

To **sleep** near Malpensa, consider **Hotel Cervo**, which offers newly renovated rooms and transport to and from the nearby airport (Sb-€62, Db-€83, CC, air-con, restaurant, parking, Via de Pinedo 1, Somma Lombardo 21019, Malpensa, tel. 0331-230-821, fax 0331-230-156, www.hotelcervo.it, e-mail: hotelcervo@malpensa.it).

**Linate:** Most European flights fly into Linate, eight kilometers (5 miles) east of Milan. The airport has a bank (just past customs, decent rates) and a TI (daily 8:30–20:00, tel. 02-7020-0443). Linate is linked by STAM buses with the central train station (Piazza Luigi di Savoia on east side of Milan's central station; buy €2.60 tickets from driver, 2/hr, runs from station 5:40–21:35, from airport 6:05–23:35, in general buses leave at :05 and :35 after the hour in either direction, tel. 02-717-106 or 02-711-6982); from the station, take the Metro or a taxi to your hotel. Taxis from Linate to the Duomo cost about €18.

**Between Malpensa and Linate:** The Malpensa Shuttle company runs a bus between the airports every 90 minutes (€7.75, from 6:00–20:00, 75 min).

# NEAR MILAN: STRESA, BORROMEO ISLANDS, AND LAKE MAGGIORE

Lake Maggiore is ringed by mountains, snow-capped in spring and fall, and lined with resort towns such as Stresa. This town is special mainly because of its boat dock—launching you to the islands of Lake Maggiore.

The three islands are named for the Borromeo family, who lovingly turned them into magical retreats with elaborate villas and fragrant gardens. Isola Bella has the palace and terraced garden; Isola Madre has a villa and sprawling garden; and Isola Pescatori is simply small, serene, and residential. The Borromeos, who made their money from banking and trading, enjoyed the arts—from paintings (hung in lavish abundance throughout the palace and villa) to plays (performed in an open-air theater on Isola Bella) and marionette shows (you'll see the puppets that performed here).

Tourists flock to the lakes in May and June (when flowers are in bloom) and in September. Concerts held in scenic settings draw music-lovers, particularly during the Musical Weeks in August

## Stresa and Borromeo Islands

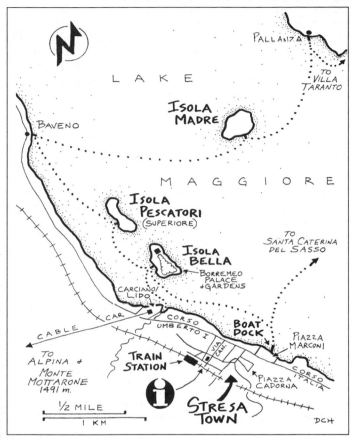

(concert schedule in English at www.stresa.net/settimanemusicali).
For fewer crowds, visit in April, July, and August (when Italians
prefer the Mediterranean beaches), and October. In winter, the
snow-covered mountains attract skiers.

## Planning Your Time
This region is best visited on a sunny day, when the mountains
are clear, the lake is calm, and the heat of the sun brings out the
scent of the blossoms.

The two top islands for sightseeing are Isola Bella and
Isola Madre. Isola Pescatori has no sights but is a peaceful place
for lunch.

**Day trip from Milan:** Catch an early train from Milan (there are two 50-min fast trains, leaving at 8:10 and 11:10, each requiring a seat reservation—can be purchased when you buy your ticket). In Stresa, walk 10 minutes downhill to the boat dock, and catch a boat to Isola Madre first (try to see it before it closes for lunch). Continue on to the Villa Taranto gardens on the mainland (if you want to see these), or backtrack to Isola Pescatori for a lazy lunch. Ideally, save Isola Bella for the afternoon, because tour groups mob it in the morning.

From Isola Bella, you have two choices: Catch the boat to the Stresa dock, see the town, and walk back to the train station. Or, if you'd like to ride the mountain cable car, take the boat from Isola Bella to Carciano (5 min) to reach the lift. From either dock, it's about a 10-minute walk to the train station.

**Overnight:** Small, touristy Stresa makes a fine first or last stop in Italy, because its connections with Milan's airport don't involve a transfer in big Milano (see "Transportation Connections," below).

## Orientation

Stresa clings to its shore, stretched thin from one end (main boat dock and a little downtown that's like an open-air shopping mall) to the other (the Lido, with the Carciano boat dock and a mountain cable car). The docks are a 15-minute walk apart. In between is a string of stately, expensive lakeside hotels. (Hemingway set part of his novel *A Farewell to Arms* in the Grand Hotel des Iles Borromées, where the luxurious "Hemingway Suite" goes for €2,750 a night.) A narrow promenade runs along most of the waterfront, offering expansive views of the lake, islands, and mountains. Market day is on Friday morning at Piazza Capucci, several blocks inland from the main square, Piazza Matteotti.

**Arrival in Stresa:** At the train station, ask for a free city map at the newsstand (marked *Libri Giornali Riviste*). To get to the downtown, exit right from the station and take your first left (on Viale Duchessa di Genova). This takes you straight down to the lake (the boat dock is about 4 blocks to your right; ask for a boat schedule at the ticket window). The TI is next door to the right. A taxi to the TI or boat dock costs about €6.

**Tourist Information:** The helpful TI, located to the right of the ticket window at the boat dock, gives out free maps and boat schedules (daily in summer 10:00–12:30 & 15:00–18:30, in winter Mon–Fri 10:00–12:30 & 15:00–18:30, Sat 10:00–12:30, closed Sun, Piazza Marconi 16, tel. 0323-30150, www.distrettolaghi.it).

**Internet Access:** It's a block off the main square, Piazza Matteotti, in the old center (€3/30 min, Mon–Fri 9:00–12:30 & 14:30–19:00, Sat 9:00–12:30, closed Sun, Via de Vit 15A).

# Getting around Lake Maggiore

Boats link the islands and towns on opposite shores, running about twice hourly (allow roughly 10 min between stops). Short hops cost €3. It's simplest to get a day pass: For the three islands, it's €6. For the islands and Pallanza (a town on the opposite shore), it's €8. For €10, add Villa Taranto (gardens).

If you're planning to tour Isola Bella and Isola Madre, you'll save money if, when you buy your boat pass, you ask to include the admission fee (*ingresso*) to the sights. The total package for the boat rides and admissions is €15—a good deal since the admissions alone total over €16. The ticket office might not display a sign advising you of this opportunity—you need to ask.

Boats run daily from March through October. (Although the boats sail in almost any weather and the rides are short, choppy water can make for a queasy ride.) The map in this chapter shows the route: Stresa, Isola Bella, Isola Pescatori, Baveno (lakeside town), Isola Madre, Pallanza, and Villa Taranto. This route is part of a longer one. To follow the boat schedule (free, available at boat docks, TI, and maybe your hotel), look at the Arona–Locarno timetable for trips from Stresa to the islands, and the Locarno–Arona timetable for the return trip to Stresa. A short five-minute boat ride connects the Carciano dock (and cable-car lift) and Isola Bella. If you're doing the lift and the islands, transfer at Isola Bella.

Go right to the dock to buy your ticket. The little booths promoting private taxi boats outside the docks will overcharge you. At the main Stresa dock, go to the ticket window inside the building in front of the dock; at Carciano, go to the booth directly next to the dock, not the booth near the stream (boat info: tel. 800-551-801).

# Sights—Stresa, Islands, and Gardens

▲▲▲**Isola Bella**—The palace dominating the island was named by Charles Borromeo for his wife, Isabella. The island itself is touristy, with a gauntlet of souvenir stands and a corral of restaurants. A few backstreets provide evidence that people actually live here.

The sight consists of the impressive palace, a chilly lower floor built to look like a series of grottos, and a formal, terraced garden nearly covering the island.

The **palace** has Murano glass chandeliers, Gobelin-covered chairs, intricate tapestries, plenty of paintings, and even some historic importance. The Conference of Stresa was held in the palace's Music Room in 1935, when Mussolini met with British and French diplomats in an attempt to scare Germany out of starting World War II; this "Stresa Front" soon fizzled when Mussolini attacked Ethiopia and joined forces with Hitler. In Napoleon's

Room in August of 1797, the emperor himself and his wife spent two nights—without a private bath, hair-dryer, or CNN. Fresh from conquering Venice, Napoleon hadn't called ahead for reservations for his party of 62. Count Borromeo wrote later: "We may thank God that the stay was a short one." The puppetry room is fun, with dragons, donkeys, King Kong, servants, and uppity upper-class puppets, each with its own personality.

The 18th-century **grotto** downstairs, decorated from ceiling to floor with shell motifs and black-and-white stones, still serves its original function of providing a cool refuge from Italy's heat.

The terraced Baroque **gardens**, which give the island the look of a stepped pyramid from the water, are topped with a nautically themed wall and a rearing unicorn—the symbol of the Borromeo family (€8.50, April–mid-Oct daily 9:00–12:30 & 13:30–18:30, last entry 1 hr before closing, English descriptions in palace, WC at entrance to garden, tel. 0323-30556).

Picnicking is not allowed in the garden, but you can picnic at the point of the island (free and open to the public); take the mosaic sidewalk to the left of the palace entrance.

▲**Isola Pescatori**—This sleepy island, the smallest and most residential of the three, has a couple of good seafood restaurants, picnic benches, views, and blissfully nothing to do—under arbors of wisteria.

▲▲▲**Isola Madre**—This island consists almost solely of this sight: An interesting, furnished villa and a lovely garden with some exotic birds and plants.

The 16th-century **villa**, which has enough furniture and art to give it warmth, is notable for its 19th-century puppet theater and many marionettes—angels, soldiers, villains, Asian visitors, and more—made out of wood, fabric, and porcelain. The smaller Hell Theater has suitably spooky skeleton puppets and devilish dragons. You'll also see canopied beds, clothes, and jewelry, along with Countess Borromeo's 19th-century doll collection (not a Barbie in the bunch).

The **gardens**, which bloom from April through October, are especially beautiful in May, when the azaleas and rhododendrons perform. Slow-moving, sleepy birds call this island home; be careful not to step on their plumage.

A one-way route of the sight is clearly signed for you, taking you through the gardens first and then the villa, ending at the chapel (€8.25, daily 9:00–12:30 & 13:30–17:30, no photos in villa, WC next to chapel outside villa, tel. 0323-31261).

Visit this island only if you intend to tour the sight, because there's nothing else here except La Piratera Ristorante Bar (daily

8:00–17:30, €18 tourist *menu*, sit-down meals and simple sandwiches to go, picnic at rocky beach a minute's walk from restaurant). Unless you go to the restaurant, it's pointless to arrive at this island between 12:30 and 13:30, when the villa and gardens are closed (though if you're already in the gardens during the lunch hour, you can stay).

▲**Villa Taranto Botanical Gardens**—Garden-lovers will enjoy this large landscaped park, located on the mainland a 10-minute boat ride from Isola Madre or a 20-minute bus ride from the boat dock in Stresa. The gardens are a Scotsman's labor of love. Starting in the 1930s, Neil MacEacharn created this garden of delights—bringing in thousands of plants from all over the world—and here he stays, in the small mausoleum. The park's highlight is the terraced garden with a series of cascading pools.

Villa Taranto is directly across the street from the boat dock on the opposite shore (€7, April–Oct 8:30–19:30, ticket office closes at 18:30, parking located on outskirts of Pallanza, tel. 0323-404-555). A simple bar is by the dock and a ristorante/bar (and WC) is at the park entrance.

**Mountain Cable Car**—From Stresa's Lido, a cable car takes you up—in two stages and a 20-minute ride—to the top of Mount Mottarone (1,491 meters, or 4,892 feet). From here, you get great views, and, by taking a short hike, a bird's-eye view of the small, neighboring Lake Orta. The biggest snowcapped mountain you see is Monte Rosa, Italy's second-highest mountain (4,600 meters/ 15,200 feet; Italy's highest is Monte Bianco/Mont Blanc on Italy– France border, 4,810 meters/15,775 feet).

Cable-car options include a round-trip (€11); a one-way up (€7) and a hike or bike ride down; or consider the midway Alpina stop, where a 10-minute walk leads to the Alpine Gardens (free, April–mid-Oct Tue–Sun 9:00–18:00, closed Mon, about 1 km, or 0.6 mile, from cable car). From the Alpine Gardens (a great picnic spot), you get an incredible view of the islands floating in the lake below, but if you love greenery, the gardens on the islands and at Taranto blow this humble collection of alpine plants out of the water. If you're hiking down, bring a good map and allow 3.5 hours from the top of Mount Mottarone, or 1.5 hours from Alpine Gardens.

You can rent a bike at the base of the cable-car lift (full-suspension mountain bike-€26/day, €21/half day, regular bikes about €5 less, helmets, tel. 0323-30295) and bring it on the cable car with you (€5.50–9.20 extra).

The cable cars run every 20 minutes, unless it's windy, lunchtime (roughly 12:10–13:50), or November. Try this well before or right after the lunch break; otherwise you'll be either rushed or bored at the top (cars run April–Oct 9:10–17:30, WCs at base and top, tel. 0323-30295).

## Side-Trips from Stresa
▲Scenic Boat and Rail Trip to Locarno and Centovalli— An enjoyable all-day excursion from Stresa involves three segments. Take the boat from Stresa to the end of Lake Maggiore past loads of small lakeside hamlets to Locarno, in the Italian-speaking Swiss canton of Ticino (bring your passport). Spend an hour or so exploring this lakeside town. Then catch the "Centovalli" train from Locarno for a 90-minute ride that links together remote mountain villages, as you return to Italy and the town of Domodossola. From here, frequent trains run to Stresa.
▲Lake Orta—Just on the other side of Mount Mottarone is the small lake of Orta. The main town, Orta San Giulia, has a beautiful lakeside piazza ringed by picturesque buildings. The piazza faces the lake with a view of Isola San Giulia. Taxi boats (€2.60 round-trip) make the five-minute trip throughout the day. The island is worth a look for the church of San Giulio and the circular "path of silence" that takes about 10 minutes. In peak season, Orta is anything but silent, but off-season or early or late in the day, this place is full of peace and magic.

The train ride from Stresa to Orta-Miasino (a short walk from the lakeside piazza) takes just under two hours and requires a change in Domodossola.

## Sleeping in Stresa
**(€1 = about $1, country code: 39)**
Because Stresa town is just a resort, I'd day-trip from Milan, but here are good options if you'd like to stay.

**HIGHER PRICED**
**Hotel Milan Speranza** is an impersonal, four-star, corporate-style hotel which caters mostly to tour groups, with 176 predictably comfortable rooms (many with lake views) in two separate buildings, both across from the boat dock (Db-€98–176, CC, air-con, elevator, tel. 0323-31178, fax 0323-32729, e-mail: hotmispe@tin.it).

**MODERATELY PRICED**
**Hotel Moderno** offers 56 soothing pastel rooms on a pedestrian street a block from the main square (Db-€120, ask for quiet room on courtyard, closed mid-Oct–mid-March, CC, elevator, Via Cavour 33, in Piazza Matteotti with your back to the lake, go right—up small street, tel. 0323-933-773, fax 0323-933-775, e-mail: hotmoder@tin.it).

**Hotel Primavera,** next door to Hotel Moderno, is run by friendly Alberto Ferraris and his family. Most of the 34 rooms have terraces, some with lake views (Sb-€63–85, Db-€85–110, tel. 0323-31286, fax 0323-33458, e-mail: hotelprimavera@stresa.it). Alberto also owns the homier **Hotel Meeting**, closer to the train station (same prices, sundeck on 3rd floor, Via Bonghi 9, tel. 0323-327-412, fax 0323-33458, e-mail: hotelmeeting@stresa.it, Web site for both hotels: www.stresahotels.net).

**LOWER PRICED**
**Hotel Saini Meuble** is a cozy, peaceful haven with 14 tidy rooms located in a pedestrian zone in the old center (Sb-€50, Db-€90, lower prices off-season, includes breakfast, CC, elevator, Via Garibaldi 10, from Piazza Matteotti head up Via Mazzini and turn left on Via Garibaldi, tel. 0323-934-519, fax 0323-31169, www.stresa.org, e-mail: hotelsaini@tiscali.it).

**Albergo Luina** is a cheap sleep without a tour group in sight. The seven rooms, above a restaurant, are basic and clean (S/Sb-€31–46, D/Db-€47–68, no CC, 10 percent discount with this book, Via Garibaldi, 2 blocks off Piazza Matteotti, with back to lake, go left up small street, tel. 0323-30285, e-mail: luinas-tresa@yahoo.it).

## Eating in Stresa
**Le Botte** offers a variety of Piemonte's regional specialties in a casual atmosphere (daily 12:00–15:00 & 18:30–22:30, Via Mazzini 6/8, tel. 0323-30462).

**Osteria degli Amici** serves up tasty risotto, pastas, and pizzas with fast and friendly service in the old center (daily 12:00–14:30 & 19:00–24:00, Via Bolongaro 33, tel. 0323-30453).

**Ristorante Pescatore,** a block away, offers a paella of mussels, calamari, shrimp, and huge prawns in saffron rice for €35 for two people (could easily serve 3), and a host of other seafood specialties (Fri–Wed 19:00–22:00, closed Thu, Vicolo del Poncivo 3, tel. 0323-31986).

**La Rosa dei Venti** is the locals' favorite pizzeria, located on the main drag, Corso Italia 50, two blocks south of the boat dock (Wed–Mon 12:00–14:00 & 19:00–22:00, closed Tue, tel. 0323-31431).

## Transportation Connections—Stresa
**By train to: Milan** (hrly, 50 min fast train, 1.25-hr slow train), **Venice** (1/day, many more with changes in Milan, 4 hrs), **Domodossola**—French border (hrly, 35 min).

**To Malpensa Airport:** For a **train/bus combination,**

take the train toward Milan (hrly), get off at Gallarate (about 40 min from Stresa), where frequent, cheap shuttle buses run to Malpensa's Terminal 1 (€2.50, pay driver, 3/hr, 45 min; from Gallarate, bus departs from train station and runs 6:00–19:15; from Malpensa's Terminal 1, bus departs outside train station and runs 5:35–19:50).

**Airport buses** run between Stresa and Malpensa (€8, 50 min, leaves airport at 8:45, 9:30, 11:30, 14:30, 17:30, 19:30, and 20:30; leaves Stresa at 6:30, 8:30, 10:30, 13:30, 16:30, 18:30, and 19:30; confirm schedule, must reserve in advance if departing from Stresa, tel. 0322-844-862).

**Taxis** to the airport cost €80 (€100 for very early or very late service) and take about an hour; your hotel can arrange the taxi for you but may charge you for it. It's easy to arrange a taxi on your own at the taxi stand at the train station or call Franco and Tiziano Ferrara's Taxi and Minibus Rental (cellular 335-644-5319).

# LAKE COMO
## (LAGO DI COMO)

Commune with nature where Italy is welded to the Alps, in the lovely Italian Lakes District. The million-euro question is: Which lake? For the best mix of accessibility, scenery, and off-beatness, Lake Como is my choice. You'll get a complete dose of Italian-lakes wonder and aristocratic-old-days romance. Bustling Milan, just an hour away, doesn't even exist. Now it's your turn to be *chiuso per ferie* (closed for vacation).

Lake Como, lined with elegant, 19th-century villas, crowned by snowcapped mountains, and busy with ferries, hydrofoils, and little passenger ships, is a good place to take a break from the intensity and obligatory turnstile culture of central Italy. It seems half the travelers you'll meet have tossed their itineraries into the lake and are actually relaxing.

Today the hazy, lazy lake's only serious industry is tourism. Thousands of lakeside residents travel daily to nearby Lugano, in Switzerland, to find work. The lake's isolation and flat economy have left it pretty much the way the 19th-century Romantic poets described it.

## Planning Your Time

If relaxation's not on your agenda, Lake Como shouldn't be either. Even though there are no essential activities, plan for at least two nights so you'll have an uninterrupted day to see how slow you can get your pulse.

Lake Como is Milan's quick getaway, and the sleepy mid-lake village of Varenna is the gateway and handiest base of operations. With good connections to Milan, Malpensa Airport, and midlake destinations, Varenna is my favorite home base.

## The Italian Lakes

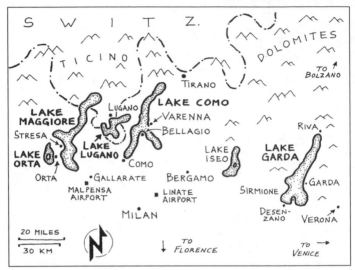

## Arrival in Varenna

I zip directly by train from Milan to Varenna, set up, and limit my activities to midlake (Varenna and Bellagio). From Milan's central station, catch a train heading for Sondrio or Tirano (often confused with Torino—wrong city). Be certain your train stops in Varenna; look at the fine print on the *Partenze* (departures) schedule posted at Milan's train station to make sure Varenna is listed. Trains leave about hourly (at :15 past the hour). Sit on the left for maximum lake-view beauty. Get off at Varenna-Esino. (Note that the name Varenna-Esino appears only at the station. Train schedules list simply Varenna. Same place.)

You can also get to Varenna from Milan via the town of Como. Trains take you from Milan to Como (50-min rides usually leave at :25 past each hour), where you can catch a boat for the two-hour ride (about hourly, last departure at 19:00, €6.70–9.60) up the lake to Varenna.

## Getting around Lake Como

**By Boat:** Lago di Como is well-served by boats and hydrofoils. The lake service is divided into three parts: south-north from Como to Colico; midlake between Varenna, Bellagio, Menaggio, and Cadenabbia (Villa Carlotta); and the southeastern arm to Lecco. Unless you're going through Como, you'll probably limit your cruising to the midlake service (boat info: tel. 031-579-211

## Lake Como

2 MILES
3 KM

N

MONTE GRONA

MENAGGIO

20 KM TO LUGANO, SWITZ. (SCENIC BUS)

CADENABBIA

VILLA CARLOTTA

JAY LENNO

TREMEZZO

OSPEDA-LETTO

CAMPO

TO COMO

ISOLA COMACINA

PUNTA BALBIONELLA

LAGO DI COMO

TO TIRANO & ST. MORITZ

BELLANO

VARENNA

TRAIL

SOURCE

FIUME-LATTE (TINY RIVER)

PUNTA SPARTI-VENTO

PESCALLO

BELLAGIO

LAGO DI LECCO

MANDELLO

TO MILANO 1 HOUR

DCH

or toll-free 800-551-801). Boats go about hourly between Varenna, Menaggio, and Bellagio (€2.50 per hop, 15 min, daily 7:00–21:00).

Passengers pay the same for car or passenger ferries, but 50 percent more for the enclosed, stuffy, speedy-but-less-scenic hydrofoil. The free schedule (available at TIs, hotels, and boat docks) lists times and prices. Stopovers aren't allowed, and there's no break for round-trips, so buy a ticket for each ride. The one-day, €6.80 midlake pass saves you money if you make three rides.

Boat schedule literacy tips: *Feriale* = workdays, Monday–Saturday. *Festivo* = Sunday and holidays. *Partenze da* = departing from. *Autotraghetto* = car ferry. *Aliscafo* = hydrofoil. *Battello* = passenger-only ferry.

**By Car:** With the parking problems, constant traffic jams, and expensive car ferries, this is no place to drive if you don't need to. While you can easily drive around the lake, the road is narrow, congested, and lined by privacy-seeking walls, hedges, and tall fences. It costs €7.50 to take your car onto a ferry. And parking is rarely easy where you need it, especially in Bellagio. Park in Varenna and cruise. Parking is free Monday through Friday near Albergo Beretta (limited to 1 hr Sat–Sun) and at the station (pay by the hour Sat–Sun). Blue lines mean metered parking (€1/hr, 2 hrs max, 8:00–19:00, overnight plus 2 hrs is OK); and yellow lines mean residents only.

## Varenna

This town of 800 people offers the best of all lake worlds. Easily accessible by train, on the less-driven side of the lake, Varenna has a romantic promenade, a tiny harbor, narrow lanes, and its own villa. It's the right place to savor a lakeside cappuccino or *aperitivo*. There's wonderfully little to do here, and it's very quiet at night. The *passerella* (lakeside walk, unlit but safe after dark) is adorned with caryatid lovers pressing silently against each other in the shadows.

**Tourist Information:** Varenna's TI is on the main square to the right of the church (Pro Varenna, Tue–Sat 10:00–12:30 & 15:30–18:30, Sun 10:00–12:30, closed Mon, Nov–April Sat–Sun 10:00–12:30 only, tel. 0341-830-367, www.varennaitaly.com).

A bank, cash machine, and small post office (Mon–Fri 8:00–13:30, Sat 8:00–11:30, closed Sun) are just off the main square (see town map). For accommodations, see "Sleeping and Eating on Lake Como," page 384.

## Hello Varenna Walk

Since you came here to relax, this short walk gives you just the town basics.

**Bridge near train station:** This main road bridge, just below the train station, spans the tiny Esino River. The river divides two communities, Perledo (which sprawls up the hill—notice the church spire high above) and the old fishing town of Varenna (huddled around its harbor). While the towns were joined in fascist times, today they are separate and not without animosity. Perledo used to have a fine beach (where the river hits the lake) until recent storms washed it away. Varenna wanted to collaborate, remaking and sharing an inviting public beach here. Perledo refused. The train station is called Varenna-Esino for a third community higher in the hills. Now, follow the river down to the lakeside promenade by the ferry dock.

**Varenna ferry landing:** Since the coming of the train, Varenna has been *the* convenient access point from "midlake" (the communities of Bellagio, Menaggio, and Varenna) to Milan. From this viewpoint, you can almost see how Lake Como is

## Varenna

(TRAIN STN. TO CHURCH IS A 10 MIN. WALK)

---- PASSERELLA (LAKESIDE WALK)
IIIII STEPPED STREETS

TRAIN STATION
TRAIN TUNNEL
TRAIL TO CASTLE VEZIO
TRAIN TUNNEL
TO MILANO
TRAVEL AGENCY ❹
TO TIRANO
MAIN ROAD
❸
TRAIL TO ❿ & FIUMELATTE
BANK
CHURCH
MAIN RD. TO LECCO
❶
❼
WC
GARDENS
PASSENGER BOAT DOCK + TICKETS
❶❶
❻
PIAZZA SAN GIORGIO
BANK
GROC.
CAR FERRY DOCK
❷
❶❷
❾
HARBOR
POST
❺
L A K E
❶❸
❽
C O M O
TO MENAGGIO
TO BELLAGIO & COMO
DCH

❶ ALBERGO OLIVEDO
❷ ALBERGO MILANO
❸ HOTEL MONTE CODENO
❹ ALBERGO BERETTA
❺ VILLA ELENA ROOMS
❻ ALBERGO DEL SOLE
❼ VILLA CIPRESSI
❽ HOTEL DU LAC
❾ HOTEL VICTORIA
❿ TO HOTEL EREMO GAUDIO
⓫ RISTORANTE IL CAVATAPPI
⓬ VECCHIA VARENNA REST.
⓭ NILUS BAR & LA FRULLERIA / IL GELATO

shaped like a man. The head is the north end (to the right, up by the Swiss Alps). Varenna is the left hip. Menaggio, across the lake, is the right hip. And Bellagio (hiding behind the wooded hill) is where the legs come together—you can see the point (Punta Spartivento—"where the wind is divided"). In a more colorful description, a local poem says "Lake Como is a man with Colico the head, Lecco and Como the feet, and Bellagio the testicles" (in the local dialect, this rhymes). Ask a local to say it for you. The ridges high above the right hip are the border of Switzerland. The region's longtime poverty shapes the local character (much like the Great Depression shaped the outlook of a generation of Americans). Many still remember that this side of the lake was the

poorest, because those on the other (Menaggio) side controlled
the lucrative cigarette smuggling business over the Swiss border.
Today, the entire region is thriving (with tourism and a booming—
if mysterious—iron and steel industry . . . convenient to secret Swiss
bank accounts). Walk past the Hotel Olivedo (Olivedo means the
place where olive trees grow—Varenna is the only such place on
this side of the lake) and past the ferry dock to the *passerella*,
Varenna's elevated shoreline walk.

*Passerella:* A generation ago, a local eccentric (who won big-
time on an Italian TV game show) and a determined town carpen-
ter successfully promoted the idea to build Varenna's elegant lakeside walk, which connects the ferry dock with the old town center.
Strolling this, you'll come to the tiny two-dinghy concrete breakwater of a local villa. Lake Como is lined with elegant 19th-
century villas. Their front doors faced the lake to welcome boats.
At this point, the modern *passerella* cuts between this villa's water
gate and its private harbor. Around the next corner and over the
hump look up at another typical old villa—with a veil of serious
wisteria and a prime lakeview terrace. Many of these villas are
owned by the region's "impoverished nobility"—bred and raised
not to work and, therefore, unable now to cover the upkeep of
their sprawling houses. From here, also enjoy a good Varenna
town view. These buildings are stringently protected. You can't
even change the color of your paint.

**Varenna harborfront:** Walk past the community harbor
and under the old-time arcades to the fisherman's pastel homes,
which face the harbor. Notice there are no streets in town . . .
just characteristic stepped lanes called *contrada*. Varenna was
originally a fishing community. Even today, old-timers enjoy
Lago di Como's counterpart to lutefisk—air-dried and salted lake
"sardines." Called *missoltino*, these sardines are served with this
region's polenta (different from Venice's because buckwheat is
mixed in with the corn). At the south end of the harbor (across
from the gelato shop), belly up to the banister for another fine
pastel town view. Another local ditty goes "If you love Lake
Como, you know Bellagio is the pearl . . . but Varenna is the
diamond." Continue straight, leaving the harbor. A lane leads
around past Hotel du Lac (its fine lakeside terrace welcomes non-
residents for a drink) to the tiny and pebbly town beach (the only
place for a swim). From here climb uphill to the town square.

**Piazza San Giorgio:** Four churches face Varenna's town
square. The main church dates from the 14th century. Romantic
Varenna is an understandably popular spot for a wedding—rice
litters the church's front yard. Stepping inside, you'll find a few
humble but centuries-old bits of carving and frescoes. The black

marble floor was quarried right in town. Outside, past the WWI monument, is the TI. From this square you can head south to the gardens, or go north to go to the train station or up to the castle.

## Sights—Varenna

**Castle**—A steep trail leads to Varenna's ruined hilltop castle, Castello di Vezio. Start at the stairs to the left of Hotel Monte Codeno and figure on 30 minutes one-way (€2.50, daily 10:00–18:00 in summer, sometimes open late into the evening, closed when rainy, Oct–March open only Sat–Sun 10:00–18:00, closed Jan, tel. 335-465-186). The castle is pretty barren, apart from a couple of medieval contraceptive devices, but comes with a sleepy café at its entrance and a peaceful, traffic-free, one-chapel town.

**Gardens**—Two manicured lakeside gardens—Villa Cipressi and the adjacent monastery—are tourable for a €2.75 combo-ticket available at Villa Cipressi or the monastery (€2 for one garden only, March–Oct daily 9:00–19:00).

**Fiumelatte**—This town, a kilometer south of Varenna, was named for its milky river. It's the shortest river in Italy at 277 meters (800 feet) and runs—like most of the local tourist industry—only April through September. The *"La Sorgente del Fiumelatte"* brochure, available at Varenna's TI, lays out a walk from Varenna to the Fiumelatte to the castle and back. It's a 30-minute hike to the source *(sorgente)* of the milky river (at Varenna's monastery, take high road, drop into peaceful and evocative cemetery, and climb steps to the wooded trail leading to peaceful and refreshing cave where the river sprouts). For a longer lakeside hike, ask the TI about the *Sentiero del Viandante* (hike one-way up the lake and return by train).

**Tours**—For bus and boat tours, consider Varenna's travel agency, I Viaggi del Tivano, next to Albergo Beretta below the train station. They book planes, trains, and automobiles and can offer half-day and day-long tours of the region and into Switzerland; book tours by 18:00 the night before (Mon–Fri 8:30–12:30 & 15:00–19:00, Sat 9:00–12:30, closed Sun, CC accepted but there may be a nominal fee for small charges, Via per Esino 3, tel. 0341-814-009, www.tivanotours.com, helpful Silvia and Luana SE). They do town walks by appointment.

## More Sights—Lake Como

▲▲**Bellagio**—The self-proclaimed "Pearl of the Lake" is a classy combination of tidiness and Old World elegance. If you don't mind that "tramp in a palace" feeling, it's a fine place to surround yourself with the more adventurous of the posh travelers and shop for ties and umbrellas. The heavy curtains between the arcades

# Bellagio

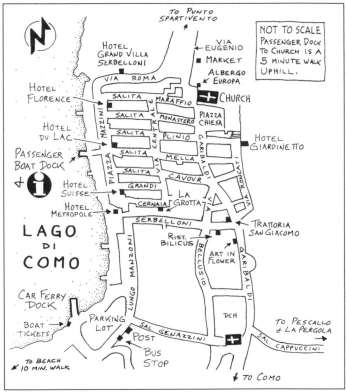

keep the visitors and their poodles from sweating. Thriving yet still cute, Bellagio is a much more substantial town than Varenna, which has almost no shops.

Steep-stepped lanes rise from the harborfront. While Johnny Walker and jewelry sell best at lake level, the locals shop up the hill. Piazza Chiesa, near the top of town, has a worth-a-look church.

The TI is right downtown at the passenger boat dock (daily 9:00–12:00 & 15:00–18:00, off-season closed Sun and Tue, tel. 031-950-204, e-mail: prombell@tin.it). If you need a destination, you can tour the Villa Serbelloni Park—overlooking the town—with a guide (€5.50, April–Oct 2 tours/day at 11:00 and 16:00, 90 min, ask at TI).

The administrative capital of the midlake region, Bellagio is located where the two southern legs of the lake split off. For an easy break in a park with a great view, wander right on out to the crotch. Meander past the rich and famous Hotel Villa Serbelloni, and walk five minutes to Punta Spartivento, literally, "the point that divides the wind." You'll find a Renoir atmosphere complete with an inviting bar/restaurant, a tiny harbor, and a chance to sit on a park bench and gaze north past Menaggio, Varenna, and the end of the lake to the Swiss Alps.

For another stroll, head south from the car-ferry dock down the tree-shaded promenade. Ten minutes later, you'll hit Bellagio's beach. The Lido di Bellagio has a chilly pool, lounge chairs, and a diving board into the lake (€3.75, daily in summer 10:00–18:00, tel. 031-950-597).

Bikers would enjoy a downhill mountain-bike run. Caval-calario Club shuttles you uphill, then lets you go (€29–34 includes bike rental, several itineraries, reservations necessary at least a day ahead, tel. & fax 031-964-814, cellular 339-530-8138, www.bellagio-mountains.it, e-mail: cavalcalarioclub@tiscalinet.it). They also offer horseback riding, paragliding, canoeing, kayaking, and trekking (see their Web site or call for details).

Bellagio has two docks a few minutes' walk apart: The northern dock is for the passenger-only ferry *(battello)* and the hydrofoil *(aliscafo)*; the southern dock is for the car ferry, which also takes foot passengers *(autotraghetto)*. To make sure you're waiting at the right dock for the boat you want to take, check the boat schedule carefully (posted near dock, free brochure from kiosk at dock). Its timetable is divided into three different schedules: *battello* (passengers only), *aliscafo* (passengers in a hurry), and *autotraghetto* (passengers and cars). Confirm your intentions at the kiosk near either dock.

▲**Menaggio**—Menaggio has more urban bulk than its neighbors. Since Lake Como is too dirty for swimming, consider its fine public pool. This is the starting point for a few hikes. Only 25 years ago, these trails were used by cigarette smugglers, sneaking at night from Switzerland back into Italy with tax-free cigarettes. The hostel (see "Sleeping," below) has information about mountain biking and catching the bus to trailheads on nearby Mount Grona.

**Villa Carlotta**—This is the best of Lake Como's famed villas (€6.50, April–Sept daily 9:00–18:00, Oct daily 9:00–12:00 & 14:00–16:30, closed Nov–March, tel. 034-440-405). I see the lakes as a break from Italy's art, but, if you're in need of a place that charges admission, Villa Carlotta offers an elegant neoclassical interior, a famous Canova statue, and a garden (its highlight, best in spring). If you plan to tour one villa on the lake, this is the best. Nearby Tremezzo and Cadenabbia are pleasant lakeside resorts an easy walk away. Boats serve all three places.

**Isola Comacina**—This remote little island (just south of Bellagio) offers peace, ancient church foundations, goats, sheep, and a lovely view of Lago di Como. It takes 30 minutes to walk around the island, but longer to savor it. Bring a picnic or try the snack bar at the dock. Look for trips to Isola Comacina on the Colico–Como schedule (listed in Lago di Como boat timetable brochure, free at ticket booths at ferry docks). The *isola* is accessible from Varenna (1 hr), Menaggio (45 min), or Bellagio (30 min). Check return times carefully (Como–Colico direction) and don't miss your boat. Usually only one trip a day each way works out for a visit.

**Como**—On the southwest tip of the lake, Como has a good, traffic-free old town, an interesting Gothic/Renaissance cathedral, and a pleasant lakefront with a promenade (TI open Mon–Thu 8:00–18:00, Fri 8:00–14:00, closed Sat–Sun, tel. 031-330-0111). It's an easy walk from the boat dock to the train station (from Milan in 30 min, usually leaving at :25 past each hour). Boats leave Como about hourly for midlake (ferries-€6.70, 2 hrs; hydrofoils-€9.60, 45 min; departures 7:00–19:00, tel. 031-579-211).

## Sleeping and Eating on Lake Como
**(€1 = about $1, country code: 39)**

Sleep Code: **S** = Single, **D** = Double/Twin, **T** = Triple, **Q** = Quad, **b** = bathroom, **s** = shower only, **CC** = Credit Cards accepted, **no CC** = Credit Cards not accepted, **SE** = Speaks English, **NSE** = No English.

To help you sort easily through these listings, I've divided the rooms into three categories based on the price for a standard double room with bath:

**Higher Priced**—Most rooms more than €120.
**Moderately Priced**—Most rooms €120 or less.
**Lower Priced**—Most rooms €80 or less.

The area is tight in August, snug in July, and wide open most of the rest of the year. Many places close in winter. All places listed (see map on page 379) are family-run and have lakeview rooms, and some English is spoken. If you're expecting friendliness, especially during peak season, you'll likely be disappointed. Enjoy the view. View rooms are given (sometimes for no extra cost) to those who telephone for reservations and request a *"camera con vista."* Prices get soft off-season (Nov–May). Varenna's TI, on the main square, can find private rooms (tel. 0341-830-367).

### Sleeping in Varenna *(zip code: 23829)*

#### HIGHER PRICED

**Albergo Milano**, located right in the old town, is great, with eight comfy, well-plumbed rooms all with balconies—rooms

1 and 2 have royal terraces—and views of the lake and gardens (Sb-€95–105, Db-€110–130, includes breakfast buffet, light lunches available, optional three-course dinner-€20 per person, CC, Via XX Settembre 29; from the station take main road to town and turn right at steep alley where sidewalk and guardrail break; tel. & fax 0341-830-298, U.S. fax 781/634-0094, www .varenna.net, e-mail: hotelmilano@varenna.net, enthusiastically run by Bettina and Egidio, SE, baby Carlotta NSE). This place whispers *luna di miele* (honeymoon) and offers a €250 three-night package including a welcome bottle of sparkling wine, candlelight dinner, and breakfast in bed.

**Hotel du Lac,** with 17 stylish and sleek rooms, overlooks the water (Db with view and balcony-€180, less without, suite Db-€217, includes breakfast, CC, parking-€11, Via del Prestino 4, tel. 0341-830-238, fax 0341-831-081, www.albergodulac.com, e-mail: albergodulac@tin.it, Ileana SE).

**Hotel Victoria**, on the main square, is a typical big hotel with a fine lakeview garden and a pool but no air-conditioning (43 rooms, Db-€147, add €34 for view, includes breakfast, CC, Piazza San Giorgio 5, tel. 0341-815-111, fax 0341-830-722, e-mail: hotelroyalvictoria@promo.it, SE).

## MODERATELY PRICED
**Albergo Olivedo**, facing the ferry dock, is a tidy, elegant, old hotel with old-time furniture and squeaky hardwood floors. Many rooms have glorious little lakeview balconies. It's a fine place to hang out and watch the children, boats, and sun come and go (prices vary with season and views: Sb-€35–58, Db-€80–110, includes breakfast, no CC, most rooms with air-con, closed mid-Nov–mid-Dec, tel. & fax 0341-830-115, www.olivedo.it, e-mail: olivedo@tin.it, hardworking Laura SE). In May, June, July, and September, half pension (dinner) is required—and rarely regretted—with the best rooms (€25 per person for dinner).

**Hotel Monte Codeno**, with 11 functional rooms and no views, is on the main road between the train station and lake (2 Sb-€70, Db-€93, includes breakfast buffet, extra bed-€16, 10 percent discount for 3 nights, CC, attached restaurant serves fresh fish and a €20 "Rick Steves" *menu*—see below, Via della Croce 2, tel. 0341-830-123, fax 0341-815-227, e-mail: ferrcas @tin.it, Marina Castelli SE). They rent a few apartments nearby (as low as €87 for 2 people, up to €195 for 6 people).

**Villa Cipressi**, in a huge, quiet garden, is a sprawling, centuries-old mansion with 32 plain, modern rooms and a garden people pay to see (Sb-€73–83, Db-€91, Db with view but no balcony-€104, Tb-€145, Qb-€176, includes breakfast,

CC, garden access, elevator, Internet access, Via IV Novembre 18, tel. 0341-830-113, fax 0341-830-401, e-mail:
villacipressi@libero.it, Elena SE).

**Eremo Gaudio**, standing isolated halfway up the hill with
a commanding lakeview high above Varenna, was once an orphan-
age (built by the Pirelli family—of tire fame), then a hermitage
(run by the Church), and—since 2000—a hotel. Perfect for monks
with champagne taste, it's peaceful, with awe-inspiring view balconies and a breakfast terrace. There are 12 bright, comfortable
rooms in the main building and 11 simpler, less expensive rooms
below in a section that still feels like a priest's dorm (open March–
Oct only, Sb-€67, Db-€83, Db with balcony-€93, Tb-€125,
Qb-€150, lower rooms: Sb-€47, Db-€62, no CC, free shuttle
service from station, Via Roma 11, tel. 0341-815-301, fax 0341-
815-314, www.eremogaudio.it, e-mail: eremogaudio@yahoo.it).
From Varenna's main square, walk south about 200 meters
(650 feet). Across from Villa Monastero, veer left up the high
road where you'll find the lower of two private, elevator-like
lifts that slide you up the mountainside to your perch.

**LOWER PRICED**

**Albergo Beretta**, on the main road a block below the station, has
10 decent rooms, several with balconies (D-€50, Db-€65, Qb-
€78, up to €18 extra for balcony, breakfast-€6, CC, coffee shop
on ground floor, Via per Esino 1, tel. & fax 0341-830-132, e-mail:
hotelberetta@iol.it, Tosca NSE, daughter Julia and Laura SE).

**Villa Elena**, a grandmotherly, low-energy place on the main
square, offers the best budget beds in town. English-speaking
Signora Vitali rents her four rooms at the same price—room
#1 has a bathroom and view terrace; the others don't even have
sinks (Db-€42 with fine breakfast, €37 without, no CC; it's
the vine-covered facade on Piazza San Giorgio #9 near Via San
Giovanni; tel. 0341-830-575). **Albergo del Sole**, a restaurant
on the same square, may rent eight rooms in 2003 (Piazza San
Giorgio 17, tel. 0341-815-218, NSE).

## Eating in Varenna

### On the Waterfront

**Albergo Olivedo's** restaurant serves fine food with no-nonsense
service across from the ferry dock. Sit either curbside under an
awning with a lake view, or in a classy old dining hall. While
Laura and her staff serve simple pasta lunches, evening meals are a
set two-course affair without an à la carte option (€25–35 dinner,
daily 12:15–14:00 & 19:30–21:15, CC, tel. 0341-830-115).

**Vecchia Varenna,** on the harbor, is respected, pricey, and the most romantic place in town. The menu features traditional cuisine and lake specialties (€25–45 meals, Tue–Sun 12:30–14:00 & 20:00–22:00, closed Mon, also closed Tue in winter, dressy indoors or on harborside deck, CC, reservations smart, tel. 0341-830-793).

The **Nilus Bar**, with a stainless steel diner interior and the best harborfront seating in town, is *the* place for a light meal. The young waitstaff serves dinner crêpes, pizzas, salads, hot sandwiches, and cocktails with a smile (daily in summer 10:00–1:30, spring and fall 12:00–23:00, Dec–Feb only Sat–Sun, Fulvia and Giovanni SE). For cold, sweet, and fruity treats, check out the harborfront **La Frulleria/Il Gelato** (next to Nilus Bar).

## Eating off the Water, on or near Piazza San Giorgio

**Ristorante del Sole**, facing the town square, serves edible meals and Naples-style pizzas (€5–8). Making few concessions to the tourist crowds, this restaurant caters to locals, providing a fun ambience and a garden in back (daily 12:00–14:30 & 19:00–22:00, closed Wed in winter, pizzas served until midnight, Piazza San Giorgio 21, tel. 0341-815-218).

**Victoria Grill**, also on the square, is more modern, with a cheery, neon-and-red-checkered-tablecloth atmosphere. They serve good, well-priced meals and pizza (daily 12:00–14:00 & 19:00–22:00, closed Mon in winter, CC, under fancy Hotel Victoria). Hotel Victoria also has a tired upscale restaurant welcoming non-guests with a set €27 *menu* and lakeview terrace seating.

**Ristorante il Cavatappi,** a five-table place on a quiet lane 30 meters (100 feet) off the town square, is the new place in town. Helpful owner-chef Mario serves old-time specialties (such as *missoltino*—the air-dried lake fish locals like more than tourists—as an antipasto). He's serious about his wine. Plan on spending €25 plus wine (daily 12:30–15:30 & 19:30–24:00, closed Wed off-season, CC, reservations smart, tel. 0341-815-349).

**Ristorante Monte Codeno,** on the main road without a hint of lake ambience, serves a special "Rick Steves" *menu* designed to give visitors a sampler of lake cuisine. For €20, you get eight different fishy appetizers, including *missoltino* and *carpione*, a *secondi* with polenta and risotto, a bit of the local *taleggio* cheese, and wine—all explained in a souvenir info sheet (12:00–14:30 & 19:00–21:00, CC, Via della Croce 2, tel. 0341-830-123).

*Picnics:* The three little grocery stores, on and just off the main square, have all you need for a classy balcony or breakwater picnic dinner (daily 7:30–12:30 & 15:30–19:30).

## Sleeping in Bellagio *(zip code: 22021)*

To locate hotels, see the map on page 382.

**HIGHER PRICED**

**Hotel du Lac**, a good waterfront splurge, comes with 48 rooms, a roof garden, and old-time elegance with no loss of comfort (Sb-€83–103, Db-€150–186, plusher superior Db-€206, includes breakfast, CC, parking-€8, air-con, TVs, minibars, closed Nov–March, Piazza Mazzini 32, tel. 031-950-320, fax 031-951-624, www.bellagiohoteldulac.com, e-mail: dulac@tin.it, Leoni family SE).

**Hotel Florence**, a few doors away and 150 years old, is family-run, with hardwood, pastels, and a rich touch of Old World elegance (30 rooms, Sb-€103–120, Db-€135–195 depending on view and balcony, Db suite-€250, includes breakfast, CC, live jazz in bar on Sun, closed Nov–March, elevator, handheld showers only, tel. 031-950-342, fax 031-951-722, www.bellagio.co.nz, e-mail: hotflore@tin.it, Ketzlar family SE).

**Hotel Metropole**, a tired but grand old place, dominates Bellagio's waterfront with 42 spacious and reasonably comfortable rooms and plush public spaces (Db-€104–129, some rooms with view balconies, CC, elevator, fridge, tel. 031-950-409, fax 031-951-534, Michela SE).

**Grand Hotel Villa Serbelloni**, a famous 19th-century palace, comes with history, doormen, two pools (inside and out), a garden, an elite clientele, and sky-high prices. While the grounds and public spaces are fancy, their 83 rooms don't quite merit the high prices (standard Db-€342, deluxe Db-€454, executive double-€585, pricier rooms have views, CC, air-con and all the comforts, tel. 031-950-216, fax 031-951-529, www.villaserbelloni.com).

**MODERATELY PRICED**

**Albergo Europa**, run with low energy, is in a concrete annex behind a restaurant, away from the waterfront. Its 10 rooms have no charm but reasonable comfort (Db-€93, CC, balconies lack views but are quiet, parking, Via Roma 21, tel. & fax 031-950-471, e-mail: albeuropa@tiscalinet.it, family Marchesi).

**LOWER PRICED**

**Hotel Suisse**, the cheapest place on the waterfront, has 10 simple rooms, hardwood floors, dim lights, fine bathrooms, unpredictable beds, and some great views and balconies (Db-€77 with this book in 2003, breakfast-€10, 10 percent discount in hotel restaurant with this book, CC, Piazza Mazzini 8/10, tel. 031-950-335, fax 031-951-755, e-mail: hsuisse@tiscalinet.it, Guido SE).

**Hotel Giardinetto**, at the top of town near the TI, 100 steps

above the waterfront, offers 14 squeaky-clean and quiet rooms.
The rooms are stark, but the breezy, peaceful garden is a joy and
available for picnics (S-€29, D-€42, Db-€52, Tb-€70, breakfast-
€6.20, no CC but personal checks and traveler's checks OK,
closed Nov–mid-Mar, Via Roncati 12, tel. 031-950-168, Eugene
and Laura Ticozzi SE).

## Eating in Bellagio

**Ristorante Bilicus**, a busy and jolly place serving regional and
lake cuisine with passion, is up a steep lane from the waterfront.
While a little pricey, the restaurant is famous for value and quality cooking (Tue–Sun 11:45–14:15 & 19:00–21:45, closed Mon,
indoor/outdoor seating, closed Nov–March, CC, Salita Serbelloni,
tel. 031-950-480).

**Trattoria S. Giacomo**, across the street, is less expensive
and respected for its traditional cuisine, such as *riso e filetto di pesce*—
rice and fish fillet (daily 12:00–14:30 & 19:00–21:30, closed Tue
off-season, CC, Salita Serbelloni 45, tel. 031-950-329).

**Hotel Metropole Ristorante**'s terrace offers the best waterfront view, though a mediocre food value.

Try **La Grotta** for pizza and pasta (daily 12:00–14:30 &
19:00–24:00, closed Mon off-season, CC OK with minimum
€25 purchase, Salita Cernaia 14, tel. 031-951-152).

**Art in Flower** serves up an assortment of quick and tasty
pastas (€3–8), sandwiches, huge salads, and creative gelato
sundaes (daily 9:00–24:00, closed Thu off-season, Via Garibaldi 21,
tel. 031-950-875).

At Punto Spartivento, the dramatic park just north of town,
you'll find **La Punta Ristorante** (daily 12:00–14:30, closed Tue
if rainy, tel. 031-951-888) and a great setting for a picnic. Pick up
picnic supplies at **Gastronomica Mini Market** (at Via Centrale
and Via Monastero, uphill from Hotel Florence). You'll find
picnic benches at the park, along the waterfront in town, and
lining the promenade south of town.

## Sleeping in or near Menaggio

### LOWER PRICED

**La Primula Youth Hostel** is a rare hostel. Run by Alberto and
Alexander, it caters to a quiet, savor-the-lakes crowd. Located 300
meters (985 feet) south of the Menaggio dock, it has a view terrace;
games galore; washing machine; bike, canoe, and kayak rentals
(€10.50/day, €15.50 for non-hostelers); and easy parking (closed
10:00–17:00 and Nov–mid-March, €11.50 per night in a 4- to
6-bed room with sheets and breakfast, €12 per bed with private

plumbing, hearty dinners for €9.30, reserve dinner by 18:00, no CC). Show this book for a free half-hour Internet connection (Ostello La Primula, Via IV Novembre 86, 22017 Menaggio, tel. & fax 0344-32356, www.hostels-aig.org/shop-uk/menaggio, e-mail: menaggiohostel@mclink.it). They have plenty of ideas for hikes and bike rides in the area.

**La Marianna B&B** is run by a husband-and-wife team, Ty and Paola (whose daughter now runs the youth hostel). They rent eight rooms and run a fine restaurant in Cadenabbia, two kilometers (1.25 miles) south of Menaggio (Db with view-€65–70, attached restaurant with lakeside terrace, CC, tel. 0344-43095, e-mail: inn@la-marianna.com). The hourly Como–Menaggio bus C-10 stops at its doorstep.

Buses run between Milan's Malpensa Airport and Menaggio (2/day year-round, 2 hrs, €13 one-way). Last year's departures: Direct from Menaggio to Malpensa at 6:30; Malpensa to Menaggio at 12:00.

*Other Hostels on Lago di Como:* The Villa Olmo hostel is at the south end of the lake in Como (€11.50/day, reception open 16:00–22:00, closed Dec–Feb, tel. 031-573-800), and another hostel is in the north at Domaso (€11/day, includes breakfast, closed Jan–Feb, tel. 0344-97449).

## Transportation Connections—Varenna

From any destination covered in this book, you'll get to Lake Como via Milan. The quickest Milan connection to any point midlake (Bellagio, Menaggio, or Varenna) is via the train to Varenna. If leaving Varenna by train, note that the Varenna station doesn't sell tickets. Purchase a ticket either at the Albergo Beretta bar or the helpful travel agency, I Viaggi del Tivano, next door. Stamp your ticket in the machine at the station before boarding.

**Milan to Varenna:** Catch a train at Milano Centrale (last year's schedule: 8:15, 9:15, 12:15, 14:15, 16:15, 18:00, 19:10, 20:15, and 21:10, 60 min, €4.20). In Milan, the large overhead train schedules list Sondrio and Tirano rather than Varenna, a small stop en route (look at the fine print in the departure schedule posted at the station to make sure Varenna is listed). Some cars on long trains don't even get a platform. Ask for help so you don't miss the stop. You may have to open the door yourself.

**Varenna to Milan:** Trains leave Varenna for Milano Centrale at 6:18, 7:24, 8:23, 10:19, 12:22, 14:22, 16:22, 18:22, 20:20, and 22:30. (Confirm these times.) Varenna makes a comfy last stop before catching the shuttle from Milan's station to the airport.

**Malpensa Airport to Varenna:** Two buses a day go direct to Varenna (€16.50, departs Terminal 1 at 11:00 and 21:30, 2 hrs).

**Varenna to Malpensa Airport:** Two buses a day go direct to Malpensa Airport (€16.50, departs Varenna at Albergo Beretta at 5:30 and 16:30, 2.25 hrs, must purchase tickets at least a day ahead at Varenna's travel agency—I Viaggi del Tivano, next to Albergo Beretta, Mon–Fri 8:30–12:30 & 15:00–19:00, Sat 9:00–12:30, closed Sun, Via per Esino 3, tel. 0341-814-009, www.tivanotours.com).

**Varenna to St. Moritz in Switzerland:** From Varenna, you have fantastic access to the Bernina Express and scenic train to St. Moritz. First take the train to Tirano and then transfer to St. Moritz (3/day, allow 6 hrs with transfer).

# THE DOLOMITES

Italy's dramatic limestone rooftop, the Dolomites, offers some of the best mountain thrills in Europe. Bolzano is the gateway to the Dolomites, and Castelrotto is a good home base for your exploration of Alpe di Siusi, Europe's largest alpine meadow.

The sunny Dolomites are well-developed, and the region's famous valleys and towns suffer from après-ski fever. The cost for the comfort of reliably good weather is a drained-reservoir feeling. Lovers of the Alps may miss the lushness that comes with the unpredictable weather farther north. But the bold limestone pillars, flecked with snow over green meadows under a blue sky, offer a worthwhile mountain experience.

A hard-fought history has left the region bicultural, with an emphasis on the German. Locals speak German first, and some wish they were still part of Austria. In the Middle Ages, as part of the Holy Roman Empire, the region faced north. Later, it was firmly in the Austrian Hapsburg realm. By losing World War I, Austria's South Tirol became Italy's Alto Adige. Mussolini did what he could to Italianize the region, including giving each town an Italian name. But even in the last decade, local secessionist groups have agitated violently for more autonomy.

The government has wooed locals with economic breaks that make it one of Italy's richest areas (as local prices attest), and today all signs and literature in the province of Alto Adige/Süd Tirol are in both languages. Many include a third language, Ladin, the ancient Latin-type language still spoken in a few traditional areas. (I have listed both the Italian and German, so the confusion caused by this guidebook will match that caused by your travels.)

In spite of all the glamorous ski resorts and busy construction cranes, the local color survives in a warm, blue-aproned,

## The Dolomites

ruddy-faced, long-white-bearded way. There's yogurt and yodel-ing for breakfast. Culturally as much as geographically, the area is reminiscent of Austria. The Austrian Tirol is named for a village that is now part of Italy.

## Planning Your Time

Train travelers should side-trip in from Bolzano (90 min north of Verona). To get a feel for the alpine culture, spend a night in Castelrotto. With two nights in Castelrotto, you can actually get out and hike. Tenderfeet ride the bus, catch a chairlift, and stroll. For mountain thrills, do a six-hour hike. And for a thrill that won't soon fade away, spend a night in a mountain hut. This means two nights in Castelrotto straddling a night in a hut.

Car hikers with a day can drive the three-hour loop from Bolzano or Castelrotto (Val Gardena–Sella Pass–Val di Fassa)

and ride one of the lifts to the top for a ridge walk. Connecting
Bolzano and Venice by the Great Dolomite Road takes two hours
longer than the autostrada but is far more scenic (see below).

Hiking season is mid-June through mid-October. The region
is packed, booming, and blooming from mid-July through mid-
September. Spring is dead, with no lifts running, huts closed,
and the most exciting trails still under snow. Many hotels and
restaurants close in April and November. Ski season (Dec–
Easter) is busiest of all.

## Helpful Hints

**Study Ahead:** The South Tirol's Web site is www.hallo.com.

**Sleeping:** Most towns offer hotels, which charge about €34
to €36 per person, and private homes, which offer beds for as low
as €16 but are often a long walk from the town centers. Beds
nearly always come with a hearty breakfast. Those traveling in
peak season or staying for only one night pay more. Local TIs
can always find budget travelers a bed in a private home *(Zimmer)*.
Drivers on a tight budget should pick remote *Zimmer*s. Most
mountain huts offer reasonable doubles, cheap dorm *(lager)* beds,
and inexpensive meals. Call any hut to secure a spot before hiking
there (most huts open mid-June–Sept only).

**Eating:** In local restaurants, there is no cover charge.
A *Jausenstation* is a place that serves cheap, hearty, and traditional mountain-style food to hikers.

## BOLZANO (BOZEN)

*Willkommen* to the Italian Tirol! If it weren't so sunny, you could
be in Innsbruck. This enjoyable old town of 100,000 is the most
convenient gateway to the Dolomites, especially if you're relying
on public transportation. It's just the place to take a Tirolean stroll.

Bolzano is easy. Everything mentioned in Bolzano is a 10-
minute walk from Piazza Walther. To get to the TI and downtown, leave the train station and veer left up the tree-lined Viale
Stazione (Bahnhofsallee), walk past the bus station (on your left)
two blocks to Piazza Walther, where you'll find the helpful TI
on your right (Mon–Fri 9:00–18:30, Sat 9:00–12:30, closed Sun,
tel. 0471-307-000, www.bolzano-bozen.it). Pick up the city map
(includes a walking tour). The excellent Dolomites information
center is one block west of Piazza Walther down Via Posta
across from the post office (Mon–Fri 9:00–12:00 & 15:00–17:00,
Parrocchia 11, tel. 0471-413-809). For Internet access, try
Happy Time at Piazza Erbe.

The medieval heart of town is just beyond Piazza Walther.
Follow your favorite Italian and head down the arcaded Via dei

Portici to Piazza Erbe, with its ancient and still-thriving open-air produce market (wash your produce in the handy drinking fountain in the middle of the market).

## Sights—Bolzano

▲▲**South Tirol Museum of Archaeology (Museo Archeologico dell'Alto Adige)**—This excellent museum features the original Ice Man. "Oetzi the Ice Man" is a 5,000-year-old body found frozen with his gear in a glacier by some German tourists a few years ago. With the help of informative displays and a great audioguide, you'll learn about life in this prehistoric period way before ATM machines. You'll see a convincing reconstruction of Oetzi, and yes, you actually get to see the man himself lying peacefully inside a specially built freezer (€6.70, €4.70 if you're 65 or over, audioguide-€1.60, Tue–Sun 10:00–18:00, Thu until 20:00, last entry 60 min before closing, closed Mon, Jan 1, May 1, and Dec 1, near the river at Via Museo 43, tel. 0471-982-098, www.iceman.it).

**Domenican Church (Chiesa dei Domenicani)**—If you're an art-lover who won't make it to Padua to see Giotto's Scrovegni Chapel, drop by this 13th-century church to see its Chapel of St. John/San Giovanni (chapel near altar to the right), frescoed by the Giotto School. It lacks the high quality and that divine "Smurf" blue of the Scrovegni Chapel, but it gives you a sense of Giotto's vision (free, Mon–Sat 9:30–17:30, also see peaceful cloisters to right of church, Piazza Domenicani).

**Cable Car to Oberbozen**—Of the three different cable cars that can whisk you out of Bolzano, the most popular is the Ritten lift to the touristy town of Oberbozen (from Bolzano train station, walk about 5 blocks down Via Renon to reach the Rittner Sielbahn cable car, which runs hourly). More interesting than Oberbozen are the nearby "earth pyramids," a 20-minute walk from the cable car station. The pyramids are Bryce-like pinnacles rising out of the ridge. A little train runs along the ridge, connecting Oberbozen nearly hourly with other villages. Both the cable car and train cost €2.50 apiece (€3.50 round-trip) and run year-round.

Many are tempted to wimp out on the Dolomites and see them from a distance by hiking from Oberbozen to the Pemmern chairlift, riding to Schwarzseespitze, and walking 45 more minutes to the Rittner Horn. You'll be atop a 2,200-meter (7,000-foot) peak with distant but often hazy Dolomite views. It's not worth the trouble. (But if you're determined to do it and it's outside of summer, call the nearby Collalbo TI at tel. 0471-356-100 to make sure the trails are clear of snow.)

**Markets**—In additon to the produce market on Piazza Erbe

(daily except Sat afternoon and all day Sun), a market is held Saturday morning on Piazza della Pace.

## Sleeping in Bolzano
**(€1 = about $1, country code: 39, zip code: 39100)**
Sleep Code: **S** = Single, **D** = Double/Twin, **T** = Triple, **Q** = Quad, **b** = bathroom, **s** = shower only, **CC** = Credit Card, **no CC** = Credit Cards not accepted, **SE** = Speaks English, **NSE** = No English.

To help you sort easily through these listings, I've divided the rooms into three categories based on the price for a standard double room with bath:

**Higher Priced**—Most rooms more than €100.
**Moderately Priced**—Most rooms €100 or less.
**Lower Priced**—Most rooms €60 or less.
All of the listed hotels are in the city center.

### HIGHER PRICED
**Stadt Hotel Città** is ideally situated on Piazza Walther. The hotel's café spills out onto the piazza, offering a prime spot for people-watching. While the hotel is expensive for singles, it's a fine value for doubles, especially if you plan to spend any time in their Wellness Center—Turkish bath, massage by appointment, Finnish sauna, whirlpool—all free to hotel guests and the perfect way to unwind after a day of hiking or skiing in the Dolomites (Sb-€85–95, Db-€113–140, Tb-€138–170, superior rooms and family apartments available, includes breakfast, CC, air-con, elevator, Piazza Walther 1, tel. 0471-975-221, fax 0471-976-688, www.citta.sudtirol.com, e-mail: citta@sudtirol.com).

**Hotel Greif** is also right on Piazza Walther. When you walk into any of their 33 rooms, designed by artists, you feel like you're in a modern art installation. It's not cozy, but it is striking (5 types of rooms: comfort/superior/deluxe/junior suite/suite—priciest, Sb-€126–180, Db-€158–225, suites €260–300, includes buffet breakfast, CC, most rooms non-smoking, air-con, computers, laundry, parking-€16/day, Piazza Walther, entrance on Via della Rena, tel. 0471-318-000, fax 0471-318-148, www.greif.it, SE).

### MODERATELY PRICED
**Hotel Figl**, warmly run by Anton and Helga Mayr, has 23 comfortable rooms and an attached café on a pedestrian square a block from Piazza Walther (Sb-€75, Db-€95, junior suite-€110, apartment available, breakfast extra, CC, air-con, elevator, Kornplatz 9, tel. 0471-978-412, fax 0471-978-413, www.figl.net, e-mail: info@figl.net, SE).

The modern, clean, church-run **Kolpinghaus Bozen** has

plenty of rooms with twin beds and all the comforts. It makes one feel thankful (Sb-€46, Db-€72, Tb-€108, includes breakfast, CC, confusing elevator, Internet access with phone card, 4 blocks from Piazza Walther, near Piazza Domenicani at Spitalgasse 3, tel. 0471 308-400, fax 0471-973-917, www.kolping.it/bz, e-mail: kolping@tin.it, SE). The lineup in front of the building at lunch-time consists mainly of workers waiting for the institutional cafeteria to open up (€8 meals, open to public, Mon–Fri 11:45–14:00 & 18:30–19:30).

**LOWER PRICED**
**Gasthof Weisses Kreuz**, with 10 basic rooms, is a great value, but it's usually booked up (S-€29, D-€48, Db-€58, Tb-€75, includes breakfast, 1 block off Piazza Walther in old town at Kornplatz 3, tel. 0471-977-552, fax 0471-972-273, e-mail: weisseskreuzbz@yahoo.it, NSE).

# Eating in Bolzano
All listings are in the downtown core.

**Weisses Rosl** offers affordable Italian, German, and veggie options in a pub-like setting (8:00–24:00, closed Sat eve and all Sun, Via Bottai 6, 2 blocks north of Piazza Municipio, tel. 0471-973-267).

The next three places cluster at the southern edge of Piazza Erbe. **Hopfen and Co.** offers delicious meals (Mon–Sat 9:30–24:00, closed Sun, Piazza Erbe 17, tel. 0471-300-788). **Vogele**, a half block south, serves German/Italian cuisine and has a rare non-smoking floor upstairs, bigger than it initially looks (Mon–Sat 9:00–24:00, closed Sun, Via Goethe 3, tel. 0471-973-938). **Enoteca Bacaro**, a wine bar a half block east, is an intriguing spot for a glass of wine and bar snacks amid locals (Mon–Sat 9:00–21:00 closed Sun, located on alley off Via Argentieri 17, tel. 0471-971-421).

**Hostaria Argentieri**, pricier than the rest, serves Italian and German cuisine plus seafood in a classy setting (Mon–Sat 12:00–14:30 & 19:00–22:30, closed Sun, Via Argentieri 14, tel. 0471-981-718).

On Sundays, when virtually all restaurants are closed, try the cheap **Restaurant Blaues Schiff** (Lauben 57, tel. 0471-979-099) or **Gasthaus Batzenhausl** (Wed–Mon 18:30–24:00, closed Tue, Andreas Hofer Strasse 30, tel. 0471-976-183).

**Picnic:** Assemble the ingredients at the **Piazza Erbe** market; dine in a superb setting in Piazza Walther or in the park along the Talvera River. A **DeSpar** supermarket is on Via della Rena near Piazza Walther (Mon–Fri 8:30–19:30, Sat 8:00–18:00, closed Sun;

from Piazza Walther, facing TI, take street to the left for 2 blocks, supermarket's at bottom of stairs on your left).

## Transportation Connections—Bolzano

**By train to: Milan** (2/day, 3.5 hrs), **Verona** (hrly, 90 min), **Trento** (hrly, 40 min), **Venice** and **Florence** (via Verona, 3–4 hrs), **Innsbruck** (hrly, 2.5 hrs). Train info: tel. 848-888-088.

**By bus to: Castelrotto** (2/hr, 50 min, leaves Bolzano at :10 and :40 virtually every hour from Bolzano's bus station 1 block west of train station; buy one-way ticket for €3.25—round-trip not available—from station ticket window or driver, reduced price of €3 for return trip—show original ticket to get discount).

# CASTELROTTO (KASTELRUTH)

Castelrotto (population 6,000, altitude 1,060 meters/3,475 feet), the ideal home base for exploring the Alpe di Siusi, has more village character than any other town I know of in the region. Friday morning is the farmers' market (June–Oct), and a crafts market fills the town square most Thursday mornings. It's touristy but not a full-blown resort—it's full of real people. Pop into the church to hear the choir practice or be on the town square weekdays at 14:45 when the moms gather their kindergartners, chat, and then head home or stop by the playground on Plattenstrasse. On Fridays, the bells peal at 15:00, commemorating Christ's sacrifice. On Sundays, townspeople and farmers attend church and linger to visit. Against a backdrop of mountains, Castelrotto conveys the powerful message that simple pleasures are enough. The folk-singing group Kastelruther Spatzen has an avid following in town, produces "more CDs than Michael Jackson" (a local told me proudly), and holds a concert here every October.

Castelrotto's medieval tournament of games on horseback—usually held in late spring—features teams of riders dressed in old-time costumes competing in contests.

The **TI** is on the main square (Mon–Sat 8:30–12:30 & 13:30–18:00, Sun 9:00–12:00, tel. 0471-706-333, www.kastelruth.com). The bus parking lot has a little building with an ATM, WC, and phones; take the stairs to the right of this building to get to the main square. Another cash machine is to the left of the TI.

For a scenic viewpoint, take a short walk uphill from the TI (facing TI, take road under arch to the right, then follow signs to Kalvarienberg/Calvario). Footpaths take you past several little chapels, each depicting a scene from Christ's passion (with the Roman soldiers looking decidedly German), culminating in the crucifixion.

## Castelrotto

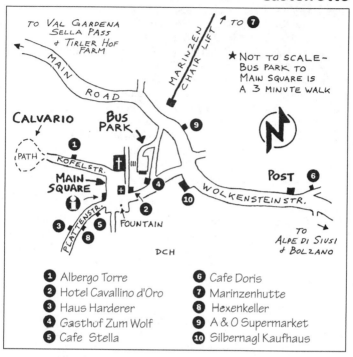

**1** Albergo Torre
**2** Hotel Cavallino d'Oro
**3** Haus Harderer
**4** Gasthof Zum Wolf
**5** Cafe Stella
**6** Cafe Doris
**7** Marinzenhutte
**8** Hexenkeller
**9** A & O Supermarket
**10** Silbernagl Kaufhaus

# Sleeping in Castelrotto
## (€1 = about $1, country code: 39, zip code: 39040)

**HIGHER PRICED**

**Albergo Torre** (in German, **Gasthof Zum Turm**) is comfortable, clean, and traditional, with great beds and modern bathrooms (Db-€50–110, Tb-€64–150, prices vary with season and amenities, includes breakfast, €3 extra for 1-night stays, CC, closed April and Nov, elevator, behind TI at Kofelgasse 8, tel. 0471-706-349, fax 0471-707-268, www.zumturm.com, e-mail: info @zumturm.com, Gabi and Günther SE). If you're driving, go right through the traffic-free town center (very likely with a police escort). Under the bell tower, enter the white arch to the right of the TI and park (free for guests) in the lot opposite the front door.

**MODERATELY PRICED**

**Hotel zum Wolf** (in Italian, **Al Lupo**) is pure Tirolean, with all the comforts (Sb-€35–50, Db-€56–85, prices vary with season and view, includes breakfast, non-smoking rooms, CNN in rooms, closed April–mid May, a block below main square at Wolkensteinstrasse 5, tel. 0471-706-332, fax 0471-707-030, www .hotelwolf.it, e-mail: info@hotelwolf.it, Arno SE).

**Hotel Cavallino D'Oro** (in German, **Goldenes Rossl**), on the main square, has plenty of Tirolean character and is run by friendly and helpful Stefan. Every room is different, and locals frequent the bar. If you love antiques by candlelight (or have only credit cards), this 600-year-old hotel is the best in town (Sb-€53–70, Db-€83–98 depending on season, discount for 3-night stay, CC, no elevator, Krausplatz 1, tel. 0471-706-337, fax 0471-707-172, www.cavallino.it, e-mail: cavallino@cavallino.it, SE). Stefan converted his 500-year-old wine cellar into a spa and sauna, complete with heated tile seats, solarium (tanning), and tropical plants.

**LOWER PRICED**

**Haus Harderer**, below Pensione Castelrotto, rents three rooms (Ss-€25, Ds-€50, includes breakfast, no CC, minimum 2 nights in summer) and a fine apartment for longer stays (€93/day, sleeps 4–6, no breakfast, no CC, Plattenstrasse 20, tel. 0471-706-702, run by Inge—SE, plus Oswald, Heinz—SE, Ida, and Mimme the cat). As you enter the driveway, the Harderer house is the one to the right.

**Tirler Hof**, the storybook Jaider family farm, has 50 cows, one friendly *hund*, four Old World–comfy guest rooms, and a great mountain view (D-€42, includes breakfast, practical only for drivers, it's the first farm outside of town on the right on road to St. Michael, Paniderstrasse 44, tel. 0471-706-017, e-mail: jaider.klaus@rolmail.net, Paola SE). The ground-floor double has a private bath. The top-floor rooms share a bathroom and a great balcony. Take a stroll before breakfast.

## Eating in Castelrotto

The hotels' restaurants are good. Consider **Cavallino D'Oro** (on one side of hotel is the *ristorante*, on the other side is the bar— each side gets the same menu; Wed–Mon 12:00–14:00 & 18:00– 2:00, closed Tue) or the less expensive **Albergo Torre** (Thu–Tue 12:00–13:30 & 18:00–20:30, closed Wed, April, and Nov). The **Hexenkellar**, or the "Witch Cellar," dishes up affordable German and Italian cooking (Mon–Sat 17:00–22:00, closed Sun, a block from TI on Plattenstrasse; facing TI, go left through arch).

For strudel, locals like the simple **Stella** (Tue–Sun 7:30–19:00, closed Mon, on Plattenstrasse; facing TI, go left through arch) and **Café Doris** (Wed–Mon 13:00–23:00, closed Tue, on main road at Wolkenstein 29, tel. 0471-706-340); both have terraces. Even better, for strudel *mit* view, take the little Marinzen cable car up the mountain to the **Marinzenhutte** café (tel. 0471-707-158, has animal park for kids). The lift runs from the end of May through October (€4.10 one-way, €6.20 return, base of lift is 2 blocks from bus park; facing A&O Supermarket, go left). You can hike down from Marinzen or return on the lift.

Castelrotto has two groceries: **Silbernagl Kaufhaus** (Mon–Sat 8:00–12:00 & 15:00–19:00, closed Sun, on Wolkenstein) and the smaller **A&O Supermarket,** two blocks away, also on the main drag (Mon–Sat 8:00–12:00 & 15:00–18:30, closed Sun, off-season closed Sat afternoon as well, Via Panider).

## Transportation Connections—Castelrotto
Catch buses to get into the heart of the Alpe di Siusi (buy tickets on bus).

**By bus to: Saltria** (4–15/day, get schedule at TI, or call toll-free tel. 800-846-047 or 0471-706-633); **Val di Fassa, Vigo di Fassa,** and **Canazei** (late June–mid-Sept only, 4/day, 2 hrs); and **Val Gardena, Ortisei/St. Ulrich,** and **St. Cristina** (summer only, 4/day, 1 hr). Buses leave Castelrotto for **Bolzano** (€3.25, reduced price of €3 for return trip, 2/hr, 50 min, runs 6:30–19:00).

**Summer Shuttle Buses:** From June through mid-October, Buxi shuttle buses go about twice hourly from Castelrotto through Alpe di Siusi to Saltria (8:00–17:00, discounted return tickets). Off-season, SAD buses take over, running four a day in both directions between Castelrotto and Saltria. Guests at some Castelrotto hotels ride free on Buxi buses—ask.

## ALPE DI SIUSI (SEISER ALM)
Europe's largest high alpine meadow, Alpe di Siusi, separates two of the most famous Dolomite ski-resort valleys. Measuring five kilometers by 12 kilometers (8 by 20 miles) and soaring up to 2,000 meters (6,500 feet) high, Alpe di Siusi is dotted by farm huts and wildflowers (mid-June–July), surrounded by dramatic— if distant—Dolomite peaks and cliffs, and much appreciated by hordes of walkers.

The Sasso Lungo (Langkofel) mountains at the head of the meadow provide a storybook Dolomite backdrop, while the spooky Schlern peak stands boldly staring into the haze of the peninsula. The Schlern, looking like a devilish *Winged Victory*, gave ancient peoples enough willies to spawn legends of supernatural forces. The Schlern witch, today's tourist brochure mascot, was the cause of many a broom-riding medieval townswoman's fiery death.

The Alpe di Siusi is my recommended one-stop look at the Dolomites because of Castelrotto's charm as a home base, its easy

## Alpe di Siusi

NOTE: THIS 3-D VIEW LOOKS
SOUTHEAST & IS NOT TO SCALE.
ELEVATIONS IN METERS

SELLA
3152

SASSOLUNGO
3181

SELLA
PASS

MARMOLADA
3342

WILLIAMS
2100

ZALLINGER
2054

TIERSER-ALPI
2441

BOLZANO
2450

MOLIGNON
2060

SALTRIA
1675

A L P E   D I   S I U S I

FLORIAN

PANORAMA
2014

SPITZBÜHL
1979

MT.
PEZ.
2563

SCHLERN

ARNIKA
2061

PUFLATSCH

COMPATSCH
1830

A.V.S.

SALTNER
SCHWAIGE
1830

FROMMER
1760

TO
VAL GARDENA
& SELLA PASS

CASTELROTTO
KASTELRUTH
1060

SEIS/SIUSI
1002

TO
BOLZANO
& AUTOSTRADA

TO PONTE
GARDENA & S-12

★ = PENSION SEELAUS

DCH

**KEY:**
- ● TOWN
- — ROAD
- ●—● LIFT
- ⋯⋯ TRAIL
- ▲ MTN. HUT
  (HUTTE / RIFUGIO)

❶ COMPATSCH HIKE
❷ PANORAMA HIKE
❸ ZALLINGER HUTTE HIKE
❹ SCHLERN SUMMIT HIKE
❺ SASSO LUNGO LOOP HIKE

accessibility for those with and without cars, its variety of walks and hikes, and its quintessentially Dolomite mountain views.

A natural preserve, Alpe di Siusi is closed to cars past Compatsch. The Buxi park bus shuttles hikers to and from key points along the tiny road all the way to Saltria at the foot of the postcard-dramatic Sasso peaks (Sasso Lungo, 3,180 meters, or 10,433 feet). Meadow walks, for flower-lovers and strollers, are pretty—or maybe pretty boring. Chairlifts are springboards for more dramatic and demanding hikes.

Trails are well-marked, and the brightly painted numbers are keyed into local maps. The Kompass Bolzano map #54 covers everything in this chapter (scale 1:50,000, €4.10). The Wander-karte map of Alpe di Siusi (produced by Tabacco) offers more detail and focuses on just Alpe di Siusi (scale 1:25,000, €2.60).

**Compatsch**, a kilometer in and as far as you're allowed to drive, is the tourist village (1,870 meters/6,135 feet) and has a TI (Mon–Sat 9:00–17:00, Sun 9:00–12:00, free WCs behind TI, tel. 0471-727-904). There's also a grocery store (open mid-June–mid-Oct), mountain bike rentals (€5.20/1 hr, €13/4 hrs), an ATM, parking (€3.10/ day), hotels, restaurants, shops, and so on. Trocker rents horses and provides guides (€13/1 hr, €23/2 hrs, €32/3 hrs, April–Oct, 100 meters, or 330 feet, before Compatsch TI, tel. 0471-727-807, NSE).

**Sleeping near the Park Entrance: Pension Seelaus**, a 10-minute walk downhill from Compatsch, is a cozy, friendly, family-run place with a Germanic feel and down comforters (Sb-€52–69, Db-€103–138, prices vary with season and type of room, includes buffet breakfast and hearty dinner, no CC, Via Compatsch 8, tel. 0471-727-954, fax 0471-727-835, www.hotelseelaus.it, e-mail: info@hotelseelaus.it, Roberto SE).

## Hikes in the Alpe di Siusi

Easy meadow walks abound, giving tenderfeet classic Dolomite views from baby-stroller trails. Experienced hikers should consider the tougher and more exciting treks. Before attempting a hike, call or stop by the local TI to confirm your understanding of the time and skills required. Many lifts operate mid-June through mid-October and during the winter ski season. The Panorama and Puflatsch lifts (both near Compatsch) run further into the off-season.

**Three Easy Walks from Compatsch:** Take a lift to Puflatsch for the two-hour loop north to Arnikahütte (has café) and back (elevation gain about 200 meters/660 feet).

**Or:** Ride the lift to Panorama, then hike 90 minutes to Molignonhütte (2,050 meters/6,725 feet) and back down to Compatsch; or continue 2.5 hours (fairly level) to Zallinger-hütte (2,050 meters/6,725 feet) and another 90 minutes to Saltria and the Buxi bus stop.

**Or:** Bus to Saltria and hike the 2.5-hour loop to Zallinger-hütte (2,050 meters/6,725 feet, 200-meter/660-foot altitude gain).

**Summit Hike of Schlern (Sciliar):** For a challenging 19-kilometer (12-mile), six-hour hike with a possible overnight in a traditional mountain refuge, consider hiking to the summit of Schlern and spending a night in Rifugio Bolzano (Schlernhaus). Start at the Spitzbühl lift (1,725 meters/5,659 feet, free parking lot, first bus stop in park). The Spitzbühl chairlift drops you at Spitzbühl

(1,935 meters/6,348 feet). Trail #5 takes you through a high
meadow, down to the Saltner Schwaige dairy farm (1,830
meters/6,004 feet), across a stream, and steeply up the Schlern
mountain. You'll meet trail #1 and walk across the rocky table-
top plateau of Schlern to the mountain hotel, Rifugio Bolzano/
Schlernhaus, three hours into your hike (2,450 meters/8,038 feet,
D-€35, dorm beds-€10, tel. 0471-612-024, call for reservation).
From this dramatic setting, you get a great view of the Rosengar-
ten range. Hike 20 more minutes up the nearby peak (Mount Pez,
2,560 meters/8,399 feet) for a 360-degree alpine panorama. From
the Schlernhaus, you can hike back the way you came or walk farther along the Schlern (12 km/7 miles, 2 hrs, past the Rifugio Alpe
di Tires, tel. 0471-727-958, 2,440 meters/8,005 feet) and descend
back into Alpe di Siusi and the road where the Buxi bus will return
you to your starting point or hotel.

**Loop around Sasso Lungo:** Another dramatic but easy
hike is the eight-hour walk around Sasso Lungo (Langkofel).
You can ride the bus to Saltria (end of the line), take the chairlift to Williamshütte, walk past the Zallingerhütte (overnight
possible, tel. 0471-727-947), and circle the Sasso group.

## More Sights in the Dolomites

▲▲**Great Dolomite Road**—This is the definitive Dolomite
drive: Belluno/Cortina/Pordoi Pass/Sella Pass/Val di Fassa/
Bolzano. Connecting Venice with Bolzano this way (the
Belluno–Venice autostrada is slick) takes two hours longer
than the Bolzano–Verona–Venice autostrada. No public
transit does this trip. In spring and early summer, passes
labeled "closed" are often bare, dry, and, as far as local
drivers are concerned, wide open.

▲▲**Abbreviated Dolomite Loop Drive**—See the biggies
in half the kilometers (allow 3 hours, Bolzano/Castelrotto/
Val Gardena/Sella Pass/Val di Fassa/Bolzano). Val Gardena
(Grodner Tal) is famous for its skiing and hiking resorts, traditional Ladin culture, and wood-carvers (the wood-carver
ANRI is from the Val Gardena town of St. Cristina). It's a bit
overrated, but even if its culture has been suffocated by the big
bucks of hedonistic European fun-seekers, it remains a good
jumping-off point for trips into the mountains. Within an hour,
you'll reach Sella Pass (2,240 meters/7,349 feet). After a series
of tight hairpin turns a kilometer or so over the pass, you'll see
some benches and cars. Pull over and watch the rock climbers.
Val di Fassa is Alberto Tomba country. The town of Canazei,
at the head of the valley and the end of the bus line, has the
most ambience and altitude (1,415 meters/4,642 feet). From

there, a lift takes you to Col dei Rossi Belvedere, where you can hike the Bindelweg trail past Rifugio Belvedere along an easy but breathtaking ridge to Rifugio Viel del Pan. This three-hour round-trip hike has views of the highest mountain in the Dolomites—the Marmolada—and the Dolo-mighty Sella range.

▲▲**Reifenstein Castle**—For one of Europe's most intimate looks at medieval castle life, let the friendly lady of Reifenstein (Frau Blanc) show you around her wonderfully preserved castle. She leads tours on the hour, in Italian and German, squeezing in whatever English she can (€3.10, open Easter–Oct, tours on Mon at 14:00 and 15:00, Tue–Thu and Sat–Sun at 9:30, 10:30, 14:00, and 15:00, closed Fri, picnic spot at drawbridge, tel. 0472-765-879).

To drive to the castle, exit the autostrada at Vipiteno (Sterzing) and follow signs toward Bolzano. The castle is just west of the freeway; park at the base of the castle's rock. Of the two castles here, Reifenstein is the one to the west. While this is easy by car, it's probably not worth the trouble by train (from Bolzano, 6/day, 70 min).

▲**Glurns**—Drivers connecting the Dolomites and Lake Como by the high road via Meran and Bormio should spend the night in the amazing little town of Glurns (45 min west of touristy Meran between Schluderns and Taufers). Glurns still lives within its square wall on the Adige River, with a church bell tower that has a thing about ringing, and real farms, rather than boutiques, filling the town courtyards. There are several small hotels in the town, but I'd stay in a private home (Family Hofer, 6 rooms, Db-€41–46 with breakfast, less for 3 nights, no CC, 100 meters, or 330 feet, from town square, near church, just outside wall on river, tel. 0473-831-597).

# NAPLES AND THE AMALFI COAST

If you like Italy as far south as Rome, go farther south. It gets better. If Italy is getting on your nerves, think twice about going farther. Italy intensifies as you plunge deeper. Naples is Italy in the extreme—its best (birthplace of pizza and Sophia Loren) and its worst (home of the Camorra, Naples' "family" of organized crime).

Serene Sorrento, without a hint of big-city Naples and just an hour to the south, makes a great home base. It's the gateway to the much-loved Amalfi Coast. From the jet-setting island of Capri to the stunning scenery of the Amalfi Coast, from ancient Pompeii to even more ancient Paestum, this is Italy's coast with the most.

## Planning Your Time

On a quick trip, give the area three days. With Sorrento as your sunny springboard, spend a day in Naples, a day exploring the Amalfi Coast, and a day split between Pompeii and the town of Sorrento. While Paestum, the crater of Vesuvius, Herculaneum, and the island of Capri are decent options, they are worthwhile only if you give the area more time.

For a blitz tour, you could have breakfast on the early Rome–Naples express train (about 7:00–9:00), do Naples and Pompeii in a day, and be back in Rome in time for *Letterman*. That's exhausting but more memorable than a fourth day in Rome. Remember that in the afternoon, Naples' street life slows and many sights close as the temperature soars. The city comes back to life in the early evening.

For a small-town vacation from your vacation, spend a few more days on the Amalfi Coast, sleeping in Positano, Atrani, or Marina del Cantone.

For most, driving south of Rome is not only stressful, it's

impractical. Take advantage of the wonderful public transportation: the slick two-hour Rome–Naples express trains (or direct
5-hour express connections with Florence); the handy Circumvesuviana commuter train (lacing together Naples, Pompeii, and
Sorrento), and the regular bus service between Sorrento and the
Amalfi Coast (where parking and car access are severely limited).

# NAPLES (NAPOLI)

Italy's third-largest city (with 1.2 million people, 2 million in
greater Naples) has almost no open spaces or parks, which makes
its position as Europe's most densely populated city plenty evident.
Watching the police try to enforce traffic sanity is almost comical
in Italy's grittiest, most polluted, and most crime-ridden city.

But Naples surprises the observant traveler with its good
humor, decency, and impressive knack for living, eating, and raising children in the streets. Overcome your fear of being run down
or ripped off long enough to talk with people—enjoy a few smiles
and jokes with the man running the neighborhood tripe shop or
the woman taking her day-care class on a walk through the traffic.
(Ask a local about the New Year's Eve tradition of tossing chipped
dinner plates off of balconies into the streets.)

Twenty-five hundred years ago, Neapolis ("new city") was a
thriving Greek commercial center. It remains southern Italy's leading city, offering a fascinating collection of museums, churches,
and eclectic architecture. The pulse of Italy throbs in Naples.
This tangled mess—the closest thing to "reality travel" you'll find
in western Europe—still somehow manages to breathe, laugh, and
sing—with a captivating Italian accent.

## Planning Your Time

For a quick visit, start with the archaeology museum, do the Slice-
of-Neapolitan-Life Walk (see "Sights," below), and celebrate your
survival with pizza. Of course, Naples is huge. But even with limited time, if you stick to the described route and grab a cab when
you're lost or tired, it's fun. Treat yourself well in Naples; the city
is cheap by Italian standards.

## Orientation

**Tourist Information:** The TI is in the central train station (Mon–
Sat 9:00–20:00, Sun 9:00–13:00; with your back to the tracks, TI is
in the lobby to your left; then, within the lobby, TI is to your right,
tel. 081-268-779). Pick up a map, and, even though the odds are
against you, ask for the *Qui Napoli* booklet—when they say they're
"finished," ask for an old one.

**Arrival in Naples:** There are several Naples stations. You

## From Naples to Paestum

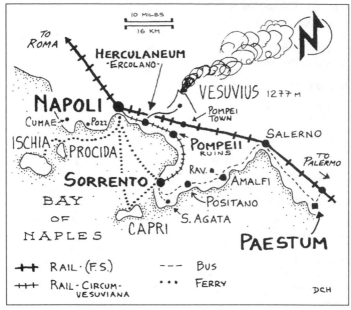

want Naples Centrale (facing Piazza Garibaldi), which has a TI, baggage check, and the Circumvesuviana stop for commuter trains to Sorrento and Pompeii. Since Centrale is a dead-end station, through trains often stop at Piazza Garibaldi (actually a subway station just downstairs from Centrale), Campi Flegrei, or Napoli Mergellina across town. The stations of Campi Flegrei and Mergellina (which also has a TI) are connected to Centrale by a direct subway route; a railpass or train ticket to Napoli Centrale covers the ride (subway trains depart about every 10 min, less often on Sun). While on the train to Naples, ask the conductor which Naples stations your train stops at. Get off at Mergellina or Campi Flegrei only if your train does not stop at Centrale or Garibaldi.

## Helpful Hints

**Tours:** Aldo Sparice, a Naples native, offers tours of Naples, Pompeii, and Herculaneum, as well as many other destinations off the worn path (€100/3 hrs, cellular 339-153-8009).

**Traffic:** In Naples, red lights are discretionary, and pedestrians need to be wary, particularly of the Vespa motorcycles.

**Theft Alert:** Lately, Naples, under a new activist mayor, has been occupied by an army of police and feels much safer. Still, err on the side of caution. Don't venture into neighborhoods that make you uncomfortable. Walk with confidence, as if you know where you're going and what you're doing. Assume able-bodied beggars are thieves. Tighten your money belt and keep it completely hidden. Stick to busy streets and beware of gangs of hoodlums. A third of the city is unemployed, and past local governments set an example the Mafia would be proud of. Assume con artists are more clever than you. Any jostle or commotion is probably a thief team smokescreen. Any bags are probably safest checked at the central train station (€2.60, *deposito bagagli* near track #24).

Perhaps your biggest risk of theft is catching or riding the Circumvesuviana commuter train. Remember, if you're connecting from a major train, you'll be stepping from a relatively secure compartment into a crowded Naples subway filled with thieves hunting disoriented American tourists with luggage. While I ride the Circumvesuviana comfortably and safely, each year I hear of many who get ripped off on this ride. You won't be mugged—just conned or pickpocketed. Con artists may say you need to "transfer" by taxi to catch the Circumvesuviana; you don't. There are no porters at the Centrale station or in the basement where the Circumvesuviana station is located; anyone offering to help you with your bags is likely a thief. Wear your money belt, hang on to your bag, and don't display any valuables. For €60–80, you can ride a **taxi** from Naples 50 kilometers (30 miles) directly to your Sorrento hotel; agree on a fixed price without the meter and pay upon arrival. As another option, consider the Naples–Sorrento **boat** (7/day, 40 min, €6.75); it's faster, safer, and more scenic than the Circumvesuviana. Naples' port (Beverello) is near Castel Nuovo at the low end of the walk described below and a quick taxi ride from the museum.

## Getting around Naples

Naples' subway, the Servizio Metropolitano, runs from the Centrale station through the center of town (direction: Pozzouli), stopping at Piazza Cavour (Archaeological Museum), Piazza Dante, and Montesanto (top of Spanish Quarter and Spaccanapoli). Tickets, which cost €0.75, are good for 90 minutes. All-day tickets cost €2.35. If you can afford a taxi, don't mess with the buses. A short taxi ride costs €3–5 (insist on the meter; supplement charged on Sun).

**Getting to the Museum:** From the Centrale train station, follow signs to *Metropolitano* (downstairs, buy tickets from window on right, ask which track—"*Binario?*" to Piazza Cavour—it's usually track 4, "*quattro*," go through a *solo metropolitano* turnstile and ride the subway one stop). As you leave the Metro, take the exit to

## Naples Transportation

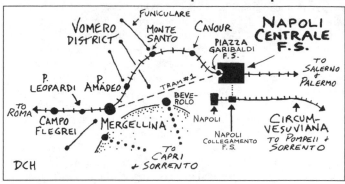

the right. Walk through the park. At the end of cluttered Piazza Cavour, you'll see several pink buildings ahead. The museum is the pink building on the right side of the street.

# Sights—Naples

▲▲▲**Archaeological Museum (Museo Archeologico)**—For lovers of antiquity, this museum alone makes Naples a worthwhile stop. It offers the only possible peek into the artistic jewelry boxes of Pompeii and Herculaneum. The actual sights are impressive but barren; the best art and all the artifacts ended up here.

**Hours, Cost, and Information:** €6.50, Wed–Mon 9:00–20:00, summer Sat until 23:00, closed Tue. Tours in English are offered weekdays at 11:30 and 15:30 (except on Tue when museum is closed) and on Sat and Sun at 10:00, 11:00, 12:00, and 15:30 (€5, 1.5 hrs, depart from entry, confirm tour times by calling 848-800-288). Audioguides cost €4 (at ticket desk, rentable for 3 hrs). Photos are allowed without a flash. The shop sells a worthwhile green guidebook, titled *National Archeological Museum of Naples* (€7.75).

**Orientation:** At the desk next to the ticket booth, you can sign up for a free 20-minute tour of the Secret Room (containing erotic art from Pompeii and Herculaneum). You'll be given a tour time; meet at the Secret Room *(Gabinetto Segreto)* on the mezzanine near the *Battle of Alexander* mosaic. These short tours, generally offered at the top and bottom of every hour, are usually given in Italian, but English tours are possible—ask.

After passing through the turnstile, follow the corridor around to the staircase. For the Farnese Collection of marble statues, continue straight, then turn right past the staircase. The Pompeii mosaics and the Secret Room are on the small mezzanine level

## Naples

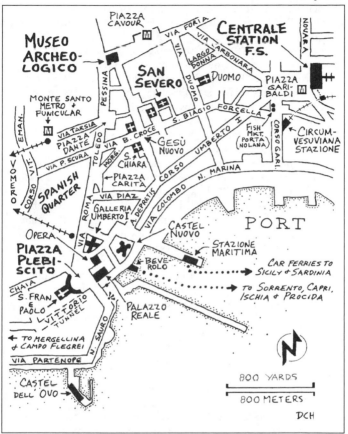

(up the grand staircase and on your left). The huge first floor (top of the grand staircase) contains bronze statues from Herculaneum, frescoes from Pompeii, and vases from Paestum. Stairs behind the grand staircase lead to the basement WCs.

**Statues, Frescoes, and Artifacts (top floor):** Climb the stairs to the top floor. Before you enter the great hall, look right to locate the entrance to the bronze statues of Herculaneum. This large collection—including a dozen bronze statues, plus busts and marble statues—came from Villa Papiri (Papyrus) in Herculaneum. Look into the lifelike blue eyes of the two intense *atleta* (athletes); they are bent on doing their best.

Step inside the great hall. With your back to the entrance,

the rooms on your left feature the Pompeii frescoes, paintings, artifacts, and an interesting model of the town of Pompeii (called *plastico di Pompeii*; near the glass objects). The rooms on your right feature ancient Greek art: a model of Paestum and ancient vases discovered on-site. (Paestum, a temple complex south of Naples, was part of a once-thriving region known as Greater Greece; for more info, see "Paestum," below.) If you contrast all of this ancient art with the darkness of medieval Europe, it becomes clear that classical art greatly inspired and enlightened the Renaissance greats.

**Mosaics (mezzanine):** On the mezzanine floor below (directly under the bronze statues from Herculaneum), you'll find a small, exquisite collection of Pompeian mosaics and the sexy Secret Room. Most of these mosaics were taken from the House of the Faun, which you'll see at Pompeii. Don't miss the house's delightful centerpiece: a bronze statue (a half-meter, or 20 inches, high) of the *Dancing Faun*. A highlight of the mosaics is the grand *Battle of Alexander* (a first-century B.C. copy of a fourth-century B.C. Greek original). It decorated a floor in the House of the Faun.

The **Secret Room**, to the left of the *Battle of Alexander* mosaic, contains a small assortment of frescoes, pottery, and statues that once decorated bedrooms, brothels, and even shops at Pompeii and Herculaneum (enter only with a guide, see "Orientation," above). If you didn't bother with making an appointment, you can still peek through the iron gate.

When this earthy art was unearthed in the mid-18th century, people were upset to find their view of the Romans as wise administrators and lawmakers upended. Actually, the meaning of an erect penis was more complex back then than today—dealing with abundance and good luck, as well as good sex.

**Farnese Collection (ground floor):** This floor has enough Egyptian, Greek, Roman, and Etruscan art to put any museum on the map. Its highlight is the Farnese Collection, a giant hall of huge, bright, and wonderfully restored statues excavated from Rome's Baths of Caracalla. The Toro Farnese—a tangled group with a woman being tied to a bull—is the largest intact statue from antiquity. Actually a third-century copy of a Hellenistic original, it was carved out of one piece of marble and restored by Michelangelo and others.

Once upon an ancient Greek time, King Lykos was bewitched by Dirce and abandoned his pregnant wife (standing regally in the background). The single mom gave birth to twin boys (shown here) who grew up to kill their deadbeat dad and tie Dirce to the horns of a bull to be bashed against a mountain.

You can almost hear the bull snorting. Read the worthwhile

descriptions on the walls. At the far end of the hall (opposite the Toro, behind Hercules), a small room contains the sumptuous Farnese Cup, a large ancient cameo made of agates (well-described).

▲▲▲**The Slice-of-Neapolitan-Life Walk**—Walk from the museum through the heart of town and back to the station (allow at least 2 hours, plus lunch and sightseeing stops). Sights are listed in the order you'll see them on this walk.

Naples, a living medieval city, is its own best sight. Couples artfully make love on Vespas, surrounded by more fights and smiles per cobble here than anywhere else in Italy. Rather than seeing Naples as a list of sights, see the one great museum and then capture its essence by taking this walk through the core of the city. Should you become overwhelmed or lost, step into a store and ask for help: "*Dov'è la stazione centrale?*" (pron. DOH-vay lah staht-zee-OH-nay chen-TRAH-lay?), or point to the next sight in this book.

**Via Toledo and the Spanish Quarter (city walk, first half):** Leaving the Archaeological Museum at the top of Piazza Cavour (Metro: Piazza Cavour), cross the street and walk through the ornate galleria (the grand, arched gallery) on your way to Via Pessina to your right. The first part of this walk is a straight 1.5-kilometer (1-mile) ramble down this boulevard to Galleria Umberto I near the Royal Palace.

Busy Via Pessina leads downhill to Piazza Dante—marked by a statue of Dante. Originally, a statue of a Spanish Bourbon king stood here. The grand red-and-gray building is typical of the Bourbon buildings from that period. In 1861 with the unification of Italy, the king, symbolic of Italy's colonial subjugation, was replaced by Dante—considered the father of the Italian language and a strong symbol of Italian nationalism.

Poor old Dante looks out over the urban chaos with a hopeless gesture. The Alba Gate, part of Naples' old wall and the entrance to a small street often lined with streetside book vendors, is to Dante's left. Via Pessina, the long, straight road we're walking, originated as a military road built by Spain around 1600. It skirted the old town wall to connect the Spanish military headquarters (now the museum) with the royal palace (down by the bay).

A new subway station has recently been built here on Piazza Dante. Construction was slowed by the city's rich underground history: four meters (13 feet) down—Roman ruins, seven meters (23 feet) down—Greek ruins.

Continue walking downhill, remembering that here in Naples, red lights are considered "decorations." Try to cross with a local. The people here are survivors; a long history of corrupt and greedy colonial overlords has taught Neapolitans to deal with authority

## Naples Walk

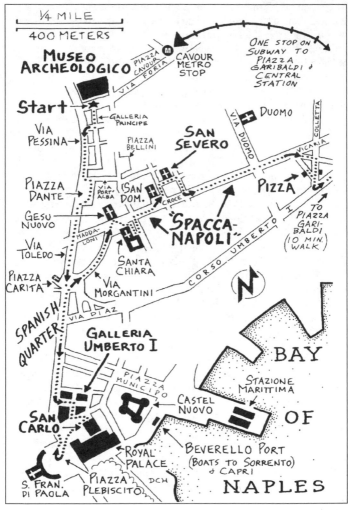

creatively. Many credit this aspect of Naples' past for the advent of organized crime here.

Via Pessina becomes Via Toledo, Naples' principal shopping street. In 1860, from the white marble balcony (on the neoclassical building) overlooking Piazza Sette Settembre, the famous revolutionary Garibaldi declared Italy united and Victor Emmanuel its first king. A year later, the dream of Italian unity was actually realized.

Continue straight on Via Toledo (even though the arterial jogs left). About five blocks below Piazza Dante, at Via Maddaloni, you cross the long, straight street called **Spaccanapoli** (literally, "split Naples"). Look left. Look right. Since ancient times, this thin street (which changes names several times) has bisected the city. (We'll be coming back to this point later. If you want to abbreviate this walk, turn left here and skip down to the Spaccanapoli section.)

Via Toledo runs through Piazza Carità (also known by its new name, Piazza Salvo D'Acquisto), with fascist architecture (from 1938, sternly straight and obedient lines) overlooking the square. Wander down Via Toledo a few blocks, past more fascist architecture—the two banks on the left. Try robbing the second one (Banco di Napoli, Via Toledo 178).

Up the hill to your right is the **Spanish Quarter**, Naples at its rawest, poorest, and most historic. Thrill-seekers (or someone in need of a prostitute) can take a stroll up one of these streets and loop back to Via Toledo.

The only thing predictable about this Neapolitan tide pool is the ancient grid plan of its streets (which survives from Greek times), the friendliness of its shopkeepers, and the boldness of its mopeds. Concerned locals will tug on their lower eyelids, warning you to be wary. Pop into a grocery shop and ask the man to make you his best ham and mozzarella sandwich. Trust him on the price—it should be around €3.

Continue down Via Toledo to Piazza Plebiscito. From here, you'll see the Church of San Francesco di Paola with its Pantheon-inspired dome and broad, arcing colonnades. A TI is in the colonnade to the right (Mon–Fri 9:00–19:00, Sat 9:00–14:00, closed Sun). Opposite is the **Royal Palace**, which has housed Spanish, French, and even Italian royalty. The lavish interior is open for tours (€4, Thu–Tue 9:00–20:00, closed Wed, shorter hours off-season). Next door, peek inside the neoclassical Teatro San Carlo, Italy's second-most-respected opera house (after Milan's La Scala). The huge castle on the harborfront just beyond the palace houses government bureaucrats and is closed to tourists.

Under the Victorian iron and glass of the 100-year-old **Galleria Umberto I**, enjoy a coffee break or sample a unique Neapolitan pastry called *sfogliatella* (crispy, scallop shell–shaped pastry filled with sweet ricotta cheese). Go through the tall yellow arch at the end of Via Toledo or across from the opera house. Gawk up.

**Spaccanapoli back to the station (city walk, second half):** To continue your walk, double back up Via Toledo past Piazza Carità to Via Maddaloni. You're back at the straight-as-a-Greek-arrow Spaccanapoli. Formerly the main thoroughfare of the Greek city of Neapolis, it starts up the hill near the Montesanto funicular.

The rest of this walk is basically a straight line down a series of streets locals nicknamed Spaccanapoli. Turn right off Via Toledo and walk down Via Maddaloni to two bulky old churches on Piazza Gesu Nuovo. The square is marked by a towering monument to the Counter-Reformation (Baroque, early 18th century). With its Spanish heritage, Jesuits were powerful in Naples. But locals never attacked Protestants with the full fury of the Spanish Inquisition.

Check out the austere, fortress-like church of **Gesu Nuovo.** The unique pyramid grill facade was from a fortress (1470), which predated the church (1600s). Step inside for a brilliant Baroque interior. The second chapel on the right features a much-kissed statue of Giuseppe Moscati, a Christian doctor famous for helping the poor. Moscati was made a saint in 1987. Continue on to the third chapel and enter the Sale Moscati for a huge room filled with Ex Voto—tiny red-and-silver plaques of thanksgiving for miracles attributed to Saint Moscati. Each has a relief symbolic of the ailment cured. Naples' practice of "Ex Voto," while incorporated into its Catholic rituals, goes back to its pagan Greek roots. A glass case displays possessions and photos of the great doctor. As you leave, notice the big bomb casing hanging in the corner. It fell through the church's dome in 1943, but never exploded...yet another miracle.

Across the street, the simpler Gothic church of **Santa Chiara** dates from a period of French Angevin rule (14th century). Notice the stark Gothic/Baroque contrast between this church and the Gesu Nuovo. The faded Trinity (from the school of Giotto, left of entry) is an example of the fine frescoes that once covered the walls (most removed during Baroque times). The altar is adorned with the finely carved Gothic tomb of an Angevin king (both churches free, Mon–Sat 8:30–13:00 & 15:30–18:30, Sun 8:30–13:00).

Continue straight down traffic-free Via B. Croce. Since this is a university district, you'll see lots of students and bookstores. This neighborhood is also extremely superstitious. You may see incense-burning women with carts of good-luck charms for sale. At Via Santa Chiara, a detour to the left leads to shops of antique musical instruments.

The next square is Piazza S. Domenico Maggiore—marked by an ornate 17th-century plague monument. The venerable **Scaturchio Pasticceria** is another good place to try Naples' *sfogliatella* pastry (€1 to go, costs double at a table in the square).

From this square, detour left (along the right side of the castle-like church, then follow yellow signs and take first right) to **Cappella Sansevero** (€5, Mon and Wed–Sat 10:00–19:00, Nov–April 10:00–17:00, Sun year-round 10:00–13:30, closed Tue, Via de Sanctis 19). No photos are allowed in the chapel (postcards available in gift shop).

This small chapel is a Baroque explosion mourning the body of Christ, who lies on a soft pillow under an incredibly realistic veil. It's also the personal chapel of Raimondo de Sangro, an eccentric Freemason. The monuments to his relatives have a second purpose: To share the Freemason philosophy of freedom through enlightenment. For example, the statue of *Despair* struggling with a marble rope net (carved out of a single piece of marble) shows how knowledge—in the guise of an angel—frees the human mind.

Study the incredible *Veiled Christ* in the center. It's all carved out of marble and is like no other statue I've seen (by Giuseppe "howdeedoodat" Sammartino, 1753). The Christian message (Jesus died for our salvation) is accompanied by a Freemason message (the veil represents how the body and ego are an obstacle to real spiritual freedom.) As you walk from Christ's feet to his head, notice how the expression of Jesus' face goes from suffering to peace. When you stand directly behind Him, the veil over the face and knees disappears.

Raimondo de Sangro, an inventor, created the deep green pigment used on the ceiling fresco. De Sangro is even credited with a crude 18th-century version of Gore-Tex.

To the right of *Despair* and the net, an inlaid Escher-esque maze on the floor leads to de Sangro's tomb. The maze is another Freemason reminder of the importance of how the quest for knowledge gets you out of the maze of life. Your Sansevero finale is downstairs: two mysterious...skeletons. Perhaps another of the mad inventor's fancies: Injecting a corpse with a fluid to fossilize the veins so they'll survive the body's decomposition.

Return to Via B. Croce, turn left, and continue your Spaccanapoli cultural scavenger hunt. At the intersection of Via Nilo, find the statue of *The Body of Naples*, with the abundant cornucopia symbolizing the abundance of Naples. (I asked a Neapolitan man to describe the local women, who are famous for their beauty. He replied simply, "Abundant.") This intersection is considered the center of old Naples.

At Via San Gregorio Armeno, a left leads you into a very colorful district (kitschy Baroque church on left with a Vesuvius lava shrine in its portico, lots of shops selling tiny components of fantastic manger scenes).

As Via B. Croce becomes Via S. Biagio dei Librai, notice the gold and silver shops. Some say stolen jewelry ends up here, is melted down immediately, and appears in a saleable form as soon as it cools. The wonderful Sr. Grassi runs the Ospedale delle Bambole (doll hospital) at #81.

Cross busy Via Duomo. The street and side-street scenes

along Via Vicaria intensify. Paint a picture with these thoughts: Naples has the most intact street plan of any ancient Roman city. Imagine this city then (retain these images as you visit Pompeii), with street-side shopfronts that close up after dark to form private homes. Today, it's just one more page in a 2,000-year-old story of a city: all kinds of meetings, beatings, and cheatings; kisses, near misses, and little-boy pisses.

You name it, it occurs right on the streets today, as it has since ancient times. People ooze from crusty corners. Black-and-white death announcements add to the clutter on the walls. Widows sell cigarettes from buckets. For a peek behind the scenes in the shade of wet laundry, venture down a few side streets. Buy two carrots as a gift for the woman on the fifth floor if she'll lower her bucket to pick them up. The neighborhood action seems best around 18:00.

At the tiny fenced-in triangular park, veer right onto Via Forcella. Turning right on busy Via Pietro Colletta, walk 50 meters (165 feet) and step into the North Pole. Reward yourself for surviving this safari with a stop at the **Polo Nord Gelateria** (Via Pietro Colletta 41, sample their *bacio* or "kiss" flavor before ordering). Via Pietro Colletta leads past Napoli's two most competitive **pizzerias** (see "Eating," below) to Corso Umberto.

Turn left on the grand-boulevardian Corso Umberto. From here to the station, it's a 10-minute walk (if you're tired, hop on a bus; they all go to the station). To finish the walk, continue on Corso Umberto—past a gauntlet of purse/CD/sunglasses salesmen and shady characters hawking stolen camcorders—to the vast, ugly Piazza Garibaldi. On the far side is the Centrale station.

**Markets**—Naples' **fish market** is fun for photos, with sawed-off swordfish, wriggly eels in pans, and mussels taking a shower. It's at Piazza Nolana, a few blocks southwest of the train station (at the piazza, follow your nose and go through the old gate; market spills down small street, Vico Sopramuro). A bigger **general market** starts at the far corner of Piazza Capuana (several blocks northwest of the train station), filling the street Via Sant' Antonio Abate with a mix of clothes, olives, bags of gnocchi, hanging hams, shoes, produce, umbrellas, and shoppers on foot or on Vespas. These colorful markets are both open daily (Mon–Sat 7:00–16:00, Sun 8:00–13:00).

## Sleeping in Naples
### (€1 = $1, country code: 39)
Sleep Code: **S** = Single, **D** = Double/Twin, **T** = Triple, **Q** = Quad, **b** = bathroom, **s** = shower only, **CC** = Credit Cards accepted, **no CC** = Credit Cards not accepted, **SE** = Speaks English, **NSE** = No English.

To help you sort easily through these listings, I've divided the rooms into three categories based on the price for a standard double room with bath:

**Higher Priced**—Most rooms more than €150.
**Moderately Priced**—Most rooms €150 or less.
**Lower Priced**—Most rooms €100 or less.

With Sorrento just an hour away, I can't imagine why you'd sleep in Naples. But, if needed, here are several places, all within 200 meters (650 feet) of the station. The area can feel unnerving, especially after dark.

**HIGHER PRICED**

**Grand Hotel Terminus**, a four-star place across the street from the station (left side), feels perfectly safe, with 168 rooms and all the comforts (Db-€185 or so, less on weekends, includes breakfast, CC, air-con, elevator, non-smoking rooms on second floor, gym, roof garden, bar, restaurants, Piazza Garibaldi 91, tel. 081-779-3111, fax 081-206-689, www.starhotels.it, e-mail: terminus.na@starhotels.it, SE).

**LOWER PRICED**

**Hotel Ginevra** is quiet, bright, and cheery, and has 21 rooms with comfortable beds and floral wallpaper. It's run by a friendly family: Bruno and son Lello speak English, Anna speaks Italian (S-€25, Sb-€45, D-€40, Db-€50–70, T-€60, Tb-€75–90, Q-€70, Qb-€90, breakfast in room-€4, CC, 10 percent discount with this book and cash, turn right out of the station onto Corso Novara and walk 2 blocks, turn right on Via Genova to #116, 2nd floor, tel. & fax 081-283-210, www.hotelginevra.it, e-mail: info @hotelginevra.it).

**Hotel Eden**, a big old establishment run with panache by English-speaking Nicola and his brother Vincenzo, rents 45 dreary rooms. Front rooms get traffic noise; request a room in the back (Sb-€32, Db-€45, Tb-€60, Qb-€80, prices good through 2003 with this book and cash, no CC, no breakfast, elevator, turn right out of the station and walk 1 block to Corso Novara 9, tel. 081-285-344, fax 081-285-690). Reserve by phone and reconfirm the day before you arrive.

# Eating in Naples

Drop by one of the two most traditional pizzerias. Naples, baking just the right combination of fresh dough, mozzarella, and tomatoes in traditional wood-burning ovens, is the birthplace of pizza. **Antica Pizzeria da Michele**, a few blocks from the train station, is for purists (Mon–Sat 11:00–23:00, closed Sun, cheap, filled with locals, 50 meters, or 165 feet, off Corso Umberto on Via Cesare Sersale, look for vertical red "Antica Pizzeria" sign, tel. 081-553-9204). It serves two kinds: *margherita* (tomato sauce and mozzarella) or *marinara* (tomato sauce, oregano, and garlic, no cheese). A pizza with beer costs €5. Some locals prefer **Pizzeria Trianon** across the street. Da Michele's archrival offers more choices, higher prices, air-conditioning, and a cozier atmosphere (daily 10:00–15:30 & 18:30–23:00, Via Pietro Colletta 42, tel. 081-553-9426).

## Transportation Connections—Naples

**By boat to: Sorrento** (7/day, 40 min, €6.75), **Capri** (6 hydrofoils/ day, 45 min, €10.50).

**By train to: Rome** (hrly, 2–3 hrs), **Florence** (6/day, 5 hrs), **Brindisi** (2/day, 7 hrs, overnight possible; from Brindisi, ferries sail to Greece), **Milan** (7/day, 7–9 hrs, overnight possible, more with a change in Rome), **Venice** (4/day, 8–10 hrs), **Nice** (4/day, 13 hrs), **Paris** (3/day, 18 hrs). Naples train information: tel. 848-888-088 (automated, in Italian).

**The Circumvesuviana:** This useful commuter train links Naples, Herculaneum, Pompeii, and Sorrento. At Naples' Central Station, signs direct you downstairs to the Circumvesuviana. In the long corridor in the basement, the ticket windows—marked Circumvesuviana—are on your left. Schedules are posted on the wall. When you buy your ticket, ask which track your train will depart from (*"Che binario?"*; pron. kay bee-NAH-ree-oh). Don't go through the turnstiles opposite the ticket windows. Instead, continue down the corridor and jog right when it does, down another long corridor that has turnstiles at the end (insert your ticket). The platforms are just beyond. (The Circumvesuviana also has its own terminal, 1 stop or a 10-min walk beyond the Central Station, but there's no reason to use it.) Two trains per hour, marked Sorrento, take you to Herculaneum (Ercolano) in 15 minutes, Pompeii in 40 minutes, and Sorrento, the end of the line, in 70 minutes (€2.85 one-way, not covered by railpass, not all of the trains go as far as Sorrento—look at the schedule carefully or confirm with a local before boarding to make sure the train is going where you want to). Express trains marked DD (12/day) get you to Sorrento 30 minutes quicker. When returning to Naples' Centrale station on the Circumvesuviana, get off at the second-to-the-last station, the Collegamento FS or Garibaldi stop (Centrale station is just up the escalator).

**Note:** Many readers report being ripped off on this train (see theft alert in "Helpful Hints," above).

## Circumvesuviana Stops between Naples and Sorrento

I list these so you can look at the scenery, rather than your watch.

Napoli
**Napoli Collegamento FS**
  (a.k.a. Piazza Garibaldi;
  below Centrale station)
Gianturco
S. Giovanni
Barra
S. Maria d. Pozzo
S. Giorgio
Cavalli di Bronzo
Bellavista
V. Liberta
**Ercolano Scavi**
  (Herculaneum site)
Ercolano
Miglio D'Oro
Torre del Greco
V.S. Antonio
V. del Monte
V. Monaci
Villa della Ginestra

Leopardi
V. Viuli
Trecase
Torre Annunziata
**Pompei Scavi**
  (Pompeii site)
Moregine
Ponte Persica
Pioppaino
V. Nocera
C. Mare Stabia
C. Mare Terme
Pozzano
Scraio
Vico Equense
Seiano
Meta
Piano di Sorrento
S. Agnello
**Sorrento**

# SORRENTO

Wedged on a ledge under the mountains and over the Mediterranean, spritzed by lemon and olive groves, Sorrento is an attractive resort of 20,000 residents and—in the summer—as many tourists. It's as well-located for regional sightseeing as it is a fine place to stay and stroll. The Sorrentines have gone out of their way to create a completely safe and relaxed place for tourists to come and spend money. (None of its 40 banks has ever been robbed.) Everyone seems to speak fluent English and work for the Chamber of Commerce. This gateway to the Amalfi Coast has an unspoiled old quarter, a lively main shopping street, and a spectacular cliffside setting. Skip the port and its poor excuse for a beach unless you're taking a ferry. Locals are proud of the many world-class romantics who've vacationed here. In 1921, the famed tenor Enrico Caruso chose Sorrento as his place to die.

## Orientation

Sorrento is long and narrow. The main drag, Corso Italia
(50 meters, or 165 feet, in front of the Circumvesuviana train
station), runs parallel to the sea from the station through the
town center and out to the cape, where it's renamed Via Capo.
Everything mentioned (except the hotels on Via Capo) is within
a 10-minute walk of the station. Sorrento hibernates in January
and February when many places close down.

**Tourist Information:** The TI, located inside the Foreigner's
Club, hands out a free *Sorrentum* magazine with a great city
map and schedules of boats, buses, and events (Mon–Sat 8:45–
19:15, closed Sun, shorter hours off-season, tel. 081-807-4033,
www.sorrentotourism.com, e-mail: info@sorrentotourism.com).
To reach the TI *(Soggiorno e Turismo)* from the train station,
go left on Corso Italia and walk five minutes to Piazza Tasso;
turn right at the end of the square, then head down Via L. de
Maio through Piazza Sant Antonino to the Foreigners' Club
mansion at #35. You'll pass fake "tourist offices" (travel agencies
selling bus and boat tours). If you arrive after the TI closes, look
for key TI handouts in the lobby of the Foreigners' Club (open
until midnight).

The **Foreigners' Club** provides reasonably priced snacks
and drinks, relaxation, views, and a handy place for visitors
to meet locals (behind TI, public WC). It's lively with concerts
or dancing every summer evening (starting at 21:00, tel. 081-
877-3263; see "Nightlife" and "Eating," below). Drop in for
an orientation view of the harbor and a commanding view of
the Bay of Naples.

**Laundry:** A handy coin-op laundry is at Corso Italia 30;
turn right down the alley for the side entrance (1 load-€8,
2 loads-€15, daily 8:00–21:00).

## Getting around Sorrento

Orange city buses all stop in the main square (Tasso). They
run to the Meta beach (bus A), the port (Marina Piccola, buses
B and C), the fishing village (Marina Grande, bus D), and
to the hotels on Via Capo (€1 tickets within the center, sold
at *tabacchi* shops, purchase before boarding and stamp upon
entering). Sorrento Rent-a-Car also rents mopeds and
Vespas (€29/3 hrs, daily 8:30–13:00 & 16:00–21:00, Corso
Italia 210, tel. 081-878-1386). In summer, forget renting a
car unless you enjoy traffic jams. Taxis are expensive, charging at least €10 for the short ride from the station to
hotels. Bikes are rentable at Sorrento Bici (Corso Italia 258,
tel. 081-807-5561).

## Sights—Sorrento

▲**Strolling**—Take time to explore the surprisingly pleasant old
city between Corso Italia and the sea. Views from the public park
next to Imperial Hotel Tramontano are worth the detour. Duck
into the Church of England. The evening *passeggiata* (along Corso
Italia and Via San Cesareo) peaks around 22:00. Check out the
old-boys' club playing cards, oblivious to the tourism, under their
portico (with great 3-D frescoes) at Via San Cesareo and Via Tasso.

**Lemon Grove Garden (L'Agruminato)**—This small park consists of an inviting lemon and orange grove lined with paths. It's
dotted with benches and a little stand often offering free tastes of
*limoncello*, a local specialty made of lemons, sugar, and pure alcohol
(May–Aug 10:00–20:00, Sept–April 10:00–16:00). Enter the garden
on Corso Italia (across from Panetteria da Franco—Corso Italia
165, see door flanked by tiles, marked "L'Agruminato, il giardino
della città") or at Via Rota (next to Hotel La Meridiana Sorrento).

## Activities—Sorrento

**Tennis**—The Sorrento Sport Snack Bar has fine courts open to the
public (daily 9:00–21:00, €9.30/hr, €12/hr after dark for 2, includes
use of rackets and balls, call for reservation, across from recommended Ambasciatori Hotel at Via Califano 5, tel. 081-807-1616).

**Swimming near Sorrento**—If you need immediate tanning,
you can rent a chair on the pier by the port. There are no great
beaches near Sorrento. The best sandy, family-friendly beach is
three kilometers (less than 2 miles) east at Meta (easy Orange
bus connection from Sorrento—take bus A from Piazza Tasso).
Tarzan might take Jane to the wild and stony beach at **Punta
del Capo**, a 15-minute bus ride west of town (2/hr from Piazza
Tasso to American Bar, then walk 10 min past ruined Roman
Villa di Pollio). Beyond that, **Marina di Poulo** is a tiny fishing
town popular in the summer for its sandy beach, surfside restaurants, and beachfront disco.

## Nightlife

This town is filled with Brit-friendly pubs. These two are most
popular and within a few blocks of each other: The **Merry Monk
Irish Pub** offers good draft beer, hamburgers, fries, darts, live
dance music nightly, noisy Internet access, and a free transfer back
to your hotel if necessary. And you haven't heard "Mustang Sally"
until you've heard it in Italian (at the west end of town at Via Capo
4, tel. 081-877-2409). **The English Inn** is another place designed
to make English guests feel right at home. Its rough-feeling pub
serves baked beans on toast, fish and chips, and draft beer with fun
music and a more refined-feeling garden out back (daily 9:00–2:00,

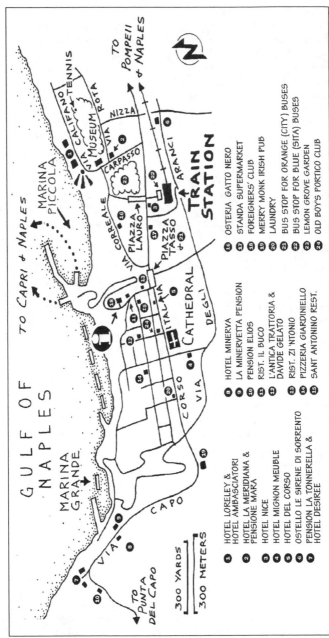

**Sorrento**

1. HOTEL LORELEY &
   HOTEL AMBASCIATORI
2. HOTEL LA MERIDIANA &
   PENSIONE MARA
3. HOTEL NICE
4. HOTEL MIGNON MEUBLE
5. HOTEL DEL CORSO
6. OSTELLO LE SIRENE DI SORRENTO
7. PENSION LA TONNERELLA &
   HOTEL DESIREE
8. HOTEL MINERVA
9. LA MINERVETTA PENSION
10. PENSION ELIOS
11. RIST. IL BUCO
12. L'ANTICA TRATTORIA &
    DAVIDE GELATO
13. RIST. ZI'NTONIO
14. PIZZERIA GIARDINIELLO
15. SANT ANTONINO REST.
16. OSTERIA GATTO NERO
17. STANDA SUPERMARKET
18. FOREIGNERS' CLUB
19. MERRY MONK IRISH PUB
20. LAUNDRY
21. BUS STOP FOR ORANGE (CITY) BUSES
22. BUS STOP FOR BLUE (SITA) BUSES
23. LEMON GROVE GARDEN
24. OLD BOY'S PORTICO CLUB

Corso Italia 53, tel. 081-807-4357). The **Foreigners' Club** has live music nightly at 21:00 and is just right for old-timers feeling frisky (in the center, see "Tourist Information," above).

# Sleeping in Sorrento
**(€1 = about $1, country code: 39, zip code: 80067)**
Sleep Code: **S** = Single, **D** = Double/Twin, **T** = Triple, **Q** = Quad, **b** = bathroom, **s** = shower only, **CC** = Credit Cards accepted, **no CC** = Credit Cards not accepted, **SE** = Speaks English, **NSE** = No English.

To help you sort easily through these listings, I've divided the rooms into three categories based on the price for a standard double room with bath:

**Higher Priced**—Most rooms more than €150.
**Moderately Priced**—Most rooms €150 or less.
**Lower Priced**—Most rooms €100 or less.

Sorrento offers the whole range of rooms. Hotels often charge the same for a room whether it has a view, balcony, or neither. At hotels that offer sea views, ask for a room *"con balcone, con vista sul mare"*—with a balcony, with a sea view. *"Tranquillo"* is taken as a request for a room off the street. Every place includes breakfast unless otherwise noted. Hotels listed are either near the station and city center or along the way to Punta del Capo, a 20-minute walk (or short bus ride) from the station. While many hotels close for the winter, you should have no trouble finding a room any time outside of August, when the place is jammed and many hotel prices go way up. Spring for a hotel with air-conditioning if you wilt in the heat. Note: The spindly, more exotic, and more tranquil Amalfi Coast town of Positano (below) is also a good place to spend the night.

## Sleeping East of the Center
A block in front of the train station, turn right onto Corso Italia, then left down Via Capasso, which winds right and becomes Via Califano. At the Loreley and Ambasciatori, the "private beach" is actually a sundeck built out over the water.

**HIGHER PRICED**
**Grand Hotel Ambasciatori** is a sumptuous four-star hotel with a cliffside setting, sprawling garden, and pool. This is Humphrey Bogart–land, with plush public spaces, a stay-awhile relaxing ambience, and an elevator to its beach (Db-€254, occasionally less, closed Jan–Feb, CC, air-con, some balconies, parking, Via Califano 18, tel. 081-878-2025, fax 081-807-1021, www .manniellohotels.it, e-mail: ambasciatori@manniellohotels.it).

**MODERATELY PRICED**

**Hotel la Meridiana Sorrento**, a fine three-star place with everything but character, offers 45 air-conditioned modern rooms and business-class public spaces (Db-€108, Tb-€145, half pension at €85 per person required Aug–mid-Sept, add €10/night for air-con, prices soft when slow, CC, big rooftop terrace with grand views, next door to public Lemon Grove Garden, Via Rota 1, tel. 081-807-3535, fax 081-807-3484, e-mail: lameridiana.sorrento@tiscalinet.it, SE).

**LOWER PRICED**

**Hotel Loreley**, a rambling, spacious, colorful, old Sorrentine villa next door to the Grand Hotel Ambasciatori, feels a bit like a sanitorium. It's ideal for those wishing to sit on the bluff and stare at the sea. Of its 27 rooms, 19 are quiet and have seaview balconies. The noisy, streetside rooms lack views but are air-conditioned. A €2.60 elevator takes you to the hotel's beach (Db-€90; from July–mid-Sept half pension at €65 per person is required but the dinner's good; CC, unpredictable management cannot guarantee view rooms but promises these prices through 2003 with this book, some free parking, Via Califano 2, tel. 081-807-3187, fax 081-532-9001, SE).

**Pensione Mara** is a dirty ashtray kind of place, with 13 simple rooms in a dull building with a good location (S-€26, D-€47, Db-€54, T-€70, Tb-€75, cheap quads and family room, prices promised through 2003, closed in March, no breakfast, no CC; from Via Capasso, turn right at Hotel La Meridiana to Via Rota 5, tel. & fax 081-878-3665, Adelle speaks a little English).

## Sleeping in the Town Center

**LOWER PRICED**

**Hotel Mignon Meuble**, with 23 big, clean, and pleasant rooms, is Old World simple on a quiet street off Corso Italia. A 10-minute walk from the station, this is the best hotel value in the town center (Db-€78, Tb-€93, CC, some balconies, no views, air-con, owned by Hotel Loreley, Via Sersale 9; from station, turn left on Via del Corso, tel. & fax 081-807-3824, Magda SE).

**Hotel del Corso**, a funky, Old World, three-star hotel, is central, family-run, and comfortable, with 26 clean and spacious rooms (Db-€110, Tb-€145, Qb-€170, ask for Rick Steves discount when you reserve, CC, air-con, cheap Internet access, rooftop sun terrace, Corso Italia 134, near Piazza Tasso, tel. & fax 081-807-3157, tel. 081-807-1016, www.hoteldelcorso.com, helpful Luca SE).

**Hotel Nice** rents 23 basic rooms 100 meters (330 feet) in front of the station on the noisy main drag. Ask for a room off the street (Sb–€47, Db–€69, Tb–€91, Qb–€106, prices increase about €5 July–Aug, CC, air-con, Corso Italia 257, tel. 081-878-1650, fax 081-878-3086, e-mail: albergo.nice@katamail.com, SE).

**Ostello le Sirene di Sorrento**, a tiny hostel four blocks from the train station, offers the cheapest beds in town (100 beds in triples and quads—€18 with bath, €16 without, Db–€57, no CC, Internet access, Via degli Aranci 160, tel. & fax 081-877-1371, e-mail: info@hostel.it, SE).

## Sleeping with a View on Via Capo

These hotels are outside of town, near the cape (straight out Corso Italia, which turns into Via Capo; from the city center, it's a 15-min walk, a €15 taxi ride, or a cheap bus ride). The bus situation is goofy because there are two competing companies. To get from the train station to Via Capo, you can catch a blue SITA bus (any except those heading for Positano/Amalfi) or an orange Circumvesuviana bus. Tickets for both are sold at the station newsstand and tobacco shops but not on the bus. Orange is more frequent (3/hr). If you're in Sorrento to stay put and luxuriate, these accommodations are ideal (although I'd rather luxuriate on the Amalfi Coast).

### MODERATELY PRICED

**Pension La Tonnarella** is a well-worn Sorrentine villa with several terraces, stylish tiles, sea views, a dreamy chandeliered dining room, and uninterested owners. Fifteen of its 21 rooms have a sea view (viewless Db–€135, Db with view-€140, Db with view balcony-€145, Db with view terrace-€155, view suite-€170, obligatory €83 per person half pension with dinner in Aug, CC, air-con, many rooms with great view balconies, small beach with free elevator access, Via Capo 31, tel. 081-878-1153, fax 081-878-2169, www.latonnarella.com, e-mail: latonnarella@libero.it, SE).

**Hotel Minerva** is like a sun worshiper's temple. Catch the elevator at Via Capo 32. Getting off at the fifth floor, you'll step into a spectacular terrace with outrageous Mediterranean views and a small, cliff-hanging swimming pool complementing 48 large, tiled *limoncello* rooms. Looking for the room numbers, you'll wonder if you're on *Candid Camera* (Db–€135, Tb–€150, Qb–€165, plus €36 in Sept, these discounted prices promised with this book through 2003 *only* if claimed at time of inquiry—fail to do this and you pay €30 more, no summer half pension requirement, CC, air-con, Via Capo 30, tel. 081-878-1011, fax 081-878-1949, www.acampora.it, e-mail: minerva@acampora.it, SE).

**ER PRICED**

**el Désirée**, run by friendly Corinna, is a simpler affair
h humbler views but no traffic noise, all the comforts, a fine
oof terrace, and no half pension requirements (maximum prices:
Sb-€54, small Db-€69, Db-€85, Tb-€100, Qb-€116, price
promised through 2003 with this book, no CC, laundry-€7.75,
shares La Tonnarella's driveway and beach, Via Capo 31, tel. &
fax 081-878-1563). Corinna is hugely helpful with tips on
exploring the peninsula, SE.

**La Minervetta Pension** rents 12 fine rooms built into the
cliff below its restaurant and far below the noisy street. Each
room comes with perfect quiet and an awesome Mediterranean
view (Db-€98, half pension—at €67 per person—is required in
Aug, extra bed–€23, bunky family rooms, price good through
2003 with this book, CC, air-con, parking, Via Capo 25, tel.
081-877-3033, fax 081-807-3069, Salvatore SE).

The humble **Pension Elios**, run by Luigi, Maria, and
daughter Gianna, offers 14 simple but spacious rooms, most with
balconies and views, and a panoramic sun terrace (Db-€47–52,
Tb-€62, family rooms, cheaper off-season, free parking, Via
Capo 33, tel. 081-878-1812, a little English spoken).

### Sleeping on Via del Mare

**MODERATELY PRICED**

**Hotel del Mare**, with modern rooms and views, is located a
15-minute walk from the center, 100 meters (330 feet) from the
Marina Grande beach (Sb-€83, Db-€135, Qb-€185, Via del Mare
30, near Via Capo hotels, tel. 081-878-3310, fax 081-807-1244,
www.hoteldelmare.com).

# Eating in Sorrento

### Dining Downtown—Splurges

In a town proud to have no McDonald's, consider eating well
for a few extra bucks. Each of these places is a worthwhile splurge
in the old center.

**Ristorante il Buco**, once the cellar of an old monastery, is now
a small, dressy restaurant serving delightfully presented, top-quality
food with good wine. The owner, Peppe, designs his menu around
whatever's fresh and travels in the winter to assemble a wine list sure
to offer connoisseurs something new and memorable (dinners run
about €40 plus wine, Thu–Tue 12:00–14:30 & 19:00–24:00, closed
Wed and Jan, CC, just off Piazza Sant Antonino at Il Rampe Marina
Piccola 5, reservations smart, tel. 081-878-2354).

**L'Antica Trattoria** serves hearty portions of more traditio
cuisine in a *romantico* candlelit ambience, full of contagiously fun
waiters and enthusiastic eaters. Its wine list is more predictable,
featuring well-known domestic wines. Walk around before you
select a place to sit (daily 12:00–15:00 & 19:00–23:30, closed Mon
off-season, air-con, shady terrace, non-smoking sections, reservations smart for eves, CC, Via P.R. Giulani 33, tel. 081-807-1082,
Aldo will take good care of you).

## Eating Well and Cheaply Downtown

**Pizzeria Giardiniello** is a family show offering good food, good
prices, friendly smiles, and a peaceful, tropical garden setting (daily
12:00–24:00, Via Accademia 7, tel. 081-878-4616). Like an old
sailor checking the lines, Franco makes sure you're well-fed.

**Osteria Gatto Nero** is a fresh, modern place catering to trendy
young locals out for good traditional cooking, especially pasta and
seafood. Chagall would eat here (Tue–Sun 19:00–24:00, closed Mon,
CC, eat indoors or out back in the garden, a few minutes' walk east
of old center at Via Correale 19, tel. 081-877-3686, Gaetano).

**Sant Antonino's** offers friendly service, red-checkered tablecloths, an outdoor patio, decent prices, and edible food (closed
Mon off-season, CC, just off Piazza Sant Antonino on Santa
Maria delle Grazie 6, tel. 081-877-1200). Nearby, the smaller
and livelier **Pizzeria Da Gigino** is better (first road to the right
of Sant Antonino as you face it, daily 12:00–15:00 & 18:30–24:00,
closed Tue off-season, CC, tel. 081-878-1927).

**Ristorante Pizzeria Zi 'Ntonio,** serving local cuisine and
homemade pasta, has a woody, hanging-hams, and happy-tiled
ambience. Its self-serve antipasto and seafood buffet makes a
quick lunch or light dinner (daily 12:00–16:00 & 18:30–1:30, CC,
air-con, Via Luigi de Maio 11, tel. 081-878-1623).

If you fancy a picnic dinner on your balcony, on the hotel
terrace, or in the public garden, you'll find many markets and
take-out pizzerias in the old town. The **Standa supermarket** at
Corso Italia 223 has it all (Mon–Wed and Fri–Sat 8:30–13:00 &
16:30–20:30, Thu 8:30–13:00 only, closed Sun, CC).

**Gelato:** A few doors downhill from L'Antica Trattoria,
**Davide Gelato** has many repeat customers—so many flavors,
so little time. Walk the most enticing chorus line in Italy before
ordering (daily and nightly, closed Mon off-season, Via P.R.
Giuliani 39, off Corso Italia).

## Cliffside Dinners with Sea Views

For a decent dinner, the following three places come with great
view terraces.

**La Minervetta**, a 10-minute walk west of town across the ~eet from the recommended Hotel Minerva, is perfect for tired ~ourists in need of a low-stress, reasonably priced, quality meal and a soothing view (closed Nov–March, Via Capo 25, tel. 081-807-3069). **Hotel Loreley's** restaurant serves reasonably priced, so-so meals with a spectacular sea view (if it's busy, non-guests may be turned away, 10-min walk east of town center, Via Califano 2, listed in "Sleeping," above).

The **Foreigners' Club Restaurant** is a place where the English Patient could recuperate. It has the best sea views in town (under breezy palms), live music nightly at 21:00, and passable meals (March–Nov daily 9:30–24:00, closed in winter, Via L. De Maio 35, tel. 081-877-3263).

## Transportation Connections—Sorrento

It's impressively fast to zip by boat from point to point during the summer, when there are many more departures. In fact, many locals get around quicker by fast boat than by car or train.

**By boat to: Naples** (7/day, 40 min, €7), **Positano** (2/day in summer only, 75 min, €8), **Capri** (at least hrly, 40 min, €6.20; quicker and pricier by hydrofoil and jet boat: 20 min, €8). For an untouristy alternative to Capri, consider the nearby island of **Ischia**, where part of *The Talented Mr. Ripley* was filmed (1/day, summer only, otherwise from Naples).

To get from Sorrento's Piazza Tasso to the port, walk or take the orange shuttle bus B or C (3/hr). Tickets are sold only at the port. Several lines compete, using boats and hydrofoils. Buy one-way tickets only (there's no round-trip discount) for schedule flexibility, so you can take any company's boat back. Prices are the same among the companies. Check times for the last return crossing upon arrival. The first boats leaving Sorrento can be jammed (either arrive early to buy your ticket or leave closer to 10:00).

**To the Amalfi Coast:** See "Amalfi Coast," below.

**To Pompeii, Herculaneum, and Naples by Circumvesuviana train:** This commuter train runs about every 40 minutes between Naples and Sorrento. From Sorrento, it's 30 minutes to Pompeii, 45 minutes to Herculaneum, and 70 minutes to Naples (€2.85 one-way). See "Transportation Connections—Naples," above, for more information on the Circumvesuviana and theft precautions. Note: The risk of theft is limited mostly to suburban Naples. Sorrento to Herculaneum is much safer.

## Sorrento Peninsula

**Marina del Cantone**, a tiny fishing village near Nerano, on a Sorrento Peninsula dead end, is the place to establish a sleepy,

fun-in-the-sun residency (10 buses/day from Sorrento to M.
del Cantone, 60 min, or a 30-min, €50 taxi ride). There are s
good hikes from here: Punto Penna is about a four-hour loop
great views. A more strenuous hike leads along the coast, past th
stunning Gulf of Salerno to Torca, where buses go to Sant Agata
(and from there, back to Sorrento). Along the trail, you might
detour down to the cliff-hugging fishing village of—get this—
Crapolla. Bring water and a good map.

**Sleeping in Marina del Cantone:** For a peaceful place to
call home, sleep literally on the beach at the friendly **Pensione
La Certosa**. This family-run place offers 16 basic, air-conditioned
rooms (6 with sea view), a great beachfront restaurant, boat
excursions, and information on a number of peaceful little
beaches nearby (Db-€83 June–Sept, otherwise Db-€66, half
pension required in Aug for €67/person, family rooms, CC,
80068 Massa Lubrense, tel. 081-808-1209, fax 081-808-1245,
www.hotelcertosa.com, run by Alfonso, SE).

# THE AMALFI COAST

The bus trip from Sorrento to Salerno along the Amalfi Coast is
a ▲▲▲ sight and one of the world's great bus rides. It will leave
your mouth open and your film exposed. You'll gain respect for
the Italian engineers who built the road—and even more respect
for the bus drivers who drive it. As you hyperventilate, notice that
the Mediterranean, a sheer 150-meter (500-foot) drop below,
really twinkles.

Cantilevered garages, hotels, and villas cling to the vertical
terrain, and beautiful sandy coves tease from far below and out
of reach. If you know where to look, you'll see the villa of Sophia
Loren. Gasp from the right side of the bus as you go out and from
the left on the way back. Those on the wrong side really miss out.
Traffic is so heavy that private tour buses are only allowed to go
east—summer traffic is infuriating. Even with a car, you may be
glad you took the bus or hired a taxi. Some enjoy doing the coast
by motorbike (rented in Sorrento).

Amalfi Coast towns are pretty but generally touristy, congested,
overpriced, and a long hike above tiny beaches. The real thrill is the
scenic drive. Catch a blue SITA bus from the Sorrento train station
(see "Transportation Connections—Amalfi Coast," below).

If you're thinking of taking a round-trip bus ride from
Sorrento along the Amalfi Coast to Salerno and back, consider
these two options instead: Get off at a prettier town (such as
Cetera) near Salerno and return from there by bus rather than go
into the big, plain town of Salerno. Or take the bus to Salerno,
then catch the ferry back to Amalfi or Positano, and from either

## Amalfi Coast

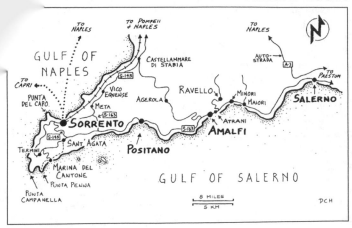

town, hop a ferry to Sorrento; Salerno's ferry dock is conveniently located at the bus stop (see "Transportation Connections—Salerno," at the end of this chapter).

This is perhaps the simplest option: Take the bus to Positano and boat from there back to Sorrento (or vice versa).

## Transportation Connections—Amalfi Coast

**From Sorrento to the Amalfi Coast by bus:** The big tourist activity from Sorrento is riding the bus along the Amalfi Coast. Blue SITA buses depart from Sorrento's train station nearly hourly (in peak season, 20/day) and stop at all Amalfi Coast towns (Positano in 45 min, €1.20; Amalfi in another 45 min, €2.25), ending up in Salerno at the far end of the coast in just under three hours (one easy transfer in Amalfi). Buses start running as early as 6:30 and run as late as 20:00 (21:00 in summer). Buy tickets at the tobacco shop nearest any bus stop before boarding. (There's a *tabacchi*/newsstand at street level at the Sorrento station.) Line up under the "Riservato SITA" sign (where a schedule is posted on the wall) in front of the station (10 steps down). Leaving Sorrento, grab a seat on the right for the best views. Returning, it's fun to sit directly behind the driver for a box seat over the hairpin twisting action.

**Crowds on the Amalfi bus:** Buses are routinely unable to handle the demand during summer months. Occasionally an extra bus is added to handle the overflow but, generally, if you don't get on, you're well-positioned to catch the next bus (bring a book). In the morning, arrive early (count the line: buses pull in empty and

seat 49). The congestion can be so bad in the summer tha
buses don't even stop in Positano (they were filled in Amalt.
those trying to get back to Sorrento have no option but extor
taxis (or, if stranded in Positano, check boat schedules).

If crowds are horrendous, consider gathering a small group
and sharing a taxi from Sorrento (4 by car one-way to Positano
for around €50, or 6 by minibus taxi for €65, 50 percent more to
Amalfi; while taxis must use meter within city, a fixed rate is okay
otherwise—negotiate; ask about a round-trip).

**Amalfi Coast tours by taxi:** Given the hairy driving, impos-
sible parking, congested buses, and potential fun, you might consider splurging to hire your own car and driver for the Amalfi day.
Fun-loving **Carmine Monetti** (a jolly, singing, in-love-with-life,
grandfatherly type who speaks "inventive English") and his son
Raffaele (much better English, fewer smiles, more information)
have long taken excellent care of my readers' transportation needs
from Sorrento. Sample trips and rates (mention this book to get
these special prices): "Amalfi Coast Day" (Positano–Amalfi–lunch
in Ravello), seven hours, €145; "Amalfi Coast and Paestum," 10
hours, €240; "Pompeii and Vesuvius," seven hours, €160; transfer
to Naples airport or train station, one hour, €80; cash only; up to
six passengers in their air-conditioned minivan, Raffaele's cellular
33-5602-9158, Carmine's cellular 33-8946-2860, "office" run by
Raffaele's Finnish (and English-speaking) wife, Susanna: tel. & fax
081-878-4795, e-mail: monettitaxi17@libero.it. Their reservation
system is simple, easygoing, and reliable. Be careful: Many cabbies
are claiming to be the Monettis. The Monettis drive taxi #17,
usually found in Piazza Tasso. Couples wanting to cut their cost
in half can tell Susanna they're open to sharing, allowing her to
try to fill the minivan. If in any kind of a jam, call Raffaele's cellular phone for information.

**Benvenuto Umberto**, run by Umberto, offers transport
and narrated excursions throughout the Amalfi Coast as well as
to Rome, Naples, Pompeii, and more (Via Roma 54, tel. 089-
874-024, cellular 330-353-294, www.taxivenvenuto.com).

# POSITANO

Specializing in scenery and sand, Positano hangs halfway between
Sorrento and Amalfi on the most spectacular stretch of the coast.
The village, a three-star sight from a distance, is a pleasant gathering of cafés and expensive women's clothing stores, with a good
but pebbly beach. Squished into a ravine, the center of town has
no main square, unless you count the beach. There's little to do
here but eat, window-shop, and enjoy the beach and views (hence
the town's popularity). Consider seeing Positano as a day trip from

...ake the bus out and the afternoon ferry home. If you
...night, save the day for the beach and the cooler morning
...ening for hiking up and down this hilly town. The town has
...al flavor at night, when the grown-ups stroll and the kids play
...cer on the church porch.

**Tourist Information:** The TI is a half block from the
beach, in a small building at the bottom of the church steps (daily
8:30–14:00 & 16:00–20:00; shorter hours off-season and closed
Sun, tel. 089-875-067).

**Arrival in Positano:** The town has only two scheduled
bus stops: Chiesa (at Bar Internazionale, nearer Sorrento) and
Sponda (nearer Amalfi Town). To minimize your descent, take
the Sponda stop (the second Positano stop if you're coming from
Sorrento). It's a 20-minute stroll/shop/munch from here to the
beach (and TI).

If you're catching the bus back to Sorrento, remember it
may leave from Sponda five minutes before the printed departure.
There's no place for the bus to wait, so in case the driver is early,
you should be, too. If the walk up is too tough, take the little
orange bus (marked Interno Positano) which does a loop from
the center of Positano (at Via Columbo and Via del Mulini, across
from Bar Mulino Verde) up to the main highway and the SITA
bus stops (€0.75, 2/hr, buy tickets for the orange bus on board;
buy tickets for SITA from Bar Mulino Verde or Positour Agency—
both are on Via Columbo).

**Drivers** must go with the one-way flow entering the town
only at the Chiesa bus stop (closest to Sorrento) and exiting at
Sponda.

## Sights—Positano

**Beach**—Positano's wide beach, colorful with beach umbrellas,
is mostly public (free) but also has a private section (April–Oct,
€9.50/person, includes use of sun beds and umbrellas). At the harbor, the nearest WC is behind the waterfront Bucca di Bacco bar.

**Boat Trips**—At the right side of the beach (as you face the
sea), you'll see a series of booths selling boat tickets. Boats to
Fornillo make three-minute, €0.75 journeys to Fornillo Beach—
a quieter beach nearby (or an easy 10-min walk, take trail near
ticket booths).

You could catch a boat to Amalfi (9/day, 30 min), Capri
(7/day, 30 min), Sorrento (4/day in afternoon, 25 min), or Naples
(1/day, 50 min on hydrofoil); fewer boats run off-season. Consider
renting a rowboat or taking various boat tours of a nearby cave
(La Grotta dello Smeraldo—Emerald Cave), fishing village
(Nerano), and small islands.

**Pos.**

Positano map legend:
- ① HOTEL MARINCANTO
- ② ALBERGO CALIFORNIA
- ③ RESIDENCE LA TAVOLOZZA
- ④ HOTEL SAVOIA
- ⑤ HOTEL BOUGAINVILLE
- ⑥ BRIKETTE HOSTEL
- ⑦ LA TRE SORRELLE REST.
- ⑧ DA VINCENZO REST.

## Sleeping in Positano
**(€1 = about $1, country code: 39, zip code: 84017)**
These hotels (but not the hostel) are all on Via Colombo, which
leads from the Sponda SITA bus stop down into the village.

### HIGHER PRICED
**Hotel Marincanto** is a newly restored four-star hotel (Db-€196,
superior Db-€227, suites-€280–375, includes breakfast, CC,
private stairs to beach, large sundeck, Via Colombo 36, tel.
089-875-130, fax 089-875-595, www.marincanto.it, SE).

### MODERATELY PRICED
**Albergo California** has great views, spacious rooms (12 of 17 with
sea views), and a grand terrace draped with vines (Db-€130–150
depending on season and amenities, viewless Db-€100, includes

,t, CC; view rooms are air-con, free parking, can arrange
Via Colombo 141, tel. 089-875-382, fax 089-812-154,
.hpe.it/california/, e-mail: albergo.california@hpe.it,
.ria, Frank SE).

**Hotel Savoia** rents 39 three-star, air-conditioned rooms
(prices vary with season: Db-€114–155, deluxe Db-€130–176,
mention this book and ask for discount, CC, some sea views,
elevator, Via Colombo 73, tel. 089-875-003, fax 089-811-844,
www.savoiapositano.com, e-mail: info@savoiapositano.it, SE).

**LOWER PRICED**
**Residence La Tavolozza** is an attractive eight-room hotel, warmly run by Celeste (pron. cheh-LES-tay). Flawlessly restored, each
room comes with a view, a balcony, fine tile, and silence (Db-€82
in 2003 with this book, breakfast extra, no CC, also has a small
apartment and royal family apartment with 6 beds, Via Colombo
10, tel. & fax 089-875-040, e-mail: celeste.dileva@tiscalinet.it, a
little English spoken).

**Hotel Bougainville** is spotless, with eager-to-please owners
and 14 basic rooms (Db-€78–93 with view balcony, Db without view-€62–78, includes breakfast only with this book, CC,
air-con, some traffic noise and fumes, Via Colombo 25, tel.
089-875-047, fax 089-811-150, www.bougainville.it, e-mail:
hotel@bougainville.it, Carlo, Luisa, and son Christian SE).

**Brikette Hostel** offers your best cheap, dorm-bed option in
this otherwise ritzy town. It's bright and clean with the normal
hostel rules: locked up from 10:00 to 16:00, curfew at midnight,
must check out by 9:00, no luggage storage or lockers (late March–
Nov only, dorm bed-€20, Db-€60, breakfast-€2.50, no CC;
Via G. Marconi 358, leave bus at Chiesa/Bar Internazionale stop
and backtrack uphill 150 meters, or 500 feet, tel. 089-812-2814,
www.brikette.com, e-mail: brikette@syrene.it).

# Eating in Positano

The pizzerias on the beach, while overpriced, are pleasant and
convenient. At the waterfront, I like **La Tre Sorelle** (daily
12:00–16:00 & 19:00–24:00, CC, tel. 089-875-452) but the
neighboring places also leave people fat and happy.

A 10-minute uphill hike rewards you with the very Italian
**Da Vincenzo**. This is a jolly festival of food with tasty surprises,
prepared by Gjosue and Marcella Porpora (Tue 19:00–24:00,
Wed–Mon 13:00–15:00 & 19:00–24:00, Viale Pasitea 172,
tel. 089-875-128).

The family-run **Da Costantino**, so high on the hill that the
restaurant sends a van to pick you up and take you home, offers

reasonably priced, simple, filling meals (closed Wed, Via Monte-pertuso 127, ask your hotel to call for the van, tel. 089-875-738).

If a picnic dinner on your balcony or the beach sounds good, Emilia at **Enogastromia Delikatessen** can supply the ingredients (daily in summer 7:00–14:00 & 16:00–22:00, in winter and on Sun closes at 20:00, just below car park at Via del Mulini 5). **Vini e Panini**, another small grocery, is a block from the beach and TI (Mon–Sat 8:00–14:00 & 16:30–21:30, Sun 8:00–14:00, just off church steps).

## AMALFI AND ATRANI

**Amalfi Town** was once a powerful maritime republic. Today, the waterfront of this most famous of the Amalfi Coast villages is dom-inated by a bus station, a parking lot, and two gas stations. But step into the town, and you find its once rich and formidable medieval shell filled with trendy shops and capped by an impressive cathe-dral. The main street through the village—hard for pedestrians to avoid—is packed with cars and bully mopeds.

Amalfi's **cathedral** is the only sight marginally worth visiting. Climb the imposing stairway. The 1,000-year-old bronze door was given to Amalfi by a wealthy local merchant, who had it made in Constantinople. When leaving the church, head right to tour the "Cloister of Paradise," the Basilica of the Crucifix (the original ninth-century church, now a museum filled with the art treasures of the cathedral), and the Crypt of St. Andrew. Andrew was the apostle who left his nets to become the original "fisher of men"; his remains were brought here in 1206 during the Crusades—an indication of the wealth and importance of Amalfi then (€2, daily in summer 9:00–21:00, winter 10:00–17:00, closed Jan–Feb, pick up the English flier).

**Atrani**, just a 15-minute stroll away, is a world apart. Amaz-ingly, it has none of the trendy resort feel of Amalfi, relatively few tourists, a delightful town square, and a free, sandy beach. For a classic Amalfi hike, walk from Atrani to Ravello (a venerable cliff-hanging resort town) and then to Amalfi.

## Sleeping in Amalfi Town or Atrani

If you're marooned in Amalfi, stay at the 40-room **Hotel Amalfi** (Db-€62–114, roof-terrace restaurant, July–Aug obligatory half pension is €78 per person, CC, no sea views, on a garden, 50 meters, or 165 feet, from cathedral, Via dei Pastai 3, 84011 Amalfi, tel. 089-872-440, fax 089-872-250, www.starnet.it/hamalfi, e-mail: hamalfi@starnet.it, SE). **Hotel La Conchiglia**, a 10-minute walk south along the harbor, is also good (11 rooms, Db-€100, no CC, packed July–Aug, Piazzale dei Protontini, tel. 089-871-856, NSE).

*In Atrani:* **A'Scalinatella** is an informal hostel—with a honeycomb of cramped two- to five-bed dorms, private rooms, family apartments, and a washer (€5.50/load). It's a small-town Amalfi hideaway, without the glitz and hill-climbing of Positano. The English-speaking owners, Filippo and Gabriele, are friendly and helpful (€13–21 per bed in D or T, D-€36–47, Db-€47–62, no CC; from the main square, hike up the ravine and look for signs, 84010 Atrani, tel. 089-871-492, www.hotelscalinatella.com, e-mail: scalinatella@amalficoast.it).

# CAPRI

Made famous as the vacation hideaway of Roman emperors Augustus and Tiberius, Capri these days is a world-class tourist trap packed with gawky visitors searching for the rich and famous, and finding only their prices. The six-by-three-kilometer (4-by-2-mile) "Island of Dreams" is a zoo in July and August—tacky low-grade group tourism at its worst. Other times of year, it provides a relaxing and scenic break from the cultural gauntlet of Italy. While Capri has some Roman ruins and an interesting 14th-century Carthusian monastery, its chief attraction is its famous Blue Grotto, and its best activity is a scenic hike.

**Tourist Information:** The TI at the ferry dock offers a room-finding service (April–Oct Mon–Sat 8:30–20:30, Sun 9:00–15:00; Nov–March Mon–Sat 9:00–13:00 & 15:30–18:45, closed Sun, tel. 081-837-0634). The Caremar baggage storage service is in front of the dock (€1.60/day per bag). As you exit the pier, the ticket windows (for your return trip) are to your right, and the funicular is across the street to your left. Bar Augusto, next to the funicular, has Internet access.

**Getting around Capri:** The buses and funicular are covered by the same ticket options: €1.25 one-way on the bus or funicular, €2.10 for 60 minutes of unlimited use, or €7.70 for an all-day pass. You can hire a convertible taxi for about €42 an hour—negotiate. From the ferry dock at Marina Grande, the funicular lifts you 150 meters (500 feet) to the town of Capri (5 min, 4/hr). From Capri, cliff-hanging buses run to Anacapri (7 min, 4/hr, note that buses can be packed returning from Anacapri to Capri; if so, guarantee a seat by catching the bus at the end of the line—a 5-min walk to your left as you face away from square).

## Sights—Capri

**Capri Town**—This is a cute but touristy shopping town. The TI is in a closet on the main square (to the left as you exit funicular, same hours as ferry dock TI—listed above, tel. 081-837-0686, WC down stairs behind TI). For a view restaurant with good seafood, try **Da**

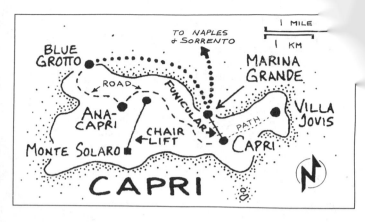

**Gemma** (daily, Via Madre Serafina 6, from town square go up stairs near church and follow the sign, tel. 081-837-0461). Overall, Capri Town is most useful as a place to catch the bus to Anacapri (from funicular exit, walk straight on shop-lined street; the bus station is about 100 meters, or 330 feet, ahead on your right).

**Anacapri**—This is the island's second town (TI tel. 081-837-1524). Oddly, there are no ocean views from the town, but there are hikes worth taking and one sight worth seeing. **St. Michael's Church** has a remarkable tile floor showing paradise on earth (€2, daily 9:30–18:00, until 17:00 off-season). **Ristorante Materita** on Piazza Diaz is good.

**Sleeping in Anacapri: Villa Eva**, a 10-minute walk from town on the Blue Grotto road, is a family-run place with 20 rooms, a lush setting, and a swimming pool (Db-€78–98 depending on season, Via la Fabbrica 8, tel. 081-837-1549, fax 081-837-2040, www.villaeva.com, e-mail: villa.eva@capri.it, SE). The cheap **Alla Bussola di Hermes** draws students and backpackers (dorm bed-€21, D-€62, laundry services, Internet access, can pick you up from port, in center of Anacapri, Via Traversa la Vigna 14, tel. 081-838-2010, e-mail: bus.hermes @libero.it, run by lovely Rita, SE).

**Hike down Monte Solaro**—From Anacapri, ride the €5.20 chair-lift to the 570-meter (1,900-foot) summit of Monte Solaro for a commanding view of the Bay of Naples and a pleasant downhill hike through lush vegetation and ever-changing views, past the 14th-century Chapel of Santa Maria Cetrella, and back into Anacapri.

**Blue Grotto**—To most, a visit to Capri's Blue Grotto is an over-rated and overpriced "must." The boat from Marina Grande costs €5.20. Once you reach the grotto, you pay €4 for a rowboat to take you in, then €4.20 to cover the admission (total €13.40).

n lop off €5.20 if you catch the bus to Anacapri and hike
.y for one hour to the grotto (instead of taking the boat from
.ina Grande). Hikers can dive in for free. And so can anyone
..er 17:00, when the boats stop running. Touristy as this is, the
grotto, with its eerily beautiful blue sunlight reflecting through
the water, is impressive (daily 9:00 until an hour before sunset,
boats don't run in stormy weather).

**Villa Jovis**—Emperor Tiberius' now-ruined villa is a scenic 45-
minute hike from Capri Town. Tiberius ruled Rome from here for a
decade in about A.D. 30 (€2, daily 9:00 until an hour before sunset).

## Transportation Connections—Capri

**By boat to: Sorrento** (nearly hrly, €6.20 for 40-min ride, €8 for
20-min jet-boat ride), **Naples** (6 hydrofoils/day, 45 min, €10.50).
Check the schedule carefully—the last boat leaves at 18:00 or 19:00.

# POMPEII, HERCULANEUM, AND VESUVIUS

▲▲▲**Pompeii**—Stopped in its tracks by the eruption of Mount
Vesuvius in A.D. 79, Pompeii offers the best look anywhere at what
life in Rome must have been like 2,000 years ago. An entire city of
well-preserved ruins is yours to explore. Once a thriving commercial port of 20,000, Pompeii grew from Greek and Etruscan roots
to become an important Roman city. Then, it was buried under
nine meters (30 feet) of hot mud and volcanic ash. For archaeologists, this was a shake-and-bake windfall, teaching them almost
all they know about daily Roman life. Pompeii was rediscovered
in the 1600s; excavations began in 1748.

**Cost, Hours, Information:** €10, or €13.50 combo-ticket
includes Herculaneum and three lesser sites (valid 3 days), April–
Oct daily 8:30–19:30, Nov–March daily 8:30–17:00. The ticket
office closes 1.5 hours before closing time. A good map is included
with admission (for more information, check www.pompeiisites
.org). A free baggage check is near the ticket window.

Stop by the bookshop. A guidebook on Pompeii makes this
site more meaningful. (Books are also on sale in Sorrento.) The
small Pompeii and Herculaneum "past and present" book has a
helpful text and allows you to re-create the ruins with plastic
overlays—with the "present" actually being 1964 (available for
€9.50 in bookstore unless they're "finished"; if you buy from a
street vendor, pay no more than €9.50). Audioguides are available
at the ticket booth for €4.

Live guides cluster near the ticket booth. If you gather 10
people, the price is reasonable when split (around €10 apiece,
total cost about €100, 2 hrs). For a local guide, consider Gaetano
Manfredi (cellular 338-725-5620, tel. 081-863-9816).

**Pom**

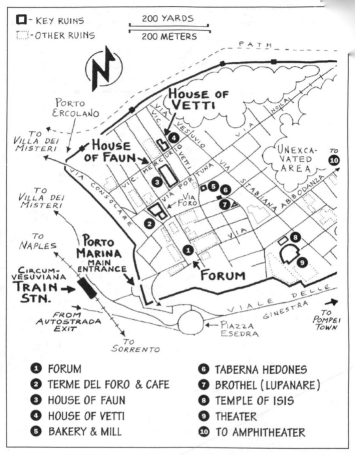

- **1** FORUM
- **2** TERME DEL FORO & CAFE
- **3** HOUSE OF FAUN
- **4** HOUSE OF VETTI
- **5** BAKERY & MILL
- **6** TABERNA HEDONES
- **7** BROTHEL (LUPANARE)
- **8** TEMPLE OF ISIS
- **9** THEATER
- **10** TO AMPHITHEATER

**Background:** Pompeii was a booming Roman trading city. Most streets would have been lined with stalls and jammed with customers from sunup to sundown. Chariots vied with shoppers for street space, and many streets were off-limits to chariots during shopping hours (you'll still see street signs with pictures of men carrying vases—this meant pedestrians only).

Fountains overflowed into the streets, flushing the gutters into the sea (thereby cleaning the streets). The stones you see at intersections allowed pedestrians to cross the constantly gushing streets. A single stone designated a one-way street (just enough room for one chariot, stone straddled by its two oxen), and two

meant a two-way chariot street. There were no posh neighborhoods. Rich and poor mixed it up, as elegant homes existed
side by side with simple homes throughout Pompeii. While nearby
Herculaneum would have been a classier place to live (traffic-free
streets, more elegant homes, far better drainage), Pompeii was
the place for action and shopping. It served its estimated 20,000
residents with more than 40 bakeries, 30 brothels, and 130 bars,
restaurants, and hotels. Rome controlled the entire Mediterranean
2,000 years ago—making it a kind of free-trade zone—and
Pompeii was a central and booming port town. With most buildings covered by brilliant, white ground-marble stucco, Pompeii in
A.D. 79 was an impressive town. Remember, Pompeii's best art is
in the Naples Archaeological Museum, described above.

**Tour of Pompeii:** Allow at least three hours to tour the site.
Consider the following route, starting at the Porta Marina (town
gate) after the ticket booth. Before Vesuvius blew, the sea came
nearly to this gate. As you approach the Porta Marina, notice the
two openings—big for chariots, small for pedestrians.

From the Porta Marina, Via Marina leads strait to Pompeii's
main square, the forum.

The **forum** (*foro*), Pompeii's commercial, religious, and political center, stands at the intersection of the city's two main streets.
While the most ruined part of Pompeii, it's grand nonetheless—
with temples, lots of pedestals that once sported statues (now in
the museum in Naples), and the basilica (Pompeii's largest building, the ancient equivalent of law courts and stock market—on
the right as you enter). The Curia (home of the government)
stands at the end of the forum. It's built of brick and mortar, a
Roman invention. While brick now, it was once faced with marble.
Note that while Pompeii was destroyed by the eruption of A.D. 79,
it was also devastated by an earthquake in A.D. 62. It's safe to
assume any brick you see dates from between A.D. 62 and A.D. 79—
restoration work done by Pompeians after the quake.

Walk (away from the Curia) along the fenced, roofed area that
runs alongside the forum. Behind the iron fence are piles of pottery
and, at the end, some eerie casts of volcano victims. With the unification of Italy in the 1860s, national spirit fueled efforts to excavate
Pompeii. During this period, archaeologists made these molds
(detecting hollows underfoot—left by decomposed bodies—as they
dug, they'd pour liquid plaster into them, let dry, and dig up).

Such a busy square needed a public toilet. Just past the warehouse, turn left into an ancient public WC. Notice the ditch that
led to the sewer (marked by an arch in the corner). The stone
supports once held wooden benches with the appropriate holes.
Even back then, this area had pay toilets.

Continue on, leaving the forum through the gate at the end. Take an immediate right, then a left. You're on Via del Foro, passing a convenient 21st-century cafeteria (decent value, gelato, books, WCs upstairs; a fancier restaurant in a more elegant ancient gymnasium setting is adjacent).

Head down Via del Foro and enter the impressive baths, **Terme del Foro** (on the left, past the cafeteria). You'll enter through the gymnasium. After working out, clients would find four rooms: a waiting room, warm bath *(tepidarium)*, hot bath *(caldarium)*, and cold-plunge bath *(frigidarium)*.

The *tepidarium* is ringed by mini-statues or *telamones* (male caryatids, figures used as supporting pillars), which divided clients' lockers. They'd undress and warm up here, perhaps stretching out on one of the benches near the bronze heater for a massage. Notice the ceiling: half crushed by the eruption and half surviving with its fine blue-and-white stucco work.

Next, in the *caldarium*, you'd get hot. Notice the engineering. The double floor was heated from below—so nice with bare feet (look into the grate to see the brick support towers). The double walls with brown terra-cotta tiles held the heat. Romans soaked in the big tub, which was filled with hot water. To keep condensation from dripping annoyingly from the ceiling, the fluting (ribbing) was added to carry the drips down the walls.

Next came the cold plunge in the *frigidarium*—a circular marble basin with the spout spewing frigid water, opposite the entry.

Exit the baths. Notice the oxcart wheel grooves and stepping stones in the street. During ancient rainstorms, streets would turn into filthy rivers. Do as the ancient Romans did. Keep your feet dry by using the stepping stones to cross the street. Directly in front of you is an ancient fast-food stand (notice the holes in the counters for pots). To your left, a few doors down, is the **House of the Tragic Poet** (Casa de Poeta Tragico), with its famous "Beware of Dog" (Cave Canum) mosaic in the entryway. On either side, grooves in the doorway indicate a shop with sliding doors.

Face the House of the Tragic Poet, then walk to your right two blocks to the House of the Faun (Casa del Fauno, Danzante). Notice the holes drilled into the curbs—to hitch your animal or perhaps to support an awning from your storefront.

Pompeii's largest home (with 40 rooms), the **House of the Faun** provided Naples' Archaeological Museum with many of its top treasures, including the original dancing faun (you'll see a copy here) and the famous mosaic of the "Battle of Alexander." Wander past the welcome mosaic (*HAVE*, or "hail to you") and through its courtyards. The back courtyard leads to the exit. It's lined by

rs rebuilt after the A.D. 62 earthquake. Take a close look
the brick, mortar, and fake marble stucco veneer.

Back on the street, turn right and look for the exposed
2,000-year-old lead pipes in the wire cage (ahead and down on
the ground to your right). The lead was imported from Roman
Britannia. A huge water tank—fed by an aqueduct—stood at the
high end of town. Three independent pipe systems supplied
water to the city from here: one each for baths, private homes,
and public water fountains. In the case of a water shortage, supply
could be limited. Democratic priorities prevailed: first the baths
were cut, then the private homes. The last water to be cut was
that which fed the public fountains (where the people got their
water for drinking and cooking).

Take your first left on Vicolo dei Vetti. Enter Pompeii's
best-preserved home, the House of the Vetti (Casa dei Vetti).

The **House of the Vetti**, which has retained its mosaics and
frescoes, was the bachelor pad of two wealthy merchant brothers.
In the entryway, see if you can spot the erection. This is not
pornography. There's a meaning here: The penis and the sack
of money balance each other on the goldsmith scale above a fine
bowl of fruit. The meaning: Only with a balance of fertility and
money can you have abundance.

Step into the atrium with its open sky to collect light and
rainwater. The pool, while decorative, was a functional water-
supply tank. It's flanked by large money boxes anchored to the
floor. They were certainly successful merchants, and possibly
moneylenders, too.

Exit on the right, passing the tight servant quarters, and go
into the kitchen, with its bronze cooking pots (and a touchable
lead pipe on the back wall). The passage dead-ends in the little
Venus Room with its erotic frescoes behind glass.

Return to the atrium and pass into the big colonnaded garden.
It was planted according to the plan indicated by traces of roots
excavated in the volcanic ash. This courtyard is ringed by richly
frescoed entertainment rooms. Circle counterclockwise. The dining room is finely decorated in "Pompeian red" (from iron rust)
and black. Study the detail. Notice the lead humidity seal between
the wall and the floor designed to keep the wet-sensitive frescoes
dry. (Had Leonardo taken this clever step, his *Last Supper* in Milan
might be in better shape today.) Continuing around, notice the
square white stones inlaid in the floor. Imagine them reflecting
like cat eyes as the brothers and their friends wandered around
by oil lamp late at night. Frescoes in the Yellow Room (near the
exit) show off the ancient mastery of perspective, which was not
matched elsewhere in Europe for nearly 1,500 years.

Leaving the House of the Vetti, go left past the pipes again. Then turn right, following Vicolo dei Vetti to Via della Fortuna. Intersections like this, with public fountains, were busy neighborhood centers, where rent was high and people gathered.

Turn left on Via della Fortuna and take a quick right on Vicolo Storto, which leads down a curving street to the **bakery and mill** *(forno e mulini)*. The ovens look like a modern-day pizza oven. And the stubby stone towers are flour grinders: After grain was poured into the top, donkeys pushed wooden bars that turned the stones, and eventually powdered grain dropped out the bottom as flour—flavored with tiny bits of rock.

Take the first left after the bakery onto Via degli Augustali, and check out the mosaics on the left at the Taberna Hedones. This must be the tavern of hedonism—see the cute welcome mosaic reading *HAVE* ("hail to you"), with the bear licking his wounds.

Next turn right, over the street dam, and follow the signs to the **brothel** *(lupanare)*, at #18. Prostitutes were nicknamed *lupas* (she-wolves). Wander into the brothel, a simple place with stone beds and pillows. The ancient graffiti includes stroke tallies and exotic names of the girls, indicating they came from all corners of the Mediterranean. The faded frescoes above the cells may have served as a kind of menu for services offered. Note the idealized portrayal of women (white, considered beautiful) and man (dark, considered horny). Outside at #17 is a laundry—likely to boil the sheets (thought to guard against venereal disease).

Leaving the brothel, go down the hill to Pompeii's main drag, Via Abbondanza. The forum (and exit) is to the right. (The huge amphitheater—which you can skip—is 10 minutes to your left.) Go straight down Via dei Teatri, then left before the columns, downhill to the **Temple of Isis** (on the right). This Egyptian temple served Pompeii's Egyptian community. The little shrine with the plastic roof housed holy water from the Nile. Pompeii must have had a synagogue, but it has yet to be excavated.

Immediately upon leaving, follow the lane at #17 to our last stop, the **theater**. Originally a Greek theater (Greeks built theirs with the help of a hillside), this marks the spot of the birthplace of the Greek port here in 470 B.C. During Roman times, it sat 5,000 in three price ranges: the five marble terraces up close (filled with romantic wooden seats for two), the main section, and the cheap nosebleed section (surviving only on the right). The square stones above the cheap seats used to support a canvas rooftop. Notice the high-profile boxes, flanking the stage, for guests of honor. From this perch, you can see the gladiator barracks—the colonnaded courtyard beyond the theater. They lived in tiny rooms, trained in the courtyard, and fought in the nearby amphitheater.

There's much more to see; 75 percent of Pompeii's 164 acres has been excavated. But this tour's over. *Ciao!*

**Getting to Pompeii:** Pompeii is halfway between Naples and Sorrento, about 30 minutes from either by direct Circumvesuviana train (runs at least hrly). Get off at the Pompei Scavi, Villa dei Misteri stop on the Naples–Sorrento train line. A different Circumvesuviana line, which does *not* go to Sorrento, has a Pompeii stop that leaves you far from the excavation site entrance. Check your bag at the Pompei Scavi train station (at the bar) for €0.75, or, better yet, at the Pompeii ruins for free. From the train station, turn right and walk down the road about a block to the entrance (first left turn). The TI is farther down the street, but not a necessary stop for your visit.

▲▲**Herculaneum (Ercolano)**—Smaller, less ruined, and less crowded than its famous big sister, Herculaneum offers a closer peek into ancient Roman life but with none of the grandeur of Pompeii. (There's barely a colonnade.) It's extremely low-tech, so you'll find no information or books at the site (guidebooks are on sale in nearby gift shops). Caked and baked by the same A.D. 79 eruption, Herculaneum is a small community of intact buildings with plenty of surviving detail (€8.25, €13.50 combo-ticket includes Pompeii and 3 lesser sites—valid 3 days, daily March–Sept 8:30–19:30, Oct–Feb 8:30–17:00, ticket office closes 90 min earlier, free baggage check, 15 min from Naples and 45 min from Sorrento on the same Circumvesuviana train that goes to Pompeii, leave station and turn right, following yellow signs, 8 blocks straight downhill from Ercolano station to end of road, tel. 081-739-0963).

▲**Vesuvius**—The 1,200-meter (4,000-foot) summit of Vesuvius, mainland Europe's only active volcano (sleeping restlessly since 1944), is accessible year-round by car, taxi (€36 round-trip), or by the blue Transporti Vesuviani bus (often 5/day but irregular, roughly hourly departures 9:00–14:00 from Herculaneum station; 60 min up with stop at bar, 40 min down). The round-trip bus ride costs about €8 (includes €1.50 site entry). Be prepared for a long wait for the return trip. Beware of expensive pit stops: the bus may make a bathroom stop at a tourist shack along the way—if you use the WC, you may be expected to purchase a candy bar or some other item at a premium.

From the bus and car park, it's a steep, often cold and windy 30-minute hike to the top for a sweeping view of the Bay of Naples. Up here, it's desolate and lunar-like. The rocks are hot. Walk the entire crater lip for the most interesting views; the far end overlooks Pompeii. Be still and alone to hear the wind and tumbling rocks in the crater. Any steam? Closed when erupting.

# PAESTUM

Paestum is one of the best collections of Greek temples any-where—and certainly the most accessible to western Europe. Serenely situated, it's surrounded by fields and wildflowers and has only a modest commercial strip.

This town was founded as Poseidonia by Greeks in the sixth century B.C. and became a key stop on an important trade route. In the fifth century B.C., the Lucans, a barbarous inland tribe, conquered Poseidonia, changed its name to Paistom, and tried to adopt the cultured ways of the Greeks. The Romans, who took over in the third century B.C., gave Paestum the name it bears today. The final conquerors of Paestum, malaria-carrying mos-quitoes, kept the site wonderfully deserted for nearly a thousand years. Rediscovered in the 18th century, Paestum today offers the only well-preserved Greek ruins north of Sicily (TI: daily in sum-mer 9:00–19:00, off-season Mon–Sat 9:00–16:30, Sun 9:00–13:00, hours may vary, tel. 082-881-1016, e-mail: aastp@oneonline.it).

**Arrival at Paestum:** Buses from Salerno (see "Transporta-tion Connections," below) stop near a corner of the ruins (at a little bar/café). Arriving by train, exit the station and walk through the old city gate; the ruins are an eight-minute walk straight ahead. Stop by the TI (next to museum) to pick up a free map of the site. If you ask politely, you can store luggage at the TI, site, or museum.

**Cost, Hours, Information:** €4 for the museum, €4 for the site, €6.50 for a combo-ticket. Both the museum and site open daily at 9:00 (except the first and third Mon of month, when museum is closed, though the site is open). Year-round, the museum closes at 19:00 (last ticket sold at 18:30). The site closes one hour before sunset (as late as 19:30 June–Aug, as early as 15:45 in Dec, last ticket sold an hour before closing). Several mediocre guidebooks are offered at the museum's bookshop, including a past-and-present guide. The book with the jumbled title, *Archaeologic Site Temples Museum Paestum*, is the most infor-mative (€7.75). The site and museum have separate entrances. The museum, just outside the ruins, is in a cluster with the TI and a small paleo-Christian basilica.

**Planning Your Time:** Allow two hours, including the museum. Depending on your interest and the heat of the day, start with either the museum or the site.

**Museum:** This offers you the rare opportunity to see artifacts—dating from prehistoric to Greek to Roman times—at the site where they were discovered. These beautifully crafted works help bring Paestum to life.

The large ground floor (the most impressive part) contains

...eek artifacts. Upstairs, you'll find the prehistory exhibits (in ...walkway hugging the walls of the building, with displays of ...pottery, blades, and arrowheads, and nothing in English) as well as the Roman Room (near the elevator; contains statues, busts, and inscriptions dating from the time of the Roman occupation). No matter where you start, you'll feel like you've come in on the middle of something, but about half of the work is described in English, and the art speaks for itself.

On the ground floor, the large carvings overhead—wrapping around the first room you see as you enter the museum—once adorned a sanctuary of the goddess Hera (wife of Zeus) outside the city. Some of the carvings show scenes from the life of Hercules. In the various ground-floor rooms, you'll see startlingly well-preserved Greek vases, crumbling armor, and paintings. The highlight of the museum is a rare example of Greek painting, known as the Diver's Tomb (480 B.C.). These slabs—showing a diver and four scenes of banqueting—originally were the sides of a tomb. The simple painting of a diver arcing down into a pool was the top of the tomb (painting faced inward). Though the deceased might have been a diver, it's thought the art more likely represents our dive from life to death. It's rare to see a real Greek statue (most are Roman copies), even rarer to see a Greek painting. The many other painted slabs in the museum date from a later time under Lucan rule. The barbarous people who conquered the Greeks tried to appropriate their art and style, but lacked the Greeks' distinct, light touch. Regardless, the Lucan paintings, as well as the crisply drawn pictures on dozens of Greek vases, are instructive and enjoyable—consider them ancient snapshots.

**Site:** The key ruins are the impossible-to-miss Temples of Neptune, Hera, and Ceres, but the scattered village ruins are also interesting. Lonely Ceres, in an evocative setting, is about a 10-minute walk from Neptune and Hera, which stand together. The entry to the site may return to its original place in front of Neptune (once the scaffolding is off) or it may be still be in front of Ceres.

The misnamed Temple of Neptune is a textbook example of the Doric style. Constructed in 450 B.C. and actually dedicated to Hera, the Temple of Neptune is simply overwhelming. Better preserved than the Parthenon in Athens, this huge structure is a tribute to Greek engineering and aesthetics. Contemplate the word "renaissance"—the rebirth of this grand Greek style of architecture. Notice how the columns angle out and the base bows up (scan the short ends of the temple). This was a trick ancient architects used to create the illusion of a perfectly straight building. All important Greek buildings were built using this technique. Now imagine it richly and colorfully decorated with marble and statues.

**Paestu**

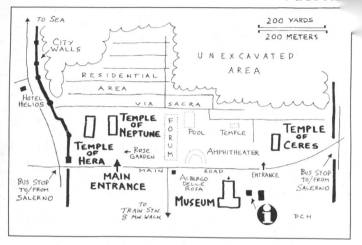

Adjacent to the Temple of Neptune is the almost-delicate Temple of Hera, dedicated to the Greek goddess of marriage in 550 B.C.

**Sleeping near Paestum:** Paestum at night, with views of the floodlit ruins, is magic. **Hotel delle Rose**, which has 12 small, fine rooms and a respectable restaurant, is near the site entry, on the street bordering the ruins (Db-€55, includes breakfast, CC, Via Magna Grecia 193, tel. 082-881-1070, www.hoteldellerose.com, NSE). The **Seliano Estate for Agritourism** offers spacious, spotless rooms on a farm, complete with horses, buffalo, a pool, and great cooking (Db-€70 with breakfast, €90 in July–Aug, CC, run by an English-speaking baroness, serves a fine €15 dinner, near beach, 1.5 kilometers, or 1 mile, from ruins, tel. 082-872-4544, fax 082-872-3634).

**Hotel Helios** is a three-star hotel with one-star rooms. After you're wowed by a classy lobby with stained glass and marble, as well as by the inviting swimming pool, the basic rooms are a disappointment (Db-€82, includes breakfast, Via Principe di Piedmonte 1, tel. 082-881-1451, fax 082-811-600, speak a little English). Ask to visit the owner's mozzarella farm, located nearby.

# Transportation Connections— Salerno and Paestum

Salerno, the big city just north of Paestum, is the nearest transportation hub. From Naples or Sorrento, you'll change buses or trains in Salerno to get to Paestum. Salerno's TI has bus, ferry, and train dules (Mon–Sat 9:00–14:00 & 15:00–20:00, closed Sun, shorter urs off-season, on Piazza Veneto, just outside train station, tel. 89-231-432, toll-free 800-213-289, www.crmpa.it/ept/).

**Salerno to Paestum by bus:** Four companies (CSTP, SCAT, Giuliano, and Lettieri) offer a Salerno–Paestum bus service, all conveniently leaving from the same stop at Piazza Concordia on the waterfront (2–3/hr, 70 min, schedules extremely sparse on Sun). Buy the €2.85 ticket on the bus, except on CSTP buses (CSTP prefers you buy a ticket at their office, next to TI at Piazza Veneto/train station, but driver will grumpily sell you a ticket on bus if necessary). No clear schedule is posted at the Salerno stop. Simply ask a local or a bus rep at the stop for the next bus to Paestum; otherwise, get a schedule at the TI (more impartial, since they don't represent a particular company and their schedule shows all companies and times). Note that orange city buses use the same stop; ignore these.

When leaving Paestum, catch a northbound bus from either of the intersections that flank the ruins (see map on page 449). Flag down any bus, ask "Salerno?", and buy the ticket on board (except for CSTP buses—try to buy ticket at bar closest to stop).

**Salerno to Paestum by train:** The train from Salerno to Paestum (3–4/day, 40 min, direction: Paola or Sapri) runs far less frequently than the buses, though it's a quicker ride because it's immune from traffic jams; check schedules at Salerno's TI or train station. Paestum's train station is an eight-minute walk from the ruins (from station, go through old city wall, ruins are straight ahead). If you plan to leave Paestum by train, buy your train ticket at the bar/café near the TI because the station is unstaffed (train schedules at TI). Leaving Paestum, trains bound for Salerno (direction: Battipaglia) usually continue to Naples.

**Naples to Salerno by train:** Hourly, 1.5-hour trip (some trains stop at Pompeii).

**Sorrento to Salerno by bus:** The scenic three-hour Amalfi Coast drive (blue SITA bus, 12/day, 3 hrs, easy transfer in Amalfi) drops you in Salerno, on the waterfront at Piazza Concordia, at the same place where the buses to Paestum depart. Salerno's train station and TI are two blocks inland.

If you plan to take a bus from Salerno to Sorrento (or points in between), buy your bus ticket at Salerno's Bar Ciofi (CHOH-fee), across the square from Piazza Concordia (see map on page 451). Ticket vendors change periodically; if Bar Ciofi no longer sells tickets, ask anyone or a clerk at a *tabacchi* shop, "Who sells bus tickets to ____?" by saying, *"Chi vendi i biglietti dell'autobus per ___?"* (pron. kee VEHN-dee ee beel-YET-tee del-OW-toh-boos pehr ___).

## Salerno Connecti

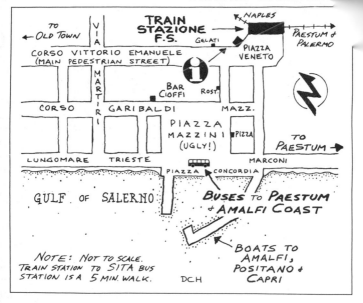

**Salerno by ferry to Amalfi towns:** If you take the bus to Salerno, consider returning by boat. Catch the ferry from Salerno's Piazza Concordia (where the SITA bus drops you off) to **Amalfi** (12/day, 35 min, €5) or **Positano** (11/day, 70 min, €5; tickets and info at TravelMar, Piazza Concordia, tel. 089-873-190 or 089-872-950).

**Sorrento to Salerno by train:** Ride the Circumvesuviana to Naples Centrale station (hrly, 70 min) and catch the Salerno train (hrly, 1 hr). Or ask about connecting in Pompeii.

**Drivers:** While the Amalfi Coast is a thrill to drive off-season, summer traffic is miserable. From Sorrento, Paestum is 100 kilometers (60 miles) and three hours via the coast and a much smoother two hours by autostrada. To reach Paestum from Sorrento via the autostrada, drive toward Naples, catch the autostrada (direction: Salerno), skirt Salerno (direction: Reggio), exit at Eboli, and drive straight through the modern town of Paestum. You'll hit the ruins just about the time you start to worry you missed the turnoff. Along the way, you'll see many signs for "*mozzarella di bufala*," the cheese made from the milk of water buffalo that graze here. Try it here— it can't be any fresher.

# APPENDIX

## Let's Talk Telephones

This is a primer on telephoning in Europe. For specifics on Italy, see "Telephones" in the Introduction.

**Making Calls within a European Country:** What you dial depends on the phone system of the country you're in. About half of all European countries have phone systems that use area codes; the other half uses a direct-dial system without area codes.

If you're calling within a country that uses a direct-dial system (Italy, Belgium, the Czech Republic, Denmark, France, Norway, Portugal, Spain, and Switzerland), you dial the same number whether you're calling across the street or across the country.

In countries that use area codes (such as Austria, Britain, Finland, Germany, Ireland, the Netherlands, and Sweden), you dial the local number when calling within a city, and you add the area code if calling long-distance within the country. Example: The phone number of a hotel in Munich is 089-264-349. To call it in Munich, dial 264-349; to call it from Frankfurt, dial 089-264-349.

**Making International Calls:** You always start with the international access code (011 if you're calling from America or Canada, or 00 from virtually anywhere in Europe), then dial the country code of the country you're calling (see list of country codes, below).

What you dial next depends on the particular phone system of the country you're calling. If the country uses area codes, you drop the initial zero of the area code, then dial the rest of the area code and the local number. Example: To call the Munich hotel (mentioned above) from Spain, dial 00, 49 (Germany's country code), then 89-264-349.

Countries that use direct-dial systems (no area codes) differ in how they're accessed internationally by phone. For instance, if you're making an international call to Italy, the Czech Republic, Denmark, Norway, Portugal, or Spain, you simply dial the international access code, country code, and the phone number in full. But if you're calling Belgium, France, or Switzerland, you drop the initial zero of the phone number. Example: The phone number of a Paris hotel is 01 47 05 49 15. To call it from Rome, dial 00, 33 (France's country code), then 1 47 05 49 15 (the phone number without the initial zero).

**Calling America or Canada from Europe:** Dial the international access code (00 for virtually all of Europe), then dial 1, the area code, and local phone number. Example: My number here at Europe Through the Back Door (in Edmonds, WA) is 425/771-8303. To call me from Europe, dial 00-1-425-771-8303.

# European Calling Chart

**Just smile and dial, using this key:**
**AC = Area Code, LN = Local Number.**

| European Country | Calling long distance within... | Calling from the U.S.A./ Canada to... | Calling from another European country to... |
|---|---|---|---|
| **Austria** | AC (Area Code) + LN (Local Number) | 011 + 43 + AC (without the initial zero) + LN | 00 + 43 + AC (without the initial zero) + LN |
| **Belgium** | LN | 011 + 32 + LN (without initial zero) | 00 + 32 + LN (without initial zero) |
| **Britain** | AC + LN | 011 + 44 + AC (without initial zero) + LN | 00 + 44 + AC . (without initial zero) + LN |
| **Czech Republic** | LN | 011 + 420 + LN | 00 + 420 + LN |
| **Denmark** | LN | 011 + 45 + LN | 00 + 45 + LN |
| **Estonia** | LN | 011 + 372 + LN | 00 + 372 + LN |
| **Finland** | AC + LN | 011 + 358 + AC (without initial zero) + LN | 00 + 358 + AC (without initial zero) + LN |
| **France** | LN | 011 + 33 + LN (without initial zero) | 00 + 33 + LN (without initial zero) |
| **Germany** | AC + LN | 011 + 49 + AC (without initial zero) + LN | 00 + 49 + AC (without initial zero) + LN |
| **Gibraltar** | LN | 011 + 350 + LN | 00 + 350 + LN From Spain: 9567 + LN |
| **Greece** | LN | 011 + 30 + LN | 00 + 30 + LN |

| European Country | Calling long distance within... | Calling from the U.S.A./ Canada to... | Calling from another European country to... |
|---|---|---|---|
| Ireland | AC + LN | 011 + 353 + AC (without initial zero) + LN | 00 + 353 + AC (without initial zero) + LN |
| Italy | LN | 011 + 39 + LN | 00 + 39 + LN |
| Morocco | LN | 011 + 212 + LN (without initial zero) | 00 + 212 + LN (without initial zero) |
| Nether-lands | AC + LN | 011 + 31 + AC (without initial zero) + LN | 00 + 31 + AC (without initial zero) + LN |
| Norway | LN | 011 + 47 + LN | 00 + 47 + LN |
| Portugal | LN | 011 + 351 + LN | 00 + 351 + LN |
| Spain | LN | 011 + 34 + LN | 00 + 34 + LN |
| Sweden | AC + LN | 011 + 46 + AC (without initial zero) + LN | 00 + 46 + AC (without initial zero) + LN |
| Switzer-land | LN | 011 + 41 + LN (without initial zero) | 00 + 41 + LN (without initial zero) |
| Turkey | AC (if no initial zero is included, add one) + LN | 011 + 90 + AC (without initial zero) + LN | 00 + 90 + AC (without initial zero) + LN |

- The instructions above apply whether you're calling a fixed phone or cell phone.
- The international access codes (the first numbers you dial when making an international call) are 011 if you're calling from the U.S.A./Canada, or 00 if you're calling from virtually anywhere in Europe. Finland and Lithuania are the only exceptions. If calling from either of these countries, replace the 00 with 990 in Finland and 810 in Lithuania.
- To call the U.S.A. or Canada from Europe, dial 00 (unless you're calling from Finland or Lithuania), then 1 (the country code for the U.S.A. and Canada), then the area code and number. In short, 00 + 1 + AC + LN = Hi, mom!

## nternational Access Codes

When dialing direct, first dial the international access code. For the United States and Canada, it's 011. Virtually all European countries use "00" as their international access code; the only exceptions are Finland (990) and Lithuania (810).

## Country Codes

After you've dialed the international access code, dial the code of the country you're calling.

Austria—43
Belgium—32
Britain—44
Canada—1
Czech Rep.—420
Denmark—45
Estonia—372
Finland—358
France—33
Germany—49
Gibraltar—350
Greece—30

Ireland—353
Italy—39
Morocco—212
Netherlands—31
Norway—47
Portugal—351
Spain—34
Sweden—46
Switzerland—41
Turkey—90
United States—1

## Useful Italian Phone Numbers

**Emergency (English-speaking police help):** 113 or 112
**Ambulance:** 118
**Road Service:** 116
**Directory Assistance** (for €0.50, an Italian-speaking robot gives the number twice, very clearly): 12
**Telephone help** (in English; free directory assistance): 170 or 176

## U.S. Embassies

**In Rome:** American Embassy at Via Veneto 119, tel. 06-46741; Canadian Embassy at Via Zara 30, tel. 06-445-981.
**In Milan:** U.S. Consulate at Via Principe Amedeo 2, tel. 02-290-351.

# Public Holidays and Festivals

Italy (including most major sights) closes down on these national holidays: January 1, January 6 (Epiphany), Easter Sunday and Monday (April 20 and 21 in 2003), April 25 (Liberation Day), May 1 (Labor Day), May 20 (Ascension Day), August 15 (Assumption of Mary), November 1 (All Saints' Day), December 8 (Immaculate Conception of Mary), and December 25 and 26.

Each town has a local festival honoring its patron saint. For more information on Italian festivals, check out

# 2003

## JANUARY
| S | M | T | W | T | F | S |
|---|---|---|---|---|---|---|
|   |   |   | 1 | 2 | 3 | 4 |
| 5 | 6 | 7 | 8 | 9 | 10 | 11 |
| 12 | 13 | 14 | 15 | 16 | 17 | 18 |
| 19 | 20 | 21 | 22 | 23 | 24 | 25 |
| 26 | 27 | 28 | 29 | 30 | 31 |   |

## FEBRUARY
| S | M | T | W | T | F | S |
|---|---|---|---|---|---|---|
|   |   |   |   |   |   | 1 |
| 2 | 3 | 4 | 5 | 6 | 7 | 8 |
| 9 | 10 | 11 | 12 | 13 | 14 | 15 |
| 16 | 17 | 18 | 19 | 20 | 21 | 22 |
| 23 | 24 | 25 | 26 | 27 | 28 |   |

## MARCH
| S | M | T | W | T | F | S |
|---|---|---|---|---|---|---|
|   |   |   |   |   |   | 1 |
| 2 | 3 | 4 | 5 | 6 | 7 | 8 |
| 9 | 10 | 11 | 12 | 13 | 14 | 15 |
| 16 | 17 | 18 | 19 | 20 | 21 | 22 |
| 23/30 | 24/31 | 25 | 26 | 27 | 28 | 29 |

## APRIL
| S | M | T | W | T | F | S |
|---|---|---|---|---|---|---|
|   |   | 1 | 2 | 3 | 4 | 5 |
| 6 | 7 | 8 | 9 | 10 | 11 | 12 |
| 13 | 14 | 15 | 16 | 17 | 18 | 19 |
| 20 | 21 | 22 | 23 | 24 | 25 | 26 |
| 27 | 28 | 29 | 30 |   |   |   |

## MAY
| S | M | T | W | T | F | S |
|---|---|---|---|---|---|---|
|   |   |   |   | 1 | 2 | 3 |
| 4 | 5 | 6 | 7 | 8 | 9 | 10 |
| 11 | 12 | 13 | 14 | 15 | 16 | 17 |
| 18 | 19 | 20 | 21 | 22 | 23 | 24 |
| 25 | 26 | 27 | 28 | 29 | 30 | 31 |

## JUNE
| S | M | T | W | T | F | S |
|---|---|---|---|---|---|---|
| 1 | 2 | 3 | 4 | 5 | 6 | 7 |
| 8 | 9 | 10 | 11 | 12 | 13 | 14 |
| 15 | 16 | 17 | 18 | 19 | 20 | 21 |
| 22 | 23 | 24 | 25 | 26 | 27 | 28 |
| 29 | 30 |   |   |   |   |   |

## JULY
| S | M | T | W | T | F | S |
|---|---|---|---|---|---|---|
|   |   | 1 | 2 | 3 | 4 | 5 |
| 6 | 7 | 8 | 9 | 10 | 11 | 12 |
| 13 | 14 | 15 | 16 | 17 | 18 | 19 |
| 20 | 21 | 22 | 23 | 24 | 25 | 26 |
| 27 | 28 | 29 | 30 | 31 |   |   |

## AUGUST
| S | M | T | W | T | F | S |
|---|---|---|---|---|---|---|
|   |   |   |   |   | 1 | 2 |
| 3 | 4 | 5 | 6 | 7 | 8 | 9 |
| 10 | 11 | 12 | 13 | 14 | 15 | 16 |
| 17 | 18 | 19 | 20 | 21 | 22 | 23 |
| 24/31 | 25 | 26 | 27 | 28 | 29 | 30 |

## SEPTEMBER
| S | M | T | W | T | F | S |
|---|---|---|---|---|---|---|
|   | 1 | 2 | 3 | 4 | 5 | 6 |
| 7 | 8 | 9 | 10 | 11 | 12 | 13 |
| 14 | 15 | 16 | 17 | 18 | 19 | 20 |
| 21 | 22 | 23 | 24 | 25 | 26 | 27 |
| 28 | 29 | 30 |   |   |   |   |

## OCTOBER
| S | M | T | W | T | F | S |
|---|---|---|---|---|---|---|
|   |   |   | 1 | 2 | 3 | 4 |
| 5 | 6 | 7 | 8 | 9 | 10 | 11 |
| 12 | 13 | 14 | 15 | 16 | 17 | 18 |
| 19 | 20 | 21 | 22 | 23 | 24 | 25 |
| 26 | 27 | 28 | 29 | 30 | 31 |   |

## NOVEMBER
| S | M | T | W | T | F | S |
|---|---|---|---|---|---|---|
|   |   |   |   |   |   | 1 |
| 2 | 3 | 4 | 5 | 6 | 7 | 8 |
| 9 | 10 | 11 | 12 | 13 | 14 | 15 |
| 16 | 17 | 18 | 19 | 20 | 21 | 22 |
| 23/30 | 24 | 25 | 26 | 27 | 28 | 29 |

## DECEMBER
| S | M | T | W | T | F | S |
|---|---|---|---|---|---|---|
|   | 1 | 2 | 3 | 4 | 5 | 6 |
| 7 | 8 | 9 | 10 | 11 | 12 | 13 |
| 14 | 15 | 16 | 17 | 18 | 19 | 20 |
| 21 | 22 | 23 | 24 | 25 | 26 | 27 |
| 28 | 29 | 30 | 31 |   |   |   |

www.italiantourism.com, www.hostetler.net, www.carnivalofvenice .com, www.festivals.com, www.whatsgoingon.com, and www .whatsonwhen.com.

Here's a partial list of events:

| **January** | Epiphany Fair—Jan 6 (religious festival), Rome |
| **February** | Carnevale—Feb 21–March 4 in 2003 (Mardi Gras), Venice |
| **April** | Vinitaly—early April (wine festival), Verona Holy Week and Good Friday (processions), All Italy; Scoppio del Carro (fireworks) on Easter, Florence |
| **May** | Florence May Music Festival—early May–mid-June, Florence |
| **June** | Battle of the Bridge—June 29 (medieval festival), Pisa |

| June | Regatta of the Great Maritime Republics—first week of June (rowing competition, parade), Venice in 2003; Calcio Fiorentino—late June (costumed soccer game, fireworks), Florence |
| July | Feast of the Redeemer—July 19 and 20 (parade, fireworks), Venice; Festa de'Noantri—mid- to late July (neighborhood fair), Rome; Il Palio—July 2 (horse race), Siena; Verona Arena Outdoor Opera, Verona |
| August | Il Palio—Aug 16 (horse race), Siena; Siena Music Week—late Aug, Siena |
| September | Historical Regatta—Sept 1–7 (boat parade), Venice; Chestnut Festivals (festival, chestnut roasts) Most towns, mainly north of Rome; Festival of San Genarro—Sept 19 (religious festival), Naples |
| December | Christmas Market, Rome, Piazza Navona |

## Numbers and Stumblers

- Europeans write a few of their numbers differently than we do. 1 = 1 , 4 = 4 , 7 = 7 . Learn the difference or miss your train.
- In Europe, dates appear as day/month/year, so Christmas is 25/12/03.
- Commas are decimal points and decimals commas. A dollar and a half is 1,50, and there are 5.280 feet in a mile.
- When pointing, use your whole hand, palm down.
- When counting with fingers, start with your thumb. If you hold up your first finger to request one item, you'll probably get two.
- What Americans call the second floor of a building is the first floor in Europe.
- Europeans keep the left "lane" open for passing on escalators and moving sidewalks. Keep to the right.

## Metric Conversion (approximate)

| | |
|---|---|
| 1 inch = 25 millimeters | 32 degrees F = 0 degrees C |
| 1 foot = 0.3 meter | 82 degrees F = about 28 degrees C |
| 1 yard = 0.9 meter | 1 ounce = 28 grams |
| 1 mile = 1.6 kilometers | 1 kilogram = 2.2 pounds |
| 1 centimeter = 0.4 inch | 1 quart = 0.95 liter |
| 1 meter = 39.4 inches | 1 square yard = 0.8 square meter |
| 1 kilometer = .62 mile | 1 acre = 0.4 hectare |

# Climate Chart

First line, average daily low; second line, average daily high; third line, days of no rain.

| | J | F | M | A | M | J | J | A | S | O | N | D |
|---|---|---|---|---|---|---|---|---|---|---|---|---|
| **Rome** | | | | | | | | | | | | |
| | 40° | 42° | 45° | 50° | 56° | 63° | 67° | 67° | 62° | 55° | 49° | 44° |
| | 52° | 55° | 59° | 66° | 74° | 82° | 87° | 86° | 79° | 71° | 61° | 55° |
| | 13 | 19 | 23 | 24 | 26 | 26 | 30 | 29 | 25 | 23 | 19 | 21 |
| **Milan** | | | | | | | | | | | | |
| | 32° | 35° | 43° | 49° | 57° | 63° | 67° | 66° | 61° | 52° | 43° | 35° |
| | 40° | 46° | 56° | 65° | 74° | 80° | 84° | 82° | 75° | 63° | 51° | 43° |
| | 25 | 21 | 24 | 22 | 23 | 21 | 25 | 24 | 25 | 23 | 20 | 24 |

## asic Italian Survival Phrases

| English | Italian | Pronunciation |
|---|---|---|
| Good day. | Buon giorno. | bwohn **jor**-noh |
| Do you speak English? | Parla inglese? | par-lah een-**glay**-zay |
| Yes. / No. | Sì. / No. | see / noh |
| I (don't) understand. | (Non) capito. | (nohn) kah-**pee**-toh |
| Please. | Per favore. | pehr fah-**voh**-ray |
| Thank you. | Grazie. | **graht**-seeay |
| I'm sorry. | Mi dispiace. | mee dee-spee**ah**-chay |
| Excuse me. | Mi scusi. | mee **skoo**-zee |
| (No) problem. | (Non) c'è un problema. | (nohn) cheh oon proh-**blay**-mah |
| Good. | Va bene. | vah **behn**-ay |
| Goodbye. | Arrivederci. | ah-ree-vay-**dehr**-chee |
| one / two | uno / due | **oo**-noh / **doo**-ay |
| three / four | tre / quattro | tray / **kwah**-troh |
| five / six | cinque / sei | **cheeng**-kway / **seh**ee |
| seven / eight | sette / otto | **seht**-tay / **ot**-toh |
| nine / ten | nove / dieci | **nov**-ay / **deeay**-chee |
| How much is it? | Quanto costa? | **kwahn**-toh **kos**-tah |
| Write it? | Me lo scrive? | may loh **skree**-vay |
| Is it free? | È gratis? | eh **grah**-tees |
| Included? | È incluso? | eh een-**kloo**-zoh |
| Where can I buy / find...? | Dove posso comprare / trovare...? | **doh**-vay **pos**-soh kohm-**prah**-ray / troh-**vah**-ray |
| I'd like / We'd like... | Vorrei / Vorremo... | vor-**reh**ee / vor-**ray**-moh |
| ...a room. | ...una camera. | **oo**-nah **kah**-meh-rah |
| ...the bill. | ...il conto. | eel **kohn**-toh |
| ...a ticket to ___. | ...un biglietto per___. | oon beel-**yeht**-toh per |
| Is it possible? | È possibile? | eh poh-**see**-bee-lay |
| Where is...? | Dov'è...? | **doh**-veh |
| ...the train station | ...la stazione | lah staht-see**oh**-nay |
| ...the bus station | ...la stazione degli autobus | lah staht-see**oh**-nay **dayl**-yee **ow**-toh-boos |
| ...tourist information | ...informazioni per turisti | een-for-maht-see**oh**-nee pehr too-**ree**-stee |
| ...toilet | ...la toilette | lah twah-**leht**-tay |
| men | uomini, signori | **woh**-mee-nee, seen-**yoh**-ree |
| women | donne, signore | **don**-nay, seen-**yoh**-ray |
| left / right | sinistra / destra | see-**nee**-strah / **dehs**-trah |
| straight | sempre diritto | **sehm**-pray dee-**ree**-toh |
| When do you open / close? | A che ora aprite / chiudete? | ah kay oh-rah ah-**pree**-tay / keeoo-**day**-tay |
| At what time? | A che ora? | ah kay **oh**-rah |
| Just a moment. | Un momento. | oon moh-**mayn**-toh |
| now / soon / later | adesso / presto / tardi | ah-**dehs**-soh / **prehs**-toh / **tar**-dee |
| today / tomorrow | oggi / domani | oh-jee / doh-**mah**-nee |

For more user-friendly Italian phrases, check out *Rick Steves' Italian Phrase Book and Dictionary* or *Rick Steves' French, Italian & German Phrase Book and Dictionary*.

# Road Scholar Feedback for ITALY 2003

*We're all in the same travelers' school of hard knocks. Your feedback helps us improve this guidebook for future travelers. Please fill this out (or use the online version at www.ricksteves.com/feedback), attach more info or any tips/favorite discoveries if you like, and send it to us. As thanks for your help, we'll send you our quarterly travel newsletter free for one year. Thanks!* **Rick**

**Of the recommended accommodations/restaurants used, which was:**

Best _____

    Why? _____

Worst _____

    Why? _____

**Of the sights/experiences/destinations recommended by this book, which was:**

Most overrated _____

    Why? _____

Most underrated _____

    Why? _____

**Best ways to improve this book:**

_____

_____

**I'd like a free newsletter subscription:**

____ Yes    ____ No    ____ Already on list

_____
Name

_____
Address

_____
City, State, Zip

_____
E-mail Address

    *Please send to: ETBD, Box 2009, Edmonds, WA 98020*

# Faxing Your Hotel Reservation

Use this handy form for your fax or find it online at
www.ricksteves.com/reservation. Photocopy and fax away.

## One-Page Fax

To: _____ @ _____
                 *hotel*                         *fax*

From: _____ @ _____
                 *name*                         *fax*

Today's date: ____ /_____ /____
              *day*  *month*  *year*

Dear Hotel _____,

Please make this reservation for me:

Name: _____

Total # of people: _____    # of rooms: _____    # of nights: _____

Arriving: ____ /_____ /____ My time of arrival (24-hr clock): _____
        *day*  *month*  *year*

(I will telephone if I will be late)

Departing: ____ /_____ /____
          *day*  *month*  *year*

Room(s):  Single___  Double___  Twin___  Triple___  Quad___

With:  Toilet___  Shower___  Bath___  Sink only___

Special needs:  View___  Quiet___  Cheapest___  Ground Floor___

Credit card:  Visa___  MasterCard___  American Express___

Card #: _____

Expiration date: _____

Name on card: _____

You may charge me for the first night as a deposit. Please fax, e-mail, or
mail me confirmation of my reservation, along with the type of room
reserved, the price, and whether the price includes breakfast. Please also
inform me of your cancellation policy. Thank you.

_____
*Signature*

_____
*Name*

_____
*Address*

_____
*City*             *State*          *Zip Code*    *Country*

_____
*E-mail Address*

# INDEX

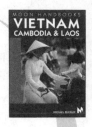

# FREE TRAVEL GOODIES FROM

*Rick Steves*

## EUROPEAN TRAVEL NEWSLETTER

My *Europe Through the Back Door* travel company will help you travel better *because* you're on a budget—not in spite of it. To see how, ask for my 64-page *travel newsletter* packed full of savvy travel tips, readers' discoveries, and your best bets for railpasses, guidebooks, videos, travel accessories and free-spirited tours.

## 2003 GUIDE TO EUROPEAN RAILPASSES

With hundreds of railpasses to choose from in 2003, finding the right pass for your trip has never been more confusing. To cut through the complexity, visit www.ricksteves.com for my online *2003 Guide to European Railpasses.* Once you've narrowed down your choices, we give you unbeatable prices, including important extras with every Eurailpass, free: my 90-minute *Travel Skills Special* video or DVD and your choice of one of my 24 guidebooks.

## RICK STEVES' 2003 TOURS

We offer 20 different one, two, and three-week tours (200 departures in 2003) for those who want to experience Europe in Rick Steves' Back Door style, but without the transportation and hotel hassles. If a tour with a small group, modest family-run hotels, lots of exercise, great guides, and no tips or hidden charges sounds like your idea of fun, ask for my 48-page 2003 Tours booklet.

## YEAR-ROUND GUIDEBOOK UPDATES

Even though the information in my guidebooks is the freshest around, things do change in Europe between book printings. I've set aside a special section at my website (www.ricksteves.com/update) listing *up-to-the-minute changes* for every Rick Steves guidebook.

*Visit **www.ricksteves.com** to get your...*

☑ **FREE EUROPEAN TRAVEL NEWSLETTER**
☑ **FREE 2003 GUIDE TO EUROPEAN RAILPASSES**
☑ **FREE RICK STEVES' 2003 TOURS BOOKLET**

## Rick Steves' Europe Through the Back Door

130 Fourth Avenue North, PO Box 2009, Edmonds, WA 98020 USA
Phone: (425) 771-8303 ■ Fax: (425) 771-0833 ■ www.ricksteves.com